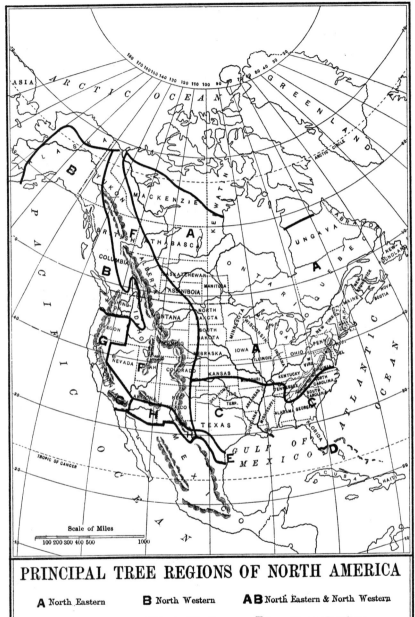

PRINCIPAL TREE REGIONS OF NORTH AMERICA

A North Eastern   **B** North Western   **AB** North Eastern & North Western

C South Eastern   **D** Tropical Florida   **E** Texas-Mexican Boundary

F Rocky Mountains   **G** Oregon & California   **H** New Mexico & Arizona Mexican Boundary

MANUAL OF THE TREES
OF NORTH AMERICA

(EXCLUSIVE OF MEXICO)

By

CHARLES
SPRAGUE SARGENT

Onetime Director of the Arnold Arboretum of Harvard University

With seven hundred and eighty-three illustrations by

CHARLES EDWARD FAXON
and
MARY W. GILL

Second Corrected Edition

In Two Volumes

VOL.
2

DOVER PUBLICATIONS, INC.
NEW YORK

TABLE OF CONTENTS
Volume Two

TABLE OF CONTENTS

SYNOPSIS

OF THE FAMILIES OF PLANTS DESCRIBED IN THIS BOOK

Class I. GYMNOSPERMÆ.

Resinous trees; stems formed of bark, wood, or pith, and increasing in diameter by the annual addition of a layer of wood inside the bark; flowers unisexual; stamens numerous; ovules and seeds 2 or many, borne on the face of a scale, not inclosed in an ovary; embryo with 2 or more cotyledons; leaves straight-veined, without stipules.

I. **Pinaceæ** (p. 1). Flowers usually monœcious; ovules 2 or several; fruit a woody cone (*in Juniperus berry-like*); cotyledons 2 or many; leaves needle-shaped, linear or scale-like, persistent (*deciduous in Larix and Taxodium*).

II. **Taxaceæ** (p. 90). Flowers diœcious, axillary, solitary; ovules 1; fruit surrounded by or inclosed in the enlarged fleshy aril-like disk of the flower; cotyledons 2; leaves linear, alternate, persistent.

Class II. ANGIOSPERMÆ.

Carpels or pistils consisting of a closed cavity containing the ovules and becoming the fruit.

Division I. MONOCOTYLEDONES.

Stems with woody fibres distributed irregularly through them, but without pith or annual layers of growth; parts of the flower in 3's; ovary superior, 3-celled; embryo with a single cotyledon; leaves parallel-veined, persistent, without stipules.

III. **Palmæ** (p. 96). Ovule solitary; fruit baccate or drupaceous, 1 or rarely 2 or 3-seeded; leaves alternate, pinnate, flabellate or orbicular, persistent.

IV. **Liliaceæ** (p. 110). Ovules numerous in each cell; fruit 3-celled, capsular or baccate; leaves linear-lanceolate.

Division II. DICOTYLEDONES.

Stems formed of bark, wood, and pith, and increasing by the addition of an annual layer of wood inside the bark; parts of the flower mostly in 4's or 5's; embryo with a pair of opposite cotyledons; leaves netted-veined.

SUBDIVISION 1. APETALÆ. Flowers without a corolla and sometimes without a calyx.

Section 1. Flowers in unisexual aments (*female flowers of Juglans and Quercus solitary or in spikes*); ovary inferior (*superior in Leitneriaceæ*) when a calyx is present.

V. **Salicaceæ** (p. 119). Flowers diœcious, without a calyx. Fruit a 2–4-valved capsule. Leaves simple, alternate, with stipules, deciduous.

VI. **Myricaceæ** (p. 163). Flowers monœcious or diœcious; fruit a dry drupe, covered with waxy exudations; leaves simple, alternate, resinous-punctate, persistent.

VII. **Leitneriaceæ** (p. 167). Flowers diœcious, the staminate without a calyx; ovary superior; fruit a compressed oblong drupe; leaves alternate, simple, without stipules, deciduous.

VIII. **Juglandaceæ** (p. 168). Flowers monœcious; fruit a nut inclosed in an indehiscent (Juglans) or 4-valved (Carya) fleshy or woody shell; leaves alternate, unequally pinnate without stipules, deciduous.

IX. **Betulaceæ** (p. 200). Flowers monœcious; fruit a nut at the base of an open leaf-like involucre (Carpinus), in a sack-like involucre (Ostrya), in the axil of a scale of an ament (Betula), or of a woody strobile (Alnus); leaves alternate, simple, with stipules, deciduous.

X. **Fagaceæ** (p. 227). Flowers monœcious; fruit a nut more or less inclosed in a woody often spiny involucre; leaves alternate, simple, with stipules, deciduous (*in some species of Quercus and in Castanopsis and Lithocarpus persistent*).

Section 2. Flowers unisexual (*perfect in Ulmus*); calyx regular, the stamens as many as its lobes and opposite them; ovary superior, 1-celled; seed 1.

XI. **Ulmaceæ** (p. 308). Fruit a compressed winged samara (Ulmus), a drupe (Celtis and Trema), or nut-like (Planera), leaves simple, alternate, with stipules, deciduous (*persistent in Trema*).

XII. **Moraceæ** (p. 328). Flowers in ament-like spikes or heads; fruit drupaceous, inclosed in the thickened calyx and united into a compound fruit, oblong and succulent (Morus), large, dry and globose (Toxylon), or immersed in the fleshy receptacle of the flower (Ficus); leaves simple, alternate, with stipules, deciduous (*persistent in Ficus*).

Section 3. Flowers usually perfect; ovary superior or partly inferior, 1-4celled; leaves simple, persistent in the North American species.

XIII. **Olacaceæ** (p. 336). Calyx and corolla 4–6-lobed; ovary 1–4-celled; fruit a drupe more or less inclosed in the enlarged disk of the flower; leaves alternate or fascicled, without stipules.

XIV. **Polygonaceæ** (p. 338). Calyx 5-lobed; ovary 1-celled; fruit a nutlet inclosed in the thickened calyx; leaves alternate, their stipules sheathing the stems.

XV. **Nyctaginaceæ** (p. 340). Calyx 5-lobed; ovary 1-celled; fruit a nutlet inclosed in the thickened calyx; leaves alternate or opposite, without stipules.

SUBDIVISION 2. PETALATÆ. Flowers with both calyx and corolla (*without a corolla in Lauraceæ, in Liquidambar in Hamamelidaceæ, in Cercocarpus in Rosaceæ, in Euphorbiaceæ, in some species of Acer, in Reynosia, Condalia, and Krugiodendron in Rhamnaceæ, in Fremontia in Sterculiaceæ, in Chytraculia in Myrtaceæ, in Conocarpus in Combretaceæ and in some species of Fraxinus in Oleaceæ*). Section 1. POLYPETALÆ. Corolla of separate petals.

A. Ovary superior (*partly inferior in Hamamelidaceæ; inferior in Malus, Sorbus, Heteromeles, Cratægus, and Amelanchier in Rosaceæ*).

XVI. **Magnoliaceæ** (p. 342). Flowers perfect; sepals and petals in 3 or 4 rows of 3 each; fruit cone-like, composed of numerous cohering carpels; leaves simple, alternate, their stipules inclosing the leaf-buds, deciduous or rarely persistent.

XVII. **Annonaceæ** (p. 353). Flowers perfect; sepals 3; petals 6 in 2 series; fruit a pulpy berry developed from 1 or from the union of several carpels; leaves simple, alternate, without stipules, deciduous or persistent.

XVIII. **Lauraceæ** (p. 356). Flowers perfect or unisexual; corolla 0; fruit a 1-seeded drupe or berry; leaves simple, alternate, punctate, without stipules, persistent (*deciduous in Sassafras*).

XIX. **Capparidaceæ** (p. 365). Flowers perfect; sepals and petals 4; fruit baccate, elongated, dehiscent; leaves alternate, simple, without stipules, persistent.

XX. **Hamamelidaceæ** (p. 366). Flowers perfect or unisexual; sepals and petals 5 (*corolla 0 in Liquidambar*); ovary partly inferior; fruit a 2-celled woody capsule opening at the summit; leaves simple, alternate, with stipules, deciduous.

XXI. **Platanaceæ** (p. 371). Flowers monœcious, in dense unisexual capitate heads; fruit an akene; leaves simple, alternate, with stipules, deciduous.

XXII. **Rosaceæ** (p. 376). Flowers perfect; sepals and petals 5 (*petals 0 in Cercocarpus*); ovary inferior in Malus, Sorbus, Heteromeles, Cratægus, and Amelanchier; fruit a drupe (Prunus and Chrysobalanus), a capsule (Vauquelinia and Lyonothamnus), an akene (Cowania and Cercocarpus), or a pome (Malus, Sorbus, Heteromeles, Cratægus, and Amelanchier); leaves simple or pinnately compound, alternate (*opposite in Lyonothamnus*), with stipules, deciduous or persistent.

XXIII. **Leguminosæ** (p. 585). Flowers perfect, regular or irregular; fruit a legume; leaves compound, or simple (Dalea), alternate, with stipules, deciduous or persistent.

XXIV. **Zygophyllaceæ** (p. 630). Flowers perfect; calyx 5-lobed; petals 5; fruit capsular. becoming fleshy; leaves opposite, pinnate, with stipules, persistent.

XXV. **Malpighiaceæ** (p. 631). Flowers usually perfect rarely dimorphous; calyx 5-lobed: petals 5, unguiculate; fruit a drupe or samara; leaves opposite, simple, entire, persistent; often with stipules.

XXVI. **Rutaceæ** (p. 633). Flowers unisexual or perfect; fruit a capsule (Xanthoxylum), a samara (Ptelea), of indehiscent winged 1-seeded carpels (Helietta), or a drupe (Amyris); leaves alternate or opposite, compound, glandular-punctate, without stipules, persistent or rarely deciduous (0 in Canotia).

XXVII. **Simaroubaceæ** (p. 641). Flowers diœcious, calyx 5-lobed; petals 5; fruit drupaceous (Simarouba), baccate (Picramnia), a samara (Alvaradoa); leaves alternate, equally pinnate, without stipules, persistent.

XXVIII. **Burseraceæ** (p. 645). Flowers perfect; calyx 4 or 5-parted; petals 5; fruit a drupe; leaves alternate, compound, without stipules, persistent.

XXIX. **Meliaceæ** (p. 648). Flowers perfect; calyx 5-lobed; petals 5; fruit a 5-celled dehiscent capsule; leaves alternate, equally pinnate, without stipules, persistent.

XXX. **Euphorbiaceæ** (p. 649). Flowers perfect; calyx 4–6-parted (Drypetes), 3-lobed (Hippomane), or 0 (Gymnanthes); petals 0; fruit a drupe (Drypetes and Hippomane), or a 3-lobed capsule (Gymnanthes).

XXXI. **Anacardiaceæ** (p. 655). Flowers usually unisexual, diœcious or polygamo-diœcious (*Pistacia without a calyx, and without a corolla in the North American species*); fruit a dry drupe; leaves simple or compound, alternate, without stipules, deciduous (*persistent in Pistacia and in one species of Rhus*).

XXXII. **Cyrillaceæ** (p. 665). Flowers perfect; calyx 5–8-lobed; petals 5–8; fruit an indehiscent capsule; leaves alternate, without stipules, persistent (*more or less deciduous in Cyrilla*).

XXXIII. **Aquifoliaceæ** (p. 668). Flowers polygamo-diœcious; calyx 4 or 5-lobed; petals 5; fruit a drupe, with 4–8 1-seeded nutlets; leaves alternate, simple, with stipules, persistent or deciduous.

XXXIV. **Celastraceæ** (p. 674). Flowers perfect, polygamous or diœcious; calyx 4 or 5-lobed; petals 4 or 5; fruit a drupe, or a capsule (Evonymus); leaves simple, opposite or alternate, with or without stipules, persistent (*deciduous in Evonymus*).

XXXV. **Aceraceæ** (p. 681). Flowers diœcious or monœciously polygamous; calyx usually 5-parted; petals usually 5, or 0; fruit of 2 long-winged samara joined at the base; leaves opposite, simple or rarely pinnate, without or rarely with stipules, deciduous.

XXXVI. **Hippocastanaceæ** (p. 702). Flowers perfect, irregular; calyx 5-lobed; petals 4 or 5, unequal; fruit a 3-celled 3-valved capsule; leaves opposite, digitately compound. long-petiolate, without stipules, deciduous.

XXXVII. **Sapindaceæ** (p. 711). Flowers polygamous; calyx 4 or 5-lobed; corolla of 4 or 5 petals; fruit a berry (Sapindus and Exothea), a drupe (Hypelate), or a 3-valved capsule (Ungnadia); leaves alternate, compound, without stipules, persistent, or deciduous (Ungnadia).

XXXVIII. **Rhamnaceæ** (p. 718). Flowers usually perfect; calyx 4 or 5-lobed; petals 4 or 5 (0 in Reynosia, Condalia, and Krugiodendron); fruit drupaceous; leaves simple, alternate (*mostly opposite in Reynosia and Krugiodendron*), with stipules, persistent (*deciduous in some species of Rhamnus*).

XXXIX. **Tiliaceæ** (p. 732). Flowers perfect; sepals and petals 5; fruit a nut-like berry; leaves simple, alternate, mostly oblique at base, with stipules, deciduous.

XL. **Sterculiaceæ** (p. 749). Flowers perfect; calyx 5-lobed; petals 0; fruit a 4 or 5-valved dehiscent capsule; leaves simple, alternate, with stipules, persistent.

XLI. **Theaceæ** (p. 750). Flowers perfect; sepals and petals 5; fruit a 5-celled woody dehiscent capsule, loculicidally dehiscent; leaves simple, alternate, without stipules, persistent or deciduous.

XLII. **Canellaceæ** (p. 753). Flowers perfect; sepals 3; petals 5; filaments united into a tube; fruit a berry; leaves simple, alternate, without stipules, persistent.

XLIII. **Kœberliniaceæ** (p. 754). Flowers perfect; sepals and petals 4, minute; leaves bract-like, alternate, without stipules, caducous.

XLIV. **Caricaceæ** (p. 755). Flowers unisexual or perfect; calyx 5-lobed; petals 5; fruit baccate; leaves palmately lobed or digitate, alternate, without stipules, persistent.

B. Ovary inferior *(partly inferior in Rhizophora)*.

XLV. **Cactaceæ** (p. 757). Flowers perfect; petals and sepals numerous; fruit a berry; leaves usually wanting.

XLVI. **Rhizophoraceæ** (p. 763). Flowers perfect; calyx 4-parted; petals 4; ovary partly inferior; fruit a 1-celled 1-seeded berry perforated at apex by the germinating embryo; leaves simple, opposite, entire, with stipules, persistent.

XLVII. **Combretaceæ** (p. 764). Flowers perfect or polygamous; calyx 5-lobed; petals 5 *(0 in Conocarpus)*; fruit drupaceous; leaves simple, alternate or opposite, without stipules, persistent.

XLVIII. **Myrtaceæ** (p. 768). Flowers perfect; calyx usually 4-lobed, or reduced to a single body forming a deciduous lid to the flower (Chytraculia); petals usually 4 *(0 in Chytraculia)*; fruit a berry; leaves simple, opposite, pellucid-punctate, without stipules, persistent.

XLIX. **Melastomaceæ** (p. 776). Flowers perfect; calyx and corolla 4 or 5-lobed; stamens as many or twice as many as the lobes of the corolla; fruit capsular or baccate, inclosed in the tube of the calyx; leaves opposite, rarely verticillate, 3–9-nerved, without stipules.

L. **Araliaceæ** (p. 777). Flowers perfect or polygamous; sepals and petals usually 5; fruit a drupe; leaves twice pinnate, alternate, with stipules, deciduous.

LI. **Nyssaceæ** (p. 779). Flowers diœcious, polygamous, diœcious or perfect; calyx 5-toothed or lobed; petals 5 or more, imbricate in the bud, or 0; stamens as many or twice as many as the petals; fruit drupaceous (Nyssa), usually 1-celled and 1-seeded; leaves alternate, deciduous, without stipules.

LII. **Cornaceæ** (p. 784). Flowers perfect or polygamo-diœcious; calyx 4 or 5-toothed; petals 4 or 5; fruit a fleshy drupe; leaves simple, opposite *(alternate in one species of Cornus)*, without stipules, deciduous.

Section 2. GAMOPETALÆ. Corolla of united petals *(divided in Elliottia in Ericaceæ, 0 in some species of Fraxinus in Oleaceæ)*.

A. OVARY SUPERIOR *(inferior in Vaccinium in Ericaceæ, partly inferior in Symplocaceæ and Styracaceæ)*.

LIII. **Ericaceæ** (p. 790). Flowers perfect; calyx and corolla 5-lobed *(in Elliottia corolla of 4 petals)*; *(ovary inferior in Vaccinium)*; fruit capsular, drupaceous or baccate; leaves simple, alternate, without stipules, persistent *(deciduous in Elliottia and Oxydendrum)*.

LIV. **Theophrastaceæ** (p. 804). Flowers perfect, with staminodia; sepals and petals 5; stamens 5; fruit a berry; leaves simple, opposite or alternate, entire, without stipules.

LV. **Myrsinaceæ** (p. 805). Flowers perfect; calyx and corolla 5-lobed; stamens 5; fruit a drupe; leaves simple, alternate, entire, without stipules, persistent.

LVI. **Sapotaceæ** (p. 808). Flowers perfect; calyx 5-lobed; corolla 5-lobed *(6-lobed in Mimusops)*, often with as many or twice as many internal appendages borne on its throat; fruit a berry; leaves simple, alternate, without stipules, persistent *(deciduous in some species of Bumelia)*.

LVII. **Ebenaceæ** (p. 820). Flowers perfect, diœcious, or polygamous; calyx and corolla 4-lobed; fruit a 1 or several-seeded berry; leaves simple, alternate, entire, without stipules, deciduous.

LVIII. **Styracaceæ** (p. 824). Flowers perfect; calyx 4 or 5-toothed; corolla 4 or 5-lobed or divided nearly to the base, or rarely 6 or 7-lobed; ovary superior or partly superior; fruit a drupe; leaves simple, alternate, without stipules, deciduous; pubescence mostly scurfy or stellate.

LIX. **Symplocaceæ** (p. 830). Flowers perfect; calyx and corolla 5-lobed; ovary inferior or partly inferior; fruit a drupe; leaves simple, alternate, without stipules, deciduous; pubescence simple.

LX. **Oleaceæ** (p. 832). Flowers perfect or polygamo-diœcious; calyx 4-lobed *(0 in some species of Fraxinus)*; corolla 2–6-parted *(0 in some species of Fraxinus)*; fruit a winged samara (Fraxinus) or a fleshy drupe (Forestiera, Chionanthus and Osmanthus); leaves pinnate (Fraxinus) or simple, opposite, without stipules, deciduous *(persistent in Osmanthus)*.

LXI. **Borraginaceæ** (p. 858). Flowers perfect or polygamous; calyx and corolla 5-lobed; fruit a drupe; leaves simple, alternate, scabrous-pubescent, without stipules, persistent or tardily deciduous.

LXII. **Verbenaceæ** (p. 864). Flowers perfect; calyx 5-lobed; corolla 4 or 5-lobed; fruit a drupe or a 1-seeded capsule; leaves simple, opposite, without stipules, persistent.

LXIII. **Solanaceæ** (p. 867).   Flowers perfect; calyx campanulate, usually 5-lobed; corolla usually 5-lobed; fruit baccate, surrounded at base by the enlarged calyx; leaves alternate, rarely opposite, without stipules.

LXIV. **Bignoniaceæ** (p. 868).   Flowers perfect; calyx bilabiate; corolla bilabiate, 5-lobed; fruit a woody capsule (Catalpa and Chilopsis) or a berry (Enallagma); leaves simple, opposite (*sometimes alternate in Chilopsis*), without stipules, deciduous (*persistent in Enallagma*).

B. Ovary inferior (*partly superior in Sambucus in Caprifoliaceæ*).

LXV. **Rubiaceæ** (p. 875).   Flowers perfect; calyx and corolla 4 or 5-lobed; fruit a capsule (Exostema and Pinckneya), a drupe (Guettarda), or nut-like (Cephalanthus); leaves simple opposite, or in verticils of 3 (Cephalanthus), with stipules, persistent (*deciduous in Pinckneya and Cephalanthus*).

LXVI. **Caprifoliaceæ** (p. 882).   Flowers perfect; calyx and corolla 5-lobed; fruit a drupe; leaves unequally pinnate (Sambucus) or simple (Viburnum), opposite, without stipules, deciduous in North American species.

ANALYTICAL KEY

TO THE GENERA OF PLANTS INCLUDED IN THIS BOOK, BASED CHIEFLY ON THE CHARACTER OF THE LEAVES

I. **Leaves parallel-veined, alternate, persistent, clustered at the end of the stem or branches. Monocotyledones.**
Stem simple; leaves stalked.
Leaves fan-shaped.
Leaf stalks unarmed.
Rachis short; leaves usually silvery white below.
Leaves 2°–4° in diameter (*green below in No. 2*), their segments undivided at
apex. **Thrinax** (p. 96).
Leaves 18′–24′ in diameter, their segments divided at apex.
Coccothrinax (p. 100).
Rachis elongated; leaves green below, their segments divided at apex.
Sabal (p. 101).
Leaf stalks armed with marginal teeth or spines.
Leaf stalks furnished irregularly with broad thin large and small, straight or hooked
spines confluent into a thin bright orange-colored cartilaginous margin; leaves
longer than wide, divided nearly to the middle into segments parted at apex and
separating on the margins into thin fibres. **Washingtonia** (p. 104).
Leaf stalks furnished with stout or slender flattened teeth; leaves suborbicular,
divided to the middle or nearly to the base into segments parted at apex; seg-
ments of the blade not separating on the margin into thin fibres.
Accœlorraphe (p. 105).
Leaves pinnate.
Leaves 10°–12° in length, their pinnæ 2½°–3° long and often 1½° wide, deep green.
Roystonea (p. 107).
Leaves 5°–6° long, their pinnæ 18′ long and 1′ wide, dark yellow-green above, pale and
glaucous below. **Pseudophœnix** (p. 109).
Stem simple or branched; leaves sessile, lanceolate, long- and usually sharp-pointed at
apex. **Yucca** (p. 110).

II. **Leaves 1-nerved, needle-shaped, linear or scale-like, persistent (deciduous in Larix and Taxodium). Gymnospermæ.**

1. LEAVES PERSISTENT.

a Leaves fascicled, needle-shaped, in 1–5-leafed clusters enclosed at base in a membranaceous sheath. **Pinus** (p. 2).
aa Leaves scattered, usually linear.
b Leaves linear, often obtuse or emarginate.
Base of the leaves persistent on the branches.
Leaves sessile, 4-sided, or flattened and stomatiferous above. **Picea** (p. 34).
Leaves stalked, flattened and stomatiferous below, or angular, often appearing 2-ranked. **Tsuga** (p. 42).
Base of the leaves not persistent on the branches; leaves often appearing
2-ranked.
Leaves stalked, flattened, stomatiferous below; winter-buds pointed, not
resinous. **Pseudotsuga** (p. 47).
Leaves sessile, flattened and often grooved on the upper side, or quadrangular,
rarely stomatiferous above, on upper fertile branches often crowded;
winter-buds obtuse, resinous (*except in No. 9*). **Abies** (p. 50).
bb Leaves linear-lanceolate, rigid, acuminate, spirally disposed, appearing 2-ranked
by a twist in the petiole.

Leaves abruptly contracted at base, long-pointed, with pale bands of stomata on the lower surface on each side of the midveins; fruit drupelike.
Torreya (p. 91).
Leaves gradually narrowed at base, short-pointed, paler, and without distinct bands of stomata on the lower surface; fruit berry-like. **Taxus** (p. 93).
bbb Leaves ovate-lanceolate and scale-like, spreading in 2 ranks or linear on the same tree, acute, compressed, keeled on the back and closely appressed or spreading at apex. **Sequoia** (p. 61).
aaa Leaves opposite or whorled, usually scale-like.
Internodes distinctly longer than broad; branchlets flattened, of nearly equal color on both sides; leaves eglandular. **Libocedrus** (p. 65).
Internodes about as long as broad, often pale below, usually glandular.
Branchlets flattened.
Branchlets in one plane, much flattened, $\frac{1}{12}'-\frac{1}{6}'$ broad. **Thuja** (p. 67).
Branchlets slightly flattened, $\frac{1}{24}'-\frac{1}{16}'$ broad. **Chamæcyparis** (p. 75).
Branchlets terete or 4-angled.
Branchlets more or less in one plane; fruit a cone. **Cupressus** (p. 69).
Branchlets not in one plane, fruit a berry (*leaves needle-shaped, in whorls of 3 in No. 1*). **Juniperus** (p. 78).

2. Leaves Deciduous.

Leaves in many-leafed clusters on short lateral spurs. **Larix** (p. 31).
Leaves spreading in 2 ranks. **Taxodium** (p. 63).

III. Leaves netted-veined, rarely scale-like or wanting. Dicotyledones.

A. LEAVES OPPOSITE. (B, see p. xvii).

1. Leaves Simple. (2, see p. xvi).

* Leaves persistent.
a Leaves with stipules.
b Leaves entire or occasionally slightly crenate or serrate.
c Leaves emarginate at apex, very short-stalked, $1\frac{1}{2}'-2'$ long.
Leaves obovate, gradually narrowed into the petiole. **Gyminda** (p. 678).
Leaves oval to oblong, rounded or broad-cuneate (*rarely alternate*).
Branchlets densely velutinous. **Krugiodendron** (p. 721).
Branchlets slightly puberulous at first, soon glabrous.
Reynosia (p. 720).
cc Leaves not emarginate at apex.
Leaves obtuse, rarely acutish or abruptly short-pointed.
Leaves elliptic, $3\frac{1}{2}'-5'$ long. **Rhizophora** (p. 763).
Leaves obovate, usually rounded at apex, $\frac{3}{4}'-2'$ long.
Byrsonima (p. 632).
Leaves acute to acuminate.
Leaves oblong-ovate to lanceolate; branchlets glabrous.
Exostema (p. 877).
Leaves broad-elliptic to oblong-elliptic; branchlets villose.
Guettarda (p. 879).
bb Leaves serrate (*often pinnate*). **Lyonothamnus** (p. 378).
a1 Leaves without stipules.
Petioles biglandular; leaves obtuse or emarginate, $1\frac{1}{2}'-2\frac{1}{2}'$ long.
Laguncularia (p. 767).
Petioles without glands.
Leaves furnished below with small dark glands, slightly aromatic; petioles short.
Leaves oblong to oblong-ovate and acuminate or elliptic and bluntly short-pointed. **Calyptranthes** (p. 769).
Leaves ovate, obovate or elliptic. **Eugenia** (p. 770).
Leaves without glands.

Leaves green and glabrous below.
Leaves obtuse or emarginate at apex (*rarely alternate*), 1'-1½' long.
Torrubia (p. 341).
Leaves acute, acuminate, or sometimes rounded or emarginate, 3'-5' long.
Leaves distinctly veined. **Citharexylon** (p. 864).
Leaves obscurely veined. **Osmanthus** (p. 856).
Leaves hoary tomentulose or scurfy below.
Leaves strongly 3-nerved, acuminate, densely scurfy below.
Tetrazygia (p. 776).
Leaves penniveined, rounded or acute at apex, hoary tomentulose below.
Avicennia (p. 865).

** Leaves deciduous.

a Leaves without lobes.
  b Leaves serrate.
    Winter-buds with several opposite outer scales.
    Leaves puberulous below, closely and finely serrate; axillary buds solitary.
Evonymus (p. 675).
    Leaves glabrous below, remotely crenate-serrulate; axillary buds several,
    superposed. **Forestiera** (p. 853).
    Winter-buds enclosed in 2 large opposite scales. **Viburnum** (p. 886).
  bb Leaves entire.
    c Leaves without stipules.
      Leaves suborbicular or elliptic to oblong.
      Leaves rounded or acutish at apex, 1'-2' long, occasionally 3-foliolate,
      glabrous; branchlets quadrangular. **Fraxinus anomala** (p. 837).
      Leaves acuminate or acute at apex, 3'-4' long.
      Leaf-scars connected by a transverse line, with 3 bundle-traces; branch-
      lets slender, appressed-pubescent. **Cornus** (p. 785).
      Leaf-scars not connected, with 1 bundle-trace; branchlets stout, villose,
      puberulous or glabrous. **Chionanthus** (p. 855).
      Leaves broad-ovate, cordate, acuminate, 5'-12' long, on long petioles.
Catalpa (p. 870).
      Leaves linear to linear-lanceolate, short-stalked or sessile (*sometimes alter-
      nate*). **Chilopsis** (p. 869).
    cc Leaves with persistent stipules, entire.
      Leaves oval or ovate; winter-buds resinous, the terminal up to ½' in length.
Pinckneya (p. 876).
      Leaves ovate to lanceolate; winter-buds minute. **Cephalanthus** (p. 878).
aa Leaves palmately lobed. **Acer** (p. 681).

2. LEAVES COMPOUND.

a Leaves persistent, with stipules.
  Leaves equally pinnate; leaflets entire. **Guaiacum** (p. 630).
  Leaves unequally pinnately parted into 3-8 linear-lanceolate segments (*sometimes
  entire*). **Lyonothamnus** (p. 378).
  Leaves trifoliate.
    Leaflets stalked. **Amyris** (p. 640).
    Leaflets sessile. **Helietta** (p. 637).
aa Leaves deciduous.
  Leaves unequally pinnate or trifoliate.
    Leaflets crenate-serrate or entire, the veins arching within the margins; stipules
    wanting; winter-buds with several opposite scales. **Fraxinus** (p. 833).
    Leaflets sharply or incisely serrate, the primary veins extending to the teeth.
      Leaflets 3-7, incisely serrate; stipules present; winter-buds with 1 pair of obtuse
      outer scales. **Acer Negundo** (p. 699).
      Leaflets 5-9, sharply serrate; stipules present; winter-buds with many opposite
      acute scales; pith thick. **Sambucus** (p. 882).
  Leaves digitate, with 5-7, sharply serrate leaflets; terminal buds large.
Æsculus (p. 702).

B. LEAVES ALTERNATE.

1. LEAVES SIMPLE. (2, see p. xxii).

*Leaves persistent. (** see p. xx).

a Leaves deeply 3–5-lobed, $\frac{1}{4}$–$\frac{1}{2}$' long, with linear lobes, hoary tomentose below.
Cowania (p. 549).

  aa Leaves palmately lobed.
    Leaves stellate-pubescent, about $1\frac{1}{2}$' in diameter, with stipules.
Fremontia (p. 749).
    Leaves glabrous, 1°–2° in diameter, without stipules. **Carica** (p. 755).

  aaa Leaves not lobed or pinnately lobed.
    b Branches spinescent.
      Leaves clustered at the end of the branches, at least 2'–3' long.
Bucida (p. 765).
      Leaves fascicled on lateral branchlets, obtuse or emarginate, pale and glabrous
        beneath. **Bumelia angustifolia** (p. 816).
      Leaves scattered.
        Leaves generally obovate, mucronate, not more than $\frac{1}{2}$'–1' long, glabrous and
          green or brownish tomentulose beneath. **Condalia** (p. 719).
        Leaves elliptic-ovate to oblong, obtuse or emarginate, glabrous, 1–2 cm. long.
Ximenia (p. 337).

    bb Branches not spinescent.
      c Leaves serrate, or lobed (*in some species of Quercus*). (*cc*, see p. xviii).
        d Juice watery. (*dd*, see p. xviii).
          e Stipules present. (*ee*, see p. xviii).
            f Primary veins extending straight to the teeth.
              Leaves and branchlets glabrous or pubescent to tomentose with
                fascicled hairs.
                Leaves fulvous-tomentose beneath, repand-dentate, 3'–5'
                  long. **Lithocarpus** (p. 236).
                Leaves glabrous or grayish to whitish tomentose beneath,
                  entire, lobed or dentate. **Quercus sp. 21–34** (p. 268).
              Leaves and branchlets coated with simpled silky or woolly
                hairs at least while young. not more than $2\frac{1}{2}$' long.
Cercocarpus (p. 550).
            ff Primary veins arching and united within the margin.
              Leaves 3-nerved from the base. **Ceanothus** (p. 726).
              Leaves not 3-nerved.
                Leaves acute.
                  Leaves sinuately dentate, with few spiny teeth (*rarely en-*
                    tire), glabrous. **Ilex opaca** (p. 669).
                  Leaves serrate.
                    Leaves tomentose below; branchlets tomentose.
                    Leaves narrow-lanceolate, glabrous and smooth above.
Vauquelinia (p. 377).
                    Leaves ovate, cordate, scabrate above. **Trema** (p. 327).
                    Leaves glabrous below. **Heteromeles** (p. 392).
                Leaves entire, very rarely toothed.
                  Leaves elliptic, glabrous. **Prunus caroliniana** (p. 579).
                Leaves oblanceolate, pubescent beneath when young.
Ilex Cassine (p. 670).
             Leaves obtuse, sometimes mucronate.
             Leaves spinose-serrate, glabrous.
                Leaves broad-ovate to suborbicular or elliptic; branch-
                lets dark red-brown, spinescent.
Rhamnus crocea (p. 723).
                Leaves ovate to ovate-lanceolate; branchlets yellow or
                orange-colored, not spinescent.
Prunus ilicifolia (p. 581).
            Leaves crenate (*often entire*), oval to oblong.
Ilex vomitoria (p. 671).

    ee Stipules wanting.
         Leaves resinous-dotted, aromatic, $1\frac{1}{2}'$–$4'$ long.   **Myrica** (p. 163).
         Leaves not resinous-dotted, crenately serrate, $4'$–$6'$ long.
            Leaves dark green, glabrous below. **Gordonia Lasianthus** (p. 751).
            Leaves yellowish green, pubescent below, sometimes nearly entire.
                 Symplocos (p. 831).
   dd Juice milky.
       Petioles $2\frac{1}{2}'$–$4'$ long; leaves broad-ovate.   **Hippomane** (p. 652).
       Petioles about $\frac{1}{4}'$ long; leaves elliptic to oblong-lanceolate.
                 Gymnanthes (p. 654).
cc Leaves entire (*rarely sparingly toothed on vigorous branchlets*).
   d Stipules present.
     e Stipules connate, at least at first.
       Stipules persistent, forming a sheath surrounding the branch above
         the node; leaves obtuse.   **Coccolobis** (p. 338).
       Stipules deciduous, enveloping the unfolded leaf.
         Leaves ferrugineous-tomentose beneath.
                 Magnolia grandiflora (p. 345).
         Leaves glabrous beneath, with milky juice.   **Ficus** (p. 333).
     ee Stipules free.
       f Juice milky; leaves oval to oblong, $3'$–$5'$ long. **Drypetes** (p. 650).
       ff Juice watery.
         g Leaves obtuse or emarginate at apex.
           Leaves with ferrugineous scales beneath, their petioles
            slender.   **Capparis** (p. 365).
           Leaves without ferrugineous scales.
            Leaves soft-pubescent on both sides.
                 Colubrina cubensis (p. 730).
            Leaves glabrous at least at maturity.
              Leaves rarely $2'$–$3'$ long, standing on the branch at
               acute angles.   **Chrysobalanus** (p. 583).
              Leaves rarely more than $1'$ long, spreading (sometimes
               3-nerved).   **Ceanothus spinosus** (p. 728).
         gg Leaves acute or acutish.
           Petioles with 2 glands.   **Conocarpus** (p. 766).
           Petioles without glands.
            Leaves and branchlets more or less pubescent, at least
            while young.
            Leaves fascicled except on vigorous branchlets.
                 Cercocarpus (p. 550).
            Leaves not fascicled.
             Winter-buds minute, with few pointed scales.
              Leaves rounded or nearly rounded at base.
                 Colubrina sp. 1, 3 (p. 729).
              Leaves broad-cuneate at base.
                 Ilex Cassine (p. 670).
             Winter-buds conspicuous, with numerous scales.
              Leaves usually lanceolate, entire, covered below
               with yellow scales.   **Castanopsis** (p. 234).
              Leaves oblong or oblong-obovate, repand-dentate,
               fibrous tomentose below. **Lithocarpus** (p. 236).
           Leaves and branchlets glabrous.
            Leaf-scar with 1 bundle-trace. **Ilex Krugiana** (p. 672).
            Leaf-scar with 3 bundle-traces. Cherry Laurels.
                 Prunus sp. 19–22 (p. 579).
  dd Stipules wanting.
     e Leaves aromatic when bruised.
       Leaves resinous-dotted.   **Myrica** (p. 163).
       Leaves not resinous-dotted.
         Leaves obtuse, obovate, glabrous.   **Canella** (p. 753).
         Leaves acute.

Leaves mostly rounded at the narrowed base, ovate to oblong, acute, glabrous.   **Annona** (p. 354).
Leaves more or less cuneate at base, elliptic to lanceolate, usually acuminate.
Leaves abruptly long-acuminate, glabrous, the margin undulate; branchlets red-brown.   **Misanteca** (p. 364).
Leaves gradually acuminate or nearly acute.
Leaves strongly reticulate beneath.
Branchlets glabrous, light grayish brown; leaves glabrous, light green beneath.   **Ocotea** (p. 359).
Branchlets pubescent while young, greenish or yellowish; leaves pale beneath, pubescent while young.
Umbellularia (p. 360).
Leaves not or slightly reticulate, glaucous, glabrous or pubescent beneath.   **Persea** (p. 356).
ee Leaves not aromatic.
  f Leaves acute or acutish.
Leaves obovate, gradually narrowed into short petioles.
Leaves 2'-2½' long.   **Schæfferia** (p. 679).
Leaves at least 6'-8' long.   **Enallagma** (p. 873).
Leaves elliptic to oblong or ovate.
Leaves rough or pubescent above, pubescent below, subcordate to cuneate at base.
Leaves stellate-pubescent.   **Solanum** (p. 867).
Leaves scabrous above.
Petiole ⅛'-¼' long; leaves oval or oblong, 1¼'-4' long.
Ehretia (p. 862).
Petiole 1'-1½' long; leaves ovate to oblong-ovate, 3'-7' long.   **Cordia** (p. 858).
Leaves smooth above.
Winter-buds scaly.
Leaves covered below with ferrugineous or pale scales, 1'-3' long.   **Lyonia** (p. 797).
Leaves glabrous or nearly so below.
Leaves ovate-lanceolate or obovate-lanceolate, 4'-12' long, usually clustered at end of branchlet, veinlets below obscure.·   **Rhododendron** (p. 792).
Leaves elliptic or oval to oblong or lanceolate.
Leaves light yellowish green below and without distinctly visible veins or veinlets, entire, 3'-4' long.
Kalmia (p. 794).
Leaves pale below and more or less distinctly reticulate, occasionally serrate or denticulate, 1'-5' long; bark of branches red.   **Arbutus** (p. 799).
Winter-buds naked.
Leaves pubescent below when unfolding.
Mature leaves nearly glabrous below.
Leaves oblong-lanceolate to narrow-obovate.
Dipholis (p. 810).
Leaves oval.   **Sideroxylum** (p. 809).
Mature leaves covered below with brilliant copper-colored pubescence.
Leaves glabrous below.   **Chrysophyllum** (p. 817).
Leaves marked by minute black dots, ovate to oblong-lanceolate.   **Ardisia** (p. 806).
• Leaves lepidote, oblong-obovate.   **Rapanea** (p. 807).
ff Leaves obtuse or emarginate at apex.
  g Leaves rounded or cordate at base, emarginate, their petioles slender.
Leaves reniform to broad-ovate, cordate; juice watery.
Cercis (p. 603).

Leaves elliptic to oblong, rounded at base; juice milky or viscid.

Leaves emarginate; petioles slender, rufous-tomentulose.
Mimusops (p. 819).

Leaves obtuse at apex; petioles stout, grayish-tomentulose or glabrous.   **Rhus integrifolia** (p. 664).

gg Leaves cuneate at base.

Petioles slender, ½' long.   **Beureria** (p. 861).

Petioles short and stout.

Leaves coriaceous, with thick revolute margins (*sometimes opposite*).   **Jacquinia** (p. 804).

Leaves subcoriaceous, slightly revolute.

Leaves reticulate-veined beneath.

Leaves oval to obovate or oblong-oval, more or less pubescent while young.   **Vaccinium** (p. 802).

Leaves oblong to oblong-obovate, glabrous.
Cyrilla (p. 666).

Leaves obscurely veined beneath, glabrous.

Leaves oblong-lanceolate, narrowed toward the emarginate apex, decurrent nearly to base of petiole.   **Cliftonia** (p. 667).

Leaves rounded at apex, distinctly petioled.
Maytenus (p. 676).

**Leaves deciduous.

† Leaves conspicuous.   (††, see p. xxii).

a Leaves entire, sometimes 3 or 4-lobed.   (*aa*, see p. xxi).

b Stipules present.

Juice milky.   **Maclura** (p. 331).

Juice watery.

Stipules connate, enveloping the young leaves, their scars encircling the branchlet.

Leaves acute or acuminate, entire; winter-buds pointed, nearly terete.
Magnolia (p. 342).

Leaves truncate, sinuately 4-lobed; winter-buds obtuse, compressed.
Liriodendron (p. 351).

Stipules distinct.

Branches spinescent; leaves glandular, caducous (*crenately serrate on vigorous shoots*).   **Dalea** (p. 621).

Branches not spinescent; leaves without glands.

Winter-buds with a single pair of connate scales.   **Salix** (p. 138).

Winter-buds with several pairs of imbricate scales.

Branchlets without a terminal bud; leaves 3-nerved.   **Celtis** (p. 318).

Branchlets with a terminal bud, leaves penniveined.
Quercus sp. 17–20 (p. 262).

bb Stipules wanting.

c Branchlets bright green and lustrous for the first 2 or 3 years; leaves sometimes 3-lobed, aromatic.   **Sassafras** (p. 362).

cc Branchlets brown or gray.

d Leaves acute or acuminate.

Leaves 10'–12' long, obovate-oblong, acuminate, glabrous, emitting a disagreeable odor.   **Asimina** (p. 353).

Leaves smaller.

Petioles very slender, 1'–2' long; leaves elliptic, acuminate.
Cornus alternifolia (p. 789).

Petioles short.

Branchlets with a terminal bud.

Leaf-scars about as long as broad; branchlets without lenticels, light reddish brown.   **Elliottia** (p. 791).

Leaf-scars crescent-shaped, broader than long, with 3 distinct bundle-traces.

Leaves pubescent on both sides, rugulose above; petioles 1′–2′ long, like the young branchlet densely pubescent.
Leitneria (p. 167).
Leaves glabrous and smooth above, glabrous or pubescent below; petioles and branchlets usually glabrous or nearly so at maturity. **Nyssa** (p. 779).
Branchlets without a terminal bud.
Pubescence consisting of simple hairs or wanting.
Leaves 4′–6′ long, pubescent beneath while young; branchlet light brown or gray. **Diospyros virginiana** (p. 821).
Leaves 1½′–3′ long, glabrous; branches light yellowish gray.
Schœpfia (p. 336)
Pubescence stellate; leaves obovate or elliptic, 2½′–5′ long, pubescent below. **Styrax** (p. 829).
dd Leaves obtuse or acute.
Branchlets not spinescent.
Leaves glabrous at maturity, their petioles slender. **Cotinus** (p. 657).
Leaves pubescent below at maturity; their petioles short and thick.
Diospyros texana (p. 823).
Branchlets spinescent; leaves often fascicled on lateral branchlets.
Bumelia (p. 812).
aa Leaves serrate or pinnately lobed.
b Stipules present. (*bb*, see p. xxii).
c Winter-buds naked.
Leaves oblique at base, the upper side rounded or subcordate, obovate, coarsely toothed. **Hamamelis** (p. 368).
Leaves equal at base, cuneate, finely serrate or crenate.
Rhamnus sp. 2, 3 (p. 724, 725).
cc Winter-buds with a single pair of connate scales.
Primary veins arching and uniting within the margins; leaves simply serrate or crenate, sometimes entire. **Salix** (p. 138).
Primary veins extending to the teeth, leaves doubly serrate, often slightly lobed. **Alnus** (p. 220).
ccc Winter-buds with several pairs of imbricate scales.
d Terminal buds wanting; branchlets prolonged by an upper axillary bud.
Juice milky; leaves usually ovate, often lobed. **Morus** (p. 328).
Juice watery; leaves not lobed.
Leaves distinctly oblique at base.
Leaves with numerous prominent lateral veins.
Leaves generally broad-ovate, simply serrate, stellate-pubescent at least while young, rarely glabrous. **Tilia** (p. 732).
Leaves never broad-ovate, usually doubly serrate, more or less pubescent with simple hairs, at least while young.
Winter-buds ovoid, usually acute, ⅓ to nearly as long as petioles; leaves 1′–7′ long, doubly serrate. **Ulmus** (p. 309).
Winter-buds subglobose, minute; leaves 2′–2½′ long, crenate-serrate. **Planera** (p. 316).
Leaves 3 or 4-nerved from the base. **Celtis** (p. 318).
Leaves slightly or not at all oblique at base.
Leaves 3-nerved from the base, glandular-crenate or glandular-serrate. **Ceanothus** (p. 726).
Leaves not or obscurely 3-nerved at base, usually doubly serrate.
Leaves blue-green; petioles ¼′–½′ long; bark smooth, gray-brown.
Carpinus (p. 201).
Leaves yellow-green.
Bark rough, furrowed; petioles ⅛′–¼′ long; leaves not resinous-glandular. **Ostrya** (p. 202).
Bark flaky or cherry-tree like; petioles ¼′–1′ long; leaves often resinous-glandular while young. **Betula** (p. 205).
dd Terminal buds present.
Primary veins arching and uniting within the margin (*extending to the margin in the lobed leaves of Malus*).

Winter-buds resinous; leaves crenate, usually truncate at base; petioles slender.   **Populus** (p. 119).
Winter-buds not resinous.
Leaf-scars with 3 bundle-traces.
Leaves involute in bud, often lobed on vigorous shoots; winter-buds obtuse, short, pubescent.   **Malus** (p. 379).
Leaves conduplicate (*or in some species of Prunus convolute*), never lobed; winter-buds acute.
Winter-buds elongated; branches never spinescent.
                                                                    Amelanchier (p. 393).
Winter-buds not elongated, ovoid; branches sometimes spinescent.   **Prunus** (p. 555).
Leaf-scars with 1 bundle-trace; leaves simply serrate.
                                                                    Ilex sp. 5-6 (p. 673).
Primary veins extending to the teeth or to the lobes.
Leaves lobed.   **Quercus sp.** 1-16, 35-50 (pp. 241, 283).
Leaves serrate-toothed.
Winter-buds with numerous scales.
Leaves lustrous beneath, remotely serrate or denticulate; winter-buds elongated, acuminate.   **Fagus** (p. 228).
Leaves pale beneath, coarsely dentate or serrate; winter-buds acute. Chestnut Oaks.   **Quercus sp.** 51-54 (p. 303).
Winter-buds with 2 pairs of scales.   **Castanea** (p. 230).
Leaves doubly or simply serrate, or lobed, with serrate lobes; branches often furnished with spines.
Leaves involute in the bud; branchlets often ending in blunt spines.
                                                                    Malus (p. 379).
Leaves conduplicate in the bud; branches usually armed with sharp-pointed single or branched axillary spines. **Cratægus** (p. 397).
bb Stipules wanting.
  c Leaves not lobed.
Leaves subcoriaceous, oblong, sometimes nearly entire, glabrous.
                                                                    Symplocos (p. 831).
  Leaves thin.
Leaves oblong-obovate, acute, pubescent beneath.
                                                                    Gordonia alatamaha (p. 752).
Leaves oblong or lanceolate, acuminate, glabrous or puberulous while young, turning scarlet in the autumn.   **Oxydendrum** (p. 796).
Leaves ovate to elliptic, stellate-pubescent or glabrous, turning yellow in the autumn.   **Halesia** (p. 824).
  cc Leaves palmately lobed.
Stipules large, foliaceous, united; branchlets without a terminal bud.
                                                                    Platanus (p. 371).
Stipules small, free, caducous; branchlets with a terminal bud.
                                                                    Liquidambar (p. 367).

†† Leaves inconspicuous or wanting; branches spiny or prickly.

Branches or stems succulent, armed with numerous prickles.
Branches and stems columnar, ribbed, continuous; leaves 0.   **Cereus** (p. 757).
Branches jointed, tuberculate; leaves scale-like.   **Opuntia** (p. 759).
Branches rigid, spinescent.
Leaves minute, narrow-obovate.
Branchlets bright green.   **Kœberlinia** (p. 754).
Branchlets red-brown.   **Dalea** (p. 621).
Leaves scale-like, caducous.   **Canotia** (p. 677).

2. LEAVES COMPOUND.

* Leaves 3-foliolate, without stipules.

Leaves persistent; leaflets obovate, entire, sessile.   **Hypelate (p. 716).**
Leaves deciduous.

Leaflets deltoid to hastate, entire, rounded at apex; branches prickly.
Erythrina (p. 627).
Leaflets ovate to oblong, acuminate, strongly scented and bitter; branches unarmed.
Ptelea (p. 639).
** Leaves twice pinnate; stipules present.

a Leaves unequally twice pinnate, 2°–4° long, deciduous; leaflets serrate, 2'–3' in length; branches and stem armed with scattered prickles. Aralia (p. 778).
aa Leaves equally twice pinnate, usually smaller; branches unarmed or armed with stipular or axillary spines (in *Parkinsonia* often apparently simply pinnate).
b Leaflets crenate; leaves simply or twice-pinnate on the same plant, deciduous, usually armed with simple or branched axillary spines. Gleditsia (p. 607).
bb Leaflets entire.
Leaflets 2–2½' long; leaves deciduous; branchlets stout, unarmed.
Gymnocladus (p. 605).
Leaflets smaller; leaves usually persistent; branchlets slender.
Branches armed with prickles or spines.
Leaves with 2 or rarely 4 pinnæ.
Branches armed with axillary spines or spiny rachises.
Pinnæ with 4–8 leaflets; branches with short axillary spines.
Cercidium (p. 613).
Pinnæ with 8–60 leaflets; branches armed with spiny rachises or rigid branchlets terminating in stout spines. Parkinsonia (p. 611).
Branches armed with stipular prickles; leaves persistent.
Pinnæ with many oblong to linear leaflets. Prosopis (p. 599).
Pinnæ with 1 pair of orbicular to broad-oblong leaflets.
Pithecolobium unguis-cati (p. 586).
Leaves with 6, or more, rarely 4, pinnæ.
Prickles usually spreading, often recurved. Acacia (p. 591).
Prickles usually more or less ascending, straight. Pithecolobium (p. 586).
Branches unarmed.
Branchlets and petioles glabrous; leaves with 2–5 pair of pinnæ, each with 40–80 leaflets. Lysiloma (p. 589).
Branchlets and petioles pubescent while young; leaves with 5–17 pair of many-foliolate pinnæ, or pinnæ 2–4 and each with 8–16 leaflets.
Leucæna (p. 596).

*** Leaves simply pinnate.

a Leaves equally pinnate.
Stipules wanting.
Leaflets 2–4, generally oblong-obovate. Exothea (p. 714).
Leaflets 6–12.
Leaflets obtuse, usually oblong-obovate.
Leaflets 8–12, 2'–3' long, pale below; leaves occasionally opposite.
Simarouba (p. 642).
Leaflets 6–8, 1'–1½' long, green below. Xanthoxylum coriaceum (p. 637).
Leaflets 6–8, acuminate. Swietenia (p. 648).
Stipules present.
Branches armed with infra-stipular spines in pairs; leaflets 10–15, usually oblong-obovate, ½'–¾' long, persistent. Olneya (p. 626).
Branches unarmed; leaflets 20–46, ovals ½'–⅔' long. Eysenhardtia (p. 620).
aa Leaves unequally pinnate.
b Stipules present.
Leaflets sharply serrate; leaves deciduous; winter-buds resinous.
Sorbus (p. 390).
Leaflets entire or crenately serrate.
Leaves deciduous.
Leaflets 7–11, 3'–4½' long; branches unarmed.
Leaflets usually alternate, thin and glabrous at maturity.
Cladrastis (p. 618).

Leaflets opposite, coriaceous, pubescent beneath at least along the veins.
Ichthyomethia (p. 628).
Leaflets 9–21, 1–2 cm. long.
Branches usually with stipular prickles, sometimes viscid.
Robinia (p. 622).
Branches unarmed, not viscid; leaflets 13–19, elliptic.
Sophora affinis (p. 617).
Leaves persistent.
Leaflets 7–9, oblong-elliptic, 1′–2½′ long; branches unarmed.
Sophora secundiflora (p. 616).
Leaflets 10–15; branches prickly. **Olneya** (p. 626).
bb Stipules wanting.
  d Leaves persistent.
Leaflets long-stalked (*sometimes nearly sessile in Xanthoxylum flavum*).
Leaflets oblong-ovate, cuneate at base.
Leaflets acuminate, glabrous. **Picramnia** (p. 643).
Leaflets obtuse, tomentose when unfolding.
Xanthoxylum flavum (p. 636).
Leaflets broad-ovate, usually rounded or subcordate at base.
Metopium (p. 658).
Leaflets sessile or nearly so.
Petiole and rachis winged.
Leaflets crenate, obovate, about ½′ long; branches prickly.
Xanthoxylum Fagara (p. 634).
Leaflets entire.
Leaflets oblong, usually acute, 3′–4′ long.
Sapindus saponaria (p. 712).
Leaflets spathulate, rounded at apex, not more than ¾′ long.
Pistacia (p. 656).
Petiole and rachis not winged.
Leaflets 7–19, acuminate, 2′–5′ long. **Sapindus marginatus** (p. 713).
Leaflets 21–41, obtuse, ½′–¾′ long. **Alvaradoa** (p. 644).
dd Leaves deciduous.
Leaflets long-stalked, 3–7, entire, acute. **Bursera** (p. 645).
Leaflets sessile or nearly so.
Branches prickly; leaflets crenate. **Xanthoxylum clava-Herculis** (p. 635).
Branches unarmed.
Juice milky or viscid; leaflets serrate or entire; rachis sometimes
winged. **Rhus species 1–3** (p. 660).
Juice watery.
Rachis without wings.
Leaflets entire, acuminate, 7–9. **Sapindus Drummondii** (p. 714).
Leaflets serrate or crenate.
Winter-buds large; leaflets 5–23, aromatic.
Winter-buds naked. **Juglans** (p. 169).
Winter-buds covered with scales. **Carya** (p. 176).
Winter-buds minute, globose, scaly; leaflets 5–7, ovate, not
aromatic. **Ungnadia** (p. 717).
Rachis winged; leaflets 10–20, entire, rounded at apex, not more than
¼′ long. **Bursera microphylla** (p. 647).

TREES OF NORTH AMERICA

III. ÆSTIVALES.

CONSPECTUS OF THE ARBORESCENT SPECIES.

Leaves glabrous with the exception of small axillary tufts of pale hairs on the lower surface, oblong-obovate; stamens 15–20; anthers pink or pale rose color.
38. **C. æstivalis** (C).
Leaves hoary-tomentose below early in the season, becoming villose with rufous hairs most
abundant on the midrib and veins; stamens 20; anthers deep rose color.
Leaves oblong-obovate, acute or broad and rounded at apex, often slightly lobed
above the middle, lustrous above; pedicels villose-pubescent.   39. **C. rufula** (C).
Leaves elliptic to oblong-cuneiform, narrowed at apex, dull above; pedicels glabrous.
40. **C. opaca** (C).

38. Cratægus æstivalis Sarg.   May Haw.   Apple Haw.

Mespilus æstivalis Walt.

Leaves oblong-obovate, rounded or acute at apex, gradually narrowed and cuneate at
base, glabrous with the exception of small axillary tufts of pale hairs, and coarsely crenately
serrate above the middle with gland-tipped teeth, beginning to unfold as the flowers open the

Fig. 390

middle of March, and when the fruit ripens at the end of May thin, dark green and lustrous
above, yellow-green below, $1\frac{1}{4}'$–$2'$ long, and $\frac{1}{3}'$–$\frac{3}{4}'$ wide, with a slender yellow midrib and obscure primary veins; petioles slender, narrow wing-margined to below the middle, rarely fur-
nished with occasional deciduous glands, about $\frac{1}{4}'$ in length; leaves at the ends of vigorous
shoots elliptic to oblong-obovate, acute and usually abruptly short-pointed at apex, concave-cuneate at base, often lobed with one or two lateral lobes.   **Flowers** $\frac{3}{4}'$ in diameter,
on pedicels about $\frac{1}{3}'$ long, in compact 2 or 3-flowered corymbs; calyx-tube narrowly obconic,
glabrous, the lobes gradually narrowed from a broad base, short, entire, without glands,
acute or acuminate and often red at apex, persistent and red on the fruit; stamens 15–20;
anthers large, pink or pale rose color; styles usually 3.   **Fruit** on a short slender erect
pedicel, about $\frac{1}{2}'$ long, usually solitary, short-oblong, scarlet, lustrous, about $\frac{1}{2}'$ in length,
the calyx persistent with erect lobes; flesh yellow, juicy, acidulous; nutlets usually 3, acute
at ends, rounded and slightly ridged on the back, $\frac{1}{4}'$ long.

A slender tree, 20°–25° high, with a tall stem 6'–8' in diameter, covered with pale flaky bark, erect or slightly spreading branches forming a narrow head, and slender straight or slightly zigzag branchlets chestnut-brown and lustrous during their first season, and dull gray-brown the following year, and armed with stout straight gray spines $\frac{1}{2}'$–$1\frac{1}{4}'$ in length.

Distribution. Low river banks, the borders of swamps and in depressions filled with water during most of the year; banks of the Ogeechee River near Meldrim, Effingham County, and near Valdosta, Lowndes County, Georgia; swamp of the Combahee River near Yemassee, Hampton County, and near Aiken, Aiken County, South Carolina; pond holes eight or nine miles west of Newbern, Craven County, North Carolina; passing into var. *maloides* Sarg. with young leaves tinged with red and villose along the upper side of the midrib, those at the end of vigorous shoots sometimes broad-obovate, rounded and divided at apex into 3 short rounded lobes, longer acuminate calyx-lobes and dark red anthers. Wet prairies, Volusia County, Florida; and into var. *cerasoides* Sarg. differing in the presence of short white hairs on the upper surface of the young leaves, in the longer acuminate calyx-lobes slightly villose on the inner surface and often minutely serrate near the middle, in the dark rose-colored anthers, and the late ripening fruit up to $\frac{1}{2}'$ in diameter, on drooping pedicels often $\frac{1}{2}'$ in length. An arborescent shrub with a round-topped head 30°–40° across, numerous large erect and spreading stems often 30° high, covered with smooth pale bark separating into thin plate-like scales, in falling disclosing the dull red inner bark, and slender nearly straight glabrous branchlets armed with straight slender spines 1'–1$\frac{1}{2}'$ in length. Fruit ripening late in July and in August. Low, wet, often inundated prairies near Sewall, Volusia County, Bradfordville, Leon County, Jasper, Hamilton County, and Quincy, Gadsden County, Florida. A form of this variety growing in Volusia County (f. *luculenta* Sarg.) differs in the more numerous hairs on the upper surface of the young leaves, in the rather smaller flowers, smaller and less juicy fruit ripening at the end of June or early in July, and in its often arborescent habit.

39. Cratægus rufula Sarg.

Cratægus æstivalis Torr. & Gray in part, not *Mespilus æstivalis* Walt.

Leaves oblong-obovate, acute or rounded at apex, gradually narrowed, cuneate and entire at base, finely crenately glandular-serrate, and often slightly lobed above the middle;

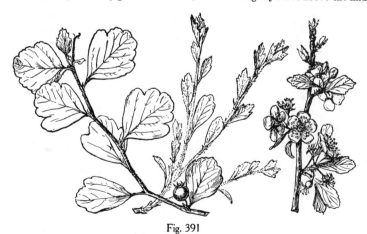

Fig. 391

with short rounded lobes, covered above with soft pale hairs and whitish tomentose below when they unfold, and at maturity thick, dark green, lustrous and glabrous or slightly pubescent along the midrib on the upper surface, rufous-pubescent especially on the midrib and veins on the lower surface, $1\frac{1}{2}'-2'$ long, and $\frac{3}{4}'-1\frac{1}{4}'$ wide, rarely not more than $1'$ long and $\frac{1}{2}'$ wide; petioles slender, villose-pubescent with rufous hairs, occasionally glandular, $\frac{1}{4}'-\frac{1}{3}'$ in length; leaves at the ends of vigorous shoots oblong-obovate, rounded and short-pointed to elliptic and acuminate, laterally lobed, or deeply 3-lobed at apex, often $2\frac{1}{2}'$ long and $1\frac{1}{2}'$ wide. **Flowers** appearing from the 10th to the end of March, $\frac{3}{4}'-1'$ in diameter, in mostly 3–5-flowered clusters, on villose-pubescent pedicels about $\frac{1}{3}'$ in length; calyx-tube broadly obconic, glabrous or villose-pubescent sometimes in the same cluster, the lobes gradually narrowed from a broad base, acuminate, entire or slightly glandular-serrate nearly to apex, glabrous or slightly pubescent on the outer surface; stamens 20; anthers dark rose color; styles 3–5, surrounded at base by a ring of white tomentum. **Fruit** ripening at the end of May, often solitary on glabrous erect pedicels $\frac{1}{4}'-\frac{1}{2}'$ long, sub-globose, scarlet, lustrous, about $\frac{1}{2}'$ in diameter, the calyx persistent with erect lobes; nutlets only slightly grooved on the back, about $\frac{1}{4}'$ long.

A tree, sometimes 30° high, with a tall trunk $8'-10'$ in diameter, covered with rough deeply furrowed dark bark, paler and less deeply furrowed on smaller and younger stems, stout ascending and spreading branches forming a broad round-topped head, and slender slightly zigzag branchlets covered when they first appear with pale tomentum, glabrous or rusty tomentose until the early summer, becoming chestnut-brown, lustrous and glabrous before autumn and dull gray in their second year, and unarmed or armed with slender or stout straight spines $\frac{1}{2}'-1\frac{1}{2}'$ in length.

Distribution. Depressions filled with water except in spring and early summer, sandy borders of ponds and streams and low wet prairies, Cottondale and Round Lake, Jackson County, and Quincy, Gadsden County, Florida; near Bainbridge, Decatur County, and Albany, Dougherty County, Georgia; near Dothan, Houston County, Alabama; pond holes along the Neuse River near Goldsboro, Wayne County, North Carolina.

40. Cratægus opaca Hook.

Cratægus æstivalis Torr. & Gray in part, not *Mespilus æstivalis* Walt.

Leaves elliptic to oblong-cuniform, gradually narrowed and acute or bluntly pointed at apex, cuneate at the often glandular base, finely crenately serrate above the middle with

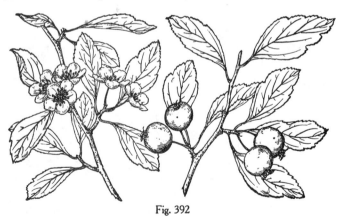

Fig. 392

minute glandular teeth, pilose above and hoary-tomentose below when they unfold, and at maturity dull dark green and glabrous or slightly hairy on the midrib on the upper surface, pubescent on the lower surface with rusty brown hairs most abundant on the midrib and veins, $2'-2\frac{1}{2}'$ long, and $\frac{1}{2}'-1'$ wide; petioles slender, villose-pubescent, about $\frac{1}{4}'$ in length; leaves at the end of vigorous shoots elliptic to oblong-ovate, often irregularly laterally lobed, and $2\frac{1}{2}'-3'$ long and wide. **Flowers** appearing in February and March before or with the unfolding of the leaves, $1'$ in diameter, on glabrous pedicels $\frac{1}{2}'$ long, in 3–5-flowered corymbs; calyx-tube broadly obconic, glabrous, the lobes narrowed from a wide base, short, nearly triangular, acute and tipped at apex with a conspicuous gland, entire or minutely serrate, glabrous, often deeply tinged with red; stamens 20; anthers large, deep rose color; styles 3–5, surrounded at base by a broad ring of pale tomentum. **Fruit** ripening early in May, in usually 2–3-fruited clusters, depressed-globose, scarlet, lustrous, dotted with pale spots, $\frac{1}{2}'-\frac{2}{3}'$ in diameter, with a small narrow cavity surrounded by the erect calyx-lobes; nutlets 3–5, rounded at the ends, rounded and slightly grooved on the back, $\frac{1}{4}'$ long.

A tree, $20°-30°$ high, with a tall stem occasionally $1°$ in diameter, covered with deeply fissured bark, divided into dark red-brown persistent scales, slender mostly erect branches forming a narrow round-topped head, and slender branchlets villose-pubescent when they first appear, soon glabrous, lustrous and bright chestnut-brown during their first season, becoming dull gray in their second year, and armed with stout straight chestnut-brown spines $\frac{1}{2}'-1'$ in length, or more often unarmed; occasionally with several stems forming a large shrub.

Distribution. In deep depressions filled with water for most of the year, low river banks and borders of swamps; near Mt. Vernon, Mobile County, and near Selma, Dallas County, Alabama; southern Mississippi (Meridian, Lauderdale County, and Hattiesburg, Forrest County); eastern Louisiana; sometimes in St. Tammany Parish covering large tracts almost to the exclusion of other plants; western Louisiana from the coast to nearly the northern border of the state, and eastern Texas to the valley of the Trinity River; rare and local east of the Mississippi River; common westward. The fruit is largely used in making preserves and jellies.

IV. VIRIDES.

CONSPECTUS OF THE ARBORESCENT SPECIES.

Stamens 20.
  Fruit not exceeding $\frac{1}{3}'$ in diameter.
    Anthers pale yellow.
      Corymbs, branchlets and leaves glabrous.
        Bark of the trunk pale gray, close and smooth.
          Leaves ovate to oblong-obovate, acute or acuminate, rarely rounded at apex; fruit depressed-globose, bright scarlet or orange. 41. **C. viridis** (A, C).
          Leaves ovate, acute, often broadly cuneate at base; fruit subglobose, orange-red. 42. **C. ovata** (A).
          Leaves oval or ovate, acute, rounded or broadly cuneate at base; fruit globose, yellow-green flushed with red. 43. **C. vulsa** (C).
        Bark of the trunk dark brown or nearly black; leaves subcoriaceous.
          Leaves oblong-ovate to semiorbicular, acute, often short-pointed or rarely rounded at apex; fruit short-oblong to obovoid or globose, dull orange color. 44. **C. glabriuscula**.
          Leaves oval to rhombic, acute or acuminate; fruit subglobose to short-oblong, bright orange-red. 45. **C. blanda** (C).
      Corymbs and branchlets villose-pubescent; leaves ovate or obovate, acute or rounded at apex; fruit subglobose, orange-red. 46. **C. velutina** (C).
    Anthers deep rose color; leaves elliptic to oblong-ovate, acute, acuminate or rarely rounded at apex; fruit globose or subglobose, orange-red. 47. **C. arborescens** (C).
  Fruit $\frac{1}{4}'-\frac{5}{16}'$ in diameter.

Anthers yellow.

Leaves cuneate at base; calyx-tube glabrous.

Leaves lanceolate to oblong-obovate, acuminate; fruit short-oblong, dull brick red covered with a glaucous bloom.   48. **C. nitida** (A).

Leaves obovate to oval or rhombic, acute or rarely rounded at apex; fruit subglobose to short-oblong, dark crimson.   49. **C. mitis** (A).

Leaves, broad and rounded at base, ovate, acute; calyx-tube villose; fruit subglobose to short-oblong, dark red.   50. **C. atrorubens** (A).

Anthers rose color; corymbs villose; fruit red.

Leaves obovate, oval or ovate, acute, scabrate above; fruit globose to subglobose, anthers deep rose color.   51. **C. ingens** (C).

Leaves broadly obovate, oval or ovate, acute or acuminate, smooth above; fruit globose or depressed-globose; anthers pale rose color.   52. **C. penita** (C).

Stamens usually 10; occasionally 12–20; anthers bright red; leaves oblong-obovate to oval, usually acute or acuminate; fruit subglobose to short-oblong, bright orange-red.
                                                                    53. **C. micracantha** (C).

41. Cratægus viridis L.

Cratægus Davisii Sarg.

Leaves ovate to oblong-obovate or oval, acute or acuminate or rarely rounded at apex, gradually narrowed to the cuneate base, finely serrate above with incurved glandular

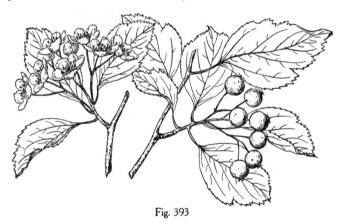

Fig. 393

teeth, and sometimes slightly 3-lobed toward the apex, tinged with red and slightly hairy above when they unfold, nearly fully grown when the flowers open in April and May, and at maturity membranaceous to subcoriaceous, dark green and lustrous on the upper surface, paler on the lower surface, with large axillary tufts of pale hairs, 1′–2′ long, and ½′–1′ wide, with a thick midrib and conspicuous primary veins; often turning brilliant scarlet late in the autumn before falling; petioles slender, 1′–1½′ in length; leaves at the end of vigorous shoots often deeply laterally lobed with narrow acuminate lobes, and 2½′–4′ long, and 1½′–2′ wide.   **Flowers** ¾′ in diameter, on long slender pedicels, in many-flowered corymbs; calyx-tube narrowly obconic, glabrous, the lobes lanceolate, entire; stamens 20; anthers pale yellow; styles 2–5, usually 5, surrounded at base by conspicuous tufts of pale hairs.   **Fruit** ripening in the autumn and mostly persistent on the branches through the winter, on long slender pedicels, in drooping many-fruited clusters, depressed-globose, bright scarlet or orange, ⅛′–¼′ in diameter; calyx little enlarged, the lobes often deciduous from the ripe fruit; nutlets usually 5, narrowed and rounded at the ends, rounded and slightly grooved or ridged on the back, $\frac{1}{16}'-\frac{1}{8}'$ long.

A tree, 20°–35° high, with a straight often fluted trunk 8°–12° tall, and 18'–20' in diameter, covered with close gray or pale orange-colored bark, small branches forming a round rather compact head, and slender glabrous branchlets ashy gray to light red-brown in their first winter, and unarmed or occasionally armed with slender sharp pale spines $\frac{3}{4}'$–1' long.

Distribution. On the often inundated borders of streams and swamps, rarely in drier ground on low slopes; southeastern Virginia (banks of the Blackwater River near Zuni, Isle of Wight County), North Carolina (Salisbury, Rowan County), South Carolina (near Aiken, Aiken County), eastern Georgia (near Augusta, Richmond County, and Macon, Bibb County), western Florida (River Junction, Gadsden County, and Tallahassee, Leon County to the swamps of the lower Apalachicola River), and westward through central and southern Alabama, southern Mississippi, and Louisiana to the valley of the San Antonio River (Sutherland Springs, Wilson County), Texas, and to central and western Arkansas, eastern Oklahoma and southeastern Missouri (Butler County), southeastern Kansas and northward in the region adjacent to the Mississippi River from Louisiana to northeastern Missouri, and to Pike County, Illinois, ranging eastward in Mississippi to Tishomingo County in the northeastern corner of the state, to northwestern Georgia, southeastern Tennessee, and to Richland County, Illinois; rare and local in the Atlantic and east Gulf states; common and often forming great thickets in western Louisiana, the coast region of eastern Texas, southern Arkansas, and in the region adjacent to the Mississippi River.

42. Cratægus ovata Sarg.

Leaves ovate, acute, broadly or acutely concave-cuneate at the entire base, coarsely often doubly serrate above with glandular teeth, and occasionally slightly divided into

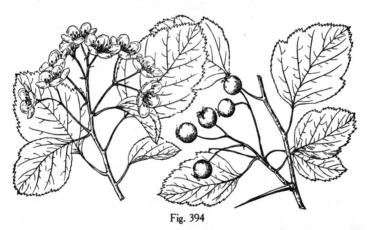

Fig. 394

short lateral lobes, nearly fully grown when the flowers open early in May and then dark green, very smooth and glabrous above with the exception of a few short scattered hairs near the base of the midrib, paler below, with small persistent axillary tufts of white hairs, and at maturity membranaceous, 2'–2½' long, and 1½'–2' wide, with a slender yellow midrib and primary veins; petioles slender, rose-colored in the autumn, about $\frac{3}{4}'$ in length; leaves at the end of vigorous shoots rounded or truncate at the broad base, coarsely serrate, and sometimes 3' long and wide. **Flowers** about $\frac{1}{2}'$ in diameter, on long slender pedicels, in broad loose many-flowered corymbs; calyx-tube narrowly obconic, glabrous, the lobes broad acute, entire or coarsely glandular-serrate toward the apex, glabrous; styles 5

Fruit ripening in October, on elongated pedicels, in long drooping clusters, subglobose or a little longer than broad, orange-red, $\frac{1}{4}$–$\frac{5}{16}'$ long; calyx enlarged, with elongated closely appressed lobes sometimes deciduous from the ripe fruit; nutlets 5, acute at the ends, rounded or slightly ridged on the back, about $\frac{3}{16}'$ long.

A tree, 25°–30° high, with a tall trunk sometimes a foot in diameter, covered with smooth gray bark, slender glabrous branchlets light reddish brown and lustrous during their first year, becoming grayish brown in their second season, and unarmed or armed with occasional dark purple slender slightly curved shining spines 1′ long.

Distribution. Low moist soil on the banks of the River Desperes, South St. Louis, St. Louis County, and near Alba, Jasper County, Missouri.

43. Cratægus vulsa Beadl.

Leaves oval or ovate, acute, broad and rounded or broad-cuneate at the entire base, irregularly and often doubly serrate above with straight or incurved gland-tipped teeth, and often divided into several short acute lateral lobes, when they unfold dark bronze-red, and pilose with scattered caducous hairs, and furnished below with tufts of pale often per-

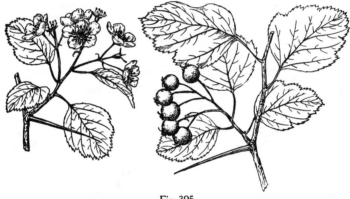

Fig. 395

sistent hairs in the axils of the principal veins, nearly fully grown when the flowers open late in April, and at maturity thin, bright green on the upper surface, paler on the lower surface, about 2′ long and 1½′ wide, with a slender midrib and 4 or 5 pairs of thin pale yellow primary veins; turning in the autumn yellow or brown; petioles slender, somewhat villose at first, soon becoming glabrous, about $\frac{3}{4}'$ in length; leaves at the end of vigorous shoots broadly ovate, acute or acuminate, broad and rounded or occasionally truncate or broadly cuneate at base, more coarsely serrate and more deeply lobed, often 3′ long and 2½′ wide, with a stout winged glandular petiole.   **Flowers** $\frac{3}{4}'$ in diameter, on slender pedicels, in compact 3–10-flowered corymbs, with linear acuminate glandular red bracts and bractlets; calyx-tube broadly obconic, glabrous, the lobes gradually narrowed from a broad base, acuminate, entire or occasionally obscurely serrate toward the apex, glabrous; stamens 20; anthers pale yellow; styles 3–5, surrounded at base by a thin ring of pale hairs.   **Fruit** ripening at the end of September or early in October, on slender pedicels, in few-fruited drooping clusters, globose, yellow-green flushed with red, $\frac{1}{2}'$ in diameter; calyx prominent, with closely appressed lobes; flesh yellow-green; nutlets 3–5, thin, rounded, sometimes slightly ridged and grooved on the back, about $\frac{3}{16}'$ long.

A tree, occasionally 20° high, with a tall trunk 5′–6′ in diameter, covered with thin fissured bark separating into light gray scales tinged with brown, and often armed with long compound spines, ascending or spreading branches forming an oval usually compact symmetrical head, and slender nearly straight glabrous chestnut-brown branchlets becoming gray, and armed with thin nearly straight bright chestnut-brown shining spines 1′–1½′ long; sometimes a shrub, with numerous stems.

Distribution. Rich moist soil in the neighborhood of streams; northwestern Georgia and northeastern Alabama.

44. Cratægus glabriuscula Sarg.

Leaves oblong-ovate to semiorbicular, acute or often short-pointed or rarely rounded at apex, gradually narrowed from below the middle to the slender entire base, coarsely and often doubly serrate usually only above the middle with broad straight gland-tipped teeth, and sometimes divided toward the apex into 2 or 3 short acute lobes, nearly fully grown when the flowers open the 1st of April, and then membranaceous and slightly pilose above with scattered hairs most abundant along the base of the midrib, and at maturity subcoriaceous, hard and firm, dark green and lustrous on the upper surface, pale on the lower surface, 1½′–2′ long, and ¾′–1′ wide, with a thin light yellow midrib, and primary

Fig. 396

veins extending obliquely toward the end of the leaf, conspicuous secondary veins and reticulate veinlets; petioles slender, wing-margined, ⅓′ in length; leaves at the end of vigorous shoots often ovate, broadly cuneate at base, much more coarsely serrate, more frequently lobed, 2′–2½′ long and wide. **Flowers** about ½′ in diameter, on long slender pedicels, in few-flowered rather compact corymbs; calyx-tube broadly obconic, glabrous, the lobes short, gradually narrowed from a broad base, entire, villose on the inner surface; stamens 20, anthers nearly white; styles 5. **Fruit** ripening in September and often persistent until late into the winter, on long slender pedicels, in compact many-fruited drooping clusters, short-oblong to obovoid or nearly globose, dull orange color, marked by minute dark dots, about ¼′ long; calyx enlarged, conspicuous, with spreading or closely appressed lobes dull red on the upper side at base, often deciduous before the fruit ripens; flesh very thin, yellow, dry and hard; nutlets 5, rounded and sometimes obscurely grooved on the back, about 3/16′ long.

A tree, 20°–25° high, with a tall straight trunk often a foot in diameter, covered with thin dark brown scaly bark, long ascending branches forming a narrow head, and slender nearly straight branchlets, unarmed or armed with occasional slender straight chestnut-brown lustrous spines ¾′–1′ long.

Distribution. Bottom-lands of the Trinity River and its branches near Dallas, Dallas County, and in Tarrant County, Texas, in forests of Elms and Nettle-trees.

45. Cratægus blanda Sarg.

Leaves oval to rhombic, acute or acuminate, and occasionally slightly lobed toward the apex, broadly cuneate or concave-cuneate at the entire base, coarsely crenately serrate above the middle with gland-tipped teeth, coated with soft pale hairs when they unfold, fully grown when the flowers open about the 1st of May, and then membranaceous, dark green and lustrous above and glabrous below with the exception of large axillary tufts of snow-white tomentum, and at maturity subcoriaceous, yellow-green and lustrous on the upper surface, paler on the lower surface, $1\frac{1}{2}'-2'$ long, and $1'-1\frac{1}{3}'$ wide, with a slender midrib, and 2 or 3 pairs of thin primary veins extending obliquely toward the end of the leaf;

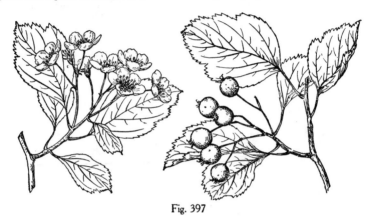

Fig. 397

petioles slender, at first villose along the upper side, soon becoming glabrous, $\frac{3}{4}'-1'$ in length; leaves at the end of vigorous shoots often broadly ovate, rounded at base, more deeply lobed above the middle, $2'-2\frac{1}{2}'$ long, and $1\frac{1}{2}'-2'$ wide. **Flowers** $1'$ in diameter, on slender elongated pedicels, in broad many-flowered corymbs, with linear entire bracts and bractlets; calyx-tube broadly obconic, glabrous, the lobes gradually narrowed from a broad base, acuminate, entire or obscurely dentate, glabrous; stamens 20; anthers canary-yellow; styles 5. **Fruit** ripening about the middle of October, on slender pedicels, in many-fruited drooping clusters, subglobose to short-oblong, bright orange-red, $\frac{1}{4}'$ in diameter; calyx prominent, with spreading lobes usually deciduous from the ripe fruit; nutlets 5, thin, narrowed at the ends, deeply grooved on the back, $\frac{1}{4}'$ long.

An unarmed tree, $25°-30°$ high, with a tall trunk $10'-12'$ in diameter, covered with dark brown or nearly black bark divided by shallow fissures and broken on the surface into small plate-like scales, stout ascending branches forming a broad irregular head, and nearly straight glabrous branchlets dark orange-green at first, becoming dull red-brown during their first season and darker brown the following year.

Distribution. Dry uplands and low rolling hills: central Arkansas to the valley of the Brazos River, Texas (Columbia and Brazoria), and to Menden, Louisiana, and Selma, Alabama.

46. Cratægus velutina Sarg.

Leaves ovate to obovate, acute or rounded at apex, gradually narrowed and cuneate at the entire base, and sharply often doubly serrate with straight glandular teeth, more than half grown when the flowers open at the end of April and then covered above by short white hairs and below with hoary pubescence, and often furnished with axillary tufts of white tomentum, and at maturity glabrous, smooth and lustrous on the upper surface and covered on the lower surface with matted pale hairs, $1\frac{3}{4}'-2'$ long, and $1\frac{1}{2}'-2'$ wide, with a thin midrib and primary veins; petioles slender, thickly covered early in the season with matted hairs, becoming glabrous, $\frac{1}{2}'-1'$ in length; leaves at the end of vigorous shoots ovate, rounded or broad-cuneate at base, coarsely serrate, usually slightly lobed above the middle, and often $2\frac{1}{2}'-3'$ long and $1\frac{1}{2}'$ wide. **Flowers** $\frac{1}{2}'$ in diameter on slender villose pedicels, in usually 7–12-flowered hairy corymbs; calyx-tube narrowly obconic, villose, the lobes gradually narrowed from a broad base, short, acute, entire, slightly villose; stamens 20; anthers yellow; styles 5. **Fruit** on long slender glabrous or nearly glabrous drooping stems in few-fruited clusters, subglobose, orange-red, marked by small pale dots, about $\frac{1}{4}'$ in diameter; calyx prominent, with a deep narrow cavity pointed in the bottom, and closely

Fig. 398

appressed lobes; flesh thin, dry and mealy; nutlets 5, acute at base, rounded at apex, ridged on the back with a low grooved ridge, about $\frac{1}{5}'$ long and $\frac{1}{8}'$ wide.

A tree, 20°–25° high, with a trunk 8′–10′ in diameter, covered with dark rough scaly bark, and slender slightly zigzag branchlets, hoary-tomentose when they first appear, light reddish brown, marked by pale lenticels and glabrous or sometimes pubescent near the end in their first autumn, and ashy gray the following year, and armed with slender nearly straight chestnut-brown spines $1'-1\frac{1}{2}'$ in length.

Distribution. Uplands in dry sandy soil, Fulton, Hempstead County, near Texarkana, Bowie County, Arkansas; and in the valley of the lower Brazos River (near Columbia, Brazoria County), Texas, and eastern Louisiana.

47. Cratægus arborescens Ell.

Leaves elliptic to oblong-obovate, acute, acuminate or rarely rounded and abruptly short-pointed and slightly lobed at apex, gradually narrowed cuneate and entire at base, and coarsely doubly serrate above the middle with incurved glandular teeth, villose on the upper side of the midrib with short white hairs when they unfold, and at maturity thin, glabrous, dark green and lustrous on the upper surface, paler and often furnished on the lower surface with small axillary tufts of pale hairs, $1'-2'$ long, and $\frac{3}{4}'-1'$ wide, with a slender midrib and primary veins; petioles slender, glabrous, $\frac{1}{2}'-1'$ in length; leaves at the end of vigorous shoots oval to oblong-ovate or elliptic, acuminate, abruptly or gradually narrowed and cuneate at base, more or less deeply lobed with acuminate lateral lobes, often $2\frac{1}{2}'$ long and $1\frac{1}{4}'$ wide, their petioles stout, and glabrous early in the season. **Flowers** $\frac{1}{2}'$ in diameter, on slender pedicels, in wide many-flowered compound corymbs; calyx-tube narrowly obconic, glabrous or slightly pilose, the lobes slender, acuminate, entire, glabrous or slightly villose on the inner surface, deciduous from the ripe fruit; stamens 20; anthers deep rose color; styles usually 5. **Fruit** on short pedicels in many-fruited drooping clusters, globose or subglobose, orange-red, $\frac{1}{4}'-\frac{1}{3}'$ in diameter; nutlets 5, pointed at the ends, slightly ridged on the back, about $\frac{1}{6}'$ long.

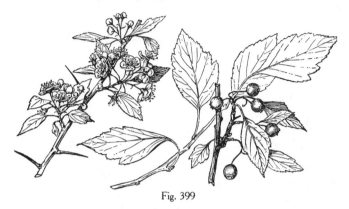

Fig. 399

A tree, 25°–30° high, with a tall trunk 12′–18′ in diameter covered with close pale gray bark, spreading and erect branches forming a broad rather open irregular head, and slender glabrous red-brown branchlets, ashy gray in their second season, and unarmed or armed with straight slender chestnut-brown spines.

Distribution. River banks, low wet woods and borders of swamps; Georgia-coast region, near Dorchester, Liberty County, in the neighborhood of Savannah, and on the Ogeechee River at Fort Argyle, Chatham County (type station); near Augusta, Richmond County, Georgia.

48. Cratægus nitida Sarg.

Leaves lanceolate to oblong-obovate, acuminate, abruptly or gradually narrowed and cuneate at the entire base, coarsely serrate above with straight or incurved glandular teeth,

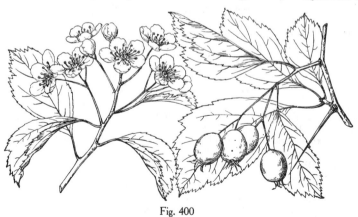

Fig. 400

and often more or less divided into 2 or 3 pairs of broad acute lobes, dark red and slightly villose along the upper side of the midrib with scattered caducous hairs when they unfold, nearly fully grown when the flowers open early in May, and at maturity thick and coriaceous, dark green and very lustrous on the upper surface, pale and dull on the lower surface, 2′–3′ long, and 1′–1½′ wide, with a prominent midrib usually red on the lower side, and few thin prominent primary veins generally extending to the point of the lobes; turning in the autumn rich orange color through shades of bronze and orange-red; petioles stout, glandular, villose while young on the upper side, soon becoming glabrous, ½′–¾′ in length; leaves at the end of vigorous shoots more deeply lobed and frequently 5′ long and 2½′ wide. **Flowers** ¾′ in diameter, on long slender pedicels, in broad compound many-flowered glabrous corymbs; calyx-tube narrowly obconic, glabrous, the lobes slender, elongated, acuminate, entire or sparingly glandular-serrate; stamens 15–20; anthers pale yellow; styles 2–5. **Fruit** ripening at the end of October, on slender elongated pedicels, in many-fruited drooping clusters, short-oblong, full and rounded at the ends, pruinose with a glaucous bloom, marked by small dark dots, ½′–⅝′ long, and about ⅓′ in diameter; calyx only slightly enlarged, the lobes dark red at the base on the upper side, usually erect, often deciduous before the fruit ripens; nutlets 2–5, rounded and ridged on the back with a broad low rounded ridge, light-colored, ¼′ long.

A tree, often 30° high, with a tall straight trunk sometimes 18′ in diameter, covered with close dark bark broken into thick plate-like scales, stout spreading lower branches and erect upper branches forming a broad often irregular head, and slender glabrous branchlets bright orange-brown and lustrous during their first and second seasons, becoming pale reddish brown in their third year, and ultimately ashy gray, and unarmed or armed with occasional straight thin bright chestnut-brown lustrous spines 1′–1½′ long.

Distribution. Bottoms of the Mississippi River, St. Clair County, and to Shawneetown, Gallatin County, Illinois, to Hannibal, Missouri, and in eastern Arkansas to Helena, Phillips County; common.

49. Cratægus mitis Sarg.

Leaves obovate to oval or rhombic, acute or rarely rounded at apex, gradually narrowed and concave-cuneate at the entire base, and coarsely serrate above with straight glandular teeth, nearly fully grown when the flowers open during the first week of May, and then light yellow-green above, paler below, and glabrous with the exception of a few short hairs on the upper side of the midrib, and at maturity subcoriaceous, dark green and lustrous on the upper surface, pale yellow-green on the lower surface, 1½′–2½′ long, and 1′–1½′ wide, with

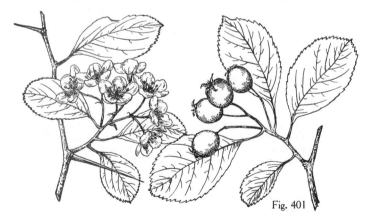

Fig. 401

a prominent midrib and slender primary veins; petioles stout, wing-margined at apex, occasionally glandular with minute glands, 1⅓′–1½′ in length. **Flowers** ½′–⅝′ in diameter, on long slender pedicels, in compact 8–15-flowered glabrous corymbs, with red glandular bracts and bractlets; calyx-tube narrowly obconic, glabrous, the lobes glabrous, abruptly narrowed from a broad base, acuminate, finely glandular-serrate below the middle with minute stipitate red glands; stamens 20; anthers yellow; styles 2–4, usually 3. **Fruit** ripening the middle of October, on slender pedicels, in many-fruited drooping clusters, subglobose to short-oblong, rounded at the ends, dark crimson, marked by occasional large dark dots, $\frac{1}{2}'$–$\frac{5}{8}'$ long, about $\frac{1}{2}'$ in diameter; calyx only slightly enlarged, the lobes serrate, closely appressed, often deciduous from the ripe fruit; flesh thick, pale orange color, and juicy; nutlets usually 3, thick, full and rounded at the ends, prominently ridged on the back, with a broad high rounded deeply grooved ridge, about $\frac{1}{4}'$ long.

A tree, 25°–30° high, with a tall trunk sometimes a foot in diameter, covered with dark scaly bark, large spreading branches forming a broad round-topped head, and glabrous branchlets dull light reddish brown during their first season, becoming dark brown or ashy gray, and armed with stout straight or slightly curved dull red-brown or purplish spines usually about $1\frac{1}{2}'$ long.

Distribution. Low moist rich soil on the bottoms of the Mississippi River near the village of Cahokia, St. Clair County and Richland County, Illinois.

50. Cratægus atrorubens Ashe.

Leaves ovate, acute, usually rounded or sometimes cuneate or truncate at the broad entire base, coarsely and usually doubly serrate above, and often divided into 2 or 3 pairs

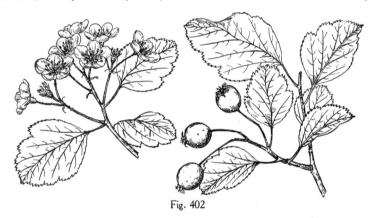

Fig. 402

of short acute lobes, about half grown when the flowers open late in April or early in May and then slightly roughened above by short scattered white hairs, and furnished below with conspicuous axillary tufts of pale tomentum, and at maturity thin, glabrous, dark dull green and smooth on the upper surface, light yellow-green on the lower surface, about $2'$ long and $1\frac{1}{2}'$ wide, or on vigorous shoots frequently $3'$ long, and $2\frac{1}{2}'$ wide, with a thin midrib and 4 or 5 pairs of slender primary veins; petioles slender, nearly terete, more or less densely villose early in the season, soon becoming glabrous, $1'$–$1\frac{1}{2}'$ in length. **Flowers** about $\frac{5}{8}'$ in diameter, on slender elongated villose pedicels, in broad loose glabrous or villose corymbs; calyx-tube narrowly obconic, densely villose throughout or only at base with pale tomentum, the lobes short, acute, finely glandular-serrate, villose particularly on the inner surface; stamens 20; styles 4 or 5, surrounded at base by a narrow ring of pale tomentum. **Fruit** ripening and falling early in October, on slender pedicels, in drooping few-fruited clusters, subglobose to short-oblong, rounded at the ends, dark red; calyx somewhat enlarged, with spreading lobes usually deciduous before the fruit ripens; nutlets 4 or 5, thin, rounded and sometimes obscurely grooved on the back, about $\frac{3}{16}'$ long.

A tree, sometimes 30° high, with a tall trunk 12'–18' in diameter, covered with dark red-brown scaly bark, thin erect and spreading branches forming a compact rather narrow head, and slender glabrous branchlets marked by occasional dark lenticels, dark green more or less tinged with red when they first appear, soon becoming dark chestnut-brown and very lustrous, and bright reddish brown in their second year, and usually unarmed.

Distribution. St. Louis County, Missouri, and rich bottom-lands of the Mississippi River, St. Clair County, Illinois; not common.

51. Cratægus ingens Beadl.

Leaves obovate-oval or ovate, broadly or acutely cuneate at the entire base, crenately serrate above, and often slightly lobed toward the acute apex, about half grown when the flowers open at the end of April or early in May and then roughened above by short rigid hairs and villose below along the midrib, and the remote slender veins extending obliquely

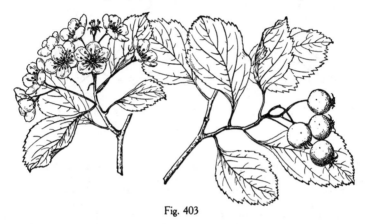

Fig. 403

to the point of the lobes, and at maturity subcoriaceous, dark green and scabrate on the upper surface, paler and nearly glabrous on the lower surface, $1\frac{1}{2}'$–$2'$ long, and $1\frac{1}{4}'$–$1\frac{1}{2}'$ wide; turning in the autumn yellow, orange, red, or brown; petioles stout, narrowly wing-margined to the middle, pubescent while young, becoming glabrous, about $\frac{3}{4}'$ in length; leaves at the end of vigorous shoots more deeply lobed and often $3'$–$3\frac{1}{2}'$ long, and $2'$ wide, with a stout broad-winged petiole sometimes $1\frac{1}{2}'$ long. **Flowers** $\frac{1}{2}'$–$\frac{5}{8}'$ in diameter, on slender hairy pedicels, in many-flowered compact hairy corymbs; calyx narrowly obconic, coated, especially toward the base with matted pale hairs, the lobes slender, elongated, acute, glandular with bright red glands, glabrous on the outer, sparingly villose on the inner surface; stamens 20; anthers deep rose color; styles 3–5. **Fruit** ripening in October, on stout puberulous pedicels, in few-fruited drooping clusters, globose to subglobose, red, about $\frac{3}{8}'$ in diameter; calyx little enlarged, with reflexed appressed nearly glabrous lobes; nutlets 3–5, rounded or slightly grooved and ridged on the back, $\frac{1}{4}'$ long.

A tree, sometimes 25° high, with a trunk a foot in diameter, spreading branches forming a wide round-topped head, and unarmed branchlets covered at first with matted pale hairs, soon becoming glabrous, dark chestnut-brown.

Distribution. Moist woods and the low banks of streams; southeastern Tennessee and northwestern Georgia.

52. Cratægus penita Beadl.

Leaves broad-obovate, oval, or ovate, acute or acuminate at apex, broadly or acutely concave-cuneate at the entire base, sharply often doubly serrate above with glandular mostly straight teeth, and often slightly lobed above the middle, deeply tinged with red and covered with pale hairs when they unfold, nearly fully grown when the flowers open about the 1st of May and then smooth above, and glabrous below with the exception of axillary tufts of pale hairs, and at maturity subcoriaceous, dark green and lustrous on the upper surface, paler on the lower surface, $1\frac{3}{4}$–$2'$ long, and $1'$–$1\frac{3}{4}'$ wide, with a prominent midrib and slender primary veins; turning orange, yellow, and brown in the autumn; petioles slender, covered while young like the upper side of the base of the midrib with pale decid-

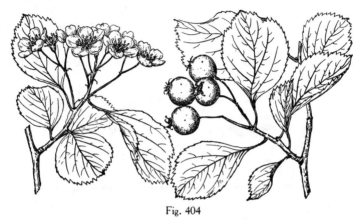

Fig. 404

uous hairs, $\frac{1}{2}'$–$\frac{3}{4}'$ in length; leaves at the end of vigorous shoots often rounded or subcordate at base, more or less deeply lobed, and $2\frac{1}{2}'$–$3'$ long and broad, with a stout broadly winged glandular petiole. **Flowers** about $\frac{5}{8}'$ in diameter, on elongated glabrous or sparingly hairy pedicels, in compact few-flowered nearly glabrous corymbs; calyx broadly obconic, glabrous, the lobes gradually narrowed from a broad base, slender, acuminate, entire, or furnished with occasional minute glandular teeth, slightly villose on the inner surface; stamens 20; anthers white faintly tinged with pink; styles 3–5. **Fruit** ripening in October, on elongated slender pedicels, in few-fruited drooping clusters, globose or depressed-globose, red, about $\frac{1}{4}'$ in diameter; calyx enlarged, with spreading or reflexed lobes villose on the upper side; nutlets 3–5, narrowed and acute at the ends rounded and broadly grooved on the back, about $\frac{1}{4}'$ long.

A tree, $18°$–$20°$ high, with a short trunk sometimes $10'$ in diameter, stout ascending or spreading branches forming a wide head, unarmed branchlets puberulous while young, soon glabrous, becoming light reddish brown.

Distribution. Low moist woods and the banks of streams; southeastern Tennessee.

53. Cratægus micracantha Sarg.

Leaves oblong-obovate to oval, acute, acuminate, or rarely rounded at apex, gradually or abruptly narrowed from above or from below the middle to the cuneate entire base, coarsely crenulate-serrate, and occasionally 3-lobed above with short broad acute lateral lobes, when they unfold villose on the upper and hoary-tomentose on the lower surface, more than half grown when the flowers open about the middle of May and then membranaceous and slightly villose above with short scattered pale hairs, and at maturity thin but firm in texture, dark yellow-green, lustrous and smooth above, paler and tomentose below on the slender midrib and 3 or 4 pairs of very obscure primary veins, $2'$–$2\frac{1}{2}'$ long, and $1'$–$1\frac{1}{4}'$ wide; petioles slender, tomentose early in the season, becoming glabrous or pubescent, $\frac{1}{2}'$–$1'$ in length; leaves at the end of vigorous shoots often broadly rhombic to obovate, acuminate, frequently deeply 3-lobed or divided into 2 or 3 pairs of short lateral lobes, usually $2\frac{1}{2}'$–$3'$ long.

Flowers cup-shaped, $\frac{1}{4}'$ in diameter, on long slender pedicels thickly coated with matted white hairs, in broad lax many-flowered compound hairy corymbs; calyx-tube narrowly obconic, villose, the lobes linear, acuminate, entire, slightly villose, tipped with minute dark glands; stamens usually 10, occasionally 12, 15, or 20; anthers small, deep bright red; styles 5. **Fruit** ripening the middle of October, on slender pubescent pedicels, in drooping many-fruited clusters, subglobose to short-oblong, full and rounded at the ends, bright orange-red, lustrous, marked by occasional large pale dots, about $\frac{1}{4}'$ long; calyx prominent,

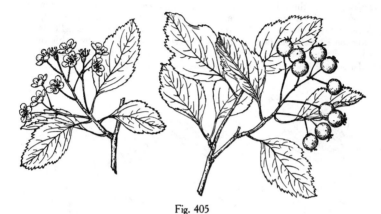

Fig. 405

with a short villose tube, and spreading erect hairy lobes often deciduous from the ripe fruit; nutlets 5, thin, acute at the narrow ends, rounded and sometimes slightly grooved on the back, about $\frac{3}{16}'$ long.

An unarmed tree, sometimes 25° high, with a tall trunk $8'–12'$ in diameter, covered with light or dark brown bark separating freely into thin narrow scales, stout spreading branches forming a broad flat-topped handsome head, and slender nearly straight branchlets coated until after the flowering time with thick hoary tomentum, bright red-brown and puberulous during their first season, becoming light or dark dull reddish brown the following year.

Distribution. Common in low woods in rich moist soil near Fulton, Hempstead County, Arkansas.

V. PRUINOSÆ.

CONSPECTUS OF THE ARBORESCENT SPECIES.

Stamens 20.
  Anthers rose color.
    Leaves elliptic; fruit subglobose, green and pruinose when fully grown, becoming dark purple-red and very lustrous; anthers large, deep rose color. 54. **C. pruinosa** (A, C).
    Leaves ovate, acute or acuminate; fruit short-oblong, dull russet-green; anthers small, light rose color. 55. **C. georgiana** (C).
  Anthers white; leaves ovate, acute, cordate at base; fruit broader than high, scarlet, pruinose, becoming lustrous. 56. **C. callicarpa** (A).
Stamens 10; anthers dark rose color; leaves broad-ovate, acuminate; fruit subglobose, green more or less tinged with red, pruinose. 57. **C. disjuncta** (A.)

54. Cratægus pruinosa K. Koch.

Leaves elliptic, acute, broadly or acutely cuneate at the entire base, irregularly and often doubly serrate above with glandular straight or incurved teeth, and divided in 3 or 4 pairs of short acute or acuminate lateral lobes, when they unfold bright red and glabrous with the exception of a few short caducous hairs on the upper side of the base of the midrib, nearly fully grown when the flowers open from the middle to the end of May and then membranaceous and bluish green, and at maturity subcoriaceous, dark blue-green and often glaucous above, pale below, $1'-1\frac{1}{2}'$ long, and $\frac{3}{4}'-1'$ wide, with a slender midrib, and 3 or 4 pairs of thin primary veins running to the point of the lobes; late in the autumn turning dull orange color; petioles slender, glandular, slightly winged at the apex, often bright red in early spring and in the autumn, $1'-1\frac{1}{2}'$ in length; leaves at the end of vigorous shoots broadovate, often rounded at base, more coarsely serrate and more deeply lobed, frequently $2\frac{1}{2}'$ long and wide, with stouter and more broadly winged petioles. **Flowers** $\frac{3}{4}'-1'$ in diameter, on long slender pedicels, in few-flowered glabrous corymbs; calyx-tube broadly obconic, glabrous, the lobes gradually narrowed from a wide base, long-pointed, finely glandular-serrate below the middle; stamens 20; anthers large, deep rose color; styles 5,

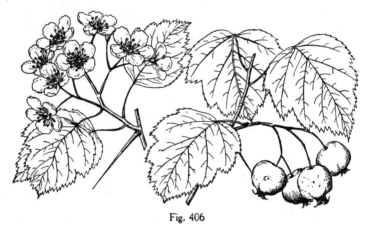

Fig. 406

surrounded at base by a thick ring of hoary tomentum. **Fruit** on long thin light green ultimately bright red pedicels, in few-fruited drooping clusters, 5-angled, apple green and covered with a glaucous bloom until nearly fully ripe, at maturity late in October subglobose but rather broader than high, barely angled, $\frac{1}{2}'-\frac{5}{8}'$ in diameter, dark purple-red, marked by many small dull dots, very lustrous; calyx prominent, with a long well-developed tube, and enlarged usually erect lobes often deciduous before the fruit ripens; flesh thick, light yellow; nutlets 5, light-colored, acute at apex, nprrowed and rounded at base, deeply grooved on the back, $\frac{1}{4}'$ long.

A tree, $15°-20°$ high, with a stem a few inches in diameter, spreading horizontal branches forming a broad open irregular head, and slender glabrous branchlets bright chestnut-brown during their first season, later becoming dark reddish brown, and armed with numerous stout straight light chestnut-brown spines $1'-1\frac{1}{2}'$ long; often shrubby, with several intricately branched stems.

Distribution. Slopes of low hills often in limestone soil; southwestern Vermont, westward through New York to southern Ontario (neighborhood of Toronto), and through Ohio and Indiana to central and northern Illinois, and southward through eastern Pennsylvania to northern Delaware.

55. Cratægus georgiana Sarg.

Leaves ovate, acute or acuminate at apex, rounded or broad-cuneate at base, finely and often doubly serrate with straight or incurved gland-tipped teeth, and divided into numerous short acute lateral lobes, glabrous with the exception of a few pale caducous hairs on the upper surface and bronze-yellow when they unfold, nearly half grown when the flowers open about the 20th of April and then thin, dark yellow-green above and pale below, and at maturity thin but firm in texture, dark blue-green on the upper surface, pale on the lower surface, $1\frac{1}{2}'-2'$ long, and $1'-1\frac{1}{4}'$ wide, with a slender yellow midrib and 3 or 4 pairs of thin primary veins; petioles slender, often short-winged at the apex, usually about $\frac{3}{4}'$ in length; leaves at the end of vigorous shoots often 3' long and 2' wide, sometimes deltoid and usually much more deeply lobed. **Flowers** $\frac{3}{4}'$ in diameter, on slender pedicels, in usually 5–7-flowered compact glabrous corymbs; calyx-tube broadly obconic, glabrous, the lobes gradually narrowed from a broad base, acuminate, entire or obscurely and irregularly serrate, glabrous; stamens 20; anthers small; light rose color; styles 5; surrounded at the base by a narrow ring of pale tomentum. **Fruit** ripening and falling early in October, on slender pedicels, in drooping few-fruited clusters, short-oblong, full and rounded at the

Fig. 407

ends, often obscurely 5-angled, dull russet-green, $\frac{3}{8}'-\frac{1}{2}'$ long; calyx-lobes only slightly enlarged, mostly deciduous before the fruit ripens, leaving a well-defined ring at the summit of the short calyx-tube; flesh thin, light green; nutlets 5, thin, rounded and irregularly grooved on the back, about $\frac{1}{4}'$ long.

A tree, sometimes 25°–30° high, with a tall trunk $10'-12'$ in diameter, stout wide-spreading branches forming a broad symmetrical round-topped head, and slender lustrous chestnut-brown branchlets armed with straight or slightly curved thin spines rarely more than $1\frac{1}{2}'$ long.

Distribution. Low rich river-bottoms and meadows in the neighborhood of Rome, Floyd County, Georgia.

56. Cratægus callicarpa Sarg.

Leaves ovate, acute, cordate at base, coarsely often doubly serrate with long straight glandular teeth, and slightly divided into 3 or 4 pairs of short broad acuminate lateral lobes, not more than a quarter grown when the flowers open late in April and then very thin, yellow-green and slightly villose above and on the midrib below, and at maturity thin, glabrous, dark yellow-green and lustrous on the upper surface, pale yellow-green on the lower surface, $4'-4\frac{1}{2}'$ long, and $2'-2\frac{1}{2}'$ wide, with a stout midrib, and 3 or 4 pairs of prominent primary veins connected by conspicuous cross veinlets; petioles stout, slightly wing-margined at apex, sparingly glandular, $1'-1\frac{1}{4}'$ in length; leaves at the end of vigorous shoots thicker, with shorter glandular petioles rose-colored toward the base. **Flowers** 1' in diameter, on short stout pedicels, in small compact 5–10-flowered corymbs, with lanceolate to linear-obovate glandular bracts and bractlets usually persistent until the flowers open; calyx-tube broadly obconic, glabrous, the lobes separated by wide sinuses, short, broad, acuminate, coarsely glandular-serrate, slightly villose on the inner surface; stamens 20; anthers white; styles 5, surrounded at base by a broad ring of pale tomentum. **Fruit** ripening early in October on short stout spreading pedicels in 2 or 3-fruited clusters, broader than high, distinctly 5-angled, rounded at the wide apex, truncate at base, with a deep depression at the insertion of the pedicel, scarlet, pruinose, becoming lustrous, marked by numerous large pale dots, $\frac{3}{4}-\frac{4}{5}'$ broad, and about $\frac{3}{4}'$ high; calyx-lobes deciduous; flesh thin, light yellow slightly tinged with red, remaining on the ground through the winter without becoming soft; nutlets 5, thin, acute at apex, rounded at base, rounded and slightly grooved or ridged with a low grooved ridge on the back, $\frac{1}{5}-\frac{1}{4}'$ long and wide.

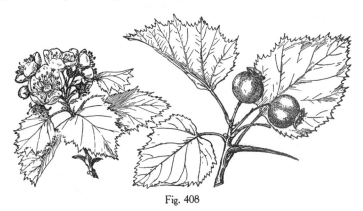

Fig. 408

A tree, 20°-25° high, with a tall stem 5'-6' in diameter covered with dark scaly bark, and stout nearly straight branchlets dark orange-green when they first appear, becoming light chestnut-brown, lustrous and marked by small pale lenticels in their first season, and dull reddish brown the following year, and armed with stout straight or slightly curved purplish spines 1'-1½' in length.

Distribution. Rich hillsides, near Shrewsbury, St. Louis County, Missouri.

57. Cratægus disjuncta Sarg.

Leaves broad-ovate, acuminate, full and rounded or concave cuneate at the entire base, sharply often doubly serrate above with straight or incurved glandular teeth, and slightly and irregularly divided above the middle into narrow acuminate spreading lobes, thin, glabrous, dark blue-green above, pale below, 2½'-3' long, and 2¼'-2½' wide, with a slender yellow midrib, and 4 or 5 pairs of thin primary veins extending obliquely to the point of the lobes; petioles slender, wing-margined at apex, glandular, 1'-1¼' in length. **Flowers** opening the first of May, ⅔' in diameter, on long stout pedicels, in glabrous compact 3-6 usually 5-flowered glabrous corymbs, with conspicuous glandular early deciduous bracts and bractlets; calyx-tube narrowly obconic, glabrous, the lobes slender, acuminate, glabrous, entire or sparingly glandular-serrate; stamens 10; anthers large, dark rose color; styles 4 or 5, surrounded at base by a narrow ring of pale tomentum. **Fruit** on stout rigid pedicels, in drooping or spreading clusters, subglobose, usually rather broader than high, angled, green more or less tinged with red, pruinose, ½'-¾' in diameter; calyx prominent, with a short tube and much enlarged spreading or erect lobes usually deciduous at midsummer; flesh thin, greenish yellow; nutlets usually 4, rounded at the ends, deeply grooved on the back, about ¼' long.

A tree, 15°-18° high, with a tall slender trunk, covered with dark slightly scaly bark, small erect and spreading branches forming an open irregular head, and stout slightly zigzag glabrous branchlets dark olive-green tinged with red when they first appear, dark dull red-

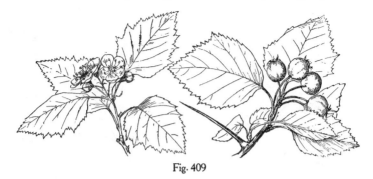

Fig. 409

dish brown or purple and marked by small pale lenticels at the end of their first season, becoming light grayish brown in their second year, and armed with numerous stout nearly straight dark purple lustrous spines $2\frac{1}{2}'-3'$ in length.

Distribution. Gravelly banks of small streams near Monteer, Shannon County, and at Carl Junction, Jasper County, Missouri, and to Heber Springs, Cleburne County, and Fayetteville, Washington County, Arkansas.

VI. SILVICOLÆ.

Medioximæ Sarg.

CONSPECTUS OF THE ARBORESCENT SPECIES.

Fruit on short erect pedicels; leaves rounded or occasionally slightly cordate at base.
58. **C. drymophila** (C).
Fruit on elongated drooping pedicels.
Leaves truncate, cordate or rounded at base; anthers, pale rose. 59. **C. diffusa** (A).
Leaves cuneate or rounded at base; anthers, dark purple. 60. **C. luxuriosa** (A).

58. Cratægus drymophila Sarg.

Cratægus silvicola Beadl.

Leaves ovate, acute or acuminate at apex, rounded at the entire base, sharply and often doubly serrate above with gland-tipped teeth, and slightly and irregularly divided into short acute lateral lobes, when they unfold dark red and coated with short soft pale hairs most abundant on the upper surface, about half grown when the flowers open at the end of April and then nearly glabrous, and at maturity thin, dark yellow-green and smooth or scabrate above, pale and glabrous below, or occasionally villose along the under side of the slender midrib, and of 3 or 4 pairs of thin primary veins extending to the point of the lobes, about $2'$ long and $1\frac{1}{2}'-1\frac{3}{4}'$ wide; petioles slender, glandular, about $1'$ in length; leaves at the end of vigorous shoots often deltoid, truncate or cordate at base, more coarsely serrate, more deeply lobed, and often $2\frac{1}{2}'$ long and wide. **Flowers** about $\frac{3}{4}'$ in diameter, on slender pedicels, in compact few-flowered thin-branched glabrous corymbs, with linear glandular bright red caducous bracts and bractlets; calyx-tube narrowly obconic, glabrous, the lobes gradually narrowed, acuminate, glabrous, entire or glandular-serrate; stamens 10; anthers large, dark rose color; styles 3–5, surrounded at base by a narrow ring of pale hairs **Fruit** ripening at the end of September and soon falling, on short pedicels, in erect few-fruited clusters, subglobose and often a little broader than long, red or greenish yellow, with a rosy cheek, about $\frac{1}{2}'$ in diameter; calyx little enlarged, with spreading lobes usually deciduous before the fruit ripens; flesh thin and yellow; nutlets 3–5, about $\frac{1}{4}'$ long.

A tree, sometimes 30° high, with a tall straight trunk 6'–8' in diameter, covered with close or slightly fissured bark broken into small gray or red-brown scales, and often armed with long stout branched gray spines, ascending or spreading branches forming a narrow irregular or round-topped head, and slender branchlets dark green tinged with red and covered with long pale scattered white hairs when they first appear, soon becoming gla-

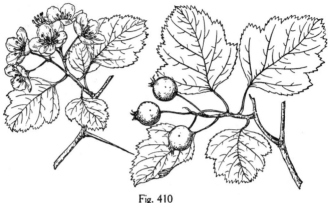

Fig. 410

brous, bright red-brown during their first year, and ultimately ashy gray, and armed with few or many thin straight or somewhat curved bright chestnut-brown spines $1\frac{1}{2}'$–$2'$ long; or in dry soil of upland forests usually a shrub, with numerous stems.

Distribution. Low moist flat woods; northern Alabama and northwestern and central Georgia, and occasionally on the drier uplands of the surrounding country; common; central Mississippi (Pelahatchee, Rankin County; Jackson, Hinds County, and in Franklin County); eastern Louisiana (Holtsville, St. Tammany Parish, anthers pink, *R. S. Cocks*).

59. Cratægus diffusa Sarg.

Cratægus Beckwithæ Sarg.

Cratægus Robbinsiana Sarg.

Leaves ovate, acute or acuminate at apex, rounded, truncate or cordate at the entire base, often doubly serrate above with straight glandular teeth, and more or less deeply divided into 4 or 5 pairs of spreading acuminate lateral lobes, deeply-tinged with red, glabrous below and covered above with short white hairs when they unfold, nearly fully grown when the flowers open from the middle to the 20th of May and then thin, pale yellow-green and hairy above and pale below, and at maturity thin and firm, smooth, dark green and glabrous on the upper surface, pale on the lower surface, $1\frac{1}{4}'$–$2'$ long, and $1'$–$1\frac{1}{2}'$ wide, with a slender yellow midrib, and thin primary veins extending obliquely to the point of the lobes; often turning orange color tinged with red in the autumn; petioles slender, slightly wing-margined at apex, glandular with minute stipitate dark glands, $\frac{1}{2}'$–$\frac{3}{4}'$ in length; leaves at the end of vigorous shoots broad-ovate, usually long-pointed, cordate or rarely truncate at base, more coarsely serrate, more deeply lobed, and frequently $2\frac{1}{2}'$–$3'$ long, and $2'$–$2\frac{1}{2}'$ wide, with a stout reddish conspicuously glandular petiole $\frac{2}{5}'$–$\frac{3}{5}'$ in length. **Flowers** $\frac{1}{2}'$–$\frac{3}{5}'$ in diameter, on slender glabrous pedicels, in 6–10-flowered corymbs, with linear glandular bracts and bractlets mostly deciduous before the flowers open; calyx-tube broadly obconic, glabrous, the lobes gradually narrowed from a wide base, acuminate at the gland-tipped apex, entire or slightly and irregularly toothed near the middle; stamens 7–10; anthers light rose color; styles 4 or 5, surrounded at base by a ring of pale tomentum.   Fruit ripening from the first to the middle of October, on slender pedicels, in few-fruited erect clusters, depressed-globose, rather broader than high, dull red and slightly pruinose, becoming lustrous, and about $\frac{1}{2}'$ in diameter; calyx little enlarged, with spreading appressed lobes bright red on the upper side below the middle and mostly persistent on the ripe fruit; flesh thin, hard, greenish white; nutlets 4 or 5, broad and rounded at base, narrowed and rounded at apex, ridged on the back with a high ridge, about $\frac{1}{4}'$ long.

A tree, occasionally 30° high with a tall trunk 8′–10′ in diameter, covered with light gray closely appressed scales, comparatively small erect branches forming an open head, and

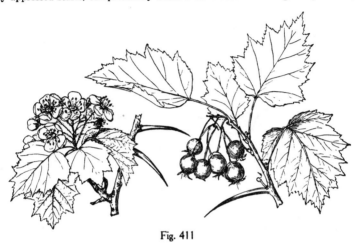

Fig. 411

slender slightly zigzag branchlets marked by numerous dark lenticels, green tinged with red and glabrous when they first appear, bright chestnut-brown and lustrous during their first winter, and pale gray-brown the following year, and armed with numerous slender or occasionally stout nearly straight bright red-brown shining spines $1\frac{1}{4}'$–$1\frac{1}{2}'$ long; usually smaller and sometimes a shrub.

Distribution.   Valley of the Connecticut River (Walpole, Cheshire County, New Hampshire, and Westminster and Putney, Windham County, Vermont), western Vermont (near Burlington, Chittenden County); eastern, central and western New York; common.

60. Cratægus luxuriosa Sarg.

Leaves oblong-ovate, acuminate, gradually narrowed and cuneate or rounded at the often unsymmetrical base, finely often doubly serrate with straight glandular teeth, and slightly divided usually only above the middle into 3 or 4 pairs of small acute lobes, about half grown when the flowers open late in May and then thin, dark yellow-green and roughened above by short white hairs and paler below, and at maturity thin, dark yellow-green and scabrate on the upper surface, pale bluish green on the lower surface, $2\frac{1}{4}'$–$2\frac{1}{2}'$ long, and $1\frac{3}{4}'$–$2'$ wide, with a slender midrib and obscure primary veins; petioles slender, slightly wing-margined at apex, occasionally glandular with minute persistent glands, $1'$–$1\frac{1}{4}'$ in length; leaves at the end of vigorous shoots broad-ovate, rounded at base, coarsely serrate, laterally lobed with numerous short broad lobes, often 3′ long and $2\frac{1}{2}'$ wide.   **Flowers** $\frac{3}{4}'$ in diameter, on short slender pedicels, in compact mostly 6–12-flowered corymbs; calyx-tube narrowly obconic, the lobes long, slender, acuminate, entire or occasionally slightly dentate near the middle, glabrous on the outer surface, slightly villose on the inner surface; stamens 8–10; anthers bright purple; styles 3–5. **Fruit** ripening and beginning to fall early in October, on short stout pedicels, in drooping usually 1–3-fruited clusters, subglobose to slightly obovoid, scarlet, lustrous, marked by pale dots, $\frac{1}{2}'–\frac{3}{4}'$ in diameter; calyx little enlarged, with a deep narrow cavity and spreading and incurved usually persistent lobes dark red on the upper side below the middle; flesh thick, yellow-green and acid; nutlets 3–5, usually 4, gradually narrowed and rounded at the ends, ridged on the back with a broad high grooved ridge, about $\frac{1}{4}'$ long.

An oval-headed tree, 20°–30° high, with a short trunk sometimes 8'–10' in diameter,

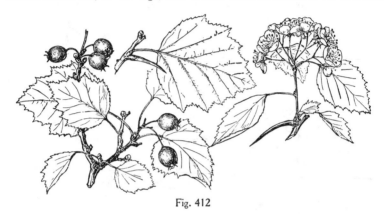

Fig. 412

covered with dark gray scaly bark, and stout zigzag often contorted branchlets dark orange-green and marked by large pale lenticels when they first appear, becoming light chestnut-brown and lustrous in their first season and dull red-brown the following year, and armed with few stout slightly curved chestnut-brown shining spines 1'–1½' long, persistent and becoming branched on old stems.

Distribution. Rich hillsides, Kittanning, Armstrong County, and on the flood plain of the Allegheny River at Whiskey Hollow across the river from Kittanning, and Linesville, Crawford County, Pennsylvania.

VII. TENUIFOLIÆ.

CONSPECTUS OF THE ARBORESCENT SPECIES.

Stamens 5–10.
 Corymbs villose.
  Leaves oblong-ovate; stamens usually 5; anthers pink; fruit obovoid to short-oblong.
                   61. **C. apiomorpha** (A).
  Leaves oblong-obovate; stamens 10; anthers reddish purple; fruit obovoid to subglobose.   62. **C. paucispina** (A).
 Corymbs glabrous; leaves oval or ovate; stamens usually 5; anthers dark reddish purple; fruit short-oblong.   63. **C. pentandra** (A).
Stamens usually 20.
 Corymbs villose.
  Leaves broad-ovate to obovate or rarely oval; fruit short-oblong to obovoid.
                   64. **C. lucorum** (A).
  Leaves rhombic to broad-ovate or rarely obovate; fruit ellipsoidal.
                   65. **C. lacera** (C).

Corymbs glabrous.
Leaves ovate; anthers pale rose color; fruit subglobose to broad-obovoid, dark red.
66. **C. depilis** (A).
Leaves ovate; stamens 15–20; anthers dark rose color; fruit subglobose.
67. **C. basilica** (A).

61. Cratægus apiomorpha Sarg.

Leaves oblong-ovate, acuminate, rounded or rarely cuneate at the entire often unsymmetrical base, finely doubly serrate above with slender glandular teeth, and slightly divided above the middle into 4 or 5 pairs of triangular acute lobes, about half grown when the flowers open early in May and then membranaceous, light yellow-green and tinged with red or bronze color, and covered above with short white hairs and pale and glabrous below, and at maturity thick and firm in texture, dark blue-green and smooth and lustrous or

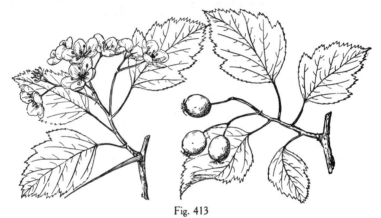

Fig. 413

sometimes dull and scabrate on the upper surface, pale blue-green on the lower surface, $1\frac{1}{2}'$–$2\frac{1}{4}'$ long, and $1\frac{1}{8}'$–$1\frac{1}{2}'$ wide, with a stout midrib, and primary veins arching obliquely to the point of the lobes; petioles slender, slightly winged at the apex, often sparingly glandular, $\frac{3}{8}'$–$1'$ in length; leaves at the end of vigorous shoots often 3' long. **Flowers** $\frac{1}{2}'$–$\frac{3}{4}'$ in diameter, on short villose or glabrous pedicels, in compact many-flowered usually hairy corymbs, their bracts and bractlets linear to oblong-obovate, glandular-serrate with stipitate dark red or purple glands, turning red before falling, mostly persistent until after the flowers open; calyx-tube narrowly obconic, glabrous, the lobes abruptly narrowed at base, slender, acuminate, entire or sparingly glandular; stamens 5–10, usually 5; anthers pink; styles 3–5, surrounded at base by tufts of pale hairs. **Fruit** ripening early in September and soon falling, on slender pedicels, in few-fruited drooping clusters, obovoid or rarely short-oblong, bright reddish purple, marked by small scattered pale dots, $\frac{3}{8}'$–$\frac{5}{8}'$ long, and $\frac{1}{4}'$–$\frac{1}{3}'$ in diameter; calyx much enlarged, with spreading lobes, their tips mostly deciduous from the ripe fruit; flesh thin, yellow, juicy, pleasantly acid; nutlets 3–5, thin, rounded and ridged on the back with a low ridge, about $\frac{1}{4}'$ long.

A tree, sometimes 25° high, with a trunk 6' in diameter and 3°–6° long, covered with dark gray bark separating into thin plates, in falling disclosing the yellow inner bark, numerous ascending branches forming an oblong or pyramidal crown, and slender branchlets dark dull red-brown during their first season, becoming dark gray-brown the following year, and unarmed, or armed with slender nearly straight dull red-brown ultimately ashy gray spines 1'–$1\frac{1}{2}'$ long; or often shrubby, with numerous stems spreading into small clumps.

Distribution. Dry open places, borders of woods, and the margins of the high banks of streams; common and generally distributed in northeastern Illinois.

62. Cratægus paucispina Sarg.

Leaves oblong-obovate, acuminate, rounded, concave-cuneate to truncate or subcordate at the entire base, sharply doubly serrate above with straight glandular teeth, and deeply divided into 4 or 5 pairs of acute lateral lobes spreading or pointing toward the apex of the leaf, about half grown when the flowers open early in May and then light yellow-green and slightly roughened above by short white hairs and paler and glabrous below, and at maturity membranaceous, dark blue-green and scabrate on the upper surface, pale blue-green on the lower surface, $2\frac{1}{2}'$–$3'$ long, and $1\frac{1}{2}'$–$2\frac{1}{2}'$ wide, with a slender yellow midrib, and thin primary veins extending obliquely to the point of the lobes; petioles slender, usually without glands, tinged with purple in the autumn, $\frac{3}{4}'$–$1\frac{1}{2}'$ in length. **Flowers** $\frac{5}{8}'$–$\frac{3}{4}'$ in diameter, on slender hairy pedicels, in broad 12–20-flowered slightly villose corymbs, their bracts and bractlets linear to oblong-obovate, glandular, red, mostly persistent until after the flowers

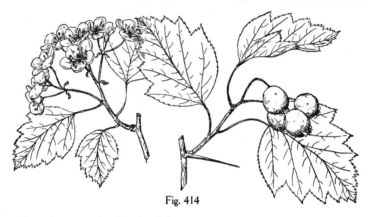

Fig. 414

open; calyx-tube narrowly obconic, glabrous, the lobes narrow, acuminate, glandular-serrate with small dark red stipitate glands, glabrous on the outer, pubescent on the inner surface; stamens 10; anthers bright reddish purple; styles 4 or 5, surrounded at base by tufts of pale hairs. **Fruit** ripening during the first half of September and soon falling, on slender glabrous pedicels, in drooping clusters, obovoid to subglobose, crimson or purplish, marked by numerous small pale dots, slightly pruinose, $\frac{1}{2}'$–$\frac{5}{8}'$ long, and about $\frac{1}{2}'$ in diameter; calyx small, with reflexed and appressed or erect and incurved serrate lobes dark red on the upper side below the middle, often deciduous from the ripe fruit; flesh thin, yellow, juicy, acid and edible; nutlets 4 or 5, thin, narrowed and acute at the ends, rounded and slightly grooved or obscurely ridged on the back, about $\frac{1}{4}'$ long.

A tree, sometimes 25° high, with a trunk $4'$–$6'$ in diameter and often 6° long, covered with dark gray or nearly black bark separating into thin plate-like scales, numerous branches forming a round-topped head, and slender glabrous branchlets dark yellow-green when they first appear, becoming dark reddish brown at the end of their first season, olive-green in their second year, and ultimately dark gray-brown, and armed with small straight light red-brown shining spines $\frac{1}{2}'$–$\frac{3}{4}'$ long.

Distribution. Woods and river banks in dry clay soil; northeastern Illinois; common.

63. Cratægus pentandra Sarg.

Leaves oval or ovate, acuminate, broadly cuneate or rarely rounded at the entire base, divided above the middle into numerous short acute or acuminate lobes, and coarsely and often doubly serrate with straight or incurved teeth tipped with small dark glands, nearly fully grown and very thin when the flowers open at the end of May, and at maturity membranaceous, dark green and roughened above by short rigid pale hairs, pale and glabrous below, 2'–2½' long, and 1½'–2' wide, with a slender yellow midrib, and thin primary veins extending to the point of the lobes; petioles slender, often winged toward the apex, glandular with minute dark glands, usually about 1' in length; leaves at the end of vigorous shoots more deeply lobed, and often 4' long and 3' wide. **Flowers** $\frac{5}{8}'$–$\frac{3}{4}'$ in diameter, on long slender pedicels, in compact few-flowered glabrous corymbs; calyx-tube narrowly obconic, glabrous, dark red, the lobes linear-lanceolate, entire or finely glandular-serrate; stamens usually 5, occasionally 6–10; anthers large, dark red-purple; styles 3, surrounded at base by a thin ring of hoary tomentum. **Fruit** ripening about the middle of September and soon falling, on stout pedicels, in drooping narrow clusters, short-oblong, full and rounded at the ends, dark crimson, lustrous, marked by minute pale dots, usually about $\frac{5}{8}'$ long and $\frac{1}{2}'$ in diameter; calyx enlarged and persistent, the lobes elongated, strongly incurved, often

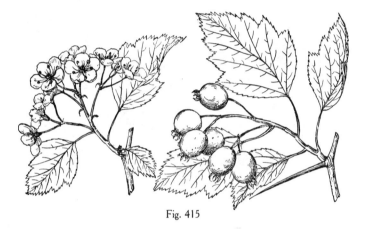

Fig. 415

deciduous before the fruit ripens; flesh thick, dry and mealy; nutlets 3, narrowed and acute at the ends, prominently ridged on the back with a high broad ridge, $\frac{1}{3}'$ long.

A tree, rarely more than 15° high, with a straight trunk 5'–6' in diameter, covered with thin bark separating into papery lustrous pale scales, stout branches forming a broad open irregular head, and slender glabrous branchlets bright chestnut-brown during their first season, becoming ashy gray the following year, and armed with many thick straight or curved bright chestnut-brown or red-brown spines 1'–1½' long.

Distribution. Low hills and limestone ridges; western and southern Vermont; southern Connecticut (rocky shore of Alewive Creek, Waterford, New London County), and eastern and central New York (Whitesboro, Oneida County).

64. Cratægus lucorum Sarg.

Leaves broad-ovate to obovate or rarely oval, broad-cuneate or rounded at the entire base, coarsely serrate above with straight teeth tipped with large persistent bright red glands, and deeply divided above the middle into 3 or 4 pairs of wide acute or acuminate lobes. rather more than a third grown when the flowers open early in May and then light yellow-bronze color, covered on the upper surface with short soft pale hairs and glabrous on the lower surface, and at maturity membranaceous, smooth, dark dull green and glabrous above, pale yellow-green below, about 2' long and 1¼' wide, with a slender yellow midrib. and 3 or 4 pairs of thin primary veins extending obliquely to the point of the lobes;

petioles slender, glandular, often somewhat winged toward the apex, $1'-1\frac{1}{2}'$ in length; leaves at the end of vigorous shoots usually ovate and rounded at the broad base, more deeply lobed, and sometimes 3' long and broad. **Flowers** $\frac{3}{4}'$ in diameter, on thin pedicels, in narrow compact few-flowered small villose corymbs; calyx broadly obconic, glabrous, the lobes narrow, acuminate. coarsely glandular-serrate, villose on the inner surface; stamens 20; anthers small, dark purple; styles 4 or 5. **Fruit** ripening about the middle of September and soon falling, on short stout pedicels, in erect few-fruited slightly villose clusters, obovoid until nearly fully grown and then short-oblong or somewhat obovoid, full and rounded at the ends, crimson, lustrous, marked by small pale dots, $\frac{1}{2}'-\frac{5}{8}'$ long; calyx enlarged, the lobes elongated, coarsely glandular-serrate, villose above, closely appressed, often deciduous before the fruit ripens; flesh thick, yellow, dry and mealy; nutlets 4 or 5, thin, rounded, and sometimes obscurely ridged on the back, about $\frac{1}{4}'$ long.

A tree, 20°–25° high, with a tall straight trunk 6'–8' in diameter, covered with close dark red-brown bark, slender ascending branches forming a narrow open head, and thin branch-

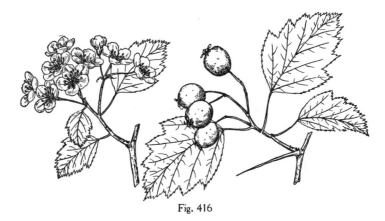

Fig. 416

lets dark green and somewhat villose when they first appear, becoming dull orange-brown in their first summer and ultimately dark gray-brown, and armed with straight or slightly curved bright red-brown lustrous spines $1'-1\frac{1}{2}'$ long.

Distribution. Rich moist soil along the margins of Oak-groves on the banks of sloughs; Barrington, Cook County, Illinois; near Ithaca, Tompkins County, New York.

65. Cratægus lacera Sarg.

Leaves rhombic to broad-ovate or rarely obovate, acute at apex, broadly cuneate and entire at base, coarsely often doubly serrate above with straight glandular teeth, and divided above the middle into numerous acute lobes, when they unfold coated below with thick hoary tomentum and villose above, nearly fully grown when the flowers open about the 20th of April and then glabrous on the lower surface and covered on the upper surface with short scattered pale hairs, and at maturity glabrous, light yellow-green, paler below than above, thin, about $1\frac{1}{2}'$ long and $1\frac{1}{4}'$ wide, with a slender yellow midrib and few remote primary veins; petioles slender, villose, becoming glabrous or puberulous, slightly winged at the apex, often red toward the base, $\frac{1}{4}'-\frac{1}{3}'$ in length; leaves at the end of vigorous shoots broad-ovate, often deeply 3-lobed, coarsely serrate, 3'–4' long and broad. **Flowers** $\frac{3}{4}'$ in diameter, on slender villose pedicels, in sparingly villose few-flowered corymbs; calyx-tube narrowly obconic, glabrous, the lobes linear-lanceolate, elongated, coarsely glandular-serrate, glabrous on the outer surface, villose on the inner surface; stamens 20; anthers small, rose color; styles 4 or 5. **Fruit** ripening toward the end of October, on short stout glabrous pedicels, in erect few-fruited clusters, ellipsoidal, rounded at the ends, bright cherry-red, lustrous, marked by occasional large dark dots, about $\frac{1}{2}'$ long; calyx only slightly

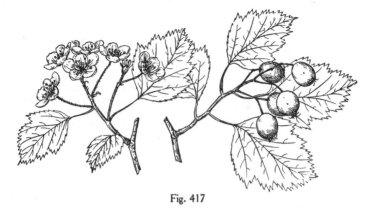

Fig. 417

enlarged, with small nearly triangular villose spreading lobes mostly deciduous before the fruit ripens; flesh thick, orange color; nutlets 3–5, thin, narrowed at the ends, only slightly ridged on the rounded back, $\frac{5}{16}'$ long.

A slender tree, 25°–30° high, with a tall trunk 4′–5′ in diameter, covered with pale scaly bark, small short branches forming a narrow head, and slender branchlets dark olive-green and villose when they first appear, becoming light red-brown and glabrous during their first summer, and ultimately dull light gray, and armed with thin straight bright chestnut-brown lustrous spines $\frac{3}{4}'$–$1\frac{3}{4}'$ long.

Distribution. Low rich forest-glades near Fulton, Hempstead County, Arkansas.

66. Cratægus depilis Sarg.

Leaves ovate, acute or acuminate, rounded or broad-cuneate and often unsymmetrical at the entire base, sharply doubly serrate above with straight glandular teeth, and often

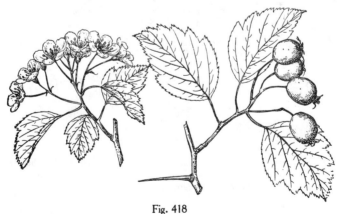

Fig. 418

divided into 4 or 5 pairs of short acute lobes, when they unfold deeply tinged with red and covered above with fine short caducous hairs, nearly half grown when the flowers open during the second week of May, and at maturity membranaceous, glabrous, smooth, yellowish to bluish green on the upper surface, pale on the lower surface, $1\frac{1}{2}'$–$2'$ long, and $1'$–$1\frac{1}{4}'$ wide, with a slender midrib and 5 or 6 pairs of thin primary veins; turning yellowish and brown or russet color in the autumn; petioles slender, glabrous, sparingly glandular with minute glands, $\frac{3}{4}'$–$1'$ in length; leaves at the end of vigorous shoots often $2\frac{1}{2}'$ long and $1\frac{1}{2}'$ wide. **Flowers** $\frac{3}{4}'$ in diameter, on slender pedicels, in broad glabrous 8–12-flowered corymbs, with linear or oblong glandular bracts and bractlets; calyx narrowly obconic, glabrous, the lobes lanceolate, glandular-serrate, deeply tinged with purple; stamens 20; anthers pale rose color; styles 4 or 5. **Fruit** ripening early in September and soon falling, on slender pedicels, in drooping few-fruited clusters, subglobose to broad-obovoid, dark red to reddish purple, lustrous, $\frac{1}{2}'$–$\frac{3}{4}'$ long, and $\frac{3}{8}'$–$\frac{5}{8}'$ in diameter; calyx only slightly enlarged, the lobes reflexed, glandular-serrate, and red on the upper side toward the base; flesh thick, yellow, sweet, juicy and slightly acid; nutlets 4 or 5, full and rounded at apex, narrowed and acute at base, and prominently but irregularly ridged on the back with a high sometimes grooved ridge, $\frac{1}{4}'$–$\frac{5}{16}'$ long.

A tree, 20°–25° high, with a trunk $4'$–$8'$ in diameter and 6°–9° long, covered with dark gray or gray-brown flaky bark, spreading branches forming an oblong or rounded open head, and slender glabrous branchlets bright red-brown and very lustrous during their first summer, becoming light gray-brown the following year, and armed with stout or slender nearly straight spines $\frac{3}{4}'$–$1\frac{1}{2}'$ long.

Distribution. Rich clay or gravelly soil in pastures and on the borders of woods; northeastern Illinois (Lake, Cook and Mill Counties).

67. Cratægus basilica Beadl.

Leaves ovate, acute or acuminate, broad-cuneate or rounded at the entire or crenate base, sharply and often doubly serrate above with straight slender glandular teeth, and

Fig. 419

divided into numerous short acute lateral lobes, more than half grown when the flowers open early in May and then roughened above by short pale hairs and glabrous below, and at maturity thin but firm in texture, bright green and scabrate above, paler below, $2\frac{1}{2}'$–$3'$ long, and $1\frac{1}{2}'$–$2'$ wide, with a slender yellow midrib, and thin veins arching to the point of the lobes; turning yellow and brown in the autumn; petioles slender, slightly winged at apex, $1'$–$1\frac{1}{2}'$ in length. **Flowers** $\frac{1}{2}'$–$\frac{5}{8}'$ in diameter, on elongated slender pedicels, in 5–15-flowered glabrous compact corymbs; calyx-tube broadly obconic, glabrous, the lobes slender, acuminate, glabrous, entire or occasionally serrate; stamens 15–20; anthers dark rose color;

styles 3–5. **Fruit** ripening and falling early in September, on slender pedicels, in few-fruited drooping clusters, subglobose, scarlet, covered with a glaucous bloom, $\frac{1}{2}'-\frac{5}{8}'$ in diameter; flesh soft, sweet, and edible; nutlets 3–5, narrowed and acute at the ends, prominently ridged on the back with a high broadly grooved ridge, $\frac{1}{4}'-\frac{5}{16}'$ long.

A tree, sometimes 20° high, with a trunk 7′–8′ in diameter, covered with dark gray or brown scaly bark, ascending or slightly spreading branches forming a narrow irregular head, and stout glabrous branchlets dark chestnut-brown in their first season becoming dark gray, and armed with numerous slender bright chestnut-brown lustrous ultimately gray spines $2'-2\frac{1}{2}'$ long.

Distribution. Open woods and the borders of fields and roads, western North Carolina, usually at altitudes of 2000°–3000° above the sea.

VIII. MOLLES.

CONSPECTUS OF THE ARBORESCENT SPECIES.

Stamens 20.
  Anthers pale yellow or white (*rose color in* 71).
    Leaves broad and rounded, truncate or cordate at base; fruit subglobose to short-oblong or obovoid, red, crimson or scarlet.
      Mature leaves glabrous on the upper surface.
        Leaves thin.
          Fruit subglobose to short-oblong, scarlet, ripening in August and September.
                              68. **C. mollis** (A).
          Fruit obovoid to short-oblong, dark red, ripening in October.   69. **C. sera** (A).
        Leaves subcoriaceous; fruit short-oblong to obovoid, crimson, ripening in October and November.   70. **C. arkansana** (C).
      Mature leaves scabrate on the upper surface; fruit depressed-globose, red, ripening in August and September.   71. **C. gravida** (A).
    Leaves broad-cuneate or rounded at base, acute or acuminate, scabrate on the upper surface at maturity.
      Fruit red.
        Leaves villose below at maturity on midrib and veins, those at the end of vigorous shoots cuneate at base; flowers in usually 7–12-flowered corymbs; fruit short-oblong, orange-red.   72. **C. invisa** (C).
        Leaves hoary-tomentose below at maturity, those at the end of vigorous shoots rounded, cordate or abruptly cuneate at the broad base; flowers in 15–20-flowered corymbs; fruit ellipsoidal, ovoid, short-oblong or subglobose, crimson.
                                      73. **C. limaria** (C).
      Fruit bright canary yellow, subglobose; leaves villose below at maturity elliptic to ovate, oval or slightly obovate.   74. **C. viburnifolia** (C).
    Leaves narrowed at base.
      Mature leaves glabrous on the upper surface; fruit short-oblong to subglobose.
        Leaves oblong-obovate or oval.   75. **C. Berlandieri** (C).
        Leaves elliptic to ovate or slightly obovate.   76. **C. meridionalis** (C).
      Mature leaves scabrate on the upper surface; fruit subglobose to short-oblong, red.
        Leaves ovate to oval; flowers in 3–10-flowered corymbs; calyx-lobes glabrous.
                                      77. **C. Treleasei** (C).
        Leaves ovate; flowers in many-flowered corymbs; calyx-lobes villose.
                                    78. **C. canadensis**.
  Anthers rose color.
    Leaves broad at base.
      Mature leaves smooth on the upper surface.
        Leaves thick, ovate, acute at apex; fruit short-oblong to obovoid, bright cherry red.   79. **C. corusca** (A).

Leaves thin, broad-ovate to suborbicular, rounded at apex; fruit subglobose to ovoid, bright yellow.   80. C. Kelloggii (A).

Mature leaves scabrate on the upper surface, oblong-obovate; fruit short-oblong, crimson.   81. C. induta (C).

Leaves narrowed at base; fruit red.

Leaves yellow-green.

Mature leaves glabrous on the upper surface; fruit short-oblong to obovoid.
           82. C. texana (C).

Mature leaves scabrate on the upper surface.

Fruit subglobose to short-oblong.   83. C. quercina (C).

Fruit obovoid.   84. C. dispersa (C).

Leaves blue-green, subcoriaceous, ovate to suborbicular, scabrate on the upper surface; fruit subglobose to short-oblong, red.   85. C. lanuginosa (C).

Stamens 10.

Anthers yellow.

Leaves broad at base.

Leaves smooth on the upper surface.

Leaves ovate or rarely oval, dark yellow-green above; fruit subglobose, crimson, ripening late in August.   86. C. arnoldiana (A).

Leaves ovate, blue-green above; fruit obovoid to short-oblong, scarlet, ripening in September.   87. C. champlainensis (A).

Leaves scabrate on the upper surface, ovate, acute, rounded or abruptly cuneate at base; anthers nearly white; fruit short-oblong, bright orange-red.
           88. C. pennsylvanica (A).

Leaves cuneate at base, scabrate on the upper surface, ovate, acute; fruit obovoid, orange-red.   89. C. submollis (A).

Anthers rose color.

Leaves broad at the rounded, abruptly cuneate or cordate base.

Leaves scabrate on the upper surface.

Leaves oval, rounded or cuneate at base; flowers in wide many-flowered corymbs; fruit short-oblong, crimson.   90. C. Ellwangeriana (A).

Leaves oblong-ovate; flowers in compact few-flowered corymbs; fruit obovoid to short-oblong, scarlet.   91. C. Robesoniana (A).

Leaves smooth on the upper surface at maturity, ovate, usually broad-cuneate at base; fruit obovoid to short-oblong, crimson.   92. C. anomala (A).

Leaves cuneate at base, smooth on the upper surface at maturity; fruit subglobose, orange-red.   93. C. noelensis (C).

68. Cratægus mollis Scheele.   Red Haw.

Leaves broad-ovate, acute, usually cordate or rounded at the wide base, coarsely and generally doubly serrate with straight glandular teeth, and more or less deeply divided into 4 or 5 pairs of acute or rounded lateral lobes, covered above with short pale hairs and hoary-tomentose below when they unfold, about half grown when the flowers open early in May and then membranaceous, light yellow-green and hairy above and pubescent or tomentose below, and at maturity firm in texture, dark yellow-green and slightly rugose on the upper surface and paler and pubescent or puberulous on the lower surface along the stout midrib, and 4 or 5 pairs of primary veins extending to the point of the lobes, 3'–4' long and broad; petioles stout, terete, at first tomentose, ultimately pubescent or nearly glabrous, often slightly glandular with small dark caducous glands, 1'–1¼' in length; leaves at the end of vigorous shoots more deeply lobed, with a deeper basal sinus, and frequently 5'–6' long and broad.   **Flowers** 1' in diameter, on stout densely villose pedicels, in broad many-flowered tomentose corymbs, with conspicuous bracts and bractlets; calyx-tube narrowly obconic, hoary-tomentose, the lobes narrow, acuminate, coarsely glandular-serrate with bright red glands, villose on the outer, tomentose on the inner surface; stamens 20: anthers large, light yellow; styles 4 or 5, surrounded at base by a broad ring of hoary tomentum. **Fruit** ripening late in August and early in September, on stout pedicels, in drooping few-fruited villose clusters, short-oblong to subglobose, rounded at the ends, more or less pubescent, scarlet marked by occasional large dark dots; $\frac{3}{4}'$–$1'$ in diameter; calyx prominent, hairy, with large erect and incurved lobes usually deciduous before the fruit ripens; flesh thick, yellow, subacid, dry and mealy; nutlets 4 or 5, thin, rounded and obscurely ridged on the back, light brown, $\frac{1}{4}'$ long.

Fig. 420

A tree, sometimes 40° high, with a tall trunk often 18′ in diameter, heavy wide-spreading smooth ashy gray branches forming a broad round-topped and often symmetrical head, and stout branchlets covered at first with a thick coat of long white matted hairs, villose during their first season, becoming glabrous in their second year, and armed with occasional straight thick bright chestnut-brown shining spines 1′–2′ long.

Distribution. Low rich soil usually on the bottom-lands of streams; northern Ohio and southwestern Ontario (Point Edward) to northern Missouri, eastern South Dakota, eastern Nebraska, eastern Kansas, and Richland County, Illinois; common; near Nashville, Davidson County, Tennessee.

69. Cratægus sera Sarg.

Leaves oblong-ovate, acute or acuminate, rounded, truncate or slightly cordate at the broad base, irregularly divided into 4 or 5 pairs of short acute lateral lobes, and sharply and sometimes doubly serrate nearly to the base with straight glandular teeth, unfolding about the 1st of May with the opening of the flowers and then covered above with short soft white hairs and tomentose below, and at maturity membranaceous, dark yellow-green and glabrous on the upper surface, pubescent on the lower surface, 2′–4′ long, and 2½′–3′ wide, with a slender midrib, and thin remote primary veins extending to the point of the lobes; petioles slender, tomentose, becoming pubescent, 1′–1½′ in length; leaves at the end of vigorous shoots more deeply lobed, and often 4′–5′ long and 3′–4′ wide. **Flowers** $\frac{3}{4}'$ in diameter, on stout densely villose pedicels, in compact many-flowered tomentose corymbs; calyx-tube broadly obconic, coated with broad matted pale hairs, the lobes broad, acute or acuminate, glandular-serrate with large dark glands, tomentose on the outer surface and villose on the inner surface; stamens 20; anthers pale yellow; styles 4 or 5, usually 5. **Fruit** ripening about the 1st of October, on stout puberulous or villose pedicels, in drooping or erect few-fruited clusters, obovoid or short-oblong, dull dark red, marked by small pale dots, usually slightly villose or pubescent at the ends, $\frac{2}{3}'$ long, and $\frac{1}{2}'$ in diameter; calyx enlarged, with erect, coarsely glandular-serrate, incurved lobes often deciduous before the ripening of the fruit; flesh thick, dry and mealy; nutlets usually 5, thin, light brown, irregularly grooved on the back with a broad shallow groove, $\frac{1}{4}'$ long.

A tree, 30°–40° high, with a tall straight trunk 12′–18′ in diameter, thick branches form-ing a broad round-topped symmetrical head, and branchlets hoary-tomentose at first, be-

Fig. 421

coming light red-brown and puberulous and ultimately pale orange-brown, and armed with occasional straight or slightly curved chestnut-brown lustrous spines $1\frac{1}{4}′–1\frac{1}{2}′$ in length.

Distribution. Walpole Island, Lamberton County, southwestern Ontario; Belle Isle in the Detroit River, near Port Huron, St. Clair County, and in the neighborhood of Grand Rapids, Kent County, Michigan; northeastern Illinois (Cook, Will, Lake and Dupage Counties), and in the neighborhood of Milwaukee, Milwaukee County, Wisconsin.

70. Cratægus arkansana Sarg.

Leaves oblong-ovate or oval, acute, rounded, broadly cuneate or truncate at base, usually divided above the middle into 3 or 4 pairs of short broad acute lobes, and serrate sometimes to the base with short straight glandular teeth, when the flowers open about the

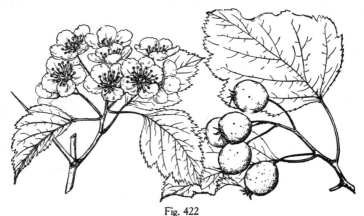

Fig. 422

middle of May nearly one third grown and coated with soft white hairs, and at maturity thick and leathery, dull dark green and glabrous on the upper surface, pale yellow-green on the lower surface, 2′–3′ long, and $1\frac{3}{4}′–2′$ wide, with a stout light yellow midrib and primary veins slightly villose below, conspicuous secondary veins and reticulate veinlets; late in October and in November turning bright clear yellow; petioles stout, deeply grooved, more or less winged toward the apex, glandular with minute usually deciduous dark glands, at first tomentose, ultimately glabrous or puberulous, turning dark red after midsummer, $1'$–$1\frac{1}{2}'$ in length; leaves at the end of vigorous shoots broad-ovate, rounded or truncate at base, often $4'$ long and $3'$ wide.   **Flowers** nearly $1'$ in diameter, on short stout pedicels, in broad rather compact many-flowered villose corymbs; calyx-tube narrowly obconic, coated with long matted pale hairs, the lobes short, acute, coarsely glandular-serrate, glabrous or slightly villose; stamens 20; anthers large, pale yellow; styles 5.   **Fruit** ripening at the end of October and falling gradually at the end of several weeks, on stout villose pedicels, in few-fruited drooping clusters, short-oblong or rarely obovoid, rounded and slightly tomentose at the ends, bright crimson, very lustrous, marked by few large dark dots, $\frac{3}{4}'$–$1'$ long, about $\frac{3}{4}$ in diameter; calyx little enlarged, with small linear-lanceolate coarsely glandular-serrate erect and persistent lobes; flesh thick, yellow, subacid; nutlets 5, small in comparison to the size of the fruit, thin, rounded or slightly and irregularly ridged on the back, $\frac{1}{3}'$ long.

A tree, $20°$ high, with a tall straight stem, thick slightly ascending wide-spreading branches forming a broad open irregular head, and stout branchlets dark green and covered early in the season with long pale hairs, becoming orange-brown, glabrous, and very lustrous in their first winter, and unarmed or armed with occasional straight light chestnut-brown shining spines, $\frac{1}{3}'$–$\frac{1}{2}'$ in length.

Distribution.   Bottom-lands of the White River near Newport, Jackson County, Arkansas; hardy as far north as eastern Massachusetts, and unsurpassed late in the autumn in the beauty of its large brilliant abundant fruits long persistent on the branches.

71. Cratægus gravida Beadl.

Leaves broad-ovate, acute, rounded or truncate at base, coarsely and often doubly serrate with incurved glandular teeth, and slightly incisely lobed, roughened above by short pale hairs and hoary-tomentose below when they unfold, nearly half grown when the

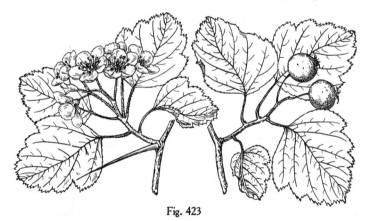

Fig. 423

flowers open about the 1st of May, and at maturity thin, firm, dark green, lustrous and scabrate above, paler and pubescent or puberulous below, particularly on the slender midrib and veins, $1\frac{3}{4}'$–$2\frac{1}{2}'$ long, and $1\frac{1}{2}'$ wide; turning in the autumn yellow, orange and brown; petioles slender, tomentose early in the season, becoming pubescent or nearly glabrous, about $\frac{1}{2}'$–$1'$ in length; leaves at the end of vigorous shoots oblong-ovate to nearly orbicular, round or cuneate at the broad base, more coarsely serrate, more deeply lobed, and often $2\frac{1}{2}'-3'$ long and wide, their petioles $\frac{3}{4}'-1'$ long. **Flowers** about $\frac{5}{8}'$ in diameter, on short hoary-tomentose pedicels, in narrow crowded many-flowered hoary-tomentose corymbs; calyx-tube broadly obconic, covered with matted pale hairs, the lobes gradually narrowed, acuminate, glandular-serrate, villose; stamens 20; anthers dark rose; styles 5. **Fruit** ripening in August and September, on elongated tomentose pedicels, in few-fruited drooping clusters, depressed-globose, red; calyx enlarged, the lobes conspicuously serrate, puberulous on the upper surface, reflexed and closely appressed, sometimes deciduous from the ripe fruit; flesh thin, yellow, dry and mealy; nutlets 5, thin, narrow and rounded at base, acute at apex, rounded and obscurely grooved on the back, about $\frac{5}{16}'$ long.

A tree, sometimes 20° high, with a trunk $8'-10'$ in diameter, heavy wide-spreading branches forming a broad round-topped head, and stout branchlets covered at first with a thick coat of matted pale hairs, orange-red and puberulous at the end of their first season, glabrous and reddish brown the following year, and armed with slender nearly straight spines about $1\frac{1}{2}'$ long.

Distribution.   Limestone hills in the neighborhood of Nashville, Davidson County, Tennessee.

72. Cratægus invisa Sarg.

Leaves ovate to oval, acute or acuminate at apex, cuneate or rounded at base, coarsely often doubly serrate with broad straight glandular teeth, and slightly divided usually only above the middle into 3 or 4 pairs of small acuminate lobes, densely tomentose below and

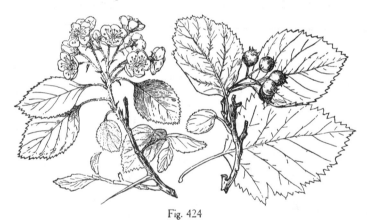

Fig. 424

villose above when they unfold, about one third grown when the flowers open at the end of March and then thin, dark yellow-green and roughened on the upper surface by short hairs and coated below with long matted white hairs, and at maturity thin, yellow-green, scabrate and lustrous above, hairy below especially on the midrib and veins, $2\frac{1}{2}'-3'$ long, and $2'-2\frac{1}{2}'$ wide; petioles slender, slightly wing-margined at apex, covered with pale hairs early in the season, becoming nearly glabrous, and $1\frac{1}{2}'-2'$ in length; leaves at the end of vigorous shoots broad-ovate, acuminate, abruptly cuneate at the wide base, more coarsely serrate, deeply divided into acute lateral lobes, and often $3\frac{1}{2}'-4'$ long and $3'-3\frac{1}{2}'$ wide; petioles slender, villose, $1\frac{1}{2}'-2'$ in length.   **Flowers** opening at the end of March, about $\frac{3}{4}'$ in diameter, on slender pedicels thickly coated like the wide calyx-tube with long matted white hairs, in broad mostly 7–12-flowered corymbs; calyx-lobes gradually narrowed from the base, short, broad, acuminate, laciniately glandular-serrate, thickly covered with long white hairs on the outer surface, villose above the middle on the inner surface; stamens 20; anthers white; styles 3–5, surrounded at base by a ring of long white hairs.   **Fruit** ripening at the end of October, on long slender slightly hairy pedicels, in erect or spreading few-fruited clusters, short-oblong, full and rounded and slightly hairy at the ends, orange-red, marked by large pale dots, and about $\frac{1}{2}'$ in diameter; calyx little enlarged, with spreading lobes dark red on the upper side below the middle and villose toward the apex; flesh thin, yellow, dry and mealy; nutlets 3–5, rounded at the ends, broader at apex than at base, rounded and only slightly grooved on the back, $\frac{1}{5}'$ long.

A tree, sometimes 30° high, with a tall trunk covered with dark brown bark broken into small closely appressed plate-like scales, large spreading branches forming a wide irregular head, and stout slightly zigzag branchlets clothed when they first appear with hoary tomentum, dull gray-brown, marked by small pale lenticels and slightly pubescent at the end of their first season and dark gray the following year, and unarmed or armed with occasional slender straight chestnut-brown spines $1'-1\frac{1}{4}'$ long.

Distribution. In dense woods on the rich bottom-lands of Red River near Fulton, Hempstead County, and near Texarkana, Miller County, Arkansas, Hugo, Choctaw County, Oklahoma, and to San Augustine, San Augustine County, Texas.

73. Cratægus limaria Sarg.

Cratægus Mackensenii Sarg.

Leaves ovate, acute, concave-cuneate or rounded at base, coarsely often doubly serrate with broad straight glandular teeth, and slightly divided into 3 or 4 pairs of small acute lateral lobes, not more than a quarter grown when the flowers open early in April and then

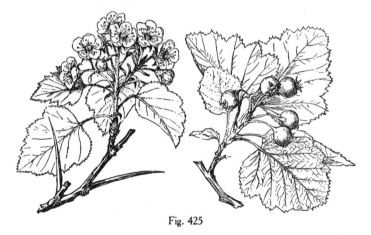

Fig. 425

thin, yellow-green and covered above with short white hairs and thickly coated below with hoary tomentum, and at maturity light green and scabrate on the upper surface, pale and tomentose on the lower surface, $2\frac{1}{2}'-3'$ long, and $1\frac{1}{2}'-2'$ wide, with a stout midrib and thin primary veins; petioles slender, slightly wing-margined at apex, covered when they first appear with long matted white hairs, villose through the season, and $1'-1\frac{1}{2}'$ in length; leaves at the end of vigorous shoots broad-ovate, rounded or cordate at the wide base, more deeply lobed, and often 4' long and broad. **Flowers** opening early in April, $\frac{4}{5}'-1'$ in diameter, on long slender pedicels coated with matted white hairs, in compact 15–20-flowered villose corymbs; calyx-tube broadly obconic, thickly covered with white hairs, the lobes gradually narrowed from the base, wide, acuminate, laciniately glandular-serrate, villose; stamens 20; anthers white; styles 3–5, surrounded at base by a narrow ring of pale tomentum. **Fruit** ripening in October, on long stout erect or spreading hairy pedicels, in few-fruited clusters, ellipsoidal to ovoid or short-oblong, rounded at apex, truncate at base, crimson, lustrous, marked by large pale dots, villose especially at the ends, $\frac{1}{2}'-\frac{3}{5}'$ in diameter; calyx prominent, with a long villose tube, and erect villose persistent lobes dark red on the upper side below the middle, their tips slightly spreading or incurved; flesh thick, yellow, dry and mealy; nutlets 3–5, narrowed and rounded at apex, rounded at the broad base, slightly grooved on the back, $\frac{1}{5}'-\frac{1}{4}'$ long.

A tree, often 30° high, with a tall trunk 8'–12' in diameter, covered with dark scaly bark, stout ascending branches forming a narrow irregular head, and slender zigzag branchlets thickly coated when they first appear with long white hairs, light orange-brown, lustrous, pubescent and marked by pale lenticels at the end of their first season, dull gray-brown and glabrous the following year, and armed with slender straight or slightly curved purple ultimately ashy gray spines 2'–2½' long.

Distribution. In dense woods on the rich bottom-lands of the Red River near Fulton, Hempstead County, Arkansas; river banks; western Texas (Guadalupe River, near Victoria, Victoria County; Cibolo River, Sutherland Springs, Wilson County; San Antonio River, Bexar County; *C. Mackensenii* Sarg.).

74. Cratægus viburnifolia Sarg.

Leaves elliptic to ovate, oval or slightly obovate, acute or rounded at apex, concave-cuneate at the entire base, coarsely often doubly serrate above with straight glandular teeth, and slightly and irregularly divided above the middle into 2 or 3 pairs of small acute

Fig. 426

lobes, half grown when the flowers open about the 20th of March and then thin, yellow-green and roughened above by short white hairs and hoary-tomentose below, and at maturity thick, deep green, very lustrous and scabrate on the upper surface, coated on the lower surface with pale hairs, 2½'–3½' long, and 2'–2½' wide, with a prominent midrib and primary veins; petioles slightly wing-margined at apex, densely hoary-tomentose early in the season, becoming glabrous, $\frac{2}{5}'-1\frac{1}{2}'$ in length. **Flowers** about $\frac{3}{4}'$ in diameter, on long slender tomentose pedicels, in wide lax mostly 5–12-flowered corymbs, with large lanceolate to spatulate foliaceous bracts and bractlets slightly serrate above the middle, and generally persistent until after the petals fall; calyx-tube narrowly obconic, thickly coated with matted white hairs, the lobes gradually narrowed from the base, long, slender, acuminate, laciniately glandular-serrate, slightly villose on the outer surface, densely villose on the inner surface; stamens 20; anthers white; styles 4 or 5. **Fruit** ripening early in October, on long slender drooping slightly hairy pedicels, in few-fruited clusters, subglobose, bright canary yellow, about 1' in diameter; calyx little enlarged, with spreading lobes; flesh thick, light yellow, soft and succulent; nutlets 4 or 5, gradually narrowed and rounded at the ends, irregularly ridged on the back with a broad grooved ridge, $\frac{1}{3}'$ long.

A tree, 30°-35° high, with a tall trunk sometimes a foot in diameter, covered with gray scaly bark, large ascending and spreading branches forming an open irregular head, and stout nearly straight unarmed branchlets thickly coated with hoary tomentum when they first appear, becoming purple, lustrous and nearly glabrous at the end of their first season and dark brown or gray-brown the following year.

Distribution. Borders of woods in low ground, valley of the Brazos River near Columbia, Brazoria County, and in low woods on the Colorado River, at Wharton, Wharton County, Texas.

75. Cratægus Berlandieri Sarg.

Leaves oblong-obovate or oval, acute or acuminate, gradually narrowed, cuneate and entire below the middle, coarsely and often doubly serrate with broad straight or incurved glandular teeth, and unequally divided above into numerous acute or acuminate lobes,

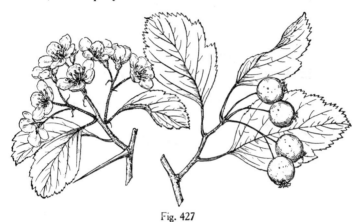

Fig. 427

when the flowers open from the middle to the end of March coated on the upper surface with short pale caducous hairs and on the lower surface with thick hoary tomentum, and at maturity thin and firm in texture, glabrous, dark green, and lustrous above, pale and pubescent below, and usually about 3′ long and 2′ wide, with a slender midrib, remote primary veins extending to the point of the lobes, conspicuous secondary veins, and reticulate veinlets; petioles more or less winged toward the apex, tomentose early in the season, becoming pubescent, $\frac{1}{2}'-\frac{3}{4}'$ in length; leaves at the end of vigorous shoots often 5′ long and 3′ wide, with rounded, acute lobes. **Flowers** $\frac{3}{4}'$ in diameter, on long stout hoary-tomentose pedicels, in broad loose many-flowered tomentose corymbs, with oblong-obovate to lanceolate finely glandular-serrate villose conspicuous bracts and bractlets; calyx-tube broadly obconic, covered with thick pale tomentum, the lobes broad, acute, very coarsely glandular-serrate, tomentose on the outer surface and villose on the inner surface; stamens 20, anthers yellow; styles 5, surrounded at base by tufts of white hairs. **Fruit** ripening after the middle of October, on slender elongated pedicels, in loose drooping clusters, short-oblong to subglobose, scarlet, about $\frac{1}{2}'$ long; calyx much enlarged, with coarsely serrate erect and persistent villose lobes; flesh thin, yellow, dry and mealy; nutlets 5, rounded and occasionally obscurely grooved on the back, about $\frac{1}{4}'$ long.

A tree, 15°-20° high, with a tall straight trunk 8′-10′ in diameter, covered with thin dark brown furrowed bark, spreading branches forming a broad open head, and branchlets hoary-tomentose at first, soon puberulous, dull reddish brown or yellow-brown by midsummer, becoming ashy gray late in the autumn, and armed with few straight gray spines about 1′ in length.

Distribution. Low rich woods on the bottom-lands of the Brazos River at Columbia and Brazoria, Brazoria County, Texas.

76. Cratægus meridionalis Sarg.

Leaves elliptic to ovate or slightly obovate, acuminate, cuneate at the entire base, and coarsely often doubly serrate above with broad straight glandular teeth, coated below with hoary tomentum and covered above with short white hairs when they unfold, more than half grown when the flowers open from the first to the middle of April, and at maturity thin, yellow-green and scabrate on the upper surface, paler and villose-pubescent on the lower surface, especially on the slender midrib and primary veins, $2'-3\frac{1}{2}'$ long, and $1'-2'$ wide; petioles slender, slightly wing-margined at apex, densely villose-pubescent with white hairs early in the season, becoming glabrous or nearly glabrous, $\frac{1}{2}'-\frac{3}{4}'$ in length; leaves at the end of vigorous shoots broad-ovate to broad-elliptic, more coarsely serrate, occasionally

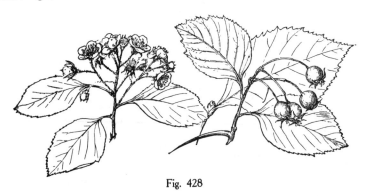

Fig. 428

slightly divided into short broad lateral lobes, often $4'$ long and $2\frac{1}{2}'$ wide, with a stout midrib and petioles broadly wing-margined at apex, and about $\frac{1}{2}'$ in length. **Flowers** $\frac{3}{4}'$ in diameter, on stout pedicels thickly covered like the narrow obconic calyx-tube with matted silvery white hairs, in broad compact many-flowered villose corymbs, with conspicuous glandular-serrate villose bracts and bractlets mostly persistent until after the flowers open; calyx-lobes narrow, acuminate, laciniately glandular-serrate, slightly villose-pubescent when the buds open; stamens 20; anthers white; styles 3–5, surrounded at base by a broad ring of white tomentum. **Fruit** ripening from the middle to the end of September, on elongated slender puberulous pedicels, in few-fruited drooping red-stemmed clusters, short-oblong to subglobose, rounded at the ends, scarlet, $\frac{1}{2}'$ to $\frac{2}{3}'$ in diameter, the calyx persistent, much enlarged, with erect or spreading conspicuous lobes; nutlets 3–5, rounded at base, acute at apex, ridged on the back with a high rounded ridge, about $\frac{1}{3}'$ long.

A tree, often $25°$ high, with a trunk $8'$ in diameter, covered with dark bark slightly divided by shallow fissures into broad thin plates, spreading ashy gray branches forming a round-topped head, and slender zigzag branchlets, covered when they first appear with long white hairs, soon glabrous, orange-brown or reddish brown during their first season and dull gray the following year, and armed with numerous straight slender purple spines $1'-2'$ in length.

Distribution. Limestone soil, in upland woods and glades; common in the limestone belt of central Alabama, from the neighborhood of Gallion, Hale County to western Mississippi (Starkville, Oktibbeha County, and Brookville, Noxubee County).

77. Cratægus Treleasei Sarg.

Leaves ovate to elliptic, acute, concave-cuneate or rounded at the narrow base, sharply doubly serrate above with straight glandular teeth, and slightly divided into 3 or 4 pairs of narrow acuminate lateral lobes, unfolding with the opening of the flowers at the end of April or early in May and then light yellow-green tinged with bronze color, lustrous and covered above with short shining caducous white hairs and hoary-tomentose below, and at maturity thin, light yellow-green and scabrate on the upper surface, paler and pubescent on the lower surface, especially on the slender midrib, and 4 or 5 pairs of thin primary veins extending obliquely to the point of the lobes, $1\frac{3}{4}'-2\frac{1}{4}'$ long, and $1\frac{1}{2}'-2'$ wide; petioles slender, more or less wing-margined at apex, villose early in the season, pubescent in the autumn, $\frac{1}{2}'-\frac{3}{4}'$ in length; leaves at the end of vigorous shoots broad-ovate, acute, cuneate at the wide base, often $2\frac{1}{2}'-3'$ long and $2'-2\frac{1}{2}'$ wide; petioles stout, wing-margined at apex $\frac{3}{4}'-1'$ long. Flowers $1'$ in diameter, on short stout pedicels covered with matted pale hairs, in 3-10-flowered compact eompound or rarely simple villose corymbs; calyx-tube broadly obconic, covered with matted pale hairs, the lobes glabrous, narrowed from the base, with wide rounded sinuses between them, slender, acuminate, tipped with a small red

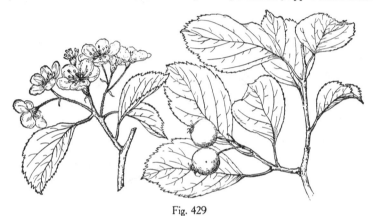

Fig. 429

gland, and glandular-serrate with stipitate red glands; stamens 20; anthers pale yellow; styles 4 or 5, usually 5. Fruit ripening at the end of September, on stout erect villose pedicels, in few-fruited clusters, subglobose, often broader than high, crimson, lustrous, marked by numerous large pale dots, pubescent at the ends, and $\frac{1}{2}'-\frac{3}{4}'$ in diameter; calyx prominent, with a short villose tube, and reflexed appressed villose lobes often deciduous from the ripe fruit; flesh thick, light yellow, dry and mealy; nutlets 4 or 5, thin, full and rounded at apex, narrowed and acute at base, grooved with a broad shallow groove and sometimes irregularly ridged on the back, about $\frac{5}{16}'$ long.

A tree, 20°-25° high, with a tall trunk sometimes 6′ in diameter, slender branches forming a narrow open head, and thin nearly straight branchlets thickly covered at first with long lustrous white hairs, dull light reddish brown and puberulous at the end of their first season, becoming dark gray-brown, and armed with stout straight or slightly curved dark purple shining spines usually about $1\frac{1}{4}'$ long, or unarmed.

Distribution. Banks of small streams in moist soil from Doe Run to Bismarck, St. François County, Missouri.

78. Cratægus canadensis Sarg.

Leaves ovate, short-pointed, slightly lobed usually only above the middle with short broad acute lobes, and coarsely and frequently doubly serrate to the broad-cuneate base with spreading glandular teeth, coated above in early spring with soft white hairs, and below with dense hoary tomentum, about a third grown when the flowers open at the end of May, and at maturity thin and firm in texture, blue-green and scabrate on the upper surface, pale and pubescent on the lower surface on the midrib and primary veins, $2'$-$2\frac{1}{2}'$ long, and $1\frac{1}{2}'$ to nearly $3'$ wide; petioles slender, glandular, often more or less winged above, at first tomentose, becoming nearly glabrous, $\frac{3}{4}'$-$1'$ in length; leaves at the end of vigorous shoots broad-ovate, truncate or slightly cordate at the broad base, more deeply lobed, often $2\frac{1}{2}'$-$3'$ long and wide, the petioles wing-margined at apex often glandular, and $1'$-$1\frac{1}{2}'$ in length. **Flowers** about $\frac{3}{4}'$ in diameter, in broad loose tomentose corymbs; calyx-tube broadly obconic, villose with long matted hairs, the lobes lanceolate, villose, and glandular with large red stipitate glands; stamens 20; anthers small, nearly white; styles 5, surrounded at base by a thin ring of pale tomentum. **Fruit** ripening early in October and falling gradually until after midwinter, on stout pedicels, in erect slightly villose few-fruited clusters, short-oblong to subglobose, crimson, lustrous, marked by large scattered pale dots, slightly hairy toward the ends, $\frac{1}{2}'$-$\frac{5}{8}'$ long, $\frac{1}{3}'$-$\frac{1}{2}'$ in diameter; calyx prominent, the lobes gradually narrowed from a broad base, elongated, glandular, villose,

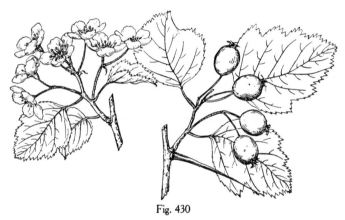

Fig. 430

spreading or reflexed, often deciduous before the fruit ripens; flesh thin, pale yellow, dry and mealy; nutlets 5, thin, rounded and irregularly ridged on the back, $\frac{1}{4}'$ long.

A tree, $18°$-$30°$ high, with a trunk $6'$-$8'$ in diameter, stout spreading branches forming a broad round-topped symmetrical head, and stout zigzag branchlets dark green and covered with matted pale hairs when they first appear, soon becoming light orange-brown and very lustrous, and armed with numerous stout straight or slightly curved dark chestnut-brown shining spines $2'$-$2\frac{1}{2}'$ long.

Distribution. Limestone ridges near the St. Lawrence River at Châteaugay, Caughnawaga, and La Tortue in the Province of Quebec.

79. Cratægus corusca Sarg.

Leaves ovate, acute, truncate, rounded or slightly cordate at the broad base, regularly divided into 4 or 5 pairs of short acute lateral lobes, and doubly serrate with straight glandular teeth, when they unfold covered above with short soft pale hairs and glabrous below, about a third grown when the flowers open the middle of May, and at maturity thin but firm and rigid in texture, glabrous, dark yellow-green, bright and lustrous above, pale yellow-green below, $2'$-$2\frac{1}{2}'$ long and wide, with a slender pale midrib and primary veins; petioles slender, villose early in the season, soon becoming glabrous and dark red below the middle, $1\frac{1}{2}'$-$2\frac{1}{2}'$ in length; leaves at the end of vigorous shoots frequently divided into narrow acute lateral lobes, and often $3\frac{1}{2}'$-$4'$ long and wide. **Flowers** $\frac{3}{4}'$ in diameter, on stout villose pedicels, in compact narrow many-flowered corymbs covered with matted pale hairs; calyx-tube narrowly obconic, glabrous, or villose toward the base, the lobes narrowed from a broad base, acute, coarsely glandular-serrate, villose on the inner surface; stamens 20; anthers small, pale pink; styles 4 or 5. **Fruit** beginning to ripen and fall about the middle of September and continuing to fall until the end of October, on stout pedicels, in glabrous few-fruited clusters, short-oblong to obovoid, bright cherry-red, lustrous, marked by dark scattered pale dots, $\frac{5}{8}'-\frac{3}{4}'$ long, and $\frac{1}{2}'-\frac{5}{8}'$ in diameter; calyx little

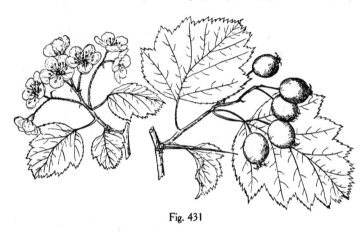

Fig. 431

enlarged, the lobes slightly glandular-serrate, usually deciduous before the fruit ripens; flesh thick, yellow, dry and mealy; nutlets 4 or 5, dark-colored, rounded on the back, $\frac{1}{4}'$ long.

A tree, 18°–20° high, with a tall trunk 8'–10' in diameter, wide-spreading branches forming a handsome symmetrical head, and stout branchlets dark green and coated with matted pale hairs when they first appear, soon becoming light red-brown, light orange-brown and lustrous in their second year, and armed with thick nearly straight bright chestnut-brown spines often 3' in length.

Distribution. Sandy shores of Lake Zurich, Lake County, Illinois.

80. Cratægus Kelloggii Sarg.

Leaves broad-ovate to suborbicular, rounded and often short-pointed at apex, rounded, broadly cuneate or truncate at the entire base, coarsely serrate above with straight gland-tipped teeth, and divided usually only above the middle into several short broad acute or acuminate lobes, about half grown when the flowers open during the last week of April and then thin, yellow-green, covered above with short pale hairs and pubescent below on the midrib and veins, and at maturity thin but firm in texture, dark yellow-green, glabrous and smooth on the upper surface, pale and glabrous on the lower surface with the exception of a few hairs near the base of the thin yellow midrib and of the 4 or 5 pairs of slender prominent primary veins arching to the point of the lobes, 2'–2½' long, 1¾'–2½' wide, and often broader than long; petioles slender, slightly winged at apex, villose while young with long matted white hairs, becoming glabrous, ¾'–1' in length. **Flowers** $\frac{5}{8}'$ in diameter, on slender hairy pedicels, in compact 5–10-flowered villose corymbs, with oblong-obovate to linear acuminate glandular bracts and bractlets mostly persistent until the flowers open; calyx-tube broadly obconic, slightly hairy at base, glabrous above, the lobes slender, acuminate, glandular with minute dark red stipitate glands, or entire, glabrous on the outer surface, sparingly villose on the inner surface; stamens 20; anthers pale rose color; styles 5. **Fruit** ripening at the end of September and soon falling, on long slender glabrous pedicels, in few-fruited drooping clusters, subglobose to short-ovoid, bright yellow, marked by many small pale dots, $\frac{3}{4}'-1'$ in diameter; calyx small, with spreading reflexed lobes slightly villose toward the apex and often deciduous from the ripe fruit; flesh thin, yellow, dry and mealy; nutlets 5, rounded and very slightly grooved on the back, about $\frac{3}{8}'$ long.

A tree, 20°–25° high, with a tall trunk 4'–5' in diameter, covered with nearly black deeply furrowed bark, erect branches, and nearly straight branchlets dark green tinged

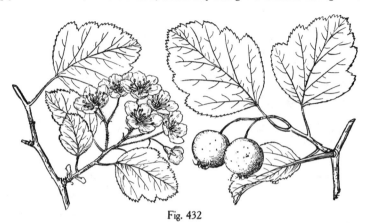

Fig. 432

with red and slightly villose when they first appear, bright red-brown and lustrous at the end of their first season, becoming dark dull reddish brown the following year, and unarmed, or armed with slender nearly straight bright chestnut-brown shining spines usually about 1' long.

Distribution. Banks of the Desperes River, South St. Louis, St. Louis County, Missouri; not common.

81. Cratægus induta Sarg.   Turkey Apple.

Leaves oblong-obovate, acute, cuneate, rounded or rarely truncate at the broad entire base, coarsely doubly serrate above with glandular teeth, and slightly and irregularly divided into broad acute lateral lobes, about a third grown when the flowers open from

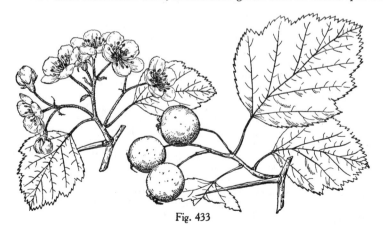

Fig. 433

the middle to the end of April and then thin, light yellow-green and roughened above by short lustrous white hairs and hoary-tomentose below, and at maturity thin, dark yellow-green and scabrate on the upper surface, pale and tomentose or pubescent on the lower surface, particularly on the stout midrib and 4 or 5 pairs of prominent primary veins, 3′–4′ long, and 2½′–3′ wide; petioles slender, more or less wing-margined at the apex, glandular, hoary-tomentose early in the season, becoming sparingly villose in the autumn, 1¼′–1½′ in length. **Flowers** ¾′ in diameter, on slender tomentose pedicels, in broad many-flowered hoary-tomentose corymbs; calyx-tube narrowly obconic, thickly coated with long densely matted white hairs, the lobes small, acuminate, glandular-serrate, villose; stamens 20; anthers small, rose color; styles 5, surrounded at base by a broad ring of snow-white hairs. **Fruit** ripening the middle of October, on stout villose pedicels, in few-fruited clusters, short-oblong, rounded and villose at the ends, crimson or reddish yellow, lustrous, marked by small pale dots, ¾′–2′ in diameter; calyx prominent, with a short tomentose tube and much enlarged coarsely glandular-serrate hairy erect incurved lobes often deciduous from the ripe fruit; flesh thick, orange-colored, with an astringent subacid flavor; nutlets 5, thin, rounded and slightly grooved on the back, $\frac{5}{16}′$–$\frac{3}{8}′$ long.

A tree, sometimes 25° high, with a trunk often a foot in diameter, covered with thick dark brown furrowed bark, large spreading and ascending branches forming an open irregular head, and stout branchlets covered at first with long matted white hairs, light orange-brown, lustrous and puberulous at the end of their first season, becoming ashy gray or light grayish brown the following year, and armed with many stout nearly straight dark purple shining spines usually about 2½′ long.

Distribution. Dry upland woods, near Fulton, Hempstead County to Texarkana, Miller County, and Prescott, Nevada County, Arkansas; common.

82. Cratægus texana Buckl.

Leaves broad-ovate, acute or rarely rounded at apex, broadly concave-cuneate at base, coarsely doubly glandular-serrate above, and usually divided above the middle into 4 or 5 pairs of broad acute lobes, covered above when they unfold with short soft pale hairs and

Fig. 434

below with a thick coat of hoary tomentum, more than half grown when the flowers open late in March, and at maturity thick and firm, dark green and lustrous above, pale and pubescent or tomentose below, particularly on the stout midrib, primary veins, prominent secondary veins and reticulate veinlets, 3′–4′ long, 2½′–3′ wide; petioles stout, deeply grooved, more or less winged above, at first tomentose, becoming nearly glabrous, ½′–¾′ in length; leaves at the end of vigorous shoots sometimes truncate or slightly cordate at the broad base, more deeply lobed, and frequently 3′ long and wide. **Flowers** ¾′ in diameter, on elongated slender densely villose pedicels, in broad open many-flowered tomentose corymbs, with oblong or oblong-obovate acute conspicuous villose bracts and bractlets often $1\frac{1}{2}'$ in length; calyx-tube broadly obconic, coated with pale tomentum, the lobes foliaceous, gradually narrowed from a broad base, acuminate, coarsely glandular-serrate, and villose with long matted pale hairs; stamens 20; anthers large, dark red; styles 5, surrounded at base by a narrow ring of pale tomentum. Fruit ripening toward the end of October, in drooping many-fruited tomentose ultimately glabrous clusters, obovoid and tomentose until nearly grown, becoming when fully ripe short-oblong or slightly obovoid, rounded at the ends, bright scarlet, marked by occasional large pale dots, puberulous at apex, $\frac{3}{4}$–1' long; calyx enlarged, with glandular-serrate usually erect lobes, dark red at base on the upper side, often deciduous before the ripening of the fruit; flesh thick, yellow, sweet, and edible; nutlets 5, slightly grooved on the back, $\frac{1}{4}$–$\frac{1}{3}'$ long.

A tree, often 30° high, with a tall trunk sometimes a foot in diameter, thick branches ascending while the tree is young, forming an open irregular crown, and spreading in old age into a broad symmetrical round-topped head, and branchlets dark bronze-green and covered with long matted white hairs when they first appear, becoming dull reddish brown and ultimately pale ashy gray, and armed with occasional thin nearly straight bright chestnut-brown lustrous spines usually about 2' long, or often unarmed.

Distribution. Rich bottom-lands, Texas coast region; valley of the lower Brazos River to those of the Navidad (Canardo, Jackson County), Guadalupe (Victoria, Victoria County), and Cibolo (Sutherland Springs, Wilson County).

83. Cratægus quercina Ashe.

Leaves elliptic to obovate, usually acute or occasionally rounded at apex, obtusely or acutely cuneate at the entire base, irregularly doubly serrate above with slender glandular teeth, and often divided above the midrib into narrow acuminate lobes, when they unfold

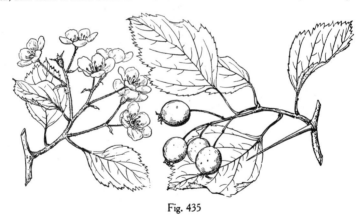

Fig. 435

conspicuously plicate, often dark red and coated above with long soft pale hairs and covered below with a thick coat of silvery white shining tomentum, about a third grown when the flowers open from the middle to the end of March, and at maturity thin but firm in texture, dark green, lustrous and scabrate above, pale and pubescent or tomentose below, and $2'$–$2\frac{1}{2}'$ long and wide, with a slender midrib, 4 or 5 pairs of thin primary veins, and conspicuous reticulate veinlets; petioles stout, tomentose, about $\frac{1}{2}'$ in length; leaves at the end of vigorous shoots broad-ovate, rounded or obtusely cuneate at the wide base, usually deeply divided into numerous acuminate lateral lobes, often 3' long and $2\frac{1}{2}'$ wide. **Flowers** $\frac{3}{4}'$ in diameter, on long slender tomentose pedicels, in broad many-flowered lax hoary-tomentose corymbs, with oblong-obovate glandular-serrate villose bracts and bractlets; calyx-tube narrowly obconic, hoary-tomentose, the lobes short, acute, coarsely glandular-serrate, tomentose; stamens 20; anthers small, dark red; styles 5, surrounded at base by tufts of long snow-white hairs. Fruit ripening after the middle of October, on slender nearly glabrous pedicels, in few-fruited tomentose spreading clusters, subglobose but often rather longer than broad, rounded at the ends, tomentose until nearly fully grown, glabrous at maturity, dark red, marked by numerous large pale dots, about $\frac{1}{2}'$ in diameter; calyx prominent, with short spreading often deciduous lobes; flesh thin, light yellow, hard and dry, generally shrivelling before the fruit falls; nutlets 5, rounded and ridged on the back, about $\frac{1}{4}'$ long.

A tree, remarkable for the lustre of its white tomentum, occasionally 25° high, with a tall trunk 6'–8' in diameter, covered with light gray scaly bark, becoming near the base of old trees deeply furrowed and nearly black, ascending branches forming a broad symmetrical head, and branchlets coated when they first appear with hoary tomentum, becoming light red-brown and more or less villose during their first season, glabrous and rather darker in their second year, and armed with numerous straight or slightly curved chestnut-brown shining spines usually 1'–1¼' long.

Distribution. Sandy bottom-lands in open Live Oak-forests on the Brazos River, near Columbia, Brazoria County, Rosenburg and Richmond, Fort Bend County, Wharton, Wharton County, and San Augustine, San Augustine County, Texas.

84. Cratægus dispersa Ashe.

Cratægus pyriformis Britt.

Leaves oval to broad-ovate, acute and often short-pointed at apex, gradually narrowed and concave-cuneate at the entire base, sharply and sometimes doubly serrate above with straight glandular teeth, and often slightly and irregularly lobed above the middle, fully

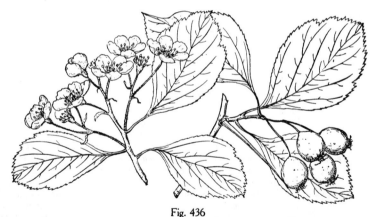

Fig. 436

grown when the flowers open about the 10th of May and then thin, light yellow-green, roughened above by short rigid pale hairs and pubescent below, particularly on the slender midrib and 5 or 6 pairs of remote primary veins, and at maturity thin and firm, lustrous and scabrate on the upper surface, pale and pubescent on the lower surface, and generally about 3' long and 2' wide; petioles slender, winged at apex, tomentose, ultimately pubescent, 1'–1¼' in length; leaves at the end of vigorous shoots usually ovate, coarsely serrate, more deeply lobed, and frequently 4'–5' long and 3'–4' wide. Flowers 1' in diameter, on long slender tomentose pedicels, in broad many-flowered lax corymbs; calyx-tube narrowly obconic, villose, the lobes narrow, acuminate, glandular-serrate, and covered more or less thickly with pale hairs; stamens 20; anthers pale rose color; styles 4 or 5, usually 5, surrounded at base by a broad ring of pale tomentum. **Fruit** ripening in October, on long slender pubescent pedicels, in drooping few-fruited clusters, obovoid, rounded at the ends, bright cherry-red, lustrous, marked by occasional large pale dots, about ⅝′ long and ½′ in diameter; calyx prominent, with linear glandular-serrate closely appressed lobes often deciduous before the fruit ripens; flesh thin, light yellow, juicy; nutlets 4 or usually 5, rounded, and deeply grooved on the back, dark brown, ⅝′ long.

A tree, 25°–30° high, with a trunk a foot in diameter, spreading branches forming a broad symmetrical head, and slender branchlets light green and villose when they first appear with long matted pale hairs, dull red-brown and pubescent in their first season, becoming glabrous the following year, and armed with occasional thin nearly straight bright chestnut-brown shining spines usually about 1½′ long.

Distribution. Rich bottom-lands of the streams of Shannon County, southern Missouri.

85. Cratægus lanuginosa Sarg.

Leaves ovate to suborbicular, acute or rounded and short-pointed at apex, broadly cuneate or rounded at the entire base, coarsely and sharply doubly serrate above with glandular teeth, and often irregularly divided above the middle into short broad acute

Fig. 437

lateral lobes, less than half grown when the flowers open during the last week of April and then dark green and villose above and covered below with a thick coat of hoary tomentum, and at maturity subcoriaceous, dark blue-green, lustrous and scabrate on the upper surface, yellow-green and tomentose on the lower surface, 1½′–2′ long, and 1′–1½′ wide, with a thick midrib, and 3–5 pairs of stout primary veins extending obliquely to the point of the lobes; petioles stout, tomentose, ½′–¾′ in length; leaves at the end of vigorous shoots often broad-ovate, very coarsely glandular-serrate, rounded or truncate at base, and frequently 3′ long and wide. **Flowers** ¾′ in diameter, on short stout pedicels covered with long matted pale hairs, in compact many-flowered hoary-tomentose corymbs, with large glandular-serrate conspicuous bracts and bractlets persistent until the flowers open; calyx-tube broadly obconic, hairy, the lobes short, broad, acute, glandular with minute stipitate glands, densely villose on the outer surface and slightly villose on the inner surface; stamens 20; anthers rose color; styles 5, surrounded at base by large tufts of snow-white hairs. **Fruit** ripening at the end of October, on short tomentose erect pedicels, in few-fruited clusters, subglobose to short-oblong, rounded and slightly hairy at the ends, ½′ in diameter; calyx enlarged, with villose coarsely serrate usually erect spreading or incurved persistent lobes bright red on the upper side near the base; flesh thin, orange color, dry and mealy; nutlets 5, thin, rounded and very irregularly ridged on the back, about ¼′ long.

A tree, sometimes 25° high, with a stout trunk covered with pale bark, spreading and erect branches, and stout zigzag branchlets light green and villose early in the season, dull red-brown and sparingly villose or pubescent at the end of their first year, becoming dark or light gray-brown, and armed with many long straight purple shining ultimately ashy gray spines $1\frac{1}{4}'-3\frac{1}{2}'$ in length.

Distribution. Southwestern Missouri; common near Webb City, Jasper County, to Gum Springs, Clark County, Arkansas; well distinguished by the distinctly blue color of the small leaves, the dark crimson hard fruits and by the remarkable development of the spines unusual in the species of this group.

86. Cratægus arnoldiana Sarg.

Leaves broad-ovate or rarely oval, acute, regularly divided above the middle into numerous short acute lobes, and coarsely doubly serrate with straight glandular teeth except at the rounded truncate or occasionally cuneate base, coated with dense matted pale hairs when they unfold, about half grown when the flowers open at the end of May or early in June and then roughened above by stout stiff hairs and soft-pubescent below, and at maturity thin, smooth, very dark green and lustrous above, paler below, and slightly villose on the under side of the slender midrib, and of the thin prominent primary veins extending

Fig. 438

to the point of the lobes, $2'-3'$ long and wide; petioles slender, densely villose early in the season, becoming puberulous, $\frac{3}{4}'-1\frac{1}{2}'$ in length; leaves at the end of vigorous shoots acute or acuminate, round or obtusely cuneate at base, more deeply lobed, often $3'-4'$ long and $3'$ wide. **Flowers** about $\frac{3}{4}'$ in diameter, on slender pedicels, in broad many-flowered tomentose corymbs; calyx-tube broadly obconic, densely tomentose, the lobes narrow, elongated, acuminate, glandular-serrate, villose on both surfaces; stamens 10; anthers, large, pale yellow; styles 3–5, usually 3 or 4, surrounded at base by a broad ring of thick hoary tomentum. **Fruit** ripening about the middle of August and mostly falling before the first of September, on stout pedicels, in erect spreading or rarely drooping few-fruited villose clusters, subglobose but rather longer than broad, bright crimson marked by many large pale dots, villose, particularly toward the ends, with long scattered white hairs, $\frac{3}{4}'$ long; calyx little enlarged, with elongated coarsely glandular-serrate spreading lobes often deciduous before the fruit ripens; flesh thick, bright yellow, subacid; nutlets 3 or 4, light-colored, prominently ridged on the back with a high rounded ridge, about $\frac{1}{4}'$ long.

A tree, $15°-20°$ high, with a short trunk $10'-12'$ in diameter, stout ascending branches forming a broad open irregular head, and slender conspicuously zigzag branchlets clothed early in the season with long matted pale hairs, becoming dark orange-brown and very lustrous before midsummer, glabrous or puberulous during their first winter, bright orange-brown or gray-brown during their second year, and armed with many stout straight or slightly curved bright chestnut-brown shining spines $2\frac{1}{2}'-3'$ long.

Distribution. Thickets on a dry bank in the Arnold Arboretum, valley of the Mystic River at West Medford, Middlesex County, Massachusetts, and near Lyme, New London County, Connecticut.

Often cultivated in the parks and gardens in the neighborhood of Boston; very conspicuous and easily recognized in winter by its ascending remarkably zigzag branchlets.

87. Cratægus champlainensis Sarg.

Leaves ovate, acute, rounded, truncate, slightly cordate or broad-cuneate at base, usually divided into 2 or 3 pairs of short narrow acute lobes, and coarsely often doubly serrate with glandular teeth, roughened above by short pale hairs and villose below when they unfold, nearly fully grown when the flowers open early in June, and at maturity thick and firm in texture, conspicuously blue-green and glabrous above, light yellow-green and somewhat pubescent below on the slender midrib and remote primary veins, $2'-2\frac{1}{2}'$ long,

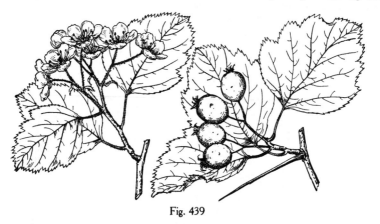

Fig. 439

and $1'-1\frac{1}{2}'$ wide; petioles slender, more or less tomentose early in the season, usually becoming glabrous and light red below the middle before autumn, and $\frac{3}{4}'-1'$ in length; leaves at the end of vigorous shoots broad-ovate, rounded or slightly cordate at base, more deeply lobed, and often $3'-4'$ long and wide. **Flowers** $\frac{3}{4}'$ in diameter, on short slender densely villose pedicels, in compact few-flowered densely villose corymbs; calyx-tube narrowly obconic, coated with thick hoary tomentum, the lobes lanceolate, finely glandular-serrate, tomentose on the outer surface usually only below the middle, villose on the inner surface; stamens 10; anthers small, light yellow; styles 5, surrounded at base by tufts of pale hairs. **Fruit** ripening early in September and usually remaining on the branches during the remainder of the year, on short slightly pubescent pedicels, in compact erect villose clusters, obovoid to short-oblong, bright scarlet, marked by scattered pale dots, more or less villose or pubescent toward the ends; calyx prominent, persistent, with a long tube, the lobes gradually narrowed from a broad base, acuminate, finely glandular-serrate, villose, dark red on the upper side below the middle, spreading or erect; flesh thick, yellow, dry and mealy; nutlets 5, ridged on the back with a broad ridge, $\frac{5}{16}'$ long.

A tree, $15°-20°$ high, with a tall trunk $8'-10'$ in diameter, covered with deeply fissured bark separating into thin loose plate-like scales, stout wide-spreading branches forming a broad round-topped often symmetrical head, and slender somewhat zigzag branchlets coated early in the season with hoary tomentum, soon becoming glabrous and light chestnut-brown and lustrous, and armed with straight or slightly curved chestnut-brown spines 1½′–2′ long.

Distribution. Limestone ridges; valley of the St. Lawrence River near Montreal, Province of Quebec, southward through the Champlain valley to eastern New York and westward through New York, and southern Ontario to the neighborhood of Toronto.

88. Cratægus pennsylvanica Ashe.

Leaves ovate, acuminate, rounded or abruptly cuneate at base, coarsely often doubly serrate with straight glandular teeth, and slightly divided into 3 or 4 pairs of short broad acuminate lobes, slightly tinged with red when they unfold, more than half grown when the flowers open the middle of May and then thin, dark yellow-green and roughened above by short white hairs and villose on the prominent midrib and primary veins below, and at maturity thin, dark yellow-green and scabrate on the upper surface, paler, scabrate and still somewhat villose on the midrib and veins below, 2½′–3½′ long, and 2′–2¾′ wide; petioles slender, slightly wing-margined at apex, villose through the season, occasionally glandular,

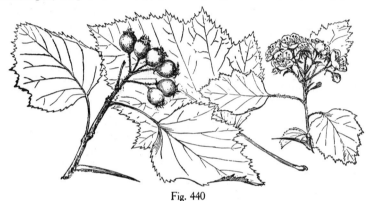

Fig. 440

1¼′–1½′ in length; leaves at the end of vigorous shoots rounded or truncate at base, coarsely serrate, more deeply lobed, and often 4′–4½′ long and broad, with a stout midrib, prominent primary veins, a conspicuously glandular petiole, and large foliaceous lunate coarsely glandular-serrate persistent stipules. **Flowers** ¾′–1′ in diameter, on slender densely villose pedicels in broad lax hairy mostly 8–15-flowered corymbs; calyx-tube narrowly obconic, covered with long white hairs, the lobes long, slender, acuminate, laciniately glandular-serrate, glabrous on the outer surface, villose on the inner surface; stamens 8–12; anthers faintly tinged with pink; styles 3–5. **Fruit** ripening and falling early in October, on short stout drooping slightly hairy pedicels, in 4–12-fruited clusters, short-obovoid, full and rounded at apex, bright orange-red marked by small pale dots, puberulous at the ends, ¾′–1′ in diameter; calyx little enlarged, with small spreading lobes dark red on the upper side, their tips often deciduous from the ripe fruit; flesh thick, orange-yellow, somewhat acidulous, edible, sometimes made into jelly; nutlets 3–5, rounded at apex, acute at base, rounded and slightly grooved or ridged on the back, about ⅓′ long.

A tree, sometimes 30° high, with a tall trunk often 18′ in diameter, covered with dark gray scaly bark, large spreading branches forming a wide symmetrical round-topped head, and stout slightly zigzag branchlets dark orange-green and more or less tinged with red when they first appear, becoming dark chestnut-brown, marked by large dark lenticels and more or less pubescent in their first season, dark red-brown the following year, and armed with stout straight or slightly curved chestnut-brown spines 1′–1½′ long.

Distribution. Meadows in low moist soil near Pittsburgh, Allegheny County, Pennsylvania.

89. Cratægus submollis Sarg.

Leaves ovate, acute, gradually narrowed and cuneate at the nearly entire base, coarsely doubly serrate above with straight glandular teeth, and divided into 3 or 4 pairs of short acute lobes, half grown at the end of May or early in June when the flowers open and then roughened above by short stiff pale hairs and soft-pubescent below, particularly on the midrib and veins, and at maturity thin, dark yellow-green and scabrate above, pale below, $3'-3\frac{1}{2}'$ long, and $2'-2\frac{1}{2}'$ wide, with a thick yellow midrib and remote primary veins puberulous on the lower side; petioles stout, nearly terete, more or less winged at apex, tomentose early in the season, becoming puberulous, often bright red toward the base, $1'-2'$ in length; leaves at the end of vigorous shoots broad-ovate, cuneate, rounded, truncate, or occasionally slightly cordate at base, often $4'$ long and $3'-3\frac{1}{2}'$ wide.   **Flowers** $1'$ in diameter, on long slender villose pedicels, in broad many-flowered tomentose corymbs; calyx-tube narrowly obconic, covered with a thick coat of long matted white hairs, the lobes gradually narrowed from a broad base, acute, glandular with large red stipitate glands, glabrous or villose on

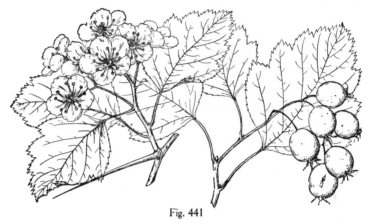

Fig. 441

the outer surface; stamens 10; anthers small, pale yellow; styles 3–5, surrounded at base by a narrow ring of long white hairs.   **Fruit** ripening and falling during the first half of September, on elongated slender slightly villose pedicels, in broad gracefully drooping many-fruited clusters, obovoid, bright orange-red, lustrous, marked by large scattered pale dots, puberulous toward the base, about $\frac{3}{4}'$ long; calyx much enlarged, with erect coarsely glandular-serrate persistent lobes; flesh yellow, thin, subacid, dry and mealy; nutlets usually 5, rounded and slightly ridged on the back, about $\frac{1}{3}'$ in length.

A tree, 20°–25° high, with a tall trunk occasionally a foot in diameter, ascending or spreading ashy gray branches forming a broad handsome head, and branchlets dark green and coated with hoary tomentum when they first appear, light or dark orange-brown and slightly tomentose at midsummer, becoming glabrous, lustrous, and light red-brown or dark orange-brown, and armed with numerous thin straight or somewhat curved bright chestnut-brown shining spines $2\frac{1}{2}'-3'$ in length.

Distribution.   Rich damp hillsides and the borders of woods and roads; valley of the St. Lawrence River from the Isle of Orleans westward; Hull County, Province of Quebec; near Ottawa, Ontario; valley of the Penobscot River and Gerrish Island, Maine to the coast of eastern Massachusetts.

90. Cratægus Ellwangeriana Sarg.

Leaves oval, acute, rounded or broad-cuneate at the entire base, irregularly divided usually only above the middle into numerous short acute lobes, and coarsely and often doubly serrate above with straight or incurved glandular teeth, about half grown when the flowers open the middle of May, and then roughened above by short pale hairs and villose below on the slender midrib and primary veins, and at maturity thin, light green and scabrate on the upper surface, pale and nearly glabrous on the lower surface, $2\frac{1}{2}'-3\frac{1}{2}'$ long, and $2'-3'$ wide; petioles slender, villose early in the season, finally glabrous, $1\frac{1}{2}'-2'$ in length; stipules oblong-obovate, acute, villose, coarsely glandular-serrate, $\frac{1}{2}'$ long, those of the upper leaves mostly persistent until after the ripening of the fruit. **Flowers** $1'$ in diameter, on short stout hairy pedicels, in many-flowered densely villose corymbs; calyx-tube broadly obconic, villose, the lobes long, lanceolate, glandular with small pale stalked glands, villose on both surfaces; stamens 10, sometimes 8; anthers small, rose color; styles 3–5. **Fruit** ripening and falling at the end of September, on slender glabrous pedicels, in drooping villose many-fruited crowded clusters, short-oblong, full and rounded at the ends, bright crimson, lustrous, covered at the ends with scattered pale hairs, $1'$ long, and $\frac{1}{2}'-\frac{3}{4}'$ in diameter; calyx little enlarged, the lobes elongated, glandular-serrate above the middle,

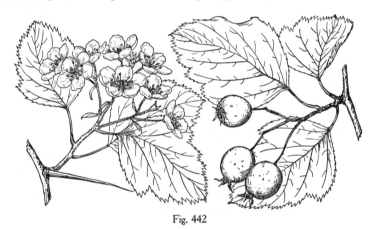

Fig. 442

villose on the inner surface, spreading, or erect and incurved; flesh thin, yellow, juicy and acid; nutlets 3–5, thick, pale brown, deeply and often doubly and irregularly grooved on the back, $\frac{1}{4}'-\frac{1}{3}'$ long.

A tree, sometimes 20° high, with a tall trunk often a foot in diameter, covered with pale gray scaly bark, stout ascending branches forming a broad symmetrical head, and slender zigzag branchlets dark green and clothed at first with long matted pale hairs, becoming in their first summer light chestnut-brown and slightly villose, dark chestnut-brown and very lustrous in their second year, and armed with stout straight or somewhat curved dark chestnut-brown shining spines $1\frac{1}{2}'-2'$ long.

Distribution. Western New York (common) to western Pennsylvania, and through southern Ontario to southern Michigan.

91. Cratægus Robesoniana Sarg.

Cratægus spissiflora Sarg.

Leaves oblong-ovate, acute or acuminate at apex, rounded broadly cuneate or rarely cordate at the entire base, sharply doubly serrate above with slender straight gland-tipped teeth, and deeply divided into numerous broad acute or acuminate lateral lobes, villose above and densely tomentose below when they unfold, about half grown when the flowers open at the end of May and then roughened above by short rigid white hairs and pubescent below on the midrib and veins, and at maturity dark yellow-green and scabrate on the upper surface, glabrous on the lower surface, 3′–3½′ long, and 2½′–3′ wide, with a slender midrib, and 4 or 5 pairs of prominent veins extending obliquely to the point of the lobes; petioles slender, more or less wing-margined at apex, slightly grooved, sparingly glandular, villose early in the season, becoming glabrous and rose color in the autumn, 1¼′–1½′ in length; leaves at the end of vigorous shoots cordate or rarely cuneate at base, deeply lobed, often 4′ long and 3½′ wide, with a stout conspicuous glandular petiole. **Flowers** ¾′ in diameter, on short slender villose pedicels, in small very compact few, usually 4–6-flowered, thin-branched villose corymbs, with oblong-obovate acuminate glandular bracts and bractlets mostly deciduous before the flowers open; calyx-tube narrowly obconic, coated with long matted white hairs, the lobes slender, acuminate, finely glandular-serrate, glabrous on the outer surface, villose on the inner surface; stamens 10; anthers dark rose color; styles 4 or 5, surrounded at base by a narrow ring of pale tomentum. **Fruit** ripening at the end of September or early in October, on short reddish pubescent pedicels, in compact drooping clusters, oblong-obovoid to short-oblong, scarlet, lustrous, marked by small pale

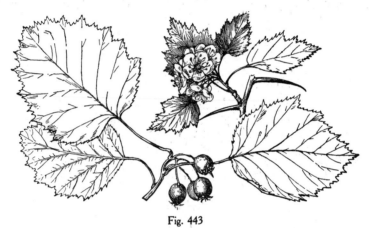

Fig. 443

dots, about ¾′ long, and ½′ in diameter; calyx little enlarged, with spreading sharply serrate lobes often deciduous from the ripe fruit; flesh thick, yellow, dry and mealy; nutlets 4 or 5, thin, acute at the ends, rounded or only slightly grooved on the back, about ⅝′ in length.

A tree, 20°–25° high, with a trunk often 1° in diameter, covered with smooth pale gray bark, and stout spreading branches forming a round-topped head, and stout slightly zigzag dark red-brown branchlets sparingly villose early in the season, soon glabrous, bright red-brown, very lustrous and marked by small pale lenticels at the end of their first season, becoming dark gray or gray-brown the following year, and armed with few stout spreading bright chestnut-brown shining ultimately gray spines 1′–1½′ long.

Distribution. Western Massachusetts through central and western New York to the neighborhood of Toronto, southern Ontario.

92. Cratægus anomala Sarg.

Leaves ovate, acute, divided above the middle into 5 or 6 pairs of short acute or acuminate lobes, and coarsely doubly serrate with spreading glandular teeth except toward the broad-cuneate or occasionally rounded base, when they unfold conspicuously plicate, covered above with short appressed pale hairs, and villose below, especially on the slender midrib, and thin remote primary veins arching to the point of the lobes, about a third grown when the flowers open at the end of May, and at maturity membranaceous, light yellow-green, smooth and glabrous above, paler and villose below, $2\frac{1}{2}'-3'$ long, and $2'-3'$ wide; petioles stout, glandular on the upper side with scattered dark glands, $\frac{3}{4}'-1'$ in length; leaves at the end of vigorous shoots, rounded or truncate at base, and often $4'-4\frac{1}{2}'$ long and $2\frac{1}{2}'-3'$ wide. **Flowers** saucer-shaped, $\frac{1}{2}'$ in diameter when fully expanded, on elongated slender hairy pedicels, in broad loose many-flowered villose corymbs; calyx-tube narrowly obconic, coated with long matted pale hairs, the lobes long, acuminate, coarsely glandular-serrate, pubescent on the outer surface and tomentose on the inner surface; stamens usually 10, occasionally 7 or 8; anthers large, bright red; styles 4 or 5, surrounded at base by a narrow ring of pale tomentum. **Fruit** ripening in October, on long slender slightly pubescent pedicels, in loose many-fruited sparingly villose clusters, obovoid to oblong, gradually narrowed to the rounded base, crimson, lustrous, marked by large pale dots, slightly villose, particularly toward the full and rounded apex, $\frac{3}{4}'-\frac{7}{8}'$ long, $\frac{1}{2}'-\frac{5}{8}'$ in diameter; calyx large and prominent, with elongated acuminate lobes abruptly narrowed from a broad base, dark red on the upper side, tomentose on the lower, finely glandular-serrate, spreading or closely

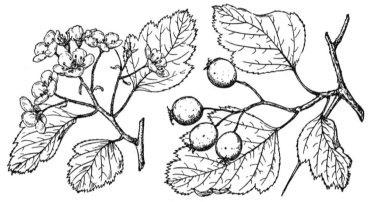

Fig. 444

appressed, often deciduous before the ripening of the fruit; flesh thin, light yellow, somewhat juicy; nutlets 4 or 5, thin, prominently and irregularly ridged on the back, $\frac{1}{4}'-\frac{5}{16}'$ long.

A bushy tree, sometimes 20° high, with a short trunk 6' in diameter, covered with pale gray-brown scaly bark, stout ascending branches, and slender somewhat zigzag branchlets at first dark green and villose with long matted white hairs, puberulous and light orange-brown during their first season, becoming glabrous and orange-brown or bright red, and armed with numerous stout straight or slightly curved bright chestnut-brown spines $1\frac{1}{4}'-2'$ long.

Distribution. Low limestone ridges near the banks of the St. Lawrence River in the Caughnawaga Indian Reservation opposite Lachine in the Province of Quebec; western Vermont (Clarendon, Rutland County); Crown Point, Essex County, and Fort Ann, Washington County, New York.

93. Cratægus noelensis Sarg.

Leaves ovate to oval, acute, acuminate or rarely rounded at apex, acutely or broadly cuneate at base, and coarsely doubly serrate with straight teeth, covered above with short white hairs and densely villose-pubescent below when they unfold, more than half grown when the flowers open at the end of April, and at maturity dark yellow-green, smooth and glabrous on the upper surface, villose-pubescent on the lower surface, $2'-3'$ long, and $1\frac{1}{4}'-2\frac{1}{2}'$ wide, with a prominent midrib and thin conspicuous primary veins; petioles slender, slightly wing-margined at apex, hoary-tomentose early in the season, becoming glabrous,

$1'-1\frac{1}{4}'$ in length; leaves at the end of vigorous shoots ovate, acuminate, rounded or cuneate at the broad base, more coarsely serrate, usually laterally lobed with short broad acuminate lobes, $3'-4'$ long, and $2\frac{1}{2}'-3'$ wide. **Flowers** $\frac{3}{4}'$ to nearly $1'$ in diameter, on short pedicels densely covered like the narrow obconic calyx-tube and the compact 5–10-flowered corymb with long matted white hairs; calyx-lobes slender, long-acuminate, minutely glandular-serrate, slightly villose; stamens 5–10, usually 10; anthers rose color; styles 3–5, surrounded at base by a broad ring of pale tomentum. **Fruit** ripening in September, on slender drooping pubescent pedicels, subglobose, orange-red, $\frac{1}{2}'-\frac{2}{3}'$ in diameter, the calyx prominent with a short tube and spreading closely appressed lobes; flesh thin, soft and yellow; nutlets 3–5, rounded at base, narrowed and rounded at apex, slightly grooved on the back, about $\frac{1}{4}'$ long.

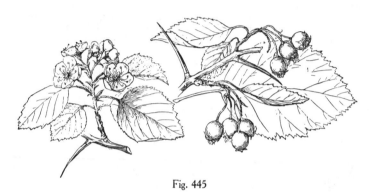

Fig. 445

A tree, $15°-18°$ high, with a trunk sometimes $1°$ in diameter, spreading branches forming a broad flat or round-topped head, and stout zigzag branchlets coated when they first appear with matted white hairs, reddish brown, pubescent or puberulous during their first season and gray the following year, and armed with few or many slender straight purple lustrous spines $1'-2\frac{1}{2}'$ in length, sometimes persistent and compound on old trunks.

Distribution. Rich alluvial soil; in the neighborhood of Noel, McDonald County, and Galena, Stone County, Missouri, and to Rogers, Benton County, Arkansas; common.

IX. COCCINEÆ.

Flabellatæ Sarg.

CONSPECTUS OF THE ARBORESCENT SPECIES.

Stamens 20; leaves yellow-green and scabrate above.
  Leaves ovate; anthers deep rose-purple; fruit obovoid to short-oblong, bright red, often slightly pruinose.   94. **C. neo-londinensis** (A).
  Leaves oblong-ovate; anthers pink; fruit obovoid, crimson, lustrous. 95. **C. Hillii** (A).
Stamens 10–20, usually 10; anthers pinkish purple, leaves broad-ovate, dull dark green and scabrate above; fruit short-oblong to slightly obovoid, dull red or crimson.
                                                                         96. **C. assurgens** (A).
Stamens usually 10.
  Fruit on short stout pedicels; leaves yellow-green and glabrous above.
    Leaves oval, drooping, conspicuously concave; anthers purple; fruit short-oblong, dark dull red, villose at the ends.   97. **C. Pringlei** (A).
    Leaves oval to oblong-ovate; anthers dark reddish purple; fruit short-oblong, crimson, lustrous.   98. **C. lobulata** (A).
  Fruit on long slender pedicels; leaves broad-ovate to obovate or rhombic, dark rich

green and scabrate above; anthers rose color; fruit short-oblong, bright scarlet, lustrous. 99. **C. pedicellata** (A).
Stamens usually 5–7, rarely 10.
Fruit obovoid to ellipsoidal; leaves oval or ovate, conspicuously yellow-green; anthers dark reddish purple; fruit crimson, lustrous. 100. **C. Holmesiana** (A).
Fruit short-oblong; leaves oblong-ovate, deep yellow-green, nearly smooth above; anthers pink; fruit yellowish red, glaucous 101. **C. acclivis** (A).
Fruit subglobose to obovoid.
Leaves glabrous above; anthers dark rose color.
Leaves broad-ovate, thin, light yellow-green and lustrous above; fruit bright red or scarlet. 102. **C. delecta** (A).
Leaves oblong-ovate, subcoriaceous, dark dull green; fruit bright cherry-red, pruinose. 103. **C. Eamesii** (A).
Leaves scabrate above, oblong-ovate, thin, dark yellow-green; anthers pale rose color, fruit crimson. 104. **C. sertata** (A).

94. Cratægus neo-londinensis Sarg.

Leaves ovate, acute or acuminate, rounded, truncate or broadly concave-cuneate at the wide entire or glandular base, sharply often doubly serrate above with straight glandular teeth, and divided into numerous short narrow acuminate lateral lobes, about half grown

Fig. 446

when the flowers open the middle of May and then very thin, light yellow-green and roughened above by short white rigid hairs and paler and sparingly hairy below, and at maturity membranaceous, dull yellow-green and scabrate on the upper surface, pale green and glabrous below, or occasionally slightly hairy on the under side of the stout yellow midrib, and of the thin remote primary veins arching to the point of the lobes, 3′–4′ long, and 2½′–3½′ wide; petioles slender, nearly terete, glandular, at first slightly hairy, becoming glabrous and purplish toward the base, 1′–2′ in length; leaves at the end of vigorous shoots only slightly larger. **Flowers** 1′–1⅛′ in diameter, on slender sparingly villose pedicels, in lax slightly drooping usually 5–12-flowered villose or nearly glabrous corymbs, with linear often slightly falcate glandular bracts and bractlets, persistent until after the flowers open; calyx-tube narrowly obconic, covered with short matted pale hairs, the lobes gradually narrowed from a broad base, acuminate, coarsely glandular-serrate below the middle, glabrous on the outer, villose on the inner surface; stamens 17–21, usually 20; anthers deep rose-purple; styles 4 or 5, usually 5, surrounded at base by a narrow ring of pale tomentum.

Fruit ripening and beginning to fall early in September, on stout villose or glabrous pedicels, in large drooping few-fruited clusters, obovoid or short-oblong, bright red, often slightly pruinose, marked by numerous minute pale dots, $\frac{5}{8}'-\frac{3}{4}'$ long, $\frac{1}{2}'-\frac{5}{8}'$ in diameter; calyx enlarged, prominent, with spreading or erect and incurved coarsely serrate persistent lobes, their upper surface bright red below the middle and covered above with soft white hairs; flesh thick, orange-yellow, soft, juicy and acidulous; nutlets 4 or 5, thin, narrowed at the ends, acute at base, rounded at apex, rounded and sometimes broadly grooved on the back, about $\frac{5}{16}'$ long.

A tree, often 20° high, with a tall trunk 8′–10′ in diameter, covered with light grayish brown slightly fissured bark, large spreading and drooping branches forming an open head often 20° across, and slender branchlets olive-green and slightly hairy when they first appear, dull red-brown and marked by many large pale lenticels during their first season, becoming light gray and rather lustrous, and armed with stout straight dark purple shining ultimately gray spines often 2′ long.

Distribution. Borders of woods near the shores of Fisher's Island Sound, Mumford's Point, Groton, and near Lyme, New London County, Connecticut.

95. Cratægus Hillii Sarg.

Leaves oblong-ovate, acuminate, rounded or rarely cuneate at the broad entire base, coarsely doubly serrate above with straight glandular teeth, and divided into numerous short acuminate lateral lobes, when they unfold coated above with short lustrous white

Fig. 447

hairs and densely tomentose below, particularly on the midrib and veins, about one fourth grown when the flowers open the middle of May and then roughened above by short hairs and villose below, and at maturity thin, light yellow-green and scabrate on the upper surface, pale yellow-green on the lower surface, $2\frac{1}{2}'-3'$ long, and $2'-2\frac{1}{2}'$ wide, with a slender midrib often slightly hairy near the base, and 4 or 5 pairs of thin primary veins extending obliquely to the point of the lobes; petioles slender, densely villose early in the season, slightly hairy in the autumn, and $\frac{5}{8}'-1\frac{1}{2}'$ in length; leaves at the end of vigorous shoots often truncate or slightly cordate at base, deeply lobed with broad triangular lobes, and $3\frac{1}{2}'-4'$ long and wide, with a stout rose-colored glandular petiole, and hairy lunate glandular-serrate stipules. **Flowers** about $\frac{3}{4}'$ in diameter, on slender densely villose pedicels, in broad many-flowered hairy compound corymbs, their large linear to oblong bracts and bractlets occasionally persistent until midsummer; calyx-tube narrowly obconic, thickly covered with long spreading white hairs, the lobes abruptly narrowed at base, broad, acuminate, coarsely glandular-serrate, glabrous on the outer surface, villose on the inner surface; stamens 20; anthers pink; styles 4 or 5, surrounded at base by a narrow ring of pale tomentum. Fruit ripening from the middle to the end of September, on slender puberulous pedicels, in drooping few-fruited clusters, obovoid, broad and rounded at apex, gradually narrowed to the rounded base, crimson, lustrous, marked by small pale dots, $\frac{1}{2}'-\frac{5}{8}'$ long, $\frac{3}{8}'-\frac{1}{2}'$ in diameter; calyx only slightly enlarged, with closely appressed coarsely serrate lobes often deciduous from the ripe fruit; flesh yellow, thin, acidulous, juicy; nutlets 4 or 5, thin, gradually narrowed and acute at the ends, irregularly ridged and sometimes grooved on the back, about $\frac{3}{8}'$ long.

A tree, 25°-30° high, with a trunk sometimes a foot in diameter and 6° or 7° long, covered with close light gray bark tinged with red and divided by shallow fissures into small plates, stout ascending branches forming an open irregular often round-topped head, and slender nearly straight branchlets densely villose when they first appear, dark orange color tinged with red and sparingly villose when the flowers open, becoming bright red-brown and lustrous at the end of their first season and dark dull reddish brown the following year, and sparingly armed with slender nearly straight red-brown shining spines $1\frac{1}{2}'-2'$ long.

Distribution. Open woods near the borders of streams in moist rich soil; northeastern Illinois, (Thatcher's Park, Glendon Park, and River Forest, Cook County); not common.

96. Cratægus assurgens Sarg.

Leaves broad-ovate, acuminate, rounded or rarely cuneate at the wide entire base, sharply doubly serrate above with straight gland-tipped teeth, and slightly divided, into 3 or 4 pairs of small acuminate lobes, about one third grown when the flowers open

Fig. 448

the middle of May and then roughened above by short white hairs and glabrous or sparingly villose below, with persistent hairs on the slender yellow midrib, and on the veins arching obliquely to the point of the lobes, and at maturity membranaceous, dull dark green and scabrate on the upper surface, light yellow-green on the lower surface, $2\frac{3}{4}'-3\frac{1}{2}'$ long, and $2\frac{1}{4}'-2\frac{3}{4}'$ wide; petioles slender, villose early in the season, becoming pubescent $1'-1\frac{1}{2}'$ in length; leaves at the end of vigorous shoots often deeply lobed, coarsely serrate sometimes 4' long and wide, with long stout glandular petioles and foliaceous lunate acuminate coarsely glandular-serrate persistent stipules. **Flowers** $\frac{3}{4}'-\frac{5}{8}'$ in diameter, on short villose pedicels, in compact 8-15-flowered hairy corymbs, with oblong, acuminate, glandular bracts and bractlets, deciduous with the opening of the flowers; calyx-tube narrowly obconic, sparingly villose, the lobes long, narrow, acuminate, tipped with minute red

glands, finely glandular-serrate, glabrous on the outer, pubescent on the inner surface; stamens 10–20, usually 10; anthers pinkish purple; styles 4 or 5, surrounded at base by tufts
of pale hairs. **Fruit** ripening from the 15th to the 20th of September, and usually falling
about the 1st of October, on short glabrous pedicels, in drooping few-fruited clusters,
short-oblong to slightly obovoid, dull red to crimson, $\frac{1}{2}'-\frac{5}{8}'$ long, about $\frac{1}{2}'$ wide; calyx
sessile, with spreading closely appressed serrate usually persistent lobes; flesh thin, pale
yellow or nearly white, acidulous; nutlets 4 or 5, broad, narrow and acute at the ends,
prominently ridged on the back with a high narrow ridge, or often grooved, about $\frac{1}{4}'$ long.

A tree, sometimes 25° high, with a trunk 2'–6' in diameter and often 6°–9° long, covered
with close dark gray bark, ascending branches forming an oblong, open head, and slender
branchlets light orange-yellow and covered when they first appear with long scattered
caducous white hairs, becoming bright red-brown and lustrous, and dark gray-brown the
following year, and armed with many stout usually slightly curved bright red-brown
shining spines, 1'–1½' long.

Distribution. River banks and low woods in rich soil; northeastern Illinois (Leyden
township, La Grange, Thatcher's Park, Cook County, Highland Park, Deerfield, Wauconda, Lake County); Fox Point, Milwaukee County, Wisconsin.

97. Cratægus Pringlei Sarg.

Leaves oval, acute, rounded or often abruptly narrowed and cuneate at base, occasionally irregularly lobed above the middle with short broad acute lobes, and coarsely and often
doubly serrate with glandular teeth, as they unfold villose on both surfaces, and often

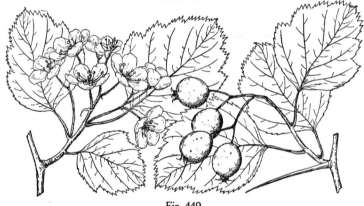

Fig. 449

more or less tinged with red, when the flowers open, usually in the last week of May,
roughened above by short closely appressed pale hairs and glabrous below with the exception of a few hairs on the slender midrib and remote primary veins, and at maturity thin,
glabrous, and bright yellow-green on the upper surface, pale below, 2'–2½' long, and 1¾'–2¼'
wide, usually conspicuously concave by the gradual turning down of the blades from the
midrib to the margins, drooping on long thin slender glandular petioles at first villose,
ultimately glabrous, 1'–1¾' in length; leaves at the end of vigorous shoots sometimes
truncate or slightly cordate at the base, and frequently 3' long and wide. **Flowers** about
¾' in diameter, on stout hairy pedicels, in many-flowered compound villose corymbs; calyx-
tube narrowly obconic, villose, particularly toward the base, the lobes narrow, acuminate,
coarsely glandular-serrate, villose on both surfaces or only on the inner surface; stamens
10, occasionally 5–10; anthers small, purple; styles 3–5, surrounded at the base by con-

spicuous tufts of pale tomentum. **Fruit** ripening and falling late in September or early in October, on stout pedicels, in erect villose mostly few-fruited clusters, short-oblong, dark dull red, marked by few dark dots, villose at the ends with long scattered pale hairs, $\frac{3}{4}'$ long and $\frac{5}{8}'$ in diameter; calyx little enlarged, the lobes gradually narrowed from a broad base, acuminate, glandular-serrate, often erect; flesh thick, yellow, dry and acid, with a disagreeable flavor; nutlets 3–5, rounded and slightly ridged on the back, $\frac{1}{3}'$ long.

A tree, occasionally 25° high, with a tall trunk 10′–12′ in diameter, covered with thin bark separating into large flakes broken into small loose dark red-brown scales, stout branches forming a wide symmetrical head, and slightly zigzag branchlets at first dark green and villose, soon becoming glabrous, chestnut-brown and lustrous, bright orange-brown during their second year, and armed with thick straight or somewhat curved chestnut-brown spines often $1\frac{1}{2}'$ long.

Distribution. Southern New Hampshire, through southern Vermont to western Massachusetts and eastern New York; through central and western New York and southern Ontario to northeastern Ohio (Plymouth, Ashtabula County), the southern peninsula of Michigan and northeastern Illinois.

98. Cratægus lobulata Sarg. Red Haw.

Leaves oval to oblong-ovate, acute at apex, broad-cuneate or rounded at the entire base, sharply and often doubly serrate above with straight glandular teeth, and deeply divided into numerous narrow acute or acuminate lobes spreading or pointing to the apex

Fig. 450

or to the base of the leaf, when they first appear and until after the opening of the flowers during the last week in May covered above with short soft pale hairs and slightly pubescent below on the slender midrib, and thin primary veins arching to the point of the lobes, and at maturity thin, dark yellow-green and glabrous on the upper surface, paler on the lower surface, with occasional short white hairs toward the base of the midrib, $2\frac{1}{2}'$–$3\frac{1}{2}'$ long and $2'$–$2\frac{1}{2}'$ wide; petioles slender, nearly terete, at first tomentose, particularly at the base, becoming pubescent or nearly glabrous and bright red, $1'$–$1\frac{1}{2}'$ in length; leaves at the end of vigorous shoots broad-ovate, rounded or truncate at the broad base, divided into numerous acuminate lateral lobes, often $3\frac{1}{2}'$–$4'$ long and $3'$–$3\frac{1}{2}'$ wide. **Flowers** $\frac{3}{4}'$ in diameter, on elongated slender pedicels, in rather compact many-flowered tomentose corymbs, with linear-lanceolate glandular-serrate bright red bracts and bractlets; calyx-tube broadly obconic, glabrous, or villose toward the base, dark red, the lobes gradually narrowed from a broad base, glabrous, coarsely glandular-serrate with large dark red stipitate glands; stamens usually 10, occasionally 5–10; anthers small, dark reddish purple; styles

3–5, sometimes surrounded at the base by a ring of pale tomentum. **Fruit** ripening and falling early in October, on short stout pedicels, in erect compact tomentulose clusters, short-oblong, somewhat flattened at the rounded ends, bright crimson, very lustrous, marked by occasional small white dots, about $\frac{3}{4}'$ long and $\frac{5}{8}'$ in diameter; calyx little enlarged, the lobes small, lanceolate, coarsely glandular-serrate, tomentose on the upper surface, erect and incurved, persistent; flesh thick, yellow, sweet and juicy; nutlets 3–5, thin, dark colored, ridged and often grooved on the back, $\frac{1}{4}'$ long.

A tree, occasionally 35° high, with a straight trunk often a foot in diameter, covered with dark red-brown fissured bark broken into small thick plate-like scales, stout generally ascending branches forming an open usually narrow irregular head, and slender branchlets, dark green and covered with matted pale hairs when they first appear, becoming bright chestnut-brown and very lustrous during their first season, and light orange-brown the following year, and armed with many stout nearly straight chestnut-brown spines rarely more than 1′ in length.

Distribution. Burlington, Chittenden County, Vermont, and southward through the Champlain valley to Crown Point, Essex County and to the neighborhood of Albany, New York; western Massachusetts to southern Connecticut (Stratford, Fairfield County); common.

99. Cratægus pedicellata Sarg.

Leaves broad-ovate or occasionally obovate or rhombic, acute or acuminate, broad-cuneate or rounded at the entire base, coarsely often doubly serrate above with spreading glandular teeth, and divided above the middle into 4 or 5 pairs of short acute or acuminate

Fig. 451

lobes, nearly two thirds grown when the flowers open during the last week in May, and then roughened above by short rigid pale hairs and glabrous below, and at maturity membranaceous, dark rich green and scabrate on the upper surface, pale on the lower surface, 3′–4′ long, and 2′–3′ wide, with a slender midrib, and thin remote primary veins arching to the point of the lobes; petioles slender, nearly terete, glandular with minute scattered dark glands, at first villose, becoming glabrous, $1\frac{1}{2}'$–$2\frac{1}{2}'$ in length; leaves at the end of vigorous shoots sometimes truncate or slightly cordate at base, more deeply lobed, often 3′–4′ long and 3′ wide. **Flowers** $\frac{1}{2}'$ in diameter, on long thin pedicels, in loose lax many-flowered slightly villose corymbs; calyx-tube narrowly obconic, glabrous, the lobes broad, acute, very coarsely glandular-serrate; stamens usually 10; anthers rose color; styles 5, surrounded at base by a conspicuous ring of pale tomentum. **Fruit** ripening and falling during September, on long slender pedicels, in few-fruited drooping glabrous clusters, obovoid until nearly fully grown, becoming short-oblong when fully ripe, rounded at the ends, bright scarlet, lustrous, marked by numerous small dark dots, $\frac{3}{4}'$ long, and $\frac{1}{2}'-\frac{5}{8}'$ in diameter; calyx large and conspicuous, the lobes much enlarged, coarsely serrate, and usually erect and incurved; flesh pale, thin, dry and mealy; nutlets 5, narrowed and acute at the ends, rounded and deeply grooved on the back, about $\frac{1}{4}'$ long.

A tree, 18°–20° high, with a tall trunk sometimes a foot in diameter, covered with close red-brown scaly bark, long comparatively slender spreading or ascending branches forming a handsome symmetrical head, and thin branchlets dark chestnut-brown and slightly villose at first, becoming very lustrous and ashy gray in their second year, and armed with straight or slightly curved shining chestnut-brown spines $1\frac{1}{2}'-2'$ long.

Distribution. Central and western New York to western Pennsylvania (Allegheny and Crawford counties), and to southern Ontario to the neighborhood of Toronto and London; common; passing into var. *gloriosa* Sarg. differing in its rather larger flowers with pink anthers, larger and more lustrous fruit often mammillate at base and ripening a few days earlier and in its convex leaves. A tree, 20°–25° high, with a trunk often 1° in diameter, and a symmetrical round-topped head; Rochester, Monroe County, New York; not common.

100. Cratægus Holmesiana Ashe.

Leaves oval or ovate, acute or acuminate at apex, rounded or broad cuneate at base, coarsely doubly serrate above the middle with straight teeth tipped at first with prominent dark red caducous glands, and usually divided into 3 or 4 pairs of short acute or acu-

Fig. 452

minate lateral lobes, when they unfold dark red, roughened by rigid pale hairs on the upper surface, and glabrous or sometimes villose on the lower surface, scabrate above, pale yellow-green and nearly half grown when the flowers open early in May, and at maturity thick and firm, almost smooth, conspicuously yellow-green, usually about 2′ long and $1\frac{3}{4}'$ wide, with a prominent midrib often bright red on the lower side toward the base, and 4–6 pairs of slender primary veins arching to the point of the lobes; petioles slender, nearly terete, glandular, glabrous or sometimes puberulous while young, $1'-1\frac{1}{2}'$ in length; leaves at the end of vigorous shoots often broad-ovate to oval, rounded, truncate or slightly cordate at base, more coarsely serrate and more deeply lobed, and frequently 4′ long and 3′ wide. **Flowers** cup-shaped, $\frac{1}{2}'-\frac{3}{4}'$ in diameter, on long slender glabrous pedicels, in loose glabrous or rarely puberulous many-flowered corymbs, with oblanceolate or linear acute glandular caducous bracts and bractlets; calyx-tube narrowly obconic, glabrous, more or less deeply tinged with red, the lobes long, acuminate, glandular-serrate, or often nearly entire; glabrous on the outer surface, villose-pubescent on the inner surface; stamens usually 5, sometimes 6–8; anthers large, dark reddish purple; styles usually 3, surrounded at base by a narrow ring of pale tomentum. **Fruit** ripening and falling early in September, on long slender pedicels, in many-fruited drooping clusters, obovoid to ellipsoidal, crimson, lustrous, marked by occasional small dark dots, about $\frac{1}{2}'$ long, and $\frac{1}{3}'$ in diameter; calyx enlarged, conspicuous, with erect and incurved glandular-serrate lobes, bright red toward the base on the upper side; flesh thin, yellow, dry and mealy, with a disagreeable flavor; nutlets usually 3, light chestnut-brown, prominently grooved and ridged on the back with a broad rounded ridge, about $\frac{1}{4}'$ long.

A tree, often 30° high, with a tall straight trunk 10′–15′ in diameter, covered with pale gray-brown or nearly white scaly bark, stout ascending branches forming an open irregular rather compact head, and stout glabrous branchlets dark green more or less tinged with red when they first appear, becoming bright chestnut-brown or orange-brown and lustrous, and ultimately ashy gray, and armed with occasional thick mostly straight bright chestnut-brown shining spines $1\frac{1}{2}'$–2′ long.

Distribution. Rich moist hillsides and the borders of streams and swamps, neighborhood of Montreal and southern Ontario to the coast of southern Maine, central and western Massachusetts, Rhode Island, western New York, and eastern Pennsylvania; most abundant and of its largest size on the hills of Worcester County, Massachusetts. In Sellersville, Bucks County, Pennsylvania, in a form of this species (var. *villipes* Ashe) the young branchlets, petioles, and corymbs are often puberulous and the under surface of the leaves more or less hairy, especially on the midrib and veins. Passing into var. *tardipes* Sarg. differing from the type in its darker green leaves somewhat rougher on the upper surface, flowers often $\frac{4}{5}'$ in diameter on villose pedicels, and in the shorter slightly hairy pedicels of the fruit ripening early in October.

A tree, in size, habit and bark similar to the species; southern Ontario (neighborhood of Toronto, common, near London, bank of the St. Clair River below Sarnia and Walpole Island, Lamberton County); Province of Quebec (Montreal, Caughnawaga, Isle Perrot, St. Ann's and Hemmingford); central and western New York.

101. Cratægus acclivis Sarg.

Leaves oblong-ovate, acuminate, broad-cuneate or rounded at the entire base, coarsely doubly serrate above with straight gland-tipped teeth, and deeply divided into numerous wide-spreading acuminate lateral lobes, when they unfold tinged with red, densely villose on the upper surface, pubescent on the midrib and veins below, about half grown when the flowers open during the last week of May and then light yellow-green, slightly roughened above by short white hairs and pubescent on the midrib and veins below, and at maturity membranaceous, dark yellow-green and nearly smooth above, pale yellow-green and glabrous below, $2\frac{1}{2}'$–3′ long, and 2′–$2\frac{1}{2}'$ wide, with a stout yellow midrib, and 5 or 6 pairs of primary veins extending obliquely to the point of the lobes; petioles slender, slightly wing-margined at apex, glandular with numerous small dark glands, densely villose early in the season, becoming puberulous or glabrous in the autumn, $1\frac{1}{2}'$–2′ in length; leaves at the end of vigorous shoots broad-ovate, acuminate, cordate at the wide base, deeply divided into wide acute lateral lobes, and often 4′–5′ long and wide, with foliaceous, lunate, coarsely glandular-serrate stipules, $1\frac{1}{2}'$ wide, and persistent throughout the season. **Flowers** $\frac{3}{4}'$ in diameter, on slender densely villose pedicels, in broad lax many-flowered long-branched hairy corymbs, their bracts lanceolate, glandular, large and conspicuous, persistent until after the flowers open; calyx-tube narrowly obconic, covered with a thick coat of long matted hairs, the lobes long slender, acuminate, serrate with occasional large gland-tipped teeth, glabrous on the outer surface, slightly villose on the inner surface; stamens usually 5; anthers pink; styles mostly 5. **Fruit** ripening the middle of September and soon falling, on long slender slightly hairy pedicels, in many-fruited drooping clusters, short-oblong, broad and rounded at the ends, yellowish red, glaucous, marked by occasional pale dots, about $\frac{3}{4}'$ long and $\frac{5}{8}'$ wide; calyx sessile, with usually erect enlarged coarsely serrate lobes villose on the upper side and often deciduous from the ripe fruit; flesh thick, yellow, rather juicy; nutlets usually 5, narrow and acute at the ends, ridged with a high broad ridge, or rounded and slightly grooved on the back, about ⅜′ long.

A tree, 25°–30° high, with a short trunk occasionally 4′–5′ in diameter, covered with smooth light gray bark, numerous erect branches forming an oblong open very irregular

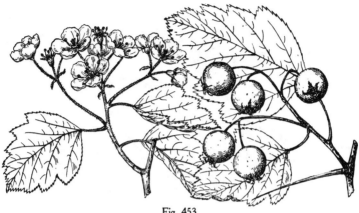

Fig. 453

head, and stout slightly zigzag branchlets coated when they first appear with long matted pale hairs, light red-brown and lustrous, marked by small pale lenticels, and pubescent at the end of their first season, becoming dull red or orange-brown the following year, and armed with stout straight or curved bright red-brown shining spines 1¼′–2′ long.

Distribution. New York: near Albany, Albany County, steep banks of the gorge of the Genesee River, Rochester, Monroe County, banks of the Niagara River, Niagara Falls, Niagara County, and near Buffalo, Erie County; common.

102. Cratægus delecta Sarg.

Leaves broad-ovate, acute or acuminate at apex, rounded or broad-cuneate at the entire base, sharply often doubly serrate above with straight glandular teeth, and divided usually only above the middle into numerous short acuminate lateral lobes, when they unfold tinged with red and covered with glistening white hairs more abundant below than above, nearly half grown when the flowers open during the first half of May and then roughened on the upper surface by short white hairs and glabrous or sparingly villose on the midrib and veins below with scattered hairs sometimes persistent through the season, and at maturity membranaceous, light yellow-green, lustrous and glabrous above, paler below, 1½′–2′ long and wide, with a stout yellow midrib, and 6 or 7 pairs of slender primary veins arching obliquely to the point of the lobes; turning purplish in the autumn before falling; petioles slender, covered early in the season with matted pale hairs, becoming glabrous, slightly glandular, often tinged with red below the middle, ¾′–1′ in length; leaves at the end of vigorous shoots sometimes long-pointed at apex and slightly cordate at base, more deeply lobed and more coarsely serrate, and often 3′–4′ long and wide. **Flowers** ¾′–1′ in diameter, on long slender slightly hairy pedicels, in broad villose 10–15-flowered sparingly villose corymbs, with glandular caducous bracts and bractlets; calyx-tube broadly obconic, villose or nearly glabrous, the lobes acuminate, coarsely glandular-serrate, glabrous on the outer surface, villose on the inner surface; stamens 5–10, usually 5; anthers dark rose color; styles 3–5, usually 5. **Fruit** ripening from the first to the middle of September and soon falling, on stout glabrous pedicels, in drooping few-fruited clusters, subglobose to slightly obovoid, bright red or scarlet, becoming purple when fully ripe, $\frac{1}{2}'-\frac{3}{4}'$ long, and $\frac{2}{3}'-\frac{3}{4}'$ in diameter; calyx prominent, with erect and incurved coarsely serrate lobes; flesh thick, yellow, juicy, mildly acid and edible; nutlets 3–5, usually 5, narrowed and acute at the ends, rounded and very irregularly ridged on the back, $\frac{1}{4}'-\frac{5}{16}'$ long.

A tree, sometimes 30° high, with a trunk rarely 1° in diameter and 6°–9° long, covered with light gray slightly fissured smooth bark, spreading or ascending branches forming an

Fig. 454

oblong open head, and slender branchlets at first slightly villose, becoming glabrous, dull red, and ultimately gray or olive-gray, and armed with stout nearly straight spines much thickened below the middle, dark chestnut-brown and lustrous, becoming dull brown or gray, and usually $1'-2'$ long.

Distribution. Pastures, open woods or their borders; northeastern Illinois (Lockport, Will County, Wauconda, Fort Sheridan, Deerfield, Lake Forest, Highland Park, Lake County).

103. Cratægus Eamesii Sarg.

Leaves oblong-ovate, acute or acuminate, concave-cuneate or rounded at the entire or glandular base, sharply often doubly serrate above with straight glandular teeth, and divided into numerous short acute lateral lobes, about half grown when the flowers open the middle of May, and then membranaceous, light yellow-green and roughened above by short rigid white hairs and pale and glabrous below with the exception of a few hairs on the midrib, and slender primary veins arching to the point of the lobes, and at maturity subcoriaceous, dark rather dull green and smooth above, pale yellow-green below, $3'-3\frac{1}{2}'$ long, and $2'-2\frac{1}{2}'$ wide; petioles slender, wing-margined above, villose at first, becoming glabrous, $1'-1\frac{1}{2}'$ in length; leaves at the end of vigorous shoots usually rounded or truncate at the broad base, more deeply lobed, often $3\frac{1}{2}'-4'$ long and $3\frac{1}{2}'$ wide. **Flowers** about $\frac{3}{4}'$ in diameter, on slender slightly hairy pedicels, in crowded compact 5–25, usually 15–18-flowered sparingly villose corymbs, with linear-obovate coarsely glandular reddish bracts and bractlets, mostly deciduous before the flowers open; calyx narrowly obconic, glabrous, the lobes long, slender, glandular with large bright red stipitate glands, glabrous on the outer, slightly villose on the inner surface; stamens 5–10, usually 5–8; anthers deep rose-purple; styles 4 or 5, surrounded at base by a narrow ring of pale pubescence. **Fruit** ripening early in September and soon falling, on stout glabrous pedicels, in large many-fruited drooping clusters, short-oblong to slightly ovoid, rounded at the ends, bright cherry-red, lustrous, pruinose, marked by few large dark dots, $\frac{5}{8}'-\frac{3}{4}'$ long, and about $\frac{1}{2}'$ in diameter; calyx only slightly enlarged, the lobes erect and incurved, coarsely serrate, dark red on the upper side below the middle, their tips deciduous from the ripe fruit; flesh thick, pale yellow, juicy; nutlets 4 or 5, narrow at the ends, irregularly ridged often with a high broad ridge, and sometimes grooved on the back, about $\frac{1}{4}'$ long.

A tree, occasionally 20° high, with a trunk a foot in diameter, ascending branches forming a narrow open head, and stout glabrous branchlets bright reddish brown and rather lus-

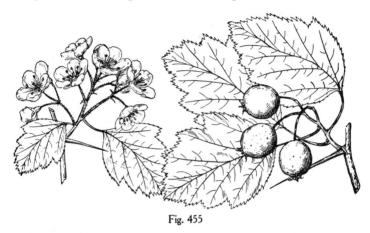

Fig. 455

trous during their first season, becoming light gray slightly tinged with red in their second year, and armed with stout straight or slightly curved spines $1'-1\frac{1}{2}'$ long; or occasionally shrubby, with a short trunk divided near the ground into several spreading stems.

Distribution. Rich moist ground, Stratford, Fairfield County (*E. H. Eames*), and Ansonia, New Haven County, Connecticut (*E. B. Harger*).

104. Cratægus sertata Sarg.

Leaves oblong-ovate, acuminate, rounded, truncate, subcordate or rarely cuneate at the broad base, finely and often doubly serrate with straight gland-tipped teeth, and deeply divided into 5 or 6 pairs of wide acuminate lobes, when they unfold coated above with short pale hairs and villose below on the midrib and veins, about half grown and villose when the flowers open during the first half of May, and at maturity membranaceous, dark yellow-green and scabrate on the upper surface, pale yellow-green and glabrous on the lower surface, $2\frac{1}{2}'-3'$ long, and $1\frac{1}{2}'-2'$ wide, with a thin yellow midrib, and slender primary veins arching obliquely to the point of the lobes; petioles slender, slightly grooved, villose early in the season, ultimately glabrous, sparingly glandular, $1\frac{1}{2}'-3'$ in length; leaves at the end of vigorous shoots broad-ovate, rounded or slightly cordate at base, often 3' long and $2\frac{1}{2}'$ wide. **Flowers** $\frac{3}{4}'-1'$ in diameter, on slender pedicels, in broad 10–15-flowered densely villose corymbs, with linear to linear-obovate glandular large and conspicuous caducous bracts and bractlets; calyx-tube broadly obconic, glabrous above, villose below, the lobes abruptly narrowed from the base, broad, acuminate, tipped with small red glands, coarsely glandular-serrate, glabrate on the outer surface, pubescent on the inner surface; stamens 5–10, usually 5; anthers pale rose color; styles 3–5, surrounded at base by tufts of pale hairs. **Fruit** ripening about the middle of September and soon falling, on slender villose or pubescent pedicels, in drooping many-fruited clusters, subglobose to slightly obovoid, rounded at the ends, bright red and lustrous, becoming darker or crimson when fully ripe, marked by occasional large pale dots, about $\frac{1}{2}'$ long and wide; calyx prominent, with enlarged mostly erect incurved serrate lobes; flesh thin, yellow, aromatic, pleasantly acid; nutlets 3–5, usually 4, thin, narrow and acute at the ends, slightly ridged on the back with a wide or narrow ridge, $\frac{3}{8}$' long.

A tree, 10°–20° high, with a trunk 6'–8' in diameter and often 4°–5° long, covered with close dark gray bark separating into long narrow thin plate-like scales, stout spreading branches forming a handsome open head, and slender nearly straight branchlets thickly coated when they first appear with matted pale hairs, light brown and lustrous at the end

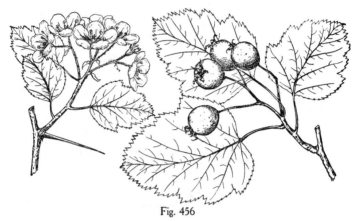

Fig. 456

of their first season, and dark gray-brown the following year, and unarmed or armed with stout nearly straight or curved spines 1'–2$\frac{1}{2}$' long.

Distribution. Open woods and pastures in rich moist soil; northeastern Illinois (Mokena, Will County, Glenellyn, Dupage County, Barrington, Glendon Park, Cook County, Highland Park, Lake Zurich, Lake County); Fox Point, Milwaukee County, Wisconsin.

X. DILATATÆ.

CONSPECTUS OF THE ARBORESCENT SPECIES.

Flowers in broad 6–12-flowered corymbs.
    Leaves broad-ovate; fruit bright scarlet.   **105. C. dilatata (A).**
    Leaves nearly orbicular to oval; fruit dull red blotched with green, or orange-red.
                                      106. C. suborbiculata (A).
    Leaves ovate to slightly obovate; fruit crimson, pruinose.   **107. C. hudsonica (A).**
Flowers in very compact 5–7-flowered corymbs; leaves broad-ovate; fruit usually broader than high, much flattened at the ends, dark crimson, very lustrous.
                                        108. C. coccinioides (A).

105. Cratægus dilatata Sarg.

Leaves broad-ovate, acute, truncate, cordate or slightly rounded at the broad base, coarsely and generally doubly and irregularly serrate above with straight teeth tipped with large dark glands, unequally lobed usually with 2 or 3 pairs of acute or acuminate lateral lobes, about one third grown when the flowers open at the end of May, and then light yellow-green, conspicuously plicate, roughened on the upper surface with short stiff white hairs and glabrous on the lower surface, and at maturity smooth and glabrous, dark green above, pale below, 2'–2$\frac{1}{2}$' long, and almost as wide as long, with a slender midrib and 4 or 5 pairs of thin primary veins; petioles slender, somewhat glandular, at first villose, soon glabrous, often dark red toward the base after midsummer, 1'–2' in length; leaves at the end of vigorous shoots often 4'-5' long, and frequently rather broader than long. Flowers 1'-1⅛' in diameter, on slender elongated hairy pedicels, in broad, loose, usually 8-12-flowered slightly villose corymbs, with lanceolate bracts and bractlets glandular like the inner bud-scales with dark red glands; calyx-tube broadly obconic, covered toward the base with matted pale hairs, nearly glabrous above, the lobes broad, acuminate, coarsely glandular with large scattered red glands, glabrous on the outer surface and generally slightly villose on the inner surface; stamens 20; anthers large, rose color; styles usually 5, surrounded at base by small tufts of white hairs. Fruit ripening and falling early in September, on slender pedicels, in many-fruited drooping clusters, subglobose, bright scarlet, marked by numerous small dark dots, about ¾' in diameter; the calyx much enlarged, with

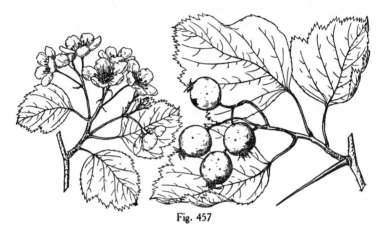

Fig. 457

spreading coarsely serrate lobes bright red on the upper side toward the base; flesh thin, sweet and yellow; nutlets 5, thin, rounded and prominently ridged on the back, about ¼' long.

A tree, occasionally 20° high, with a tall straight trunk, covered with light gray-brown scaly bark, branches spreading into a wide round-topped symmetrical head, and short glabrous slightly zigzag branchlets armed with few stout straight light brown shining spines 1'-2' long.

Distribution. Eastern Massachusetts, coast of Rhode Island, western Vermont, in the neighborhood of Albany, New York, and near Montreal, Province of Quebec.

106. Cratægus suborbiculata Sarg.

Leaves nearly orbicular to oval or rarely to oblong, short-pointed at apex, broad and rounded or broad-cuneate at the entire base, sharply doubly serrate above with slender straight or incurved glandular teeth, and often divided above the middle into 3 or 4 pairs of short acute lobes, when they unfold pale yellow-green and somewhat villose on the upper surface toward the base and below in the axils of the principal veins, about a third grown when the flowers open during the first week of June, and at maturity thin and firm in texture, dull dark green above, paler below, usually about 1½' long and broad, with a slender midrib and 4 or 5 pairs of thin primary veins; petioles slender, slightly glandular, more or less winged above, ⅝'-1' in length; leaves at the end of vigorous shoots nearly orbicular to oval, more coarsely serrate and more deeply lobed, and frequently 3' long and wide, their petioles often broadly winged and conspicuously glandular. Flowers ¾' in diameter, on short stout pedicels, in compact 6-12-flowered glabrous corymbs; calyx broadly obconic, the lobes gradually narrowed from a broad base, long, acuminate, entire or occasionally obscurely denticulate; stamens 20; anthers small, rose color; styles 5, surrounded at base by a broad ring of hoary tomentum. **Fruit** falling in October without becoming mellow, on short rigid pedicels, in few-fruited erect clusters, subglobose, often rather longer than broad, about $\frac{5}{8}'$ in diameter, dull red more or less blotched with green, or often wholly green on one face, or scarlet in one form; calyx enlarged, prominent, with a broad deep

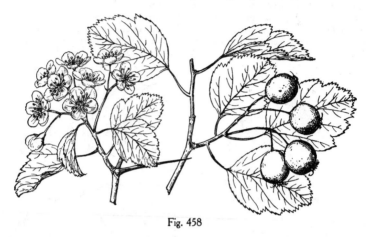

Fig. 458

cavity and nearly entire wide-spreading lobes; flesh yellow, thin, dry and hard; nutlets 5, broad and thick, narrow and rounded at the ends, obscurely and unequally grooved on the back, about $\frac{1}{4}'$ long.

A tree, rarely more than 15°–20° high, with a well-developed trunk 5′–6′ in diameter, stout spreading branches forming a broad low flat-topped head, and stout branchlets orange-brown in their first season, becoming dark gray-brown the following year, and armed with thick straight or slightly curved bright chestnut-brown shining spines 1′–2′ in length.

Distribution. Low limestone ridges opposite Lachine near the south bank of the St. Lawrence River, and on the Island of Montreal, Province of Quebec; near Cornwall, Ontario.

107. Cratægus hudsonica Sarg.

Leaves ovate or slightly obovate, acute, gradually and abruptly narrowed and mostly concave-cuneate at the entire base, sharply and often doubly serrate above with straight or incurved glandular teeth, and frequently slightly divided above the middle into short acute lobes, nearly fully grown when the flowers open at the end of May, and then thin, light yellow-green, smooth and glabrous above with the exception of a few short white scattered hairs on the midrib, and pale and glabrous below, and at maturity thin and firm in texture, glabrous, 2′–2½′ long, and 1½′–1¾′ wide, with a slender yellow midrib, and 5 or 6 pairs of thin primary veins extending obliquely to the point of the lobes; petioles slender, wing-margined above, glandular, at first slightly hairy, becoming glabrous and rose color toward the base, $\frac{3}{4}'$–1′ in length; leaves at the end of vigorous shoots broad-ovate to suborbicular, full and rounded or broad-cuneate at the wide base, deeply divided into broad lateral lobes, and 2′–3′ long and wide. **Flowers** about $\frac{3}{4}'$ in diameter, on long slender pedicels, in broad usually 10–12-flowered glabrous corymbs; calyx-tube narrowly obconic, glabrous, the lobes gradually narrowed from a broad base, acuminate, glandular-serrate often only below the middle, glabrous on the outer surface, slightly hairy on the inner surface; stamens 20; anthers rose color; styles 3–5. **Fruit** ripening early in September, in few-fruited drooping clusters, subglobose, crimson, pruinose, marked by numerous pale dots, about $\frac{5}{8}'$ in diameter; calyx enlarged, with a deep broad cavity, and closely appressed serrate lobes villose on the upper side; flesh thick, yellow, dry and mealy; nutlets 3–5, rounded at base and narrowed and rounded at apex, rounded and sometimes ridged on the back with a high rounded ridge, about $\frac{5}{16}'$ long.

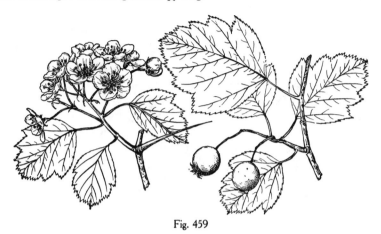

Fig. 459

A tree, sometimes 20° high, with a tall trunk 8'–10' in diameter, covered with pale scaly bark, heavy ascending and spreading branches forming a broad open head, and stout ascending glabrous branchlets dark orange color when they first appear and light orange-brown and lustrous during their first winter, and armed with numerous slender straight or slightly curved bright red-brown shining spines $1\frac{1}{2}'$–2' long; sometimes a broad bush, with numerous stout spreading stems.

Distribution. Rolling hills in the valley of the Hudson River, near Albany, Albany County, New York.

108. Cratægus coccinioides Ashe.

Leaves broad-ovate, acute, full and rounded or truncate at base, sharply and often doubly serrate with straight glandular teeth, and divided above the middle into short acute lobes, as they unfold conspicuously plicate, very lustrous, yellow-green, and villose on the lower side of the midrib with a few short pale hairs usually persistent during the season, about half grown when the flowers open early in May, and at maturity thin and firm in texture, rather rigid, dull dark green and smooth on the upper surface, pale on the lower surface, $2\frac{1}{2}'$–3' long, and 2'–$2\frac{1}{2}'$ wide, with a thin pale yellow midrib deeply impressed above and often bright red toward the base after midsummer, and slender primary veins arching to the point of the lobes; turning late in October gradually bright orange and scarlet; petioles glandular on the upper side with minute-stalked dark red glands, at first villose, soon glabrous, often bright red or pink toward the base, $\frac{3}{4}'$–1' in length; leaves at the end of vigorous shoots more or less cordate at base and usually $3\frac{1}{2}'$–4' long and wide. **Flowers** $\frac{3}{4}'$ in diameter, in very compact 5–7-flowered glabrous or slightly villose corymbs, with coarsely serrate oblong-obovate acute bracts and bractlets, conspicuously glandular with large bright red glands; calyx-tube broadly obconic, glabrous, the lobes gradually narrowed from a broad base, acute and coarsely glandular-serrate; stamens 20; anthers large, deep rose color; styles 5, surrounded at base by a ring of pale tomentum. **Fruit** ripening early in October and falling gradually during a month or six weeks, on stout pedicels, in few-fruited compact erect clusters, subglobose, much flattened at the ends, often obscurely angled, dark crimson, very lustrous, marked by numerous large pale dots, $\frac{3}{4}'$ long, and $\frac{7}{8}'$ wide; calyx much enlarged and conspicuous, with spreading or erect lobes bright red on the upper side near the base; flesh thick, firm, subacid, more or less deeply tinged with red; nutlets 5, comparatively small, light-colored, narrow at the ends, acute at apex, rounded at base, rounded and slightly ridged on the back, about $\frac{1}{3}'$ long.

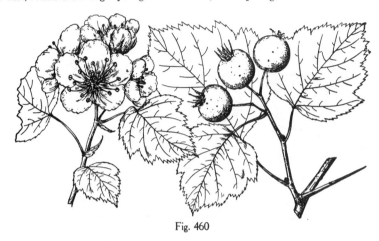

Fig. 460

A tree, sometimes 20° high, with a stem 8'–10' in diameter, covered with dark brown scaly bark, stout spreading light gray branches forming a broad handsome head, and stout nearly straight glabrous bright chestnut-brown very lustrous branchlets armed with thick dark reddish purple shining spines $1\frac{1}{2}'$–2' long.

Distribution. Dry woods in the neighborhood of St. Louis, to southwestern Missouri and to Farmington, Washington County, Arkansas, in eastern Kansas.

XI. ROTUNDIFOLIÆ.

Coccineæ Sarg.

CONSPECTUS OF THE ARBORESCENT SPECIES.

Stamens 10; leaves coriaceous.
  Leaves elliptic or obovate; fruit subglobose, dark crimson; anthers pale yellow.
    109. C. rotundifolia (A).
  Leaves elliptic or ovate; fruit short-oblong to oblong-obovoid, bright carmine-red; anthers rose color. 110. C. Jonesæ (A).
Stamens 20; leaves subcoriaceous, rhombic to oblong-obovate; fruit short-oblong to subglobose, dark dull red or rusty orange-red; anthers pale yellow.
    111. C. Margaretta (A, C).

109. Cratægus rotundifolia Moen.

Cratægus coccinea var. *rotundifolia* Sarg.

Leaves elliptic or obovate, acute or acuminate, gradually narrowed from above the middle to the cuneate entire base, finely and often doubly serrate above with incurved or straight teeth tipped with minute dark glands, and divided above the middle into several short acute lateral lobes, about half grown when the flowers open at the end of May, and then thin, light yellow-green and glabrous, and at maturity coriaceous, dark green, smooth and lustrous on the upper surface, paler on the lower surface, $1\frac{1}{2}'$–2' long, and 1'–$1\frac{1}{2}'$ wide, with a thin midrib, and 4 or 5 pairs of primary veins extending to the point of the lobes; petioles slender, glandular, slightly winged at apex, glabrous, often dark red toward the base, $\frac{3}{4}'-1'$ in length; leaves at the end of vigorous shoots oblong-ovate, oval or often nearly orbicular, more deeply lobed, and frequently $2\frac{1}{2}'-3'$ long and wide. **Flowers** $\frac{1}{2}'-\frac{3}{4}'$ in diameter, on slender pedicels, in broad loose many-flowered glabrous corymbs; calyx-tube

Fig. 461

broadly obconic, glabrous, the lobes gradually narrowed from a broad base, acute, coarsely glandular-serrate, glabrous, often bright red toward the apex; stamens 10; anthers small, pale yellow; styles 3 or 4. **Fruit** ripening and falling late in October, on short stout pedicels, in drooping many-fruited glabrous clusters, subglobose but occasionally rather longer than broad, dark crimson, marked by scattered dark dots, about $\frac{1}{2}'$ in diameter; calyx enlarged, conspicuous, the lobes bright red on the upper side toward the base, wide-spreading or erect; flesh thin, yellow, dry and sweet; nutlets 3 or 4, rounded at the ends, about $\frac{1}{4}'$ long.

A bushy tree, occasionally 20° high, with a short trunk 8'–10' in diameter, covered with dark red-brown scaly bark, stout ascending branches forming a broad round-topped symmetrical head, and slender glabrous branchlets light green when they first appear, bright red-brown and lustrous during their first year, and ultimately ashy gray, and armed with many stout straight or slightly curved chestnut-brown shining spines 1'–1$\frac{1}{2}'$ long.

Distribution. Nova Scotia, southern Quebec and Ontario to Manitoba and Saskatchewan (Saskatoon), and southward through New England, eastern and northern New York, the southern peninsula of Michigan and northern Indiana; in Pennsylvania (Lackawanna, Bucks, Northampton and Blair Counties); common in the New England coast region; a form (var. *pubera* Sarg.) with young leaves covered above with soft pale hairs and pubescent on the under side of the midrib and veins and villose petioles, flowers with a pubescent calyx-tube, in villose corymbs, becoming pilose when the fruit ripens, and young branchlets covered with long matted pale hairs, ranges from Newfoundland to the shores of Lake St. John, Province of Quebec, northern Ontario, Winnepeg and Manitoba, and southward through the maritime provinces of Canada. New England to southern Connecticut, northern and western New York (near Buffalo, Erie County), the northern peninsula of Michigan, northeastern Wisconsin : in central Minnesota (St. Cloud, Stearns County); common northward.

110. Cratægus Jonesæ Sarg.

Leaves elliptic to ovate, acute, gradually narrowed or broad-cuneate at the entire base, coarsely doubly serrate above with spreading or incurved teeth tipped with deciduous dark red glands, and usually divided above the middle into 2 or 3 pairs of short acute or acuminate lobes, more than half grown when the flowers open during the first week of June, and then membranaceous and coated with soft pale hairs most abundant on the under side of the midrib and principal veins, and at maturity thick and coriaceous, dark green and lustrous on the upper surface, pale and puberulous on the lower surface, 3′–4′ long and 2′–3′ wide, with a stout midrib, 4–6 pairs of primary veins and conspicuous secondary veinlets; petioles stout, more or less winged toward the apex, villose, ultimately glabrous, tinged with red below the middle, 1½′–2′ in length, after midsummer often twisted at base, bringing the lower surface of the leaf to the light; leaves at the end of vigorous shoots usually more coarsely serrate and much more deeply lobed, with broadly winged petioles, and falcate coarsely glandular-serrate stipules sometimes 1′ in length. **Flowers** 1′ in diameter, on long slender pedicels, in broad loose lax many-flowered tomentose corymbs; calyx-

Fig. 462

tube narrowly obconic, tomentose, the lobes abruptly narrowed from a broad base, long, acute, entire, villose; stamens 10; anthers large, rose color; styles 2, or generally 3, surrounded at base by a narrow ring of pale tomentum. **Fruit** ripening usually early in October, on slender elongated pedicels, in broad many-fruited drooping glabrous or puberulous clusters, short-oblong to oblong-obovoid, rounded at the ends, bright carmine-red, marked by occasional large dots, ¾′–1′ long, and ¾′ in diameter; calyx conspicuous, with enlarged and elongated closely appressed lobes; flesh thick, yellow, sweet and mealy; nutlets 3 or rarely 2, thick, narrowed and acute at base, full and broad at apex, rounded and ridged on the back with a high broad ridge, about $\frac{7}{16}$′ long.

A tree, sometimes 20° high, with a tall trunk often a foot in diameter, covered with dark brown scaly bark, ascending or spreading branches forming a broad open irregular head, and stout branchlets tomentose early in the season, becoming orange-brown, glabrous and very lustrous during their first summer, and light gray the following year, and armed with stout straight or curved chestnut-brown shining spines 2′–3′ long and usually pointed toward the base of the branch.

Distribution.   Rocky shores of sounds and bays; coast of Maine, Islesboro and Belfast Bay to the island of Mount Desert (Waldo and Hancock Counties); in hedges, near Fredericton, York County, New Brunswick; Rivière du Loup, Kamouraska County, Province of Quebec (*Brother Victorin*).

111. Cratægus Margaretta Ashe.

Leaves broad-rhombic, oblong-obovate or rarely ovate, acute or rounded at apex, gradually narrowed and usually entire below, coarsely often doubly crenately-serrate above with usually glandless teeth, and divided above the middle or frequently only at apex into short broad rounded or acute lobes; when the flowers open in May thin and roughened above by short pale hairs and glabrous below, and at maturity firm and rather leathery in texture, or subcoriaceous, glabrous, smooth, dark green and somewhat lustrous on the upper surface, pale on the lower surface, $1'-1\frac{1}{4}'$ long, and $1'$ wide, with a yellow midrib, and 3–5 pairs of primary veins extending obliquely to the point of the lobes; petioles slender, often slightly winged toward the apex, glandular at first with minute dark red caducous glands, $\frac{1}{2}'-1'$ in length; leaves at the end of vigorous shoots broad-ovate or semi-orbicular, usually more deeply and more generally lobed, often $3'$ long and $2'-3'$ wide. Flowers about $\frac{3}{4}'$ in diameter, on long slender pedicels, in 3–12-flowered thin-branched slightly villose corymbs; calyx-tube narrowly obconic, slightly villose toward the base, or glabrous, the lobes gradually narrowed from below, acuminate or short-pointed at apex, finely and irregularly glandular-serrate, glabrous or villose on the inner surface; stamens

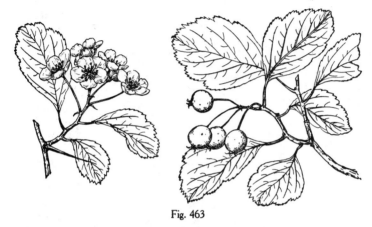

Fig. 463

usually 20; anthers small, light yellow; styles 2 or 3, surrounded at the base by a narrow ring of pale tomentum, and villose below the middle with occasional long spreading hairs. Fruit ripening and falling at the end of September, in few-fruited drooping clusters, short-oblong, rounded at the ends, or subglobose and flattened at the ends, dull dark red or rusty orange-red or rarely yellow, marked by occasional dark dots, and about $\frac{1}{2}'$ long; calyx only slightly enlarged, the lobes spreading or erect and frequently deciduous before the fruit ripens; flesh thin, yellow, dry and mealy; nutlets 2 or 3, broad and rounded at base, acute at apex, conspicuously grooved and ridged on the back with a broad rounded ridge, about $\frac{1}{4}'$ long.

A tree, occasionally 25° high, with a straight trunk $4'-6'$ in diameter, covered with thin dark gray-brown bark, small rather erect branches forming a narrow open head, and slender branchlets, orange-green, glabrous or sometimes pubescent when they first appear, becoming bright chestnut-brown and lustrous, and ashy gray or gray tinged with red during their second year, and armed with thin straight or slightly curved bright chestnut-brown spines $\frac{3}{4}'-1\frac{1}{2}'$ long.

Distribution. Central Iowa (Steamboat Rock, Harden County, Cedar Rapids, Linn County), southward to Missouri (Hannibal, Marion County, Webster, St. Louis County to the neighborhood of Springfield, Greene County), and eastward to northeastern Illinois (Downers Grove, Dupage County); through north central Indiana to southern Michigan (Kalamazoo and Ingham Counties); through central and southern Ohio to the southeastern part of the state (Washington County); southeastern Ontario (London and Oakwood); in central Tennessee (West Nashville, Davidson County).

XII. INTRICATÆ.

CONSPECTUS OF THE ARBORESCENT SPECIES.

Stamens 10; leaves broad-ovate to oval.
    Fruit depressed-globose, yellow-green flushed with russet-red; anthers pale yellow; calyx-lobes eglandular.   112. **C. Boyntonii** (A, C).
    Fruit subglobose, red or russet-red; anthers pale rose color; calyx-lobes glandular with stalked glands.   113. **C. Buckleyi** (A).
Stamens 20.
    Leaves oval to ovate or oblong-obovate; fruit short-oblong, dull red, often with a bright russet face; stamens usually 5–15; anthers small, pale yellow.   114. **C. venusta** (C).
    Leaves oblong-ovate to elliptic or ovate; fruit subglobose to short-oblong, yellow or orange-yellow, more or less flushed with red; anthers large, purple.
                                   115. **C. Sargentii** (C).

112. Cratægus Boyntonii Beadl.

Leaves broad-ovate to oval, acute, rounded or cuneate at the entire glandular base, sharply and often doubly serrate above with glandular teeth, and frequently divided into 2 or 3 pairs of short broad acute lateral lobes, when they unfold deep bronze-red, slightly

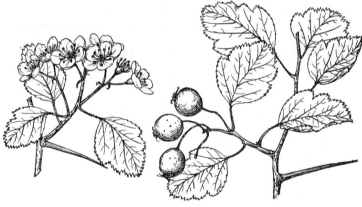

Fig. 464

glandular and viscid, nearly fully grown when the flowers open early in May, and then membranaceous and glabrous or occasionaly slightly pilose, and at maturity subcoriaceous, glabrous, yellow-green on the upper surface, pale on the lower surface, 1′–2½′ long, and 1′–2′ wide, with a thin pale yellow midrib and 4–7 pairs of slender veins; petioles stout, glandular often to the base with bright red glands, slightly winged above, usually about ½′ in length; leaves at the end of vigorous shoots often as broad as long, truncate or cordate at base, and more coarsely dentate and more deeply lobed. **Flowers** about ¾′ in diameter, on short slender pedicels, in compact 4–10-flowered compound corymbs; calyx-tube broadly obconic, the lobes abruptly narrowed from a broad base, acute or rounded at apex, entire or obscurely and irregularly glandular-serrate above the middle; stamens 10; anthers large, pale yellow; styles 3–5, surrounded at base by a broad thick ring of hoary tomentum. **Fruit** ripening and falling early in October, on short stout pedicels, in few-fruited erect clusters, depressed-globose, more or less angled, yellow-green flushed with russet-red, marked with small dark dots, usually about ½′ in diameter; calyx prominent, the large spreading lobes often deciduous before the fruit ripens; nutlets 3–5, acute or acuminate at apex, rounded at the narrow base, about ¼′ long.

A tree, occasionally 20° high, with a tall straight trunk 6′–8′ in diameter, sometimes armed with long gray compound spines, stout ascending branches forming a narrow open irregular or occasionally a round-topped head, and glabrous branchlets furnished with many thin nearly straight light chestnut-brown spines 1½′–2′ long; or more often a shrub, with numerous stems.

Distribution. Banks of streams, the borders of fields and upland woods in the southern Appalachian foothill region from southern Virginia to northern Georgia; in northern Alabama, southeastern Kentucky, and eastern Tennessee; sometimes ascending to altitudes of 3000° above the sea.

113. Cratægus Buckleyi Beadl.

Leaves broad-ovate or oval, acute, rounded or subcordate or narrowed and concave-cuneate at the entire base, coarsely often doubly serrate above with straight glandular teeth, and more or less incisely lobed with acuminate lateral lobes, more than half grown

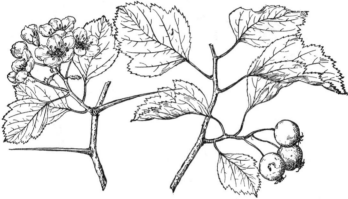

Fig. 465

when the flowers open about the middle of May and then pale green and glabrous with the exception of a few caducous hairs on the upper side of the base of the midrib, and at maturity dark green above, paler below, 1½′–2′ long, and 1½′–2′ wide; petioles stout, conspicuously glandular above the base, wing-margined at the apex, glabrous, ½′–¾′ in length. **Flowers** about ¾′ in diameter, on slender glabrous pedicels, in compact 3–7-flowered simple corymbs, with conspicuously glandular bracts and bractlets; calyx-tube broadly obconic, glabrous, the lobes broad, acuminate, laciniately cut toward the apex, and glandular with stipitate glands; stamens 10; anthers pale rose color; styles 3–5, surrounded at base by tufts of pale hairs. **Fruit** ripening late in September or in October, subglobose, usually angled, red or russet-red, about ½′ in diameter; calyx little enlarged, with spreading or reflexed lobes; flesh thin, dry and mealy; nutlets 3–5, broad and rounded at base, rounded at the slightly narrowed apex, prominently ridged on the back, with a broad grooved ridge, about ₁₆⁵′ long.

A tree, often 25° high, with a trunk 4′–7′ in diameter and sometimes 10°–12° long, covered with gray or often dark brown scaly bark, stout spreading or ascending branches, and thick glabrous red-brown branchlets armed with thin straight shining spines ½′ long, becoming much longer and branched on the trunk and large branches.

Distribution. Southwestern Virginia, through western North Carolina to eastern Tennessee; usually at altitudes between 2000° and 3000°; common on wooded slopes with Oaks, Hickories, and Pines.

114. Cratægus venusta Beadl.

Leaves oval to ovate or occasionally to oblong-ovate, acute, gradually or abruptly narrowed and cuneate or rounded at the entire base, finely serrate above with usually incurved glandular teeth, and frequently slightly and irregularly divided above the middle into 1–3 pairs of short broad acute lobes, when they unfold dark bronze color, with a few scattered pale caducous hairs on the upper surface, about half grown when the flowers open from the 20th to the end of April, and then yellow-green, smooth and glabrous, and at maturity dark dull green above, pale below, $2\frac{1}{2}'$ long, and $1\frac{1}{2}'$ wide, with a stout midrib and 4–7 pairs of thin primary veins; late in the autumn turning, especially those on leading shoots deep orange or scarlet; petioles stout, glandular, more or less winged above, $\frac{1}{2}'-\frac{3}{4}'$ in length; leaves at the end of vigorous shoots generally broad-ovate, rounded at base, deeply lobed with broad lobes, and often $3\frac{1}{2}'$ long and $3'$ wide. **Flowers** $1'$ in diameter, on short pedicels, in 4–9-flowered compact corymbs, their bracts and bractlets like the inner bud-

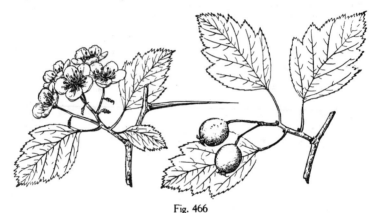

Fig. 466

scales coarsely glandular-serrate and bright red before falling; calyx-tube broadly obconic, the lobes gradually narrowed from a broad base, acute, coarsely glandular-serrate often only below the middle; stamens 15–20, usually 15–17; anthers small, pale yellow; styles 3–5, surrounded at the base by a ring of pale hairs. **Fruit** ripening and falling from the 1st to the middle of October, on stout pedicels often $1'$ long, in few-fruited clusters, short-oblong, rounded at the ends, dull red, often with a bright russet face, and marked by occasional large dark dots; calyx prominent, with a long tube, and spreading lobes often deciduous before the fruit ripens; flesh thick, yellow, dry and mealy; nutlets 3–5, narrow and acute at base, broad, about $\frac{1}{4}'$ long.

A bushy tree, often 25° high, with a short trunk a foot in diameter, furnished like the large branches with innumerable stout much-branched spines frequently $6'$ long, and slender nearly straight glabrous dark chestnut-brown branchlets, armed with many stout straight or slightly curved dark chestnut-brown shining spines frequently pointing toward the base of the branch, and $1\frac{1}{2}'-2\frac{1}{2}'$ long.

Distribution. Open Oak and Hickory-woods on the dry slopes of Red Mountain in the southern part of the city of Birmingham, Jefferson County, Alabama.

115. Cratægus Sargentii Beadl.

Leaves oblong-ovate to elliptic or rarely to ovate, acute or acuminate at apex, gradually or abruptly cuneate or rounded at the nearly entire base, irregularly doubly serrate above with straight or incurved glandular teeth, and usually irregularly divided into 3 or 4 pairs of short broad acute or acuminate lobes, nearly fully grown when the flowers open late in April, and then subcoriaceous, pale yellow-green, and villose on the midrib with scattered pale caducous hairs, and at maturity lustrous, dark yellow-green above, pale below, $2'–3'$ long, and $1\frac{1}{2}'–2'$ wide, with a thin midrib, 5–7 pairs of thin light yellow veins and conspicuous reticulate veinlets; turning in the autumn bright yellow and red; petioles slender, glandular, more or less broadly winged toward the apex, $\frac{1}{2}'–\frac{3}{4}'$ in length; leaves at the end of vigorous shoots oblong-ovate, concave-cuneate at base, often 3' long and 2' wide, their petioles broadly wing-margined to below the middle. **Flowers** nearly 1' in diameter, on long thin slightly villose pedicels, in 2–5 usually 3-flowered simple corymbs, with coarsely glandular-serrate bracts and bractlets; calyx-tube narrowly obconic, glabrous or slightly villose, the lobes foliaceous, acute, coarsely glandular-serrate above the middle; stamens 20; anthers large, dark rose color; styles 3–5, usually 4, surrounded at base by a narrow ring of pale hairs. **Fruit** ripening and falling about the middle of September, often only a single fruit maturing from a flower-cluster, subglobose to short-oblong, rounded at the

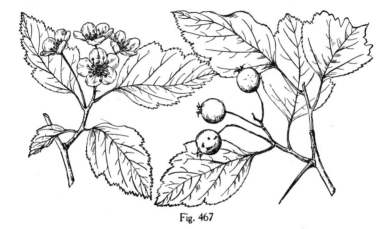

Fig. 467

ends, yellow or orange-yellow, generally more or less flushed with red, marked by occasional large dark dots, $\frac{1}{3}'–\frac{1}{2}'$ long; calyx prominent, with an elongated tube and closely appressed lobes; flesh yellow, thin and hard; nutlets 3–5, usually 4, about $\frac{1}{4}'$ long.

An intricately branched tree, rarely more than 20° high, with a tall trunk 6'–7' in diameter, stout ascending branches forming a narrow or sometimes a round flat-topped head, and glabrous branchlets armed with thin straight or slightly curved dark chestnut-brown shining spines, $\frac{3}{4}'–1\frac{1}{2}'$ long; often a large shrub, with few or many stems.

Distribution. Rocky woods and bluffs in the foothill region of northwestern Georgia (cliffs of the Coosa River near Rome, Floyd County), southeastern Tennessee (near Chatanooga, Hamilton County, and Tracy City, Grundy County), and northeastern Alabama; very abundant in Alabama at Valley Head, De Kalb County, and on the low ridges extending southward to the neighborhood of Birmingham, Jefferson County.

XIII. PULCHERRIMÆ.

CONSPECTUS OF THE ARBORESCENT SPECIES.

Leaves oval to ovate or nearly orbicular, their lobes acute or rounded; fruit bright red.
116. **C. opima** (C).
Leaves ovate to oval or obovate, their lobes acute; fruit orange-red. 117. **C. robur** (C).

116. Cratægus opima Beadl.

Leaves oval to ovate or nearly orbicular, acute, gradually or abruptly narrowed and cuneate at the entire base, finely serrate above with incurved teeth, and usually divided above the middle into short acute, acuminate or rounded lobes, half grown when the flowers open the middle of April, and then glabrous with the exception of a few short caducous hairs on the midrib and veins, and at maturity light green on the upper surface, pale on the lower surface, $1\frac{1}{2}'$ long, and $1\frac{1}{4}'$ wide, with a slender midrib, and 5 or 6 pairs of arcuate primary veins spreading to the point of the lobes; petioles narrowly winged at the apex, usually about $\frac{3}{4}'$ in length; leaves at the end of vigorous shoots sometimes rounded or nearly truncate at base and $1\frac{1}{2}'-2\frac{1}{2}'$ long and broad. **Flowers** about $\frac{2}{3}'$ in diameter, on short slender pedicels, in compact few-flowered glabrous corymbs; calyx-tube broadly obconic, glabrous, the lobes gradually narrowed from a broad base, acute, entire or sparingly glandular-serrate, tipped with dark red glands, glabrous on the outer surface, puberulous on the inner surface; stamens 20; anthers dark rose color; styles 3–5, surrounded at base by a narrow ring of snowy white tomentum. **Fruit** ripening about the 1st of October and

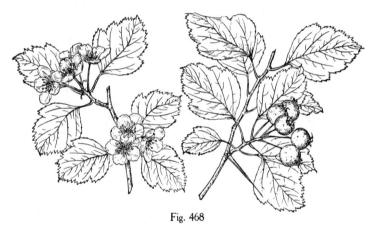

Fig. 468

then remaining on the branches for several weeks, on short stout pedicels, in compact few-fruited erect or drooping clusters, subglobose, often rather longer than broad, bright red, about $\frac{1}{4}'$ in diameter; calyx prominent, with a well-developed tube, and much enlarged closely appressed lobes often deciduous with the tube before the fruit becomes entirely ripe; flesh thin, yellow, dry and mealy; nutlets 3–5, thin, $\frac{1}{8}'$ long.

A tree, 20°–25° high, with a tall, slender often spiny trunk covered with ashy gray bark nearly black at the base of old trees, spreading and ascending branches forming a rounded or oval usually open head, and thin nearly straight bright red-brown glabrous branchlets becoming gray tinged with red or brown in their second season, and armed with thin nearly straight bright chestnut-brown lustrous spines, $1'-1\frac{1}{2}'$ long.

Distribution. Open woods in clay soil in the neighborhood of Greenville, Butler County, Alabama; common near Tallahassee, Leon County, Florida.

117. Cratægus robur Beadl.

Leaves ovate, oval or obovate, acute or acuminate, entire or sparingly glandular below, finely serrate above with incurved glandular teeth, and incisely lobed above the middle with numerous short acute lobes, nearly fully grown when the flowers open at the end of March, and then membranaceous and dark yellow-green and lustrous, and at maturity yellow-green, $1\frac{1}{2}'-2'$ long, and $1'-1\frac{1}{2}'$ wide, with a slender yellow midrib, and thin primary veins extending very obliquely to the point of the lobes; turning in the autumn orange, yellow, or brown; petioles slender, slightly wing-margined toward the apex, sparingly glandular, $\frac{1}{2}'-1'$ in length; leaves at the end of vigorous shoots broadly ovate, cuneate or nearly truncate at the wide base, deeply divided into broad lateral lobes, often $2'-3'$ long and broad, with a stout broadly winged petiole frequently $1'$ long. **Flowers** $1\frac{1}{8}'-1\frac{1}{4}'$ in diameter, on long slender pedicels, in 5–10-flowered glabrous corymbs, with large conspicuously glandular bracts and bractlets; calyx-tube narrowly obconic, glabrous, the lobes gradually narrowed from a broad base, glabrous, entire or sparingly serrate; stamens 20; anthers pale rose color; styles 3–5, surrounded at base by a narrow ring of pale hairs. **Fruit** ripening in September and October, on elongated, slender pedicels, in few-fruited drooping clusters, subglobose, orange-red, about $\frac{1}{2}'$ in diameter; calyx-lobes deciduous before the maturity of the fruit leaving a narrow ring round the shallow cavity; flesh thin and firm; nutlets 3–5, broad, rounded at the ends, barely grooved on the rounded back, $\frac{3}{16}'$ long and nearly as broad.

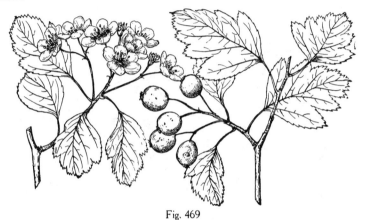

Fig. 469

A tree, $20°-25°$ high, with a trunk $4'-6'$ in diameter, covered with gray or brown scaly bark, spreading or ascending branches, and slender red-brown branchlets unarmed or armed with stout spines $\frac{3}{4}'-1'$ long; more often a large much-branched shrub, with one or more stems.

Distribution. Woods and borders of fields, northwestern Florida; common in the neighborhood of Tallahassee, Leon County.

XIV. BRACTEATÆ.

CONSPECTUS OF THE ARBORESCENT SPECIES.

Leaves oval to broad-obovate, subcoriaceous; corymbs many-flowered; stamens 10–20, usually 20; fruit bright red or orange-red. 118. **C. Harbisonii** (C).

Leaves broad-ovate or rarely obovate, thin; corymbs 3–10-flowered; stamens 20; fruit bright red. 119. **C. Ashei** (C)

118. Cratægus Harbisonii Beadl.

Leaves oval to broad-obovate, acute at apex, cuneate or rounded at the entire base, and coarsely serrate above with straight glandular teeth, when they unfold roughened above by stout, rigid pale hairs, and soft and pubescent below, nearly fully grown early in

May when the flowers open, and then thin, dark yellow-green above and pale below, and at maturity subcoriaceous; pale on the lower surface, 2'–2½' long, and 1'–1½' wide, with a stout midrib and primary veins deeply impressed on the upper side of the leaf, and conspicuous reticulate veinlets; petioles stout, villose, more or less winged above, ¼'–½' in length; leaves at the end of vigorous shoots broad-ovate, cuneate and decurrent on their stouter petiole, 3'–4' long, and 2½'–3' wide, with lunate coarsely glandular-dentate stipules frequently ½' long. **Flowers** ¾' in diameter, in broad loose usually 10–12-flowered corymbs, with broad acute conspicuous glandular-serrate bracts and bractlets; calyx-tube broadly obconic, densely villose at the base and glabrous or pubescent above, the lobes elongated, gradually narrowed from a broad base, acute, bright green, more or less hairy, coarsely glandular-serrate, with large stipitate dark red glands; stamens 10–20, usually 20; anthers large, light yellow; styles 3–5. **Fruit** ripening and falling early in October, subglobose, often rather longer than broad, bright red or orange-red, marked by numerous large dark dots; calyx enlarged, with spreading glandular lobes often deciduous before the fruit ripens; flesh yellow, thick, dry and mealy; nutlets 3–5, narrowed at the ends, ¼' long.

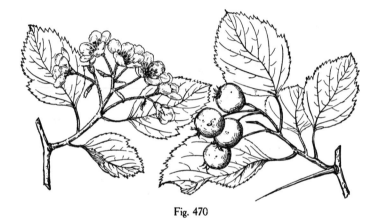

Fig. 470

A tree, sometimes 25° high, with a trunk 10'–12' in diameter, covered with light gray or gray-brown bark, and often armed with straight or much-branched spines, wide-spreading light gray or reddish branches forming a rather open symmetrical head, and slender branchlets coated when they first appear with long spreading white hairs, pubescent or glabrous and light red-brown or orange-brown during their first season, becoming dark or light gray the following year, and furnished with numerous usually stout straight dark reddish brown shining spines 1½'–2' long.

Distribution. Dry limestone hills and ridges; West Nashville, Davidson County, Tennessee; common.

119. Cratægus Ashei Beadl.

Leaves broad-ovate or occasionally obovate, acute and generally short-pointed at apex, gradually or abruptly narrowed and cuneate and usually entire at base, coarsely and occasionally doubly serrate above with straight or incurved teeth tipped with small dark glands, when they unfold roughened on the upper surface with short pale hairs and pubescent below, nearly fully grown and membranaceous when the flowers open early in May, and at maturity thin but firm in texture, pale and puberulous on the lower surface on the slender midrib and primary veins, about 2' long and 1½' wide; petioles stout, broadly winged above, glandular, pubescent early in the season but ultimately nearly glabrous, about ½' in length;

leaves at the end of vigorous shoots usually broadly oval or nearly orbicular, rounded or short-pointed at apex, $2\frac{1}{2}'-3'$ long, and $2'-2\frac{1}{2}'$ wide. Flowers $\frac{3}{4}'$ in diameter, on slender hairy pedicels, in 3–10-flowered simple or compound corymbs, with broad conspicuous glandular bracts and bractlets; calyx-tube broadly obconic, thickly coated with long matted reflexed white hairs, the lobes broad, acute, nearly glabrous on the outer surface, villose on the inner surface, glandular with small stout stipitate glands; stamens 20; anthers small, yellow; styles 3–5, surrounded at base by a narrow ring of pale hairs. Fruit ripening and falling late in September or early in October, on stout villose or glabrous pedicels, in few-fruited clusters, subglobose or rather longer than broad, bright red, marked by large scattered dots, more or less villose toward the ends, about 1' in diameter; calyx conspicuous, with elongated coarsely glandular-serrate, erect incurved or reflexed lobes; flesh thick and yellow; nutlets 3–5, thin, acute at the ends, $\frac{1}{3}'$ long.

A tree, rarely more than 20° high, with a slender trunk covered with smooth light gray or red-brown bark becoming fissured and scaly on old individuals, stout ascending branches

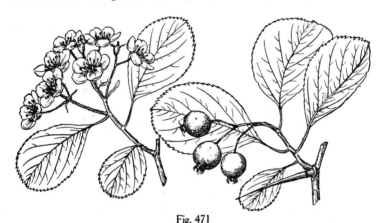

Fig. 471

forming a pyramidal or oval head, and slender branchlets coated when they first appear with long pale matted reflexed hairs, soon becoming nearly glabrous, lustrous, orange-brown or reddish brown, and light gray or gray tinged with red during their second season, and armed with straight or slightly curved thin dark red-brown shining spines $1'-1\frac{1}{2}'$ long.

Distribution. Abandoned fields, and woods, growing usually on clay soils; near Montgomery, Montgomery County, and Gallion, Hale County, Alabama.

XV. FLAVÆ.

CONSPECTUS OF THE ARBORESCENT SPECIES.

Stamens 20.
    Anthers pink or purple.
        Corymbs usually 3–6-flowered.
            Leaves elliptic to broad-ovate, yellow-green; fruit dark orange-brown.

                                        120. **C. flava** (C).
            Leaves ovate to obovate or orbicular, bright yellow-green; fruit obovoid, dark orange color with a red cheek.   121. **C. visenda** (C).
            Leaves obovate or ovate, dark green; fruit subglobose to short-oblong, red or orange-red.   122. **C. ignava** (C).

Corymbs 1–5-flowered.
 Leaves broad-obovate to nearly orbicular, bright green; fruit globose or depressed-
  globose, bright red.   123. C. consanguinea.
  Leaves obovate, bright green; fruit ellipsoidal to short-oblong, orange-red; anthers
   pink.   124. C. tristis.
Anthers yellow (doubtful in 128, 133).
 Leaves yellow-green.
  Leaves 3-nerved.
   Leaves obovate-cuneate, often 3-lobed at apex; fruit obovoid to subglobose,
    bright orange-red and lustrous; corymbs tomentose.   125. C. floridana.
   Leaves obovate; fruit subglobose to short-oblong, dull brownish yellow; corymbs
    glabrous.   126. C. lacrimata.
  Leaves with numerous primary veins.
   Leaves thin.
    Leaves scabrate above at maturity, obovate, rounded or abruptly short-
     pointed at apex; fruit subglobose to short-oblong, bright orange-red.
                   127. C. Ravenelii (C).
    Leaves smooth above at maturity.
     Leaves obovate to obovate-cuneiform; fruit subglobose, bright red.
                   128. C. senta (A).
     Leaves obovate to oval or orbicular; fruit subglobose to ellipsoidal, orange-red
      or red and orange.   129. C. annosa (C).
    Leaves subcoriaceous.
     Flowers in 3–5-flowered corymbs.
      Leaves obovate; fruit globose or depressed-globose, orange-yellow with a
       red cheek.   130. C. panda (C).
      Leaves obovate to oblong-ovate, minutely serrate; fruit globose, red or
       yellow.   131. C. integra (C).
     Flowers in 1 or 2-flowered corymbs; leaves spathulate; fruit obovoid, red.
                   132. C. recurva (C).
 Leaves conspicuously blue-green, broad-ovate to orbicular; fruit subglobose to
  short-oblong, light red, puberulous at the ends.   133. C. dispar (C).
Stamens 10; anthers yellow; leaves broad-obovate to oval or rhombic, dark yellow-green;
 fruit subglobose, dull orange-red, often slightly villose at the ends. 134. C. aprica (C).

120. Cratægus flava Ait.

Leaves elliptic to broad-obovate, acute or rarely rounded at apex, gradually narrowed
and cuneate at the glandular base, and coarsely doubly serrate above with broad straight
or incurved teeth tipped with large dark red stipitate glands, when they unfold bronze
color, villose above with short pale caducous hairs most abundant near the base of the midrib and pubescent below on the midrib and veins, about half grown when the flowers open
from the 10th to the 20th of April, and at maturity membranaceous, yellow-green, usually
about 2′ long and 1½′ wide, with a slender yellow midrib and 3 or 4 pairs of primary veins
usually puberulous on the under side and only slightly impressed above; petioles slender,
glandular, winged nearly to the base, generally more or less villose, after midsummer often
light red on the lower side, and about ½′ in length; leaves at the end of vigorous shoots frequently 3′ long and 2′ wide, and sometimes broad-ovate, 3-lobed or divided into 2 or 3 pairs
of lateral lobes, their petioles 1′–1½′ long, broadly winged and conspicuously glandular,
and foliaceous lunate or elliptic coarsely glandular-serrate stipules. **Flowers** about ¾′ in
diameter, on short slender pedicels, in few-flowered simple or compound slightly villose
compact corymbs, with lanceolate acute coarsely glandular-serrate bracts and bractlets;
calyx-tube broadly obconic, glabrous, the lobes wide, acute, usually laciniately divided, very
glandular; stamens 20; anthers large, dark rose color. **Fruit** ripening early in October and
soon falling, in few-fruited drooping clusters, short-oblong, full and rounded at the ends,

dark orange-brown, $\frac{1}{2}'-\frac{5}{8}'$ long, and $\frac{1}{3}'-\frac{1}{2}'$ in diameter; calyx prominent, with a long narrow tube, and enlarged closely appressed lobes often deciduous before the fruit ripens; flesh thick, orange color, dry and mealy; nutlets 5, gradually narrowed and rounded at the ends. ridged and deeply grooved on the back with a high narrow ridge, about $\frac{1}{2}'$ long.

Fig. 472

A tree, 15°–20° high, with a tall trunk 8′–10′ in diameter, covered with thin dark brown bark tinged with red and divided into narrow rounded ridges, stout ascending branches forming an open and somewhat irregular head sometimes 20° across, and slender slightly zigzag glabrous branchlets dark green deeply tinged with red when they first appear, becoming dull red-brown or orange-brown during their first season, darker the following year, and ultimately dark gray-brown, and armed with thin nearly straight bright chestnut-brown spines $\frac{3}{4}'-1\frac{1}{4}'$ long.

Distribution. Dry sandy soil on the sand hills of Summerville, near Augusta, Richmond County, Georgia, and at River Junction, Gadsden County, Florida.

121. Cratægus visenda Beadl.

Leaves ovate, obovate, or orbicular, short-pointed and acute or occasionally broad and rounded at apex, concave-cuneate and gradually narrowed at the mostly entire base, finely

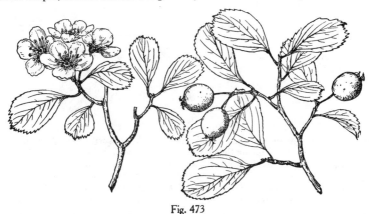

Fig. 473

serrate above with rounded teeth, glandular with bright red glands, and divided above the middle into short acute lobes, nearly fully grown when the flowers open at the end of March, and then glabrous with the exception of a few short pale hairs on the two surfaces near the base of the midrib, and at maturity thin and firm in texture, bright yellow-green and lustrous above, pale below, glabrous, $1'-1\frac{1}{2}'$ long, and $\frac{3}{4}'-1'$ wide, with a slender midrib, and thin primary veins extending very obliquely to the point of the lobes; turning yellow, orange, or brown in the autumn; petioles slender, broadly wing-margined above the middle, conspicuously glandular, sparingly villose early in the season, becoming nearly glabrous, $\frac{1}{2}'-\frac{3}{4}'$ in length.   **Flowers** about $\frac{3}{4}'$ in diameter, on short villose pedicels, in simple 3–6-flowered corymbs; calyx-tube broadly obconic, hairy near the base with scattered pale hairs, glabrous above, the lobes broad, acuminate, glandular-serrate, glabrous on the outer, pilose on the inner surface; stamens 20; anthers pale purple; styles 3–5, surrounded at base by small tufts of white hairs.   **Fruit** ripening and falling late in August and early in September, on stout pedicels, usually in 1 or 2-fruited clusters, obovoid, dark orange-colored, with a red cheek, $\frac{1}{2}'-\frac{5}{8}'$ long, nearly $\frac{1}{2}'$ in diameter; calyx enlarged, the lobes coarsely glandular-serrate, puberulous on the upper surface, closely appressed; flesh soft and yellow; nutlets 3–5, obtuse and rounded at the ends, rounded and slightly ridged on the back, about $\frac{3}{8}'$ long.

A tree, sometimes 30° high, with a trunk $10'-12'$ in diameter, covered with dark gray or brownish bark, crooked horizontal or ascending branches forming a broad irregular head, and stout often contorted branchlets villose when they first appear, soon glabrous, dull reddish brown to ashy gray, and armed with slender straight spines $\frac{1}{2}'-\frac{5}{8}'$ long.

Distribution.   Sandy soil near Bristol, Liberty County, Florida.

122. Cratægus ignava Beadl.

Leaves obovate to ovate, acute, gradually narrowed from near the middle to the concave-cuneate glandular base, sharply often doubly serrate above with glandular teeth, and usually divided toward the apex into short acute lobes, nearly fully grown when the flowers

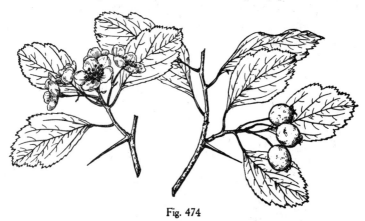

Fig. 474

open at the end of April, and then membranaceous, glabrous with the exception of a few hairs on the midrib above and on the midrib and slender veins below, and at maturity subcoriaceous, bright green and lustrous on the upper surface, pale and still hairy on the lower surface, $1\frac{1}{2}'-2'$ long, and $1'-1\frac{1}{2}'$ wide; turning in the autumn yellow and brown sometimes flushed with red; petioles slender, wing-margined at the apex, glandular, $\frac{1}{4}'-\frac{1}{2}'$ in length. **Flowers** about $\frac{3}{4}'$ in diameter, on slender glabrous pedicels, in 3–6-flowered simple corymbs, with lanceolate conspicuously glandular reddish bracts and bractlets; calyx-tube broadly

obconic, glabrous, the lobes abruptly narrowed from the base, wide, glabrous, glandular with dark red stipitate glands, and often coarsely serrate above the middle; stamens 20; anthers large, dark rose color; styles 3–5, surrounded at base by a ring of pale hairs. **Fruit** ripening and falling at the end of September and early in October, on slender erect pedicels, in few-fruited clusters, subglobose to short-oblong, orange-red, marked by numerous pale dots, about $\frac{3}{8}'$ long; calyx enlarged and prominent, with spreading lobes often deciduous from the ripe fruit; flesh thick and soft; nutlets 3–5, rounded at the ends, prominently but irregularly ridged and grooved on the back, $\frac{1}{4}'$ long.

A tree, sometimes 10°–12° high, with a slender trunk covered with ashy gray fissured scaly bark often tinged with brown and frequently nearly black near the ground, stout ascending branches, and slender zigzag glabrous branchlets bright red-brown during their first season, becoming dark gray-brown, and armed with many very slender red-brown lustrous ultimately ashy gray spines $1'-1\frac{1}{2}'$ long.

Distribution. Northeastern Alabama; common on Lookout Mountain above Valley Head and at Collinsville, DeKalb County, and at Gadsden, Etowah County.

123. Cratægus consanguinea Beadl.

Leaves broad-obovate to nearly orbicular, occasionally oval or rhombic, acute and generally short-pointed at apex, gradually narrowed and concave-cuneate or sometimes rounded at the entire base, finely and often doubly serrate with glandular teeth, and fre-

Fig. 475

quently irregularly divided above the middle into short acute lobes, nearly fully grown when the flowers open at the end of March or early in April, and then very thin, blue-green, slightly villose, especially on the midrib and veins, and at maturity thin, bright green, glabrous with the exception of a few hairs on the under side of the slender midrib, and thin primary veins extending very obliquely toward the end of the leaf, about 1' long, and $\frac{3}{4}-\frac{7}{8}'$ wide; petioles slender, glandular, wing-margined above, villose early in the season, becoming glabrous, $\frac{3}{4}-\frac{3}{4}'$ in length; leaves at the end of vigorous shoots often $1\frac{1}{2}'-2'$ long and wide. **Flowers** $\frac{3}{4}'$ in diameter, on long slender hairy pedicels, in simple 1–5-flowered corymbs, with oblanceolate acuminate bright red caducous bracts and bractlets; calyx-tube broadly obconic, sparingly hairy with long pale caducous hairs, the lobes gradually narrowed from a broad base, acute, glandular with minute bright red glands, glabrous; stamens 20; anthers small, deep rose color; styles 3–5, surrounded at base by a narrow ring of short pale hairs. **Fruit** ripening and falling about the middle of September, on slender glabrous pedicels, often only a single fruit in a cluster developing, globose to depressed-globose, bright red, marked by small dark dots, nearly $\frac{1}{2}'$ in diameter; calyx prominent, with enlarged appressed lobes; flesh thin, yellow, dry and mealy; nutlets 3–5, thick, narrowed and rounded at base, broad and rounded at apex, ridged on the back with a broad low rounded ridge, about $\frac{5}{16}'$ long.

A tree, often 20° high, with a tall trunk 6′–8′ in diameter, covered with nearly black deeply furrowed bark broken into short thick closely appressed scales, wide-spreading often pendulous branches forming a broad symmetrical handsome head, and slender slightly zigzag branchlets covered when they first appear with pale caducous hairs, soon becoming bright red-brown and lustrous, and dull reddish brown in their second season, and armed with short nearly straight gray or chestnut-brown spines $\frac{1}{3}'–\frac{3}{4}'$ long.

Distribution. Dry upland Oak-woods in middle Florida from the neighborhood of Tallahassee, Leon County to the Apalachicola River; common in the neighborhood of River Junction, Gadsden County, and at Aspalaga, Liberty County.

124. Cratægus tristis Beadl.

Leaves obovate, acute, acuminate, or rounded and often more or less undulate-lobed at the broad apex, gradually narrowed from above the middle and concave-cuneate at the glandular base, and serrate above with blunt glandular teeth, about half grown when the

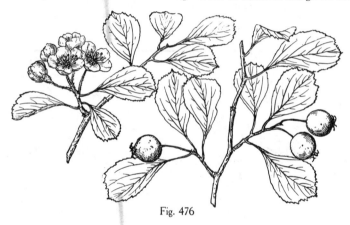

Fig. 476

flowers open at the end of April, and then slightly pilose on the upper and villose on the lower surface on the thin midrib and in the axils of the slender veins extending obliquely to the point of the lobes, and at maturity thin and firm in texture, bright green and glabrous, $1\frac{1}{4}'–1\frac{1}{2}'$ long, and about $\frac{3}{4}'$ wide; turning in the autumn yellow, brown, and orange; petioles slender, wing-margined above, conspicuously glandular, slightly puberulous, $\frac{1}{2}'–\frac{3}{4}'$ in length; leaves at the end of vigorous shoots oblong-obovate, often deeply and irregularly divided into broad acute lateral lobes, and frequently $1\frac{1}{2}'–2'$ long and nearly as broad. **Flowers** $\frac{5}{8}'–\frac{3}{4}'$ in diameter, on slender villose pedicels, in simple 3–5-flowered corymbs, with rose-colored and conspicuously glandular bracts and bractlets; calyx-tube broadly obconic, hairy toward the base with long scattered pale hairs, the lobes gradually narrowed from a broad base, acuminate, glandular with large dark red glands, and entire or coarsely serrate above the middle; stamens 20; anthers pink; styles 3–5. **Fruit** ripening and falling late in August or early in September, ellipsoidal or short-oblong, orange-red, about $\frac{1}{2}'$ long, with soft flesh; calyx little enlarged, with recurved persistent lobes; nutlets 3–5, broad and rounded at base, gradually narrowed and acute at apex, rounded and ridged on the back with a broad low slightly grooved ridge, about $\frac{5}{16}'$ long.

A tree, sometimes 25° high, with a trunk 8′–10′ in diameter, covered with dark sometimes nearly black deeply furrowed bark, stout pendulous branches forming a broad shapely handsome head, and slender branchlets hoary-tomentose when they first appear, bright red-brown and puberulous at the end of their first season, becoming dark gray-brown, and armed with few slender straight spines $1\frac{1}{4}'$–$1\frac{1}{2}'$ long; or often a large shrub.

Distribution. Slopes of low hills, northwestern Georgia; common in the neighborhood of Rome, Floyd County.

125. Cratægus floridana Sarg.

Leaves obovate-cuneate, frequently 3-lobed at apex with short rounded lobes, gradually narrowed and cuneate at the entire base, finely serrate above with straight or incurved teeth tipped with conspicuous ultimately dark persistent glands, 3-nerved with slender nerves, numerous thin secondary veins and reticulate veinlets, slightly villose above as they unfold, nearly fully grown when the flowers open about the middle of March, and then light yellow-green and glabrous with the exception of a few persistent hairs on the upper side of the nerves and in their axils, and at maturity thick and firm, dark green and lustrous

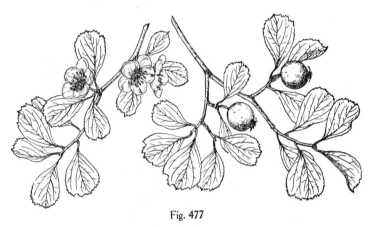

Fig. 477

on the upper surface, pale on the lower surface, $1'$–$1\frac{1}{2}'$ long, and about $\frac{1}{2}'$ wide; petioles slender, glandular, more or less winged toward the apex, tomentose, becoming pubescent or glabrous, usually about $\frac{1}{2}'$ in length; leaves at the end of vigorous shoots frequently $2'$ long, and sometimes divided by deep rounded sinuses into numerous narrow lateral lobes, their stipules lunate, foliaceous, pointed, coarsely glandular-serrate. **Flowers** about $\frac{5}{8}'$ in diameter, on slender tomentose pedicels, in few usually 1-3-flowered simple compact corymbs; calyx-tube broadly obconic, coated with long matted white hairs, the lobes narrow, acuminate, glandular with bright red stipitate glands, villose toward the base on the outer surface and on the inner surface; stamens 20; anthers small, pale yellow; styles 4 or 5, surrounded at the base by a broad ring of long shining white hairs. **Fruit** ripening from the middle to the end of August, on short stout pubescent pedicels, solitary or in 2 or 3-fruited drooping clusters, obovoid to short-oblong, usually about $\frac{3}{4}'$ long, bright orange-red, lustrous, marked by numerous pale dots; calyx prominent, with an elongated tube puberulous on the outer surface, and reflexed glandular-serrate lobes; flesh thin, yellow, dry and mealy; nutlets 4 or 5, acute at base, broad and rounded at apex, rounded and occasionally slightly ridged on the back, about $\frac{1}{3}'$ long.

A tree, rarely more than 15° high, with a long straight trunk $6'$–$8'$ in diameter, covered with thick nearly black deeply furrowed bark broken into short thick plate-like scales, small drooping branches forming a handsome symmetrical head, and slender conspicuously zigzag pendulous branchlets coated when they first appear with long pale matted hairs, becoming during their first season dark red-brown and more or less villose, and dark brown the following year, and armed with thin straight spines $\frac{3}{4}'$–1' long, or unarmed.

Distribution. Dry sandy soil of the Pine-barrens of northeastern Florida; abundant in the neighborhood of Jacksonville, Duval County.

126. Cratægus lacrimata Small.

Leaves obovate, rounded or acute and glandular-serrate at apex usually with incurved teeth, entire and glandular below, gradually narrowed from above the middle to the base, and 3-nerved with slender yellow nerves, numerous thin secondary veins and reticulate veinlets, when the flowers open early in April nearly fully grown, light yellow, glabrous, with the exception of small tufts of pale caducous hairs in the axils of the nerves below, and at maturity subcoriaceous, lustrous, $\frac{1}{4}'$–$\frac{3}{4}'$ long, and about $\frac{1}{3}'$ wide; petioles slender, wing-margined toward the apex, dark orange-brown, at first puberulous, soon becoming glabrous, $\frac{1}{4}'$–$\frac{1}{2}'$ in length. **Flowers** about $\frac{2}{3}'$ in diameter, on short stout glabrous pedicels, in 3–5-flowered simple corymbs, with long linear entire caducous bracts and bractlets turning

Fig. 478

red in fading; calyx-tube broadly obconic, glabrous, the lobes gradually narrowed from a broad base, acuminate, entire, tipped with large dark glands; stamens 20; anthers large, light yellow; styles usually 3, surrounded at base by a narrow ring of pale hairs. **Fruit** ripening toward the end of August, on slender pedicels, in 1 or 2-fruited clusters, subglobose to short-oblong, rounded at the ends, dull brownish yellow marked by occasional dark dots, about $\frac{1}{3}'$ in diameter; calyx prominent, with an elongated tube, and spreading lobes usually deciduous before the fruit ripens; flesh thin, yellow, dry and mealy; nutlets 3, broad, rounded at the broad ends, rounded and sometimes obscurely grooved on the back, about $\frac{3}{8}'$ long.

A tree, occasionally 20° but usually not more than 10° high, with a tall trunk 4'–6' in diameter, covered with thick deeply furrowed black bark broken on the surface into thick plate-like closely appressed scales, long slender drooping branches forming a handsome symmetrical round-topped head; and thin glabrous very zigzag branchlets light orange-brown when they first appear, soon becoming reddish brown and lustrous, and dark gray-brown in their second year, and armed with many small nearly straight dark chestnut-brown spines $\frac{1}{2}'$–$\frac{3}{4}'$ long.

Distribution. Western Florida, Walton and Santa Rosa Counties (Pensacola to De Funiak Springs); sometimes in moist sand; more often in dry barrens; common and often a conspicuous feature of the vegetation.

127. Cratægus Ravenelii Sarg.

Leaves obovate, rounded and abruptly short-pointed or acute at the broad sometimes slightly lobed apex, gradually narrowed from above the middle to the elongated cuneate base, more or less undulate on the margins, and coarsely and usually doubly glandular-serrate above with large bright red ultimately dark persistent glands, nearly fully grown when the flowers open the middle of April, and then coated with long pale caducous hairs, and at maturity thin and firm in texture, yellow-green, scabrous on the upper surface, pale, and pubescent on the lower surface on the slender veins, $1'-1\frac{1}{2}'$ long, and about $\frac{3}{4}'$ wide; petioles slender, glandular, winged above, tomentose when they first appear, becoming pubescent, $\frac{1}{4}'-\frac{1}{2}'$ in length; leaves at the end of vigorous shoots often $2'$ long and $1\frac{1}{2}'$ wide, and frequently divided above the middle into 2 or 3 pairs of broad lateral lobes. **Flowers** about $\frac{3}{4}'$ in diameter, on slender tomentose pedicels, in simple corymbs; calyx-tube narrowly obconic, thickly coated with long white hairs, the lobes lanceolate, villose on the outer, glabrous on the inner surface, glandular with small red glands; stamens 20; anthers

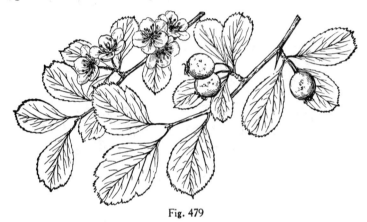

Fig. 479

small, pale yellow; styles 5, surrounded at base by a broad ring of pale tomentum. **Fruit** ripening early in October, on short thick pedicels, in few-fruited drooping or spreading clusters, globose to short-oblong, bright orange-red, marked by occasional dark dots, puberulous at the ends, $\frac{1}{3}'-\frac{1}{2}'$ in diameter; calyx prominent, with enlarged spreading and appressed lobes; flesh thick, yellow, subacid; nutlets 5, narrowed and acute at the ends, ridged on the back with a high narrow ridge, $\frac{1}{2}'$ long.

A tree, $25°-30°$ high, with a trunk often $14'$ or $15'$ in diameter, covered with thick dark brown bark deeply divided into narrow interrupted ridges broken on the surface into short thick plate-like scales, heavy ascending or spreading branches forming an open irregular head, and stout zigzag branchlets thickly coated at first with hoary tomentum, dark purple or red-brown and pubescent during their first summer, becoming dark red-brown and glabrous the following season, and armed with thick straight dull gray-brown spines usually about $1\frac{1}{2}'$ long.

Distribution. Sand hills near Aiken, Aiken County, South Carolina, and in Summerville near Augusta, Richmond County, Georgia.

128. Cratægus senta Beadl.

Leaves obovate or obovate-cuneiform, acute or sometimes rounded and frequently slightly divided into several short acute lobes at the broad apex, gradually narrowed from the middle to the entire base, and serrate or doubly serrate above with incurved conspicuously glandular teeth, when they unfold often dark red, covered above with long pale caducous hairs and villose below on the midrib and veins, nearly fully grown when the flowers open from the 1st to the 10th of May and then bright yellow-green and almost glabrous with the exception of the persistent tufts of pale hairs in the axils of the veins, and at maturity thin and firm, dark green and lustrous above, paler below, usually about $1\frac{1}{2}'$ long and $1'$ wide, with an orange-colored midrib, generally 3 pairs of slender primary veins extending obliquely to the point of the lobes, and dark conspicuous reticulate veinlets; turning red, yellow, or brown in the autumn; petioles slender, glandular, wing-margined above, at first tomentose, becoming pubescent or nearly glabrous, about $\frac{3}{4}'$ in length; leaves at the end of vigorous shoots broad-ovate, often nearly orbicular, more deeply lobed with broad rounded or acute lobes, $2'-2\frac{1}{2}'$ in diameter, their stipules lunate, coarsely glandular-dentate, sometimes $\frac{1}{2}'$ long. **Flowers** $\frac{3}{4}'$ in diameter, on long slender pedicels coated with matted pale hairs, in lax compound 3–6-flowered villose corymbs, with lanceolate straight or falcate glandular bracts and bractlets; calyx-tube broadly obconic, villose particularly toward the base, the lobes narrow, elongated, acuminate,

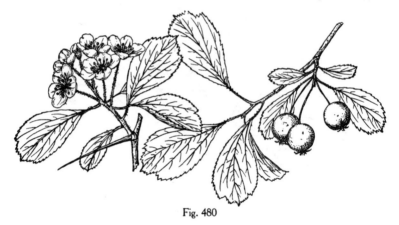

Fig. 480

nearly glabrous, coarsely and irregularly glandular-serrate; stamens 20; styles 3–5, surrounded at base by a broad ring of hoary tomentum. **Fruit** ripening and falling at the end of September or early in October, on slender slightly hairy elongated pedicels, in few-fruited drooping clusters, globose, bright red, $\frac{1}{3}'-\frac{1}{2}'$ in diameter; calyx enlarged, with closely appressed lobes; flesh yellow, dry and mealy; nutlets 3–5, broad and rounded at apex, narrowed and acute at base, slightly grooved on the back, about $\frac{1}{2}'$ long.

Distribution. Abandoned fields and open Pine-woods near Asheville, Buncombe County, North Carolina, at altitudes of about 2200°.

129. Cratægus annosa Beadl.

Leaves obovate, oval, or oblanceolate, cuneate and glandular at base, sharply and often doubly glandular-serrate above, and usually slightly lobed toward the short-pointed acute apex, more than half grown when the flowers open early in April and then pale yellow-green and scurfy above, with a few short pale hairs above and below near the base of the midrib, and at maturity thin, glabrous, bright green, $1'-1\frac{1}{2}'$ long, and $\frac{3}{4}'-1'$ wide, with a prominent pale yellow midrib, and remote slender veins extending very obliquely to the point of the lobes; turning in the autumn yellow, orange, or brown; petioles slender, narrowly winged above, conspicuously glandular with large dark glands, $\frac{1}{2}'-\frac{3}{4}'$ in length; leaves at the end of vigorous shoots broad-ovate to obovate or suborbicular, coarsely serrate, conspicuously reticulate-venulose, sometimes $2'$ long and wide, with broadly winged petioles and foliaceous coarsely dentate persistent stipules often ¾′ long. **Flowers** ¾′ in diameter, on stout villose pedicels, in simple 3–5-flowered villose corymbs; calyx-tube narrowly obconic, sparingly villose toward the base, the lobes acute, glandular-serrate, glabrous on the outer surface, puberulous on the inner surface; stamens 20; anthers almost white; styles 3–5, surrounded at base by a broad ring of snow-white tomentum. **Fruit** ripening and falling late in August or early in September, subglobose or ellipsoidal, orange-red or red and orange,

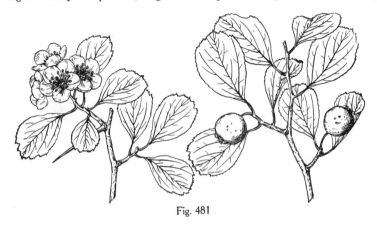

Fig. 481

about ½′ long; calyx little enlarged, the lobes puberulous on the upper side and reflexed; flesh thick and soft; nutlets 3–5, broad and rounded at base, narrowed and rounded at apex, rounded and ridged on the back with a broad low rounded ridge, about $\frac{5}{16}$′ long.

A tree, 20°–25° high, with a trunk sometimes a foot in diameter, covered with dark rough often black bark, stout spreading or ascending branches, and thick dull red-brown ultimately dark gray or nearly black branchlets armed with straight rather stout spines 1′–1½′ long.

Distribution. Eastern central Alabama; common near Phœnix, Lee County, and Girard, Russell County.

130. Cratægus panda Beadl.

Leaves obovate, rounded and short-pointed or abruptly narrowed and acute at the broad occasionally slightly lobed apex, concave-cuneate and glandular at the entire base, and finely serrate above with minute incurved glandular teeth, when they unfold tinged with red and sparingly villose, nearly fully grown when the flowers open the 1st of April and then roughened above by short pale rigid hairs and villose above and below on the midrib and on the veins below, and at maturity glabrous, or puberulous on the under surface of the slender midrib, subcoriaceous, light green and lustrous, glandular, 1′–1¼′ long, and ¾′–1′ wide, with slender primary veins extending very obliquely toward the end of the leaf; turning yellow-brown or orange color in the autumn before falling; petioles slender, slightly wing-margined at apex, villose early in the season, becoming glabrous, glandular, about ⅜′ in length; leaves at the end of vigorous shoots broad-ovate, rounded, apiculate and lobed at apex, puberulous and villose on the midrib and veins on the lower surface, often 1¾′ long and 2′ wide. **Flowers** ⅝′–¾′ in diameter, on slender hairy pedicels, in compact 3–5-flowered simple corymbs; calyx-tube narrowly obconic, covered with matted white hairs, the lobes gradually narrowed from a broad base, acuminate, glandular-serrate, more or less villose; stamens 20; anthers nearly white; styles 3–5, surrounded at base by a narrow ring of pale hairs. **Fruit** ripening and falling at the end of August or early in September, on stout pedicels, in erect few-fruited clusters, globose or depressed-globose, orange-yellow, with a red cheek, $\frac{3}{8}'$–$\frac{3}{4}'$ in diameter; calyx slightly enlarged, with closely appressed often deciduous lobes; flesh thick, succulent, orange-yellow; nutlets 3–5, narrowed and acute at the ends, grooved on the rounded back with a broad shallow groove, about $\frac{1}{4}'$ long.

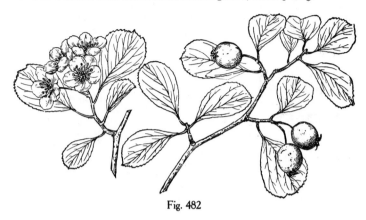

Fig. 482

A tree, 20°–25° high, with a trunk sometimes a foot in diameter, covered with dark rough bark, crooked recurved branches forming an open irregular head, and stout branchlets covered at first with matted pale hairs, reddish brown and puberulous during their first season, becoming gray and unarmed or occasionally armed with stout spines $\frac{1}{2}'$–1' long.

Distribution. Dry sandy soil near Tallahassee, Leon County, Florida.

131. Cratægus integra Beadl.

Leaves obovate to oblong-obovate, narrowed from near the middle to the acute apex, concave-cuneate and gradually narrowed to the slender base, and finely serrate, nearly half

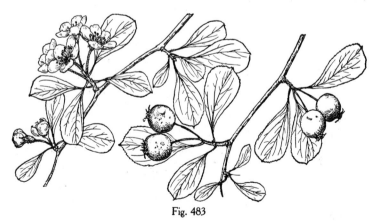

Fig. 483

grown when the flowers open about the 20th of March, and then glandular on the margins, slightly hairy on the midrib and on the under side of the veins, and at maturity subcoriaceous, bright green, lustrous, and glabrous above, paler below, 1'–1$\frac{1}{4}'$ long, and about $\frac{3}{4}'$ wide, with a thin yellow midrib puberulous below, slender primary veins extending very obliquely to the end of the leaf, with 1 or 2 pairs near the middle of the blade more prominent than those below and above them; turning in the autumn yellow, orange and brown; petioles slender, narrowly wing-margined above, glandular, at first hoary-tomentose, becoming pubescent or puberulous, $\frac{1}{2}'-\frac{3}{4}'$ in length; leaves at the end of vigorous shoots broadly obovate, short-pointed at apex, slightly undulate-lobed above the middle, sometimes $1\frac{1}{2}'$ long and broad. **Flowers** $\frac{5}{8}'-\frac{3}{4}'$ in diameter, on slender elongated hoary-tomentose pedicels, in 3–5-flowered simple corymbs; calyx-tube narrowly obconic, thickly covered with matted white hairs, the lobes gradually narrowed from a broad base, acuminate, glandular, pilose on the outer, sparingly pilose on the inner surface; stamens 20; anthers pale yellow; styles 3–5, surrounded at base by a thick ring of white hairs. **Fruit** ripening and falling in August, on slender erect pubescent pedicels, globose, red, about $\frac{1}{2}'$ in diameter; calyx deciduous; flesh thin, orange-yellow, and succulent; nutlets 3–5, narrowed and acute at the base, rounded at the apex, flat and grooved on the back with a narrow shallow groove, about $\frac{5}{16}'$ long.

A tree, 12°–15° high, with a trunk sometimes 8' in diameter, covered with thick nearly black checkered bark, drooping branches forming a handsome symmetrical head, and slender very zigzag branchlets clothed when they first appear with hoary tomentum, rather bright reddish brown and roughened by minute tubercles at the end of their first season, becoming gray or grayish brown, and unarmed or armed with occasional short slender spines.

Distribution. Sandy woods and abandoned fields; central Florida; common near Eustis, Lake County, and Orlando, Orange County.

132. Cratægus recurva Beadl.

Leaves spatulate, rounded or acute or sometimes obovate and obtusely 3-lobed at apex, and finely glandular-serrate with bright red glands, nearly half grown when the flowers

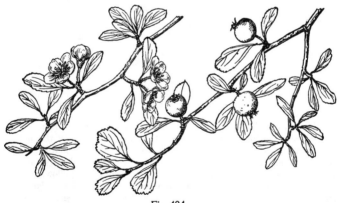

Fig. 484

open about the 20th of March and then almost glabrous above, slightly hairy near the base below, and at maturity subcoriaceous, glabrous, about 1' long and $\frac{1}{4}'-\frac{1}{2}'$ wide, with a slender yellow midrib and one pair of veins often more prominent than the others and nearly parallel with the margins of the blade; turning in the autumn yellow, orange, and brown; petioles slender, conspicuously glandular, villose when they first appear, becoming glabrous, $\frac{1}{4}'-\frac{1}{2}'$ in length; leaves at the end of vigorous shoots broad-obovate, deeply divided into narrow lateral ascending rounded lobes, concave-cuneate at base, with a stouter midrib, and veins arching to the point of the lobes, and often 1' long and $\frac{3}{4}'$ wide. **Flowers**

$\frac{1}{2}'-\frac{5}{8}'$ in diameter, on stout pedicels thickly covered with matted pale hairs, solitary or in 2-flowered simple corymbs; calyx-tube broadly obconic, pilose below, nearly glabrous above, the lobes slender, acuminate, glandular-serrate, slightly hairy on the outer surface, glabrous on the inner surface; stamens 20; anthers pale yellow; styles 3–5. **Fruit** ripening in August, erect on short stout pedicels, obovoid, red, $\frac{1}{2}'$ long; calyx little enlarged, often deciduous; flesh thick and soft; nutlets 3–5, broad and rounded at the ends, rounded and obscurely grooved on the back, about $\frac{1}{4}'$ long.

A tree, 15°–18° high, with a short trunk 5′–6′ in diameter, covered with gray or brownish rough bark, slender pendulous branches forming a broad symmetrical head, and slender very zigzag branchlets, villose early in the season, becoming bright chestnut-brown and very lustrous and ultimately dark reddish brown, and armed with numerous slender straight spines usually about $\frac{1}{2}'$ long.

Distribution. Dry sandy soil, Ocala, Marion County, Florida.

133. Cratægus dispar Beadl.

Leaves broad-ovate or orbicular, 3-nerved, acute or rounded at apex, generally narrowed and cuneate or concave-cuneate at the glandular entire base, serrate or doubly serrate above with straight or incurved glandular teeth, and mostly divided above the middle into

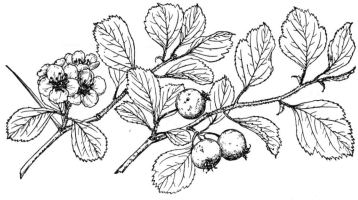

Fig. 485

short acute lobes, when they unfold coated with long matted white hairs most abundant on the lower surface, more than half grown when the flowers open about the middle of April and then blue-green and villose above and tomentose below, and at maturity thin and firm in texture, blue-green and glabrous on the upper surface, pale and slightly pubescent on the lower surface, usually about 1′ long and $\frac{3}{4}'$–1′ wide; turning red, yellow, or brown in the autumn; petioles slender, tomentose, becoming pubescent or villose, glandular, slightly wing-margined above, usually about $\frac{1}{3}'$ in length; leaves at the end of vigorous shoots broad-ovate or suborbicular, rounded at the broad base, coarsely serrate, and often deeply divided above the middle into 3 wide acute lobes broader than long. **Flowers** about $\frac{5}{8}'$ in diameter, on slender hoary-tomentose pedicels, in simple 3–7-flowered corymbs, with narrow-obovate acute glandular bracts and bractlets; calyx-tube narrowly obconic, coated with hoary tomentum, the lobes narrow, acute, glandular-serrate with minute bright red glands, tomentose on the outer surface below the middle, glabrous above, tomentose on the inner surface; stamens 20; styles 3–5, surrounded at base by a ring of pale tomentum. **Fruit** ripening late in August or early in September, on slender pubescent pedicels, in few-fruited clusters, subglobose to short-oblong, light red, puberulous toward the ends, about $\frac{3}{4}'$ in diameter; calyx prominent, with reflexed closely appressed lobes tomentose at base;

flesh thin, yellow, subacid; nutlets 3–5, rounded at the ends, ridged on the back with a broad low ridge, dark brown, ¼′ long.

A tree, 20°–25° high, with a short trunk a foot in diameter, heavy ascending branches forming a broad irregular head, and stout zigzag branchlets at first hoary-tomentose, dark red-brown and pubescent during their first summer, becoming darker colored and glabrous the following season, and armed with thick or thin nearly straight dark red-brown ultimately gray spines 1½′–2′ long.

Distribution. Dry sand hills near Aiken, Aiken County, and Trenton, Edgefield County, South Carolina; more abundant at Summerville, west of Augusta, Richmond County, Georgia.

134. Cratægus aprica Beadl.

Leaves broad-obovate, oval, or rhombic, acute and short-pointed or rounded and often somewhat lobed at apex, gradually or abruptly narrowed and cuneate at the entire base, and serrate usually only above the middle with small incurved teeth terminating in con-

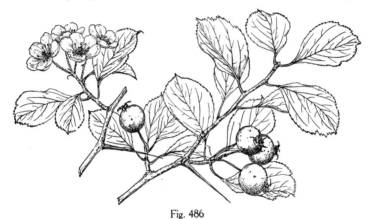

Fig. 486

spicuous rose-colored ultimately dark red persistent glands, when they unfold deep orange color, roughened above by short pale appressed hairs and sparingly villose below, especially on the slender midrib and remote primary veins, nearly fully grown when the flowers open about the 10th of May, and at maturity thick and firm, glabrous, smooth, and dark yellow-green on the upper surface, pale on the lower surface, 1′–1¼′ long, and 1′ wide; petioles stout, conspicuously glandular, more or less winged toward the apex, villose early in the season, becoming nearly glabrous, usually bright red on the lower side toward the base after midsummer, about ½′ in length; leaves at the end of vigorous shoots often nearly orbicular, frequently more deeply lobed, and 1½′–2′ long and wide, with a stout broadly winged petiole, and foliaceous lunate stipules. **Flowers** ¾′ in diameter, on slender villose pedicels, in small 3–6-flowered compact simple corymbs; calyx-tube broadly obconic, villose at base, glabrous above, the lobes gradually narrowed from a broad base, acuminate, glabrous, coarsely glandular-serrate; stamens 10; anthers small, bright yellow; styles 3–5, surrounded at base by a narrow ring of pale hairs. **Fruit** ripening late in the autumn, on stout glabrous or slightly villose pedicels, in erect or drooping usually 2 or 3-fruited clusters, subglobose, rarely rather longer than broad, about ½′ in diameter, dull orange-red, often slightly villose at the ends, marked by numerous small dark dots; calyx much enlarged, with wide-spreading coarsely glandular acuminate lobes bright red at base on the upper side; flesh thin, light yellow, sweet and rather juicy; nutlets 3–5, broad and rounded at the ends, rounded and ridged on the back with a broad low ridge, about ¼′ long.

A tree, occasionally 20° high, with a stem 6′–8′ in diameter, covered with deeply furrowed dark gray bark broken irregularly into small persistent plate-like scales, and becoming on old stems often nearly black, spreading often elongated contorted branches forming a broad open head, and slender zigzag branchlets dark green tinged with red and villose when they first appear, soon becoming nearly glabrous, light orange-brown at midsummer, dark reddish brown or purple before winter, and ultimately ashy gray, and armed with thin nearly straight chestnut-brown spines 1′–1½′ long; or frequently a much-branched shrub, with several stout spreading stems.

Distribution. Dry woods in the foothill region of the southern Appalachian Mountains; southwestern Virginia through western North Carolina to eastern Tennessee and northern Georgia; in northern Alabama; usually at altitudes between 1500° and 3500°; common.

XVI. MICROCARPÆ.

CONSPECTUS OF THE ARBORESCENT SPECIES.

Fruit short-oblong; leaves orbicular to broad-ovate, pinnately 5–7-cleft.

135. **C. apiifolia** (C).

Fruit subglobose.

Leaves broad-ovate to triangular, long-stalked; calyx deciduous from the fruit.

136. **C. Phænopyrum** (A, C).

Leaves spatulate to oblanceolate, short-stalked; calyx generally persistent on the fruit.

137. **C. spathulata** (C).

135. Cratægus apiifolia Michx.   Parsley Haw.

Leaves broad-ovate to orbicular, acute at apex, truncate, slightly cordate or cuneate at the broad base, and pinnately 5–7-cleft with shallow acute or deep wide sinuses, and incisely lobed with broad or acute segments serrate toward the apex with spreading glandu-

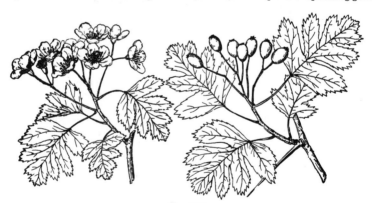

Fig. 487

lar teeth, when they unfold pilose above with long pale hairs, and mostly glabrous below, fully grown when the flowers open late in March or early in April, and at maturity thin, bright green and rather lustrous above, paler and glabrous or pilose below on the prominent midrib and primary veins, or on occasional plants pubescent on both surfaces, ⅔′–1½′ wide; petioles slender, pubescent, becoming glabrous, 1′–1½′ in length; leaves at the end of vigorous shoots often divided nearly to the midrib, with foliaceous lunate coarsely glandular-serrate short-stalked stipules sometimes ½′ long.   **Flowers** ½′ in diameter, on long slender hairy pedicels, in crowded densely villose usually 10–12-flowered corymbs; calyx-tube narrowly obconic, glabrous or covered with long matted pale hairs, the lobes lanceolate, acute, glabrous, usually glandular-serrate, often tinged with red toward the apex; stamens 20; anthers bright rose color; styles 1–3. **Fruit** ripening in October and persistent on the branches until the beginning of winter, short-oblong, bright scarlet, $\frac{1}{3}'$ long; calyx prominent, the lobes elongated, reflexed, often deciduous from the ripe fruit; flesh thin; nutlets 1–3, rounded at the ends, about $\frac{1}{3}'$ long.

A tree, occasionally 20° high, with a trunk rarely 6'–8' in diameter, branches spreading nearly at right angles and forming a wide irregular open head, and slender more or less zigzag often contorted branchlets covered when they first appear with long pale hairs, light red or pale orange-brown and usually puberulous in their first winter, ultimately light brown or ashy gray, and armed with stout straight chestnut-brown spines 1'–1½' long.

Distribution. Borders of streams and swamps or in hummocks in Pine-barrens in the coast and Piedmont regions of the south Atlantic States from southeastern Virginia to Georgia; in western Florida south to Dixie County (near Old Town), north-central and southern Alabama, Louisiana and the coast region of Texas to the valley of the lower Colorado River (low woods, Peyton's Creek, Matagorda County), and through Arkansas to eastern Oklahoma (Page, Le Flore County) and to southeastern Missouri; most abundant and of its largest size in southern Arkansas and western Louisiana.

136. Cratægus Phænopyrum Med. Washington Thorn.

Cratægus cordata Ait.

Leaves broad-ovate to triangular, acute or acuminate, truncate, broad-cuneate, rounded or cordate at the entire base, coarsely serrate above with acute spreading often gland-tipped teeth, and more or less incisely lobed or often 3-lobed, tinged with red when they

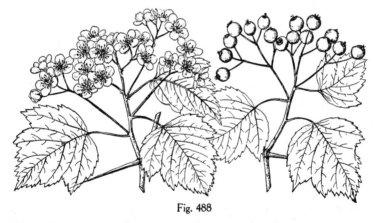

Fig. 488

unfold and sparingly pilose above with long pale caducous hairs, fully grown when the flowers open at the end of May, and at maturity thin and firm, dark green and lustrous above, pale and rarely pubescent on the lower surface, especially on the conspicuous orange-colored midrib and primary veins, 1½'–2' long, and 1'–1½' wide; turning late in the autumn bright scarlet and orange; petioles slender, terete, glabrous, $\frac{3}{4}'$–1½' in length. **Flowers** on slender pedicels, in rather compact many-flowered glabrous corymbs; calyx-tube broadly obconic, glabrous, the lobes short, nearly triangular, entire, abruptly contracted at apex into a minute point, glabrous on the outer, pubescent on the inner surface, ciliate on the margins; stamens 20; anthers rose color; styles 2–5, surrounded at base by conspicuous tufts of pale hairs. Fruit ripening in September and October and persistent on the branches until the spring of the following year, depressed-globose, scarlet, lustrous, $\frac{1}{4}'$ in diameter; calyx deciduous from the ripe fruit, leaving a wide circular scar surrounding the persistent erect tips of the carpels; nutlets 3–5, narrowed and acute at base, broad and rounded at apex, about $\frac{1}{8}'$ long.

A tree, 20°–30° high, with a straight trunk sometimes a foot in diameter, generally dividing 4°–5° above the ground into slender usually upright branches forming an oblong or occasionally round-topped head, slender zigzag glabrous bright chestnut-brown lustrous branchlets, becoming dark gray or reddish brown, and armed with slender sharp spines $1\frac{1}{2}'$–$2'$ long; often much smaller, and sometimes a broad spreading bush.

Distribution. Banks of streams in rich soil; western North Carolina at altitudes of about 2000°, to middle Tennessee and southern Kentucky; in southern Missouri (St. Francois, Wayne, Shannon, Carter and Ripley Counties), and in Richland County, Illinois; now often naturalized in the middle and Ohio valley states; nowhere common. Often cultivated in the eastern states and in western Europe; hardy as far north as eastern Massachusetts.

137. Cratægus spathulata Michx.

Cratægus spathulata var. *flavanthera* Sarg.

Leaves spatulate to oblanceolate, rounded or acuminate and sometimes 3-lobed at apex, gradually narrowed from above the middle to the slender concave-cuneate entire base, and crenately serrate above, nearly fully grown when the flowers open from March to May and

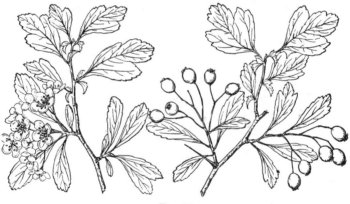

Fig. 489

then sparingly villose above with long white caducous hairs, and at maturity subcoriaceous, glabrous, dark green and lustrous above, paler below, reticulate-venulose, with an obscure yellow midrib and primary veins, $1'$–$2'$ long, and $1'$–$1\frac{1}{2}'$ wide, clustered at the end of short lateral branchlets; petioles slender, wing-margined to the base, $\frac{1}{2}'$–$1'$ in length; leaves at the end of vigorous shoots often deeply 3-lobed above the middle with rounded coarsely crenately serrate lobes, and narrowed below into a long winged petiole, $1'$–$2'$ long, and $1'$–$1\frac{1}{2}'$ wide, with a broad thick midrib often pilose on the lower surface, their stipules foliaceous, lunate, sharply serrate, stalked, often $\frac{1}{2}'$ broad. Flowers $\frac{1}{2}'$ in diameter, on long slender pedicels, in glabrous many-flowered narrow corymbs; calyx-tube broadly obconic, glabrous, the lobes short, nearly triangular, almost entire, minutely glandular-apiculate; stamens 20; anthers pale yellow; styles 2–5. Fruit ripening in October, subglobose, bright scarlet, lustrous, about $\frac{1}{8}'$ in diameter; calyx only slightly enlarged, with reflexed lobes; flesh thin, dry and mealy; nutlets 3–5, broad and rounded at apex, narrowed at base, $\frac{1}{16}'-\frac{1}{8}'$ long.

A tree, 18°–25° high, with a straight trunk occasionally 8'–10' in diameter, slender upright and spreading branches forming a broad open head, and thin zigzag glabrous light reddish brown branchlets, unarmed, or armed with straight stout light brown spines 1'–1$\frac{1}{2}'$ long; more often a shrub, with numerous spreading stems.

Distribution. Rich soil usually near the banks of streams or swamps, or low depressions in Pine-forests; North Carolina (near Albemarle, Stanly County) to central South Carolina, central, northwestern (Rome, Floyd County), and southwestern Georgia to northern Florida (Ocala, Marion County, to River Junction, Gadsden County); northern Alabama southward to Dallas County; eastern and western Mississippi (near Natchez, Adams County) eastern and northwestern Louisiana (Richland, Rapides, Caddo and Natchitoches Parishes); eastern Texas to the valley of the Guadalupe River (near Seguin, Guadalupe County), southeastern Oklahoma (Bennington, Bryan County), and through southern and western Arkansas to southwestern Missouri (Taney and Jasper Counties); probably most abundant in central Georgia.

XVII. BRACHYACANTHÆ.

CONSPECTUS OF THE ARBORESCENT SPECIES.

Leaves oblong-lanceolate to ovate or rhombic; broad-ovate to nearly triangular on vigorous shoots; fruit subglobose to obovoid, bright blue covered with a glaucous bloom.
138. **C. brachyacantha** (C).

Leaves narrow-rhombic to oval; lanceolate, acuminate on vigorous shoots; fruit globose, blue-black, very lustrous. 139. **C. saligna** (F).

138. Cratægus brachyacantha Sarg. & Engelm. Pomette Bleue.

Leaves oblong-lanceolate to ovate or rhombic, acute or rounded at apex, gradually narrowed to the concave-cuneate entire base, and crenulate-serrate above with minute incurved glandular teeth, slightly puberulous when they unfold on the upper surface and glabrous

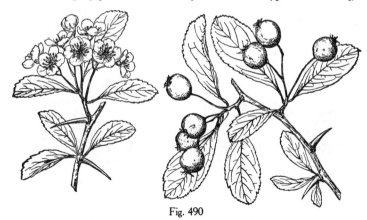

Fig. 490

on the lower surface, nearly fully grown when the flowers open at the end of April and early in May, and at maturity subcoriaceous, glabrous, dark green and lustrous, 1'–2' long, and $\frac{1}{2}'$ to nearly 1' wide, with a thin inconspicuous midrib and veins; petioles slender, narrowly wing-margined above, $\frac{1}{2}'-\frac{3}{4}'$ in length; leaves at the end of vigorous shoots sometimes broad-ovate or almost triangular, cuneate, truncate or cordate at the broad base, more or less deeply lobed, frequently $2\frac{1}{2}'$ long and $2'$ wide, with foliaceous broadly ovate to triangular acute stalked stipules sometimes $1'$ long. **Flowers** $\frac{1}{3}'$ in diameter, on slender pedicels, in crowded glabrous many-flowered corymbs; calyx-tube narrowly obconic, glabrous, the lobes short, nearly triangular, gradually narrowed to the gland-tipped apex, entire; petals turning bright orange color in fading; stamens 15–20; anthers yellow; styles 3–5. **Fruit** ripening and falling the middle of August, on erect pedicels, in few-fruited clusters, sub-globose or obovoid, bright blue, covered with a glaucous bloom, $\frac{1}{3}'-\frac{1}{2}'$ in diameter; calyx slightly enlarged, with spreading lobes; flesh thin; nutlets 3–5, narrowed and acute at base, full and rounded at apex, rounded and slightly grooved on the back, about $\frac{1}{4}'$ long.

A tree, 40°–50° high, with a trunk 18′–20′ in diameter, covered with thick dark brown deeply furrowed scaly bark, and divided usually 5°–10° from the ground into stout spreading light gray branches forming a broad compact round-topped head, and branchlets light green and slightly pubescent early in the season, soon becoming glabrous and pale red-brown, and ultimately ashy gray, and armed with numerous short stout generally curved or sometimes straight slender spines $\frac{1}{3}'-\frac{2}{3}'$ long, and also often terminal on the lateral branchlets of vigorous shoots.

Distribution. Borders of streams in rich moist soil; southwestern Arkansas (Ashdown, Little River County, and Texarkana, Miller County) to the valley of the Trinity River (Livingston, Polk County), eastern Texas, and to western Louisiana (Caddo, Webster, Ouachita, Natchitoches, St. Landry and Jefferson Davis Parishes); in eastern Louisiana (Glen Gordon, Covington, St. Tammany Parish; common); a few miles west of Opelousas, Louisiana, surrounding with dense groves low wet prairies and a conspicuous and beautiful feature of arborescent vegetation.

139. Cratægus saligna Greene.

Leaves narrow-rhombic to oval, gradually narrowed at the ends, acute or acuminate and apiculate at apex, entire toward the base, finely serrate above with incurved teeth tipped with minute bright red glands, nearly fully grown when the flowers open toward the middle

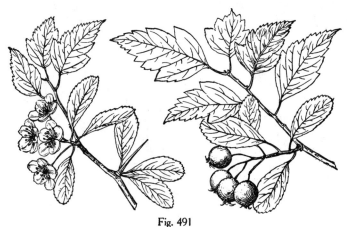

Fig. 491

of June, and then light yellow-green, covered above with short pale hairs and pale and gla-brous below, and at maturity thick and firm, dark green, glabrous and lustrous above, pale below $1\frac{1}{2}'-2'$ long, and $\frac{3}{4}'-1'$ wide, with a stout midrib rose color on the upper side, dark ob-scure forked veins, and reticulate veinlets; turning late in the autumn to brilliant shades of orange and bright scarlet; petioles slender, glandular near the base, with 2 or 3 large stipitate dark red caducous glands, and about $\frac{1}{3}'$ in length; leaves at the end of vigorous shoots lanceolate, acuminate, coarsely serrate, often irregularly and deeply divided into 2 or 3 acute lateral lobes, $3'-3\frac{1}{2}'$ long, and $1\frac{1}{4}'-1\frac{1}{2}'$ wide. **Flowers** about $\frac{5}{8}'$ in diameter, on short slender pedicels, in compact glabrous few or many-flowered corymbs; calyx-tube glabrous, the lobes nearly triangular, entire, often bright red toward the apex; stamens 20; anthers small, yellow; styles 5. **Fruit** ripening toward the end of September, on stout pedicels, in compact drooping clusters, globose, $\frac{1}{4}'$ in diameter, dull vinous red and very lustrous when fully grown, ultimately blue-black; calyx small, with reflexed persistent lobes; flesh thin, yellow, dry and sweet; nutlets 5, thick, rounded and slightly ridged on the back, $\frac{1}{8}'-\frac{3}{16}'$ long.

A tree, occasionally 20° high, with a short stem, long slender spreading branches gracefully drooping at the ends, covered with bright red or reddish brown bark, separating on old trunks near the ground into long slightly attached narrow plate-like gray scales, and slender glabrous bright red lustrous branchlets armed with numerous straight slender spines $\frac{3}{4}'-1\frac{1}{2}'$ long; often forming clumps or small thickets with numerous stems 8°-15° tall springing from a single root.

Distribution. Banks of the Cimarron, Gunnison, White, Tomichi, Eagle, San Juan, and other Colorado streams on both slopes of the continental divide at altitudes of 6000°-8000° above the sea.

XVIII. MACRACANTHÆ.

Tomentosæ Sarg.

CONSPECTUS OF THE ARBORESCENT SPECIES.

Leaves thin, with midrib and veins only slightly impressed on their upper surface; anthers rose color or red.
  Mature leaves pale pubescent below.
    Leaves ovate to ovate-oblong; fruit in erect clusters, obovoid, orange-red; stamens 20.   140. **C. tomentosa** (A, C).
    Leaves ovate, oval, or obovate, fruit in drooping clusters, globose to subglobose, bright red or orange-red; stamens 5-10.   141. **C. Chapmanii** (A, C).
  Mature leaves glabrous (*slightly pubescent on the midrib and veins below in* 142).
    Stamens 20.
      Leaves elliptic to suborbicular, smooth above; fruit in drooping clusters, subglobose to short-oblong.   142. **C. Gaultii** (A).
      Leaves elliptic, scabrate above; fruit in erect clusters, subglobose.
          143. **C. vegeta** (A).
    Stamens 10; leaves ovate, scabrate above; fruit short-oblong.   144. **C. Deweyana** (A).
Leaves subcoriaceous to coriaceous, with midrib and veins deeply impressed on their upper surface and pubescent below.
  Anthers rose color.
    Stamens 20.
      Leaves elliptic, acute at the ends; fruit globose.   145. **C. succulenta** (A).
      Leaves broadly oval or obovate; fruit subglobose to short-oblong.
          146. **C. gemmosa** (A).
    Stamens 10.
      Leaves broad-obovate or oval; fruit globose, villose at the ends; calyx-lobes coarsely glandular-serrate.   147. **C. illinoiensis** (A).
      Leaves broad-obovate to oval or rhombic; fruit subglobose; calyx-lobes entire.
          148. **C. integriloba** (A).
  Anthers yellow; stamens 10; leaves broad-obovate to elliptic or oval; fruit in erect clusters, globose.   149. **C. macracantha** (A).

140. Cratægus tomentosa L.

Leaves ovate, oblong-ovate, rhombic or elliptic, acute, acuminate or rarely rounded at apex, gradually narrowed to the cuneate entire base, sharply and usually doubly serrate above with broad spreading usually glandular teeth, and often divided above the middle into several short lateral lobes, nearly fully grown when the flowers open from the 1st to the middle of June, and at maturity thin and firm, gray-green, coated below with pale persistent pubescence, puberulous or ultimately glabrous above, conspicuously reticulate-venulose, 2′–5′ long, and 1′–3′ wide, with a broad midrib and slender primary veins; turning brilliant orange and scarlet in the autumn before falling; petioles stout, glandular, wing-margined, $\frac{1}{2}′$–$\frac{3}{4}′$ in length; leaves at the end of vigorous shoots sometimes broad-obovate to semi-orbicular, rounded and abruptly short-pointed at apex, rounded at base, and 3′–4′ long and wide; more often oblong-obovate, acuminate, and 5′–6′ in length. **Flowers** $\frac{1}{2}′$ in diameter, on slender villose pedicels, in villose corymbs; calyx-tube obconic, hoary-tomentose,

Fig. 492

the lobes lanceolate, acute, coarsely or pinnately serrate, usually glandular, stamens 20; anthers pale rose color; styles 2–5. **Fruit** ripening in October, on slender erect pubescent pedicels, in broad many-fruited clusters, obovoid or rarely subglobose, $\frac{1}{2}′$ in diameter, erect, dull orange-red, translucent when fully ripe, mostly persistent on the branches until the following spring; flesh thick, orange-yellow, sweet and succulent; nutlets about $\frac{1}{4}′$ long and broad, rounded at the ends, the ventral cavities broad and deep.

A tree, 15°–20° high, with a trunk 5′–6′ in diameter, covered with smooth pale gray or dark brown furrowed bark, slender spreading often nearly horizontal smooth gray branches forming a wide flat head, and slender branchlets covered when they first appear with thick hoary tomentum, becoming dark orange color and puberulous in their first winter, and ashy gray in their second season, and unarmed, or armed with occasional slender straight dull ashy gray or very rarely bright chestnut-brown spines 1′–1$\frac{1}{2}′$ long.

Distribution. Near Troy, Rensselaer County, New York, westward through New York to southwestern Ontario, through Ohio, southern Michigan, Indiana and Illinois to central Minnesota and southward to Pennsylvania and along the Appalachian Mountains to northeastern Georgia, and to central Iowa, northeastern Missouri to the valley of the Meramec River, and to eastern Kansas; near Nashville, Davidson County, Tennessee; in the neighborhood of Augusta, Richmond County, Georgia; and in Dallas County, Alabama (*R. S. Cocks*).

Occasionally cultivated as an ornamental tree in the gardens of western Europe.

141. Cratægus Chapmanii Ashe.

Cratægus mollita Sarg.

Leaves ovate, oval, or obovate, acuminate, gradually narrowed and acute or concave-cuneate at the entire base, sharply serrate above with glandular teeth, and often slightly lobed above the middle, about half grown when the flowers open early in June and then covered above with short soft pale hairs and pale-tomentose below, and at maturity dark dull green and smooth or scabrate above, pale-tomentulose below, especially on the slender yellow midrib and primary veins, $2\frac{1}{2}'-3'$ long, and $1\frac{1}{2}'-2\frac{1}{2}'$ wide; turning yellow or brown in the autumn before falling; petioles stout, wing-margined at apex, tomentose early in the season, becoming nearly glabrous, $\frac{1}{2}'-\frac{3}{4}'$ in length; leaves at the end of vigorous shoots sometimes $6'$ long and $4'$ wide. **Flowers** about $\frac{3}{8}'$ in diameter, on long stout hoary-tomen-

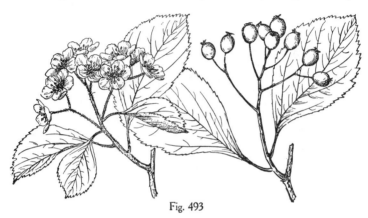

Fig. 493

tose or pubescent pedicels, in broad many-flowered tomentose corymbs; calyx-tube narrowly obconic, tomentose, the lobes acuminate, glandular-serrate, sparingly villose; stamens 10; anthers rose color; styles 2 or 3. **Fruit** ripening the middle of September, on elongated slightly villose pedicels, in broad lax drooping many-fruited clusters, globose to subglobose, bright red, about $\frac{5}{8}'$ in diameter; calyx only slightly enlarged, with reflexed coarsely glandular-serrate lobes; flesh juicy, succulent, yellow; nutlets 2 or 3, about $\frac{3}{4}'$ long and nearly as broad, thin, rounded at the obtuse ends, rounded and obscurely ridged on the back, the ventral cavities broad and deep.

A tree, sometimes $20°$ high, with a short trunk $6'-8'$ in diameter, covered with gray scaly bark, erect branches forming a broad open head, and slender branchlets hoary-tomentose early in the season, becoming bright red-brown and lustrous, and armed with occasional stout straight or curved bright chestnut-brown spines $1\frac{1}{2}'-2'$ long.

Distribution. Banks of streams in the Appalachian region from Virginia to northern Georgia and eastern Tennessee; in southern Missouri (Taney County, *C. mollita*).

142. Cratægus Gaultii Sarg.

Leaves elliptic to suborbicular, acute or rounded at apex, concave-cuneate or rounded at the entire base, coarsely doubly serrate above with straight glandular teeth, and occasionally divided above the middle into short acute lobes, nearly fully grown when the flowers open at the end of May and then very thin, yellow-green and sparingly villose above, pale and slightly pubescent below, and at maturity thin and firm in texture, glabrous, dark dull green on the upper surface, pale on the lower surface, $2\frac{1}{2}'-3'$ long, and $2'-2\frac{3}{4}'$ wide, with a stout yellow midrib deeply impressed above, and 6 or 7 pairs of primary veins extending obliquely to the point of the lobes; petioles stout, wing-margined to below the middle, villose on the upper side early in the season with matted white hairs, becoming nearly glabrous, $\frac{1}{2}'$–$1'$ in length. Flowers $\frac{5}{8}'$ in diameter, on long slender slightly villose pedicels, in broad many-flowered hairy corymbs, their bracts and bractlets linear, acuminate, glandular, mostly persistent until the flowers open; calyx-tube narrowly obconic, glabrous, the lobes broad, acuminate, coarsely glandular-serrate, glabrous on the outer, villose on the inner surface; stamens 18–20; anthers pale pink; styles 2 or 3. Fruit ripening from the middle to the end of September, on slender slightly hairy pedicels, in few-fruited drooping clusters, subglobose to short-oblong, $\frac{1}{2}'$–$\frac{5}{8}'$ long; calyx prominent, with spreading appressed coarsely serrate lobes; flesh thick, yellow, soft and juicy; nutlets 2 or 3, rounded at the ends, about $1\frac{3}{8}'$ long and nearly as wide, the ventral cavities long, deep, and narrow.

A tree, 20°–25° high, with a trunk often 10' in diameter and 6°–7° long, spreading

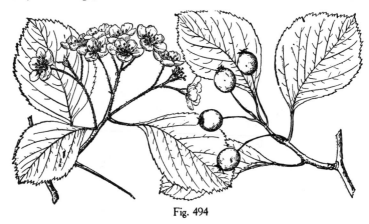

Fig. 494

branches forming a broad round-topped head, and slender slightly zigzag glabrous light red-brown lustrous branchlets, unarmed, or armed with occasional straight slender dark purple shining spines $1\frac{1}{4}'$–$1\frac{3}{4}'$ long.

Distribution. Open pastures, Milton Township and Gleneilyn, Du Page County, and Mokena, Will County, northeastern Illinois.

143. Cratægus vegeta Sarg.

Leaves elliptic, acuminate, gradually narrowed and concave-cuneate at the entire base, finely often doubly serrate above, with straight glandular teeth, and slightly divided above the middle into numerous short acute lobes, nearly fully grown when the flowers open at the end of May and then membranaceous, dark yellow-green and roughened above by short rigid pale hairs and densely pubescent below, and at maturity thin and firm in texture, dark dull green and scabrate on the upper surface, pale and pubescent on the lower surface on the slender midrib, and 5 or 6 pairs of thin primary veins arching obliquely to the point of the lobes, $3\frac{1}{4}'$–$4'$ long, and $1\frac{3}{4}'$–$2\frac{1}{2}'$ wide; petioles slender, broadly wing-margined at apex, villose on the upper side early in the season, becoming glabrous and rose color in the autumn, $\frac{1}{2}'$–$\frac{3}{4}'$ long. Flowers $\frac{5}{8}'$–$\frac{3}{4}'$ in diameter, on long slender villose pedicels, in usually 10–12-flowered hairy corymbs, with linear to linear-obovate acute glandular bracts and bractlets becoming reddish and mostly persistent until after the flowers open; calyx-tube narrowly obconic, villose, the lobes slender, acuminate, glandular-serrate, villose; stamens 20; anthers small, light pink or red; styles 2 or 3, usually 3. Fruit ripening late in September, on slender elongated rigid slightly villose pedicels, in few-fruited erect clusters, subglobose, scarlet, lustrous, marked by small pale dots, about $\frac{3}{8}'$ in diameter; calyx prominent, with a short tube and spreading reflexed serrate lobes; flesh thin, yellow, dry and mealy; nutlets 2 or 3, $\frac{1}{4}'$ long and nearly as broad, full and rounded at the ends, the ventral cavities broad and deep.

A tree, 20°–25° high, with a tall straight trunk sometimes 8′ in diameter, stout wide-spreading branches forming a symmetrical round-topped head, and very slender nearly

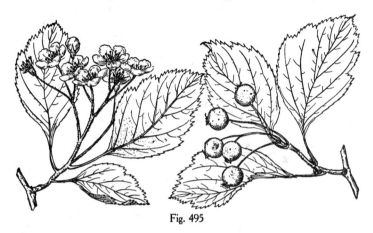

Fig. 495

straight branchlets, light orange-green when they first appear, becoming bright red-brown and lustrous at the end of their first season and darker the following year, and unarmed, or sparingly armed with slender nearly straight purple shining spines about 4′ long.

Distribution. Oak-woods in moist rich soil near the banks of the Calumet River, Calumet, Cook County, Illinois.

144. Cratægus Deweyana Sarg.

Leaves ovate, acuminate or abruptly long-pointed at apex, abruptly narrowed and concave-cuneate at the entire often unsymmetric base, coarsely doubly serrate above with straight or incurved gland-tipped teeth, and slightly divided above the middle into several pairs of small acuminate spreading lobes, about one third grown when the flowers open during the last week of May and then membranaceous, dark yellow-green, and covered above with short lustrous white hairs, and light yellow-green and glabrous below, and at maturity thin, yellow-green and scabrate on the upper surface, pale on the lower surface, 3′–4′ long, and 2′–$\frac{3}{4}'$ wide, with a stout midrib deeply impressed on the upper side, and 6 or 7 pairs of thin primary veins arching to the point of the lobes; petioles stout, wing-margined at apex, deeply grooved, sparingly villose on the upper side, soon glabrous, glandular with occasional minute dark glands, usually dull orange color in the autumn, $\frac{3}{4}'$–1′ in length; leaves at the end of vigorous shoots more deeply lobed and more coarsely serrate, subcoriaceous, often 4′ long and 3$\frac{1}{2}'$ wide, and gradually narrowed into stout broad-winged coarsely glandular petioles, their stipules foliaceous, stipitate, lunate, acutely lobed, glandular-serrate with minute dark red glands, sometimes $\frac{1}{2}'$ long, persistent through the season. **Flowers** about $\frac{1}{2}'$ in diameter, on slender hairy pedicels, in wide lax slightly villose corymbs; calyx-tube narrowly obconic, villose at base, glabrous above, the lobes slender, elongated, acuminate, finely glandular-serrate usually only above the middle, dark green and glabrous on the outer surface, villose on the inner surface; stamens 7–10, usually 10; anthers small, dark rose color; styles 2 or 3, usually 2. **Fruit** ripening from the first to the middle of October and falling a few weeks later, on long slender puberulous pedicels, in wide many-fruited drooping clusters, subglobose to short-oblong, rounded at the ends, scarlet, lustrous, marked by occasional large pale dots, $\frac{1}{2}'$ in diameter; calyx prominent, with elongated glandular-serrate lobes dark red on the upper side near the base, usually erect and incurved, mostly persistent on the ripe fruit; flesh when fully ripe thick, yellow and sweet; nutlets usually 2, occasionally 3, about $\frac{3}{16}'$ long and $\frac{1}{8}'$ wide, rounded at the ends, rounded and conspicuously ridged on the back, the ventral cavities broad and shallow.

A tree, 20°–25° high, with a tall trunk sometimes 10' in diameter, covered with light gray

Fig. 496

bark becoming rough and scaly near the base, slender branches, the lower horizontal and wide-spreading, the upper ascending and forming a wide open irregular head, and stout glabrous branchlets dark orange-brown when they first appear, deep red-brown and lustrous on the upper, gray-brown and lustrous on the lower side during their first winter, becoming gray slightly tinged with red the following year, and armed with numerous stout curved chestnut-brown or purple spines $1\frac{1}{2}'$–2' long and occasionally persistent on old stems.

Distribution. Western and central New York; Hagaman swamp near Rochester, and Rush, Monroe County, Portage, Livingston County, Castile and Silver Springs, Wyoming County, and near Ithaca, Tompkins County; not common.

145. Cratægus succulenta Link.

Leaves elliptic, acute or acuminate at apex, gradually narrowed from near the middle to the entire base, coarsely and usually doubly serrate above with spreading glandular teeth, and divided above the middle into numerous short acute lobes, nearly fully grown when the flowers open at the end of May or early in June and then membranaceous, covered above with soft pale hairs, and puberulous or rarely nearly glabrous below, and at maturity coriaceous, dark green, glabrous and somewhat lustrous above, pale yellow-green and mostly puberulous below on the stout yellow midrib, and 4–7 pairs of slender veins extending obliquely to the point of the lobes and deeply impressed on the upper side, usually $2'$–$2\frac{1}{2}'$ long and $1'$–$1\frac{1}{2}'$ wide; petioles stout, more or less winged above, frequently bright red after midsummer, generally about $\frac{1}{2}'$ in length; leaves at the end of vigorous shoots occasionally ovate, and often $2\frac{1}{2}'$ long and 3' wide. **Flowers** about $\frac{2}{3}'$ in diameter, on long slender hairy pedicels, in broad lax villose corymbs; calyx-tube narrowly obconic, villose or glabrous, the lobes broad, acute, laciniate, glandular with bright red glands, and generally villose; stamens usually 20, sometimes 15; anthers small, rose color; styles 2 or 3, surrounded at base by a ring of pale hairs. **Fruit** beginning to ripen about the middle of September and sometimes remaining on the branches until the end of October, on slender elongated pedicels, in broad loose many-fruited drooping clusters, globose, bright scarlet, marked by large pale dots, $\frac{1}{2}'$–$\frac{2}{3}'$ in diameter; calyx prominent, with a broad shallow depression, and much enlarged coarsely serrate closely appressed persistent lobes; flesh thick, yellow, becoming juicy, sweet and pulpy; nutlets 2 or 3, $\frac{1}{3}'$ long, $\frac{1}{4}'$ broad, prominently ridged on the back, the ventral cavities wide and deep.

A tree, occasionally 20° high, with a short trunk 5′–6′ in diameter, covered with dark red-brown scaly bark, stout ascending branches forming a broad irregular head, and stout more or less zigzag glabrous dark orange-brown lustrous branchlets becoming dull gray-brown

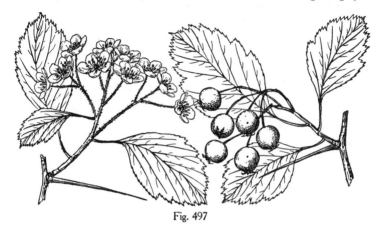

Fig. 497

in their second season and ultimately ashy gray, and armed with numerous stout slightly curved bright chestnut-brown shining spines $1\frac{1}{2}'$–$2\frac{1}{2}'$ long; or usually shrubby and much smaller, and often flowering when only a few feet high.

Distribution. Coast of northeastern Massachusetts; southwestern Vermont; eastern and western New York; near London, Ontario; widely distributed in Pennsylvania; northeastern Illinois.

146. Cratægus gemmosa Sarg.

Leaves broad-oval or rarely broad-obovate, gradually narrowed and cuneate or occasionally rounded at the entire base, sharply and usually doubly serrate from below the middle with straight glandular teeth, and often slightly lobed toward the acute or acuminate apex with short acute lobes, dark red and villose as they unfold, nearly fully grown when the flowers open from the middle to the end of May and then membranaceous, light yellow-green, nearly glabrous above and pale and villose below, and at maturity thick and firm in texture, very dark dull green on the upper surface, pale on the lower surface and pubescent on the under side of the stout yellow midrib deeply impressed and occasionally puberulous above, and on the 4 or 5 pairs of slender primary veins extending obliquely to the end of the leaf, $1\frac{1}{2}'$–$2\frac{1}{2}'$ long, and 1′–2′ wide; petioles stout, villose or pubescent, more or less winged above, glandular while young with minute bright red caducous glands, usually pink in the autumn, $\frac{1}{4}'$–$\frac{1}{2}'$ in length; leaves at the end of vigorous shoots more coarsely serrate, frequently divided into short acute lateral lobes, and often 4′ long and 3′ wide, with a rose-colored midrib and stout spreading primary veins. **Flowers** $\frac{1}{2}'$–$\frac{3}{4}'$ in diameter, on slender hairy pedicels, in broad open compound villose many-flowered corymbs, with lanceolate or oblanceolate acuminate glandular-serrate conspicuous bracts and bractlets; calyx-tube narrowly obconic, more or less villose with matted pale hairs, or nearly glabrous, the lobes lanceolate, acuminate, glabrous or villose on the outer surface, villose on the inner surface, coarsely glandular-serrate with bright red glands; stamens 20; anthers small, rose color; styles 2 or 3, surrounded at the base by a narrow ring of pale tomentum. **Fruit** ripening early in October and becoming very succulent just before falling, on long slender pedicels, in drooping many-fruited glabrous or puberulous clusters, subglobose to short-oblong, scarlet, lustrous, $\frac{1}{2}'$ in diameter; calyx prominent, with an elongated narrow tube, and reflexed villose lobes bright red toward the base on the upper side; flesh thick, bright yellow, sweet and succulent; nutlets usually 3, or 2, $\frac{1}{4}'$ long, broad and flat, full and rounded at the ends, ridged on the back with a prominent rounded ridge, the ventral cavities broad and deep.

A tree, occasionally 30° high, with a tall trunk $10'-12'$ in diameter, covered with dark brown scaly bark, stout spreading or ascending branches forming a broad rather open

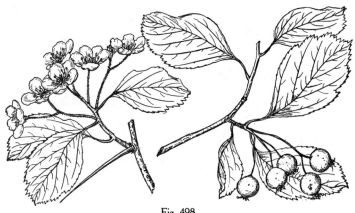

Fig. 498

symmetrical head, stout zigzag glabrous red-brown or gray-brown lustrous branchlets armed with straight or slightly curved thick chestnut-brown spines usually about $2'$ long, and winter-buds sometimes $\frac{1}{4}'$ in diameter.

Distribution. Rich forest glades, or the margins of woods, usually in low rich soil; eastern New York, near Albany, Albany County; western New York (Monroe and Livingston Counties); southern Ontario (La Salle on the Niagara River and near London); northwestern Ohio (Oak Harbor, Ottawa County); southern Michigan; common; Illinois (Calumet, Cook County, and Manley, Fulton County); southern Wisconsin (Waukesha, Waukesha County and near Madison, Dane County).

147. Cratægus illinoiensis Ashe.

Leaves broad-obovate to oval, rounded or rarely acute at the wide apex, broad-cuneate and entire at the base, coarsely and often doubly serrate above, with straight or incurved teeth tipped with minute deciduous glands, and sometimes slightly and irregularly divided toward the apex into short acute lobes, when they unfold covered below with a thick coat of hoary tomentum and pilose above, and when the flowers open about the 20th of May membranaceous, yellow-green, covered above with short pale hairs and pubescent below, and at maturity thick and firm in texture, dark green and glabrous on the upper surface, pale and pubescent on the lower surface, particularly on the stout midrib and 4–6 pairs of primary veins deeply impressed on the upper side, $2'-2\frac{1}{2}'$ long, and $1\frac{1}{2}'-2'$ wide; petioles stout, slightly winged toward the apex, generally bright red below the middle after midsummer, and usually $\frac{1}{2}'-\frac{2}{3}'$ in length; leaves at the end of vigorous shoots usually elliptic, acute or acuminate, more coarsely dentate and more often lobed, sometimes decurrent nearly to the base of the stout petiole, $3'-4'$ long, and $2\frac{1}{2}'-3'$ wide. **Flowers** about $\frac{5}{8}'$ in diameter, on slender slightly hairy pedicels, in broad compact villose corymbs; calyx-tube narrowly obconic, coated with long matted pale hairs, the lobes broad, acuminate, very coarsely glandular-serrate with large stipitate bright red glands, glabrous on the outer surface except at the base, villose on the inner surface; stamens 10; anthers rose color; styles 2 or usually 3. **Fruit** ripening early in October and persistent on the branches until after the beginning of winter, on stout bright red pedicels, in few-fruited drooping villose clusters, globose, scarlet, lustrous, marked by occasional dark dots, more or less villose at the ends, $\frac{1}{2}'$ in diameter; calyx prominent, with a short villose tube, and spreading lobes gradually narrowed from a broad base, sparingly glandular-serrate or nearly entire, villose, mostly deciduous before the fruit ripens; flesh thin, yellow, dry and mealy; nutlets 2 or 3, $\frac{1}{4}'$ long, broad and thick, rounded at the ends, the ventral cavities broad and deep.

Fig. 499

A tree, rarely more than 18° high, with a trunk 4'–5' in diameter, covered with thin close bark broken on the surface into pale plate-like scales, and divided into several long erect and spreading slender branches forming a wide open-topped head, and stout somewhat zigzag branchlets covered at first with scattered pale caducous hairs, bright orange-brown and lustrous during their first season, becoming dark brown in their second year and ultimately ashy gray, and armed with numerous slender straight or curved bright chestnut-brown shining spines $1\frac{1}{2}'$–3' long.

Distribution. Open woods along the gravelly banks of small streams in Stark and Peoria Counties, Illinois; not common.

148. Cratægus integriloba Sarg.

Leaves broad-obovate, oval or rhombic, acute, gradually or abruptly narrowed below the middle, entire at the cuneate base, coarsely doubly serrate above with spreading glandular teeth, and irregularly divided into numerous short acute or acuminate lobes, coated in early spring with soft pale caducous hairs, nearly fully grown when the flowers open during the first week in June, and at maturity glabrous, thin and firm in texture, dark green and lustrous on the upper surface, pale yellow-green on the lower surface, $1\frac{1}{2}'$–2' long, and 1'–$1\frac{1}{2}'$ wide, with a slender midrib often dark red at the base, and 4–6 pairs of slender primary veins deeply impressed on the upper side; petioles stout, more or less broadly winged toward the apex, at first puberulous, soon glabrous, often red on the lower side, $\frac{1}{3}'$–$\frac{3}{4}'$ in length; leaves at the end of vigorous shoots more coarsely serrate, more deeply lobed, often 3' long and $2\frac{1}{2}'$ wide, with stout broadly winged petioles. **Flowers** $\frac{3}{4}'$ in diameter, on long slender villose pedicels, in broad open crowded villose corymbs; calyx-tube broadly obconic, coated toward the base with long matted white hairs and glabrous above, the lobes linear-lanceolate, elongated, entire or very rarely furnished with occasional caducous glands; stamens 10; anthers large, rose color; styles 2 or 3, surrounded at base by a narrow ring of snow-white hairs. Fruit ripening at the end of September or early in October, on short stout pedicels, in drooping or erect many-fruited slightly villose clusters, subglobose, bright scarlet, lustrous, marked by large pale dots, $\frac{1}{3}'-\frac{1}{2}'$ in diameter; calyx enlarged, prominent, with elongated entire lobes, dark red on the upper side at base, much reflexed and persistent; flesh thin, yellow, sweet and pulpy; nutlets 2 or 3, about $\frac{1}{4}'$ long, thick and broad, rounded at the narrow ends, the ventral cavities broad and deep.

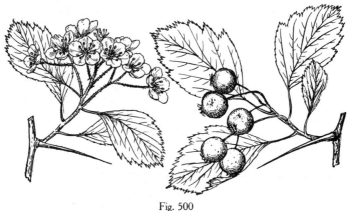

Fig. 500

A tree, occasionally 18°–20° high, with a straight erect trunk 6′–8′ in diameter, wide-spreading or erect branches forming an open irregular head, and stout nearly straight or occasionally slightly zigzag glabrous branchlets, lustrous and red-brown or orange-brown during their first summer and ultimately dull ashy gray, and armed with stout nearly straight bright chestnut-brown shining spines $1\frac{1}{2}'-2\frac{1}{2}'$ long and often pointed toward the base of the branch.

Distribution. Low limestone ridges, Province of Quebec, south of the St. Lawrence River near the Lachine Rapids, and at Caughnawaga, Rockfield, and Adirondack Junction.

149. Cratægus macracantha Koehne.

Leaves broad-obovate to elliptic or oval, acute or rounded and sometimes short-pointed at apex, gradually or abruptly narrowed and cuneate at the entire base, coarsely and often doubly serrate above with straight or incurved gland-tipped teeth, and usually divided above the middle into numerous short acute or acuminate lobes, when they unfold often bright red and coated on the upper surface with soft pale hairs, more than half grown when the flowers open late in May and then dull yellow-green, nearly glabrous on the upper surface and pale and puberulous on the lower surface, and at maturity coriaceous, dark green and glabrous above, frequently puberulous below on the midrib, and on the 4–6 pairs of slender primary veins extending obliquely to the point of the lobes and deeply impressed on the upper side, usually $2'-2\frac{1}{2}'$ long and $1\frac{1}{2}'-2'$ wide; petioles stout, more or less winged above, frequently bright red after midsummer and usually about $\frac{1}{2}'$ in length; leaves at the end of vigorous shoots often broad and rounded at base, coarsely dentate, 3′–4′ long, and $2\frac{1}{2}'-3'$ wide. Flowers about $\frac{3}{4}'$ in diameter, on long slender hairy pedicels, in broad more or less villose corymbs; calyx-tube narrowly obconic, more or less villose or nearly glabrous, the lobes long, narrow, acuminate, glandular with minute dark glands, glabrous on the outer surface, slightly villose on the inner surface; stamens usually 10, occasionally 8–12; anthers pale yellow; styles 2–3, surrounded at the base by a broad ring of hoary tomentum.

Fruit ripening at the end of September and often remaining on the branches for several weeks longer, on erect slender pedicels, in broad open many-fruited usually slightly villose clusters, globose, often hairy at the ends until nearly ripe, crimson, very lustrous, $\frac{1}{4}'-\frac{1}{3}'$ in diameter; calyx large and conspicuous, the lobes coarsely serrate, reflexed and persistent; flesh thin, dark yellow, dry and mealy; nutlets 2 or 3, about $\frac{1}{4}'$ long and wide, broad and rounded at the ends, the ventral cavities deep and irregular.

A tree, occasionally 15° high, with a tall stem $5'-6'$ in diameter, covered with pale close bark, stout wide-spreading branches forming an open rather irregular head, and stout

Fig. 501

slightly zigzag glabrous light chestnut-brown very lustrous branchlets, becoming dull reddish brown in their second year, and armed with numerous slender usually curved very sharp bright chestnut-brown shining spines $2\frac{1}{2}'-4'$ long.

Distribution. Western Vermont (near Middlebury, Addison County); central and western New York; southern Ontario (near Toronto); northeastern Illinois (Barrington, Cook County); and eastern Pennsylvania (Bucks and Northampton Counties).

XIX. DOUGLASIANÆ.

CONSPECTUS OF THE ARBORESCENT SPECIES.

Leaves subcoriaceous, lustrous above, obovate to broad-ovate, coarsely serrate, usually lobed; stamens 5–20, normally 10; spines numerous, short and stout.

150. **C. Douglasii.**

Leaves thinner, dull bluish green, lanceolate to oblong-obovate or elliptic, acute at the ends, finely serrate, not lobed; stamens 10–20; spines few, long and slender or wanting.

151. **C. rivularis.**

150. Cratægus Douglasii Lindl.

Leaves broad-obovate to ovate, gradually narrowed below to the cuneate entire base, coarsely serrate above with minute glandular teeth, and often incisely lobed toward the acute apex, nearly fully grown and coated above and on the midrib and veins below with short pale hairs when the flowers open in May, and at maturity thin, glabrous, dark green and lustrous above, paler below, $1'-2'$ long, and $\frac{1}{2}'-1\frac{1}{2}'$ wide; petioles slender, wing-margined above, sparingly glandular, villose early in the season, becoming glabrous, $\frac{1}{2}'-\frac{3}{4}'$ in length; leaves at the end of vigorous shoots broad-obovate, incisely lobed at the broad apex, often deeply divided into lateral lobes, or occasionally 3-lobed, 3'–4' long, and 2'–3' wide. **Flowers** $\frac{1}{2}'–\frac{7}{12}'$ in diameter, on long slender glabrous pedicels, in broad glabrous corymbs, with linear caducous bracts and bractlets; calyx-tube broadly obconic, glabrous, the lobes gradually narrowed from a broad base, entire or occasionally minutely dentate, acute and bright red at apex, glabrous on the outer surface, villose on the inner surface; stamens 10 or rarely 5 by abortion; anthers small, pale rose color; styles 2–5, surrounded at base by tufts of long pale hairs. **Fruit** ripening and falling in August and September, on slender pedicels, in compact, many-fruited drooping clusters, short-oblong, truncate at apex, black and lustrous, very rarely chestnut-colored (f. *badia* Sarg.), about $\frac{1}{2}'$ long; calyx persistent; flesh thick, sweet and succulent, light yellow; nutlets usually 5, about $\frac{1}{4}'$ long, narrowed at base, broad and rounded at apex, ridged on the back with a narrow ridge, the ventral cavities irregular, small and shallow.

A tree, 30°–40° high, with a long trunk 18'–20' in diameter, stout branches spreading and ascending and forming a compact round-topped head, and slender rigid glabrous bright red

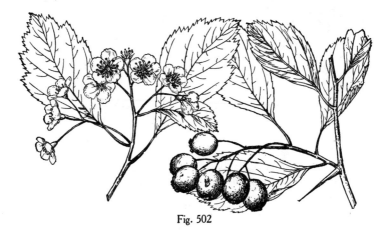

Fig. 502

or orange-red lustrous branchlets unarmed, or armed with straight or slightly curved blunt or rarely acute bright red ultimately ashy gray spines $\frac{1}{3}'–1'$ long; often shrubby and spreading into wide thickets.

Distribution. Banks of mountain streams; valley of the Parsnip River, British Columbia, through Washington and Oregon to the valley of the Pitt River, California, and eastward in the United States through the northern Rocky Mountain region to the Bighorn Mountains, Wyoming; passing into the var. *Suksdorfii* Sarg. differing in its 20 stamens, fruit not more than $\frac{1}{3}'$ in diameter, usually in few-fruited clusters and ripening from the 1st of July to the middle of August. A shrub with numerous stems occasionally 25° high; banks of the Columbia River and borders of bottom-lands, western Klickitat County, Washington.

151. Cratægus rivularis Nutt.

Leaves lanceolate to narrowly oblong-obovate or elliptic, acute, acuminate or abruptly acuminate at apex, gradually narrowed and concave-cuneate at the long entire base, and very finely crenately serrate above with glandular teeth, when they unfold tinged with red, villose above and coated below with matted pale hairs, more than half grown when the flowers open late in May and then hairy on the midrib and veins above and pale and glabrous below, and at maturity thin, dull bluish green and smooth on the upper surface, pale yellow-green on the lower surface, about 2' long and $\frac{3}{4}'$ wide, with a slender yellow midrib and 3 or 4 pairs of thin obscure primary veins; petioles slender, slightly winged at apex, at first villose, becoming glabrous and rose-colored below the middle, and about $\frac{1}{2}'$ in length; leaves at the end of vigorous shoots often rhombic, coarsely serrate, often slightly incisely lobed, coriaceous, 3' long, and 2' wide, with a stout broadly winged petiole. **Flowers** $\frac{1}{2}'$ in diameter, on long slender pedicels, in rather compact glabrous corymbs; calyx-tube broadly obconic, glabrous, the lobes linear, entire or glandular with minute caducous glands, glabrous on the outer surface, sparingly villose on the inner surface, often tinged with red; stamens 10–20; anthers pale rose color. **Fruit** ripening in September, on long pedicels, in drooping few-fruited clusters, short-oblong, full and rounded at the ends, dark crimson and marked by many large white dots when fully grown, becoming black and lustrous at maturity, $\frac{1}{3}'-\frac{1}{2}'$ long; calyx slightly enlarged, persistent, with elongated closely appressed entire lobes slightly villose and dark red on the upper side below the middle; flesh thin, yellow, dry and mealy; nutlets 3–5, $\frac{1}{4}'$ long, narrowed and rounded at the ends, slightly ridged on the back, the ventral cavities broad and shallow.

Fig. 503

A tree, occasionally 20° high, with a slender trunk covered with dark brown scaly bark, erect branches forming a narrow rather open head, and slender bright red-brown lustrous branchlets marked by numerous pale lenticels, and unarmed or armed with straight slender spines usually about 1' long.

Distribution. Banks of mountain streams, often forming thickets; southeastern Idaho, (Pocatello and Inkom, Bannock County); northeastern Nevada (Lee, Elk County) to southwestern Wyoming, eastern Utah, southwestern Colorado, and northern New Mexico.

XX. ANOMALÆ.

CONSPECTUS OF THE ARBORESCENT SPECIES.

Stamens 5–15; corymbs glabrous; leaves scabrate above. 152. **C. scabrida** (A).
Stamens 20; corymbs villose; leaves glabrous above. 153. **C. virilis** (A).

152. Cratægus scabrida Sarg.

Leaves oval to obovate, acuminate, gradually narrowed from near the middle to the acuminate base, irregularly glandular-serrate nearly to the base, and divided above into numerous short spreading lobes coated above when the flowers open at the end of May with short pale hairs, and at maturity thick and firm, dark green and scabrate on the upper surface, pale yellow-green and glabrous on the lower surface, 2'–3' long, and $1\frac{1}{2}'-2'$ wide; petioles slender, occasionally glandular, often slightly winged toward the apex, $\frac{1}{2}'-1\frac{1}{4}'$ in length. **Flowers** $\frac{3}{4}'$ in diameter, on slender glabrous pedicels, in broad glabrous corymbs;

calyx narrowly obconic, glabrous, the lobes linear-lanceolate, long-acuminate, finely gland-ular-serrate; stamens 5–15; anthers small, pale yellow; styles 3, surrounded at base by a thick tuft of pale tomentum. **Fruit** in loose drooping clusters, subglobose, scarlet, $\frac{1}{2}'$ in diameter, only the base of the reflexed calyx-lobes persistent on the ripe fruit; flesh yellow, thick, dry and mealy; nutlets 3, rounded and prominently ridged on the back, $\frac{1}{3}'$ long, the ventral depression wide, shallow, irregular, often obscure.

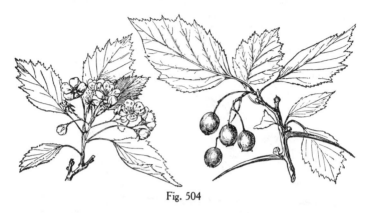

Fig. 504

A tree, 15°–20° high, with a trunk 6′ to 8′ in diameter, spreading horizontal branches forming a broad round-topped head, and stout slightly zigzag glabrous branchlets marked by oblong pale lenticels, dark chestnut-brown during their first season, becoming ashy gray during their second year, and armed with slender straight or curved spines $1\frac{1}{2}'$–2′ in length; or often a tall intricately branched shrub.

Distribution. Valley of the St. Lawrence River, near Montreal, Province of Quebec to the neighborhood of Toronto, southern Ontario; northern and western Vermont; southern New Hampshire (slopes of Little Monadnock Mountain); western Massachusetts, and western New York.

153. Cratægus virilis Sarg.

Leaves oblong-obovate, acuminate or rounded and short-pointed at apex, concave-cuneate and gradually narrowed to the acute entire base, finely doubly serrate above with straight glandular teeth, and slightly divided above the middle into 3 or 4 pairs of small acuminate lobes, nearly fully grown when the flowers open during the first week of June and then thin, yellow-green, smooth and slightly hairy above and pale. bluish green and covered below with short white hairs most abundant on the stout yellow midrib and slender primary veins, and at maturity thin, glabrous, dark green and lustrous on the upper surface, slightly villose on the lower surface, $2\frac{1}{2}'$–3′ long, and $1\frac{3}{4}'$–2′ wide; petioles stout, wing-margined often to below the middle, slightly villose on the upper side early in the season, soon glabrous, $\frac{3}{5}'$–1′ in length; leaves at the end of vigorous shoots subcoriaceous, oval to rhombic, acuminate, often long-pointed, 3′–4′ long, and 2′–$2\frac{1}{2}'$ wide, with a rose-colored midrib and stout broadly winged petiole. **Flowers** about $\frac{1}{2}'$ in diameter, on slender villose pedicels, in broad lax hairy usually 15–18-flowered corymbs; calyx-tube narrowly obconic, coated with long matted pale hairs, the lobes slender, acuminate, irregularly glandular-serrate near the middle, glabrous on the outer, slightly villose on the inner surface, reflexed after anthesis; stamens 20, anthers slightly tinged with pink, styles 4 or 5. **Fruit** ripening from the middle to the end of September, on puberulous reddish pedicels, in erect or spreading few-fruited clusters, short-oblong to ovoid, scarlet, lustrous, pubescent especially near the rounded ends, marked by small dark dots, $\frac{2}{5}'$–$\frac{1}{2}'$ long, and about $1\frac{1}{3}'$ in diameter; calyx prominent, with long slender spreading and reflexed coarsely serrate usually persistent lobes villose on the upper surface; flesh thin, yellow, rather dry; nutlets 4 or 5, acute at the ends, prominently ridged on the back with a broad deeply grooved ridge, generally furnished with obscure ventral depressions, about $\frac{1}{4}'$ long.

A tree, sometimes 30° high, with a short trunk frequently 1° in diameter, covered with dark scaly bark, stout ascending branches forming a narrow open irregular head, and slen-

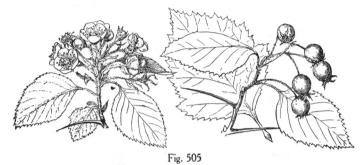

Fig. 505

der nearly straight glabrous branchlets dark orange-green when they first appear, becoming light chestnut-brown, lustrous and marked by pale lenticels in their first season, and armed with stout straight or slightly curved bright chestnut-brown shining spines $1\frac{1}{2}'-2'$ in length, long persistent and becoming branched on old stems.

Distribution. Fence rows, southwest of the village of Weston, near Toronto, Ontario.

8. COWANIA D. Don.

Trees or shrubs with scaly bark and rigid terete branchlets. Leaves alternate, simple, lobed or rarely linear, subcoriaceous, straight-veined, glandular-dotted on the upper surface, tardily deciduous or persistent, short-petiolate; stipules adnate to the base of the petiole. Flowers solitary at the end of short lateral branches; calyx-tube turbinate, persistent, the limb 5-lobed, deciduous, the lobes imbricated in the bud; disk thin, adnate to the tube of the calyx, its margins thickened; petals 5, obovate, spreading, larger than the calyx-lobes; stamens numerous, inserted in two rows in the mouth of the calyx-tube, incurved, persistent; anthers peltate, eglandular, 2-celled, opening longitudinally; carpels 5-12, inserted in the bottom of the calyx-tube, free, villose, 1-celled; style short, villose, stigma simple, filiform; ovule solitary, ascending: raphe linear, dorsal; micropyle inferior. Fruit composed of 5-12 1-celled ellipsoidal akenes, included in the tube of the calyx, and tipped with the much elongated persistent styles covered with long white hairs; seed filling the cavity of the carpel, linear-obovoid, erect; hilum basal, minute; testa membranaceous; albumen thin; cotyledons oblong, radicle inferior.

Cowania is confined to the dry interior region of the United States and Mexico. Three species can be distinguished; of these the type of the genus, *Cowania mexicana* D. Don, sometimes attains the size and habit of a small tree. The genus was named in honor of James Cowan (died 1823), an English merchant who traveled in Mexico and Peru and sent plants to England.

1. Cowania mexicana D. Don.

Cowania Stansburiana Torr.

Cowania Davidsonii Rydb.

Leaves short-petioled, cuneate, revolute on the margins, 3 or rarely 5-lobed above the middle, the lobes linear, entire or slightly divided, coriaceous, dark green above, hoary-tomentose below, $\frac{1}{3}'-\frac{1}{2}'$ long, tardily deciduous or persistent until spring; leaves on vigorous shoots and on flower-bearing branchlets occasionally linear and entire; stipules ciliate on the margins, united below and adnate to the short persistent petiole, free above the middle and acute at apex, persistent and becoming woody on the flower-bearing branchlets. Flowers appearing in early spring, 1' in diameter; calyx-tube more or less tomentose and covered with rigid glandular hairs, the lobes rounded at apex, hoary-tomentose; petals broad-obovate, rounded and emarginate at apex, cuneate and short-stipitate below, pale yellow or nearly white. Fruit ripening in October, about $\frac{1}{4}'$ long and as long as the calyx-tube, the elongated style often 2' in length.

A tree, occasionally 20°–25° high, with a tall trunk 6'–8' in diameter, short spreading branches forming a narrow head, and slender rigid branchlets red and glandular during

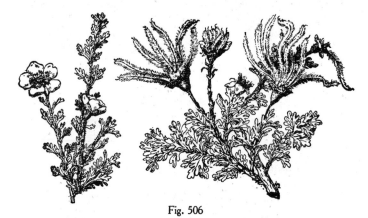

Fig. 506

their first season, becoming dark reddish brown and glabrous the following year. Bark of the trunk pale gray, separating freely into long narrow thin loosely attached plates; more often a shrub with spreading stems often only a few feet tall.

Distribution. Dry rocky slopes and mesas, usually at altitudes between 6000° and 8000°; northern Utah and central Nevada, through Arizona and western New Mexico to northern Mexico; common and probably of its largest size near the southern rim of the Grand Cañon, and on the lower slopes of the San Francisco Mountains, Arizona.

9. CERCOCARPUS H. B. K.   Mountain Mahogany.

Trees or shrubs, with scaly bark, rigid terete branches, short lateral spur-like branchlets conspicuously roughened for many years by the crowded narrow horizontal scars of fallen leaves, minute buds, the scales of the inner rows accrescent on the growing shoots and often colored. Leaves alternate, simple, entire or serrate, coriaceous, straight-veined, short-petiolate, persistent; stipules minute, adnate to the base of the petiole, deciduous. Flowers axillary on the short lateral branchlets, sessile or short-pedicellate, solitary or fascicled, the pedicels sometimes lengthening before the fruit ripens; calyx-tube long, cylindric, abruptly expanded at apex into a cup-shaped, 5-lobed deciduous limb, the lobes imbricated in the bud; disk thin, slightly glandular, adnate to the tube of the calyx; petals 0; stamens 15–30, in 2 or 3 rows; filaments incurved in the bud, free, short, terete; anthers oblong, pubescent or tomentose, distinct and united by a broad connective; ovary composed of a single carpel inserted in the bottom and included in the tube of the calyx, acute, terete, smooth, striate or sulcate, sericeous, rarely bicarpellate; style terminal, filiform, villose or glabrate, crowned with a minute obtuse stigma; ovule solitary, subbasilar, ascending; raphe dorsal; micropyle inferior. Fruit a linear-oblong coriaceous slightly ridged angled or sulcate akene, included in the persistent tube of the spindle-shaped calyx more or less deeply cleft at the apex, and tipped with the elongated persistent style clothed with long white hairs. Seed solitary, linear, acute, erect; hilum conspicuous lateral above the oblique base; testa membranaceous; embryo filling the cavity of the seed; cotyledons ovate-oblong, elongated, fleshy; radicle inferior.

Cercocarpus is confined to the dry interior and mountainous regions of North America. Twenty-one species, often of doubtful value, have been distinguished; seventeen are credited to the territory of the United States and the others to Mexico. The heavy hard brittle wood of all the species makes valuable fuel and is occasionally used in the manufacture of small articles for domestic and industrial use.

The generic name, from κέρκος and καρπός, refers to the peculiar long-tailed fruit.

CONSPECTUS OF THE ARBORESCENT SPECIES OF THE UNITED STATES.

Flowers usually in many-flowered clusters.
> Leaves coarsely serrate above the middle.
>> Leaves oval to semiorbicular or obovate, hoary-tomentose below, sinuate-dentate; flowers short-pedicellate.   **1. C. Traskiæ.**
>> Leaves oval to slightly obovate, green and glabrous below, denticulate with broad apiculate teeth; flowers long-pedicellate.   **2. C. alnifolius.**
> Leaves finely serrate above the middle, obovate to oval, pale and villose below; flowers short-pedicellate.   **3. C. betuloides.**
Flowers solitary or rarely in 2 or 3-flowered clusters, nearly sessile.
> Leaves narrow-lanceolate, lance-elliptic or oblanceolate, acute at the ends, entire, pale or rufous below.   **4. C. ledifolius.**
> Leaves oblong-obovate to narrow-elliptic, entire or slightly dentate below the apex, villose-pubescent.   **5. C. paucidentatus.**

2. Cercocarpus Traskiæ Eastw.

Leaves oval to semiorbicular or obovate, rounded or acute at apex, cuneate, rounded or occasionally somewhat cordate at the narrow base, revolute on the margins, entire below,

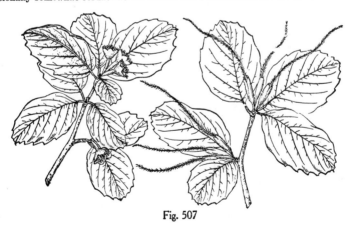

Fig. 507

coarsely sinuate-dentate above the middle with slender teeth tipped with minute dark glands, when they unfold covered above with soft pale hairs and below with thick hoary tomentum, and at maturity coriaceous, dark green, lustrous and villose or nearly glabrous on the upper surface, pale-tomentose on the lower surface, $1\frac{1}{2}'-2'$ long, and $1'-1\frac{1}{2}'$ wide, with prominent primary veins running obliquely to the point of the teeth, and, like the stout midrib, conspicuously impressed on the upper side; petioles stout, hoary-tomentose, about $\frac{1}{4}'$ in length; stipules acuminate, scarious, covered on the margins with long white hairs, $\frac{1}{4}'$ long. **Flowers** appearing early in March, nearly sessile, in 1–5 usually 4 or 5-flowered clusters, hoary-tomentose, $\frac{1}{2}'-\frac{3}{4}'$ long; calyx broad, glabrous on the inner surface; anthers tomentose. **Fruit:** mature calyx, light reddish brown, villose-pubescent, deeply cleft at apex, $\frac{1}{2}'$ long; akene slightly ridged on the back, $\frac{1}{3}'$ in length, covered with long lustrous white hairs; style $1\frac{1}{2}'-2'$ in length.

A tree, occasionally 25° high, with a trunk often inclining, usually much contorted, $2'-10'$ in diameter and 6°–8° long, stout wide-spreading branches, and stout branchlets, hoary-tomentose when they first appear, marked by numerous small scattered lenticels, bright reddish brown during two or three years, ultimately dark gray-brown and conspicuously roughened by the enlarged ring-like leaf-scars. **Bark** light gray, sometimes slightly broken by shallow fissures and marked by irregular cream-colored blotches.

Distribution. Steep sides of a deep narrow arroyo on the south coast of Santa Catalina Island, California.

2. Cercocarpus alnifolius Rydb.

Cercocarpus parvifolius Sarg., in part, not Nutt.

Leaves occasionally persistent until late in the spring, oval to slightly obovate, rounded or rarely acute at apex, rounded or cuneate at base, and coarsely serrate above the middle with broad apiculate teeth, when they unfold covered above with soft white hairs and pale and

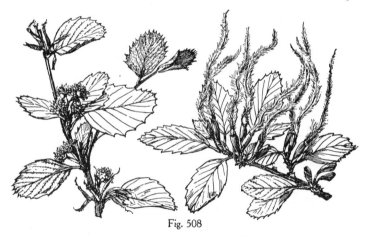

Fig. 508

villose on the midrib and veins below, and at maturity thick, glabrous, dark green and lustrous on the upper surface, pale and yellow-green on the lower surface, $1\frac{1}{2}'-2\frac{1}{2}'$ long, and $1'-2'$ wide, with a stout midrib and 6–7 pairs of slender prominent veins; petioles stout, sparingly villose early in the season, soon glabrous, $\frac{1}{3}'-\frac{1}{2}'$ long; stipules ovate, abruptly long-pointed, covered with silky white hairs. **Flowers** on slender hairy pedicels $\frac{1}{3}'-\frac{1}{2}'$ long, in 2–15 usually 4 or 5-flowered clusters; calyx-tube villose, about $\frac{5}{12}'$ long, the limb villose on the outer surface, $\frac{1}{4}'$ broad. **Fruit:** mature calyx-tube many-nerved, deeply cleft at apex, villose-pubescent, dark chestnut-brown, $\frac{1}{3}'-\frac{1}{2}'$ long; akene covered with long silky hairs; style $2'-2\frac{1}{2}'$ in length.

A tree, 12°–20° high, with one or two or three trunks, occasionally 8' in diameter, small erect and spreading branches forming a narrow round-topped head, and slender branchlets green and sparingly villose when they first appear, soon becoming glabrous, and in their second year chestnut-brown and lustrous and marked by minute pale lenticels. **Bark** about ¼′ thick, dark reddish brown, fissured and divided into small closely appressed scales.

Distribution. Hillsides, Descanso Cañon, about a mile and a half up the coast west of Avalon, Santa Catalina Island, and on Santa Cruz Island, California.

3. Cercocarpus betuloides Nutt.

Cercocarpus parvifolius var. *betuloides* Sarg.

Leaves obovate to oval, acute or rounded at apex, cuneate at base, finely serrate above the middle with straight or incurved glandular teeth, dark green on the upper surface, pale and villose-pubescent or tomentose sometimes becoming nearly glabrous on the lower

Fig. 509

surface, 1′–1¼′ long, and ⅓′–½′ wide, with a thin midrib, and 5–8 pairs of slender primary veins more or less deeply impressed on the upper side of the leaf; petioles densely villose, often becoming glabrous, about ¼′ in length; stipules scarious, acuminate. **Flowers** nearly sessile, in 1–3-flowered clusters; calyx-tube densely villose, about ⅓′ long, the limb turbinate, villose on the outer surface, glabrous on the inner surface, ¼′ wide. **Fruit** on slender slightly villose pedicels ¼′–⅓′ in length; mature calyx-tube often slightly gibbous, deeply cleft at apex, light chestnut-brown, sparingly villose, ¹⁄₁₂′ in diameter; akene covered with stiff spreading hairs; style 2′–3′ in length.

A tree, occasionally 25° high, with a single trunk, small ascending and spreading branches forming an open irregular head, and slender red-brown branchlets covered when they first appear with loose pubescence, soon becoming glabrous; more often a tall or low shrub with several stems. **Bark** smooth, separating into thin deciduous scales.

Distribution. Common and widely distributed over the California coast ranges from Siskiyou County to the Santa Monica and San Bernardino Mountains.

4. Cercocarpus ledifolius Nutt.

Leaves narrow-lanceolate, lance-elliptic or oblanceolate, acute at the ends, apiculate, entire with thick revolute margins, coriaceous, reticulate-veined, puberulous while young, and at maturity dark green, lustrous and glabrous on the upper surface and pale or rufous and tomentulose on the lower surface, resinous, ½′–1′ long, and ⅛′–⅔′ wide, with a broad thick midrib deeply grooved on the upper side, and obscure primary veins; persistent until the end of their second summer; petioles broad, about $\frac{1}{8}'$ in length; stipules nearly triangular. **Flowers** solitary, sessile in the axils of the clustered leaves, $\frac{2}{3}'$ long; calyx hoary-tomentose. **Fruit**: mature calyx-tube almost $\frac{1}{2}'$ long, nearly cylindric, rather larger above than below, 10-ribbed, obscurely 10-angled, slightly cleft at apex, hoary-tomentose; akene pointed at the ends, obscurely angled, chestnut-brown, $\frac{1}{4}'$ long, covered with long pale or tawny hairs; style $2'-3'$ in length, generally contracted by 1 or 2 partial corkscrew twists.

A resinous slightly aromatic tree, occasionally 40° high, with a short trunk sometimes $2\frac{1}{2}°$ in diameter, stout spreading usually contorted branches forming a round compact head, and red-brown branchlets coated at first with pale pubescence, soon becoming glabrous, frequently covered with a glaucous bloom, silver gray or dark brown in their second year, and for many years marked by the conspicuous elevated leaf-scars. **Bark** red-brown, divided by deep broad furrows, and broken on the surface into thin persistent plate-like

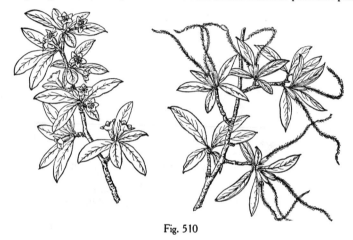

Fig. 510

scales, becoming on old trunks 1' thick. **Wood** bright clear red or rich dark brown, with thin yellow sapwood of 15–20 layers of annual growth.

Distribution. Dry gravelly arid slopes at altitudes of 5000°–9000°; mountain ranges of the interior region of the United States from eastern Washington and Oregon, to lower Green and Snake River valleys, Wyoming, and through Utah and Nevada to southwestern Colorado; in California to the eastern slope of the Sierra Nevada, the northern slopes of the San Bernardino Mountains, on Mt. Pinos, San Diego County, and on the northern coast mountains (Snow Mountain to Scott Mountain, *Jepson*).

5. Cercocarpus paucidentatus Britt.

Cercocarpus eximius Rydb.

Leaves oblong-obovate to narrow-elliptic, acute or rounded and often apiculate at apex, gradually narrowed from above the middle and acute at base, their margins revolute, often undulate, and entire or dentate toward the apex with few small straight or incurved apiculate teeth, when they unfold coated with hoary tomentum, and at maturity thick, gray-green and covered with soft white hairs or nearly glabrous on the upper surface, pale and tomentulose on the lower surface, $\frac{1}{2}'-1'$ long and $\frac{1}{4}'-\frac{1}{2}'$ wide, with a thin prominent midrib and primary veins; petioles stout, tomentose, ultimately pubescent or nearly glabrous, $\frac{1}{16}'-\frac{1}{8}'$ in length; stipules linear-lanceolate, tomentose, about half as long as the petioles. **Flowers** appearing from March to May and often again in August, nearly sessile, solitary, in pairs or rarely in 3-flowered clusters in the axils of the crowded leaves; calyx-tube slender, $\frac{1}{6}'-\frac{1}{4}'$ long, thickly covered on the outer surface, like the short rounded lobes, with long white hairs. **Fruit:** mature calyx-tube short-stalked, light red-brown, villose, deeply cleft at apex, about $\frac{1}{4}'$ long; akene nearly terete, covered with long white hairs; style $1'-1\frac{1}{2}'$ in length.

A tree, 20°–25° high, with a long straight trunk sometimes 6′–8′ in diameter, erect rigid branches forming a narrow open or irregular head, and slender bright red-brown lustrous branchlets marked irregularly by large scattered pale lenticels, covered at first with a thick coat of hoary tomentum, villose or pubescent for two or three years and ultimately ashy

Fig. 511

gray or gray tinged with red, the spur-like lateral branchlets much roughened by the ring-like scars of fallen leaves. **Bark** about $\frac{1}{8}'$ thick, divided by shallow fissures and broken on the surface into small light red-brown scales.

Distribution. In forests of Pines and Oaks usually at altitudes of about 5000°, on the dry ridges of the mountains of western Texas, and of southern New Mexico and Arizona; in Arizona ranging northward to Oak Creek Cañon, near Flagstaff, Coconino County (*P. Lowell*); and southward over the mountains of northern Mexico.

10. PRUNUS B. & H. Plum and Cherry

Trees or shrubs, with bitter astringent properties, slender branchlets, marked by the usually small elevated horizontal leaf-scars with 2 or 3 fibro-vascular bundle-scars, and small scaly buds, their scales imbricated in many rows, those of the inner rows accrescent and often colored. Leaves convolute or conduplicate in the bud, alternate, simple, usually serrate, petiolate, deciduous or persistent; stipules free from the petiole, usually lanceolate and glandular, often minute, early deciduous. Flowers in axillary umbels or corymbs, or in terminal or axillary racemes, appearing from separate buds before, with, or later than the leaves, or on leafy branches; calyx 5-lobed, the lobes imbricated in the bud; disk thin, adnate to the calyx-tube, glandular, often colored; petals 5, white, deciduous; stamens usually 15–20, inserted with the petals in 3 rows, those of the outer row 10, opposite the petals, those of the next row alternate with them and with those of the inner row, sometimes 30 in 3 rows; filaments filiform, free, incurved in the bud; anthers oval, attached on the back; ovary inserted in the bottom of the calyx-tube, 1-celled; style terminal, dilated at apex into a truncate stigma; ovules 2, suspended; raphe ventral; the micropyle superior. Fruit a 1-seeded drupe; flesh thick and pulpy or dry and coriaceous; stone bony, smooth, rugose, or pitted, compressed, indehiscent.   Seed filling the cavity of the nut, suspended; seed-coat thin, membranaceous, pale brown; cotyledons thick and fleshy; radicle superior.

Prunus with about one hundred and twenty species is generally distributed over the temperate regions of the northern hemisphere, and is abundant in North America, eastern Asia, western and central Asia and central Europe, ranging southward in the New World into tropical America, and to southern Asia in the Old World.   Of the twenty-five or thirty species which occur in the United States, twenty-two are arborescent in habit.   Several of the species bear fruits which are important articles of human food; many contain in the seeds and leaves hydrocyanic acid, to which is due their peculiar odor, and the fruit of some of the species is used to flavor cordials.   The wood of Prunus is close-grained, solid, and durable, and a few of the species are important timber-trees.

Prunus is the classical name of the Plum-tree.

CONSPECTUS OF THE NORTH AMERICAN ARBORESCENT SPECIES.

Flowers in sessile axillary umbels; fruit usually slightly 2-lobed by a ventral groove, generally more than $\frac{1}{2}'$ in diameter, red to nearly black or yellow, often covered with a glaucous bloom.   PRUNOPHORA.   PLUMS.
  Leaves convolute in the bud, their petioles usually without glands.
    Leaves broad-ovate to orbicular; fruit often 1′ or more in diameter, red or yellow,
      nearly destitute of bloom.   1. **P. subcordata** (G).
    Leaves ovate-lanceolate to oblong or obovate; fruit $\frac{1}{2}'$ in diameter or less, blue, nearly
      black, red or yellow, covered with a glaucous bloom.   **2. P. umbellata** (C).
  Leaves conduplicate in the bud.
    Leaves dull dark green, usually abruptly pointed at apex.
      Fruit red, rarely yellow, or blue in one form of 2 and 5; leaves oblong to obovate;
        stone of the fruit compressed.
        Leaves crennate-serrate, their petioles biglandular; calyx-lobes glandular.
                                                          3. **P. nigra** (A).
        Leaves sharply serrate with slender often apiculate teeth.
          Leaves narrowed and usually cuneate at base.
            Leaves glabrous or villose on the midrib below; petioles and calyx-lobes usu-
              ally without glands.   4. **P. americana** (A, C, F).
            Leaves pubescent below; fruit covered with a thick glaucous bloom.
              Petioles eglandular or with a single gland near the apex; pedicel of the
                flower glabrous; calyx-tube puberulous; stone of the fruit rounded at
                base.   5. **P. lanata** (A, C).
              Petioles glandular near the apex with 1-3 prominent glands; pedicel of
                the flower furnished near the apex, like the glabrous calyx-tube, with
                long white hairs; stone of the fruit pointed at base.
                                                          6. **P. tenuifolia** (C).
          Leaves usually broad and rounded at base, ovate to elliptic or obovate, con-
            spicuously reticulate-venulose; petioles glandular.   7. **P. mexicana** (C).
      Fruit purple, covered with a glaucous bloom; leaves lanceolate to oblong-ovate; peti-
        oles and calyx-lobes without glands; stone of the fruit turgid.
                                                          8. **P. alleghaniensis** (A).
    Leaves thin and lustrous, acute or acuminate, narrowed at base; petioles usually glan-
      dular; fruit red or yellow, the stone turgid.
      Calyx-lobes glandular.
        Leaves oblong-obovate to oblong-oval or rarely oblong-lanceolate.
                                                          9. **P. hortulana** (A).
        Leaves elliptic to lanceolate.   10. **P. Munsoniana** (A, C).
      Calyx-lobes without glands; leaves lanceolate to oblong-lanceolate.
                                                          11. **P. angustifolia** (A, C).

Flowers in axillary umbels or corymbs; fruit bright red and lustrous, $\frac{1}{2}'$ in diameter or less; leaves conduplicate in the bud. MAHALEB. BIRD CHERRIES.

Leaves oblong-lanceolate, acuminate or rarely acute at apex.

12. P. pennsylvanica (A, B, F).

Leaves oblong-obovate to oblanceolate, usually obtuse, occasionally acute at apex.

13. P. emarginata (B, F, G).

Flowers in terminal racemes on leafy branches of the year; fruit globose, red or rarely yellow; leaves conduplicate in the bud. PADUS. WILD CHERRIES.

Calyx-lobes deciduous from the fruit; leaves oblong-oval or obovate, abruptly pointed, cuneate, rounded or in one form cordate at base. 14. P. virginiana (A, B, F, G).

Calyx-lobes persistent on the fruit.

Petioles biglandular near the apex.

Leaves oblong to oblong-lanceolate, acuminate, glabrous, or rarely pubescent on the midrib below. 15. P. serotina (A, C).

Leaves oval, broad-ovate or rarely obovate, acute, short-pointed or rounded at apex, villose-pubescent below. 16. P. alabamensis (C).

Leaves obovate, oval or elliptic, short-pointed or rounded at apex, covered below with rufous hairs. 17. P. australis (C).

Petioles without glands; leaves elliptic to ovate or slightly obovate, acute, rounded or abruptly short-pointed at apex, in one form rusty pubescent on the midrib below.

18. P. virens (E, F, H).

Flowers in racemes from the axils of persistent leaves of the previous year; fruit globose or slightly three-lobed; leaves conduplicate in the bud. LAUROCERASUS. CHERRY LAURELS.

Calyx-lobes rounded, undulate on the margins; leaves oblong-lanceolate, acuminate, entire or rarely remotely spinulose-serrate; fruit black, the stone broad-ovoid, acute, cylindric. 19. P. caroliniana (C).

Calyx-lobes acute, minute.

Leaves elliptic to oblong-ovate, entire; fruit orange-brown, the stone subglobose.

20. P. myrtifolia (D).

Leaves ovate to ovate-lanceolate, acute, rounded or emarginate at apex, conspicuously spinulose-dentate; fruit red, becoming purple or nearly black, the stone ovoid, short-pointed. 21. P. ilicifolia (G).

Leaves ovate to lanceolate, acuminate or abruptly short-pointed at apex, usually entire; fruit dark purple or nearly black, the stone ovoid to obovoid, short-pointed.

22. P. Lyonii (G).

1. Prunus subcordata Benth. Wild Plum.

Leaves broad-ovate or orbicular, usually cordate, sometimes truncate or rarely cuneate at base, and sharply often doubly serrate, when they unfold puberulous on the upper surface and pubescent on the lower surface, and at maturity glabrous, or puberulous below, slightly coriaceous, dark green above and pale below, $1'-3'$ long and $\frac{1}{2}-2'$ wide, with a broad midrib and conspicuous veins; northward turning brilliant scarlet and orange or red and yellow in the autumn before falling; petioles slender, usually eglandular, $\frac{1}{4}-\frac{3}{4}'$ in length; stipules lanceolate, acute, glandular-serrate. Flowers appearing before the leaves in March and April, $\frac{2}{3}'$ in diameter, on slender glabrous or pubescent pedicels $\frac{1}{4}-\frac{1}{2}'$ long, in 2-4-flowered umbels; calyx-tube campanulate, glabrous or puberulous, the lobes oblong-obovate, rounded at apex, pubescent on the outer surface, more or less clothed with pale hairs on the inner surface, half as long as the obovate white petals rounded above and narrowed below into a short claw. Fruit ripening in August and September, on stout pedicels $\frac{1}{2}-\frac{2}{3}'$ long, short-oblong, $\frac{1}{2}-1\frac{1}{4}'$ long, with dark red or sometimes bright yellow skin, and more or less subacid flesh; stone flattened or turgid, acute at the ends, $\frac{1}{3}-1'$ long, narrowly wing-margined on the ventral suture, conspicuously grooved on the dorsal suture.

A tree, $20°-25°$ high, with a trunk sometimes a foot in diameter, dividing $6°-8°$ from the ground into stout almost horizontal branches, and glabrous or pubescent bright red more or less spinescent branchlets marked by occasional minute pale lenticels, becoming darker red or purple in their second year, and ultimately dark brown or ashy gray; or often a bush, with stout ascending stems 10°–12° tall, or a low much-branched shrub. **Winter-buds** acute, $\frac{1}{8}'$ long, with chestnut-brown scales, scarious on the margins, those of the inner rows

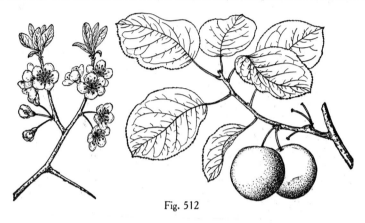

Fig. 512

$\frac{1}{4}'$ long at maturity, oblong, acute, and generally bright red. **Bark** about $\frac{1}{4}'$ thick, gray-brown, deeply fissured, and divided into long thick plates broken on the surface into minute persistent scales. **Wood** heavy, hard, close-grained, pale brown, with thin lighter colored sapwood of 5 or 6 layers of annual growth.

Distribution. Dry rocky hills and open woods usually in the neighborhood of streams, sometimes forming thickets of considerable extent; central Oregon to northeastern California in the region east of the Cascade and Sierra Nevada Mountains, and common to central California; on the foothills of the western slopes of the Sierra Nevada up to altitudes of 4000° south to the Yosemite Valley, and on the coast ranges to Black Mountain, Santa Clara County; of its largest size on the borders of small streams in southern Oregon and northern California; at high altitudes, and in the arid regions of southeastern Oregon a low shrub producing sparingly small sometimes pubescent fruit (var. *oregona* Wight); Klamath Indian Reservation, near Klamath Falls and in Sprague River Valley, Klamath County.

2. Prunus umbellata Ell. Sloe. Black Sloe.

Leaves obovate-lanceolate to oblong, acute at the ends or sometimes rounded or slightly cordate at base, finely and sharply serrate with remote incurved glandular teeth, and usually furnished with 2 large dark glands at the base, when they unfold bright bronze-green, with red margins, midrib, and petiole, glabrous above and pubescent or glabrous below with the exception of a few hairs along the prominent orange-colored midrib and primary veins, and at maturity thin, dark green above, paler below, $2'–2\frac{1}{2}'$ long and $1'–1\frac{1}{2}'$ wide, petioles stout, glabrous or pubescent, about $\frac{1}{3}'$ in length; stipules lanceolate, setaceous, glandular-serrate, $\frac{1}{4}'–\frac{2}{3}'$ long. **Flowers** opening in March and April before the appearance of the leaves, $\frac{2}{3}'$ in diameter, on slender glabrous pedicels $\frac{1}{2}'$ long, in 3 or 4-flowered umbels; calyx-tube broad-obconic, glabrous or puberulous, the lobes sometimes slightly clavate at the acute red apex, scarious on the margins, and hoary-tomentose on the inner surface; petals nearly orbicular, contracted at the base into a short claw. **Fruit** ripening from July to September, on slender stems $\frac{1}{2}'$ to nearly $1'$ long, globose, without a basal depression, about $\frac{1}{2}'$ in diameter, with a tough thick black or on some individuals yellow, and on others bright red skin covered with a glaucous bloom, and thick acid flesh; stone flattened with thin brittle walls, $\frac{1}{2}'$ long, $\frac{1}{4}'-\frac{5}{16}'$ wide and half as thick, acute at the ends, slightly rugose, conspicuously ridged on the ventral suture, and slightly grooved on the dorsal suture.

A tree, sometimes 15°–20° high, with a short often crooked or inclining trunk 6′–10′ in diameter, slender unarmed branches forming a wide compact flat-topped head, and slender branchlets more or less densely coated at first with pale pubescence, soon becoming glabrous, lustrous and bright red, and in their second year dark dull brown and marked by

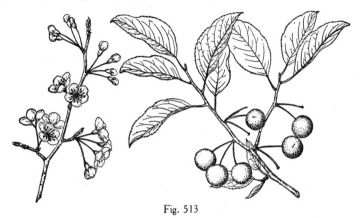

Fig. 513

occasional orange-colored oblong lenticels; or frequently a low shrub. **Winter-buds** about $\frac{1}{16}'$ long, with acute chestnut-brown apiculate scales, those of the inner rows at maturity $\frac{1}{4}'$ long and red at the apex. **Bark** $\frac{1}{4}'$ thick, dark brown, separating into small appressed persistent scales. **Wood** heavy, hard, close-grained, dark reddish brown, with thick lighter colored sapwood of about 30 layers of annual growth. The fruit is used in large quantities in making jellies and jams.

Distribution. Stanly County (near Albemarle, *J. S. Holmes*), North Carolina, and South Carolina southward, usually in the neighborhood of the coast, to Orange County, Florida, and westward to eastern Texas and southern Arkansas. The form with red fruit common in the interior of the Florida peninsula (Orange County). Variable in the amount of its pubescence and slightly variable in the shape of the fruit, and passing into var. *injucunda* Sarg. (*Prunus mitis* Beadl.) A small tree with branchlets hoary tomentose when they first appear, becoming pubescent, and puberulous in their second season, leaves more or less tomentose below, villose pedicels, calyx and ovary, and subglobose to short-oblong fruit. Central and southern Georgia (base of Stone Mountain and Little Stone Mountain, De Kalb County, and near Augusta, Richmond County), and eastern Alabama (near Auburn, Lee County). More distinct is

Prunus umbellata var. tarda Wight

Prunus tarda Sarg.

Differing from the type in the more oblong stone of the later-ripening fruit, lighter-colored bark and larger size.

Leaves oblong or oval, or occasionally obovate, acute or acuminate and short-pointed at apex, gradually narrowed and cuneate at base, and finely serrate with straight or incurved teeth tipped with dark minute persistent glands, when they unfold glabrous or rarely scabrous or puberulous above and cinereo-tomentose below, and at maturity thick and firm, dark yellow-green and glabrous on the upper surface, pale and pubescent or puberulous on the lower surface, especially along the prominent light yellow midrib and thin primary veins, $1\frac{1}{2}'$–$3'$ long and $\frac{3}{4}'$–$1\frac{1}{4}'$ wide; petioles stout, tomentose or ultimately pubescent, $\frac{1}{3}'$–$\frac{1}{2}'$ in length, glandular at apex with 2 large round stalked dark glands, or often eglandular; stipules acicular, often bright red, about $\frac{1}{3}'$ long. **Flowers** appearing early in April with or before the leaves, about $\frac{3}{4}'$ in diameter, on slender glabrous pedicels, in 2 or 3-flowered umbels; calyx-tube narrow-obconic, glabrous toward the base, villose above, the lobes acute, entire, villose on the outer surface, hoary-tomentose on the inner surface; petals oblong-obovate, gradually contracted below into a short claw. **Fruit** ripening late in October or early in November, on stout rigid pedicels, short-oblong to subglobose, $\frac{1}{3}'$–$\frac{1}{2}'$ long, clear bright yellow on some trees, bright red on others, and on others purple, dark blue, or black, with tough thick skin, and thick very acid flesh; stone ovoid more or less compressed, very rugose, obscurely ridged on the ventral suture and slightly grooved on the dorsal suture, acute and apiculate at apex, and rounded at base.

A tree, 20°–25° high, with a tall trunk 18′–20′ in diameter, wide-spreading branches forming an open symmetrical head, and slender branchlets marked by small scattered dark lenticels, light-green and hoary-tomentose when they first appear, becoming glabrous, light

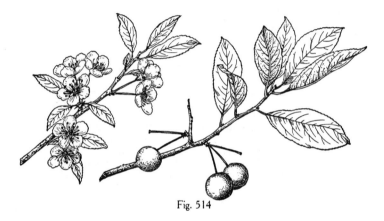

Fig. 514

red-brown and lustrous during their first summer and darker at the end of their second year. **Winter-buds** narrow, acute, the color of the branchlets, $\frac{1}{16}'$–$\frac{1}{8}'$ long. **Bark** $\frac{1}{2}'$–$\frac{5}{8}'$ thick, light brown tinged with red, and divided by shallow interrupted fissures into flat ridges broken on the surface into small loose plate-like scales.

Distribution. Glades and open woods in the neighborhood of Marshall, Harrison County, Texas, to western Louisiana, southern Arkansas, and western Mississippi.

3. Prunus nigra Ait   Red Plum.   Canada Plum.

Leaves oblong-ovate to obovate, abruptly contracted at apex into a long narrow point, cuneate, truncate or slightly cordate at base, and doubly crenate-serrate with small dark glandular teeth, when they unfold faintly tinged with red and pubescent on the under surface or glabrous with the exception of conspicuous tufts of slender white or rufous hairs in the axils of the primary veins, and at maturity thick and firm, dull dark green on the upper surface, pale on the lower surface, $3'$–$5'$ long and $1\frac{1}{2}'$–$3'$ wide, with a conspicuous pale midrib and slender veins; petioles stout, biglandular at apex with 2 large dark glands, $\frac{1}{2}'$–$1'$ in length; stipules lanceolate or on vigorous shoots often 3–5-lobed, glandular-serrate, $\frac{1}{2}'$ long. **Flowers** appearing in early spring with or before the leaves, $1\frac{1}{4}'$ in diameter, on slender glabrous dark red pedicels, $\frac{1}{2}'$–$\frac{2}{3}'$ long, in 3 or 4-flowered umbels; calyx-tube broad-obconic, dark red on the outer surface, bright red on the inner surface, the lobes narrow, acute, glandular, glabrous or occasionally pubescent on the outer surface, reflexed after the flowers open;

petals broad-ovate, rounded at apex, more or less erose on the margins, contracted at base into a short claw, white, turning pink in fading. **Fruit** ripening from the middle to the end of August, oblong-oval, $1'-1\frac{1}{4}'$ long, with a tough thick orange-red skin nearly destitute of bloom, and yellow rather austere flesh; stone oval, compressed, $1'$ long, $\frac{2}{3}'$ wide, thick-walled, acutely ridged on the ventral suture and slightly grooved on the dorsal suture.

A tree, $20°-30°$ high, with a trunk sometimes $8'-10'$ in diameter, divided usually $5°-6°$ from the ground into a number of stout upright branches forming a narrow rigid head, stout slightly zigzag branchlets marked by numerous pale excrescences, bright green, glabrous or puberulous at first, and dark brown tinged with red in their second season, and stout spiny lateral spur-like secondary branchlets. **Winter-buds** acuminate, $\frac{1}{8}'-\frac{1}{4}'$ long, with chestnut-brown, triangular scales pale and scarious on the margins. **Bark** about $\frac{1}{8}'$ thick, light gray-brown, with a smooth outer layer exfoliating in large thick plates of several papery layers, and in falling exposing the darker slightly fissured scaly inner bark. **Wood** heavy, hard, close-grained, rich bright red-brown, with thin lighter colored sapwood.

Distribution. In the alluvial soil of river valleys and on limestone hills; western New Brunswick (near the mouth of the Aroostook River) to the valley of the Saint Lawrence River and westward to the southern shore of Georgian Bay, the northern shore of Lake Superior (west of Port Arthur, Ontario), the valley of the Winnipeg River, Manitoba, and

Fig. 515

southward to northern New England, central and western New York, northern Ohio (Lorraine County), southern Michigan, northern Indiana (*C. C. Deam*), northeastern Illinois, southeastern and western Wisconsin (valley of the Wisconsin River), eastern Minnesota and North Dakota.

Often cultivated in Canadian gardens and occasionally in those of the northern states as a fruit-tree or for the beauty of its flowers. Varieties are propagated by pomologists.

4. Prunus americana Marsh. Wild Plum.

Leaves oval to oblong-oval or slightly obovate, acuminate at apex, narrowed and cuneate or rounded at base, and sharply often doubly serrate with slender apiculate teeth, when they unfold glabrous or slightly pubescent, and often furnished below with conspicuous axillary tufts of pale hairs, and at maturity thick and firm, more or less rugose, dark green on the upper surface, pale and glabrous on the lower surface, $3'-4'$ long and $1\frac{1}{2}'-1\frac{3}{4}'$ wide, with a thin midrib glabrous or villose-pubescent on the lower side, and slender primary veins; petioles slender, eglandular or furnished near the apex with one or two glands, glabrous or puberulous, $\frac{1}{2}'-\frac{3}{4}'$ in length. **Flowers** appearing in early spring before or with the unfolding of the leaves, $1'$ in diameter, bad-smelling, on slender glabrous pedicels

$\frac{1}{3}$–$\frac{2}{3}$' long, in 2–5-flowered umbels; calyx-tube narrow-obconic, bright red, glabrous or puberulous, green on the inner surface, the lobes lanceolate to oblong-lanceolate, obtuse or acute, eglandular or obscurely glandular above the middle, usually dentate toward the apex, glabrous or puberulous on the outer surface, soft-pubescent on the inner surface; petals rounded and irregularly laciniate at apex, contracted below into a long narrow claw, bright red at base, $\frac{1}{2}$' long and $\frac{1}{4}$' wide. **Fruit** ripening in June at the south and from the middle of August to early October at the north, subglobose or slightly elongated, usually rather less than 1' in diameter, in ripening turning from green to orange often with a red cheek, becoming bright red when fully ripe, usually destitute of bloom and more or less conspicuously marked by pale spots, with a thick tough acerb skin and bright yellow succulent rather juicy acid flesh; stone oval slightly rugose rounded at apex, more or less narrowed at base, $\frac{3}{4}$–1' long and $\frac{2}{3}$–$\frac{3}{5}$' wide, often as thick as broad, slightly and acutely ridged on the ventral suture and obscurely grooved on the dorsal suture.

A tree 20°–35° high, with a trunk rarely exceeding 1° in diameter and dividing usually 4° or 5° from the ground into many spreading branches often pendulous at the end and forming a broad graceful head and slender glabrous branchlets at first bright green, light orange-brown during their first winter, becoming darker and often tinged with red and marked by minute circular raised lenticels, and furnished with long slender remote sometimes spinescent lateral branchlets; usually spreading by shoots from the roots into broad thickets, or in the Gulf States growing with a single stem. **Winter-buds** acute, $\frac{1}{8}$–$\frac{1}{4}$' long, the chestnut-brown scales more or less erose on the margins, the inner scales when fully grown foliaceous, $\frac{1}{2}$' long, oblong, acute, remotely serrate, with 2 narrow acuminate lateral lobes. **Bark** about $\frac{1}{2}$' thick, dark brown tinged with red, the outer layer separating into long thin persistent plates, southward often lighter-colored. **Wood** heavy, hard, close-grained, strong, dark rich brown tinged with red, with thin lighter-colored sapwood. The fruit is sometimes used in the preparation of jellies and preserves, and is eaten raw or cooked.

Distribution. In the middle and northern states in rich soil, growing along the borders of streams and swamps; in the south Atlantic states often in river swamps; west of the

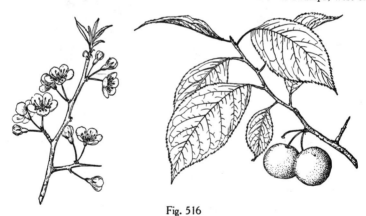

Fig. 516

Mississippi on bottom-lands, dry uplands and low mountain slopes; western Connecticut (Gaylordsville, Litchfield County), Eastern Greenbush, Rensselaer County and central New York to southern Ontario, central Michigan and northern Indiana, and northwestward to North Dakota, Manitoba (near Brandon), the Bitter Root Mountains, Wyoming and western Montana (Dixon, Sanders County), and southward to western Florida, central Mississippi, Alabama, eastern Louisiana, Missouri, southern Arkansas, eastern Kansas and Oklahoma, and in the Rocky Mountain region along the eastern foothills of Colorado to northern New Mexico (near Las Vegas, San Miguel County); and northeastern Utah (near Logan, Cache County); on the southern Appalachian Mountains ascending to altitudes of 3000°, and in South Carolina and Georgia extending to the immediate neighborhood of the coast; in the Rocky Mountain region usually a low shrub forming large thickets. Passing into the var. *floridana* Sarg., differing in its much thinner finely serrate leaves and purple fruit. A small tree without root suckers; low rich woods near St. Marks, Wakulla County, middle Florida; common.

5. Prunus lanata Mack. & Bush.

Prunus americana lanata Sudw.

Prunus Palmeri Sarg.

Leaves ovate to oblong-obovate, elliptic or rarely slightly obovate, abruptly acuminate and long-pointed at apex, gradually narrowed and cuneate or rarely rounded at base, and coarsely often doubly serrate with apiculate spreading teeth, when they unfold sparingly

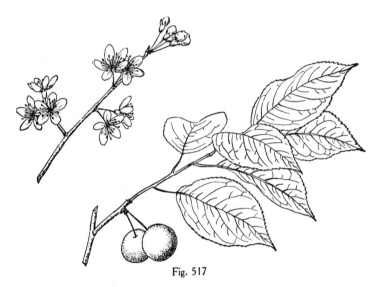

Fig. 517

covered above by short caducous hairs and below by long white spreading hairs, and at maturity thin, light yellow-green and glabrous on the upper surface, pale and more or less densely covered below with close soft pubescence at the south often becoming fuscous late in the season, and villose on the midrib and primary veins, $2\frac{1}{2}'-4'$ long and $1\frac{1}{2}'-2\frac{1}{2}'$ wide; petioles slender, pubescent, eglandular or furnished with a gland near the apex, $\frac{1}{2}'-\frac{2}{3}'$ in length, stipules linear, acuminate, occasionally 3-lobed, villose, sparingly glandular. **Flow-ers** about $\frac{3}{4}'$ in diameter, on slender glabrous pedicels $\frac{1}{2}'-\frac{2}{3}'$ in length, in 2–5-flowered umbels; calyx-tube narrow-obconic, puberulous, the lobes long, acuminate, entire or rarely slightly serrate toward the apex, ciliate on the margins, puberulous and more or less tinged with red on the outer surface, pubescent on the inner surface; petals oblong-oval, narrowed and rounded at apex, gradually narrowed below into a long claw, about $\frac{1}{4}'$ wide; stamens about 25; style elongated, exceeding the stamens. **Fruit** on drooping glabrous pedicels, ellipsoid, deep crimson covered with a glaucous bloom, often $1'$ long and $\frac{4}{5}'$ in diameter, with thick succulent flesh; stone oblong, compressed, rounded at base, pointed and apiculate at apex, ridged on the dorsal edge with a thin narrow ridge, thin and slightly grooved on the ventral edge.

A tree 20°–30° high, with a trunk 12′–18′ in diameter, small erect branches and slender unarmed branchlets light yellow-green and puberulous or pubescent when they first appear, usually becoming glabrous before the end of their first season, light orange-brown during their first season and dark red-brown the following year; sometimes a shrub only a few feet tall; usually growing with a single well-developed trunk; occasionally spreading by suckers from the roots into small thickets. **Winter-buds** acute, $\frac{1}{8}′-\frac{1}{5}′$ long, with light chestnut-brown puberulous scales ciliate on the margins. **Bark** pale gray-brown, exfoliating in large thin scales.

Distribution. Hillsides and river-bottom lands; southern Indiana (near Columbus, Bartholomew County, and Gordon Hills, Gibson County), through southern Illinois (Gallatin, Pope, Richland and Johnson Counties) to western Kentucky (Ballard and Hickman Counties); through Missouri and Arkansas to eastern Oklahoma, western Louisiana and eastern Texas to Wilson County (Southerland Springs); through eastern Louisiana (West Feliciana and Tammany Parishes), and near Selma, Dallas County, Alabama.

6. Prunus tenuifolia Sarg.

Leaves oblong to oblong-obovate or elliptic, gradually narrowed and acute or acuminate and often abruptly long-pointed at apex, cuneate or often narrowed and rounded at base, finely doubly serrate with teeth pointing to the apex of the leaf, at maturity thin, dark yellow-green and sparingly covered above with short soft white hairs, paler and soft pubes-

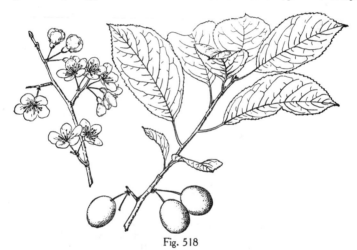

Fig. 518

cent below, especially on the slender midrib, and 7 or 8 pairs of thin primary veins connected by occasional cross veinlets, 3′–4′ long and $1\frac{1}{4}′$–2′ wide; petioles slender, pubescent, becoming puberulous or nearly glabrous, glandular near the apex with 1–3 prominent dark glands, or eglandular. **Flowers** $\frac{4}{5}′$ in diameter, opening from the middle to the end of March, on slender pedicels $\frac{2}{5}′$–$\frac{4}{5}′$ long, furnished near the apex with a few long white hairs, in 2–4-flowered sessile umbels; calyx-tube narrow-obconic, glabrous with the exception of occasional long scattered white hairs near the base, the lobes narrow, entire, or minutely dentate near the rounded apex, ciliate on the margins, pubescent on the outer surface, densely villose on the inner surface, reflexed after anthesis; petals white, ovate-oblong, narrowed and rounded at apex, crenulate above the middle, gradually narrowed below into a short claw. **Fruit** on stout slightly hairy or glabrous stems, oblong to oblong-obovoid, red, covered with a thick glaucous bloom, $\frac{3}{5}'-\frac{3}{4}'$ long and $\frac{1}{2}'-\frac{3}{5}'$ in diameter, with a thick skin and thin flesh; stone oblong, compressed, pointed at the ends, slightly sulcate at apex, unsymmetric, ridged on the full and rounded dorsal edge with a broad thin ridge, thin nearly straight and only slightly grooved on the ventral edge, $\frac{2}{5}'-\frac{3}{5}'$ long and about $\frac{1}{2}'$ wide.

A tree 30° high, with a tall trunk usually about 12' but occasionally 18' in diameter, stout spreading branches and stout or slender glabrous branchlets light orange green when they first appear, becoming light gray or red-brown and lustrous at the end of their first season, and dark dull red-brown the following year. **Bark** of the trunk and large branches thick, pale gray, and broken into long platelike scales.

Distribution. Dry Oak-woods near Jacksonville and Larissa, Cherokee County, Texas.

7. Prunus mexicana S. Wats. Big Tree Plum.

Prunus arkansana Sarg.

Leaves ovate to elliptic or obovate, abruptly long-pointed and acuminate at apex, rounded or rarely cuneate and often glandular at base, and finely doubly serrate with apiculate slender straight or slightly incurved teeth, at maturity thick, dark yellow-green,

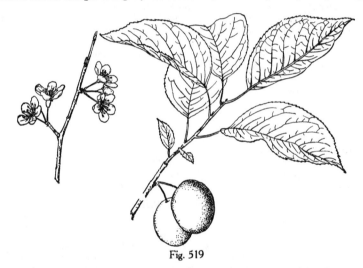

Fig. 519

glabrous and lustrous on the upper surface, paler and sparingly covered on the lower surface with long soft white hairs most abundant on the prominent midrib and primary veins and on the numerous conspicuous reticulate veinlets, $1\frac{3}{4}'-3\frac{1}{4}'$ long and $1\frac{1}{4}'-2'$ wide; petioles stout, pubescent or puberulous, glandular at apex with large dark glands, or eglandular, $\frac{2}{5}'-\frac{3}{5}'$ in length. **Flowers** appearing in March before the leaves, 1' in diameter, on slender glabrous pedicels in 3 or 4-flowered sessile umbels; calyx-tube narrow-obconic, glabrous, the lobes oblong or oblong-ovate, about as long as the tube, rounded and laciniate at apex or entire, ciliate and glandular on the margins with small sessile glands, puberulous on the outer surface, hoary-tomentose on the inner surface, reflexed after anthesis; petals sometimes puberulous on the outer surface toward the base, ovate-orbicular to oblong-ovate, rounded at the narrow apex, crenulate, abruptly or gradually narrowed below into a short claw, about 3 times as long as the calyx-lobes; style longer than the stamens. **Fruit** ripening from the end of August to early October, subglobose to short-oblong, rounded at the ends, dark purple-red with a slight glaucous bloom, $1\frac{1}{4}'$–$1\frac{1}{3}'$ long and $1'$–$1\frac{1}{4}'$ in diameter, with thick succulent flesh; stone smooth obovoid to nearly circular, turgid, unsymmetric, narrowed and rounded at base, rounded or short-pointed at apex, ridged on the rounded dorsal edge with a broad thin ridge, thin, less rounded and grooved on the ventral edge, $\frac{3}{4}'$–$1'$ long and about $\frac{1}{2}'$ wide.

A tree from $20°$–$25°$ high, with a trunk sometimes $8'$–$10'$ in diameter, stout branches forming an open irregular head, and slender glabrous branchlets light orange-brown, very lustrous and marked by dark lenticels during their first winter and dull gray-brown the following year. **Winter-buds** ovoid, acute, glabrous, $\frac{1}{4}'$ long. **Bark** dark, nearly black or light gray, exfoliating in platelike scales on young stems and large branches, becoming rough and deeply furrowed on old trunks.

Distribution. Open woods on rich alluvial bottom-lands, upland prairies and hillsides; southeastern Kansas (near Parsons, Labette County), through Arkansas to western Oklahoma (Navina, Logan County, Minca, Grady County), western Louisiana, northern and eastern Texas to the valley of the San Antonio River, ranging westward in Texas over the Edwards Plateau and to Brown and Palo Pinto Counties; in West Feliciana Parish, eastern Louisiana; in Coahuila and Nuevo Leon.

Passing into the following varieties:

Prunus mexicana var. **reticulata** Sarg. Differing in its thicker leaves more often narrowed at base, with more prominent reticulate veinlets, pubescent pedicels, globose fruit ripening late in September or in October, with thin, bitter, astringent flesh and dark deeply furrowed bark.

Distribution. Uplands and along the margins of river bottoms; neighborhood of Denison and Sherman, Grayson County, northern Texas.

Prunus mexicana var. **polyandra** Sarg. Differing in the narrowed base of the leaves, the more numerous stamens, in its earlier ripening fruit, with an obovoid compressed stone pointed at apex and gradually narrowed and acute at base.

Distribution. Rich woods near Fulton, Hempstead County, Arkansas.

Prunus mexicana var. **fultonensis** Sarg. Differing in its thinner leaves pubescent below over the whole surface, and in its smaller dark bluish-purple fruit, ripening in June, with thin flesh and a compressed stone pointed at apex and gradually narrowed and acute at base.

Distribution. Rich woods near Fulton, Hempstead County, Arkansas.

8. Prunus alleghaniensis Porter. Sloe.

Leaves lanceolate to oblong-ovate, often long-pointed, finely and sharply serrate with glandular teeth, and furnished at base with 2 large rather conspicuous glands, when they unfold covered with soft pubescence, and at maturity puberulous on the upper surface, and glabrous with the exception of a few hairs in the axils of the veins, or covered, especially along the broad midrib and conspicuous veins, with rufous pubescence on the lower surface, rather thick and firm in texture, dark green above and paler below, $2'$–$3\frac{1}{2}'$ long and $\frac{2}{3}'$–$1\frac{1}{4}'$ wide; petioles slender, grooved, pubescent or puberulous, $\frac{1}{4}'$–$\frac{1}{3}'$ in length. **Flowers** appearing in May with the unfolding of the leaves, $\frac{1}{2}'$ in diameter, on slender puberulous pedicels $\frac{1}{2}'$–$\frac{2}{3}'$ long, in 2–4-flowered umbels; calyx-tube narrow-obconic, pubescent or puberulous on the outer surface, the lobes ovate-oblong, rounded at apex, scarious on the margins, and coated with pale tomentum on the inner surface; petals rounded at apex, contracted at base into a short claw, turning pink in fading. **Fruit** ripening the middle of August, on stout puberulous pedicels, subglobose or slightly oval to obovoid, $\frac{1}{4}'$–$\frac{2}{3}'$ in diameter, with thick rather tough dark reddish-purple skin covered with a glaucous bloom, and yellow juicy austere flesh; stone thin-walled, turgid, two thirds as thick as broad, $\frac{1}{4}'$–$\frac{1}{2}'$ long, pointed at the ends, ridged on the ventral suture, and slightly grooved on the dorsal suture.

A slender tree, occasionally $18°$–$20°$ high, with a trunk sometimes $6'$–$8'$ in diameter, dividing into numerous erect rigid branches, and branchlets at first coated with pale caducous pubescence, becoming dark red and rather lustrous in their first winter, and ultimately nearly black, and unarmed, or sometimes armed with stout spinescent lateral spur-like branchlets. **Winter-buds** acuminate or obtuse, $\frac{1}{16}'$ long, their inner scales accrescent, scarious, oblong, acute, $\frac{2}{3}'$ long, bright red at apex. **Bark** $\frac{1}{4}'$ thick, dark brown, fissured and

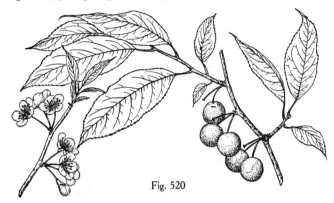

Fig. 520

broken on the surface into thin persistent scales. **Wood** heavy, hard, close-grained, brown tinged with red, with thin pale sapwood of 10–12 layers of annual growth. The fruit is made into preserves, jellies and jams.

Distribution. Low moist soil, often forming shrubby thickets sometimes of considerable extent, and dry ridges; slopes of Tusseys Mountain in the northwestern part of Huntingdon County, and over the main range of the Alleghany Mountains into Clearfield and Elk Counties, Pennsylvania; rocky ridges near the Natural Bridge, Rockbridge County, Virginia, and lower slopes of Peak Mountain on South Fork of Buffalo Creek, Ashe County, North Carolina (*W. W. Ashe*), and in southern Connecticut; of its largest size on limestone bluffs south of the Little Juniata River, Pennsylvania. A shrubby variety with leaves broader in proportion to their length and less acuminate at apex (var. *Davisii* Wight) occurs in Roscommon and Montmorency Counties, Michigan.

9. Prunus hortulana Bailey.   Wild Plum.

Leaves oblong-obovate to oblong-oval or rarely to oblong-lanceolate, acuminate and contracted at apex into a long slender point, cuneate or more or less rounded at the narrow base, and finely serrate with incurved lanceolate glandular teeth, when they unfold pilose with slender white hairs, and at maturity glabrous above, pilose below in the axils of the primary veins and along the midrib with tawny hairs, thin but firm, dark green and lustrous on the upper surface paler on the lower surface, $4'$–$6'$ long and $1'$–$1\frac{1}{2}'$ wide, with a broad conspicuous orange-colored midrib, primary veins connected near the margins of the leaf, and prominent reticulate veinlets; petioles slender, orange-colored, $1'$–$1\frac{1}{2}'$ in length and furnished above the middle with numerous scattered dark glands; stipules lanceolate, acuminate, glandular-serrate, early deciduous. **Flowers** appearing in April or early in May when the leaves are about one-third grown, $\frac{2}{3}'$–$1'$ in diameter, on slender puberulous pedicels $\frac{1}{2}'$ long, in 2–4-flowered umbels; calyx-tube narrow-obconic, the lobes about as long as the tube, oblong-ovate, acute or rounded at apex, glandular-serrate, glabrous or puberulous on the outer surface, pubescent or tomentose on the inner surface chiefly toward the base, reflexed after the unfolding of the narrow oval or oblong-orbicular petals rounded and occasionally emarginate at apex, contracted below into a long narrow claw, entire, erose, or occasionally serrate, and white often marked with orange toward the base. **Fruit** ripening in September and October, on stout stems, globose or rarely ellipsoid, $\frac{3}{4}'$–$1'$ in diameter, with thick deep red or sometimes yellow lustrous skin, and hard austere thin flesh; stone turgid, $\frac{2}{3}'-\frac{3}{4}'$ long, compressed at the ends, abruptly short-pointed or rounded at apex, rounded or truncate at base, conspicuously ridge-margined on the ventral suture and broadly and deeply grooved on the dorsal suture, thick-walled, usually conspicuously or rarely obscurely rugose and pitted.

A tree 20°-30° high, without suckers from the roots, with a slender often inclining trunk, frequently 5'-6' or occasionally 10'-12' in diameter, dividing usually several feet above the ground into thick spreading branches forming a broad round-topped head, and stout rigid branchlets marked by minute pale lenticels, glabrous or slightly puberulous during their first summer, rather dark red-brown, and usually unarmed or on vigorous trees armed with stout spinescent lateral chestnut-colored branchlets; or often a shrub, with many stems forming thicket-like clumps. **Winter-buds** minute, obtuse, with chestnut-brown scales slightly ciliate on the margins, those of the inner ranks becoming oblong-lanceolate, acute, glandular-serrate, sometimes $\frac{1}{2}'$ in length. **Bark** thin, dark brown, separating into large thin persistent plates, and displaying the light brown inner layers.

Distribution. Low banks of streams in rich moist soil; southwestern Illinois to Scott County, Iowa, and to eastern Kansas and northeastern Oklahoma, and to central Ken-

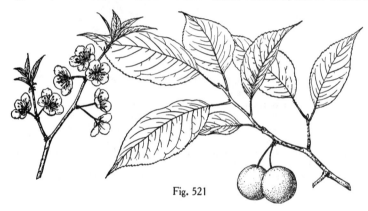

Fig. 521

tucky and northwestern Tennessee; most abundant and of its largest size in Missouri. The handsomest of American Plum-trees, and hardy as far north as eastern Massachusetts. Several selected forms are grown and valued by pomologists. Passing into var. *Mineri* Bailey, with darker green duller leaves, and sometimes more scaly bark. Southwestern Illinois to central Missouri; and into var. *pubens* Sarg. differing from the type in its pubescent leaves, petioles and young branchlets. In the neighborhood of Webb City, Jasper County, and to northeastern Missouri and southeastern Kansas.

Often cultivated by pomologists in many selected forms.

10. Prunus Munsoniana Wight & Hedrick

Leaves elliptic to lanceolate, acute or acuminate at apex, gradually narrowed and cuneate or rounded at base and finely glandular-serrate, when they unfold densely villose-pubescent above and glabrous below, and at maturity thin, light green and lustrous on the upper surface, pale on the lower surface, $2\frac{1}{2}'-4'$ long and $\frac{3}{4}'-1\frac{1}{4}'$ wide, with a slender midrib often red and usually pubescent or sparingly villose on the lower side, and slender primary veins often furnished with small axillary clusters of white hairs; petioles slender, usually biglandular toward the apex, the groove on the upper side covered with white pubescence, often bright red, $\frac{3}{4}'$ in length; stipules linear, glandular-serrate. **Flowers** appearing in Texas before the leaves at the end of March and as late as May after the appearance of the leaves at

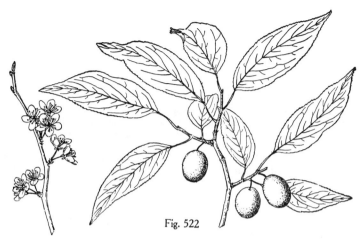

Fig. 522

the northern limits of its range, $\frac{1}{2}'-\frac{3}{5}'$ in diameter, on slender glabrous pedicels $\frac{2}{5}'-1'$ long, in 2–4-flowered umbellike clusters; calyx-tube broad-obconic, glabrous, obscurely nerved, the lobes ovate, acute or acuminate, minutely glandular-serrate, glabrous or rarely slightly pubescent on the outer surface, pubescent on the inner surface below the middle; petals about $\frac{1}{4}'$ long, obovate to oblong-obovate, entire or sparingly erose, white, about $\frac{1}{4}'$ long, abruptly contracted into a short claw. **Fruit** ripening in July and August, subglobose to short-oblong, $\frac{3}{4}'$ long, bright red with a slight bloom, marked by pale dots and occasionally by yellow blotches, rarely yellow, with a thin skin and light or dark yellow juicy aromatic fibrous flesh often of good quality; stone oval, compressed, pointed at apex, truncate or obliquely truncate at base, thick-margined and grooved on the ventral suture, grooved on the dorsal suture, irregularly roughened on the surface, about $\frac{1}{2}'$ long.

A tree spreading into dense thickets, the oldest central stem sometimes 20° high and 5′ or 6′ in diameter, diminishing in height and size to the margin of the thicket, with erect, rarely slightly spinescent branches, and slender glabrous red-brown lustrous branchlets marked by numerous pale lenticels. **Winter-buds** obtuse, chestnut brown, glabrous, rarely more than $\frac{1}{8}'$ long. **Bark** thin, usually smooth and reddish or chestnut-brown on young stems, becoming gray or grayish brown and separating into thin platelike scales on older trunks.

Distribution. Usually in rich soil; southern Illinois (Alexander, Gallatin, Pope, Johnson and Richland Counties); southwestern Kentucky; central Tennessee; northern Mississippi; central Missouri to southeastern Kansas, and through Arkansas to eastern Oklahoma, western Louisiana (Natchitoches and Lincoln Parishes), and northern Texas west to Clay and Lampasas Counties); now occasionally naturalized from cultivated trees in eastern Texas, and eastward to Georgia, eastern Kentucky, southern Ohio, and in northern Missouri. Hardy in eastern Massachusetts and western New York.

Cultivated in orchards, a tree sometimes 20°–30° tall with a trunk 6′–8′ in diameter, and rather small wide-spreading branches forming a handsome round-topped head. Selected forms of the wild plants are valued by pomologists who have produced several hybrids by crossing *Prunus Munsoniana* with other American and with Old World species. The "Wild Goose Plum," one of the best known forms of *Prunus Munsoniana*, has flowered and produced fruit for many years in the Arnold Arboretum.

11. Prunus angustifolia Marsh. Chickasaw Plum.

Leaves lanceolate to oblong-lanceolate, pointed at the ends, apiculate at apex, and sharply serrate with minute glandular teeth, glabrous or at first sometimes furnished with axillary tufts of long pale hairs, bright green and lustrous on the upper, paler and rather dull on the lower surface, $1'-2'$ long and $\frac{1}{3}'-\frac{2}{3}'$ wide; petioles slender, glabrous or puberulous, biglandular near the apex with 2 conspicuous red glands, bright red, $\frac{1}{4}'-\frac{1}{2}'$ in length; stipules linear or lobed, glandular-serrate, $\frac{1}{2}'$ long. **Flowers** appearing before the leaves from the beginning of March at the south to the middle of April at the north, $\frac{1}{3}'$ in diameter, on slender glabrous pedicels $\frac{1}{4}'-\frac{1}{2}'$ long, in 2–4-flowered umbels; calyx-tube campanuiate, glabrous, the lobes oblong, obtuse, entire ciliate on the margins with slender hairs, pale-pubescent on the inner surface, reflexed at maturity; petals obovate, rounded at apex, contracted at base into a short broad claw, white or creamy white. **Fruit** ripening between the end of May and the end of July, globose or subglobose, about $\frac{1}{2}'$ in diameter, bright red or yellow, rather lustrous, nearly destitute of bloom, with a thin skin, and juicy subacid flesh; stone turgid, rugose, compressed at the ends, nearly $\frac{1}{2}'$ long, more or less thick-margined on the ventral suture and grooved on the dorsal suture.

A tree, $15°-25°$ high, with a trunk rarely exceeding $8'$ in diameter, slender spreading branches, and bright red and lustrous branchlets glabrous or covered at first with short caducous hairs, becoming in their second year dull, darker and often brown, marked with

Fig. 523

occasional horizontal orange-colored lenticels, and frequently armed with long thin spinescent lateral branchlets; spreading into thickets. **Winter-buds** acuminate, $\frac{1}{16}'$ long, with chestnut-brown scales. **Bark** about $\frac{1}{8}'$ thick, dark reddish brown and slightly furrowed, the surface broken into long thick appressed scales. **Wood** heavy, although rather soft, not strong, light brownish red with lighter colored sapwood. The fruit is often sold in the markets of the middle and southern states.

Distribution. Widely naturalized especially in the south Atlantic and Gulf states from southern Delaware and Kentucky to central Florida and eastern Texas, occupying the margins of fields and other waste places near human habitations usually in rich soil; probably native in central Texas and Oklahoma. Passing into var. *varians* Wight & Hedrick, differing from the type in its usually larger leaves occasionally up to $2\frac{1}{2}'$ in length and to $1'$ in width, in the longer pedicels of the flowers and in the ovoid to ellipsoid often pointed stone of the red or yellow later ripening fruit. A tree usually spreading into thickets, occasionally $12°$ high with a trunk $4'$ or $5'$ in diameter, small branches and slender often spinescent chestnut-brown branchlets. Usually in richer soil than the type, southwestern Kansas (Arkansas City, Desha County), through eastern Oklahoma and southern Arkansas to northern and central Texas (Cherokee County); now occasionally naturalized in the eastern Gulf States and possibly indigenous in Dallas County, Alabama, and Orange County, Florida.

A number of selected forms of this variety, including most of those formerly referred to *Prunus angustifolia*, are grown and valued in southern orchards but are not hardy in the north.

12. Prunus pennsylvanica L. Wild Red Cherry. Bird Cherry.

Leaves oblong-lanceolate, sometimes slightly falcate, acuminate or rarely acute, and finely and sharply serrate with incurved teeth often tipped with minute glands, when they unfold bronze-green, pilose below and slightly viscid, soon becoming green and glabrous, and at maturity bright and lustrous on the upper surface, rather paler on the lower surface, $3'-4\frac{1}{2}'$ long and $\frac{3}{4}'-1\frac{1}{4}'$ wide; turning bright clear yellow some time before falling in the autumn; petioles slender, glabrous or slightly pilose, $\frac{1}{2}'-1'$ in length, and often glandular above the middle; stipules acuminate, glandular-serrate, early deciduous. **Flowers** appearing in early May when the leaves are about half grown, or at the extreme north and at high altitudes as late as the 1st of July, $\frac{1}{2}'$ in diameter, on slender pedicels nearly 1' long, in

Fig. 524

4 or 5-flowered umbels or corymbs; calyx-tube broad-obconic, glabrous, marked in the mouth of the throat by a conspicuous light orange-colored band, the lobes obtuse, red at apex, and reflexed after the flowers open; petals $\frac{1}{4}'$ long, nearly orbicular, contracted at base into a short claw, creamy white. **Fruit** ripening from the 1st of July to the 1st of September, globose, $\frac{1}{4}'$ in diameter, with a thick light red skin, and thin sour flesh; stone oblong, thin-walled, slightly compressed, pointed at apex, rounded at base, about $\frac{3}{16}'$ long, and ridged on the ventral suture.

A tree, with bitter aromatic bark and leaves, 30°–40° high, with a trunk often 18'–20' in diameter, regular slender horizontal branches forming a narrow usually more or less rounded head, and slender branchlets light red and sometimes slightly puberulous when they first appear, soon glabrous, bright red, lustrous and covered with pale raised lenticels in their first winter, and developing in their second year short thick spur-like lateral branchlets and then covered with dull red bark marked by bright orange-colored lenticels, the outer coat easily separable from the brilliant green inner bark; at the extreme north often a low shrub. **Winter-buds** ovoid to ellipsoid, acute, about $\frac{1}{12}'$ long, with bright red-brown acute scales, ciliate on the margins. **Bark** of young stems and of the branches smooth and thin, bright reddish brown, becoming on old trunks $\frac{1}{4}'-\frac{1}{2}'$ thick, and separating horizontally into broad persistent papery dark red-brown plates marked by irregular horizontal bands of orange-colored lenticels and broken into minute persistent scales. **Wood** light, soft, close-grained, light brown, with thin yellow sapwood. The fruit is often used domestically and in the preparation of cough mixtures.

Distribution. Newfoundland to the shores of Hudson's Bay, and westward in British America to the eastern slopes of the coast range of British Columbia in the valley of the Frazer River, and southward through New England, New York, northern Pennsylvania, central Michigan, northern Indiana, northern Illinois, central Iowa, and on the Appalachian Mountains, North Carolina and Tennessee; common in all the forest regions of the extreme northern states, growing in moist rather rich soil; often occupying to the exclusion of other trees large areas cleared by fire of their original forest-covering; common and attaining its largest size on the western slopes of the Big Smoky Mountains in Tennessee. Passing into var. *saximontana* Rehd. differing from the type in its shorter and broader, more coarsely serrate leaves, usually fewer flowered sessile umbels, larger fruit, and smaller size. The Rocky Mountain form; common from Manitoba, the Flathead Lake region, Montana, and northern Wyoming, southward through Colorado.

13. Prunus emarginata Walp.   Wild Cherry.

Leaves oblong-obovate to oblanceolate, rounded and usually obtuse or sometimes acute at apex, cuneate and furnished at base with 1 or 2 and sometimes 3 or 4 large dark glands, and serrate with minute subulate glandular teeth, when they unfold puberulous or pubescent on the lower surface and slightly viscid, and at maturity glabrous or pubescent below (var. *mollis* S. Wats.), 1'–3' long, $\frac{1}{3}$'–1$\frac{1}{2}$' wide, dark green above and paler below; petioles usually pubescent, $\frac{1}{8}$'–$\frac{1}{4}$' in length; stipules lanceolate, acuminate, glandular-serrate, deciduous.   **Flowers** appearing when the leaves are about half grown, at the end of April at the level of the ocean or as late as the end of June at high altitudes, $\frac{1}{3}$'–$\frac{1}{2}$' in diameter, on slender pedicels from the axils of foliaceous glabrous glandular-serrate bracts, in

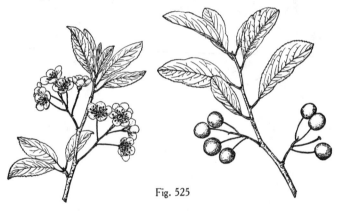

Fig. 525

6–12-flowered glabrous or pubescent corymbs 1'–1$\frac{1}{2}$' long; calyx-tube obconic, glabrous or puberulous, bright orange-colored in the throat, the lobes short, rounded, emarginate or slightly cleft at apex, sometimes slightly glandular on the margins, reflexed after the flowers open; petals obovate, rounded or emarginate at apex, contracted below into a short claw, white faintly tinged with green.   **Fruit** ripening from June to August, on slender pedicels, in long-stalked corymbs often 2' long, globose, $\frac{1}{4}$'–$\frac{1}{2}$' in diameter, more or less translucent, with a thick skin bright red at first when fully grown, becoming darker and almost black, and thin bitter astringent flesh; stone ovoid, turgid about $\frac{1}{8}$' long, pointed and compressed at the ends, with thick brittle slightly pitted walls, ridged and prominently grooved on the ventral suture and rounded and slightly grooved on the dorsal suture.

A tree, occasionally 30°–40° high, with exceedingly bitter bark and leaves, a trunk 12'–14' in diameter, slender rather upright branches forming a symmetric oblong head, and slender flexible branchlets coated at first with pale pubescence, dark red-brown during their first winter, bright red, conspicuously marked by large pale lenticels in their second season, and furnished with short lateral branchlets; frequently a shrub especially at high altitudes, with spreading stems 3°–10° tall forming dense thickets.   **Winter-buds** acute, $\frac{1}{8}$' long, with chestnut-brown scales often slightly scarious on the margins, those of the inner ranks becoming acuminate, glandular-serrate above the middle, with bright red tips, scarious, and ½' long. **Bark** about ¼' thick, with a generally smooth dark brown surface marked by horizontal light gray interrupted bands and by rows of oblong orange-colored lenticels. **Wood** close-grained, soft and brittle, brown streaked with green, with paler sapwood of 8-10 layers of annual growth.

Distribution Usually near the banks of streams in low rich soil, or less commonly on dry hillsides; valley of the upper Jocko River, Montana, on the mountain ranges of Idaho and Washington and of southern British Columbia to Vancouver Island, and southward on the coast and interior ranges to the neighborhood of the bay of San Francisco, on the western slopes of the Sierra Nevada up to altitudes of 5000°–6000° above the sea to the head of Kern River, on the Santa Lucia, San Rafael, and San Bernardino Mountains, California, on the Washoe Mountains, Nevada, and the mountains of northern Arizona; of its largest size on Vancouver Island, in western Oregon and Washington, and on the Santa Lucia Mountains; on the coast ranges of middle California and on the Sierra Nevada commonly a shrub 5°–8° high.

14. Prunus virginiana L. Choke Cherry.

Leaves oval, oblong or obovate, abruptly short-pointed at apex, cuneate, rounded or rarely slightly cordate at base, and sharply often doubly serrate with spreading subulate teeth, glabrous when they unfold or furnished below with axillary tufts of pale hairs, and at maturity dark green and lustrous on the upper surface, light green or pale on the lower sur-

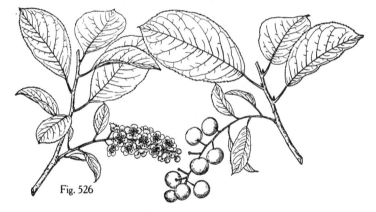

Fig. 526

face, 2'–4' long and 1'–2' wide; turning bright clear yellow in the autumn before falling; petioles slender, biglandular near apex, or on vigorous shoots sometimes many-glandular, ½'–1' in length; stipules lanceolate, about ½' long, early deciduous. **Flowers** opening from April to the end of June, ⅓'–½' in diameter, on slender glabrous pedicels from the axils of scarious caducous bracts, in erect or nodding racemes 3'–6' in length; calyx-tube cup-shaped, globose, the lobes short, obtuse, laciniate and more or less glandular on the margins; petals orbicular, contracted into a short claw, white; filaments and pistil glabrous, the short thick style abruptly enlarged into a broad orbicular stigma. **Fruit** globose or occasionally slightly elongated, ¼'–⅓' in diameter, lustrous, bright red at first when fully grown, becoming at maturity scarlet, dark vinous red or nearly black, or rarely bright canary color (var. *leucocarpa* S. Wats.), with a thick lustrous skin, and dark juicy flesh, austere and astringent, becoming at maturity less astringent and sometimes edible; stone oblong-ovoid broadly ridged on one suture and acute on the other.

A tree occasionally 20°–25° high, with a straight trunk sometimes 6'–8' in diameter, small erect or horizontal branches, and slender glabrous red-brown or orange-brown lustrous branchlets marked by pale lenticels, becoming dark red-brown in their second year; more often a large or small shrub, at the north frequently not more than 2°–3° tall. **Winter-buds** acute or obtuse, with pale chestnut brown scales rounded at apex and more or less scarious on the margins, those of the inner rank becoming lanceolate or ligulate, sharply and often glandular-serrate, and $\frac{1}{2}'$–1' in length. **Bark** strongly and disagreeably scented, about $\frac{1}{8}'$ thick, slightly and irregularly fissured, separating on the surface into small persistent dark red-brown scales, and often marked by pale irregular excrescences. **Wood** heavy, hard, close-grained, not strong, light brown, with thick lighter-colored sapwood of 15–20 layers of annual growth.

Distribution.   Margins of the forest, generally in rich rather moist soil, and along highways and fence-rows; Newfoundland, through Labrador to the shores of Hudson's Bay, and southward to the valley of the Potomac River and northern Kentucky; in Buncombe and Iredell Counties, North Carolina, and Talladega County, Alabama, and westward to Saskatchewan, eastern North and South Dakota and Nebraska, northern Missouri and Kansas; more often a tree southward and in cultivation. Passing into the var. *melanocarpa* Sarg. with rather thicker rarely lanceolate leaves, and usually darker often less astringent rarely yellow (*f. xanthocarpa* Sarg.) fruit.

Distribution.   Low valleys and the slopes of mountain ranges; Manitoba, western North and South Dakota, Nebraska, Kansas and Oklahoma, westward to northern British Columbia, and southward in the Rocky Mountain region through Wyoming, Montana and Idaho, Colorado, Utah and Nevada to southern New Mexico and Arizona, and through Washington, Oregon and California to San Diego County; in the rich soil of valleys a tree sometimes 30° tall; on dry mountain slopes a shrub 2° or 3° high.   More distinct is

Prunus virginiana var. demissa Sarg.

Cerasus demissa Nutt.

Differing in its often cordate leaves covered below with pale pubescence.
Distribution.   Prairies and valleys of western Washington and Oregon, southward to

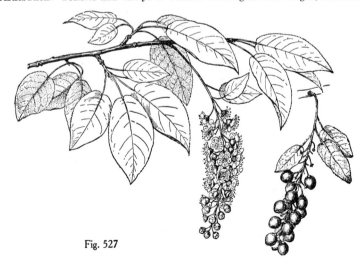

Fig. 527

Siskiyou, Napa, Santa Cruz and Kern Counties, California, in northern Nebraska, central Iowa, Stark County, Illinois (*V. H. Chase*), Laporte County, Indiana (*C. C. Deam*), western Texas (Gamble's Ranch, Armstrong County, with pubescent leaves cuneate at base), and in New Mexico.

Passing into var. *demissa* f. *pachyrrachis* Sarg. (*Padus valida* Woot. & Stanl.) differing in the cuneate or rounded base of the leaves, villose pubescent on the midrib and veins below, in the stouter pubescent rachis and pedicels, and in the pubescent branchlets usually becoming glabrous at the end of their second season.

Distribution. Common on the mountains of southwestern New Mexico (Sierra County) and rarely in southern California.

15. Prunus serotina Ehrh. Wild Black Cherry. Rum Cherry.

Prunus eximia Small.

Leaves oval, oblong or oblong-lanceolate, gradually or sometimes abruptly acuminate at apex, cuneate at base, finely serrate with appressed incurved callous teeth, and furnished at the very base with 1 or more dark red conspicuous glands, when they unfold slightly

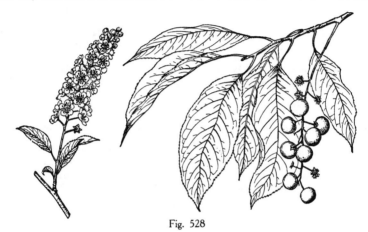

Fig. 528

hairy below on the midrib, and often bronze-green, and at maturity glabrous, thick and firm, subcoriaceous, dark green and very lustrous above, paler below, 2′–6′ long and 1′–1½′ wide, with a thin conspicuous midrib rarely furnished toward the base with a fringe of rusty tomentum and slender veins; in the autumn turning clear bright yellow before falling; petioles slender, ½′–¾′ in length; stipules lanceolate, acuminate, glandular-serrate, ½′–¾′ in length, early deciduous. **Flowers** appearing when the leaves are about half grown, from the end of March in Texas to the first week of June in the valley of the St. Lawrence River, ¼′ in diameter, on slender glabrous or puberulous pedicels from the axils of minute scarious caducous bracts, in erect or ultimately spreading narrow many-flowered racemes 4′–6′ long; calyx-tube saucer-shaped, glabrous or puberulous, the lobes short, ovate-oblong, acute, slightly laciniate on the margins, reflexed after the flowers open, persistent on the ripe fruit; petals broad-obovate, pure white. **Fruit** ripening from June to October, in drooping racemes, depressed-globose, slightly lobed, ⅓′–½′ in diameter, dark red when fully grown, almost black when ripe, with a thin skin, and dark purple juicy flesh of a pleasant vinous flavor; stone oblong-obovoid thin-walled, about ⅓′ long, acute at apex, gradually narrowed at base, broadly ridged on the ventral suture and acute on the dorsal suture.

A tree, with bitter aromatic bark and leaves, sometimes 100° high, with a trunk 4°–5° in diameter, small horizontal branches forming a narrow oblong head, and slender rather rigid glabrous branchlets at first pale green or bronze color, soon becoming bright red or dark brown tinged with red, red-brown or gray-brown and marked by minute pale lenticels during their first winter, and bright red the following year; usually much smaller and occasionally toward the northern limits of its range shrub-like in habit. **Winter-buds** obtuse, or on sterile shoots acute, with bright chestnut-brown broad-ovate scales keeled on the back and apiculate at apex, those of the inner ranks becoming scarious at maturity, acuminate, and $\frac{1}{2}'-\frac{2}{3}'$ long. **Bark** $\frac{1}{2}'-\frac{3}{4}'$ thick, broken by reticulated fissures into small irregular plates scaly on the surface, and dark red-brown, or near the Gulf-coast light gray or nearly white. **Wood** light, strong, rather hard, close straight-grained, with a satiny surface, light brown or red, with thin yellow sapwood of 10–12 layers of annual growth; largely used in cabinet-making and the interior finish of houses. The bark, especially that of the branches and roots, yields hydrocyanic acid used in medicine as a tonic and sedative. The ripe fruit is used to flavor alcoholic liquors.

Distribution. Nova Scotia westward through the Canadian provinces to Lake Superior, and southward through the eastern states to central (Lake County) Florida, and westward to eastern South Dakota, southeastern Nebraska, eastern Kansas, central Oklahoma and the valley of the east fork of the Frio River, Texas; usually in rich moist soil; once very abundant in all the Appalachian region, reaching its greatest size on the slopes of the high Alleghany Mountains from West Virginia to Georgia, and in Alabama; sometimes on low sandy soil, and often in New England on rocky cliffs within reach of the spray of the ocean; not common in the coast region of the southern states.

A form from the summits of White Top Mountain, Virginia, with larger and rather thicker leaves pale below and rather larger fruit, has been described as var. *montana* Britt.

16. Prunus alabamensis Mohr.   Wild Cherry.

Leaves oval, broad-ovate, or occasionally obovate, acute, short-pointed or rounded at apex, cuneate, rounded or rarely slightly obcordate at base, and finely serrate with incurved teeth tipped with minute or sometimes near the base of the blade with larger dark glands, when they unfold coated below and on the upper side of the midrib with fine pubescence, and at maturity thick and firm in texture, $4'-5'$ long, about $2'$ wide, dark dull green and glabrous on the upper surface, dull and covered on the lower surface with short simple or

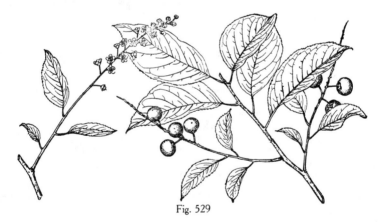

Fig. 529

forked accrescent hairs most abundant and sometimes rufescent on the slender midrib and primary veins; petioles stout, tomentose, becoming pubescent, eglandular or occasionally furnished near the apex with 1 or 2 large dark glands, $\frac{1}{4}'-\frac{1}{2}'$ in length; stipules lanceolate, acuminate, glandular-serrate, bright red, $\frac{1}{2}'$ long, caducous. **Flowers** appearing during the first week of May, when the leaves are about half grown, $\frac{1}{4}'$ in diameter, on pubescent pedicels from the axils of ovate or obovate acuminate bright pink caducous bracts, in spreading or erect slender pubescent racemes 3′–4′ long; calyx-tube broad, cup-shaped, puberulous, with short almost triangular lobes persistent on the fruit; petals white, nearly orbicular. **Fruit** ripening late in September, subglobose to short-oblong, ⅓′ in diameter, dark red or finally nearly black, with thin acid flesh; stone ovoid somewhat compressed, pointed at the ends, ¼′ long, ridged on the ventral suture with a broad low ridge, and slightly grooved on the dorsal suture.

A tree, 25°–30° high, with a short trunk rarely 10′ in diameter, spreading somewhat drooping branches, and slender branchlets coated at first with pale tomentum, dark red-brown during their first season, becoming nearly glabrous before winter, and much darker in their second year. **Bark** of the trunk dark, rough, separating freely into small thin scales.

Distribution. Summits of the low mountains of central Alabama; rare and local.

17. Prunus australis Beadl. Wild Cherry.

Leaves obovate, oval or elliptic, gradually narrowed and obtusely short-pointed or sometimes acute at apex, rounded or occasionally cuneate at the narrowed base, and finely serrate with slender teeth tipped with minute dark red glands, when they unfold membranaceous,

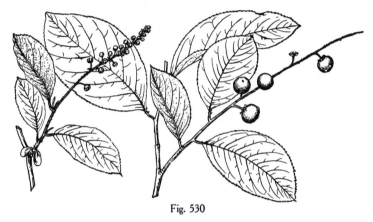

Fig. 530

pale yellow-green and glabrous above, with the exception of occasional pale hairs along the midrib, and coated below with pale or ferrugineous pubescence, and at maturity thin but firm, dark dull green above, covered below with rufous hairs most abundant on the thin broad midrib, and on the slender primary veins extending nearly to the margins of the leaf, conspicuously reticulate-venulose, 2½′–4′ long and 1½′–2½′ wide; petioles rusty-tomentose, biglandular at apex with large dark glands, about ¼′ in length; stipules linear to linear-lanceolate, glandular, bright rose color, ¼′–½′ long. **Flowers** probably opening toward the end of April, on short pedicels from the axils of minute rose-colored caducous bracts, in slender spreading hoary-pubescent racemes 3′–4′ long; the expanded flowers not known. **Fruit** ripening and falling late in July, on pedicels ¼′ long, globose, surrounded at base by the calyx-lobes and remnants of the stamens, dark purple when fully ripe, and about ¼′ in diameter, with thin flesh; stone ovoid, compressed, rounded at base, pointed at apex, about ⅙′ long and broad, ridged on the ventral suture, with a low broad ridge, slightly grooved on the dorsal suture.

A tree, sometimes 60° tall, with a trunk 12′–16′ in diameter, spreading or ascending branches forming an oblong head, and slender branchlets coated at first with pale pubescence, becoming puberulous, dull red-brown, and roughened by numerous small pale elevated lenticels at the end of their first season, and glabrous or puberulous in their second year. **Winter-buds** ovoid, obtuse, about $\frac{1}{12}'$ long, with acute dark red-brown glabrous scales. **Bark** of young stems and of the branches thin, silvery gray, and roughened by long horizontal lenticels, becoming on older trunks $\frac{1}{3}'$ thick, ashy gray or brownish black, deeply fissured and broken into thick persistent platelike scales.

Distribution. Clay soil at Evergreen, Conecuh County, Alabama; common.

18. Prunus virens Shrive. Wild Cherry.

Padus virens Woot. & Stanl.

Prunus serotina, ed. 1, in so far as relates to western Texas, New Mexico and Arizona.

Leaves elliptic, ovate or rarely slightly obovate, acute, rounded or occasionally acuminate or abruptly narrowed into a short obtuse point at apex, rounded or broad-cuneate at base, finely crenately serrate, glabrous, light green and lustrous on the upper surface,

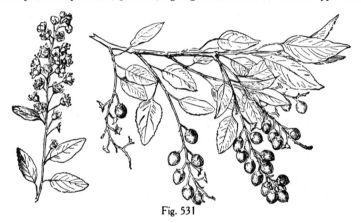

Fig. 531

lighter green and glabrous on the lower surface, $1\frac{1}{2}'-2'$ long and $\frac{3}{4}'-1'$ wide, with a slender midrib, thin veins and reticulate veinlets; petioles slender, glabrous or rarely slightly villose, without glands, $\frac{1}{4}'-\frac{1}{2}'$ in length. **Flowers** appearing when the leaves are nearly fully grown from the first to the middle of May, $\frac{1}{4}'$ in diameter, on slender glabrous pedicels, in erect or spreading many-flowered glabrous or puberulous racemes $3'-6'$ long; calyx-tube saucer-shaped, glabrous, $\frac{3}{16}'$ wide, persistent under the fruit, the lobes short-pointed, acute, persistent; petals broad-obovate, pure white. **Fruit** ripening in August and September, in erect or spreading racemes, subglobose to short-oblong, purplish black and lustrous at maturity, $\frac{1}{4}'-\frac{1}{2}'$ in diameter, with thin juicy acrid flesh; stone compressed, slightly obovoid $\frac{1}{4}'$ in diameter, with a low broad ridge on the ventral suture, and rounded on the dorsal suture.

A tree in sheltered cañons sometimes $25°-30°$ high, with a trunk $18'$ or $20'$ in diameter, small, usually drooping or occasionally wide-spreading branches, and slender glabrous red-brown pendulous branchlets marked by small pale lenticels, becoming gray-brown in their second year; on open mountain slopes a shrub with numerous erect stems and usually smaller leaves. **Winter-buds** acute or acuminate, $\frac{1}{16}'-\frac{1}{8}'$ long, with slightly villose red-brown scales. **Bark** near the base of old trunks $\frac{1}{4}'$ thick, nearly black, deeply fissured and broken on the surface into thin persistent scales, higher on the trunk and on small stems thin, smooth, reddish or gray-brown, lustrous and marked by many narrow oblong pale horizontal lenticels.

Distribution. Guadalupe Mountains, western Texas, over the mountain ranges of southern New Mexico and Arizona, extending northward in Arizona to the cañons of the

Colorado plateau south of the Colorado River; widely and generally distributed at altitudes between 5000° and 8000°, but nowhere abundant. Passing into var. *rufula* Sarg., differing in the rusty brown pubescence on the lower side of the midrib of the leaves, in the pubescent petiole and lower part of the rachis, in the puberulous ovary, and in the rusty brown pubescence of the young branchlets.

Distribution. With the species on many of the mountain ranges of southern New Mexico and Arizona at altitudes between 5400° and 6000°.

19. Prunus caroliniana Ait. Wild Orange. Mock Orange.

Leaves oblong-lanceolate, acuminate, mucronate, with entire thickened slightly revolute margins, or rarely remotely spinulose-serrate, glabrous, coriaceous, dark green and lustrous on the upper surface, paler on the lower surface, 2'–4½' long and ¾'–1½' wide, and obscurely veined, with a narrow pale midrib; persistent until their second year; petioles stout, broad, orange-colored; stipules foliaceous, lanceolate, acuminate. **Flowers** appearing from February to April, on slender pedicels about ½' long, from the axils of long-acuminate scarious red-tipped bracts, in dense racemes shorter than leaves; calyx-tube narrow-obconic, the lobes small, thin, rounded, undulate on the margins, reflexed after the flowers open, deciduous; petals boat-shaped, minute, cream-colored; stamens exserted, orange-colored, with glabrous filaments and large pale anthers; ovary gradually narrowed into a slender erect style enlarged above into a club-shaped stigma. **Fruit** ripening in the autumn, remaining on the branches until after the flowering period of the following year, oblong, short-pointed, black and lustrous, ½' long, with a thick skin, and thin dry flesh; stone short-ovoid, pointed, nearly cylindric, about ½' long, full and rounded at base, with thin fragile walls, obscurely ridged on the ventral suture and deeply grooved on the dorsal suture.

A tree, 30°–40° high, with a straight or inclining trunk sometimes 10' in diameter, slender horizontal branches forming a narrow oblong or sometimes a broad head, and glabrous branchlets marked by occasional pale lenticels, slightly angled, at first light green, becoming bright red, and in the second season light brown or gray. **Winter-buds** acuminate, ⅛'

Fig. 532

long, covered with narrow pointed dark chestnut-brown scales rounded on the back. **Bark** about ⅛' thick, gray, smooth or slightly roughened by longitudinal fissures, and marked by large irregular dark blotches. **Wood** heavy, hard, strong, close-grained, light red-brown or sometimes rich dark brown, with thick lighter colored sapwood. The partially withered leaves and young branches are often fatal to animals browsing upon them, owing to the considerable quantities of hydrocyanic acid which they contain.

Distribution. Deep rich moist bottom-lands; valley of the Cape Fear River, North Carolina, to the shores of Bay Biscayne and the valley of the Kissimee River, Florida, and through southern Alabama, Mississippi, and Louisiana to the valley of the Guadalupe River, Texas; in Bermuda; in the Atlantic and eastern Gulf states usually only in the immediate neighborhood of the sea, rarely ranging inland more than fifteen or twenty miles; common along the borders of hummocks in the center of the Florida peninsula and a characteristic tree on those in the region of Lake Apopka, Orange County; in Alabama ranging inland to Dallas County (Pleasant Hill, *T. G. Harbison*); most abundant and of its largest size in the valleys of eastern Texas, and here often forming great impenetrable thickets.

Often cultivated in the southern states as an ornamental plant and to form hedges; and when cultivated occasionally 50°–60° high, with a trunk 3° in diameter.

20. Prunus myrtifolia Urb.

Prunus sphærocarpa Sw.

Leaves elliptic to oblong-ovate, gradually or abruptly contracted into a broad obtuse point, or less commonly rounded or rarely emarginate at apex, cuneate at base, entire, with

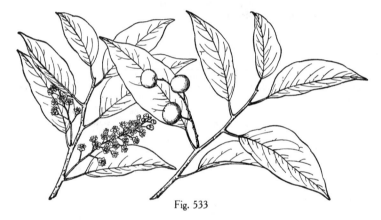

Fig. 533

slightly thickened undulate margins, glabrous, eglandular, subcoriaceous, yellow-green and lustrous on the upper surface, paler on the lower surface, obscurely veined, 2′–4½′ long and 1′–1½′ wide; persistent; petioles slender, orange-brown, ½′ to 1′ in length; stipules foliaceous, lanceolate, acuminate, entire, ¼′ long, early deciduous. **Flowers** opening in Florida in November, ⅛′ in diameter, on thin orange-colored pedicels ¼′–⅔′ long, in slender many-flowered erect racemes shorter than the leaves; calyx-tube obconic, bright orange-colored on the outer surface, marked by an orange band in the throat, the lobes thin, minute, acute, laciniate on the margins, deciduous, much shorter than the obovate rounded or acuminate white petals marked with yellow on the inner surface toward the base, contracted below into a short claw, reflexed at maturity; stamens exserted, with slender orange-colored subulate filaments and small yellow anthers; ovary sessile, contracted into a short stout style, terminating in a large club-shaped stigma. **Fruit** produced in Florida very sparingly, ripening either in the spring or early summer, subglobose to short-oblong, apiculate, orange-brown, ⅓′–½′ long, with thin dry flesh; stone thin-walled, cylindric, slightly narrowed at apex, and obscurely ridged on the ventral suture.

A glabrous tree, in Florida rarely 30°–40° high, with a trunk 5′–6′ in diameter, thin upright branches and slender orange-brown branchlets, becoming ashy gray or light brown tinged with red and marked by small circular pale lenticels. **Bark** of the trunk thin, smooth or slightly reticulate-fissured, light brown tinged with red. **Wood** heavy, hard, close-grained, light clear red, with thick pale sapwood.

Distribution. Florida, rich hummock land, occasionally in the neighborhood of small streams and ponds near the shore of Bay Biscayne and on Long Key in the Everglades, Dade County; through the West Indies to Brazil.

21. Prunus ilicifolia Walp. Islay

Leaves ovate to ovate-lanceolate, acute, rounded or emarginate at apex, narrowed and rounded or truncate at base, with thickened coarsely spinosely toothed margins, the stout teeth near the base of the leaf often tipped with large dark glands, thick and coriaceous, dark green and lustrous above, paler and yellow-green below, $1'-2\frac{1}{2}'$ long, and $1'-1\frac{1}{2}'$ wide, with a slender yellow midrib and obscure veins; deciduous during their second summer; petioles broad, $\frac{1}{8}'-\frac{1}{2}'$ in length; stipules acuminate, obscurely denticulate, $\frac{1}{4}'$ long. **Flowers** opening from March to May, $\frac{1}{3}'$ in diameter, on short slender pedicels from the axils of acuminate scarious bracts $\frac{1}{4}'$ in length and mostly deciduous before the opening of the flower-buds, in slender erect racemes $1\frac{1}{2}'-3'$ long; calyx-tube cup-shaped, orange-brown, the lobes minute, acuminate, reflexed at maturity, deciduous, about one third as long as the obovate white petals rounded above and narrowed below into a short claw; stamens slightly exserted, with slender incurved filaments and minute yellow anthers; ovary sessile, abruptly contracted into a slender style usually bent near the summit at a right angle or rarely erect, and surmounted by a large orbicular stigma. **Fruit** ripening in November and December, subglobose, often compressed, $\frac{1}{2}'-\frac{2}{3}'$ in diameter, dark red when fully grown, purple or sometimes nearly black at maturity, with thin slightly acid astringent flesh; stone ovoid slightly compressed, $\frac{1}{2}'-\frac{5}{8}'$ long, short-pointed at apex, with thin brittle walls, light yellow-brown, conspicuously marked by reticulate orange-colored vein-like lines and with 3 orange bands radiating from the base to the apex along one suture, and with a single narrow band along the other suture.

A glabrous tree, $20°-30°$ high, with a trunk rarely $2°$ in diameter or more than $10°-12°$ long, stout spreading branches forming a dense compact head, and branchlets at first yel-

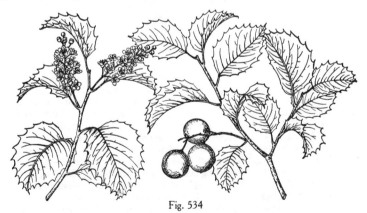

Fig. 534

low-green or orange color, soon becoming gray or reddish brown and more or less conspicuously marked by minute pale lenticels, and in their second or third years by the large leaf-scars; usually much smaller and often a shrub sometimes only a foot or two high. **Winter-buds** acuminate, with dark red scales contracted into a long slender point, those of the inner ranks accrescent and persistent on the young branchlets until these have reached a length of several inches. **Bark** $\frac{1}{3}'-\frac{1}{2}'$ thick, dark red-brown, and divided by deep fissures into small square plates. **Wood** heavy, hard, strong, close-grained, light red-brown, with thin lighter colored sapwood of 8–10 layers of annual growth; occasionally used for fuel.

Distribution. Borders of streams and moist sandy soil in the bottoms of cañons, and as a low shrub on dry hillsides and mesas from Solano County and the shores of the Bay of San Francisco southward through the coast ranges of California to the foothills of the San Bernardino Mountains, and the valley of the San Jacinto River; in Lower California southward to the western slopes of the San Pedro Mártir Mountains.

Generally cultivated as an ornamental plant in California and occasionally in western and southern Europe.

22. Prunus Lyonii Sarg.

Prunus integrifolia Sarg.

Leaves ovate to lanceolate, acuminate or abruptly narrowed into a short point at apex, cuneate, truncate or rounded at base, with thickened revolute undulate entire or occasionally, especially on vigorous shoots, remotely and minutely spinulose-dentate margins, gla-

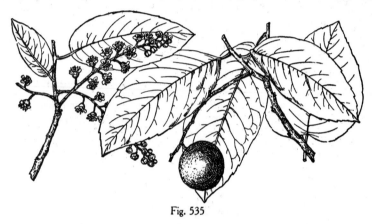

Fig. 535

brous, coriaceous, dark green and lustrous above, paler below, reticulate-venulose, 2′–3′ long and ½–2½′ wide, with a stout midrib and obscure veins; persistent; petioles stout, yellow, ¼–½′ in length. **Flowers** appearing from March to June, about ¼′ in diameter, on slender pedicels from the axils of acuminate caducous bracts, in crowded many-flowered glabrous racemes 3′–4′ long; calyx-tube cup-shaped, orange-brown, the lobes acute, apiculate, reflexed after the flowers open, deciduous, about one third as long as the obovate petals rounded and undulate above and narrowed below into a short claw; stamens slightly exserted, with incurved filaments and small yellow anthers; ovary raised on a short stipe, the style bent near the apex and terminating in a large orbicular stigma. **Fruit** ripening late in the autumn, on stout pedicels, in drooping few-fruited racemes, subglobose to short-oblong, dark purple or nearly black at maturity, 1′–1¼′ in diameter, with thick luscious flesh sometimes ¼′ thick; stone ovoid to obovoid, slightly compressed, thin-walled, about ¾′ long, pointed at apex, pale yellow-brown, conspicuously marked by reticulate orange-colored lines, and by 3 dark bands radiating from base to apex along one suture, and by a single narrow line on the other suture.

A bushy tree, sometimes 25°–30° high, with one or several stout erect or spreading stems 1°–3° in diameter, spreading branches forming a broad compact head, and stout branchlets light yellow-green when they first appear, becoming light and ultimately dark reddish brown, and much roughened by the large elevated leaf-scars. **Winter-buds** acute or obtuse, with dark red scales. **Bark** of the trunk $\frac{1}{4}'-\frac{1}{2}'$ thick and dark reddish brown. **Wood** heavy, hard, very close-grained, pale reddish brown, with hardly distinguishable sapwood.

Distribution. Islands of southern California, in all situations from the fertile valleys and cañons at the water's edge up to altitudes of 3000° on the dry interior ridges; in Lower California.

11. CHRYSOBALANUS L.

Trees or shrubs, with stout branchlets covered with pale lenticels, and fibrous roots. Leaves alternate, entire, coriaceous, short-petiolate, persistent; stipules minute, deciduous. Flowers perfect, short-pedicellate, small, creamy white, in axillary or terminal dichotomously branched slender canescent cymes, with conspicuous deciduous bracts; calyx turbinate-campanulate, 5-lobed, the lobes imbricated in the bud, without bracts, deciduous; disk thin, adnate to the calyx-tube; petals 5, alternate with the lobes of the calyx, spatulate, deciduous; stamens (in the arborescent species) indefinite in a single continuous series, inserted with the petals on the margin of the disk; filaments filiform, hairy, free or slightly united at base; anthers ovoid, ovary sessile in the bottom of the calyx-tube, pubescent or glabrous, 1-celled; style rising from the base of the ovary, filiform, terminated by a minute truncate stigma; ovules 2, collateral, ascending; raphe dorsal; the micropyle inferior. Fruit a fleshy 1-seeded drupe with pulpy flesh, a coriaceous or crustaceous stone 5 or 6-angled toward the base and imperfectly 5 or 6-valved, the valves reticulate-veined. Seed erect; seed-coat chartaceous, light brown; embryo filling the cavity of the seed; cotyledons thick and fleshy; radicle inferior, very short.

Chrysobalanus is represented in the south Atlantic states by a shrubby species confined to the coast region from Georgia to Alabama, and by an arborescent species, an inhabitant of the shores of southern Florida, and widely distributed through the maritime regions of tropical America, and found in various forms on the coast of western tropical Africa. The insipid fruit of the arborescent species is sometimes eaten; the seeds contain a considerable quantity of oil; and the astringent bark, leaves and roots have been used in medicine.

The generic name is from χρυσός and βάλανος, in allusion to the supposed golden fruit of one of the species.

1. Chrysobalanus icaco L. Cocoa Plum.

Leaves broad-elliptic or round-obovate, rounded or slightly emarginate at apex, cuneate

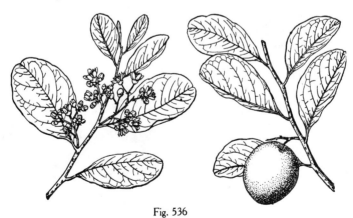

Fig. 536

at base, glabrous, coriaceous, obscurely reticulate-veined, dark green and lustrous on the upper surface, light yellow-green on the lower surface, $1'-3\frac{1}{2}'$ long and $1'-2\frac{1}{2}'$ wide, with a broad conspicuous midrib rounded on the upper side and thin primary veins, standing on the branches at an acute angle and appearing to be pressed against them; petioles stout, $\frac{1}{8}'-\frac{1}{4}'$ in length; stipules acuminate, $\frac{1}{8}'$ long. **Flowers** $\frac{1}{4}'$ long, on short thick club-shaped hoary-tomentose pedicels, in cymes $1'-2'$ in length; appearing in Florida continuously during the spring and summer months on the growing branches; calyx hoary-tomentose, the lobes nearly triangular, acute, more or less pubescent on the inner surface and about half as long as the narrow white petals; ovary hoary-pubescent; style long and slender, clothed nearly to the apex with pale hairs. **Fruit** nearly globose or oval-ovoid, $1\frac{1}{2}'-1\frac{3}{4}'$ in diameter, with a smooth bright pink, yellow, or creamy white skin, white sweet juicy flesh often $\frac{1}{4}'$ thick, and more or less adherent to the stone rounded at base, acute or acuminate at apex, 5 or 6-angled below the middle, about a$'$ long and twice as long as broad, indehiscent or finally separating into 5 or 6 valves, the walls composed of a thin red-brown dry outer layer and a thick interior layer of hard woody fibre; seed-coat lined with a thick white reticulated fibrous coat.

Usually a broad shrub $10°-12°$ high, forming dense thickets, with erect branches and dark red-brown branchlets thickly covered for four or five years with lenticels, occasionally on the borders of low hummocks arborescent with reclining or rarely erect stems $20°-30°$ long and $1°$ in diameter, or on the margins of ocean beaches often not more than $1°$ or $2°$ tall. **Bark** dark red-brown and scaly, separating into long thin scales. **Wood** heavy, hard, strong, close-grained, light brown often tinged with red, with thin lighter colored sapwood of about 10 layers of annual growth.

Distribution. Florida, saline shores, river banks and low hummocks, Cape Canaveral to Bay Biscayne, and on the west coast from the mouth of the Caloosahatchee River to the southern keys; through the West Indies to southern Brazil, and on the tropical west coast of Africa. Passing into

Chrysobalanus icaco var. pellocarpa DC.

Differing from the type in its rather larger leaves spreading and less crowded on the branches, its oblong to oblong-obovoid dark purple or nearly black usually rather smaller fruit, and in its long-acuminate and more prominently angled stone.

A tree, $20°-30°$ or rarely $50°$ high, with an erect trunk $12'-16'$ in diameter, erect and

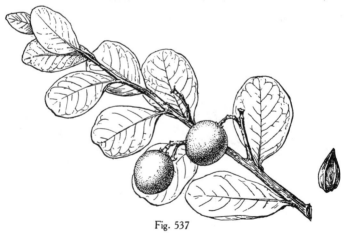

Fig. 537

spreading branches forming a wide open head, and slender branchlets marked by scattered pale lenticels; often smaller and occasionally a shrub. **Bark** gray slightly tinged with red and covered with small closely appressed scales.

Distribution. Florida, banks of streams and borders of the Everglades, near Little River to the Everglade keys, Dade County; on the Bahama Islands and in Jamaica.

XXIII. LEGUMINOSÆ.

Trees or shrubs, with alternate usually compound leaves, regular or papilionaceous usually perfect flowers; stamens 10 or indefinite, with diadelphous or distinct filaments and 2-celled anthers, the cells opening longitudinally; ovary superior, 1 or many-celled, inserted on the bottom of the calyx. Fruit a legume. Of the four hundred and thirty genera of the Pea-family now recognized and widely distributed in all temperate and tropical regions, eighteen have arborescent representatives in the United States.

CONSPECTUS OF THE NORTH AMERICAN ARBORESCENT GENERA.

Subfamily 1. MIMOSOIDEÆ. Calyx 4–6-toothed, the teeth valvate in the bud; petals as many as the teeth of the calyx, valvate in the bud; ovules numerous, suspended in 2 ranks from the inner angle of the ovary, superposed, anatropous, the micropyle superior; stamens much exserted; leaves twice pinnate; cotyledons oval or orbicular, flat; radicle straight.

Stamens numerous (more than 10); seeds without albumen.
  Filaments more or less united into a tube.
    Filaments united.
      Valves of the legume not separating at maturity from the margins.
        1. Pithecolobium.
      Valves of the legume separating at maturity from the persistent margins.
        2. Lysiloma.
    Filaments free or the inner ones slightly united at base.   **3. Acacia.**
  Stamens 10; filaments free; seeds with albumen.
    Legume plano-compressed, dehiscent; flowers in globose heads.   **4. Leucæna.**
    Legume terete or compressed, indehiscent; flowers in cylindric spikes.   **5. Prosopis.**

Subfamily 2. CÆSALPINIOIDÆ. Calyx 5-lobed or toothed, the divisions usually valvate in the bud; corolla imperfectly papilionaceous or nearly regular; petals 5, imbricated in the bud, the upper petal inside and inclosed by the others; stamens 10 or less; filaments free; anthers introrse; ovules numerous (*sometimes 2 in one species of Gleditsia*), superposed, anatropous, the micropyle superior; seeds albuminous.

Flowers imperfectly papilionaceous; calyx 5-toothed; legume flat, wing-margined; leaves simple.   **6. Cercis.**
Flowers regular.
  Flowers polygamous or diœcious.
    Calyx-tube elongated, 5-lobed; petals 5; stamens 10, shorter than the petals; legume thick and woody; leaves twice pinnate.   **7. Gymnocladus.**
    Calyx-tube short, 3–5-lobed; petals 3–5; stamens 3–5, longer than the petals; legume leathery; leaves once and twice pinnate.   **8. Gleditsia.**
  Flowers perfect.
    Legume linear, torulose, acuminate at the ends, the valves contracted between the seeds; rachis of the leaf spinescent.   **9. Parkinsonia.**
    Legume oblong, compressed; rachis of the leaf not spinescent.   **10. Cercidium.**

Subfamily 3. PAPILIONATÆ. Calyx of 5 more or less united sepals; corolla of 5 irregular petals, papilionaceous, the upper petal (*standard*) larger than the others and inclosing them in the bud, usually turned backward or spreading, the 2 lateral petals (*wings*) oblong, exterior to the 2 lower connivent more or less united petals (*keel*) inclosing the stamens and pistil; stamens 10, 9 of them united into a tube cleft on the upper side, the 10th and upper stamen separate, or all distinct; ovary 1 or many-celled by cross partitions; ovules amphitropous, the micropyle superior; seeds usually without albumen; leaves once pinnate.

Stamens distinct.
Flowers in racemes; legume terete, contracted between the seeds.   11. **Sophora.**
Flowers in panicles; legume compressed.   12. **Cladrastis.**
Stamens diadelphous (9 and 1).
  Flowers in racemes.
    Leaves glandular-dotted.
      Leaves many-foliolate; petals free and distinct.   13. **Eysenhardtia.**
      Leaves simple; wings and keel-petals adnate to the tube of the stamens. 14. **Dalea.**
    Leaves without glandular dots.
      Legume compressed; stipules becoming spinescent, persistent.   15. **Robinia.**
      Legume turgid, the valves unequally convex by the growth of the seeds.
        Leaves 10–15-foliolate, without stipules or stipels; petals purple or violet.
          16. **Olneya.**
        Leaves 3-foliolate, with minute stipules and gland-like stipels; petals usually
          scarlet.   17. **Erythrina.**
Flowers in axillary panicles; pod linear, longitudinally 4-winged.   18. **Ichthyomethia.**

1. PITHECOLOBIUM Mart.

Trees or shrubs, with slender branches armed with the persistent spinescent stipules. Leaves petiolate, bipinnate, the pinnæ few-foliolate, their rachis generally marked by numerous glands between the pinnæ and between the leaflets. Flowers perfect or polygamous, from the axils of minute bracts, in pedunculate globose heads or oblong cylindric spikes, their peduncles in terminal panicles or axillary fascicles; calyx campanulate, short-toothed; corolla funnel-shaped, the petals as many as the teeth of the calyx, joined for more than half their length; stamens numerous, united at base into a tube free from the corolla; anthers minute, versatile; ovary stipitate, contracted into a slender filiform style, with a minute terminal stigma. Legume compressed, 2-valved, dehiscent, the valves continuous or interrupted within. Seeds compressed, suspended transversely; funicle filiform or expanded into a fleshy aril; hilum near the base of the seed; seed-coat thin or thick, marked on each of the 2 surfaces of the seed by a faint oval ring or oblong depression; embryo filling the cavity of the seed; the radicle included or slightly exserted.

Pithecolobium with more than a hundred species is widely distributed through the tropical and subtropical regions of the two worlds, and is most abundant in tropical America. Of the four species found within the territory of the United States three are arborescent.

The generic name, from πίθηξ and ἑλλόβιον, relates to the contorted fruit of some of the species.

CONSPECTUS OF THE NORTH AMERICAN ARBORESCENT SPECIES.

Pinnæ with 1 pair of leaflets; valves of the legume much **contorted** after opening; seed
  surrounded by the enlarged ariloid funicle.   1. **P. unguis-cati** (D).
Pinnæ with more than 1 pair of leaflets; valves of the legume not contorted after opening;
  funicle of the seed not enlarged and ariloid.
    Pinnæ with 3–5 pairs of leaflets; legume short-stalked, the valves submembranaceous;
      seeds not in separate compartments.   2. **P. brevifolium** (E).
    Pinnæ with 2–3 pairs of leaflets; legume sessile, the valves thick and woody, tardily
      dehiscent; seeds in separate compartments.   3. **P. flexicaule** (E).

1. Pithecolobium unguis-cati Mart.   Cat's Claw.

Zygia Unguis-Cati Sudw.

Leaves persistent, long-petiolate, with a single pair of bifoliolate pinnæ and a slender petiole $\frac{1}{2}$'–1' long and slightly and abruptly enlarged at base; rachis glandular between the short stout petiolules and between the orbicular or broad-oblong leaflets, rounded and rarely emarginate at apex, rounded on one side and cuneate on the other of the oblique base, entire, thin or somewhat coriaceous, reticulate-veined, bright green and lustrous on the upper surface and paler on the lower surface, $\frac{1}{2}'-2'$ long, and $\frac{1}{2}'-1\frac{1}{2}'$ wide. **Flowers** polygamous, pale yellow, glabrous or slightly puberulous, opening in Florida in March and continuing to appear until midsummer, in globular heads on slender peduncles $1'-1\frac{1}{2}'$ long fascicled in the axils of upper leaves or collected in ample terminal panicles, their bracts lanceolate, acuminate, chartaceous, $\frac{1}{4}'$ long, caducous; calyx rather less than $\frac{1}{12}'$ long broadly toothed, one quarter as long as the acuminate petals barely exceeding the tube formed by the union of the filaments; stamens purple, $\frac{1}{2}'$ long; ovary glabrous. long-stalked, minute or rudimentary in the sterile flower. **Fruit** slightly torulose, stipitate, rounded or acute at apex, $2'-4'$ long, $\frac{1}{4}'-\frac{1}{2}'$ wide, the valves reticulate-veined, thickened on the margins, bright reddish brown and after opening greatly and variously contorted; **seeds** irregularly obovoid or sometimes nearly triangular, compressed or thickened, dark chestnut-brown, lustrous, marked by faint oval rings, $\frac{1}{3}'$ long, surrounded at base by the enlarged bright red ariloid funicle; seed-coat thin, cartilaginous.

A tree, sometimes $20°-25°$ high, with a slender trunk $7'-8'$ in diameter, ascending and spreading branches forming a low flat irregular head, and slender somewhat zigzag branchlets slightly striately angled when they first appear, becoming terete, light gray-brown or dark reddish brown, covered with minute pale lenticels, and armed with the straight persistent rigid stipular spines broad at base and $\frac{1}{4}'$ long, or rarely minute; more often a shrub,

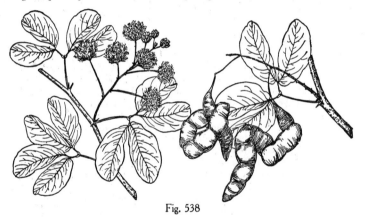

Fig. 538

with many vine-like almost prostrate stems. **Bark** of the trunk $\frac{1}{4}'$ thick, reddish brown and divided by shallow fissures into small square plates. **Wood** very heavy, hard, close-grained, rich red varying to purple, with thin clear yellow sapwood. The bark is astringent and diuretic, and was once used in Jamaica as a cure for many diseases.

Distribution. Florida, Captive and Sanibel Islands and Caloosa, Lee County to the southern keys; most abundant in its arborescent form on the larger of the eastern keys, and probably of its largest size in Florida on Elliott's Key; often forming shrubby thickets; on the Bahamas, and common and widely distributed through the Antilles to Venezuela and New Granada.

2. Pithecolobium brevifolium Benth. Huajillo.

Zygia brevifolia Sudw.

Leaves $2'-3'$ long, $2'$ wide, with eight to ten 10–20-foliolate pinnæ and slender terete petioles $1'$ in length and furnished near the middle with a dark oblong gland, when they unfold coated with pale tomentum and at maturity glabrous with the exception of the puberulous petiole and rachis; persistent or tardily deciduous; leaflets oblong-linear, obtuse or acute at apex, oblique at base, very short-petiolulate, light green on the upper surface, paler on the lower surface, $\frac{1}{8}'-\frac{1}{4}'$ long. **Flowers** white to violet-yellow, in globose or oblong heads

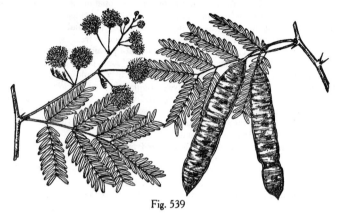

Fig. 539

$\frac{1}{2}'$ in diameter, on thin pubescent peduncles bracteolate at apex, coated at first, like the flower-buds, with thick white tomentum, developed usually in pairs from the axils of lance-olate acute scarious deciduous bracts, and arranged in short terminal racemes; calyx shortly 5-lobed, puberulous on the outer surface, about $\frac{1}{24}'$ long and one fourth the length of the puberulous petals persistent with the stamens at the base of the mature legume; stamens nearly $\frac{1}{2}'$ long. **Fruit** ripening at midsummer and often persistent on the branches after opening until the trees flower the following year, straight, slightly torulose, short-stalked, contracted at apex into a short slender point, $4'-6'$ long and $\frac{2}{3}'$ wide, its valves thin, thick-margined, reddish brown on the outer surface, yellow tinged with red on the inner surface, reticulate-veined; **seeds** suspended by a slender coiled and somewhat dilated funi-cle, compressed, ovoid to nearly orbicular, dark chestnut-brown, very lustrous, $\frac{1}{4}'$ long, and faintly marked by large oval depressions; seed-coat thin, cartilaginous.

A tree, $25°-30°$ high, with a trunk rarely $5'-6'$ in diameter, slender upright branches forming a narrow irregular head, and branchlets slightly striately angled, covered with minute white lenticels, light gray and puberulous when they first appear, becoming dark brown in their second year, and armed with stout rigid stipular spines sometimes $\frac{1}{2}'$ long and persistent for many years; more often a shrub, sometimes only $2°-3°$ tall. **Bark** of the trunk smooth, light gray somewhat tinged with red, and often marked by large pale blotches. **Wood** dark-colored, hard, and heavy.

Distribution. Bluffs and bottom-lands of the lower Rio Grande, and on the upper Nueces River in Uvalde County, Texas; usually a low shrub spreading into broad clumps, but occasionally in the rich and comparatively moist soil of the banks of river-lagoons a slender tree; in Mexico more abundant, and of its largest size from the mouth of the Rio Grande to the Sierra Madre of Nuevo Leon.

3. Pithecolobium flexicaule Coult. Ebony.

Zygia flexicaulis Sudw.

Leaves persistent, $1\frac{1}{2}'-2'$ long, $2\frac{1}{2}'-3'$ wide, long-petiolate with slender puberulous petioles glandular near the middle and furnished at apex with small orbicular solitary glands, and 4–6 usually 6-foliolate pinnæ, the lowest pair often the shortest; leaflets oblong-ovate, rounded at apex, reticulate-veined, thin or subcoriaceous, glabrous, dark green and lustrous on the upper surface, paler on the lower surface, $\frac{1}{4}'-\frac{1}{3}'$ long; petiolules short and broad. Flowers light yellow or cream color, very fragrant, sessile in the axils of minute caducous bracts, appearing from June until August, in cylindric dense or interrupted spikes $1\frac{1}{2}'$ long, on stout pubescent peduncles fascicled in the axils of the upper leaves of the previous year; corolla four or five times as long as the calyx and like it puberulous on the outer surface, and about as long as the tube formed by the union of the filaments; stamens $\frac{1}{8}'$ long; ovary glabrous, sessile. Fruit ripening in the autumn and remaining on the branches until after the flowering season of the following year, sessile, tardily dehiscent, thick, straight or slightly falcate, oblique at base, rounded and contracted into a short broad point at apex, pubescent, $4'-6'$ long and $1'-1\frac{1}{4}'$ wide, with thick

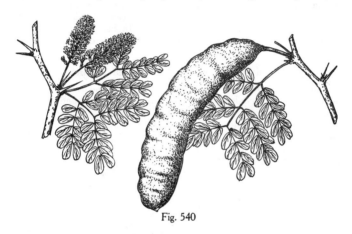

Fig. 540

woody valves lined with a thick pithy substance inclosing and separating the seeds; seeds suspended on a very short straight funicle, bright red-brown, $\frac{1}{2}'$ long and $\frac{1}{4}'$ wide, irregularly obovoid, faintly marked by short oblong depressions; seed-coat thick, crustaceous.

A tree, $20°-30°$ high, with a straight trunk $2°-3°$ in diameter, separating $8°-10°$ from the ground into short spreading branches forming a wide round head, and stout zigzag branchlets, puberulous, light green or dark reddish brown when they first appear, becoming in their second year glabrous or rarely puberulous, dark reddish brown or light gray, and armed with the persistent stipular pale chestnut-brown spines $\frac{1}{4}'-\frac{1}{2}'$ long. Wood exceedingly heavy, hard, compact, close-grained, dark rich red-brown slightly tinged with purple, with thin clear bright yellow sapwood; almost indestructible in contact with the ground and largely used for fence-posts; valued by cabinet-makers and for fuel, and considered more valuable than that of any other tree of the lower Rio Grande valley. The seeds are palatable and nutritious, and are boiled when green or roasted when ripe by the Mexicans, who use their thick shells as a substitute for coffee.

Distribution. Shores of Matagorda Bay, Texas, to the Sierra Nevada of Nuevo Leon, and in Lower California; common on the bluffs of the Gulf-coast and on both banks of the lower Rio Grande; south of the Rio Grande one of the commonest and most beautiful trees of the region.

2. LYSILOMA Benth.

Trees or shrubs, with slender unarmed branchlets, abruptly bipinnate long-petiolate persistent leaves, their petioles marked by large conspicuous glands, and small leaflets in many pairs; stipules large, membranaceous, persistent or deciduous. Flowers perfect or rarely polygamous, minute, usually white or greenish white, from the axils of minute bractlets more or less dilated at apex, in globose many-flowered heads, on axillary solitary or fascicled peduncles; calyx campanulate, 5-toothed; corolla funnel-shaped, of 5 petals united for more than half their length; stamens generally 12–30, exserted; filaments fili-form, united at base into a tube free from the corolla; anthers minute, ovoid, versatile; ovary sessile, contracted into a slender subulate style, with a minute terminal stigma. Legume broad, straight, compressed, submembranaceous, the valves at maturity separat-ing from the undivided margins, continuous within, their outer layer thin and papery, dark-colored, the inner rather thicker, pale yellow.   Seeds compressed, transverse, sus-pended by a long slender funicle, the hilum near the base; seed-coat thin, crustaceous; radicle slightly exserted.

Lysiloma with about ten species inhabits tropical America from southern Florida and the Bahama Islands, the West Indies, Mexico and Lower California, to Central America and Bolivia.   Several of the species produce valuable timber.

The generic name, from λύσις and λῶμα, refers to the separation of the valves from the margins of the legume.

1. Lysiloma bahamensis Benth.   Wild Tamarind.

Leaves 4′–5′ long, glabrous or sometimes slightly puberulous, with slender petioles 1′ long, marked near the middle with an elevated gland, enlarged and slightly glandular at base, and 2–6 pairs of short-stalked 40–80-foliolate pinnæ; stipules foliaceous, ovate or ovate-oblong, acuminate, auriculate and semicordate at base, $\frac{1}{2}$′ long, usually cadu-cous; leaflets obliquely ovate or oblong, obtuse or acute, more or less united at base by the greater development of one of the sides, sessile or short-petiolulate, entire, retic-ulate-veined, light green, paler on the lower than on the upper surface, $\frac{1}{4}$′–$\frac{1}{2}$′ long, and $\frac{1}{8}$′–$\frac{1}{4}$′ wide.   **Flowers** about $\frac{1}{4}$′ long, in heads appearing in Florida early in April, coated before the flowers open with thick pale tomentum, and after the exsertion of the stamens $\frac{2}{3}$′ in diameter, on peduncles $\frac{3}{4}$′–1$\frac{1}{2}$′ long, solitary or fascicled in the axils of upper

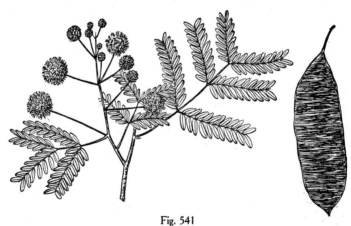

Fig. 541

leaves, their bracts and bractlets acute, membranaceous, caducous; calyx 5-toothed, pilose on the outer surface, especially above the middle, $\frac{1}{12}$′ long, and half as long as the 5-lobed corolla with reflexed lobes; stamens about 20, twice as long as the corolla, united for one fourth of their length into a slender tube.   **Fruit** ripening in the autumn and persistent on the branches until after the flowering period of the following year, stipi-tate, gradually narrowed and acute at the ends, 4′–5′ long, 1′ broad, with a slender stem 1′–

2′ long, in clusters of 2 or 3 on short peduncles abruptly and conspicuously enlarged at the apex; valves thin and papery, bronze-green when fully grown, becoming dark red-brown, separating slowly from the margins; **seeds** oval or obovoid, dark brown, lustrous, $\frac{1}{2}'$ long.

A tree, 50°–60° high, with a trunk 2°–3° in diameter, stout spreading branches forming a wide flat head, and glabrous or somewhat pilose conspicuously verrucose branchlets, bright red-brown when they first appear, becoming pale or light reddish brown in their second year. **Bark** of the trunk of young trees and of the branches smooth, light gray tinged with pink, becoming on old trunks $\frac{1}{4}'-\frac{1}{2}'$ thick, dark brown and separating into large plate-like scales. **Wood** heavy, hard, not strong, tough, close-grained, rich dark brown tinged with red, with nearly white sapwood $1'-1\frac{1}{2}'$ thick, of 4 or 5 layers of annual growth; in Florida occasionally used and valued for boat and shipbuilding.

Distribution. Florida; shores of Bay Biscayne near Miami, and the Everglade Keys, Dade County, common, and on Key Largo, Elliott's, Plantation, and Boca Chica Keys, not common; on the Bahama Islands and in Cuba.

3. ACACIA Adans.

Trees or shrubs, with slender branches armed with spinescent stipules or infrastipular spines. Leaves alternate on young branchlets and fascicled in earlier axils, bipinnate, with usually small leaflets, persistent. Flowers perfect or polygamous, small, in the axils of minute linear bractlets more or less dilated and often peltate at apex, in globose heads or cylindric spikes on axillary solitary or fascicled peduncles; calyx campanulate, 5 or 6-toothed; petals as many as the divisions of the calyx, more or less united; stamens numerous, usually more than 50, exserted, free or slightly and irregularly united at base, inserted under or just above the base of the ovary; filaments filiform; anthers small, attached on the back, versatile; ovary contracted into a long slender style terminating in a minute stigma. Legume nearly cylindric or flat, indehiscent, continuous or divided within. Seeds transverse, compressed; seed-coat thick, crustaceous, marked on each face of the seed by an oval depression or ring; radicle straight, included, or slightly exserted.

Acacia with more than four hundred species is widely distributed through Australia, where it is most largely represented, tropical and southern Africa, northern Africa, southwestern China, the warmer regions of southern Asia, the islands of the south Pacific, tropical and temperate South America, the West Indies, Central America and Mexico to the southwestern boundaries of the United States where ten or twelve species occur; of these five are arborescent. Acacia is astringent, and many species yield valuable tan bark. Gum arabic is produced by different Old World species; many of the species yield hard heavy durable wood, and some of the Australian Acacias are large and valuable timber-trees. Many species are cultivated for their graceful foliage and handsome fragrant flowers.

The generic name, from ἀκακία, relates to the spines with which the branches are usually armed.

CONSPECTUS OF THE ARBORESCENT SPECIES OF THE UNITED STATES.

Flowers in globose heads; corolla 5-lobed; ovary sessile; stipules persistent, becoming spines.
    Legume cylindric, glabrous, its sutures conspicuously thickened and grooved; seeds in 2 ranks.   1. **A. Farnesiana** (E).
    Legume flattened, pubescent, its sutures not thickened, slightly grooved; seeds in 1 rank.   2. **A. tortuosa** (E).
Flowers in short, often interrupted, spikes; legume flattened, pubescent, its sutures thickened; seeds in one rank.   3. **A. Emoriana** (E).
Flowers in elongated slender spikes; corolla of 5 petals only slightly united at base; ovary stalked; stipules caducous; branchlets armed with infrastipular spines.

Legume 1'-1¼' wide, straight or slightly contracted between the seeds, not becoming
    twisted and contorted at maturity; seeds narrow-obovoidor ovoid; leaflets green,
    glabrous, with prominent veinlets.   4. **A. Wrightii** (E).
Legume ½'-¾' wide, often conspicuously contracted between the seeds, becoming twist-
    ed and contorted at maturity; seeds nearly orbicular; leaflets blue-green, pubes-
    cent, with obscure veinlets.   5. **A. Greggii** (E, G, H).

1. Acacia Farnesiana Willd. Huisache. Cassie.

Leaves 2'-4' long, with 2-8, usually 4 or 5, pairs of pinnæ, generally somewhat puberulous on the short petiole and rachis; in Texas mostly falling at the beginning of winter;
pinnæ sessile or short-stalked, remote or close together, with 10-25 pairs of linear acute

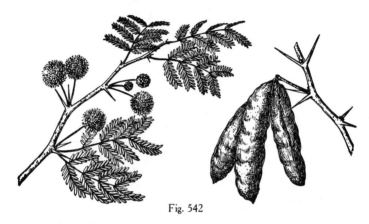

Fig. 542

leaflets tipped with a minute point, unequal at base, sessile or short-petiolulate, glabrous
or puberulous, bright green, ⅛'-¼' long. **Flowers** bright yellow, very fragrant, ¹⁄₁₆' long,
opening during the summer and autumn from the axils of minute clavate pilose bractlets,
in heads ⅔' in diameter, on axillary thin puberulous peduncles, solitary or most often 2 or
3 together and 1'-1½' in length, with two minute dentate connate bracts forming an involucral cup immediately under the flower-head; calyx about half as long as the petals and
like them somewhat pilose on the outer surface; stamens two or three times as long as the
corolla; ovary short-stipitate, covered with long pale hairs. **Fruit** oblong, cylindric or
spindle-shaped, thick, turgid, straight or curved, slightly contracted between the seeds,
short-stalked, narrowed at apex into a short thick point, 2'-3' long, ½'-2' broad, dark
red-purple, lustrous, and marked by broad light-colored bands along the thickened grooved
sutures, the outer coat of the walls thin and papery, inclosing a thick pithy pulp-like
substance surrounding the seeds, each in a separate thin-walled compartment; **seeds**
ovoid, thick, flattened on the inner surface by mutual pressure, ¼' long, suspended transversely in 2 ranks on a short straight funicle, light brown, lustrous, and faintly marked by
large oval rings.

A tree, 20°-30° high, with a straight trunk 12'-18' in diameter, separating 6°-8° from
the ground into numerous long pendulous branches forming a wide round spreading head,
and slender terete or slightly striate angled branchlets, glabrous or at first puberulous, and
armed with straight rigid terete spines developed from the persistent stipules and sometimes 1½' long. **Bark** of the trunk thin, reddish brown, irregularly broken by long reticulated ridges, exfoliating in large thin scales. **Wood** heavy, hard, close-grained, rich reddish brown, with thin pale sapwood; in India used for the knees of small vessels and in
agricultural implements.

Distribution. Now widely spread by cultivation through the tropical and subtropical regions of the two worlds and probably a native of America from western Texas to northern Chili; growing in Texas apparently naturally in the arid and almost uninhabited region between the Nueces and Rio Grande; naturalized and now covering great areas in the valley of the Guadalupe River near Victoria, Victoria County, Texas.

Largely cultivated in southern Europe for its fragrant flowers used in the manufacture of perfumery, as an ornament of gardens in all warm countries, and in India as a hedge plant.

2. Acacia tortuosa Willd.

Leaves generally less than 1' long, short-petiolate, with a slender puberulous rachis and usually 3 or 4 pairs of pinnæ; early deciduous; pinnæ sessile or short-stalked, remote, with 10–15 pairs of linear somewhat falcate leaflets, acute, tipped with a minute point, subsessile, light green, glabrous, $\frac{1}{20}'$–$\frac{1}{18}'$ long. **Flowers** minute, bright yellow, very fragrant, in the axils of clavate pilose bracts, in heads $\frac{1}{4}'$–$\frac{3}{8}'$ in diameter, appearing in March with or just before the unfolding leaves, on clustered or solitary slender puberulous peduncles $\frac{1}{2}'$–$\frac{3}{4}'$ long, and furnished at apex with 2 minute connate bracts; calyx only about one third as long as the corolla, with short puberulous lobes; corolla puberulous at apex, less than half as long as the filaments; ovary covered with short close pubescence. **Fruit** elongated, linear, slightly compressed, somewhat constricted between the seeds, dark red-brown and cinereo-puberulous, 3'–5' long and about $\frac{1}{4}'$ wide; **seeds** in 1 series, obovoid, compressed, dark red-brown, lustrous, about $\frac{1}{4}'$ long, faintly marked by large oval rings.

A tree, occasionally 15°–20° high, with a straight trunk 5'–6' in diameter, stout wide-spreading branches forming an open irregular head, and slender somewhat zigzag slightly angled reddish brown branchlets roughened by numerous minute round lenticels, villose with short pale hairs, and armed with thin terete puberulous spines occasionally $\frac{3}{4}'$ long; in Texas usually shrubby, with numerous stems forming a symmetric round-topped bush only a few feet high. **Bark** dark brown or nearly black, and deeply furrowed.

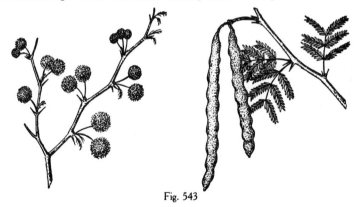

Fig. 543

Distribution. Valley of the Rio Cibolo to Eagle Pass on the Rio Grande, Maverick County, Texas; and in northern and southern Mexico, the West Indies, Venezuela, and on the Galapagos Islands; in Texas probably arborescent only on the plains of the Rio Grande near Spofford, Kinney County.

3. Acacia Emoriana Benth.

Leaves $3\frac{1}{2}'$–4' long, with a slender petiole and rachis, villose-pubescent early in the season, becoming nearly glabrous; and 4 or 5 pairs of pinnæ; falling late in the autumn;

pinnæ on slender stalks $\frac{1}{4}'$ in length, with 5–7 pairs of oblong leaflets rounded and apiculate at apex, obliquely rounded at base, short-petiolulate, pointing forward, when they unfold densely villose above and on the margins, and hoary-tomentose below, becoming glabrous, gray-green rather darker above than below, $\frac{1}{3}'$ long. **Flowers** subsessile, puberulous, in interrupted spikes, $\frac{3}{4}'$–1$'$ in length, densely hoary-tomentose when they first appear late in March, on villose peduncles $\frac{1}{2}'$–1$'$ in length, and furnished near the apex with lanceolate caducous bracts; calyx about half the length of the ovate acute petals ciliate on the margins, about $\frac{1}{12}'$ long and much shorter than the stamens; ovary stipitate, glabrous. **Fruit** fully grown in July, stipitate much compressed, rounded and sometimes slightly emarginate at apex, gradually narrowed and obliquely cuneate at base, with much thickened revolute undulate margins, densely pubescent early in the season, becoming puberulous,

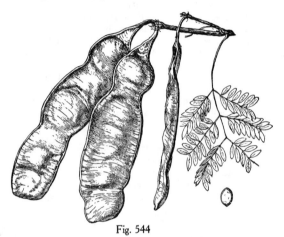

Fig. 544

5$'$ or 6$'$ long, 1$\frac{1}{4}'$–1$\frac{1}{2}'$ wide and many-seeded, or nearly orbicular and 1 or 2-seeded; **seeds** in one series, oval, the two sides unsymmetric, obliquely pointed at base, rounded at apex, compressed, dark chestnut-brown and lustrous, $\frac{1}{2}'$ long and $\frac{1}{4}'$ wide.

A tree, sometimes 25$°$ high, usually smaller, with slender red-brown branchlets pubescent or puberulous when they first appear, becoming glabrous in their second year, and armed with small curved stipular spines; often a shrub.

Distribution. Texas; creek banks and cañons, near Montell and Uvalde, Uvalde County, and rocky banks of Devil's River, Valverde County (*E. J. Palmer*).

4. Acacia Wrightii Benth. Cat's Claw.

Leaves 1$'$–2$'$ long, slightly pubescent, especially on the petiole and rachis, with 1–3 pairs of pinnæ, slender petioles 1$\frac{1}{3}'$ in length, and eglandular or glandular with small convex glands, and linear acute caducous stipules $\frac{1}{16}'$ long; pinnæ short-stalked, with 2–5 pairs of obovate-oblong leaflets, obliquely rounded and often apiculate at apex, sessile or short-petiolulate, 2 or sometimes 3-nerved, glabrous, or rarely pubescent, reticulate-veined, rigid, bright green and rather paler on the lower surface than on the upper surface, $\frac{1}{4}'$–$\frac{5}{8}'$ long. **Flowers** light yellow, fragrant, appearing from the end of March to the end of May, on slender pubescent pedicels from the axils of minute caducous bracts, in narrow spikes 1$\frac{1}{2}'$ long, often interrupted below the middle, on slender fascicled pubescent or sometimes glabrous peduncles; calyx obscurely 5-lobed, pubescent on the outer surface, half as long as the spatulate petals slightly united at base, and ciliate on the margins; stamens $\frac{1}{4}'$ long; ovary long-stalked, covered with long pale hairs. **Fruit** fully grown early in the summer, deciduous in the autumn, slightly falcate, compressed, stipitate, oblique at base, rounded and short-pointed at apex, $2'-4'$ long, $1'-1\frac{1}{4}'$ wide, with thick straight or irregularly contracted margins and thin papery walls conspicuously marked by narrow horizontal reticulate veins; seeds narrow-obovoid, compressed, $\frac{1}{4}'$ long, suspended transversely on a long slender funicle, light brown, marked by large oval depressions.

A tree, occasionally $25°-30°$ high, with a short trunk $10'-12'$ in diameter, spreading branches forming a low wide or irregular head, and branchlets when they first appear somewhat striately angled, glabrous, pale yellow-brown or dark red-brown, turning pale gray in their second year, and armed with occasional stout recurved infrastipular chestnut-brown spines $\frac{1}{4}'$ long, compressed toward the broad base and sharp-pointed, or rarely unarmed. **Bark** of the trunk about $\frac{1}{8}'$ thick, divided by shallow furrows into broad

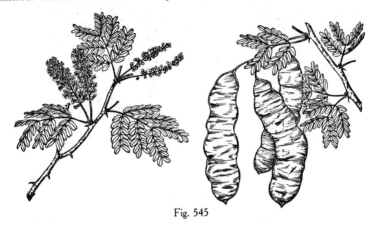

Fig. 545

ridges separating on the surface into thin narrow scales. **Wood** very heavy, hard, close-grained, bright clear brown streaked with red and yellow, with thin clear yellow sapwood of 6 or 7 layers of annual growth; valued and largely used as fuel.

Distribution. Valley of the Guadalupe River in the neighborhood of New Braunfels, Comal County, Texas, to the Sierra Madre of Nuevo Leon; most abundant and of its largest size south of the Rio Grande on dry gravelly mesas and foothills.

5. Acacia Greggii A. Gray. Cat's Claw. Una de Gato.

Leaves $1'-3'$ long, pubescent or puberulous, with 1–3 pairs of pinnæ, a short slender petiole furnished near the middle with a minute oblong chestnut-brown gland, and linear caducous stipules $\frac{1}{16}'$ long; pinnæ short-stalked, with 4–5 pairs of obovate oblique leaflets rounded or truncate at apex and unequally contracted at base into a short petiolule, thick and rigid, 2-3-nerved, inconspicuously reticulate-veined, hoary-pubescent, $\frac{1}{16}'-\frac{1}{4}'$ long. **Flowers** fragrant, bright creamy yellow, in dense oblong pubescent spikes, on a peduncle $\frac{1}{2}'-\frac{2}{3}'$ long, and fascicled usually 2 or 3 together toward the end of the branches; calyx obscurely 5-lobed, puberulous on the outer surface, half as long as the petals slightly united at base and pale-tomentose on the margins; stamens $\frac{1}{4}'$ long; ovary long-stalked, covered with long pale hairs. **Fruit** fully grown at midsummer and hanging unopened on the branches until winter or the following spring, compressed, straight or slightly falcate, obliquely narrowed at base into a short stalk, acute or rounded at apex, more or less contracted between the seeds, $2'-4'$ long, $\frac{1}{2}'-\frac{3}{4}'$ wide, curling and often contorted when fully ripe, the valves thin and membranaceous, thick-margined, light brown, conspicuously transversely reticulate-veined; **seeds** nearly orbicular, compressed, dark brown and lustrous, $\frac{1}{4}'$ in diameter, marked by small oval depressions.

A tree, rarely 30° high, with a trunk 10'–12' in diameter, numerous spreading branches, and striately angled puberulous or in Texas glabrous pale brown branchlets faintly tinged with red and armed with stout recurved infrastipular spines flat at base, and ¼ long and broad. Bark of the trunk about ⅜' thick, furrowed, the surface separating into thin nar-

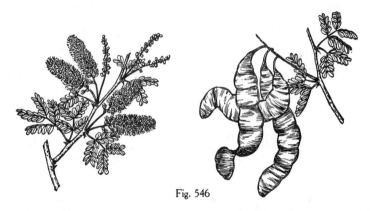

Fig. 546

row scales. Wood heavy, very hard, strong, close-grained, durable, rich brown or red, with thin light yellow sapwood of 5 or 6 layers of annual growth.

Distribution. Dry gravelly mesas, the sides of low cañons and the banks of mountain streams; valley of the Rio Grande, western Texas, through southern New Mexico and Arizona to southern California, ranging northward in Arizona to the rim of the Grand Cañon of the Colorado River, and to Clark County, Nevada; in northern Mexico, and in Lower California to the eastern base of the San Pedro Mártir Mountains.

4. LEUCÆNA Benth.

Trees or shrubs, with slender unarmed branches. Leaves persistent, abruptly bipinnate, with numerous pinnæ and small leaflets in many pairs, petiolate, the petioles often furnished with a conspicuous gland below the lower pair of pinnæ; stipules minute and caducous, or becoming spinescent and persistent. Flowers minute, white, mostly perfect, sessile or short-pedicellate, in the axils of small peltate bracts villose at apex, in globose many-flowered pedunculate heads, the peduncles in axillary fascicles or in leafless terminal racemes; calyx tubular-campanulate, minutely 5-toothed; petals 5, free, acute or rounded at apex, narrowed at base; stamens 10, free, inserted under the ovary, exserted; filaments filiform; anthers oblong, versatile; ovary stipitate, contracted into a long slender style, with a minute terminal slightly dilated stigma. Legume many-seeded, stipitate, linear, compressed, dehiscent, the valves thickened on the margins, rigid, thin, continuous within, their outer coat thin and papery, dark-colored, the inner rather thicker, woody, pale brown. Seeds obovoid, compressed, transverse, the hilum near the base, suspended on a long slender funicle; seed-coat thin, crustaceous, brown and lustrous; embryo inclosed on its two sides by a thin layer of horny albumen; radicle slightly exserted.

Leucæna with nine or ten species is confined to the warmer parts of America from western Texas to Venezuela and Peru, and to the islands of the Pacific Ocean from New Caledonia to Tahiti, where one species has been recognized. Of the indigenous species found in the territory of the United States, three are arborescent. *Leucæna glauca* L., a small tree or shrub, cultivated in all warm countries, and a native probably of tropical America, is now naturalized on Key West, Florida.

The generic name, from λευχαίνω, refers to the color of the flowers.

CONSPECTUS OF THE NORTH AMERICAN SPECIES.

Peduncles bibracteolate at apex; stipules becoming spinescent.
Leaves 10–14-pinnate; pinnæ with 15–30 pairs of leaflets; blade of the bract of the flower
produced into a short point. 1. L. Greggii (E).
Leaves 2–4-pinnate; pinnæ with 4–8 pairs of leaflets; blade of the bract of the flower
produced into a long slender villose tip. 2. L. retusa (E).
Peduncles without bracts; stipules minute, caducous; leaves 30–36-pinnate; pinnæ with
30–60 pairs of leaflets. 3. L. pulverulenta (E).

1. Leucæna Greggii S. Wats.

Leaves 6'–7' long and broad, with a slender rachis furnished on the upper side with a
single elongated bottle-shaped gland between the stalks of each pair of pinnæ; pinnæ 10–14,
remote, short-stalked, with 15–30 pairs of leaflets; stipules gradually narrowed into a long
slender point, becoming rigid and spinescent, $\frac{1}{3}'$ to nearly $\frac{1}{2}'$ long and persistent for two
or three years; leaflets lanceolate, acute or acuminate, often somewhat falcate, nearly
sessile or short-petiolulate, full and rounded toward the base on the lower margin, nearly
straight on the upper margin, gray-green, ultimately nearly glabrous, $\frac{1}{4}'–\frac{1}{3}'$ long, about $\frac{1}{8}'$
wide, with a narrow midvein and obscure lateral nerves. **Flowers** on slender pedicels,
in heads $\frac{3}{4}'–1'$ in diameter, on stout peduncles 2'–3' long furnished at apex with 2 irregularly 3-lobed bracts, and solitary or in pairs; calyx coated with hairs only near the apex,
much shorter than the spatulate glabrous more or less boat-shaped petals; ovary villose
with a few short scattered hairs. **Fruit** 6'–8' long, $\frac{1}{3}–\frac{1}{2}'$ wide, narrowed below into a
short stout stipe, acuminate and crowned at apex with the thickened style, $\frac{1}{3}'–\frac{3}{4}'$ long,

Fig. 547

cinereo-pubescent until nearly fully grown, becoming nearly glabrous at maturity, much
compressed, with narrow wing-like margins; **seeds** conspicuously notched by the hilum,
$\frac{1}{2}'$ long and $\frac{1}{4}'$ wide.

A tree, 15°–20° high, with a stem 4'–5' in diameter, and stout zigzag red-brown branchlets marked by numerous pale lenticels, coated at first with short spreading lustrous
yellow deciduous hairs found also on the young petioles and lower surface of the unfolding
leaflets, the peduncles of the flower-heads and their bracts. **Bark** about $\frac{3}{8}'$ thick, dark
brown, divided into low ridges and broken on the surface into small closely appressed
persistent scales. **Wood** heavy, hard, close-grained, rich brown streaked with red, with
thin clear sapwood.

Distribution. Mountain ravines and the steep banks of streams; western Texas from the
valley of the upper San Saba River to that of Devil's River; and southward into Mexico.

2. Leucæna retusa Benth.

Leaves 3′ or 4′ long and 4′ or 5′ wide, with a slender petiole and rachis and 2–4 pairs of pinnæ 6′–10′ long, remote, long-stalked, with 4–8 pairs of short-stalked leaflets furnished between their stems with a single globose white gland found also occasionally on the upper side of the rachis between the stems of the pinnæ; stipules ovate, gradually narrowed into a long slender tip, ½′ in length, often persistent through the season; leaflets obliquely obovate or elliptic, rounded and apiculate at apex, obliquely rounded or cuneate at the unsymmetric base, entire, short-petiolulate, villose-pubescent like the rachis and petiole when they first appear, soon glabrous, and at maturity thin, blue-green, ¾′–1′ long and ⅓′–½′ wide, with a slender midrib, and prominent veins extending obliquely toward the apex of the leaflet, those of the lowest pair more prominent and starting from near its base.

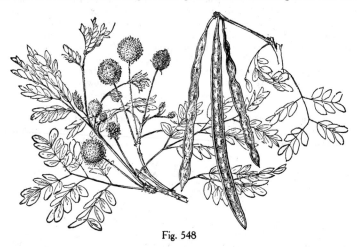

Fig. 548

Flowers short-stalked in the axil of a peltate bract, its blade produced into a long slender villose tip, appearing continuously from April until October in dense globose heads ¾′ in diameter, on villose bibracteolate axillary, single or fascicled peduncles 1½′–3′ in length; calyx thin, tubular, 5-toothed at apex; petals narrow-oblong, hardly longer than the calyx; stamens 10, shorter than the bract of the flower; anthers glabrous. **Fruit** solitary or clustered, on a puberulous peduncle 3′–5′ in length, 6′–10′ long, ⅓′–½′ wide, gradually narrowed below into a stout stipe, the acuminate apex terminating in the thickened persistent style, glabrous and dark reddish brown; seeds ⅓′ long and ¼′ wide.

A tree, occasionally 25° high, with a trunk 6′–8′ in diameter, and slender branchlets pubescent when they first appear, becoming puberulous and orange-brown or reddish brown at the end of their first season; more often a shrub.

Distribution. Texas; steep rocky hillsides, and on the summits of limestone bluffs; (Uvalde, Valverde, Kemble, Real and Jeff Davis Counties).

3. Leucæna pulverulenta Benth. Mimosa.

Leaves 4′–7′ long and 3′–4′ wide, with a slender petiole usually marked by a large dark oblong gland between the somewhat enlarged base and the lowest pair of the 30–36 nearly sessile crowded pinnæ, each with 30–60 pairs of leaflets, and minute caducous stipules, when they unfold covered like the peduncles and flower-buds with dense hoary tomentum, and at maturity puberulous on the petiole and rachis; leaflets linear, acute, rather oblique at base by the greater development of the upper side, sessile or very short-petiolulate, pale bright green, $\frac{1}{8}$–$\frac{1}{4}$' long. **Flowers** sessile, fragrant, in heads $\frac{1}{2}$' in diameter, appearing in succession as the branches grow from early spring to midsummer, on slender peduncles 1'–1$\frac{1}{2}$' long and fascicled in the axils of upper leaves; calyx one fourth as long as the acute petals and like them pilose on the outer surface; stamens twice as long as the petals; ovary coated with long pale hairs. **Fruit** conspicuously thick-margined, 4'–14' long, long-stalked, tipped with a short straight or recurved point, usually in pairs on a peduncle thickened at apex; **seeds** $\frac{5}{16}$' long.

A tree, 50°–60° high, with a straight trunk 18'–20' in diameter, separating 20°–30° from the ground into slender spreading branches forming a loose round head, and branch-lets at first more or less striately grooved and thickly coated with pulverulent caducous tomentum, becoming at the end of a few weeks terete, pale cinnamon-brown and puberu-lous. **Bark** about $\frac{1}{4}$' thick, bright cinnamon-brown, and roughened by thick persistent

Fig. 549

scales. **Wood** heavy, hard, very close-grained, rich dark brown, with thin clear yellow sapwood of 2 or 3 layers of annual growth; considered valuable, and sometimes manufac-tured into lumber.

Distribution. Rich moist soil of river banks and the borders of lagoons and small streams; valley of the lower Rio Grande; in Texas only for a few miles near its mouth; more abundant from Matamoras to Monterey in Nuevo Leon; and southward to the neighborhood of the City of Mexico.

Occasionally planted as a shade and ornamental tree in the towns of the lower Rio Grande valley and in New Orleans, Louisiana.

5. PROSOPIS L. Mesquite.

Trees or shrubs, with branches without a terminal bud and armed with geminate supra-axillary persistent spines, and small obtuse axillary buds covered with acute apiculate dark brown scales. Leaves alternate on branches of the year and fascicled in earlier axils, deciduous, usually 2 rarely 3–4-pinnate, with many-foliolate pinnæ; petioles glandular at apex with a minute gland, and tipped with the small spinescent rachis; stipules linear, membranaceous or spinescent, deciduous. Flowers greenish white, nearly sessile, in axillary pedunculate spikes; calyx campanulate, 5-toothed, or slightly 5-lobed, deciduous; petals 5, connate below the middle or ultimately free, glabrous or tomentose on the inner surface toward the apex, sometimes puberulous on the outer surface; stamens 10, free, inserted with the petals on the margin of a minute disk adnate to the calyx-tube, those opposite the lobes of the calyx rather longer than the others; filaments filiform; an-thers oblong, versatile, their connective tipped with a minute deciduous gland, the cells opening by marginal sutures; ovary stipitate, villose; style filiform, with a minute terminal stigma. Legume linear, compressed or subterete, straight or falcate, or contorted or twisted into a more or less regular spiral, indehiscent; the outer coat thin, woody, pale yellow, inclosing a thick spongy inner coat of sweet pulp containing the seeds placed obliquely and separately inclosed, their envelopes forming nut-like joints. Seeds oblong, compressed, the hilum near the base; seed-coat crustaceous, light brown, lustrous; embryo surrounded by a layer of horny albumen; radicle short, slightly exserted.

Prosopis is distributed in the New World from southern Kansas to Patagonia, and in the Old World is confined to tropical Africa, and to southwestern and tropical Asia. Sixteen or seventeen species have been distinguished. Of the three species found in the territory of the United States two are small trees.

Prosopis produces hard durable wood, particularly valuable as fuel, and the pods are used as fodder.

The generic name is from προσωπίς, employed by Dioscorides as a name of the Burdock.

CONSPECTUS OF THE NORTH AMERICAN ARBORESCENT SPECIES.

Legume compressed or ultimately convex; pinnæ 12–22-foliolate.
1. **P. juliflora** (C, E, G, H).
Legume thick, spirally twisted; pinnæ 10–16-foliolate. 2. **P. pubescens** (E, F, G, H).

1. **Prosopis juliflora** DC. Mesquite. Honey Locust.

Leaves with 2 or rarely 4 pinnæ, and slender terete petioles abruptly enlarged and glandular at base; stipules linear, acute, membranaceous, deciduous. **Flowers** appearing in successive crops from May to the middle of July, fragrant, about $\frac{1}{12}'$ long, on short

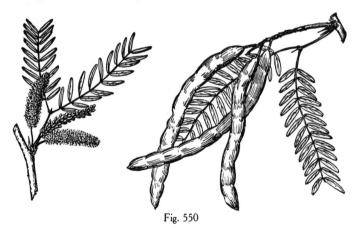

Fig. 550

pedicels, in slender cylindric spikes $1\frac{1}{2}'-4'$ long, on stout peduncles $\frac{1}{2}'-\frac{3}{4}'$ in length; calyx glabrous or puberulous, about one fourth as long as the narrowly oblong acute petals, glabrous or puberulous on the outer surface and covered on the inner surface toward the apex with hoary tomentum; stamens twice as long as the corolla, the dark-colored connective of the anther-cells furnished at apex with a stalked gland; ovary short-stalked, clothed with silky hairs. **Fruit** in drooping clusters, linear, at first flat, becoming subterete at maturity, constricted between the 10–20 seeds, straight or falcate, contracted at the ends, $4'-9'$ long, $\frac{1}{4}'-\frac{1}{2}'$ wide; **seeds** about $\frac{1}{4}'$ long.

A low tree, with a large thick taproot descending frequently to the depth of 40°–50°, and furnished with radiating horizontal roots spreading in all directions and forming a dense mat, a trunk 6′–8′ in diameter, divided a short distance above the ground into many irregularly arranged crooked branches forming a loose straggling head, and slender branchlets at first pale yellow-green, turning darker in their second year, furnished in the axils of the leaves of their first season with short spur-like excrescences covered with chaffy scales, and armed with stout straight terete supra-axillary persistent spines ½′–2′ long, or rarely unarmed; more often a shrub, with numerous stems only a few feet high. **Bark** of the trunk thick, dark reddish brown, divided by shallow fissures, the surface separating into short thick scales. **Wood** heavy, close-grained, rich dark brown or sometimes red, with thin clear yellow sapwood; almost indestructible in contact with the soil, and largely used for fence-posts, railway-ties, the underpinnings of buildings, and occasionally in the manufacture of furniture, the fellies of wheels, and the pavements of city streets; the best fuel of the region, and largely made into charcoal. The ripe pods supply Mexicans and Indians with a nutritious food, and are devoured by most herbivorous animals. A gum, resembling gum-arabic, exudes from the stems.

Distribution. Western Texas and eastern New Mexico, and on the island of Jamaica; eastward and westward diverging into two extreme forms. These are

Prosopis juliflora var. glandulosa Cock.

Leaves 8′–10′ long, 2-pinnate, with long slender petioles, the pinnæ 12–20-foliolate; leaflets distant, linear, mostly acute, glabrous, dark green, often 2′ long and ⅛′–¼′ wide.

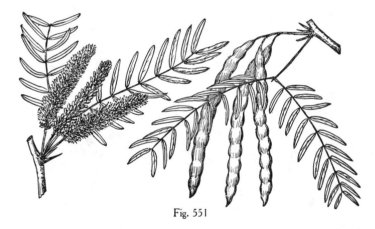

Fig. 551

Flowers with a usually glabrous calyx. **Fruit** occasionally conspicuously constricted between the seeds (f. *constricta* Sarg.).

A round-topped tree, often 20° high, with a trunk a foot in diameter, and long gracefully drooping branches forming a symmetrical round-topped head.

Distribution. Eastern Texas to western Louisiana (near Shreveport, Caddo Parish), western Oklahoma and southern Kansas, and southward into northern Mexico. The common Mesquite of eastern Texas; reappearing with rather shorter and more crowded leaflets in Arizona, southern California, and Lower California.

Prosopis juliflora var. velutina Sarg.

Leaves 5′–6′ long, often fascicled, 2–4-pinnate, cinereo-pubescent, with short petioles, the pinnæ 12–22-foliolate; leaflets oblong or linear-oblong, obtuse or acute, crowded, pale green, ¼′–½′ long. **Flowers** in densely-flowered spikes 2′–3′ long; calyx villose.

A tree, often 50° high, with a trunk 2° in diameter, covered with rough dark brown bark, and heavy irregularly arranged usually crooked branches.

Distribution. Dry valleys of southern Arizona and of Sonora.

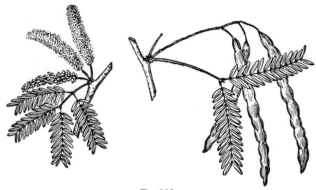

Fig. 552

2. Prosopis pubescens Benth.   Screw Bean.   Screw Pod Mesquite.

Leaves canescently pubescent, 2′–3′ long, with a slender petiole $\frac{1}{3}$′–$\frac{2}{3}$′ in length, and pinnæ $1\frac{1}{2}$′–2′ long and 10–16-foliolate; stipules spinescent, deciduous; leaflets oblong or somewhat falcate, acute, sessile or short-petiolulate, often apiculate, conspicuously reticulate-veined, $\frac{1}{3}$′–$\frac{2}{3}$′ long, $\frac{1}{8}$′ wide. **Flowers** beginning to open in early spring, and produced

Fig. 553

in successive crops from the axils of minute scarious bracts, in dense or interrupted cylindric spikes 2′–3′ long; calyx obscurely 5-lobed, pubescent on the outer surface, one third to one fourth as long as the narrow acute petals coated on the inner surface near the apex with thick white tomentum, and slightly puberulous on the outer surface; ovary and young fruit hoary-tomentose. **Fruit** ripening throughout the summer and falling in the autumn, in dense racemes, sessile, twisted with from 12–20 turns into a narrow straight spiral 1′–2′ long; seeds $\frac{1}{16}$′ long.

A tree, 25°-30° high, with a slender trunk sometimes a foot in diameter, and terete branches canescently pubescent or glabrate when they first appear, becoming glabrous and light red-brown in their third year, and armed with stout spines $\frac{1}{4}$-$\frac{1}{2}$' long. **Bark** of the trunk thick, light brown tinged with red, separating in long thin persistent ribbon-like scales. **Wood** heavy, exceedingly hard, close-grained, not strong, light brown, with thin lighter colored sapwood of 6 or 7 layers of annual growth; used as fuel and occasionally for fencing. The sweet, nutritious legumes are valued as fodder.

Distribution. Sandy or gravelly bottom-lands; valley of the Rio Grande in western Texas, and through New Mexico and Arizona to southern Utah and Nevada, and to San Diego County, California, and northern Mexico; attaining its largest size in the United States in the valleys of the lower Colorado and Gila Rivers, Arizona.

6. CERCIS L.

Trees or shrubs, with scaly bark, slender unarmed branchlets prolonged by an upper axillary bud, marked by numerous minute pale lenticels, and in their first winter by small elevated horizontal leaf-scars showing the ends of two large fibro-vascular bundles, and small scaly obtuse axillary buds covered by imbricated ovate chestnut-brown scales. Leaves simple, entire, 5-7-nerved with prominent nerves, long-petiolate, deciduous; petioles slender, terete, abruptly enlarged at apex; stipules ovate, acute, small, membranaceous, caducous. Flowers appearing in early spring before or with the leaves on thin jointed pedicels, in simple fascicles or racemose clusters produced on branches of the previous or earlier years, or on the trunk, with small scale-like bracts often imbricated at the base of the inflorescence, and minute bractlets; calyx disciferous, short-turbinate, purplish, persistent, the tube oblique at base, campanulate, enlarged on the lower side, 5-toothed, the short broad teeth imbricated in the bud; corolla subpapilionaceous; petals nearly equal, rose color, oblong-ovate, rounded at apex, unguiculate, slightly auricled on one side of the base of the blade, the upper petal slightly smaller and inclosed in the bud by the wing-petals encircled by the broader slightly imbricated keel-petals; stamens 10, inserted in 2 rows on the margin of the thin disk, free, declinate, those of the inner row opposite the petals and rather shorter than the others; filaments enlarged and pilose below the middle, persistent until the fruit is grown; anthers uniform, oblong, attached on the back near the base; ovary short-stalked, inserted obliquely in the bottom of the calyx-tube; style filiform, fleshy, incurved, with a stout obtuse terminal stigma; ovules 2-ranked, attached to the inner angle of the ovary. Legume stalked, oblong or broad-linear, straight on the upper edge, curved on the lower edge, acute at the ends, compressed, tipped with the thickened remnants of the style, many-seeded, 2-valved, the valves coriaceo-membranaceous, many-veined, tardily dehiscent by the dorsal and often by the wing-margined ventral suture, dark red-purple and lustrous at maturity. Seeds suspended transversely on a slender funicle, ovoid or oblong, compressed, the small depressed hilum near the apex; seed-coat crustaceous, bright reddish brown; embryo surrounded by a thin layer of horny albumen, compressed; cotyledons oval, flat, the radicle short, straight or obliquely incurved, slightly exserted.

Cercis is confined to eastern and western North America, southern Europe, and to southwestern, central and eastern Asia. Of the eight species now distinguished, three occur in North America. Two of these are arborescent.

The generic name is from κερκίς, the Greek name of the European species, from a fancied resemblance of the fruit to the weaver's implement of that name.

CONSPECTUS OF THE NORTH AMERICAN ARBORESCENT SPECIES.

Flowers in sessile clusters; leaves ovate, acute, cordate or truncate at base.

1. C. canadensis (A, C).

Flowers fascicled or slightly racemose; leaves reniform. 2. C. reniformis (C).

1. Cercis canadensis L.   Redbud.   Judas-tree.

Leaves broad-ovate, acute or acuminate and often abruptly contracted at apex into a short broad point, truncate or more or less cordate at base, entire, glabrous with the exception of axillary tufts of white hairs, or sometimes more or less pubescent below, $3'-5'$ long and broad; turning in the autumn before falling bright clear yellow; petioles $2'-5'$ in length. **Flowers** $\frac{1}{2}'$ long, on pedicels $\frac{1}{3}'-\frac{1}{2}'$ in length and fascicled 4–8 together; rarely white (var. *alba* Rehdr.).   **Fruit** fully grown in the south by the end of May and at the north at midsummer, and then pink or rose color, $2\frac{1}{2}'-3\frac{1}{2}'$ long, falling late in the autumn or in early winter; **seeds** about $\frac{1}{4}'$ long.

A tree, sometimes $40°-50°$ high, with a straight trunk usually separating $10°-12°$ from the ground into stout branches covered with smooth light brown or gray bark, and form-

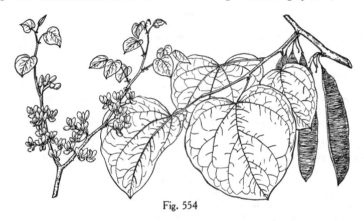

Fig. 554

ing an upright or often a wide flat head, and slender glabrous somewhat angled branchlets, brown and lustrous during their first season, becoming dull and darker the following year and ultimately dark or grayish brown.   **Bark** of the trunk about $\frac{1}{3}'$ thick and divided by deep longitudinal fissures into long narrow plates, the bright red-brown surface separating into thin scales.   **Wood** heavy, hard, not strong, close-grained, rich dark brown tinged with red, with thin lighter colored sapwood of 8–10 layers of annual growth.

Distribution. Borders of streams and rich bottom-lands, forming, especially west of the Alleghany Mountains, an abundant undergrowth to the forest; valley of the Delaware River, New Jersey, central and southern Pennsylvania southward to northern Florida, northern Alabama and southern Mississippi (Crystal Springs, Copiah County), and westward to southwestern Ontario (Point Pelee, Essex County), and through southern Michigan to southern Iowa, southeastern Nebraska, eastern Kansas, to western Oklahoma (Major and Dewey Counties), Louisiana, and the valley of the Brazos River, Texas; and on the Sierra Madre of Nuevo Leon; common and of its largest size in southwestern Arkansas, Oklahoma and eastern Texas, and in early spring a conspicuous feature of the landscape.

Often cultivated as an ornamental tree in the northeastern states, and occasionally in western Europe.

2. Cercis reniformis Engl.   Redbud.

Cercis texensis Sarg.

Leaves reniform, when they unfold light green and slightly pilose, and at maturity subcoriaceous, dark green and lustrous on the upper surface, paler, glabrous or pubescent on the lower surface, and $2'-3'$ in diameter; petioles $1\frac{1}{2}'-2'$ in length.   **Flowers** about $\frac{1}{2}'$

long, on slender pedicels $\frac{1}{2}'-\frac{3}{4}'$ in length and fascicled in sessile clusters, or occasionally racemose. **Fruit** $2'-4'$ long, $\frac{1}{2}'-1'$ wide; **seeds** $\frac{1}{4}'$ long.

A slender tree, occasionally 20° or rarely 40° high, with a trunk $6'-12'$ in diameter, and glabrous branchlets marked by numerous minute white lenticels, light reddish brown during their first and second years, becoming dark brown in their third season; more often a shrub, sending up numerous stems and forming dense thickets only a few feet high.

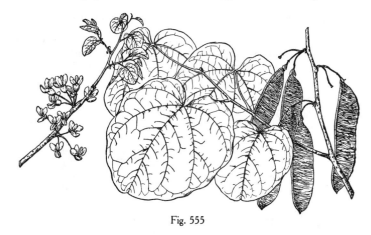

Fig. 555

Bark of the trunk and branches thin, smooth, light gray. **Wood** heavy, hard, close-grained, brown streaked with yellow, with thin lighter colored sapwood of 5 or 6 layers of annual growth.

Distribution. Limestone hills and ridges; neighborhood of Dallas, Dallas County, Texas to the Sierra Madre of Nuevo Leon; common in the valley of the upper Colorado River, Texas; of its largest size on the mountains of northeastern Mexico.

7. GYMNOCLADUS Lam.

Trees, with stout unarmed blunt branchlets with a thick pith, prolonged by axillary buds, rough deeply fissured bark, thick fleshy roots, and minute buds depressed in pubescent cavities of the bark, 2 in the axil of each leaf, superposed, remote, the lower and smaller sterile and nearly surrounded by the enlarged base of the petiole, their scales 2, ovate, rounded at apex, coated with thick dark brown tomentum, infolded one over the other, accrescent with the young shoots. Leaves deciduous, unequally bipinnate; pinnæ many-foliolulate, with 1 or 2 pairs of the lowest pinnæ reduced to single leaflets; pinnæ and leaflets usually alternate; leaflets thin, ovate, entire, petiolulate; stipules foliaceous, early deciduous. Flowers regular, diœcious, greenish white, long-pedicellate, the slender pedicels from the axils of long lanceolate scarious caducous bracts, bibracteolate near the middle; staminate flowers in a short terminal racemose corymb; pistillate flowers in elongated terminal racemes, on pedicels much longer than those of the staminate flowers; calyx tubular, elongated, 10-ribbed, lined with a thin glandular disk, 5-lobed, the lobes lanceolate, acute, nearly equal, erect; petals 4 or 5, oblong, rounded or acute at apex, pubescent, as long as the calyx-lobes or rather longer and twice as broad, inserted on the margin of the disk, spreading or reflexed; stamens 10, free, inserted with the petals, erect, included; filaments filiform, pilose, those opposite the petals shorter than the others; anthers oblong, uniform, small and sterile in the pistillate flower; ovary sessile or slightly stipitate, acute; styles short, erect, obliquely dilated into 2 broad lobes stigmatic on their inner surface, rudimentary or 0 in the sterile flower; ovules numerous, suspended from the angle opposite the posterior petals. Legume oblong, subfalcate, turgid or slightly compressed, several-seeded, 2-valved, tardily dehiscent, the thin tough woody valves thickened on the margins into narrow wings, pulpy between the seeds. Seeds ovoid or slightly obovoid, suspended by a long slender funicle; seed-coat thick, bony, brown and opaque, of 3 layers; embryo surrounded by a thin layer of horny albumen; cotyledons ovate, orange-colored, thick and fleshy, the radicle short, erect.

Gymnocladus, with two species, is confined to eastern North America and to central China.

Gymnocladus is slightly astringent and purgative, and the detersive pulp surrounding the seeds of the Asiatic species is used in China as a substitute for soap.

The generic name, from γυμνός and κλάδος, relates to the stout branchlets destitute of spray.

1. Gymnocladus dioicus K. Koch. Kentucky Coffee-tree. Mahogany.

Leaves 1°–3° long, 18′–24′ wide, obovate, 5–9 pinnate, the pinnæ 6–14-foliolate, covered when they unfold with hoary tomentum except on the upper surface of the ovate acute

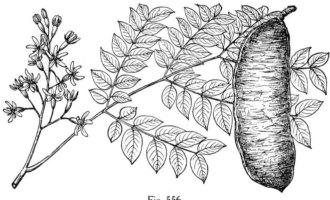

Fig. 556

leaflets, often mucronate, especially while young, cuneate or irregularly rounded at base, pink at first, soon becoming bronze-green and lustrous, glabrous on the upper surface with the exception of a few scattered hairs along the midrib, and at maturity thin, obscurely veined, dark green above, pale yellow-green and glabrous below, with the exception of a few short hairs scattered along the narrow midrib, 2′–2½′ long and 1′ wide, or those replacing the lowest or occasionally the 2 lower pairs of pinnæ sometimes twice as large; turning bright clear yellow in the autumn before falling; petioles abruptly and conspicuously enlarged at base, at first hoary-tomentose, becoming glabrous at maturity; stipules lanceolate or slightly obovate, glandular-serrate toward the apex, ¼′ long. **Flowers:** inflorescence of the staminate tree 3′–4′ long, the lower branches usually 3 or 4-flowered; inflorescence of the pistillate tree 10′–12′ long, the flowers on stout pedicels 1′–2½′ long or twice to five times as long as those of the staminate flowers; flowers hoary-tomentose in the bud; calyx ⅔′ long, covered on the outer surface when the flowers open with pale hairs and on the inner surface with hoary tomentum; petals keeled, pilose on the back, slightly grooved, tomentose on the inner surface; anthers bright orange color; ovary hairy. **Fruit** 6′–10′ long, 1½′–2′ wide, dark red-brown, covered with a glaucous bloom, on stout stalks 1′–2′ in length, remaining unopened on the branches through the winter; **seeds** separated by a thick layer of dark-colored sweet pulp, ¾′ long.

A tree, 75°–110° high, with a trunk 2°–3° in diameter, usually dividing 10°–15° from the ground into 3 or 4 principal stems spreading slightly and forming a narrow round-topped head, or occasionally sending up a tall straight shaft destitute of branches for 70°–80°, and branchlets coated when they first appear with short dense pubescence faintly tinged with red, bearing at their base the conspicuous orange-green obovate pubescent bud-scales, $\frac{1}{4}'$–$\frac{1}{3}'$ thick at the end of their first season, very blunt, dark brown, often slightly pilose, marked by orange-colored lenticels, and roughened by the large pale broadly heart-shaped leaf-scars displaying the ends of 3 or 4 conspicuous fibro-vascular bundles. **Bark** of the trunk $\frac{3}{4}'$–1' thick, deeply fissured, dark gray tinged with red, and roughened by small persistent scales. **Wood** heavy although not hard, strong, coarse-grained, very durable in contact with the soil, rich light brown tinged with red, with thin lighter colored sapwood of 5 or 6 layers of annual growth; occasionally used in cabinet-making and for fence-posts, rails, and in construction. The seeds were formerly used as a substitute for coffee; a decoction of the fresh green pulp of the unripe fruit is used in homœopathic practice.

Distribution. Bottom-lands in rich soil; central and western New York and Franklin County, Pennsylvania, through southern Ontario and southern Michigan to southeastern Minnesota, northeastern and southern Iowa, southeastern South Dakota, eastern and northeastern Nebraska, eastern Kansas, northern and western Arkansas and northeastern Oklahoma (with isolated stations in Woods and Custer Counties and in the western parts of Cimarron County); in eastern Kentucky, and western and middle Tennessee; nowhere common.

Occasionally cultivated in the gardens and parks of the eastern United States, and of northern and central Europe.

8. GLEDITSIA L.

Trees, with furrowed bark, slender terete slightly zigzag branchlets thickened at the apex and prolonged by axillary buds, thick fibrous roots, the trunk and branches often armed with stout simple or branched spines or abortive branchlets developed from supra-axillary or adventitious buds imbedded in the bark. Winter-buds minute, 3 or 4 together, superposed, the 2 or 3 lower without scales and covered by the scar left by the falling of the petiole, the upper larger, nearly surrounded by the base of the petiole and covered by small scurfy scales. Leaves long-petiolate, often fascicled in earlier axils, abruptly pin-nate or bipinnate, the pinnæ increasing in length from the base to the apex of the leaf, the lowest sometimes reduced to single leaflets; deciduous; leaflets thin, their mar-gins irregularly crenate, without stipels; stipules minute, caducous. Flowers regular, polygamous, minute, green or white on short pedicels, in axillary or lateral simple or fascicled racemes, with minute scale-like caducous bracts; calyx campanulate, lined with the disk, 3–5-lobed, the narrow lobes nearly equal; petals as many as the lobes of the calyx, nearly equal; stamens 6–10, inserted with the petals on the margin of the disk, exserted; filaments free, filiform, erect; anthers uniform, much smaller and abortive in the pistillate flower; ovary subsessile, rarely bicarpellary, rudimentary or 0 in the staminate flower; styles short; stigma terminal, more or less dilated, often oblique; ovules 2 or many, sus-pended from the angle opposite the posterior petal. Legume compressed, many-seeded, elongated, straight and indehiscent, or 1–3-seeded, ovoid and tardily dehiscent. Seeds transverse, ovoid to suborbicular, flattened, attached by a long slender funicle; seed-coat thin, crustaceous, light brown; embryo surrounded by a layer of horny orange-colored albumen; cotyledons subfoliaceous, compressed; radicle short, erect, slightly exserted.

Gleditsia is confined to eastern North America, where three species occur, southwestern Asia, China, Formosa, Japan, and west tropical Africa. It produces strong, durable, coarse-grained wood. In Japan the pods are used as a substitute for soap.

The generic name is in honor of Johann Gottlieb Gleditsch (1714–1786), professor of botany at Berlin.

CONSPECTUS OF THE NORTH AMERICAN ARBORESCENT SPECIES.

Legume linear-oblong, elongated, many-seeded, indehiscent.
 Legume 12′–18′ long, with pulp between the seeds; ovary hoary-tomentose.
                  1. **G. triacanthos** (A, C).
 Legume 4′–5′ long, without pulp between the seeds.   2. **G. texana** (C).
Legume oval, oblique, 1–3-seeded, without pulp, tardily dehiscent; ovary glabrous.
                  3. **G. aquatica** (A, C).

1. Gleditsia triacanthos L. Honey Locust.

Leaves 7′–8′ long, 18–28-foliolulate or sometimes bipinnate, with 4–7 pairs of pinnæ, those of the upper pair 4′–5′ long, when they unfold hoary-tomentose, and at maturity pubescent on the petiole and rachis, the short stout petiolules, and the under surface of the midrib of the oblong-lanceolate leaflets, unequal at base, acute or slightly rounded

Fig. 557

at apex, remotely crenulate-serrate, dark green and lustrous above, dull yellow-green below, 1′–1½′ long and ½′ wide; turning in the autumn pale clear yellow. **Flowers** appearing in June when the leaves are nearly fully grown from the axils of leaves of previous years; the staminate in short many-flowered pubescent racemes 2′–2½′ long and often clustered; the pistillate in slender graceful few-flowered usually solitary racemes 2½′–3½′ long; calyx campanulate, narrowed at base, the acute lobes thickened, revolute and ciliate on the margins, villose with pale hairs, rather shorter than and half as wide as the erect acute petals; filaments pilose toward the base; anthers green; pistil rarely of 2 carpels, hoary-tomentose. **Fruit** 12′–18′ long, dark brown, pilose and slightly falcate, with straight thickened margins, 2 or 3 together in short racemes on stalks 1′–1½′ long, their walls thin and tough, contracting in drying by a number of corkscrew twists, and falling late in the autumn or early in winter; **seeds** oval, ⅓′ long, separated by thick succulent pulp.

A tree, 75°–140° high, with a trunk 2°–3° or occasionally 5°–6° in diameter, slender spreading somewhat pendulous branches forming a broad open rather flat-topped head, and branchlets marked by minute lenticels, at first light reddish brown and slightly puberulous, soon becoming lustrous and red tinged with green, and in their second year greenish brown and armed with stout rigid long-pointed simple or 3-forked spines at first red, and bright chestnut-brown when fully grown, or rarely unarmed (var. *inermis* Pursh.). **Bark** of the trunk ½′–¾′ thick, divided by deep fissures into long narrow longitudinal ridges and roughened on the surface by small persistent scales. **Wood** hard, strong, coarse-grained, very durable in contact with the ground, red or bright red-brown, with thin pale sapwood of 10–12 layers of annual growth; largely used for fence-posts and rails, for the hubs of wheels, and in construction.

Distribution. Borders of streams and intervale lands, in moist fertile soil, usually growing singly or occasionally covering almost exclusively considerable areas; less commonly on dry sterile gravelly hills; western slope of the Alleghany Mountains of Pennsylvania, westward through southern Ontario and southern Michigan to southeastern Minnesota, southern Iowa, southeastern South Dakota, eastern Nebraska, eastern Kansas, and Oklahoma to the Salt Fork of the Arkansas River (near Alva, Woods County) and to creek valleys near Cache, Comanche County (*G. W. Stevens*), and southward to northern Alabama, Mississippi and middle Florida (St. Marks, Wakulla County), and to the valley of the Brazos River, eastern Texas; and in the cañon of Paloduro Creek near Canyon, Randall County, northwestern Texas (*E. J. Palmer*); in Pennsylvania and West Virginia occasionally on the eastern slopes of the Appalachian Mountains; attaining its largest size in the valleys of small streams in southern Indiana and Illinois; now often naturalized in the region east of the Alleghany Mountains. The var. *inermis*, the prevailing form in Richland County, Illinois, and in Taney County, southern Missouri.

Often cultivated as an ornamental and shade tree in all countries of temperate climates.

2. Gleditsia texana Sarg. Locust.

Gleditsia brachycarpa Nutt., not Pursh.

Leaves 6′–7′ long, 12–22-foliolulate, with a slender rachis at first puberulous, ultimately glabrous, or often bipinnate, usually with 6 or 7 pairs of pinnæ, the lower pairs frequently reduced to single large leaflets; leaflets oblong-ovate, often somewhat falcate,

Fig. 558

rounded or acute or apiculate at apex, obliquely rounded at base, finely crenately serrate, thick and firm in texture, dark green and lustrous above, pale below, ½′–1′ long, with a short petiolule coated while young, like the base of the slender orange-colored midrib, with soft pale hairs. **Flowers** appearing toward the end of April, the staminate dark orange-yellow, in slender glabrous often clustered racemes lengthening after the flowers begin to open and finally 3′–4′ in length; calyx campanulate, with acute lobes thickened on the margins, villose-pubescent and rather shorter and narrower than the puberulous petals; stamens with slender filaments villose near the base and green anthers; pistillate flowers unknown. **Fruit** 4′–5′ long, 1′ wide, straight, much compressed, rounded and short-pointed at apex, full and rounded at the broad base, thin-walled, dark chestnut-brown, puberulous, slightly thickened on the margins, many-seeded, without pulp; **seeds** oval, compressed, dark chestnut-brown, very lustrous, $\frac{1}{2}'$ long.

A tree, 100°–120° high, with a trunk rarely exceeding $2\frac{1}{2}°$ in diameter, ascending and spreading branches forming a narrow head, and comparatively slender more or less zigzag branchlets roughened by numerous small round lenticels, light orange-brown when they first appear, gray or orange-brown during their first year, ashy gray the following season, and unarmed. **Bark** thin and smooth.

Distribution. In a group on the bottom-lands of the Brazos River, near the town of Brazoria, Brazoria County, Texas; Louisiana, near Shreveport, Caddo Parish (*R. S. Cocks*, 1907); Mississippi, Yazoo City, Yazoo County (*S. M. Tracey*, 1911); Indiana (Knox and Gibson Counties, *J. Schneck*, Plant World, vii. 252 [1904]), Gibson County (*C. C. Deam*, 1921).

Perhaps best considered a hybrid between *G. triacanthos* and *G. aquatica*.

3. Gleditsia aquatica Marsh. Water Locust.

Leaves 5′–8′ long, 12–20-foliolate, or bipinnate, with 3 or 4 pairs of pinnæ; leaflets ovate-oblong, usually rounded or rarely emarginate at apex, unequally cuneate at base,

Fig. 559

slightly and remotely crenate or often entire below the middle, glabrous with the exception of a few hairs on the short stout petiolule, dull yellow-green and lustrous on the upper surface, dark green on the lower surface, about 1′ long and $\frac{1}{3}$–$\frac{1}{2}'$ wide. **Flowers** appearing in May and June after the leaves are fully grown on short stout purple puberulous pedicels, in slender racemes 3′–4′ long; calyx-tube covered with orange-brown pubescence, the lobes narrow, acute, slightly pilose on the two surfaces, as long as but narrower than the green erect petals rounded at apex; filaments hairy toward the base; anthers large, green; ovary long-stipitate, glabrous. **Fruit** fully grown in August, pendent in graceful racemes, obliquely ovoid, long-stalked, crowned with a short stout tip, thin, 1′–2′ long, 1′ broad, without pulp, its valves thin, tough, papery, bright chestnut-brown, lustrous and somewhat thickened on the margins; **seeds** 1 or rarely 2 or 3, flat, nearly orbicular, orange-brown, $\frac{1}{2}'$ in diameter.

A tree, 50°–60° high, with a short trunk 2°–$2\frac{1}{2}°$ in diameter, usually dividing a few feet from the ground into stout spreading often contorted branches forming a wide irregular flat-topped head, and glabrous orange-brown branchlets becoming in their second year gray or reddish brown, marked by occasional large pale lenticels, and armed with usually flattened simple or short-branched straight or falcate sharp rigid spines 3′–5′ long, about $\frac{1}{2}'$ broad at the base, and dark red-brown and lustrous. **Bark** $\frac{1}{8}$–$\frac{1}{4}'$ thick, smooth, dull gray or reddish brown, and divided by shallow fissures into small plate-like scales. **Wood** heavy, very hard and strong, coarse-grained, rich bright brown tinged with red, with thick light clear yellow sapwood of about 40 layers of annual growth.

Distribution. Eastern South Carolina to Florida, through the coast region of the Gulf states except in Alabama to the valley of the Brazos River, Texas, and northward through western Louisiana and southern Arkansas to northwestern Mississippi, middle Kentucky and Tennessee, the bottoms of the Mississippi, southeastern Missouri, western and southern Illinois and southwestern Indiana; rare east of the Mississippi River and only in deep river swamps; very abundant and of its largest size westward on rich bottom-lands; in Louisiana and Arkansas often occupying extensive tracts submerged during a considerable part of the year.

9. PARKINSONIA L.

Trees or shrubs, with smooth thin bark and terete branches often armed with simple or 3-forked spines. Leaves abruptly bipinnate, alternate or fascicled from earlier axils, short-petiolate, the rachis short and spinescent, with 2–4 secondary elongated rachises bearing numerous minute opposite entire leaflets without stipels; stipules short, persistent and spinescent, or caducous. Flowers perfect on thin elongated jointed pedicels from the axils of minute caducous bracts, in slender axillary solitary or fascicled racemes; calyx short-campanulate, 5-lobed, the lobes slightly inbricated or subvalvate in the bud, narrow, membranaceous, nearly equal, becoming reflexed, deciduous; petals bright yellow, unguiculate, much longer than the lobes of the calyx, spreading, the upper petal rather broader than the others and glandular at the base of the claw; stamens 10, inserted in 2 rows on the margin of the thin disk, free, slightly declinate, those of the outer row opposite the sepals and rather longer than the others; filaments villose below the middle, the upper filament enlarged at base and gibbous on the upper side; anthers uniform, versatile; ovary short-stipitate, pilose, contracted into a slender filiform incurved style infolded in the bud and tipped with a minute stigma; ovules numerous, suspended from the inner angle of the ovary. Legume linear, torulose, acuminate at the ends, 2-valved, the valves thin, convex by the growth of the seeds, contracted between and beyond them, longitudinally striate. Seeds oblong, suspended longitudinally on a slender funicle; hilum minute, near the apex; seed-coat thin, crustaceous, light brown; embryo inclosed on the sides only by thick layers of horny albumen; cotyledons oval, flat, slightly fleshy, the radicle very short and straight.

Parkinsonia, with four species, is confined to the warm parts of America and to southern Africa. Two species occur within the limits of the United States.

The genus is named for John Parkinson (1567–1650), an English botanical author, and herbalist to James I.

CONSPECTUS OF THE NORTH AMERICAN SPECIES.

Flowers in long slender racemes; petals imbricated in the bud; stamens shorter than the petals; legume 1–8-seeded, 12′–18′ long; leaves 7′–8′ long; rachis of the pinnæ flat, wing-margined, 50–60-foliolate; branches with spines.   1. **P. aculeata** (G, H).

Flowers in short racemes; petals valvate in the bud; stamens longer than the petals; legume 1–2-seeded; leaves about 1′ long; rachis of the pinnæ terete, 8–12-foliolate; branches without spines.   2. **P. microphylla** (G, H).

1. Parkinsonia aculeata L.   Retama.   Horse Bean.

Leaves of two forms, short-petiolate, persistent, light green and glabrous, except for a few hairs on the lower part of the young secondary rachis, 12′–18′ long; primary leaves on young branches, with 2–4 pinnæ, and a spinescent rachis developing into a stout ridged persistent short-pointed chestnut-brown spine 1′–1½′ long and marked near the base by the prominent scars left by the fall of the pinnæ; stipules persistent, appearing as lateral spiny branches on the spines; secondary leaves fascicled from the axils of the primary leaves, nearly sessile with a short terete spinescent rachis and 2 pinnæ; pinnæ flat, 12′–18′ in length, wing-margined, acute at apex, with 25–30 pairs of ovate or obovate petiolulate leaflets, $\frac{1}{16}'-\frac{1}{8}'$ long. **Flowers** appearing on the growing branches during the spring and summer, and in the tropics throughout the year, on slender pedicels $\frac{1}{3}'-\frac{1}{2}'$ in length, in slender erect racemes 5′–6′ long; petals bright yellow, the upper one marked near the base on the inner surface with conspicuous red spots; stamens shorter than the petals. **Fruit** hanging on pedicels $\frac{1}{2}'-\frac{3}{4}'$ in length, in graceful racemes, 2′–4′ long, long-pointed, dark orange-brown, slightly pilose, compressed between the remote seeds; **seeds** $\frac{1}{3}'$ long, nearly terete, with thick albumen and a bright yellow embryo.

A tree, 18°–30° high, with a trunk sometimes a foot in diameter, usually separating 6°–8° from the ground into slender spreading somewhat pendulous branches forming a wide graceful head, and slightly zigzag branchlets puberulous and yellow-green during their first season, becoming glabrous, gray or light orange color and roughened by lenticels in their second and third years. **Bark** of the trunk about $\frac{1}{8}'$ thick, brown tinged with red, the generally smooth surface broken into small persistent plate-like scales. **Wood**

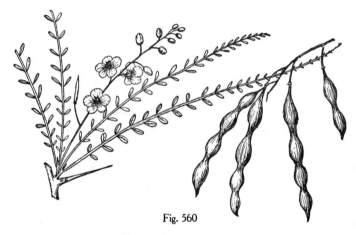

Fig. 560

heavy, hard, close-grained, with very thick lighter colored sapwood tinged with yellow.

Distribution. Low moist soil, valley of the lower Rio Grande, Texas; common in northern Mexico and in the valley of the lower Colorado River, Arizona; widely distributed in Lower California; naturalized on Key West, the Bahamas, the West Indian islands, and in many other tropical countries.

Cultivated in most warm countries as an ornament of gardens, and to form hedges.

2. Parkinsonia microphylla Torr.

Leaves 1′ long, pale, densely tomentose when they unfold, pubescent at maturity, deciduous at the end of a few weeks; petiole $\frac{1}{4}'$ long; rachis short, rarely spinescent; leaflets in 4–6 pairs, distant, entire, sessile, broad-oblong or nearly orbicular, obtuse or somewhat acute at apex, oblique at base, $\frac{1}{6}'$ long; stipules caducous. **Flowers** opening in May or early June before the leaves, on slender pedicels, in racemes 1′ or less long from the axils of leaves of the previous year, pale yellow; stamens longer than the petals. **Fruit** persistent on the branches for at least a year, frequently 1 or 2, rarely 3-seeded, 2′–3′ long, slightly puberulous, especially toward the base, with a long acuminate often falcate apex; **seeds** compressed, $\frac{1}{3}'$ long, with a bright green embryo.

An intricately branched tree, occasionally 20°–25° high, with a trunk a foot in diameter, and stout pale yellow-green rigid branchlets terminating in a stout spine, covered at first with deciduous tomentum, slightly puberulous during their first and second seasons, and often marked by the persistent scales of undeveloped buds. **Bark** dark orange color, generally smooth, although sometimes roughened by scattered clusters of short pale gray horizontal ridges, becoming on old trees $\frac{1}{4}'$ thick; more often a shrub, frequently only a few feet tall. **Wood** heavy, hard, close-grained, dark orange-brown streaked with red, with thick light brown or yellow sapwood of 25–30 layers of annual growth.

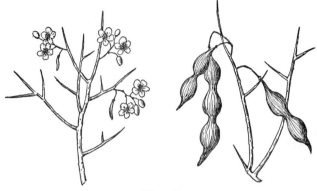

Fig. 561

Distribution. Deserts of southern Arizona and adjacent regions of California and Sonora, and in northern Lower California; known to attain the size and habits of a tree only in the neighborhood of Wickenburg, Maricopa County, Arizona.

10. CERCIDIUM Tul.

Trees or shrubs, with stout tortuous branches, covered with bright green bark and armed with slender straight axillary spines, and minute obtuse buds. Leaves alternate, abruptly pinnate, petiolate, early deciduous; pinnæ 2 or occasionally 3, 6–8-foliolate; stipules inconspicuous or 0; leaflets ovate or obovate, without stipels. Flowers perfect in short few-flowered axillary racemes, solitary or fascicled, with minute membranaceous early deciduous bracts; calyx 5-lobed, the lobes equal, acute, reflexed at maturity, their margins scarious, slightly revolute; petals orbicular or short-oblong, unguiculate, bright yellow, the upper petal broader and longer clawed than the others, slightly auriculate at base of the blade, the claw conspicuously glandular at base; stamens 10, inserted with the petals on the margin of the disk, free, slightly declinate, exserted; filaments filiform, pilose below, the upper filament enlarged at base and gibbous on the upper side; anthers uniform, ovoid, versatile; ovary short-stalked, inserted at the base of the calyx-tube; styles slender, involute, infolded in the bud, with a minute terminal stigma; ovules suspended from the angle of the ovary opposite the posterior petal. Legume linear-oblong, compressed or somewhat turgid, straight or slightly contracted between the seeds, thickened on the margins, the ventral suture acute, or slightly grooved, tipped with the remnants of the style, tardily dehiscent, 2-valved, the valves membranaceous or subcoriaceous, obliquely veined. Seeds suspended longitudinally on a long slender funicle, ovoid, compressed, the minute hilum near the apex; seed-coat thin, crustaceous; embryo compressed, light green, covered on the sides only by a thin layer of horny albumen; cotyledons oval, flat, rather fleshy; radicle very short, erect, near the hilum.

Cercidium is confined to the warmer parts of the New World, where it is distributed with four or five species from the southern borders of the United States through Mexico, Central America, and Venezuela to Mendoza. Of the three species found within the territory of the United States two are small trees.

Cercidium produces hard wood sometimes used as fuel.

The generic name, from κερκίδιον, refers to the fancied resemblance of the legume to the weaver's instrument of that name.

CONSPECTUS OF THE NORTH AMERICAN ARBORESCENT SPECIES.

Legume compressed, with straight margins; leaflets green, slightly glandular.

1. C. floridum (E).

Legume somewhat turgid, the margins often slightly contracted between the seeds; leaflets glaucous. 2. C. Torreyanum (G, H).

1. Cercidium floridum Benth. Green-barked Acacia.

Leaves 1'–1½' long, with 2 or rarely 3 pinnæ, a broad pubescent petiole and rachis, and oval or somewhat obovate dull green puberulous minutely glandular leaflets about $\frac{1}{16}'$ in length, rounded or slightly emarginate at apex, and when they unfold covered on the lower surface with scattered white hairs; petiolules short, stout, pubescent; appearing in April and deciduous in October. **Flowers** opening with the leaves, and produced in suc-

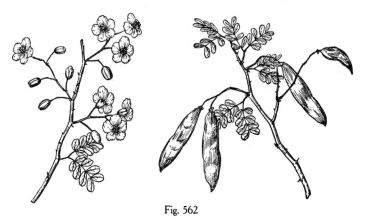

Fig. 562

cessive crops during three or four months, $\frac{3}{4}'$ in diameter, on slender pedicels, in 4 or 5-flowered racemes 1½'–2' long, with small acute minute membranaceous caducous bracts. **Fruit** compressed, oblong, straight or slightly falcate, acute, narrowly and acutely margined on the ventral suture, glabrous, 2 or 3-seeded, 2'–2½' long, ½' broad, tardily dehiscent, the valves papery, yellow tinged with brown on the outer surface, and bright orange color within; **seeds** ⅓' long.

A tree, 18°–20° high, with a short crooked trunk 8'–10' in diameter, stout spreading branches covered with thin smooth bright green bark, forming a low wide head, and branchlets light or dark olive-green, slightly puberulous at first, soon glabrous, marked by occasional black lenticels, and armed with slender spines 1' or less in length. **Bark** $\frac{1}{16}'$ thick, light brown tinged with red, with numerous short horizontal light gray ridge-like excrescences. **Wood** light, soft, close-grained, pale yellow tinged with green, with thick lighter colored sapwood.

Distribution. Shores of Matagorda Bay to Hidalgo and Valverde Counties, Texas, and in northern Mexico; not common in Texas; very abundant and a conspicuous feature of vegetation in Mexico from the mouth of the Rio Grande to the foothills of the Sierra Madre.

2. Cercidium Torreyanum Sarg.   Green-barked Acacia.   Palo Verde.

Leaves few and scattered, 1′ long, hoary-tomentose when they first appear, puberulous at maturity, with a slender petiole and 2 pinnæ, with 2 or 3 pairs of oblong obtuse glaucous leaflets narrowed toward the somewhat oblique base, $\frac{1}{12}′-\frac{1}{8}′$ long; unfolding in March and April and falling almost immediately when fully grown.   **Flowers** $\frac{3}{4}′$ in diameter, on slender pedicels $\frac{3}{4}′-1′$ long, in 4 or 5-flowered racemes about 1′ in length, with small acute membranaceous caducous bracts.   **Fruit** ripening and falling in July, 3′–4′ long, $\frac{1}{4}′-\frac{1}{3}′$ wide, 2–8-seeded, slightly turgid, often somewhat contracted between the seeds, frequently grooved on the ventral suture; **seeds** turgid, $\frac{1}{3}′$ long.

A low intricately branched tree, leafless for most of the year, 25°–30° high, with a short often inclining trunk 18′–20′ in diameter, stout spreading branches covered with yellow

Fig. 563

or olive-green bark, forming a wide open irregular head, and glabrous slightly zigzag light yellow or pale olive-green and glaucous branchlets armed with thin straight or curved spines $\frac{1}{4}′$ long.   **Bark** thin, smooth, pale olive-green, becoming near the base of old trunks reddish brown, $\frac{1}{8}′$ thick, furrowed and separating into thick plate-like scales.   **Wood** heavy, not strong, soft, close-grained, light brown, with clear light yellow sapwood.

Distribution.   Sides of low cañons and depressions, and sandhills of the desert; valley of the lower Gila River, Arizona, to the Colorado Desert of southern California, and southward into Sonora and Lower California; when in flower in early spring the conspicuous and most beautiful feature of the vegetation of the Colorado Desert.

11. SOPHORA L.

Trees or shrubs, with minute scaly buds, unarmed terete branches prolonged by an upper axillary bud, and fibrous roots.   Leaves unequally pinnate, with numerous small or few and ample thin or coriaceous leaflets; stipules minute, deciduous; stipels often 0. Flowers in terminal or axillary racemes, with linear minute deciduous bracts and bractlets; calyx broad-campanulate, often slightly turbinate or obconic at base, obliquely truncate, the short teeth nearly equal or the 2 upper subconnate and often somewhat larger than the others; disk cupuliform, glandular, adnate to the calyx-tube; corolla papilionaceous; petals white or violet blue, unguiculate; standard obovate or orbicular, usually shorter than the oblong, suberect keel-petals, as long or rather longer than the oblong-oblique wings, overlapping each other at the back, barely united; stamens free, or 9 of them slightly united at base, uniform; anthers attached on the back near the middle; ovary short-stipitate, contracted into an incurved style, with a minute truncate or slightly rounded capitate stigma; ovules numerous, suspended from the inner angle of the ovary, superposed, amphitropous. Legume terete, much contracted between the seeds, woody or fleshy, usually many-seeded, each seed inclosed in a separate cell, indehiscent. Seed oblong or oval, sometimes somewhat compressed; seed-coat thick, membranaceous or crustaceous; cotyledons thick and fleshy; radicle short and straight or more or less elongated and incurved.

Sophora is scattered over the warmer parts of the two hemispheres, with about twenty species of trees, shrubs or herbs; of the six North American species two are small trees. Several of the species produce valuable wood, and from the pods and flower-buds of the Chinese *Sophora japonica* L., a dye is obtained used to dye white cloth yellow and blue cloth green. This tree is often cultivated as an ornament of parks and gardens in northern China, Japan, the eastern United States, and in western, central, and southern Europe.

The generic name is from *Sophera*, the Arabic name of some tree with pea-shaped flowers.

CONSPECTUS OF THE NORTH AMERICAN ARBORESCENT SPECIES.

Flowers violet blue, in terminal racemes; the upper calyx-lobes larger than the others and united; legume woody; seeds without albumen; leaves coriaceous, persistent.
1. S. secundiflora (C, E, H).
Flowers white, in axillary racemes; calyx-lobes equal; legume fleshy; seeds with albumen; leaves thin, deciduous.   2. S. affinis (C).

1. Sophora secundiflora DC.   Frijolito.   Coral Bean.

Leaves persistent, covered when they unfold, especially on the lower surface of the leaflets, with silky white hairs, and at maturity 4'-6' long, with a stout puberulous petiole slightly enlarged at base, and 7-9 oblong-elliptic leaflets rounded, emarginate or sometimes

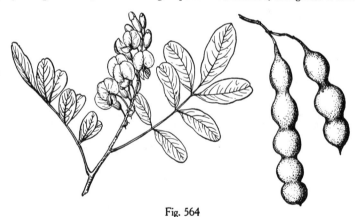

Fig. 564

mucronate at apex, gradually contracted at base into a short thick petiolule, coriaceous, lustrous and dark yellow-green above, rather paler below, glabrous or sometimes slightly puberulous along the under side of the stout midrib, entire, with thickened margins, conspicuously reticulate-veined, 1'-2½' long, ½'-1½' wide, without stipels. **Flowers** with a powerful and delicious fragrance, appearing with the young leaves in very early spring, 1' long, on stout pedicels sometimes 1' in length, from the axils of subulate deciduous bracts ½' or more long, and bibracteolate with 2 acute bractlets, in terminal 1-sided canescent racemes 2'-3' in length; calyx campanulate, slightly enlarged on the upper side, the 3 lower teeth triangular and nearly equal, the 2 upper rather larger and united almost throughout; petals shortly unguiculate, violet blue or rarely white, the broad erect standard marked on the inner surface near the base with a few darker spots; ovary coated with long silky white hairs. Fruit terete, 1′–7′ long, ½′ thick, stalked, crowned with the thickened remnants of the style, covered with thick hoary tomentum, indehiscent, 1–8-seeded, with hard woody walls ¼′ thick; seeds short-oblong, rounded, ¼′ long, bright scarlet, with a small pale hilum and a bony seed-coat; albumen 0; cotyledons thick, orange-colored, filling the cavity of the seed; radicle short and straight.

A tree, 25°–35° high, with a straight trunk 6′–8′ in diameter, separating several feet from the ground into a number of upright branches forming a narrow head, and branchlets coated when they first appear with fine hairy tomentum, becoming glabrous or nearly glabrous in their second year and pale orange-brown; more often a shrub, with low clustered stems. Wood very heavy, hard, close-grained, orange-colored, streaked with red, with thick bright yellow sapwood of 10–12 layers of annual growth. The seeds contain a poisonous alkaloid, sophorin, with strong narcotic properties.

Distribution. Borders of streams, forming thickets or small groves, in low rather moist limestone soil; shores of Matagorda Bay, Texas, to the mountain cañons of New Mexico, and to those of Nuevo Leon and San Luis Potosí; of its largest size in the neighborhood of Matagorda Bay; south and west, especially west of the Pecos River, rarely more than a shrub.

Occasionally cultivated in the gardens of the southern states.

2. Sophora affinis T. & G.

Leaves deciduous, coated when they unfold with hoary pubescence, 6′–9′ long, with a slender puberulous petiole, and 13–19 elliptic, acute or obtuse slightly mucronate leaflets contracted into short stout pubescent petiolules, entire or with slightly wavy thickened

Fig. 565

margins, thin, pale yellow-green and glabrous above, paler and covered with scattered hairs or nearly glabrous below, 1′–1½′ long and ½′ wide, with a prominent orange-colored midrib, slender primary veins, and conspicuous reticulate veinlets. **Flowers** ½′ long, appearing in early spring with the young leaves, on slender canescent pedicels nearly ¼′ long, from the axils of minute deciduous bracts, in slender pubescent semipendent racemes, 3′–5′ long, from the axils of the leaves at the end of the branches; calyx short-campanulate, abruptly narrowed at base, somewhat enlarged on the upper side, slightly pubescent, especially on the margins of the short nearly triangular teeth; petals short-unguiculate, white tinged with rose color; standard nearly orbicular, slightly emarginate, reflexed, as long and twice as broad as the ovate auriculate wing-petals and the keel-petals; ovary conspicuously stipitate, villose.   **Fruit** $\frac{1}{2}'$–$3'$ long, indehiscent, black, more or less pubescent, crowned with the thickened remnants of the style, 4–8-seeded, or rarely 1-seeded and then subglobose, with thin fleshy rather sweet walls; persistent on the branches during the winter; **seeds** oval, slightly compressed, with a thin crustaceous bright chestnut-brown seed-coat; cotyledons surrounded by a thin layer of horny albumen, bright green; radicle long and incurved.

A tree, 18°–20° high, with a trunk 8′–10′ in diameter, dividing into a number of stout spreading branches forming a handsome round-topped head, and slender terete slightly zigzag branchlets, orange-brown or dark brown and slightly puberulous when they first appear, becoming bright green marked by narrow brown ridges, and in their second year by the elevated tomentose leaf-scars.   **Winter-buds** depressed, almost surrounded by the base of the petiole, with broad scales coated on the outer surface with dark brown tomentum and on the inner surface with thicker pale tomentum, and persistent on the base of the growing shoot.   **Bark** of the trunk about $\frac{1}{8}'$ thick, dark reddish brown, and broken into numerous oblong scales, the surface exfoliating in thin layers.   **Wood** heavy, very hard and strong, light red in color, with thick bright clear yellow sapwood of 10–12 layers of annual growth.

Distribution.   Usually on limestone hills, or on the borders of streams, ravines, or depressions in the prairie, often forming small groves; valley of the Red River at Shreveport, Caddo Parish, Louisiana, to southwestern Arkansas, and to southern Oklahoma (Choctaw and Love Counties), and southward in Texas to the valley of the San Antonio and upper Guadalupe Rivers (Kerrville, Kerr County).

12. CLADRASTIS Raf.

A tree, with copious watery juice, smooth gray bark, slender slightly zigzag terete branchlets without a terminal bud, fibrous roots, and naked axillary buds 4 together, superposed, flattened by mutual pressure into an acuminate cone, and inclosed collectively in the hollow base of the petiole, the largest and upper one only developing, the lowest minute and rudimentary.   Leaves unequally pinnate, petiolate, with a stout terete petiole abruptly enlarged at base, 7–11-foliolate, deciduous; leaflets usually alternate, broadly oval, the terminal one rhombic-ovate, contracted at apex into a short broad point, cuneate at base, entire, petiolulate, without stipels, covered at first like the young shoots with fine silvery pubescence, and on the midrib with lustrous brown tomentum, at maturity thin, glabrous, dark yellow-green on the upper surface, pale on the lower surface, the midrib and numerous primary veins conspicuous, light yellow below; stipules 0.   Flowers on slender puberulous pedicels, bibracteolate near the middle, with scarious caducous bractlets, in long gracefully nodding stalked terminal panicles, the lower branches racemose, and often springing from the axils of 1-flowered pedicels, the main axis slightly zigzag, and, like the branches, covered at first with a glaucous bloom and slightly pilose; bracts lanceolate, scarious, pale, caducous; calyx cylindric-campanulate, enlarged on the upper side, and obliquely obconic at base, puberulous, 5-toothed, the teeth imbricated in the bud, nearly equal, short and obtuse, the 2 upper slightly united; disk cupuliform, adnate to the interior of the calyx-tube; corolla papilionaceous; petals white, unguiculate; standard nearly orbicular, entire or slightly emarginate, reflexed above the middle, barely longer than the straight oblong wing-petals, slightly biauriculate at the base of the blade, marked on the inner surface with a pale yellow blotch; keel-petals free, oblong, nearly straight, obtuse, slightly subcordate or biauriculate at base; stamens 10, free; filaments filiform, slightly incurved near the apex, glabrous; anthers versatile; ovary linear, stipitate, bright red, villose with long pale hairs, contracted into a long slender glabrous slightly incurved subulate style; stigma terminal, minute; ovules numerous, suspended from the inner angle of the ovary, superposed.   Legume glabrous, short-stalked, linear-compressed, the upper margin slightly thickened, tipped with the remnants of the persistent style, 4–6-seeded, ultimately dehiscent, the valves thin and membranaceous.   Seeds short-oblong, compressed, attached by a slender funicle; without albumen; seed-coat thin, membranaceous, dark brown; embryo filling the cavity of the seed; cotyledons fleshy, oblong, flat; radicle short, inflexed.

Four species are now known. One inhabits the southern United States, two occur in western China and one in Japan.

Cladrastis, from κλάδος and θραυστός, relates to the brittleness of the branches.

1. Cladrastis lutea K. Koch. Yellow Wood. Virgilia.

Leaves 8'-12' in length, with leaflets 3'-4' long and 1½'-2' wide, the terminal leaflet rather shorter than the others and 3'-3½' wide; turning bright clear yellow rather late in the autumn some time before falling. **Flowers** appearing about the middle of June, slightly fragrant, in panicles 12'-14' long and 5'-6' wide. **Fruit** fully grown by the middle of August, ripening in September and soon falling.

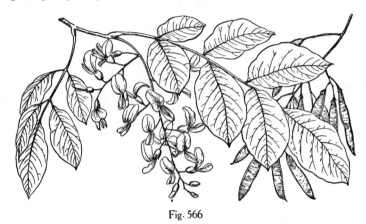

Fig. 566

A tree, sometimes 50°-60° high, with a trunk 1½°-2° or exceptionally 4° in diameter, usually divided 6°-7° from the ground into 2 or 3 stems, slender wide-spreading more or less pendulous brittle branches forming a wide graceful head, and zigzag branchlets clothed with pubescence when they first appear, soon becoming glabrous, during their first season light brown tinged more or less with green, very smooth and lustrous, and covered by numerous darker colored lenticels, bright red-brown in their first winter and marked by large elevated leaf-scars surrounding the buds, and dark dull brown the following year. **Bark** of the trunk ⅛'-¼' thick, with a silvery gray or light brown surface and rather darker colored than that of the branches. **Wood** heavy, very hard, strong and close-grained, with a smooth satiny surface, bright clear yellow changing to light brown on exposure, with thin nearly white sapwood; used for fuel, occasionally for gun-stocks, and yielding a clear yellow dye.

Distribution. Limestone cliffs and ridges generally in rich soil, and often overhanging the banks of mountain streams; Cherokee County, North Carolina, and the western slopes of the high mountains of eastern Tennessee; central Tennessee and Kentucky; near Florence, Lauderdale County, and cliffs of the Warrior River, Tuscaloosa County, Alabama; Forsyth, Taney County, Galena, Stone County, and Eagle Rock, Barry County, Missouri, to northern and central Arkansas; rare and local; most abundant in the neighborhood of Nashville, Tennessee, and in Missouri.

Often planted in the eastern United States as an ornamental tree, and hardy as far north as New England; and rarely in western and southern Europe; usually only flowering in alternate years.

13. EYSENHARDTIA H. B. K.

Small glandular-punctate trees or shrubs, with slender terete branchlets. Leaves alternate, equally pinnate, petiolate; leaflets oblong, mucronate or emarginate at apex, short-petiolulate, numerous, stipellate; stipules subulate, caducous. Flowers short-pedicellate, in long spicate racemes, terminal or axillary, with subulate caducous bracts; calyx-tube campanulate, conspicuously glandular-punctate, 5-toothed, the acute teeth nearly equal, persistent; disk cupuliform, adnate to the base of the. calyx-tube; corolla subpapilionaceous; petals erect, free, nearly equal, oblong-spatulate, rounded at apex, unguiculate, creamy white; standard concave, slightly broader than the wing and keel-petals; stamens 10, inserted with the petals, the superior stamen free, shorter than the others united to above the middle into a tube; anthers uniform, oblong; ovary subsessile, contracted into a long slender uncinate style geniculate and conspicuously glandular below the apex; stigma introrse, oblique; ovules 2 or 3, rarely 4, attached to the inner angle of the ovary, superposed. Legume small, oblong or linear-falcate, compressed, tipped with the remnants of the style, indehiscent, pendent. Seeds usually solitary, rarely 2, oblong-reniform, without albumen; seed-coat coriaceous; embryo filling the cavity of the seed; cotyledons flat, fleshy; radicle superior, short and erect.

Eysenhardtia is confined to the warmer parts of the New World, and is distributed from western Texas and southern New Mexico and Arizona to southern Mexico, Lower California, and Guatemala. Four species are distinguished; of these three species occur within the territory of the United States, and in northern Mexico, and one species is found only in Guatemala. Lignum nephriticum formerly celebrated in Europe for its reputed medical properties and for the fluorescence of its infusion in spring water is the wood of the shrubby *Eysenhardtia polystachya* Sarg. of western Texas and Mexico.

Of the North American species one is a small tree.

The generic name is in honor of Karl Wilhelm Eysenhardt (1794–1825), Professor of Botany in the University of Königsberg.

1. Eysenhardtia orthocarpa S. Wats.

Leaves 4'–5' long, with a pubescent rachis grooved on the upper side, 10–23 pairs of leaflets, and small scarious deciduous stipules; leaflets oval, rounded or slightly emarginate at apex, with a stout petiolule and minute scarious deciduous stipels, pale gray-green,

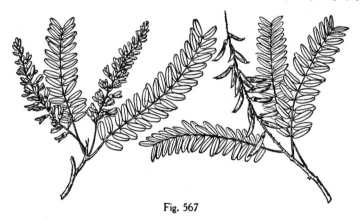

Fig. 567

glabrous or slightly puberulous on the upper surface, conspicuously glandular, with chestnut-brown glands, and pubescent especially on the prominent midrib on the lower surface, reticulate-veined, $\frac{1}{2}'-\frac{2}{3}'$ long, $\frac{1}{8}'-\frac{1}{4}'$ wide, with thickened slightly revolute margins. **Flowers** opening in May, nearly $\frac{1}{2}'$ long, on slender pubescent pedicels, in axillary pubescent spikes $3'-4'$ long; calyx many-ribbed, pubescent, conspicuously glandular, half as long as the white petals ciliate on the margins, and of nearly equal size and shape. **Fruit** $\frac{1}{2}'$ long, pendent, nearly straight or slightly falcate, thickened on the edges, with usually a single seed near the apex; seed compressed, light reddish brown, $\frac{1}{4}'$ long.

A tree, occasionally 18°–20° high, with a trunk $6'-8'$ in diameter, separating 3° or 4° above the ground into a number of slender branches, and branchlets coated when they first appear with ashy gray pubescence disappearing during the second year, and then reddish brown and roughened by numerous glandular excrescences; or more often a low rigid shrub. **Bark** of the trunk about $\frac{1}{16}'$ thick, light gray, and broken into large plate-like scales, exfoliating on the surface into thin layers. **Wood** heavy, hard, close-grained, light reddish brown, with thin clear yellow sapwood of 7 or 8 layers of annual growth.

Distribution. Dry gravelly soil, on arid slopes and dry ridges; valley of the upper Guadalupe River, western Texas, to the Santa Catalina and Santa Rita Mountains, southern Arizona, and southward into northern Mexico; arborescent in the United States only near the summit of the Santa Catalina Mountains.

14. DALEA L.

Glandular-punctate herbs, small shrubs, or rarely trees. Leaves alternate, unequally pinnate, or simple in the arborescent species; stipules generally minute, subulate, deciduous. Flowers in racemes, their bracts membranaceous or setaceous, broad, concave above, glandular-dentate; calyx 5-toothed or lobed, persistent, the divisions nearly equal; corolla papilionaceous; petals unguiculate; standard cordate, free, inserted in the bottom of the tubular disk connate to the calyx-tube, rather shorter than the wing- and keel-petals, the claws adnate to and jointed upon the staminal tube; stamens 10, sometimes 9 through the suppression of the superior stamen, united into a tube cleft above and cup-shaped toward the base; anthers uniform, often surmounted by a gland; ovary sessile or short-stalked, contracted into a slender subulate style, with a minute terminal stigma; ovules 4–6 attached to the inner angle of the ovary, superposed. Legume ovoid, sometimes conspicuously ribbed, more or less inclosed in the calyx, membranaceous, indehiscent, 1-seeded; seed reniform, without albumen; testa coriaceous; embryo filling the cavity of the seed; cotyledons broad and flat; radicle superior, accumbently reflexed.

Dalea is confined to the New World, where it is distributed from the central, western, and southwestern regions of the United States through Mexico and Central America to Peru, Chili, and the Galapagos Islands; usually herbs or low undershrubs, one species of the United States occasionally assumes the habit and attains the size of a small tree.

The generic name is in honor of Samuel Dale (1659–1739), an English botanist and writer on the materia medica.

1. Dalea spinosa A. Gray. Smoke Tree.

Leaves few, simple, irregularly scattered near the base of the spinose branchlets, cuneate or linear-oblong, sessile or nearly sessile, marked by few large glands, especially on the entire wavy margins, hoary-pubescent, $\frac{3}{4}'-1'$ long, $\frac{1}{8}'-\frac{1}{2}'$ wide, with a broad midrib and three pairs of lateral ribs, on vigorous young shoots or seedling plants remotely and coarsely serrate; remaining only for a few weeks on the branches; stipules minute, ovate, acute, pubescent. **Flowers** $\frac{1}{2}'$ long, appearing in June on short pedicels from the axils of minute bracts, in racemes $1'-1\frac{1}{2}'$ long, their rachis slender, spinescent, hoary-pubescent; calyx-tube 10-ribbed, with usually 5 glands between the dorsal ribs, the lobes short, ovate, rounded or more or less ciliate on the margins, reflexed at maturity; petals dark violet blue, standard cordate, reflexed, furnished at base of the blade with two conspicuous glands, wing- and keel-petals attached to the staminal tube by their base only and nearly equal in size, rounded at apex, more or less irregularly lobed at base; ovary pubescent, glandular punctate. **Fruit** ovoid, pubescent, glandular, twice as long as the calyx, tipped with the remnants of the recurved style; **seed** ⅛′ long, pale brown irregularly marked with dark spots.

A tree, 18°–20° high, with a short stout contorted trunk sometimes 20′ in diameter and divided near the ground into several upright branches, and branchlets reduced to slender sharp spines coated with fine pubescence, bearing minute nearly triangular scarious caducous bracts, marked by occasional glandular fistules, and developed from stouter branches hoary-pubescent when young, becoming glabrous in their third year and covered with

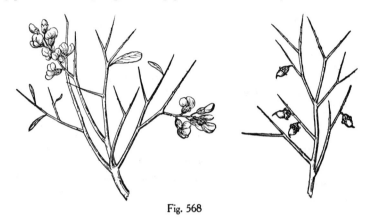

Fig. 568

pale brown bark roughened with lenticels and as it exfoliates showing the pale green inner bark; more often a low rigid intricately branched shrub. **Bark** of the trunk dark gray-brown, nearly ¼′ thick, deeply furrowed, and roughened on the surface by small persistent scales. **Wood** light, soft, rather close-grained, walnut-brown in color, with nearly white sapwood of 12–15 layers of annual growth.

Distribution. Valley of the lower Gila River, Arizona, through the Colorado Desert to San Felipe and Palm Springs, Riverside County, California, and southward into Sonora and Lower California.

15. ROBINIA L. Locust.

Trees or shrubs, with slender terete or slightly many-angled zigzag branchlets, without a terminal bud, minute naked subpetiolar depressed-globose axillary buds 3 or 4 together, superposed, protected collectively in a depression by a scale-like covering lined on the inner surface with a thick coat of tomentum and opening in early spring, its divisions persistent during the season on the base of the branchlet developed usually from the upper bud. Leaves unequally pinnate, petiolate, deciduous; leaflets entire, penniveined, stipellate, reticulate-venulose, petiolulate; stipules setaceous, becoming spinescent at maturity, persistent. Flowers on long pedicels, in short pendulous racemes from the axils of leaves of the year, with small acuminate caducous bracts and bractlets; calyx campanulate, 5-toothed or cut, the upper lobes shorter than the others, cohering for part of their length; corolla papilionaceous, petals shortly unguiculate, inserted on a tubular disk glandular on the inner surface and connate with the base of the calyx-tube; standard large, reflexed, barely longer than the wing- and keel-petals, naked on the inner surface, obcordate, reflexed; wings oblong-falcate, free; keel-petals incurved, obtuse, united below; stamens 10, inserted with the petals, the 9 inferior united into a tube often enlarged at base and cleft on the upper side, the superior stamen free at the base and connate in the middle with the staminal tube, or finally free; anthers ovoid; ovary inserted at the base of the calyx, linear-oblong, stipitate; style subulate, inflexed, bearded along the inner side near the apex, with a small terminal stigma; ovules numerous, suspended from the inner angle of the ovary, in two ranks, superposed. Legumes in drooping many-fruited racemes, many-seeded, linear, compressed, almost sessile, 2-valved, the seed-bearing suture narrow-winged; valves thin and membranaceous. Seed oblong-oblique, transverse, attached by a stout persistent incurved funicle enlarged at the point of attachment to the placenta; seed-coat thin, crustaceous; albumen thin, membranaceous; cotyledons oval, fleshy; radicle short, much reflexed, accumbent.

Robinia with seven or eight species is confined to the United States and Mexico; of the species found in the United States three are arborescent.

The generic name commemorates the botanical labors of Jean and Vespasien Robin, arborists and herbalists of the kings of France in the sixteenth and seventeenth centuries.

CONSPECTUS OF THE ARBORESCENT SPECIES OF THE UNITED STATES.

Legume without glandular hairs; flowers white. 1. **R. Pseudoacacia** (A, C).
Legume glandular-hispid (in the arborescent form of No. 2); flowers rose color.
  Glands not viscid. 2. **R. neo-Mexicana** (F, H).
  Glands exuding a clammy sticky substance. 3. **R. viscosa** (A).

1. Robinia Pseudoacacia L. Locust. Acacia. Yellow Locust.

Leaves 8'–14' long, with a slender puberulous petiole, and 7–19 leaflets; turning pale clear yellow late in the autumn just before falling; stipules ½' long, linear, subulate, mem-

Fig. 569

branaceous, at first pubescent and tipped with small tufts of caducous brown hairs, becoming straight or slightly recurved spines persistent for many years and ultimately often more than 1' in length; leaflets oval, rounded or slightly truncate and minutely apiculate at apex, when they unfold covered with caducous silvery pubescence, at maturity very thin, dull dark blue-green above, pale below, glabrous with the exception of the slight pubescence on the under side of the slender midrib, 1½'–2' long and ½'–¾' wide; petiolules stout, ⅛'–¼' in length; stipules minute, linear, membranaceous, early deciduous. **Flowers** opening in May or early in June, filled with nectar, very fragrant, on slender pedicels ½' long and dark red or red tinged with green, in loose puberulous racemes 4'–5' long; calyx conspicuously gibbous on the upper side, ciliate on the margins, dark green blotched with red, especially on the upper side, the lower lobe acuminate and much longer than the nearly triangular lateral and upper lobes; petals pure white, with a large pale yellow blotch marking the inner surface of the standard. **Fruit** ripening late in the autumn, $3'-4'$ long and $\frac{1}{2}'$ wide, with bright red-brown valves, usually 4–8-seeded, mostly persistent until the end of winter or early spring; **seeds** $\frac{3}{16}'$ long, dark orange-brown, with irregular darker markings.

A tree, $70°-80°$ high, with a trunk $3°-4°$ in diameter, small brittle usually erect branches forming a narrow oblong head, and slender terete or sometimes slightly many-angled branchlets marked by small pale scattered lenticels, coated at first with short appressed silvery white deciduous pubescence, pale green and puberulous during their first summer, becoming light reddish brown and glabrous or nearly glabrous toward autumn. **Bark** of the trunk $1'-1\frac{1}{2}'$ thick, deeply furrowed, dark brown tinged with red, and covered by small square persistent scales. **Wood** heavy, exceedingly hard and strong, close-grained, very durable in contact with the ground, brown or rarely light green, with pale yellow sapwood of 2 or 3 layers of annual growth; formerly extensively used in shipbuilding, for all sorts of posts, in construction and turnery; preferred for treenails, and valued as fuel.

Distribution. Slopes of the Appalachian Mountains, central and southern Pennsylvania, to northern Georgia; in southern Illinois, and westward to the Ozark region of southern Missouri, Arkansas and Oklahoma; now widely naturalized in the United States east of the Rocky Mountains, and nowhere common; in the Appalachian forest growing singly or in small groups up to altitudes of $3500°$; most abundant and of its largest size on the western slopes of the Alleghanies of West Virginia; often spreading by underground stems into broad thickets of small and often stunted trees.

Formerly much planted as an ornamental and timber tree in the eastern states; very frequently used in Europe, with numerous seminal varieties of peculiar foliage or habit, for the decoration of parks and gardens, and to shade the streets of cities.

2. Robinia neo-mexicana A. Gray. Locust.

In its typical form a shrub only a few feet high. The hairs on the fruit not glandular-hispid.

Distribution. Mountain cañons and plains, Grant County, New Mexico. Passing into

Robinia neo-mexicana var. luxurians Dieck.

Leaves $6'-12'$ long, with a stout pubescent petiole, and 15–21 leaflets; stipules chartaceous, covered with long silky brown hairs, becoming at maturity stout slightly recurved

Fig. 570

flat brown or bright red spines sometimes $1'$ or more long; leaflets elliptic-oblong, rounded or sometimes slightly emarginate at the mucronate apex, cuneate or sometimes rounded at base, 1½′ long, and 1′ broad, coated at first on the lower surface and on the margins with soft brown hairs, and silvery-pubescent on the upper surface, and at maturity thin, pale blue-green, conspicuously reticulate-veined, and glabrous with the exception of the slightly puberulous lower side of the slender midrib and stout petiolule; stipels membranaceous, ¼′ long, often recurved, sometimes persistent through the season. **Flowers** appearing in May, 1′ long, on slender pedicels ½′ in length and covered with stout glandular hairs, in short compact many-flowered glandular-hispid long-stemmed racemes; corolla pale rose color or sometimes almost white (f. *albiflora* Kusche), with a broad standard and wing-petals. **Fruit** 3′–4′ long, about ⅓′ wide, glandular-hispid, with a narrow wing; seeds dark brown, slightly mottled, ₁₆′ long.

A tree, sometimes 20°–25° high, with a trunk 6′–8′ in diameter, and branchlets at first pale and coated with rusty brown glandular hairs increasing in length during the summer, and slightly puberulous, bright reddish brown, often covered with a glaucous bloom, and marked by a few small scattered pale lenticels during their first winter. **Bark** of the trunk thin, slightly furrowed, light brown, the surface separating into small plate-like scales. **Wood** heavy, exceedingly hard, strong, close-grained, yellow streaked with brown, with light yellow sapwood of 4 or 5 layers of annual growth.

Distribution. Banks of mountain streams; valley of the Purgatory River, Colorado, through northern New Mexico and Arizona to southern Utah; on the Santa Catalina and Santa Rita Mountains, southern Arizona up to altitudes of 7000°; probably of its largest size near Trinidad, Las Animas County, Colorado.

Occasionally cultivated as an ornamental tree in the eastern states, and in western Europe.

× *Robinia Holdtii* Beiss, a hybrid of *Robinia neo-mexicana* var. *luxurians* and *R. Pseudoacacia*, has appeared in a Colorado nursery and is occasionally cultivated.

3. Robinia viscosa Vent.   Clammy Locust.

Leaves 7′–12′ long, with a stout nearly terete dark glandular-hispid clammy petiole, and 13–21 leaflets; stipules subulate, chartaceous, often deciduous or developing into short slender spines; leaflets ovate, sometimes acuminate, mucronate, rounded or pointed

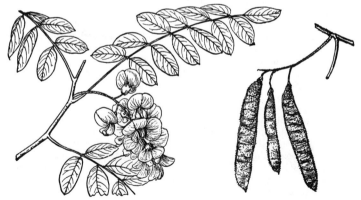

Fig. 571

at apex, and cuneate at base, when they unfold covered below with soft white pubescence, and slightly puberulous above, and at maturity dark green and glabrous on the upper surface, pale and pubescent on the lower surface, especially on the slender yellow midrib and primary veins and on the stout glandular-hispid petiolule, 1½′–2′ long and ⅔′ wide; stipels slender, deciduous. **Flowers** ⅔′ long, almost inodorous, appearing in June, on slender hairy pedicels from the axils of large lanceolate acuminate dark-red bracts contracted at apex into a long setaceous point exserted beyond the flower-buds and mostly deciduous before the flowers open, in short crowded glandular-hispid racemes; calyx dark red, coated on the outer surface and on the margins of the subulate lobes with long pale hairs; corolla pale rose or flesh color, with a narrow standard marked on the inner face by a pale yellow blotch, and broad wing-petals. **Fruit** narrow-winged, glandular-hispid, $2'-3\frac{1}{2}'$ long; **seeds** $\frac{1}{8}'$ long, dark reddish brown and mottled.

A tree, $30°-40°$ high, with a trunk $10'-12'$ in diameter, slender spreading branches, and dark reddish brown branchlets covered with conspicuous dark glandular hairs exuding, like those on the petioles and legumes, a clammy, sticky substance, during the first winter bright red-brown, covered with small black lenticels and very sticky, becoming in their second year light brown and dry; or a shrub, often only $5°-6°$ tall. **Bark** of the trunk $\frac{1}{8}'$ thick, smooth, dark brown tinged with red. **Wood** heavy, hard, close-grained, brown, with light yellow sapwood of 2 or 3 layers of annual growth.

Distribution. Mountains of North and South Carolina up to altitudes of $4000°$, and now naturalized in many parts of the United States east of the Mississippi River and as far north as eastern Massachusetts.

Often planted as an ornament of parks and gardens in all countries with a temperate climate.

16. OLNEYA A. Gray.

A tree, with thin scaly bark, and stout terete hoary-canescent slightly angled branchlets armed with stout infrastipular spines. Leaves equally or unequally pinnate, hoary-canescent, persistent, 10–15-foliolulate, destitute of stipules and stipels, short-petiolate, often fascicled in earlier axils; leaflets oblong or obovate, entire, obtuse, often mucronate at apex, cuneate at base, rigid, short-petiolulate, reticulate-veined, with a broad conspicuous midrib. Flowers on stout pedicels rather longer than the calyx, in short axillary few-flowered hoary-canescent racemes, with acute minute bracts and bractlets deciduous before the expansion of the flowers; calyx hoary-canescent, the lobes ovate, obtuse, almost equal, the two upper lobes connate nearly throughout; disk cupuliform, adnate to the tube of the calyx; corolla papilionaceous; petals unguiculate, purple or violet, inserted on the disk; standard orbicular, deeply emarginate, reflexed, furnished at base of the blade with two infolded ear-shaped appendages covering 2 prominent callosites; wing-petals oblique, oblong, slightly auriculate at base of blade on the upper side, free, as long as the broad obtuse incurved keel-petals; stamens 10, the superior stamen free, filling the slit in the tube formed by the union of the others; filaments filiform; anthers of the same length, oblong, uniform; ovary sessile or slightly stipitate, pilose; style inflexed, bearded above the middle; stigma thick and fleshy, depressed-capitate; ovules numerous, suspended from the inner angle of the ovary, superposed. Legume oblique, compressed, glandular-hairy, light brown, 2-valved, often tipped with the remnants of the long persistent style, 1–5-seeded, the valves thick and coriaceous, becoming unequally and interruptedly convex at maturity. Seeds broad-ovoid, slightly angled on the ventral side, suspended by a short thick funicle, without albumen; seed-coat thin, membranaceous, bright chestnut-brown and lustrous; embryo filling the cavity of the seed; cotyledons thick and fleshy, accumbent on the short incurved radicle.

The genus is represented by a single species of southern Arizona, California, and northwestern Mexico.

Olneya is in memory of Stephen T. Olney (1812–1878), author of a catalogue of the plants of Rhode Island.

1. Olneya tesota A. Gray. Ironwood.

Leaves $1'-2\frac{1}{2}'$ long, with leaflets $\frac{1}{2}'-\frac{3}{4}'$ in length, appearing in June and persistent until the following spring. **Flowers** unfolding with the leaves, nearly $\frac{1}{2}'$ long. **Fruit** light brown, very glandular, fully grown at midsummer, ripening before the end of August, $2'-2\frac{1}{2}'$ long.

A tree, sometimes 25°–30° high, with a short trunk occasionally 18′ in diameter and usually divided 4°–6° above the ground into a number of stout upright branches, and slender branchlets thickly coated at first with hoary-canescent pubescence disappearing early in their second year, and then pale green and more or less spotted and streaked with red, becoming pale brown in their third season, their spines straight or slightly curved, very sharp and rigid, $\frac{1}{8}'-\frac{1}{4}'$ long, and persistent at least during two years. **Bark** of the

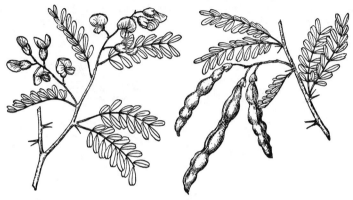

Fig. 572

trunk thin, exfoliating in long longitudinal dark red-brown scales. **Wood** very heavy, hard and strong, although brittle, rich dark brown striped with red, with thin clear yellow sapwood; valued as fuel and sometimes manufactured into canes and other small objects.

Distribution. Sides of low depressions and arroyos in the desert; valley of the Colorado River south of the Mohave Mountains, California, to southwestern Arizona, and to Sonora and Lower California; most abundant and of its largest size in Sonora.

17. **ERYTHRINA** L.

Trees or shrubs with erect terete stems and branches, often armed with recurved prickles, or rarely herbaceous. Leaves alternate, pinnately 3-foliolate; stipules small, the stipels gland-like. Flowers papilionaceous, showy, in pairs or fascicled on the rachis of axillary leafless racemes, or in terminal racemes furnished at base with leaf-like bracts; calyx oblique, truncate or 5-toothed; corolla usually scarlet; petals free; standard broad or elongated, erect or spreading, nearly sessile or raised on a long stalk; wing-petals small or wanting, longer or shorter than the keel-petals; stamens 10, united into a tube split on the upper side, the tenth and upper stamen separate or all 10 united; anthers uniform; ovary stipitate, 1-celled; styles subulate, incurved, naked; stigmas small, terminal; ovules numerous, amphitropous, the micropyle superior. Fruit a stipitate linear-falcate pod narrowed at ends, compressed or subterete, constricted or undulate between the seeds, 2-valved; seeds reniform, attached by an oblong basal hilum, exalbuminous.

From twenty-five to thirty species are recognized, all inhabitants of tropical and semitropical regions. In the gardens of warm countries several of the species are cultivated for the beauty of their large and brilliant flowers.

The name is from ἐρυθρός, in allusion to the color of the flowers.

1. Erythrina herbacea var. arborea Chapm.

Leaves persistent, usually 6'-8' long, with a slender petiole and rachis occasionally armed with small recurved prickles; leaflets thin, deltoid to hastate, concave-cuneate at the broad base, the lateral lobes broad and rounded and much shorter than the elongated terminal lobe gradually narrowed and rounded at apex, thin, yellow-green, smooth and glabrous, $2\frac{1}{4}'$-$3\frac{1}{2}'$ long and $1\frac{1}{2}'$-$2\frac{1}{4}'$ wide; petiolules slender, about $\frac{1}{4}'$ in length, with minute gland-like stipels. **Flowers** $2'$-$2\frac{1}{4}'$ long on short slender pedicels, in narrow leafless racemes 8'-13' long, the lower flowers fading before those at the apex of the raceme open; calyx dark red, truncate and ciliate at the mouth, $\frac{1}{4}'$ in length; corolla scarlet; the standard narrow, oblanceolate, gradually narrowed into the long base, about $\frac{1}{4}'$ long, closely infolded and then more or less falcate; wing-petals slightly longer than the calyx and longer than

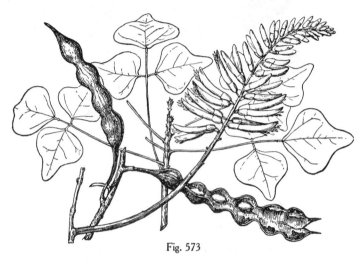

Fig. 573

the keel-petals; stamens diadelphous. **Fruit** compressed, constricted between the seeds, apiculate at apex, from 4'-6' long, gradually narrowed into a stout stipitate base often $\frac{3}{4}'$ in length; **seeds** compressed, bright scarlet, lustrous, $\frac{5}{12}'$ long and about $\frac{1}{8}'$ wide, with a dark hilum.

A tree, rarely 25°-30° high, with a tall trunk occasionally a foot in diameter, small erect and spreading branches, and slender yellow-green branchlets armed with short broad recurved spines; more often shrubby and, except in size and habit, not distinguishable from *Erythrina herbacea* L., an herb with slender spreading stems occasionally 3° long, and common in sandy soil from the coast region of North Carolina to Florida, western Mississippi and Louisiana, and in the valley of the lower Rio Grande, Texas. **Bark** thin red-brown marked by longitudinal rows of large circular elevated lenticle-like excrescences.

Distribution. Florida, coast region from Miami, Dade County, to the southern shores of Tampa Bay, and on the southern keys.

18. ICHTHYOMETHIA P. Brown.

Trees or shrubs with thin scaly bark and stout terete branchlets without a terminal bud. **Leaves** unequally pinnate, long-petiolate; leaflets opposite. **Flowers** papilionaceous, on slender pedicels enlarged at the end, bibracteolate, in lateral panicles, appearing before the leaves; bracts and bractlets minute, scarious; calyx campanulate, 2-lipped, the upper lip emarginate, the lower 3-lobed, persistent, the lobes imbricated in the bud, short and broad; petals inserted on an annular glandular disk adnate to the interior of the calyx-tube, unguiculate, white tinged with red, rarely yellowish white; stamens 10, the filament of the upper stamen free at base only, united above with the others into a long tube; anthers oblong, uniform, versatile; ovary sessile, contracted into a filiform incurved style, with a capitate stigma; ovules numerous, suspended from the inner angle of the ovary, 2-ranked. Legume linear, compressed, raised on a stalk longer than the calyx, slightly contracted between the numerous seeds, tomentose-canescent or glabrate, thin-walled, indehiscent, longitudinally 4-winged, the wings developed from the dorsal and ventral sutures, broad or narrow, continuous or interrupted by the abortion of some of the ovules, membranaceous, their margins undulate or irregularly cut; seeds oval, compressed, without albumen, laterally attached by a short thick funicle; seed-coat thin, crustaceous, red-brown, not lustrous; embryo filling the cavity of the seed; cotyledons plano-convex, oval, fleshy; radicle short, inflexed.

Seven or eight species are now recognized, inhabitants of tropical America where they are distributed from southern Florida, through the West Indies to southern Mexico and Guatemala. Piscidia from the bark of the roots of Ichthyomethia is sometimes used medicinally.

The generic name, from ιχθύς and μέθυ, indicates the Carib use of one of the species.

1. Ichthyomethia piscipula A. S. Hitch. Jamaica Dogwood.

Leaves 4′-9′ long, 5-11-foliolate, with stout petioles; leaflets oval, obovate or broad-oblong, obtuse or short-acuminate at apex, rounded or cuneate at base, with thick pubescent petiolules, when they first appear coated like the petioles with rufous hairs, at ma-

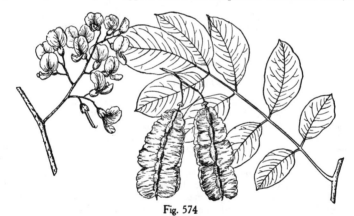

Fig. 574

turity coriaceous, glabrous and dark green above, pale and more or less clothed below with rufous or canescent pubescence along the elevated conspicuous midrib, and numerous thin veins arching and united at the entire undulate thickened margins, or covered with soft pubescence below; deciduous in spring. **Flowers** opening in May, ¾′ long, on slender pedicels sometimes 1½′ in length, in canescent ovoid densely flowered or elongated thyrsoid panicles, with short 3-12-flowered branches, from the axils of the fallen leaves of the previous year; calyx canescent, 5-lobed; petals white tinged with red, the standard hoary-canescent on the outer surface, marked with a green blotch on the inner surface, its claw as long as the calyx; ovary sericeous. **Fruit** ripening in July and August, broad-winged, light brown, 3′-4′ long and 1′-1½′ across the wings.

A tree, 40°-50° high, with a trunk often 2°-3° in diameter, stout erect sometimes contorted branches forming an irregular head, and branches coated when they first appear with thick rufous pubescence disappearing during their first summer, becoming glabrous or glabrate, bright reddish brown, conspicuously marked by oblong longitudinal lenticels, and large elevated horizontal slightly obcordate leaf-scars marked by the ends of numerous small scattered fibro-vascular bundles. **Winter-buds** ovoid, acute, $\frac{1}{8}'$–$\frac{1}{4}'$ long, with thin hoary-pubescent scales. **Bark** of the trunk about $\frac{1}{8}'$ thick, gray more or less blotched with olive and covered with small square scales. **Wood** very heavy, hard, close-grained, clear yellow-brown, with thick lighter colored sapwood, very durable, in contact with the ground; largely used in Florida in boat-building, and for firewood and charcoal. In the West Indies the bark of the roots, young branches and powdered leaves were used by the Caribs to stupefy fish and facilitate their capture.

Distribution. One of the common tropical trees of Florida from the shores of Bay Biscayne to the southern keys, and on the west coast from the neighborhood of Peace River to Cape Sable; on many of the Antilles and in southern Mexico. Sterile branches collected by *C. T. Simpson* in the neighborhood of Cape Sable indicate that a second species occurs in Florida.

XXIV   ZYGOPHYLLACEÆ.

Trees or shrubs, with hard resinous wood, and opposite pinnate leaves, with stipules. Flowers perfect, regular; calyx 5-lobed, the lobes imbricated in the bud; petals as many as the calyx-lobes, imbricated in the bud, hypogynous; stamens twice as many as the petals, hypogynous; filaments distinct; anthers introrse, 2-celled, the cells opening longitudinally; ovary 5-celled; styles united, terminating in a minute 5-lobed or entire stigma; ovules numerous, suspended, anatropous; raphe ventral. Fruit capsular, angled or winged, separating at maturity into 5 indehiscent carpels. Seeds solitary or in pairs in each cell; seed-coat thick and fleshy; embryo straight or nearly so; cotyledons oval, foliaceous; radicle short, superior.

Of the fourteen genera of this family, mostly confined to the warmer parts of the northern hemisphere, one only, Guaiacum, has an arborescent representative in the United States.

1. GUAIACUM L.   Lignum-vitæ.

Trees or shrubs, with scaly bark, and stout terete alternate branchlets often with swollen nodes. Leaves petiolate, abruptly pinnate, with 2–14 entire reticulate-veined leaflets, and minute mostly deciduous stipules. Flowers terminal, solitary or umbellate-fascicled, pedicellate, from the axils of minute deciduous bracts; calyx-lobes slightly united at base, unequal, deciduous; petals broad-obovate, more or less unguiculate; stamens inserted on the inconspicuous elevated disk opposite to and alternate with the petals; filaments filiform, naked or bearing at base on the inner surface a minute membranaceous scale; anthers oblong; ovary raised on a short thick stalk, obovoid or clavate, 5-lobed, contracted into a slender subulate acute style; ovules 8–10 in each cell, suspended in pairs from the inner angle. Fruit fleshy, 5-celled, smooth, coriaceous, narrowed at base into a short stem, with 5 wing-like angles, ventrally and sometimes dorsally dehiscent. Seeds suspended, ovoid; seed-coat easily separable from the hard bony nucleus closely invested with a thin indistinct tegumen.

Guaiacum is confined to the New World, and is distributed from southern Florida through the Antilles, Mexico, and Central America to the Andes of Peru. Seven or eight species are distinguished.

Guaiacum produces heavy close-grained wood, the cells of the heartwood filled with dark-colored resin. The lignum-vitæ of commerce, largely used for the sheaths of ship-blocks, mallets, skittle-balls, ten-pin balls, etc., is produced principally by *Guaiacum officinale* L., of the Antilles and South America, and by *Guaiacum sanctum* L. Guaiacum resin is a stimulating diaphoretic sometimes used in the treatment of gout and rheumatism.

The generic name is from the Carib Guaiaco or Guayacon, the aboriginal name of the Lignum-vitæ.

1. Guaiacum sanctum L.

Leaves 3' or 4' long, with 3 or 4 pairs of obliquely oblong or obovate mucronate subsessile leaflets, membranaceous, light green and puberulous below when they first appear, becoming subcoriaceous, glabrous, dark green and lustrous on both surfaces, 1' long and nearly ½' wide, persistent until the appearance of the new growth in March or early April of the following year; stipules acuminate, tipped with a short mucro, pubescent, ¼' long, usually caducous, but sometimes persistent during the season. **Flowers** ⅔' in diameter, opening almost immediately after the appearance of the new growth, and continuing to open during several weeks, solitary on a slender pubescent pedicel shorter than the leaves and usually produced 3 or 4 together at the end of the branches from the axils of the upper leaves, their bracts acuminate, minute, the 2 lateral rather smaller than the others; calyx-lobes obovate, slightly pubescent, especially on the outer surface near the base, and smaller

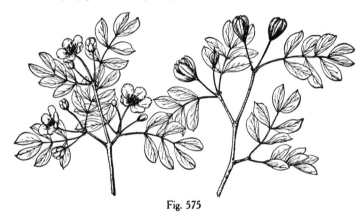

Fig. 575

than the blue petals twisted below from left to right, and thus appearing to be obliquely inserted; filaments naked; ovary obovoid, prominently 5-angled, glabrous, contracted at base into a short stout stalk. **Fruit** broad-obovoid, ¾' long, ½' wide, bright orange color, opening at maturity by the splitting of the thick rather fleshy valves; **seeds** black, with a thick fleshy scarlet aril-like outer coat.

A gnarled round-headed tree, sometimes 25°–30° high, with a short stout trunk occasionally 2½°–3° in diameter, slender pendulous branches, and branchlets conspicuously enlarged at the nodes, slightly angled, pubescent when they first appear, becoming in their second year glabrous, nearly white, and roughened by numerous small excrescences. **Bark** of the trunk rarely more than ⅛' thick, separating on the surface into thin white scales. **Wood** dark green or yellow-brown, with thin clear yellow sapwood.

Distribution. Keys of southern Florida from Key West eastward; on the Bahama Islands and on several of the Antilles.

XXV. MALPIGHIACEÆ.

Trees, shrubs or vines with opposite simple entire often stipulate persistent leaves; stipules deciduous or 0. Flowers usually perfect or dimorphous, on pedicels articulate near their base from the axils of a bract and furnished below the articulation with two bractlets, in terminal racemes, corymbs or umbels; calyx 5-lobed, the lobes generally imbricated in the bud, usually glandular; petals 5, convolute in the bud, unguiculate; disk inconspicuous; stamens usually 10; filaments generally united at base; anthers short, 2-celled, introrse; ovary of 3 rarely of 2 carpels more or less united into a 3-celled ovary; styles usually 3, distinct, rarely united; stigma terminal or sublateral, inconspicuous; ovule solitary, between orthotropous and anatropous, often uncinate, ascending on the pendulous funicle; raphe ventral; micropyle superior. Fruit drupaceous or samaroid; seeds without albumen, suspended from below the apex of the cell; testa thin; embryo curved or coiled, rarely straight; cotyledons often unequal; radicle short, superior.

This family of nearly sixty genera is confined to tropical and subtropical America, with one arborescent species in the United States.

1. BYRSONIMA Rich.

Trees, or shrubs often scandent, with astringent bark and leaves; stipules usually connate, rarely partly connate or free. Flowers in terminal racemes; lobes of the calyx furnished on the back with two glands; petals unguiculate, their slender claws reflexed in anthesis, the limb concave, penniveined; stamens 10, filaments short, united and bearded at base; ovary 3-celled; styles 3, distinct, oblong or subulate, gradually narrowed into the acute stigma. Fruit a 3-celled drupe; endocarp bony or woody, angled; seeds ovoid to subglobose; embryo circinate, with slender coiled cotyledons; radicle oblong.

Byrsonima with nearly one hundred species is widely distributed in tropical America from southern Florida, where one species occurs, and the Bahama Islands through the West Indies, Mexico, Brazil and Bolivia.

The generic name is from βύρς, a hide, in allusion to the use of the bark in tanning.

1. Byrsonima lucida DC.

Leaves oblong-obovate, rounded or occasionally abruptly short-pointed at apex, gradually narrowed and cuneate at base, coriaceous, glabrous, dark green and lustrous above,

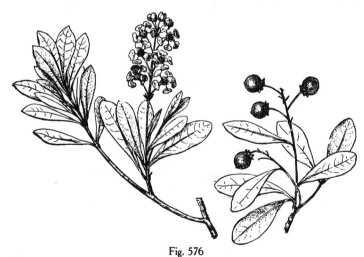

Fig. 576

paler, dull and reticulate-venulose beneath, $1'$–$1\frac{1}{2}'$ long and $\frac{1}{4}'$–$\frac{1}{2}'$ wide, with thickened revolute margins, a slender midrib and obscure primary veins; petioles stout, $\frac{1}{8}'$–$\frac{1}{4}'$ in length; stipules free, minute, acute, deciduous. **Flowers** $\frac{1}{4}'$ in diameter, appearing throughout the year on slender puberulous pedicels $\frac{1}{4}'$ to nearly $\frac{1}{3}'$ long from the axils of acuminate caducous bracts a third longer than their acuminate bractlets, in terminal 5–12-flowered erect racemes $\frac{3}{4}'$–$1\frac{1}{2}'$ in length; calyx cup-shaped, persistent under the fruit, with short nearly triangular lobes much shorter than the white petals turning yellow, pink or rose color; styles elongated and persistent on the fruit. **Fruit** subglobose, greenish, about $\frac{1}{4}'$ in diameter, the flesh thin and dry; stone woody, rugose, thick-walled, lustrous on the inner surface; seed ovoid, acute, filling the cavity of the stone, pale yellow.

A small tree, rarely 20° high with a trunk 10′ in diameter, covered with pale bark, spreading branches forming a flat-topped head and slender terete pale gray branchlets; more often a many-stemmed shrub.

Distribution. Florida, in limestone soil on the Everglade Keys, Dade County, and on several of the southern keys; on the Bahamas and many of the Antilles; in Florida arborescent on Long Key in the Everglades, and on Big Pine Key.

XXVI. RUTACEÆ.

Trees or shrubs, abounding in a pungent or bitter aromatic volatile oil, with simple or compound usually glandular-punctate leaves, without stipules or rarely with stipular spines. Flowers regular, perfect or unisexual, in paniculate or corymbose cymes; calyx 3–5-lobed, the lobes more or less united at base, imbricated in the bud; petals 3–5, imbricated in the bud; stamens as many or twice as many as the petals; filaments distinct or united below; anthers introrse, 2-celled, the cells opening longitudinally; pistils 1–4, separate or united into a compound ovary sessile or stipitate on a glandular disk; styles mostly united; ovules usually 2 in each cell of the ovary, pendulous, anatropous or amphitropous; raphe ventral; micropyle superior. Fruit of 2-valved carpels, a samara, drupe or capsule. Seeds solitary or several; seed-coat bony or crustaceous, furrowed or punctate; embryo axile in fleshy albumen; radicle short, superior.

Of this large family, widely distributed over the warm and temperate parts of the earth's surface, four genera only have arborescent representatives in the United States. *Citrus Aurantium* L., the Bitter-sweet Orange, a native of Asia, has long been naturalized in the peninsula of Florida, where other species of this genus have escaped from cultivation and are now growing spontaneously.

CONSPECTUS OF THE ARBORESCENT GENERA OF THE UNITED STATES.

Fruit of 1–5, 2-valved 1-seeded carpels; flowers diœcious or polygamous. 1. **Xanthoxylum.**
Fruit of 3 or 4-winged indehiscent 1-seeded carpels; flowers perfect. 2. **Helietta.**
Fruit a winged samara; flowers polygamous. 3. **Ptelea.**
Fruit a 1-seeded drupe; flowers perfect or polygamous. 4. **Amyris.**

1. XANTHOXYLUM L.

Trees or shrubs, with acrid aromatic bark, pellucid aromatic-punctate fruit and foliage, scaly buds, and usually stipular spines. Leaves alternate, unequally or rarely equally pinnate; leaflets generally opposite, often oblique at the base, entire or crenulate. Flowers small, diœcious or polygamous, in axillary or terminal broad or contracted pedunculate cymes; calyx and petals hypogynous; disk small or obscure; stamens as many as the petals and alternate with them, hypogynous, effete, rudimentary or wanting in the female flower; filaments filiform or subulate; pistils 1–5, oblique, raised on the summit of a fleshy gynophore, connivent, sometimes slightly united below, rudimentary, simple or 2–5-parted in the sterile flower; ovaries 1-celled; styles short and slender, more or less united toward the summit; stigmas capitate; ovules collateral, pendulous from the inner angle of the cell. Fruit of 1–5 coriaceous or fleshy 1-seeded carpels, broad-obovoid, sessile or stipitate, ventrally dehiscent. Seed solitary oblong or globose, suspended on a slender funicle, often hanging from the carpel at maturity; seed-coat black, shining, conspicuously marked by the broad hilum; cotyledons oval or orbicular, foliaceous.

Xanthoxylum is widely distributed through tropical and extratropical regions and is most abundant in tropical America.   It is represented in North America by one shrub and by four arborescent species of the southern states.   The resin contained in the bark, especially in that of the roots, is a powerful stimulant and tonic occasionally used in medicine.

The generic name is from ξανθός and ξύλον.

CONSPECTUS OF THE ARBORESCENT SPECIES OF THE UNITED STATES.

Flowers in axillary contracted cymes; branches armed with stipular spines.

                                                                1. **X. Fagara** (D, E).
Flowers in terminal cymes.
   Calyx-lobes and petals 5; leaves unequally pinnate.
      Leaves deciduous; branches armed with stout spines.   2. **X. clava-Herculis** (C).
      Leaves persistent; branches without spines.   3. **X. flavum** (D).
   Calyx-lobes and petals 3; leaves equally pinnate, persistent.   4. **X. coriaceum** (D).

1. Xanthoxylum Fagara Sarg.   Wild Lime.

Fagara Fagara Small.

Leaves persistent, 3′–4′ long, with a broad-winged jointed petiole, and 7–9 obovate leaflets rounded or emarginate at apex, minutely crenulate-toothed above the middle, sessile,

Fig. 577

½′ long or less, coriaceous, glandular-punctate, bright green and lustrous, with minute hooked deciduous stipular prickles.   **Flowers** on short pedicels from the axils of minute ovate obtuse deciduous bracts, in short axillary contracted cymes, appearing singly or in pairs from April until June, on branches of the previous year, from minute dark brown globular buds, the staminate and pistillate flowers on different trees; sepals 4, membranaceous, much shorter than the 4 ovate yellow-green petals; stamens 4, with slender exserted filaments, 0 in the pistillate flower; pistils 2, with ovate sessile ovaries gradually contracted into long slender subulate exserted styles united near apex and crowned with obliquely spreading stigmas, rudimentary in the staminate flower.   **Fruit** ripening in September, obovoid, rusty brown and rugose, ⅛′–¼′ long; **seed** dark and lustrous.

A tree, occasionally 25°–30° high, with a slender often inclining trunk, fastigiate branches, and more or less zigzag slender dark gray branchlets armed with sharp hooked stipular spines; more frequently a tall or low shrub. **Bark** of the trunk about $\frac{1}{8}'$ thick, the smooth light gray surface broken into small appressed persistent scales. **Wood** heavy, hard, very close-grained, brown tinged with red, with thin yellow sapwood of 10–12 layers of annual growth.

Distribution. Coast and islands of southern Florida, and Texas from Matagorda Bay to the Rio Grande and in San Saba, Bandera, and Brown Counties; one of the commonest of the south Florida plants, and arborescent on the rich hummock soil of Elliott's Key and the shores of Bay Biscayne; in Texas generally shrubby; common in northern Mexico, and widely distributed through the Antilles, southern Mexico, and Central and South America to Brazil and Peru.

2. Xanthoxylum clava-Herculis L. Prickly Ash. Toothache-tree.

Fagara clava-Herculis Small.

Leaves 5′–8′ long, with a stout pubescent or glabrous spiny petiole, and 3–9 pairs of ovate or ovate-lanceolate sometimes slightly falcate subcoriaceous leaflets usually oblique at base, crenulate-serrate, sessile or short-stalked, 1′–2½′ long, green and lustrous above, paler and often somewhat pubescent below, especially when they unfold; persistent until

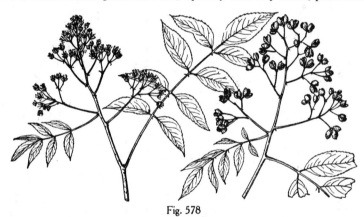

Fig. 578

late in the winter or until the appearance of the new leaves in the early spring. **Flowers** on slender pedicels $\frac{1}{3}'-\frac{1}{4}'$ long, from the axils of minute lanceolate deciduous bracts, in ample wide-branched cymes 4′–5′ long and 2′–3′ wide, appearing in very early spring, when the leaves are about half grown, the staminate and pistillate flowers on different individuals; sepals minute, membranaceous, persistent, barely one fourth the length of the oval green petals $\frac{1}{8}'-\frac{1}{4}'$ long; stamens 5, with slender filiform filaments, conspicuously exserted from the male flowers, rudimentary or wanting in the female flowers; pistils 3, rarely 2, with sessile ovaries and short styles crowned by a slightly 2-lobed stigma. **Fruit** ripening in May and June, in dense often nearly globose clusters; mature carpels obliquely ovoid, 1-seeded, chestnut-brown, $\frac{1}{4}'$ long, with a rugose or pitted surface; **seeds** hanging at maturity outside the carpels.

A round-headed tree, 25°–30°, or exceptionally 50° high, with a short trunk 12′–18′ in diameter, numerous branches spreading nearly at right angles, and stout branchlets covered when they first appear with brown pubescence, becoming glabrous and light gray in their second year, and marked by small glandular spots and by large elevated obcordate leaf-scars displaying a row of large fibro-vascular bundle-scars, and armed with stout straight or sometimes slightly curved sharp chestnut-brown spines $\frac{1}{2}'$ or more long, with a flattened enlarged base; or often a low shrub. **Winter-buds** short, obtuse, dark brown or nearly black. **Bark** of the trunk barely $\frac{1}{16}'$ thick, light gray, and roughened by corky tubercles, with ovoid dilated bases sometimes 1′ or more across and thick and rounded at apex. **Wood** light, soft, close-grained, and light brown, with yellow sapwood. The bark, which is collected in large quantities by negroes in the southern states, is used as a cure for toothache and in the treatment of rheumatism.

Distribution. Southeastern Virginia southward near the coast to the shores of Bay Biscayne and Bocagrande, Lee County, Florida, and westward through the Gulf states to northern Louisiana, southern Arkansas (near Arkadelphia, Clark County), and eastern Oklahoma, and through Texas to the valley of the Colorado River ranging northward to Tarrant and Dallas Counties; in the Atlantic states not abundant, and confined to the immediate neighborhood of the coast, growing in light sandy soil and often on the low bluffs of islands or on river banks; from the Gulf coast ranging farther inland, especially west of the Mississippi River; most abundant in eastern Texas, and of its largest size on the rich intervale lands of the streams flowing into the Trinity River. In western Texas a form occurs (var. *fruticosum* Gray), with short sometimes 3-foliolate more or less pubescent leaves, with small ovate or oblong blunt and conspicuous crenulate rather coriaceous leaflets; this is the common form of western Texas, growing usually as a low shrub.

3. Xanthoxylum flavum Vahl. Satinwood.

Fagara flava Kr. & Urb.

Leaves unequally pinnate, persistent, usually 6′–9′ long, with a stout glandular petiole enlarged at base, and usually 5, sometimes 3, or rarely 1 leaflet, unfolding in Florida during the month of June, and then densely covered with tomentum, and at maturity sparingly

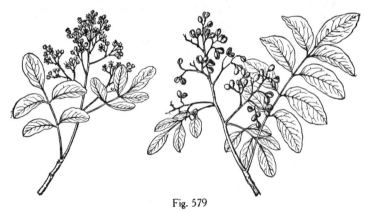

Fig. 579

hairy on the petiole and on the midrib of the ovate-lanceolate or elliptic, obtuse, often slightly falcate leaflets, sometimes oblique at base, nearly sessile or long-stalked, 2′–3′ long, 1½′–2′ broad, entire or slightly crenulate, coriaceous, pale yellow-green and conspicuously marked by large pellucid glands. **Flowers** appearing in Florida in June, on a slender pubescent pedicel $\frac{1}{4}'$ or more long, in wide-spreading pubescent sessile cymes, the male and female on different trees; calyx-lobes 5, minute, acuminate, ciliate on the margins, barely one eighth of the length of the ovate greenish white petals reflexed when the flowers are fully expanded; stamens 5, with slender filaments much longer than the petals, 0 in the pistillate flower; pistils 2 or sometimes 1, with a stipitate obovate ovary and a short style with a spreading entire stigma, minute and depressed in the staminate flower. **Fruit** ripening in autumn and early winter and sometimes persistent until the spring of the following year; mature carpels obliquely obovoid, short-stalked, 1-seeded, pale chestnut-brown at maturity, about $\frac{1}{3}'$ long, faintly marked by minute glands.

A round-headed tree, 30°-35° high, with a trunk 12'-18' in diameter, and stout brittle branchlets coated at first with thick silky pubescence, becoming light gray, rugose, conspicuously marked by large triangular leaf-scars, and puberulous during their second and third years. **Winter-buds** narrow-acuminate, $\frac{1}{2}'$ long, coated with short thick pale tomentum. **Bark** of the trunk $\frac{1}{4}'$ thick, with a smooth light gray surface divided by shallow furrows and broken into numerous short appressed scales. **Wood** very heavy, exceedingly hard, brittle, not strong, light orange-colored, with thin rather lighter colored sapwood; occasionally used in southern Florida in the manufacture of furniture, for the handles of tools, and other objects of domestic use.

Distribution. Florida, on the Marquesas Keys and on South Bahia Honda and Boca Chica Keys; on Bermuda, the Bahama Islands, San Domingo, and Porto Rico.

4. Xanthoxylum coriaceum A. Richard.

Fagara coriacea Kr. & Urb.

Leaves equally pinnate, persistent, 2'-3' long, with a stout grooved petiole, and 6-8 oblong-obovate stalked coriaceous dark yellow-green lustrous leaflets rounded or rarely emarginate at apex, 1'-1¾' long and ⅝'-¾' wide, with much-thickened revolute entire margins,

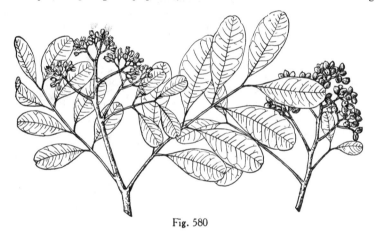

Fig. 580

a stout midrib, slender obscure spreading primary veins, and reticulate veinlets. **Flowers** yellow, appearing in March on short stout pedicels, in densely flowered terminal cymes; sepals 3, minute, united below, free above, much shorter than the 3 oval or obovate petals rounded at apex; stamens 3; filaments about as long as the petals; anthers ovoid or oval; ovary 3-celled, globose-ovoid; styles thick, 3 (*teste Urban*). **Fruit:** mature fruit not seen.

A glabrous tree, sometimes 18°-20° high, with a slender stem, and stout red-brown branches unarmed in Florida specimens, or in the West Indies furnished with short recurved spines; more often shrubby.

Distribution. Florida, shores of Bay Biscayne and near Fort Lauderdale, Dade County; rare; on the Bahama Islands and in Cuba.

2. HELIETTA Tul.

Trees or shrubs, with slender terete branchlets. Leaves opposite, long-petiolate, trifoliolate, persistent; leaflets sessile, obovate-oblong, obtuse, entire or crenate, subcoriaceous, grandular-punctate, the terminal the largest. Flowers regular, perfect, on slender bibracteolate pedicels, in terminal or axillary panicles; calyx 3 or 4-parted, the divisions imbricated in the bud, slightly united at base, persistent; petals 3 or 4, imbricated in the bud, hypogynous, oblong, concave, glandular-punctate, reflexed at maturity; stamens as many as the petals inserted under the disk; filaments shorter than the petals, slightly flattened, glabrous; anthers ovoid, cordate at base, attached on the back below the middle; disk free, cup-shaped, erect, subcorrugated, with a sinuate margin, 4-lobed, the lobes entire or crenate and opposite the petals; ovary minute, sessile, depressed, 3 or 4-lobed, glandular-verrucose or minutely pilose, the lateral lobes slightly compressed, 4-celled; styles united into a single slender column crowned by the globose 3–4-lobed stigma; ovules collateral, anatropous. Fruit obconic, composed of 3 or 4 dry woody 1-seeded indehiscent carpels with a cartilaginous endocarp and with a prominent horizontal wing, separating at maturity. Seed linear-oblong, seed-coat crustaceous, fragile, black; cotyledons straight, obtuse.

Helietta is distributed from the valley of the lower Rio Grande in Texas to Brazil and Paraguay. Four species are recognized, one species extending across the Rio Grande into western Texas.

The generic name is in honor of Lewis Théodore Hélie (1804–1867), a distinguished French physician.

1. Helietta parvifolia Benth.

Leaves $1\frac{1}{2}'$–$2'$ long, with a stout slightly club-shaped petiole, at first puberulent, soon becoming glabrous, and oblong or narrow-obovate leaflets rounded or sometimes slightly

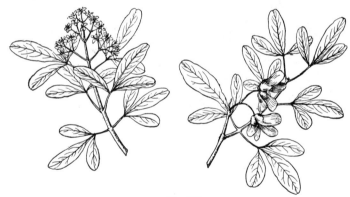

Fig. 581

emarginate at apex, gradually and regularly contracted at base, entire or slightly and remotely crenulate-serrate, yellow-green and lustrous above, paler below, conspicuously marked by black glandular dots, the terminal leaflet $\frac{1}{2}'$–$1\frac{1}{2}'$ long, sometimes $\frac{1}{2}'$ wide, and nearly twice as large as the others; persistent on the branches until early spring. Flowers appearing in April and May, on slender pedicels covered at first like the petioles and calyx with short dense pubescence, with minute acuminate early deciduous bracts, in dichotymously branched subsessile panicles on branchlets of the year from the axils of the upper leaves; petals 4, white, ovate, $\frac{1}{8}'$ long, with scattered hairs on the outer surface, and thin scabrous margins, and four or five times longer than the 4 calyx-lobes; stamens 4; ovary 4-lobed, glandular-punctate like the slender style. Fruit ripening in October, oblong, $\frac{1}{4}'$–$\frac{1}{3}'$ long, with a rigid broad-ovate sometimes slightly falcate wing rounded at apex, $\frac{1}{2}'$ long, and conspicuously reticulate-veined.

A slender tree, 20°–25° high, with a trunk 5'–6' in diameter, rather erect branches forming a small irregular head, and slender pale branchlets covered with minute wart-like excrescences, slightly puberulous when they first appear, soon becoming glabrous, and marked during their second year by small inconspicuous leaf-scars; or a low shrub. **Bark** of the trunk about ⅛′ thick, covered with dark brown closely appressed scales separating in large irregular patches and leaving when they fall a smooth pale yellow surface. **Wood** hard, very heavy, close-grained, light orange-brown, with rather lighter colored sapwood.

Distribution. Often forming thickets of considerable extent and abundant near Rio Grande, Starr County, Texas; mesas south of the lower Rio Grande; of its largest size and tree-like in habit on the limestone ridges of the Sierra Madre of Nuevo Leon.

3. PTELEA L.

Small unarmed trees or shrubs, with smooth bitter bark, slender terete branchlets, without terminal buds, small depressed lateral buds covered with pale tomentum, and nearly inclosed by the narrow obcordate leaf-scars marked by the ends of 2 or 3 small fibro-vascular bundles, and thick fleshy acrid roots. Leaves alternate or rarely opposite, without stipules, long-petiolate, usually trifoliolate, the leaflets conduplicate in the bud, ovate or oblong, entire or crenulate-serrate, punctate with pellucid dots. Flowers polygamous, on slender bracteolate pedicels, in terminal or compound cymes, greenish white; calyx 4 or 5-parted; petals 4 or 5, hypogynous; stamens 3 or 4, alternate with and as long as the petals, hypogynous, much shorter in the pistillate flower with imperfect or rudimentary anthers; filaments subulate, more or less pilose, especially toward the base; anthers ovoid or cordate; pistil raised on a short gynophore, abortive and nearly sessile in the staminate flower; ovary compressed, 2-3-celled; style short; stigma 2-3-lobed; ovules superposed, amphitropous, the upper ovule only fertilized. Fruit a 2 or 3-celled broad-winged indehiscent samara surrounded by a reticulate wing or rarely wingless. Seed oblong, acute at apex, rounded at base, ascending; seed-coat smooth or slightly wrinkled, coriaceous; cotyledons ovate-oblong.

Ptelea is confined to the United States and Mexico, where four or five species are known; of these one is a small tree. The bark and foliage of Ptelea is bitter and strong-scented and possesses tonic properties.

The generic name is from πτελέα, a classical name of the Elm-tree.

1. Ptelea trifoliata L. Hop-tree. Wafer Ash.

Leaves rarely 5-foliolate on vigorous shoots; leaflets sessile, ovate or oblong, pointed, the terminal leaflet generally larger and more gradually contracted at base than the others,

Fig. 582

entire or finely serrate, covered at first with short close pubescence, becoming glabrous and rather coriaceous at maturity, dark green and lustrous above, pale below, 4′–6′ long, 2½′–3′ wide, with a prominent midrib and primary veins; turning clear yellow in the autumn before falling; petioles stout, thickened at base, 2½′–3′ in length. **Flowers** appearing in early spring on slender pubescent pedicels 1′–1½′ long, the pistillate and staminate flowers produced together, the staminate usually less numerous and falling soon after the opening of the anther-cells; calyx and petals pubescent; ovary puberulous. **Fruit** with a thin almost orbicular sometimes slightly obovate wing, nearly 1′ across, on a long slender reflexed pedicel, in dense drooping clusters remaining on the branches through the winter; **seeds** ⅓′ long, dark red-brown.

A round-headed tree, rarely 20°–25° high, with a straight slender trunk 6′–8′ in diameter, small spreading or erect branches, and slender branchlets covered at first with short fine pubescence, becoming glabrous, dark brown and lustrous, and marked by wart-like excrescences and by the conspicuous leaf-scars; more often a low spreading shrub. **Winter-buds** depressed, nearly round, pale or almost white. **Wood** heavy, hard, close-grained, yellow-brown, with thin hardly distinguishable sapwood of 6–8 layers of annual growth. The bitter bark of the roots is sometimes used in the form of tinctures and fluid extracts as a tonic, and the fruit is occasionally employed domestically as a substitute for hops in brewing beer.

Distribution. Generally on rocky slopes near the borders of the forest, often in the shade of other trees; Long Island, New York, Pennsylvania, and westward through southwestern Ontario (Point Pelee) and southern Michigan to southern Iowa, southeastern Nebraska, and southward to Georgia, Alabama, eastern Louisiana and through Missouri and Arkansas to southeastern Kansas, eastern Oklahoma and eastern Texas. A form with leaflets soft-pubescent on the lower surface (var. *mollis* T. & G.) occurs in the south Atlantic states from North Carolina to Florida.

Often planted as an ornament of parks and gardens.

4. AMYRIS L.

Glabrous glandular-punctate trees or shrubs, with balsamic resinous juices. Leaves opposite or rarely opposite and alternate, 3-foliolate, without stipules, persistent; leaflets opposite, petiolulate, entire or crenate. Flowers white, minute, on slender bibracteolate pedicels, usually in 3-flowered corymbs in terminal or axillary branched panicles; calyx 4-toothed, persistent; petals 4, hypogynous, much larger than the calyx-lobes, spreading at maturity; disk of the staminate flower inconspicuous, that of the pistillate and perfect flowers thickened and pulvinate; stamens 8, hypogynous, opposite and alternate with the petals; filaments filiform, exserted; anthers ovoid, attached on the back below the middle; ovary ellipsoid or ovoid, 1-celled, rudimentary in the staminate flower; style short, terminal, or wanting; stigma capitate; ovules collateral, suspended near the apex of the ovary, anatropous. Fruit a globose or ovoid aromatic drupe; stone 1-seeded by abortion, chartaceous. Seed pendulous, without albumen; seed-coat membranaceous; cotyledons plano-convex, fleshy, glandular-punctate.

Amyris is confined to tropical America and northern Mexico. Of the twelve or fourteen species which have been distinguished two extend into the territory of the United States; one of these is a small West Indian tree common on the shores of southern Florida, and the other, *Amyris parvifolia* A. Gray, a Mexican shrub, grows in Texas near Corpus Christi, Neuces County, and near the mouth of the Rio Grande. Amyris is fragrant and yields a balsamic aromatic and stimulant resin, and heavy hard close-grained wood valuable as fuel and sometimes used in cabinet-making.

The generic name, from μύρρα, relates to the balsamic properties of the plants of this genus.

1. Amyris elemifera L. Torch Wood.

Leaves 3-foliolate, with slender petioles 1′–1½′ long, and broad-ovate or rounded obtuse acute or acuminate leaflets cuneate at base, or sometimes ovate-lanceolate or rhombic-lanceolate, entire or remotely crenulate, coriaceous, lustrous, dark yellow-green, conspicuously reticulate-veined, covered below with minute glandular dots, $1'-2\frac{1}{2}'$ long, with slender petiolules, that of the terminal leaflet often $1'$ or more long and twice as long as those of the lateral leaflets. **Flowers** in terminal pedunculate or nearly sessile panicles appearing in Florida from August to December. **Fruit** ripening in the spring, ovoid, often nearly $\frac{1}{2}'$ long, black covered with a glaucous bloom, with thin flesh filled with an aromatic oil and of rather agreeable flavor.

A slender tree, $40°-50°$ high, with a trunk sometimes, although rarely, a foot in diameter, and slender terete branchlets covered with wart-like excrescences, at first light brown, be-

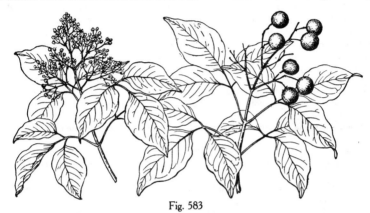

Fig. 583

coming gray during their second season. **Bark** of the trunk thin, gray-brown, slightly furrowed and broken into short appressed scales. **Winter-buds** acute, flattened, $\frac{1}{8}'$ long, with broad-ovate scales slightly keeled on the back. **Wood** heavy, exceedingly hard, strong, close-grained, very resinous, extremely durable, light orange color, with thin rather lighter colored sapwood of 12–15 layers of annual growth; often used as fuel.

Distribution. Florida, Mosquito Inlet, Volusia County, to the southern keys; common in the immediate neighborhood of the coast to the rich hummocks of the interior, and of its largest size on Umbrella Key; on the Bahama Islands and on many of the Antilles.

XXVII. SIMAROUBACEÆ.

Trees or shrubs, with bitter juice. Leaves alternate, pinnate, persistent, without stipules. Flowers regular, diœcious; calyx 5-lobed, the lobes imbricated in the bud; petals 5, imbricated in the bud, hypogynous; stamens 10, inserted under the disk; pistil of 5 united carpels; ovary 5-celled; ovule solitary in each cell, anatropous; raphe ventral; micropyle superior. Fruit a drupe.

Of the thirty genera of this family, confined chiefly to the tropics and to the warmer parts of the northern hemisphere, three have arborescent representatives in the flora of North America. *Ailanthus altissima* Swing., the so-called Tree of Heaven, a native of northern China, has been largely planted as an ornament and shade tree in the eastern United States, and is now sparingly naturalized southward.

CONSPECTUS OF THE ARBORESCENT GENERA OF THE UNITED STATES.

Fruit a drupe or berry.
    Ovary deeply 5-lobed; fruit drupaceous.   1. **Simarouba** (D).
    Ovary not lobed; fruit baccate.   2. **Picramnia** (D).
Fruit a 3-winged samara.   3. **Alvaradoa** (D).

1. SIMAROUBA Aubl.

Trees, with resinous juice and tonic properties.   Leaves long-petiolate, abruptly pinnate; leaflets usually alternate, long-petiolulate, conduplicate in the bud, entire, coriaceous, glabrous or slightly puberulous below, feather-veined.   Flowers in elongated
widely branched axillary and terminal panicles; disk cup-shaped, depressed in the sterile
flower, pubescent; stamens as long as the petals, in the pistillate flower reduced to minute
scales; filaments free, filiform, thickened toward the base, inserted on the back of a minute
ciliate scale; anthers oblong, slightly emarginate, introrse, attached on the back below
the middle, 2-celled, the cells opening longitudinally; ovary sessile on the disk, deeply
lobed, the lobes opposite the petals, rudimentary, lobulate, minute or wanting in the
staminate flower; styles united into a short column, with a 3–5-lobed spreading stigma.
Fruit composed of 1–5 sessile spreading drupes; flesh thin; stone crustaceous.   Seeds inverse, without albumen; seed-coat membranaceous; cotyledons plano-convex, fleshy, the
radicle very short, partly included between the cotyledons, superior.

Simarouba with four species is confined to tropical America, and is distributed from the
coast of southern Florida to Brazil and Guatemala.   The plants of this genus contain a
small amount of resin, a volatile oil, and an exceedingly bitter principle, quasin, with
tonic properties.

The generic name is formed from Simarouba, the Carib name of one of the species.

1. Simarouba glauca DC.   Paradise-tree.

Leaves 6′–10′ long, glabrous, with a stout petiole 2′–3′ in length, and usually 6 pairs of
opposite or alternate oblong-obovate or oval leaflets, rounded or slightly mucronate at
apex, usually oblique at base, membranaceous and dark red when they first unfold,
soon becoming coriaceous, dark green and very lustrous above, pale and glaucous below,
2′–3′ long and 1′–1½′ wide, with revolute margins, a prominent midrib, remote conspicuous
primary veins, and stout petiolules ¼′–⅓′ in length.   **Flowers** appearing in early spring, ⅛′–¼′
long, on short stout club-shaped pedicels, in panicles 12′–18′ long, and 18′–24′ broad, with a

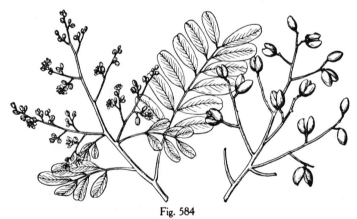

Fig. 584

stout pale glaucous stem and spreading branches from the axils of small acute scarious
deciduous bracts; petals fleshy, oval, often acute, pale yellow, and four or five times as
long as the glaucous calyx.   **Fruit** nearly fully grown by the end of April and then bright
scarlet, about 1′ long, ovoid, sometimes falcate, and slightly angled on the ventral suture,
becoming dark purple when fully ripe; **seeds** papillose, orange-brown, about ¾′ long.

A round-headed tree, growing occasionally in Florida to the height of 50°, with a straight trunk 18'–20' in diameter, slender spreading branches, and stout glabrous branchlets pale green when they first appear, becoming light brown before the end of the summer, rugose and conspicuously marked during their second season by the large oval leaf-scars. **Bark** of the trunk $\frac{1}{2}'$–$\frac{3}{4}'$ thick, light red-brown and broken on the surface into broad thick appressed scales. **Wood** light, soft, close-grained, light brown, with thick rather darker colored sapwood.

Distribution. Florida, from Cape Canaveral and the shores of Bay Biscayne to the southern keys; in Cuba, Jamaica, Nicaragua, and Brazil.

2. PICRAMNIA Sw.

Trees or shrubs, with bitter principles and slender terete branchlets. Leaves alternate, unequally pinnate, persistent, the leaflets subopposite to alternate, entire. Flowers diœcious, occasionally perfect, small, glomerate on long pendulous spikes or racemes opposite the leaves; calyx 3–5-parted, the lobes imbricated in the bud; petals 3–5, imbricated in the bud, rarely wanting; stamens 3–5, opposite the petals, inserted under the lobed depressed disk, in the pistillate flower reduced to linear scales or wanting; filaments naked; anthers 2-celled, introrse, the cells opening longitudinally; ovary inserted on the disk, 2 or 3-celled, rudimentary in the staminate flower; style 2 or 3-lobed, the lobes recurved and stigmatic on the inner surface, or crowned by a 2 or 3-lobed sessile stigma; ovules 2 in each cell, collateral, attached at the inner angle of the cell near its apex, anatropous; raphe narrow; micropyle superior. Fruit baccate, oblong to oblong-obovoid, 2 or by abortion 1-celled, the cells 1-seeded. Seeds filling the cavity of the cell, plano-convex, pendulous from the apex of the cell; hilum minute, apical, the raphe conspicuous; testa membranaceous, adherent to the exalbuminous undivided embryo; radicle superior, inconspicuous.

Picramnia, with about twenty species, is confined to the tropical and subtropical regions of the New World, one species extending into southern Florida. The bitter principle in the plants of this genus makes the bark of several of them useful in domestic remedies.

The generic name, from πικρός and θάμνος, is in reference to this bitter principle.

1. Picramnia pentandra Sw.

Leaves 8'–12' long, 5–9-foliolate, with a slender rachis and petiole; leaflets ovate-oblong, abruptly acuminate at apex, gradually narrowed and cuneate at base, coriaceous, glabrous,

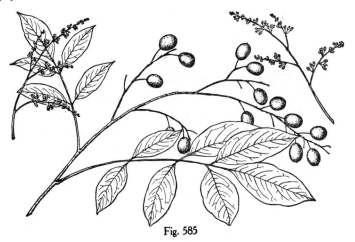

Fig. 585

dark green and lustrous above, $1\frac{1}{2}'-2\frac{1}{2}'$ long and $\frac{3}{4}'-1'$ wide, with thickened slightly revolute margins, a prominent midrib, slender primary veins and thin reticulate veinlets; petiolules stout, $\frac{1}{12}'-\frac{1}{6}'$ long, that of the terminal leaflet often $\frac{3}{4}'$ in length. **Flowers** green on short slender pedicels, in slender pubescent racemes $6'-8'$ in length; calyx 5-lobed, the lobes oblong-ovate, acuminate, coated on the outer surface with pale hairs; petals 5, acuminate, hirsute, narrower and longer than the calyx-lobes; stamens 5 in the pistillate flower; filaments slender, glabrous, exserted; anthers short-oblong, obtuse; stigma sessile, 2 or 3-lobed. **Fruit** red becoming nearly black when fully ripe, $\frac{1}{3}'-\frac{1}{2}'$ in length, about $\frac{1}{4}'$ in diameter; seeds light brown and lustrous.

A slender tree in Florida, occasionally $18°-20°$ high, with a straight trunk $4'$ or $5'$ in diameter, and slender light yellow-green or pale brown branchlets slightly pubescent during their first season; more often a shrub. Bark thin, close, yellowish brown.

Distribution. Florida, shores of Bay Biscayne to the Everglade Keys, Dade County, and on the southern keys; on the Bahama Islands and several of the Antilles, and in Colombia.

3. ALVARADOA Liebm.

Trees or shrubs, with bitter juices and slender terete pubescent branchlets. Leaves alternate, crowded at the end of the branches, unequally pinnate, long-petiolate, many-foliolulate, persistent; leaflets alternate, entire; stipules and stipels small. Flowers in many-flowered axillary or terminal racemes. Fruit a 2 or 3-winged samara, 3-celled below the middle, 2-celled above, crowned with remnants of the styles. Seed erect, compressed; testa membranaceous; albumen none; embryo oblong-compressed; cotyledons flat; radicle inferior, very short.

An anomalous genus, by several authors doubtfully referred to Sapindaceæ, but chiefly on account of its bitter properties now placed in Simaroubaceæ. It consists of three species; of these the widely distributed *Alvaradoa amorphoides* Liebmann, the type of the genus, occurs in southern Florida. The other species appear to be confined to the islands of Jamaica and Cuba.

1. Alvaradoa amorphoides Liebm.

Leaves $4'-12'$ long, with 21-41 leaflets and slender petioles; leaflets oblong-obovate, obtuse or occasionally minutely mucronate at apex, gradually narrowed below into a short

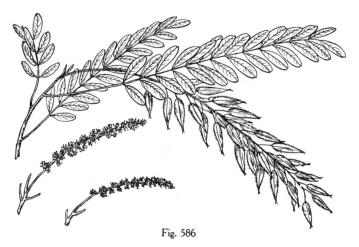

Fig. 586

slender pubescent petiolule, slightly thickened and revolute on the margins, dark green above, pale pubescent below, $\frac{1}{2}$–$\frac{3}{4}'$ long, about $\frac{1}{4}'$ wide, with a slender midrib and obscure primary veins. Flowers regular, minute, diœcious, on slender accrescent pubescent pedicels from the axils of ovate minute deciduous bracts, in many-flowered hoary-tomentose racemes 3'–4$\frac{1}{2}'$ long, the pistillate accrescent, becoming 4'–8' in length; calyx campanulate, 5-parted, the lobes ovate, acute, hoary-tomentose on the outer surface; disk 5-lobed; staminate flowers appearing sessile in the bud; their pedicels only slightly accrescent; petals filiform; filaments slender, elongated, slightly villose toward the base, inserted between the lobes of the disk and alternate with the calyx-lobes, anthers introrse, 2-celled, united except at apex, opening longitudinally by marginal slits, their connective orbicular, conspicuous; pistillate flowers on short accrescent pedicels; petals 0 or very rarely present; stamens 0; ovary compressed, unequally 3-angled, villose-hirsute on the margins, 3-celled at base, with two small compressed empty cells, the third larger with two anatropous ovules; styles 2, subulate or recurved, often of unequal length, stigmatic above the middle. Fruit lanceolate, acuminate, narrowly 2-winged, ciliate on the margins with long spreading hairs, slightly tinged with red, $\frac{3}{4}'$ in length and about two-thirds as long as its slender hairy pedicel; seeds acute at ends, pale yellow, $\frac{1}{4}'$ long.

A slender tree, in Florida occasionally 30° high, with a trunk 6'–8' in diameter, and slender branchlets hoary-pubescent during their first year becoming dull red-brown, glabrous and marked by numerous small pale lenticels and by the large obovate obcordate scars of fallen leaves showing the ends of three conspicuous equidistant fibro-vascular bundles; in Florida more often a shrub.

Distribution. Florida, Everglade Keys (Timbo Hummock near Gozman's Homestead, Caldwell's Hummock and Long Key), Dade County; in the Bahama Islands, and in Cuba, southern Mexico, Central America and Argentina.

XXVIII. BURSERACEÆ.

Trees or shrubs, with resinous bark and wood. Leaves alternate, pinnate, without stipules. Flowers perfect or polygamous, in clustered racemes or panicles; calyx 4–5-lobed, the lobes imbricated in the bud, persistent; petals 4–5, imbricated in the bud, distinct or slightly united, deciduous; stamens twice as many as the petals, inserted under the annular or cup-shaped disk; filaments distinct, subulate; anthers introrse, 2-celled, the cells opening longitudinally; pistil of 2–5 united carpels; ovary 2–5-celled; styles united; stigma 2–5-lobed; ovules 2 in each cell, pendulous, collateral, anatropous; micropyle superior; raphe ventral. Fruit drupaceous. Seeds without albumen; seed-coat membranaceous; embryo straight; cotyledons foliaceous; radicle short, superior.

Of the sixteen genera of this family, which is widely distributed through the tropics of the two hemispheres, one only, Bursera, occurs in the United States, reaching the shores of southern Florida with an arborescent species, and southern California and Arizona with another species.

1. BURSERA Jacq.

Trees, with balsamic resinous juices. Leaves unequally pinnate; leaflets opposite, petiolulate, entire or subserrate, thin, or coriaceous. Flowers polygamous, small, on fascicled or rarely solitary pedicels, in short or elongated lateral simple or branched panicles; calyx minute, membranaceous; petals inserted on the base of an annular crenate disk, reflexed at maturity above the middle; stamens inserted on the base of the disk; anthers oblong, attached on the back above the base, usually effete in the pistillate flower; ovary sessile, ovoid, 3-celled, rudimentary in the staminate flower; style short; stigma capitate, obtuse, 3-lobed; ovules suspended below the apex from the central angle. Fruit with a valvate epicarp, globose or oblong-oblique, indistinctly 3-angled; flesh coriaceo-carnose, 2–3-valved; nutlets 1–3, usually solitary, adnate to a persistent fleshy axis, 1-celled,

1-seeded, covered with a thin membranaceous coat. Seed ovoid, without albumen; seed-coat membranaceous; hilum ventral, below the apex; embryo straight; cotyledons contortuplicate.

Bursera with about forty species is confined to southern Florida, the Antilles, the southwestern United States and to Mexico, and Central and South America.

The generic name is in honor of Joachim Burser (1593–1649), a German botanist and physician.

CONSPECTUS OF THE ARBORESCENT SPECIES OF THE UNITED STATES.

Leaves 5–7 rarely 3-foliolate, their rachis and petiole without wings; staminate flowers in elongated many-flowered racemes.   1. B. Simaruba (D).

Leaves usually 10–22-foliolate, their rachis and petiole wing-margined; staminate flowers in short, usually 3-flowered clusters.   2. B. microphylla (G, H).

1. Bursera Simaruba Sarg.   Gumbo Limbo.   West Indian Birch.

Leaves confined to the end of the branchlets, 6′–8′ long, 4′–8′ wide, with a long slender petiole, and usually 5, rarely 3 or 7 leaflets coriaceous at maturity, oblong-ovate, oblique

Fig. 587

at base, contracted at apex into a long or short point, $2\frac{1}{2}′$–3′ long, $1\frac{1}{2}′$–2′ broad, with stout petiolules often $\frac{1}{2}′$ long; deciduous in early winter or occasionally persistent until the following spring. Flowers about $\frac{3}{16}′$ in diameter, appearing before the leaves or as they unfold, on slender pedicels $\frac{1}{4}′$–$\frac{1}{2}′$ long, in slender raceme-like panicles, those of the staminate plant 4′–5′ long or nearly twice as long as those of the pistillate plant; calyx-lobes and petals 5; petals ovate-lanceolate, acute, revolute on the margins, and nearly four times as long as the slender acute calyx-lobes; stamens of the staminate flower as long as the petals and in the pistillate flower not more than half as long, with smaller often effete anthers. Fruit in short raceme-like clusters, $\frac{1}{4}′$–$\frac{1}{2}′$ long, 3-angled, with a thick dark red outer coat, separating readily into 3 broad-ovate valves, and containing 1 or rarely 2 bony triangular nutlets rounded at base, pointed at apex, and covered with a thin membranaceous light pink coat; seeds 1 or 2, triangular, rose color.

A glabrous tree, 50°–60° high, with a trunk $2\frac{1}{2}°$–3° in diameter, massive primary branches spreading nearly at right angles, and stout terete branchlets light gray during their first season, becoming during their second year reddish brown, covered with lenticular spots and conspicuously marked by large elevated obcordate yellow leaf-scars. Winter-buds short, rounded, obtuse, with broad-ovate dark red scales slightly scarious on the margins. **Bark** of the trunk and large branches 1' thick, glandular dotted, separating freely into thin papery bright red-brown scales exposing in falling the dark red-brown or gray inner bark. **Wood** spongy, very light, exceedingly soft and weak, light brown, with thick sapwood, soon becoming discolored by decay. Pieces of the trunk and large branches set in the ground soon produce roots and grow rapidly into large trees. The aromatic resin obtained by incisions cut in the trunk was formerly used in the treatment of gout, and in the West Indies is manufactured into varnish. An infusion of the leaves is sometimes used in Florida as a substitute for tea.

Distribution. Florida, from Cape Canaveral to the southern keys, and on the west coast from Terra Ceia Island, Manatee County, Placida, Charlotte County, and Gasparilla Island southward; one of the largest and most common of the south Florida trees, and the only one which sheds its foliage during the autumn and winter; on most of the West Indian islands, in tropical Mexico, Guatemala, New Granada, and Venezuela.

2. Bursera microphylla A. Gray.

Leaves glabrous, deciduous, 1'–1¼' long, with a slender narrowly winged rachis and petiole and usually 10–20 oblong or oblong-obovate leaflets rounded at apex, obliquely cuneate at base, sessile, about ¼' long and $\frac{1}{12}$' wide. **Flowers** appearing in June before

Fig. 588

the leaves, ⅙' long on slender pedicels from the axils of minute acuminate caducous bracts, in mostly 3-flowered clusters ¼' in length; staminate, calyx-lobes ovate, acute; petals 5, lanceolate, acuminate, revolute on the margins, 3 or 4 times longer than the calyx-lobes, white; stamens shorter than the petals; pistillate flower not seen. **Fruit** ripening in October, ellipsoid or slightly obovoid, solitary, drooping on the thickened pedicel ⅕' in length, 3-angled, ¼' long, red, glabrous, splitting into three valves; nutlets usually ovoid, acute, narrow at base, thin walled, 3-angled, gray with a deep depression at base.

A tree, rarely 10°–12° high, with a short trunk 2½'–3' in diameter, stout erect and spreading branches, forming a wide round-topped head, and slender glabrous red branchlets, roughened during their first year by the crowded scars of fallen leaves; more often a low shrub. **Bark** of the trunk pale yellow, separating into membranaceous scales, the outer layer thin and firm, the inner layer corky, reddish brown, ½' thick. **Wood** hard, close-grained, pale yellow.

Distribution. Colorado Desert, between Fish Creek and Carriso Creek about twenty-five miles from the Mexican Boundary, on "banks of dry washes, in hard sterile soil covered with boulders" (*E. H. Davis*), Imperial County, California; near Maricopa, Pinal County, Arizona, and in Lower California and Sonora; reported as a tree only from California.

XXIX. MELIACEÆ.

Trees or shrubs, with hard wood and alternate pinnate leaves, without stipules. Flowers in panicles, perfect, regular; calyx 5-lobed, the lobes contorted (in *Swietenia*) in the bud, persistent; petals 5, convolute in the bud; stamens inserted at the base of the disk; filaments united into a tube; anthers introrse, 2-celled, the cells opening longitudinally; ovary 3-5-celled, free, surrounded at base by an annular or cup-shaped disk; styles united, dilated into a 5-lobed stigma; ovules numerous in each cell, suspended, semi-anatropous; raphe ventral; micropyle superior. Fruit a capsule (in *Swietenia*) or drupe. Seeds often winged; embryo with leafy cotyledons.

A family with about forty genera chiefly confined to the tropics, with a single representative, Swietenia, in southern Florida. *Melia Azedarach* L., of this family, the China-tree or Pride of India, with drupaceous fruits, has long been cultivated in the southern states, where it now often grows spontaneously.

1. SWIETENIA Jacq.

Trees, with heavy dark red wood. Leaves abruptly pinnate, glabrous, long-petiolate, persistent; leaflets opposite, petiolulate, usually oblique at base. Flowers small, in axillary or subterminal panicles produced near the end of the branches; calyx minute; petals spreading; staminal tube urn-shaped, connate with the petals, 10-lobed, the lobes convolute in the bud; anthers 10, fixed by the back below the sinuses of the staminal tube, included; ovary ovoid, 5-celled, the cells opposite the petals; style erect, longer than the tube of the stamens; stigma discoid, 5-rayed. Fruit a 5-celled 5-valved capsule septicidally dehiscent from the base, the valves separating from a persistent 5-angled axis thickened toward the apex and 5-winged toward the base. Seeds suspended from near the summit of the axis, imbricated in 2 ranks, compressed, emarginate, produced above into a long membranaceous wing with the hilum at its apex and transversed by the raphe; embryo transverse; cotyledons conferruminate with each other and with the thin fleshy albumen; radicle short, papillæform.

Swietenia with five species is confined to tropical America from southern Florida where one species occurs, to Venezuela, western and southwestern Mexico, and the east coast of Central America.

The generic name is in honor of Baron von Swieten (1700–1772), the distinguished Dutch physician, founder of the Botanic Garden and of the Medical School at Vienna.

1. Swietenia mahagoni Jacq. Mahogany.

Leaves 4'–6' long, with a slender glabrous petiole thickened at base and 3 or 4 pairs of ovate-lanceolate leaflets rounded at base on the upper side, narrow-cuneate or nearly straight on the lower side, entire, coriaceous, pale yellow-green or slightly rufous on the under surface, 3'–4' long, 1'–1½' wide, with a prominent reddish brown midrib, conspicuous reticulate veins, and a stout grooved petiolule ¼' long. **Flowers** appearing in July and August on slender puberulous pedicels, bibracteolate near the middle, 1 or 2 together at the end of the branches of slender panicles in the axils of leaves of the year; calyx glabrous, cup-shaped, much shorter than the ovate elliptic petals ⅛' long and slightly emarginate at apex. **Fruit** ripening in the autumn or early winter, long-stalked, ovoid, rounded at apex narrowed at base, 4'–5' long and 2½' broad, with thick dark brown valves rugose and pitted on the surface, its axis obovoid 3' or 4' long, 1'–1½' thick, dark red-brown, marked near the apex by the dark scars left by the falling seeds; **seeds** $\frac{3}{4}'$ long, almost square, thickened at base and nearly one fourth as long as their ovate rugose red-brown wings rounded or truncate at apex and gradually contracted below.

A tree, in Florida rarely more than 40°–50° high or with a trunk exceeding 2° in diameter, and slender glabrous angled branchlets covered during their first season with pale red-brown bark, becoming lighter or gray faintly tinged with red and thickly covered with lenticels during their second year; much larger in the West Indies. **Winter-buds** about $\frac{1}{8}'$ long, with broad-ovate minutely apiculate loosely imbricated light red scales. **Bark** of the trunk in Florida $\frac{1}{2}'-\frac{2}{3}'$ thick, with a dark red-brown surface broken into short broad rather thick scales. **Wood** heavy, exceedingly hard and strong, close-grained, very

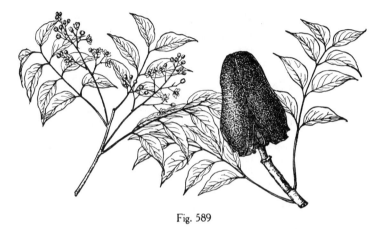

Fig. 589

durable, rich red-brown, becoming darker with age and exposure, with thin yellow sapwood of about 20 layers of annual growth; the most esteemed of all woods for cabinet-making, and also largely used in the interior finish of houses and railroad cars, and formerly in ship and boatbuilding. The bark is bitter and astringent and has been used as a substitute for quinine in the treatment of intermittent fevers.

Distribution. Florida, hummocks, shores of Bay Biscayne on the Everglade Keys and near Flamingo on White Water Bay, Dade County, on Elliotts Key, Key Largo and Upper Matacombe Key; rare and now nearly exterminated except in the region of Cape Sable; on the Bahama and many of the West Indian islands.

XXX. EUPHORBIACEÆ.

Trees, shrubs, or herbs, with acrid juice, and alternate stipular leaves. Flowers monœcious or diœcious; calyx 3–6-lobed or parted, the divisions imbricated in the bud, or wanting; corolla 0; stamens 2 or 3, or as many or twice as many as the calyx-lobes; anthers 2-celled, opening longitudinally; ovules 1 or 2 in each cell, suspended, anatropous; raphe ventral; micropyle superior. Fruit a drupe or capsule. Seeds albuminous; cotyledons flat, much longer than the superior radicle.

The Euphorbia family, widely distributed over tropical and temperate regions, with some one hundred and thirty genera and over three thousand species, is represented in the United States by three arborescent genera, with only five species, and by many shrubby herbaceous and annual plants.

CONSPECTUS OF THE ARBORESCENT GENERA OF THE UNITED STATES.

Fruit drupaceous.

Nutlets usually 1-celled and 1-seeded; stamens as many or twice as many as the calyx-lobes, free. 1. **Drypetes.**

Nutlets 6–8-celled and 6–8-seeded; stamens 2 or 3, united into a column.
2. **Hippomane.**

Fruit a 3-lobed capsule splitting into three 2-valved 1-seeded carpels. 3. **Gymnanthes.**

1. DRYPETES Vahl.

Trees or shrubs, with thick juice, and terete branchlets. Leaves involute in the bud, petiolate, penniveined, coriaceous, persistent; stipules minute, caducous. Flowers axillary, sessile or pedicellate, their pedicels from the axils of minute deciduous bracts, ebracteolate, the males in many-flowered clusters, the females solitary or in few-flowered clusters; calyx divided nearly to the base into 4 or 5 lobes rounded or acute at apex, deciduous or persistent under the fruit; stamens inserted under the margin of a flat or concave slightly lobed disk, 0 in the pistillate flower; filaments filiform; anthers ovoid, emarginate, attached on the back near the base, extrorse or introrse, 2-celled, the cells affixed to a broad oblong connective; ovary sessile, ovoid, 1 or rarely 2-celled, with 1 or 2 sessile or subsessile peltate or reniform stigmas, rudimentary or wanting in the staminate flower; ovules collateral, descending, attached to the central angle of the cell, operculate, with a hood-like body developed from the placenta. Fruit drupaceous, ovoid or subglobose, tipped with the withered remnants of the stigmas; flesh thick and corky or thin and crustaceous; stone thick or thin, bony or crustaceous, 1-celled and 1-seeded, or rarely 2-celled and 2-seeded. Seed filling the cavity of the nut; seed-coat crustaceous or membranaceous; embryo erect in thin fleshy albumen.

Drypetes is confined to the tropical regions of the New World, and is distributed from southern Florida through the West Indies to eastern Brazil. Of the eleven species now distinguished, two inhabit the coast-region of southern Florida.

The generic name, from δρύππα, relates to the character of the fruit.

CONSPECTUS OF THE NORTH AMERICAN SPECIES.

Calyx 5-lobed; stamens 8; ovary 1-celled; fruit oblong, ivory-white; outer coat thick and mealy; stone thick-walled. 1. **D. diversifolia** (D).

Calyx 4-lobed; stamens 4; ovary 2-celled; fruit subglobose, bright red; outer coat thin, crustaceous; stone thin-walled. 2. **D. lateriflora** (D).

1. Drypetes diversifolia Krug & Urb. White Wood.

Drypetes keyensis Krug & Urb.

Leaves appearing in early spring and falling during their second year, entire, oval or oblong, often more or less falcate, acute, acuminate, rounded or rarely emarginate at apex, rounded or cuneate at base, on young plants often spinose-dentate, when they unfold thin and membranaceous, light green or green tinged with red and pilose with scattered pale hairs, and at maturity coriaceous, dark green and lustrous, rather paler on the lower surface than on the upper surface, 3′–5′ long and 1′–2′ wide, with a broad thick pale midrib raised and rounded on the upper side and obscure primary veins arcuate and united near the thick revolute cartilaginous margins and connected by conspicuous coarsely reticulated veinlets; petioles stout, yellow, grooved above, $\frac{1}{2}$′ long; stipules nearly triangular, rather less than $\frac{1}{16}$′ long, caducous. **Flowers** on pedicels rather shorter than the petioles, opening in early spring from the axils of leaves of the previous year, the staminate in many-flowered clusters, the pistillate usually solitary or occasionally in 2–3-flowered clusters; calyx yellow-green, hirsute on the outer surface, $\frac{1}{16}'$ long, and divided nearly to the base into 5 ovate acute boat-shaped lobes deciduous from the fruit; stamens about 8, inserted on the borders of the slightly lobed pulvinate concave disk; filaments unequal in length, rather longer than the calyx-lobes and a little longer than the broad-ovoid emarginate pilose extrorse anthers, with broad ovate acute connectives; ovary sessile, hirsute, 1-celled, crowned with a broad sessile slightly stalked oblique pulvinate stigma, wanting in the staminate flower. **Fruit** ripening in the autumn, deciduous at maturity from its stout erect stalk much enlarged at apex and $\frac{1}{3}'$ long, ovoid, $1'$ long, ivory-white, with thick dry

Fig. 590

mealy flesh closely investing the light brown stone narrowed at base into a long point, with bony walls $\frac{1}{8}'$ thick and penetrated longitudinally by large fibro-vascular bundle-channels; seed oblong, rounded at the ends, nearly $\frac{1}{2}'$ long, covered with a thin membranaceous light brown coat marked by conspicuous veins radiating from the small hilum.

A tree, occasionally 30°–40° high, with a trunk sometimes a foot in diameter, stout usually erect branches forming an oblong round-topped head, and stout branchlets light green tinged with red and covered with pale scattered caducous hairs when they first appear, becoming ashy gray and roughened by numerous elevated circular pale lenticels and later by the large prominent orbicular leaf-scars displaying the ends of 3 conspicuous fibrovascular bundles. **Winter-buds** minute, obtuse, partly immersed in the bark and coated with brown resin. **Bark** of the trunk about $\frac{1}{2}'$ thick, smooth, milky white and often marked by large irregular gray or pale brown patches. **Wood** heavy, hard, not strong, brittle, close-grained, and brown streaked with bright yellow, with thick yellow-brown sapwood.

Distribution. Florida, Flamingo near Cape Sable (*C. T. Simpson*), Cocoanut Grove (*Miss O. Rodham*), Dade County, on Key West, Key Largo, Elliotts, Lower Metacombe and Umbrella Keys. One of the rarest of the tropical trees of Florida; on the Bahamas.

2. Drypetes lateriflora Urb. Guiana Plum.

Leaves appearing in Florida in early spring and falling during their second year, oblong, acute or acuminate at apex, gradually narrowed at base, and entire, when they unfold thin and covered with scattered pale hairs, and at maturity subcoriaceous, dark green and lustrous, $3'–4'$ long and $\frac{1}{2}'–1\frac{1}{2}'$ wide, with a conspicuous light-colored midrib, rounded above, and pale obscure primary veins arcuate and united near the slightly thickened revolute margins and connected by slender reticulate veinlets; petioles slender, grooved, $\frac{1}{4}'$ in length. **Flowers** on pedicels shorter than the petioles, opening late in the autumn or in early winter on branches one or two years old, in the axils of leaves or from leafless nodes, in many or few-flowered clusters; calyx greenish white, hirsute on the outer surface, divided to the base into 4 ovate rounded lobes, persistent under the fruit; stamens 4, inserted under the margin and between the lobes of the flat tomentose disk; filaments slender, exserted; anthers introrse, emarginate, pilose, wanting in the pistillate flower; ovary ovoid, tomentose, 2-celled, with 2 nearly sessile oblique spreading cushion-like stigmas. **Fruit** ripening during the spring and early summer, subglobose, $\frac{1}{3}'$ in diameter, tipped with the conspicuous blackened remnants of the stigmas, bright red, covered with soft pubescence, solitary or in clusters of 2 or 3, deciduous at maturity from its stout stalk enlarged at apex and $\frac{1}{4}'$

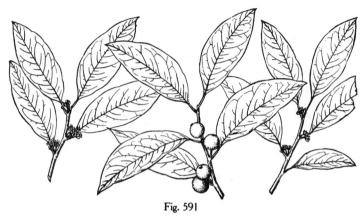

Fig. 591

long; flesh thin and crustaceous, closely investing the thin-walled crustaceous stone; **seed** usually solitary by abortion, obovoid, gibbous, $\frac{1}{8}'$ long, narrowed below, narrowed and marked at apex by the elevated pale hilum and on the inner surface of the seed-coat by the broad conspicuous raphe.

A tree, 20°–30° high, with a short trunk 5′–6′ in diameter, small erect branches, and slender branchlets, light green tinged with red when they first appear, becoming in their first winter ashy gray and marked by scattered pale lenticels, and at the end of their second year by the small elevated oval leaf-scars displaying the ends of 3 fibro-vascular bundles. **Winter-buds** minute, acute or obtuse, chestnut-brown, and covered with pale hairs. **Bark** of the trunk about $\frac{1}{16}'$ thick, light brown tinged with red, the generally smooth surface separating into small irregular scales. **Wood** heavy, hard, brittle, close-grained, rich dark brown, with thick yellow sapwood.

Distribution. Florida, Palm Beach, Palm Beach County, shores of Bay Biscayne, Dade County, and on many of the southern keys; common on the Bahama Islands and on several of the Antilles.

2. HIPPOMANE L.

A glabrous tree, with thick acrid juice, scaly bark, and stout pithy branchlets marked by circular raised lenticels, and oblong or semiorbicular horizontal elevated leaf-scars displaying a row of obscure fibro-vascular bundle-scars, and nearly encircled at the nodes by ring-like scars left by the falling of the stipules. Winter-buds ovoid, acute, covered by many loosely imbricated long-pointed chestnut-brown scales. Leaves alternate, involute in the bud, tardily deciduous, broad-ovate, rounded and abruptly narrowed at apex into a broad point terminating in a slender mucro, rounded or subcordate at base, remotely crenulate-serrate with minute gland-tipped teeth, penniveined, long-petiolate, at first pilose with occasional long pale hairs, soon becoming glabrous, and at maturity thick and coriaceous, dark yellow-green and lustrous above, paler and dull below, with a stout light yellow midrib raised and rounded on the upper side, and slender primary veins remote, arcuate, and united at some distance from the margins and connected by conspicuous coarsely reticulate veinlets more prominent on the upper than on the lower side; their petioles elongated, slender, rigid, light yellow, rounded below, obscurely grooved above, marked at the apex by large orbicular dark red glands; stipules ovate-lanceolate, abruptly narrowed from a broad base, slightly laciniate near the apex, membranaceous, light chestnut-brown, caducous. Inflorescence terminal, spicate, appearing in early spring usually before the unfolding leaves, the stout fleshy rachis often bearing at the base acute sterile deciduous bracts, or 1 or 2 small leaves, the minute pistillate flowers solitary in their axils or in the axils of ovate acute lanceolate bracts furnished with 2 lateral glandular bractlets; staminate flowers minute, articulate on slender pedicels clustered in 8–15-flowered fascicles in the axils of simple bracts higher on the rachis and extending to its apex; calyx usually 3-lobed, the lobes imbricated in the bud, that of the staminate flower yellow-green, membranaceous, divided below into 3 or sometimes into 2 acute lobes; calyx of the pistillate flower, ovoid, yellow-green, divided nearly to the base into 3 ovate acute concave divisions rounded on the back; stamens 2 or often 3, exserted, more or less connate by their filaments into a stout column, free and spreading at apex; anthers ovoid, light yellow, surmounted by the short prolonged connective, attached on the back below the middle, erect, extrorse; ovary 6–8-celled, narrowed at base, gradually contracted above into a short simple cylindric style separating into 6–8 long radiating flattened abruptly reflexed lobes stigmatic on the inner face; ovule solitary in each cell. Fruit drupaceous, pome-shaped, obscurely 6–8-lobed, raised on a thickened woody stem; skin thin, light yellow-green or yellow and red; flesh thick, lactescent, adherent to the thick-walled rugose deeply winged 6–8-celled, 6–8-seeded subglobose stone flattened at the ends, the cells divided throughout by thin dark radial plates, ultimately separable, penetrated near the summit by oblique canals filled by the funicles of the seeds. Seeds oblong-ovoid, marked by a minute slightly elevated hilum and on the ventral face by an obscure raphe; seed-coat membranaceous, separable into 2 layers, the outer dark, the inner thinner, light brown; embryo surrounded by thick fleshy albumen.

The genus is represented by a single species abounding in exceedingly poisonous caustic sap which produces cutaneous eruptions and when taken internally destroys the mucous membrane; formerly employed by the Caribs to poison arrows.

The generic name is from ἵππος and μανία, and was first used by the Greeks to distinguish some plant with properties excitant to horses.

1. Hippomane Mancinella L. Manchineel.

Leaves 3′–4′ long, 1½′–2′ wide, unfolding in early spring and persistent in Florida until the spring of the following year; petioles 2½′–4′ in length. **Flowers** opening in March

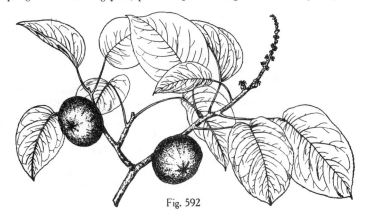

Fig. 592

before the leaves of the year; rachis of the inflorescence 4′–6′ long, dark purple, more or less covered with a glaucous bloom. **Fruit** ripening in the autumn or early winter and often persistent on the branches until after the appearance of the flowers of the following year, 1′–1½′ in diameter, light yellow-green, with a bright red cheek; seeds about ¼′ long.

A tree, in Florida rarely more than 12°–15° high, with a short trunk 5′–6′ in diameter, long spreading pendulous branches forming a handsome round-topped head; in the West Indies often 50°–60° tall, with a trunk occasionally 3° in diameter. **Bark** of the trunk ¼′–½′ thick, dark brown and broken on the surface into small thick appressed irregularly shaped scales; in the West Indies sometimes smooth, light gray or nearly white. **Wood** light and soft, close-grained, dark brown, with thick light brown or yellow sapwood.

Distribution. Florida, sandy beaches and dry knolls in the immediate neighborhood of the ocean, shores of White Water Bay and on many of the southern keys; on the Bahama Islands, through the Antilles to the northern countries of South America, and to southern Mexico and the eastern and western coasts of Central America.

3. GYMNANTHES Sw.

Glabrous trees or shrubs, with milky juice and slender terete branchlets. **Leaves** conduplicate in the bud, petiolate, entire or crenulate-serrate, coriaceous, penniveined, persistent; stipules membranaceous, minute, caducous. Flowers monœcious or rarely diœcious; inflorescence buds covered with closely imbricated chestnut-brown scales, lengthening in anthesis, bearing in the upper axils numerous 3-branched clusters of staminate flowers, their branches furnished with minute ovate bracts, and in the lower axils 2 or 3 long-stalked pistillate flowers; calyx of the staminate flower minute or 0; stamens 2 or rarely 3; filaments filiform, inserted on the slightly enlarged torus, free or slightly connate at base; anthers attached on the back below the middle, erect, ovoid, 2-celled, the cells parallel; calyx of the pistillate flower reduced to 3 bract-like scales; ovary ovoid, 3-celled, narrowed into 3 recurved styles free or slightly united at base, stigmatic on their inner face; ovule solitary in each cell. Fruit a 3-lobed capsule separating from the persistent axis into three 2-valved 1-seeded carpels dehiscent on the dorsal suture and partly dehiscent on the ventral suture. Seed ovoid or subglobose, strophiolate; seed-coat crustaceous; embryo erect in fleshy albumen.

Gymnanthes with about ten species is confined to the tropics of the New World and is distributed from southern Florida, where one species occurs, through the West Indies to Mexico and Brazil.

The generic name, from γυμνός and ἄνθος, relates to the structure of the naked flowers.

1. Gymnanthes lucida Sw.   Crab Wood.

Leaves oblong-ovate or ovate-lanceolate, obscurely and remotely crenulate-serrate or often entire, when they unfold thin and membranaceous, deeply tinged with red, and glandular on the teeth with minute caducous dark glands, and at maturity coriaceous, dark green and lustrous on the upper surface and pale and dull on the lower surface, 2′–3′ long, ⅔′–1½′ wide, with a broad pale midrib raised and rounded on the upper side, obscure primary veins arcuate and united near the margins and connected by prominent coarsely reticulate veinlets; appearing in Florida in early spring and remaining on the branches through their second summer; petioles broad, slightly grooved, about ¼′ in length; stipules ovate, acute, light brown, clothed on the margins with long pale hairs, about 1/16′ long. **Flowers:** inflorescence buds appearing in Florida late in the autumn in the axils of leaves of the year and beginning to lengthen in spring, the inflorescence becoming 1½′–2′ long, with a slender glabrous angled rachis, the scales broad-ovate, pointed, concave, rounded and thickened at apex, puberulous and ciliate on the margins, those inclosing the male flowers connate with the flowers and persistent under the calyx, those subtending the female flowers at the base of the inflorescence and not raised on their peduncle. **Fruit** produced in Florida sparingly, ripening in the autumn, slightly obovoid, dark reddish brown or nearly black, ⅓' in diameter, covered with thin dry flesh, and pendent on a slender stem 1' or more in length; seeds ovoid.

A tree, occasionally 20°–30° high, with a trunk 6'–8' in diameter and often irregularly ridged, the rounded ridges spreading near the surface of the ground into broad buttresses, slender erect branches forming a narrow open oblong head, and slender upright branchlets light green more or less deeply shaded with red when they first appear, becoming in their first winter light gray-brown faintly tinged with red and roughened by numerous oblong pale lenticels, ultimately ashy gray and marked at the end of their second year by the

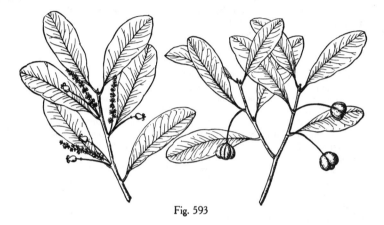

Fig. 593

semiorbicular elevated leaf-scars displaying the ends of 4 fibro-vascular bundle-scars superposed in pairs. Winter-buds ovoid, obtuse, covered with chestnut-brown scales, about 1/16' long. Bark of the trunk dark red-brown, about 1/16' thick, separating into large thin scales, in falling displaying the light brown inner bark. Wood very heavy, hard, close-grained, rich dark brown streaked with yellow, with thick bright yellow sapwood; in Florida occasionally manufactured into canes, and used as fuel.

Distribution. Florida, common in low woods from the shores of Bay Biscayne to the Everglade Keys, Dade County, and on many of the southern keys to those of the Marquesas group; on the Bahama Islands, and on many of the Antilles.

XXXI. ANACARDIACEÆ.

Trees or shrubs, with terete pithy branchlets, resinous juice, and alternate simple or pinnate leaves, without stipules, and scaly or naked buds. Flowers regular, minute, diœcious, polygamo-diœcious, or polygamo-monœcious; calyx-lobes and petals 5, imbricated in the bud or 0; stamens as many as the petals and alternate and inserted with them on the margin or under an hypogynous annular fleshy slightly 5-lobed disk; filaments filiform; anthers oblong, introrse, 2-celled, the cells opening longitudinally; ovary 1-celled; styles 1–3; ovule solitary, suspended from the apex of a slender funicle rising from the base of the cell, anatropous; micropyle superior; styles 3, united or spreading; stigmas terminal. Fruit drupaceous. Seed without albumen; seed-coat thin and membranaceous; embryo filling the cavity of the seed; cotyledons flat, accumbent on the short radicle.

The Sumach family with some sixty genera is mostly confined to the warmer parts of the earth's surface and contains the Mango, Pistacia, and other important trees. In the flora of the United States four genera have arborescent representatives.

CONSPECTUS OF THE ARBORESCENT GENERA OF THE UNITED STATES.

Flowers without petals, and in the species of the United States, without a calyx. 1. **Pistacia.**
Flowers with a calyx and petals.

Flowers usually diœcious by abortion; styles lateral, spreading; pedicels of the abortive flowers becoming long and plumose at maturity; fruit compressed, very oblique; leaves simple, deciduous. 2. **Cotinus.**

Flowers mostly diœcious; styles terminal, short, united; stigma 3-lobed; fruit ovoid, glabrous; leaves unequally pinnate, persistent. 3. **Metopium.**

Flowers polygamo-diœcious or polygamo-monœcious; styles terminal, spreading; fruit usually globose, naked or clothed with acrid hairs; leaves unequally pinnate, trifoliolate or rarely simple, deciduous or rarely persistent. 4. **Rhus.**

1. PISTACIA L.

Balsamic trees or shrubs. Leaves 3-foliolate or equally or unequally pinnate, petiolate, deciduous or persistent. Flowers small, diœcious, subtended by a bract and 2 branchlets, short pedicellate in panicles or racemes; calyx 1 or 2-lobed or in the pistillate flower 3–5-lobed, or 0; petals 0, stamens 3–5, 0 in the pistillate flower; filaments short, their base connate with the disk; anthers large; ovary subglobose or short-ovoid, rudimentary or 0 in the staminate flower; style 3-lobed, shorter than the 3 obovate-oblong or oblong stigmas. Drupe ovoid, oblique, compressed; exocarpa thin; the stone bony, 1-seeded; seed compressed; cotyledons thick plano-convex.

Pistacia with eight or nine species is confined to the valley of the lower Rio Grande, southern Mexico; the Canary Islands, the countries adjacent to the Mediterranean, and northern and central China, with one species growing on the northern banks of the Rio Grande in Texas.

The Pistacio-nuts of commerce, the green or yellow seeds of *P. vera* L. are largely used in confectionery, and some of the species are valued for the decoration of parks and gardens.

Pistacia from πιστ and ἀκεομαι, in reference to the healing properties of its resinous exudations.

1. Pistacia texana Swing.

Leaves persistent or tardily deciduous, 9–19-foliolate, with a slightly winged rachis pubescent above and a flattened narrow-winged petiole $\frac{1}{2}'–\frac{3}{4}'$ in length; leaflets spatulate,

Fig. 594

rounded and often mucronate at apex, gradually narrowed below into a deltoid or sub-cuneiform base, entire, more or less curved and unequilateral, wine-red when they unfold, and at maturity thin, dark green and sparingly pubescent along the midrib above, pale and glabrous below, nearly sessile or the terminal leaflet raised on a short petiolule, $\frac{5}{12}'-\frac{3}{4}'$ long and about $\frac{1}{4}'$ wide, with a slender midrib often near one side of the leaflet and reticulate veinlets. **Flowers** small, without a calyx, appearing just before or with the new leaves, in simple nearly glabrous panicles, their bracts and bractlets ciliate on the margins and wine-red at apex; staminate flowers more crowded than the pistillate, in compact panicles $\frac{3}{4}'-1\frac{1}{2}'$ long; anthers reddish yellow or wine color; pistillate flowers in loose panicles $1\frac{1}{2}'-2\frac{1}{2}'$ in length; ovary ovoid or subglobose, two of the three styles with 2-lobed stigmas, the third with a 3-lobed stigma. **Fruit** oval, dark reddish brown and slightly glaucescent, about $\frac{1}{4}'$ long and $\frac{1}{8}'$ broad, usually striate.

A small tree, occasionally 30° high with a short trunk 15'–18' in diameter, with stout erect and spreading branches forming a head sometimes 30°–35° across, and slender slightly pubescent reddish branchlets becoming grayish brown by the end of their first year; more often a large shrub with numerous stout stems.

Distribution. Texas, limestone cliffs and the rocky bottoms of cañons periodically swept by floods, and in deep narrow ravines, along the lower Pecos River and in the neighborhood of its mouth, Valverde County; and in northeastern Mexico.

2. COTINUS L.

Small trees or shrubs, with scaly bark, small acute winter-buds, with numerous imbri-cated scales, fleshy roots, and strong-smelling juice. Leaves simple, petiolate, oval, obo-vate-oblong or nearly orbicular, glabrous or more or less pilose-pubescent, deciduous. Flowers regular, diœcious by abortion or rarely polygamo-diœcious, greenish yellow, on slender pedicels accrescent after the flowering period, mostly abortive and then becoming conspicuously tomentose-villose at maturity, in ample loose terminal or lateral pyramidal or thyrsoidal panicles, the branches from the axils of linear acute or spatulate deciduous bracts; calyx-lobes ovate-lanceolate, obtuse, persistent; disk coherent with the base of the calyx and surrounding the base of the ovary; petals oblong, acute, twice as long as the calyx, inserted under the free margin of the disk opposite its lobes, deciduous; stamens shorter than the petals, usually rudimentary or wanting in the pistillate flower; ovary sessile, obovoid, compressed, rudimentary in the staminate flower; styles 3, short and spreading from the lateral apex of the ovary; stigmas large, obtuse. Fruit oblong-oblique, compressed, glabrous, conspicuously reticulate-veined, light red-brown, bearing on the side near the middle the remnants of the persistent styles, the outer coat thin and dry; stone thick and bony.

Cotinus is widely distributed through southern Europe and the Himalayas to central China with a single species, and is represented in the southern United States by one species.

The Old World *Cotinus coggygria* Scop., the Smoke-tree of gardens, is often cultivated in the United States.

The generic name is from Κότινος, the classical name of a tree with red wood.

1. Cotinus americanus Nutt. Chittam Wood.

Leaves oval or obovate, rounded or sometimes slightly emarginate at apex, gradually contracted at base, and entire, with slightly wavy revolute margins, when they unfold light purple and covered below with fine silky white hairs, and at maturity dark green on the upper surface, pale on the lower surface, and puberulous along the under side of the broad midrib and primary veins, 4'–6' long and 2'–3' wide; turning in the autumn brilliant shades of orange and scarlet; petioles stout, $\frac{1}{2}'-\frac{3}{4}'$ in length. **Flowers** appearing late in April or early in May on pedicels $\frac{1}{2}'-\frac{3}{4}'$ long, and usually collected 3 or 4 together in loose umbels near the end of the principal branches of puberulous terminal slender long-branched few-flowered panicles 5′–6′ long and 2½′–3′ broad, the staminate and pistillate flowers on different individuals. **Fruit** produced very sparingly, about ⅛′ long, on stems 2′–3′ in length; the sterile pedicels becoming 1½′–2′ long at maturity and covered with short not very abundant rather inconspicuous pale purple or brown hairs; **seed** kidney-shaped, pale brown, about 1/16′ long.

A tree, 25°–35° high, with a straight trunk occasionally 12′–14′ in diameter, usually dividing 12°–14° from the ground into several erect stems separating into wide-spreading often slightly pendulous branches, and slender branchlets purple when they first appear, soon becoming green, bright red-brown and covered with small white lenticels and marked by large prominent leaf-scars during their first winter, and dark orange-colored in their second year. **Winter-buds** ⅛′ long, and covered with thin dark red-brown scales. **Bark** of the trunk ⅛′ thick, light gray, furrowed, and broken on the surface into thin oblong scales.

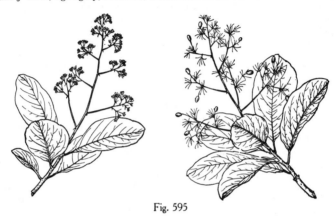

Fig. 595

Wood light, soft, rather coarse-grained, bright clear rich orange color, with thin nearly white sapwood; largely used locally for fence-posts and very durable in contact with the soil; yielding a clear orange-colored dye.

Distribution. Banks of the Ohio River, Owensboro, Daviess County, Kentucky (*E. J. Palmer*); near Huntsville, Madison County, Alabama; valley of White River in Stone and Taney Counties, southern Missouri; near Cotter, Baxter County, and Van Buren, Crawford County, Arkansas, and eastern Oklahoma; valleys of the upper Guadalupe and Medina Rivers, western Texas; usually only in small isolated groves or thickets scattered along the sides of rocky ravines or dry slopes; very abundant as a small shrub and spreading over many thousand acres of the mountain cañons, and high hillsides in the neighborhood of Spanish Pass, Kendall County, Texas.

Occasionally cultivated in the eastern United States and rarely in Europe: hardy as far north as eastern Massachusetts.

3. METOPIUM P. Br.

Trees or shrubs, with naked buds, fleshy roots, and milky exceedingly caustic juice. Leaves unequally pinnate, persistent; leaflets coriaceous, lustrous, long-petiolulate. Flowers dioecious, yellow-green, on short stout pedicels, in narrow erect axillary clusters at the ends of the branches, with minute acute deciduous bracts and bractlets, the males and females on different trees; calyx-lobes semiorbicular, about half as long as the ovate obtuse petals; stamens 5, inserted under the margin of the disk; filaments shorter than the anthers, minute and rudimentary in the pistillate flower; ovary ovoid, sessile, minute in the staminate flower; style terminal, short, undivided; stigma 3-lobed. Fruit ovoid, compressed, smooth and glabrous, crowned with the remnants of the style; outer coat thick and resinous; stone crustaceous. Seed nearly quadrangular, compressed; seed-coat smooth, dark brown and opaque, the broad funicle covering its margin.

Metopium with two species is confined to southern Florida and the West Indies.

The generic name, from ὅπος, was the classical name of an African tree now unknown.

1. Metopium toxiferum Kr. & Urb. Poison Wood. Hog Gum.

Metopium Metopium Small.

Leaves clustered near the end of the branches, 9'–10' long, with stout petioles swollen and enlarged at base, and 5–7 leaflets, or often 3-foliolate; unfolding in March and persistent until the following spring; leaflets ovate, rounded or usually contracted toward

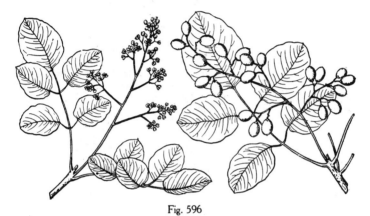

Fig. 596

the acute or sometimes slightly emarginate apex, rounded or sometimes cordate or cuneate at base, 3'–4' long, 2'–3' broad, with thickened slightly revolute margins, a prominent midrib, primary veins spreading at right angles, and numerous reticulate veinlets; petiolules stout, $\frac{1}{2}'$–1' long, that of the terminal leaflet often twice as long as the others. **Flowers** about $\frac{1}{8}'$ in diameter, in clusters as long or rather longer than the leaves; petals yellowgreen, marked on the inner surface by dark longitudinal lines; stamens rather shorter than the petals. **Fruit** ripening in November and December, pendent in long graceful clusters, orange-colored, rather lustrous, $\frac{3}{4}'$ in length; seed about $\frac{1}{4}'$ long.

A tree, frequently 35°–40° high, with a short trunk sometimes 2° in diameter, stout spreading often pendulous branches forming a low broad head, and reddish brown branchlets marked by prominent leaf-scars and numerous orange-colored lenticels; or often a shrub flowering when only a few feet tall. **Winter-buds** $\frac{1}{3}'$–$\frac{1}{2}'$ in length, with acuminate scales ciliate on the margin with rufous hairs. **Bark** of the trunk about $\frac{1}{8}'$ thick, light reddish brown tinged with orange, often marked by dark spots caused by the exuding of the resinous gum, and separating into large thin plate-like scales displaying the bright orange color of the inner bark. **Wood** heavy, hard, not strong, rich dark brown streaked with red, with thick light brown or yellow sapwood of 25–30 layers of annual growth. The resinous gum obtained from incisions made in the bark is emetic, purgative, and diuretic.

Distribution. Florida, shores of Bay Biscayne, on the Everglade Keys, and on Coot Bay in the rear of Cape Sable, Dade County, and on the southern keys; very abundant; in the Bahamas, Cuba, Jamaica, and Honduras.

4. RHUS L.

Trees or shrubs, with pithy branchlets, fleshy roots, and milky sometimes caustic or watery juice. Leaves unequally pinnate, or rarely simple. Flowers mostly dioecious, rarely polygamous, white or greenish white, in more or less compound axillary or terminal panicles, the staminate and pistillate usually produced on separate plants; calyx-lobes united at base only, generally persistent; disk surrounding the base of the free ovary, coherent with the base of the calyx; petals longer than the calyx-lobes, inserted under the margin of the disk, opposite its lobes, deciduous; stamens 5, inserted on the margin of the disk alternate with the petals; filaments longer than the anthers; ovary ovoid or subglobose, sessile; styles 3, terminal, free or slightly connate at base, rising from the centre of the ovary. Fruit usually globose, smooth or covered with hairs; outer coat thin and dry, more or less resinous; stone crustaceous or bony. Seed ovoid or reniform, commonly transverse; cotyledons foliaceous, generally transverse; radicle long, uncinate, laterally accumbent.

Rhus is widely distributed, with more than one hundred species, in the extra-tropical regions of the northern and southern hemispheres. In North America the genus is widely and generally distributed from Canada to southern Mexico and from the shores of the Atlantic to those of the Pacific Ocean, with sixteen or seventeen species within the territory of the United States. Of these, four obtain the habit of small trees. The acrid poisonous juice of *Rhus vernicifera* DC., of China, furnishes the black varnish used in China and Japan in the manufacture of lacquer, and other species are valued for the tannin contained in their leaves or for the wax obtained from their fruit.

The name of the genus is from 'Poôs, the classical name of the European Sumach.

CONSPECTUS OF NORTH AMERICAN ARBORESCENT SPECIES.

Flowers in terminal thyrsoid panicles; fruit globular, clothed with acrid hairs; leaves unequally pinnate, deciduous; SUMACHS.
Branches and leaf-stalks densely velvety hairy; leaflets 11–31, pale on the lower surface; fruit covered with long hairs; buds inclosed in the enlarged base of the petioles; juice milky. 1. R. typhina (A, C).
Branches and leaf-stalks pubescent; rachis winged; leaflets 9–21, green on the lower surface; fruit pilose; buds not inclosed by the petioles; juice watery.
2. R. copallina (A, C).
Flowers in axillary slender panicles; fruit glabrous, white; leaves unequally pinnate, deciduous; leaflets 7–13. 3. R. vernix (A, C).
Flowers in short compact terminal panicled racemes; fruit pubescent; leaves ovate, entire or serrate, simple or rarely trifoliolate, persistent. 4. R. integrifolia (G).

1. Rhus typhina L. Staghorn Sumach.

Rhus hirta Sudw.

Leaves 16′–24′ long, with a stout petiole usually red on the upper side and covered with soft pale hairs, enlarged at base and surrounding and inclosing the bud developed in its axil, and 11–31 oblong often falcate rather remotely and sharply serrate or rarely laciniate long-pointed nearly sessile or short-stalked leaflets rounded or slightly heart-shaped at base, covered above like the petiole and young shoots when they first appear with red caducous hairs, bright yellow-green until half grown, and at maturity dark green and rather opaque on the upper surface, pale or often nearly white on the lower surface, glabrous with the exception of the short fine hairs on the under side of the stout midrib, and primary veins forked near the margins, opposite, or the lower leaflets slightly alternate, those of the 3 or 4 middle pairs considerably longer than those at the ends of the leaf, 2′–5′ long, and 1′–1½′ wide; turning in the autumn before falling bright scarlet with shades of crimson, purple, and orange. **Flowers** opening gradually and in succession in early summer, the pistillate a week or ten days later than the staminate, on slender pedicels from the axils of small acute pubescent bracts, in dense panicles, with a pubescent stem and branchlets, and acuminate bracts $\frac{1}{2}'$ to nearly 2' long and deciduous with the opening of the flowers; panicle of the staminate flowers 8'–12' long and 5'–6' broad, with wide-spreading branches and nearly one third larger than the more compact panicle of the pistillate plant; calyx-lobes acute, covered on the outer surface with long slender hairs, much shorter than the petals in the staminate flower, and almost as long in the pistillate flower; petals of the staminate flower yellow-green sometimes tinged with red, strap-shaped, rounded at apex, becoming reflexed above the middle at maturity; petals of the pistillate flower green, narrow and acuminate, with a thickened and slightly hooded apex, remaining erect; disk bright red and conspicuous; stamens slightly exserted, with slender filaments and large bright orange-colored anthers; ovary ovoid, pubescent, the 3 short styles slightly connate at base, with large capitate stigmas, in the staminate flower glabrous, much smaller, unusually rudimen-

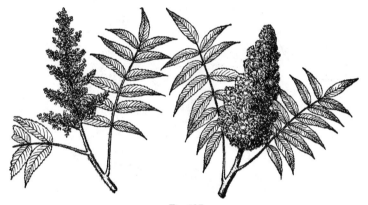

Fig. 597

tary. **Fruit** fully grown and colored in August and ripening late in the autumn in dense panicles 6'–8' long and 2'–3' wide, depressed-globose, with a thin outer covering clothed with long acrid crimson hairs and a small pale brown bony stone; **seed** slightly reniform, orange-brown.

A tree, occasionally 35°–40° high, with copious white viscid juice turning black on exposure, a slender often slightly inclining trunk occasionally 12'–14' in diameter, stout upright often contorted branches forming a low flat open head, and thick branchlets covered with long soft brown hairs gathered also in tufts in the axils of the leaflets, becoming glabrous after their third or fourth year, and in their second season marked by large narrow leaf-scars and by small orange-colored lenticels enlarging vertically and persistent for several years; more frequently a tall shrub, spreading by underground shoots into broad thickets. **Winter-buds** conic, thickly coated with long silky pale brown hairs, about $\frac{1}{4}'$ long. **Bark** of the trunk thin, dark brown, generally smooth, and occasionally separating into small square scales. **Wood** light, brittle, soft, coarse-grained, orange-colored, streaked with green, with thick nearly white sapwood. From the young shoots pipes are made for drawing the sap of the Sugar Maple. The bark, especially that of the roots, and the leaves are rich in tannin. A form with narrow deeply divided leaflets (f. *dissecta* Rehdr.) occasionally occurs.

Distribution. Usually on uplands in good soil, or less commonly on sterile gravelly banks and on the borders of streams and swamps, New Brunswick and through the valley of the St. Lawrence River to southern Ontario and westward to eastern North Dakota and eastern and northeastern Iowa, and southward through the northern states and along the Appalachian Mountains; more abundant on the Atlantic seaboard than in the region west of the Appalachian Mountains.

Occasionally cultivated as an ornamental plant in the United States, and very commonly in central and northern Europe.

✕ *Rhus hybrida* Rehdr. a hybrid of *R. typhina* and *R. glabra* L. has been found in Massachusetts.

2. Rhus copallina L.   Sumach.

Leaves 6′–8′ long, with a slender pubescent petiole and rachis more or less broadly wing-margined between the leaflets, the wings increasing in width toward the apex of the leaf, and 9–21 oblong or ovate-lanceolate leaflets entire or remotely serrate above the middle, sharp-pointed or rarely emarginate at apex, acute or obtuse and often unequal at

Fig. 598

base, those of the lower pairs short-petiolulate and smaller than those above the middle of the leaf, the others sessile with the exception of the terminal leaflet sometimes contracted into a long winged stalk, when they unfold dark green and slightly puberulous above, especially along the midrib, and covered below with fine silvery white pubescence, at maturity subcoriaceous, dark green and lustrous above, pale and pubescent below, 1½′–2½′ long and about ¾′ wide, with slightly thickened revolute margins, a prominent midrib and primary veins; turning in the autumn before falling dark rich maroon color on the upper surface.   **Flowers** appearing from June in the south to August in the north, those of the staminate plant opening in succession during nearly a month and continuing to unfold long after the petals of the pistillate plant have fallen, on stout pubescent pedicels ⅛′–¼′ long, in short compact pubescent panicles, the lower branches from the axils of the upper leaves, 4′–6′ long, 3′–4′ broad, and usually smaller on the female than on the male plant, their bracts and bractlets ovate or oblong, densely cinereo-pilose, deciduous before the expansion of the flowers; calyx puberulous on the outer surface, with ovate acute lobes one third as long as the ovate greenish yellow petals rounded at apex, becoming reflexed above the middle; disk red and conspicuous; stamens somewhat longer than the petals, with slender filaments and large orange-colored anthers, in the pistillate flower much shorter than the petals, with minute rudimentary anthers; ovary ovoid, pubescent, glabrous, much smaller in the staminate flower.   **Fruit** ripening in five or six weeks and borne in stout compact often nodding pubescent clusters sometimes persistent on the branches until the beginning of the following summer, ⅛' across, slightly obovoid, more or less flattened, with a thin bright red coat covered with short fine glandular hairs, and a smooth bony orange-brown stone; seed reniform, smooth, orange-colored, with a broad funicle.

A tree, 25°-30° high, with colorless watery juice, a short stout trunk 8'-10' in diameter, erect spreading branches, and branchlets at first dark green tinged with red and more or less densely clothed with short fine or sometimes ferrugineous pubescence, appearing slightly zigzag at the end of their first season from the swellings formed by the prominent leaf-scars, and then pale reddish brown, slightly puberulous and marked by conspicuous dark-colored lenticels; or at the north usually a low shrub rarely more than 4°-5° tall. **Winter-buds** minute, nearly globose, and covered with dark rusty brown tomentum. **Bark** of the trunk ⅓'-½' thick, light brown tinged with red, and marked by large elevated dark red-brown circular excrescences, and separating into large thin papery scales. **Wood** light, soft, coarse-grained, light brown streaked with green and often tinged with red, with thin lighter colored sapwood of 4 or 5 layers of annual growth. The leaves are rich in tannin and are gathered in large quantities and ground for curing leather and for dyeing.

Distribution. Dry hillsides and ridges; widely and generally distributed from northern New England southward to eastern Kentucky, Tennessee and to southern Florida, and to southeastern Iowa, southeastern Nebraska, eastern Kansas and the valley of the San Antonio River, Texas; in Cuba; in the United States arborescent only southward; at the north rarely more than a few feet high and spreading by underground stems on gravelly sterile soil into broad thickets; varying considerably in the size and form of the leaflets. The most distinct and probably the most constant of these varieties is var. *lanceolata* A. Gray, a small tree growing on the prairies of eastern Texas to the valley of the Rio Grande and to southeastern New Mexico, often forming thickets on river bluffs or on the banks of small streams, and distinguished by its narrow acute often falcate leaflets and by its larger inflorescence and fruit. A tree sometimes 25°-30° high, with a trunk occasionally 8' in diameter, covered by dark gray bark marked by lenticular excrescences. The flowers appear in July and August and the dull red or sometimes green fruit ripens in early autumn and falls before the beginning of winter.

Occasionally cultivated as an ornamental plant in the eastern United States, and in western and northern Europe.

3. Rhus vernix L. Poison Dogwood. Poison Sumach.

Leaves 7'-14' long, with a slender usually light red or red and green petiole, and 7-13 obovate-oblong entire leaflets slightly unequal at base and narrowed at the acute or rounded apex, bright orange color and coated, especially on the margins and under surface, with fine pubescence when they unfold, soon becoming glabrous, and at maturity 3'-4' long, 1½'-2' wide, dark green and lustrous above, pale below, with a prominent midrib scarlet above, primary veins forked near the margins, conspicuous reticulate veinlets, and revolute margins: turning early in the autumn before falling to brilliant shades of scarlet or orange and scarlet. **Flowers** about ⅛' long, appearing in early summer on slender pubescent pedicels bibracteolate near the middle, in long narrow axillary pubescent panicles crowded near the end of the branches, with acute pubescent early deciduous bracts and bractlets; calyx-lobes acute, one third the length of the yellow-green acute petals erect and slightly reflexed toward the apex; stamens nearly twice as long as the petals, with slender filaments and large orange-colored anthers, in the fertile flower not more than half the length of the petals, with small rudimentary anthers; ovary ovoid-globose, with short thick spreading styles terminating in large capitate stigmas. **Fruit** ripening in September and often persistent on the branches until the following spring, in long graceful racemes, ovoid, acute, often flattened and slightly gibbous, tipped with the dark remnants of the styles, glabrous, striate, ivory-white or white tinged with yellow, very lustrous, and about ¼' long; stone conspicuously grooved, the wall thin, membranaceous; seed pale yellow.

A tree, with acrid poisonous juice turning black on exposure, occasionally 25° high, with a trunk 5'–6' in diameter, slender rather pendulous branches forming a narrow round-topped head, and slender glabrous branchlets reddish brown and covered with minute orange-colored lenticels when they first appear, orange-brown at the end of their first season, becoming light gray and marked by large elevated conspicuous leaf-scars; more

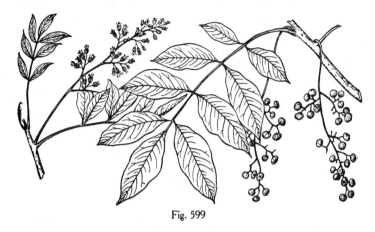

Fig. 599

often a shrub, with several slender clustered stems. **Winter-buds** acute and covered with dark purple scales puberulous on the back, and ciliate on the margins with short pale hairs, the terminal ⅛'–¾' long and two or three times larger than the axillary buds. **Bark** of the trunk thin, light gray, smooth or sometimes slightly striate. **Wood** light, soft, coarse-grained, light yellow streaked with brown, with lighter colored sapwood.

Distribution. Wet swamps often inundated during a portion of the year; Quebec south to Sebring, Highlands County, Florida (*R. M. Harper*), southern Alabama, and westward to Ontario and southeastern Minnesota, western Louisiana and the valley of the Neches River (San Augustine County) eastern Texas; common and one of the most dangerous plants of the North American flora. An infusion of the young branches and leaves is employed in homœopathic practice, and the juice can be used as a black lustrous durable varnish.

4. Rhus integrifolia B. & H.   Mahogany.

Leaves simple or very rarely 3-foliolate, persistent, acute or rounded at apex, with thickened revolute, or spinosely toothed margins (var. *serrata* Engler), puberulous when young, and at maturity 1½'–3' long, 1'–1½' wide, thick and coriaceous, dark yellow-green above, paler below, and glabrous with the exception of the stout petiole, broad thick midrib, and prominent reticulate veins. **Flowers** appearing from February to April, ¼' in diameter when expanded, on short stout pedicels, with 2–4 broad-ovate pointed persistent scarious ciliate pubescent bractlets, in short dense racemes forming hoary-pubescent terminal panicles 1'–3' in length; sepals rose-colored, orbicular, concave, ciliate on the margins, rather less than half the length of the rounded ciliate reflexed rose-colored petals; stamens as long as the petals, with slender filaments and pale anthers, minute and rudimentary in the pistillate flower; ovary broad-ovoid, pubescent, with 3 short thick connate styles and very large 3-lobed capitate stigmas, rudimentary in the staminate flower. **Fruit** ½' long, ovoid, flattened, more or less gibbous, thick, dark red, densely pubescent; stone kidney-shaped, smooth, light chestnut-brown, with thick walls; seed flattened, pale, with a broad dark-colored funicle covering its side.

A tree, rarely 30° high, with a short stout trunk 2°–3° in diameter, numerous spreading branches, and stout branchlets covered when they first appear with thick pale pubescence disappearing in their second and third years, and bright reddish brown and marked by numerous small elevated lenticels; or usually a small often almost prostrate shrub. **Winter-buds** small, obtuse, covered with a thick coat of pale tomentum. **Bark** of the trunk $\frac{1}{4}'-\frac{1}{2}'$ thick, bright reddish brown, exfoliating in large plate-like scales. **Wood** hard, heavy,

Fig. 600

bright clear red, with thin pale sapwood of 8–10 layers of annual growth; valued and largely used as fuel. The fruit is occasionally employed in the preparation of a cooling beverage.

Distribution. Sandy sterile soil along sea beaches, and bluffs in the immediate vicinity of the ocean; neighborhood of Santa Barbara, Santa Barbara County, California, to the shores of Magdalena Bay, Lower California, and on the Santa Barbara and Cedros islands; on the mainland usually shrubby, forming close impenetrable thickets; in more sheltered situations and on the islands becoming arborescent; probably of its largest size on the shores of Todos Santos Bay, Lower California.

XXXII. CYRILLACEÆ.

Trees or shrubs, with small scaly buds and watery juice. Leaves alternate, entire, subcoriaceous, without stipules, persistent or tardily deciduous. Flowers small, regular, perfect, on slender bibracteolate pedicels, in terminal or axillary racemes; calyx 5–8-lobed, persistent, the lobes imbricated in the bud; petals 5–8, hypogynous; stamens 5–10, hypogynous, those opposite the petals shorter than the others; anthers oblong, introrse, 2-celled, the cells laterally dehiscent, opening longitudinally; ovary 2–4-celled; ovules suspended, anatropous; raphe dorsal; micropyle superior. Fruit an indehiscent capsule. Seed suspended; seed-coat membranaceous; albumen fleshy, radicle superior.

A family confined to the warmer parts of America, with three genera, of which two are represented by small trees in the southern states.

CONSPECTUS OF THE GENERA OF THE UNITED STATES.

Flowers in axillary racemes; calyx 5-lobed; petals 5 contorted in the bud; fruit without wings, 2-celled, with 2 seeds in each cell.   **1. Cyrilla.**

Flowers in terminal racemes; calyx 5–8-lobed; petals 5–8 imbricated in the bud; fruit with 2–4 wings, 3 or rarely 4-celled, with 1 seed in each cell.   **2. Cliftonia.**

1. CYRILLA L.

A glabrous tree or shrub, with spongy bark, slender terete branchlets conspicuously marked by large leaf-scars, and narrow acute winter-buds covered with chestnut-brown scales. Leaves usually clustered near the end of the branches, oblong or oblong-obovate, pointed, rounded, or slightly emarginate at apex, conspicuously reticulate-veined, short-petiolate. Flowers on pedicels from the axils of narrow alternate persistent bracts, in slender racemes from the axils of fallen leaves or of small deciduous bracts near the end of the branches of the previous year; calyx minute, divided nearly to the base into 5 ovate-lanceolate acute coriaceous lobes; petals 5, contorted in the bud, white or rose color, inserted on an annular disk, three or four times longer than the calyx-lobes, oblong-lanceolate, acute, concave, subcoriaceous, furnished below the middle on the inner surface with a broad glandular nectary; stamens 5, opposite the divisions of the calyx, inserted with and shorter than the petals; filaments subulate, fleshy; anther-cells united above the point of attachment, free below; ovary ovoid, free, sessile, pointed, 2-celled; styles short, thick; stigma 2-lobed, with spreading lobes; ovules 3 in each cell, suspended from an elongated placental process developed from the apex of the cell. Fruit 2-celled, broad-ovoid, crowned with the remnants of the persistent style; pericarp spongy. Seeds 2 in each cell, elongated, acuminate; embryo minute, cylindric, 2-lobed.

Cyrilla is represented by a single species of the coast region of the south Atlantic and Gulf states and of the Antilles and eastern tropical South America.

The name commemorates the scientific labors of Dominico Cirillo (1734–1799), the distinguished Italian naturalist and patriot.

1. Cyrilla racemiflora L.   Ironwood.   Leather Wood.

Leaves 2′–3′ long and $\frac{1}{4}$′–1′ wide, with a stout petiole $\frac{1}{8}$′–1′ in length; turning late in the autumn and early winter to brilliant shades of orange and scarlet and then deciduous, or southward persistent with little change of color until the beginning of the following sum-

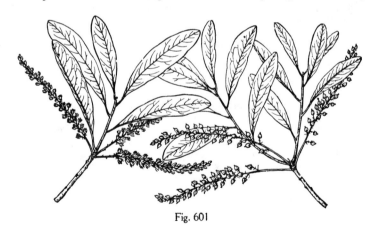

Fig. 601

mer. **Flowers** appearing late in June or early in July, in racemes usually 6–10 together and 4′–6′ long, at first erect, becoming pendulous before the fruit ripens. **Fruit** ripening in August and September, rarely more than $\frac{1}{16}$′ long; seeds light brown.

A slender tree, occasionally 30°–35° high, with a stout often eccentric trunk 10′–14′ in diameter, dividing several feet above the ground into numerous wide-spreading branches, and slender branchlets bright brown during their first season and ultimately ashy gray;

often a broad bush sending up many slender stems 15°–20° high. **Winter-buds** about ⅛′ long. **Bark** of the trunk rarely more than ½′ thick except near the base of old trees, and covered by large thin bright red-brown scales. **Wood** heavy, hard, close-grained, not strong, brown tinged with red, with rather lighter colored sapwood. The spongy bark at the base of the trunk is pliable, absorbent, and astringent, and has been recommended as a styptic.

Distribution. Rich shaded river-bottoms, the borders of sandy swamps and shallow ponds of the coast Pine-belt, or on high sandy exposed ridges rising above streams near the Gulf coast; southeastern Virginia southward near the coast to northern Florida and westward along the Gulf coast to the valley of the Neches River, Texas; in Lake County, Florida, and ranging northward in Mississippi to Forrest County (near Hattiesburg, *T. G. Harbison*), and in Alabama to Dallas County; in swamps near the coast of western Florida often a low shrub with smaller leaves and shorter racemes (var. *parviflora* Sarg.); in Cuba, Jamaica, Porto Rico, Demarara, and Brazil (var. *racemifera* Sarg.).

2. CLIFTONIA Gærtn. f.

A glabrous tree or shrub, with thick dark brown scaly bark, slender terete branchlets marked by conspicuous leaf-scars, and small acuminate buds covered by chestnut-brown scales. Leaves oblong-lanceolate, rounded or slightly emarginate at apex, glandular-punctate, short-petiolate, persistent. Flowers on pedicels from the axils of large acuminate membranaceous alternate bracts deciduous before the opening of the flowers, in short terminal erect racemes; calyx 5–8-lobed, equal or unequal, broad-ovoid, rounded or acuminate at apex, much shorter than the 5–8 obovate unguiculate concave white or rose-colored sepals; stamens 10, opposite and alternate with the sepals, inserted with and shorter than the petals, 2-ranked, those of the outer rank longer than the others; filaments laterally enlarged near the middle, flattened below, subulate above; disk cup-shaped, surrounding the base of the oblong 2–4-winged 2–4-celled ovary; stigma subsessile, obscurely 2–4-lobed; ovules 2 in each cell, suspended from its apex. Fruit oblong, 2–4-winged, crowned with the remnants of the persistent style, 3 or rarely 4-celled; pericarp spongy, the wings thin and membranaceous. Seed 1 in each cell, terete, tapering to the ends, suspended; cotyledons very short.

Cliftonia is represented by a single species of the south Atlantic and Gulf states.

The generic namé is in honor of Dr. Francis Clifton (d. 1736), an English physician.

1. Cliftonia monophylla Britt. Titi. Ironwood.

Leaves 1½′–2′ long, ½′–1′ wide, bright green and lustrous on the upper surface, paler on the lower surface; persistent until the autumn of their second year. **Flowers** fragrant,

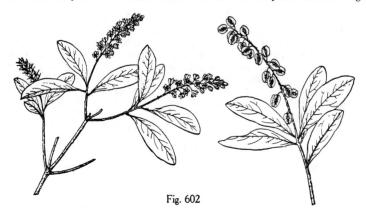

Fig. 602

appearing in February and March, in racemes at first nodding, and conspicuous from the long exserted dark red-brown caducous bracts, becoming erect as the flowers open. **Fruit** about $\frac{1}{4}'$ long, ripening in August and September; seeds $\frac{1}{16}'-\frac{1}{8}'$ long, light brown.

A tree, occasionally 40°–50° high, with a stout often crooked or inclining trunk, occasionally 15'–18' in diameter, and usually divided 12°–15° from the ground into a number of stout ascending branches, and slender rigid bright red-brown branchlets, becoming paler during their second and third seasons; or sometimes a shrub, with numerous straggling stout or slender stems frequently only a few feet high or occasionally 30°–40° high. **Winter-buds** about $\frac{1}{4}'$ long. **Bark** of young stems and of large branches thin, the surface separating into small persistent scales 1'–2' long, becoming near the base of old trees deeply furrowed, dark red-brown, $\frac{1}{4}'$ thick, and broken on the surface into short broad scales. **Wood** heavy, close-grained, moderately hard, brittle, not strong, brown tinged with red, with thick lighter colored sapwood of 40–50 layers of annual growth; burning with a clear bright flame, and valued as fuel.

Distribution. Damp sandy peat soil in alluvial swamps and bays free from mud, lime, sulphur and salt, or often in shallow rarely overflowed swamps; coast region of the south Atlantic states from the valley of the Savannah River to the coast of western Florida, and through the maritime Pine-belt of the Gulf coast to eastern Louisiana.

XXXIII. AQUIFOLIACEÆ.

Trees or shrubs, with terete branchlets, scaly buds, and alternate simple entire crenate or pungently toothed petiolate persistent or deciduous leaves, with minute stipules. Flowers axillary, solitary or cymose, small, greenish white, diœcious; calyx 4–6-lobed, the lobes imbricated in the bud, hypogynous; petals 4–6, oval or oblong, obtuse, free or united at base, imbricated in the bud; disk 0; stamens as many as and alternate with the petals and adnate to the base of the corolla; anthers introrse, 2-celled, the cells opening longitudinally, small and sterile in the pistillate flower; pistil compound; ovary 4–8-celled, minute and rudimentary in the staminate flower; style short or 0; stigmas as many as the cells of the ovary, nearly confluent; ovule generally solitary in each cell, suspended, anatropous; raphe usually dorsal, the micropyle superior. Fruit a drupe, with as many indehiscent bony or crustaceous 1-seeded nutlets as carpels; sarcocarp thin and fleshy. Seed narrowed at the ends, suspended; seed-coat membranaceous, pale brown; embryo minute in the apex of the copious fleshy albumen; cotyledons plain; the radicle superior.

The Holly family with five genera is distributed in temperate and tropical regions of the two hemispheres. Of the five genera now recognized, only Ilex is important in the number of species or is widely distributed.

1. ILEX L.

Characters of the family.

Ilex with about one hundred and seventy-five species is found in all tropical and temperate regions of the world with the exception of western North America, Australia, New Zealand, Tasmania, and New Guinea, the largest number of species occurring in Brazil and Guiana. Of the thirteen species which inhabit eastern North America, six are trees. Ilex contains a bitter principle, ilicin, and possesses tonic properties. *Ilex paraguariensis* St. Hilaire, of South America, furnishes the maté or Paraguay tea, and is the most useful of the species. The European *Ilex Aquifolium* L. is a favorite garden plant, and is sometimes planted in the middle, southern, and Pacific United States.

Ilex is the classical name of the Evergreen Oak of southern Europe.

CONSPECTUS OF THE NORTH AMERICAN ARBORESCENT SPECIES.

Parts of the flower in 4's; pedicels with bractlets at the base; nutlets prominently ribbed on the back and sides; leaves persistent.
Leaves armed with spiny teeth; young branchlets glabrous or sparingly pubescent.
1. **I. opaca** (A, C).

Leaves serrate or entire; fruit bright red.
 Leaves oblanceolate or oblong-obovate, mostly entire; young branchlets pubescent; calyx-lobes acuminate.   2. **I. Cassine** (C).
 Leaves elliptic or oblong-elliptic, coarsely crenulate-serrate; young branchlets puberulous; calyx-lobes obtuse.   3. **I. vomitoria** (C).
Leaves entire, ovate, ovate-elliptic or ovate-lanceolate; fruit brownish purple.
                   4. **I. Krugiana** (D).
Parts of the flower in 4's or 5's, rarely in 6's; pedicels without bractlets; nutlets striate, many-ribbed on the back; leaves deciduous.
 Leaves oblong-spatulate or obovate-lanceolate, remotely crenulate-serrate; calyx-lobes broad-triangular.   5. **I. decidua** (A, C).
 Leaves ovate or oblong-lanceolate, sharply serrate; calyx-lobes acute.
                   6. **I. monticola** (A).

1. Ilex opaca Ait. Holly.

Leaves elliptic to obovate-oblong, pungently acute, with thickened undulate margins and few stout spinose teeth, or occasionally entire, especially on upper branches, thick, coriaceous, dull yellow-green, paler and often yellow on the lower surface, 2′–4′ long, with a prominent midrib and conspicuous veins; persistent on the branches for three years,

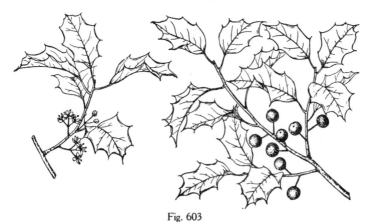

Fig. 603

finally deciduous in the spring; petioles short, stout, thickened at base, grooved above, slightly puberulent; stipules minute, broad-acute or nearly deltoid, persistent. **Flowers** appearing in spring on slender puberulous pedicels, with minute acute bractlets, in short pedunculate cymes from the axils of young leaves or scattered along the base of the young shoots, 3–9-flowered on the staminate and 1 or rarely 2 or 3-flowered on the pistillate plant; calyx-lobes acute, ciliate on the margins; stigmas broad and sessile. **Fruit** ripening late in the autumn, persistent on the branches during the winter, spherical or ovoid, dull red or rarely yellow, ¼′ in diameter; **nutlets** prominently few-ribbed on the back and sides, rather narrower at apex than at base.

A tree, often 40°–50° and occasionally 80°–100° high, with a trunk 2°, 3°, or exceptionally 4° in diameter, short slender branches forming a narrow pyramidal head, and stout branchlets covered when they first appear with fine rufous pubescence disappearing during their first season, and becoming glabrous and pale brown. **Winter-buds** obtuse or acuminate, ⅛′–¼′ long, with narrow acuminate ciliate scales. **Bark** about ½′ thick, light gray and roughened by wart-like excrescences. **Wood** light, tough, not strong, close-grained, nearly white when first cut, turning brown with age and exposure, with thick rather lighter colored sapwood; valued and much used in cabinet-making, in the interior finish of houses, and in turnery. The branches are used in large quantities for Christmas decoration.

Distribution. Coast of Massachusetts, in the city of Quincy, Norfolk County, south-ward generally near the coast to the shores of Mosquito Inlet and Charlotte Harbor, Flor-ida; valley of the Mississippi River from southeastern Missouri and eastern and southern Arkansas, eastern Oklahoma, and Louisiana to the valley of Cibolo Creek (Southerland Springs, Wilson County), Texas; rare and of small size east of the Hudson River and rare in the Appalachian Mountain region and the country immediately west of it; most abundant and of its largest size on the bottom-lands of the streams of northern Louisiana, southern Arkansas and eastern Texas; at the north in dry rather gravelly soil often on the margins of Oak-woods, southward on the borders of swampy river-bottoms, in rich humid soil.

Occasionally cultivated in the eastern states as an ornamental plant.

2. Ilex Cassine L. Dahoon.

Leaves oblanceolate to oblong-obovate, acute, mucronate or rarely rounded and occa-sionally emarginate at apex, gradually narrowed and cuneate at base, revolute and entire, or sometimes serrate above the middle with sharp mucronate teeth, puberulous above and

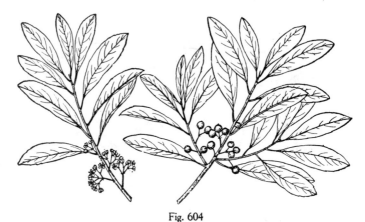

Fig. 604

densely pubescent below when they first unfold, becoming glabrous at maturity with the exception of scattered hairs on the lower surface of the broad midrib, dark green and lus-trous above, pale below, $1\frac{1}{2}'-3'$ long and $\frac{1}{2}'-1'$ wide; petioles short, stout, thickened at the base, sparingly villose. **Flowers** on hairy pedicels, with acute scarious bractlets, in pedun-culate clusters, 3–9-flowered on the staminate plant, usually 3-flowered on the pistillate plant sometimes nearly 1' long, from the axils of leaves of the year or occasionally of the previous year; calyx-lobes acute, ciliate. **Fruit** ripening late in the autumn, persistent until the following spring, globose, sometimes $\frac{1}{4}'$ in diameter, bright or occasionally dull red or nearly yellow, solitary or often in clusters of 3's; **nutlets** prominently few-ribbed on the back and sides; rounded at base, acute at apex.

A tree, $25°-30°$ high, with a trunk $12'-18'$ in diameter, and branches coated at first with dense silky pubescence persistent until the end of the second or third year, ultimately dark brown and marked by occasional lenticels; or often a low shrub. **Winter-buds** minute, acute, with lanceolate scales thickly coated with pale silky pubescence. **Bark** of the trunk about $\frac{1}{16}'$ thick, dark gray, thickly covered and roughened by lenticels. **Wood** light, soft, close-grained, not strong, pale brown, with thick nearly white sapwood.

Distribution. Cold swamps and on their borders, in rich moist soil, or occasionally on the high sandy banks of Pine-barren streams; South Carolina southward in the immediate neighborhood of the coast to the shores of Bay Biscayne and the Everglade Keys, Dade County, and in the interior of the peninsula in Polk and De Soto Counties, Florida, and along the Gulf coast to western Louisiana; on the Bahama Islands and in Cuba (var. *latifolia* Ait.); nowhere abundant on the Atlantic coast; most common in western Florida and southern Alabama; passing through forms with elongated narrow leaves (var. *angustifolia* Ait., the common form of southern Alabama) into the variety *myrtifolia* Sarg. This is a low shrub or occasionally a slender wide-branched tree, with pale nearly white bark, puberulous branchlets, and crowded generally entire mucronate leaves $\frac{1}{2}'-1'$ long, $\frac{1}{8}'$ wide, with strongly reflexed margins, a very short petiole, and a broad prominent midrib; an inhabitant of Cypress-swamps and Pine-barren ponds or their margins, in the neighborhood of the coast, North Carolina to Louisiana.

Ilex Cassine is occasionally cultivated in Europe.

3. Ilex vomitoria Ait. Cassena. Yaupon.

Leaves elliptic to elliptic-oblong, obtuse, coarsely and remotely crenulate-serrate, coriaceous, dark green and lustrous above, pale and opaque below, $1'-2'$ long and $\frac{1}{4}'-1'$ wide, persistent for two or three years, generally falling just before the appearance of the new

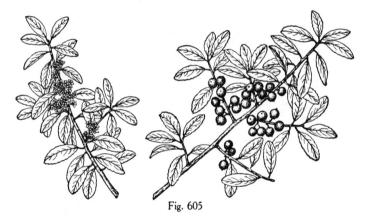

Fig. 605

growth of their third season; petioles short, broad, and grooved. **Flowers** on slender club-shaped glabrous pedicels, with minute bractlets at the base, in short glabrous cymes on branchlets of the previous year, those of the staminate plant short-stemmed and many-flowered, those of the pistillate plant sessile and 1 or 2-flowered; calyx-lobes rounded, obtuse, often slightly ciliate; ovary contracted below the broad flat stigma. **Fruit** produced in great abundance, on stems not more than $\frac{1}{4}'$ long, ripening late in the autumn or in early winter, soon deciduous, or persistent until spring, scarlet, nearly globose, about $\frac{1}{4}'$ in diameter; **nutlets** obtuse at the ends, and prominently few-ribbed on the back and sides.

A small much-branched tree, $20°-25°$ high, with a slender often inclining trunk rarely more than $6'$ in diameter, and stout branchlets standing at right angles with the stem, slightly angled and puberulous during their first season, becoming glabrous or nearly glabrous, terete and pale gray in their second year; generally a tall shrub, with numerous stems forming dense thickets. **Winter-buds** minute, obtuse, with narrow dark brown or often nearly black scales. **Bark** of the trunk $\frac{1}{16}'-\frac{1}{8}'$ thick, the light red-brown surface broken into thin minute scales. **Wood** heavy, hard, close-grained, nearly white, turning yellow with exposure, with thick lighter colored sapwood.

Distribution. Southeastern Virginia to the St. John's River and Cedar Keys, Florida, and westward to the shores of Matagorda Bay and the valleys of the upper Rio Blanco and the Guadalupe River, Texas, and to southern Arkansas; in the Atlantic and east Gulf states rarely far from salt water (in Alabama northward to Autauga County), and usually not more than 10°–15° high; of its largest size and of tree-like habit only on the rich bottom-lands of eastern Texas. The branches covered with the fruit are sold during the winter months for decorative purposes. An infusion of the leaves, which are emetic and purgative, was used by the Indians, who formerly visited the coast in large numbers every spring to drink it.

Occasionally used in the southern states for hedges.

4. Ilex Krugiana Loesen.

Leaves ovate, ovate-elliptic or ovate-lanceolate, acuminate and abruptly long-pointed or acute at apex, rounded or obtusely cuneate at base, entire, with slightly thickened margins subcoriaceous or coriaceous, glabrous, dark yellow-green and lustrous above, dull beneath,

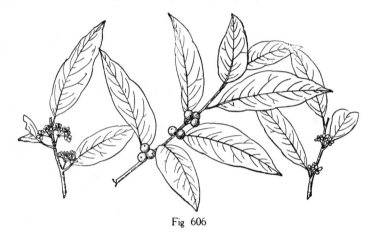

Fig 606

persistent, $2\frac{1}{2}'$–$4'$ long and $1'$–$1\frac{1}{2}'$ wide, with a prominent midrib deeply impressed on the upper side and pale on the lower side, and 6–9 pairs of slender primary veins connected by thin reticulate veinlets; petioles slender, $\frac{1}{3}'$–$\frac{3}{4}'$ in length; stipules minute, whitish, persistent. Flowers on slender pedicels, $\frac{1}{12}'$–$\frac{1}{6}'$ long, in the axils of minute acute scarious deciduous bractlets, in crowded clusters, the staminate 1–3-flowered on short peduncles, the pistillate 1-flowered; calyx about $\frac{1}{12}'$ in diameter, 4-lobed, the lobes triangular, suberect, about as long as the tube, imbricated in the bud; corolla rotate, greenish white, petals 4, ovate or slightly obovate in the pistillate flower, imbricated in the bud; stamens 4 in the staminate flower, nearly as long as the petals; filaments slender, about as long as the oval anthers; in the pistillate flower much smaller and abortive; ovary 4-celled, ellipsoid; stigma small, discoid, obscurely 4-lobed; ovary of the staminate flower subconic, minute and abortive. Fruit on a stout pedicel up to $\frac{1}{5}'$ in length, globose, brownish purple, lustrous, $\frac{1}{6}'$ in diameter; sarcocarp thin; nutlets 4, irregularly 3-seeded, obtusely angled, dark brown.

In Florida a tree, sometimes 30°–40° high, with a tall often crooked trunk occasionally $4'$ in diameter and covered with thin smooth nearly white bark, becoming on old individuals darker-colored and broken into narrow scales, and small ascending branchlets green when they first appear, becoming light gray and finally white, and marked by numerous round elliptic lenticels; often a shrub.

Distribution. Florida, Homestead and Paradise Keys in the Everglades, Dade County; in the Bahama Islands, Hayti and San Domingo.

5. Ilex decidua Walt.

Leaves deciduous, except on vigorous shoots, fascicled at the end of short spur-like lateral branchlets, oblong-spatulate or spatulate-lanceolate, acuminate, obtuse or emarginate at apex, gradually narrowed below, remotely crenulate-serrate, $2'-3'$ long, $\frac{1}{3}'-1'$ wide, thin early in the season, becoming thick and firm at maturity, light green above and pale and sparingly hairy along the narrow midrib below; petioles slender, grooved, pubescent, about $\frac{1}{4}'$ in length; stipules filiform, membranaceous. **Flowers** on slender pedicels, those of the staminate plant often $\frac{1}{2}'$ long and longer than those of the pistillate plant, in 1 or 2-flowered glabrous cymes crowded at the end of the lateral branches of the previous season, or rarely solitary on branchlets of the year; calyx-lobes triangular, with smooth or sometimes ciliate margins. **Fruit** on short stout stems, ripening in the early autumn, often remaining on the branches until the appearance of the leaves the following spring, globose or depressed-

Fig. 607

globose, orange or orange-scarlet, $\frac{1}{4}'$ in diameter; **nutlets** narrowed and rounded at base, acute or acuminate at apex, many-ribbed on the back.

A tree, $20°-30°$ high, with a slender trunk $6'-10'$ in diameter, stout spreading branches, and slender glabrous pale silver gray branchlets; more often a tall straggling shrub. **Winter-buds** minute, obtuse, with ovate light gray scales. **Bark** of the trunk rarely more than $\frac{1}{16}'$ thick, light brown, and roughened by wart-like excrescences. **Wood** heavy, hard, close-grained, creamy white, with rather lighter colored sapwood.

Distribution. Borders of streams and swamps in low moist soil; Gloucester County, Virginia, to western Florida in the region between the eastern and southern base of the Appalachian Mountains and the neighborhood of the coast, and through the Gulf states to the valley of the Colorado River, Texas, and through Arkansas, eastern Oklahoma, and southern and eastern (St. Louis, Pike and Marion Counties) Missouri to southern Illinois, and southwestern Indiana (common in bottoms, Posey County, *C. C. Deam*); usually shrubby east of the Mississippi River and only arborescent in Missouri, southern Arkansas, and eastern Texas. In Florida a form (var. *Curtissii* Fern.) occurs with leaves only $\frac{1}{3}'-\frac{2}{3}'$ long and fruit about $\frac{1}{4}'$ in diameter.

6. Ilex monticola Gray.

Leaves deciduous, ovate to oblong-lanceolate, abruptly narrowed and acuminate or rarely acute at apex, cuneate or rarely rounded at base, sharply and rather remotely serrate with minute glandular incurved teeth, thin, glabrous, or sparingly hairy along the prominent midrib and veins, 2'-5' long, ½'-2½' wide, light green above and pale below; petioles slender, ⅓'-½' in length. **Flowers** appearing in June when the leaves are more than half grown, on slender pedicels ½' long on the staminate plant and much longer on the pistillate plant, in 1-2-flowered cymes crowded at the end of lateral spur-like branchlets of the previous year, or solitary on branchlets of the year; calyx-lobes acute, ciliate; ovary contracted below the broad flat stigma. **Fruit** globose, bright scarlet, nearly ½' in diameter; **nutlets** narrowed at the ends, prominently ribbed on the back and sides.

A tree, 30°-40° high, with a short trunk sometimes 10'-12' in diameter, slender branches forming a narrow pyramidal head, and more or less zigzag glabrous branchlets pale red-

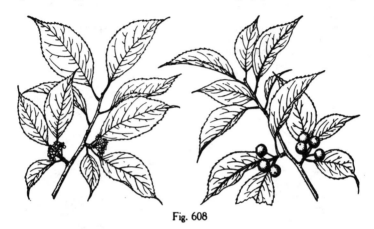

Fig. 608

brown at first, becoming dark gray at the end of their first season; more often a low shrub, with spreading stems. **Winter-buds** broad-ovoid to subglobose, about ⅛' long, with ovate keeled apiculate light brown scales. **Bark** of the trunk usually less than ₁₆' thick, with a light brown surface roughened by numerous lenticels. **Wood** hard, heavy, close-grained, and creamy white.

Distribution. Central and western New York, southward along the Appalachian Mountains to eastern Tennessee; northern and central Georgia; coast of South Carolina near Charleston; western Florida (Mariana, Jackson County, and Wakulla Springs, Wakulla County); Dallas County, Alabama; northeastern Mississippi (Tishomingo County), and in West Feliciana and Wynn Parishes, Louisiana; a shrubby form with leaves soft pubescent beneath (var. *mollis* Britt.) occurs in western Massachusetts and Connecticut, and southward to North Carolina.

XXXIV. CELASTRACEÆ.

Trees or shrubs, with watery juice, and opposite or alternate simple persistent or deciduous leaves, with or without stipules. Flowers regular, perfect, polygamous or diœcious, pedicellate in axillary clusters; calyx 4-5-lobed, the lobes imbricated in the bud; petals 4 or 5, imbricated in the bud; stamens 4 or 5; anthers introrse, 2-celled, the cells opening longitudinally; ovary 2-5-celled; ovules 2 or solitary in each cell (*6 in Canotia*), anatropous, or subhorizontal (*in Canotia*). Fruit a capsule or drupe. Seed with copious albumen; embryo axile.

A family of about thirty-eight genera widely distributed over the tropical and warm temperate parts of the world, with five arborescent representatives in the United States.

CONSPECTUS OF THE ARBORESCENT GENERA OF THE UNITED STATES.

Leaves opposite, deciduous; parts of the flower in 4's; fruit a fleshy capsule enclosed in a
colored aril. 1. Evonymus.
Leaves alternate, persistent (0 in 3).
Fruit capsular; parts of the flower in 5's.
Capsule 3–4-valved, loculicidal, its outer coat woody, the valves apiculate at
apex; base of the seed enclosed in a colored aril. 2. Maytenus.
Capsule 5-valved, septicidal, its outer coat thin and fleshy, the valves 2-lobed at
apex; seed without an aril. 3. Canotia.
Fruit drupaceous; parts of the flower in 4's; seed without an aril.
Leaves often crenately serrate above the middle; stipules minute, caducous; fruit
usually 1-seeded; branchlets quadrangular. 4. Gyminda.
Leaves entire; stipules 0; fruit 2-seeded; branchlets terete. 5. Schæfferia.

1. EVONYMUS L.

Small generally glabrous trees or shrubs, with usually square sometimes wing-margined
branchlets, bitter drastic bark, slender obtuse or acuminate winter-buds, and fibrous roots.
Leaves opposite, petiolate, entire, crenate or dentate, deciduous or rarely persistent;
stipules minute, caducous. Flowers perfect or polygamo-diœcious, in dichotomous axillary usually few-flowered cymes; calyx 4-lobed (in the North American arborescent
species); disk thick and fleshy, cohering with and filling the short tube of the calyx, flat,
4-angled or lobed, closely surrounding and adhering to the ovary; petals inserted in the
sinuses of the calyx under the free border of the disk, as many as and much longer than the
calyx-lobes, spreading, deciduous; stamens as many as the petals and alternate with them,
inserted on the summit of the disk; filaments very short, subulate, erect or recurved; anthers 2-celled, the cells nearly parallel or spreading below; ovary 4-celled; styles short,
terminating in a depressed stigma; ovules usually 2 in each cell, ascending from the central
angle; raphe ventral, micropyle inferior, or pendulous, the raphe then dorsal and the micropyle superior. Fruit capsular, 4-lobed and celled, fleshy, angled or winged, smooth (in
the North American arborescent species), loculicidally 4-valved, the valves septicidal.
Seeds 2 in each cell, or commonly solitary by abortion, ascending, surrounded by a colored aril; seed-coat chartaceous; albumen fleshy; embryo axile; cotyledons broad, coriaceous, parallel with the raphe; the radicle short, inferior.

Evonymus is widely distributed through the northern hemisphere, extending south
of the equator to the islands of the Indian Archipelago and to Australia. About forty
species are distinguished, the largest number occurring in the tropical regions of southern
Asia, and in China and Japan. Of the four species found within the territory of the
United States one only is a small tree. Many of the species are rich in bitter and astringent principles, and are drastic and slightly stimulant. Many are valued as ornaments of gardens and parks.

The generic name is from the classical name of one of the European species.

1. Evonymus atropurpureus Jacq. Burning Bush. Wahoo.

Leaves ovate-elliptic, acuminate, minutely serrate or biserrate, thin, puberulous below,
2'–5' long and 1'–2' wide, with a stout midrib and primary veins; turning pale yellow in
the autumn and falling in October; petioles stout, $\frac{1}{2}'$–1' in length. Flowers appearing
from May to the middle of June, nearly $\frac{1}{2}'$ across, in twice or thrice dichotomous usually
7–15-flowered cymes borne on slender peduncles 1'–2' long and conspicuously marked by
the scars of minute bracts; calyx-lobes 4, rounded or rarely acute at apex, mostly entire;
petals broad-obovate, undulate, often erose on the margins; anthers spreading. Fruit
ripening in October, usually persistent on the branches until midwinter, deeply lobed,
$\frac{1}{2}'$ across, with light purple valves; seeds sometimes gibbous on the dorsal side, broad and

rounded above, narrowed below, ¼′ long, with a thin light chestnut-brown wrinkled coat and a thin scarlet aril.

A tree, rarely 20°–25° high, with a trunk 4′–6′ in diameter, spreading branches, and slender terete branchlets dark purple-brown at first, becoming lighter colored in their second season, often covered with small crowded lenticels, and marked by prominent leaf-scars, occasionally slightly or on vigorous shoots rarely broadly wing-margined; more often a shrub, 6°–10° tall. Winter-buds ⅛′ long, acute, with narrow purple apiculate

Fig. 609

scales scarious on the margins and covered by a glaucous bloom. **Bark** thin, ashy gray, and covered by thin minute scales. **Wood** heavy, hard, very close-grained, white tinged with orange.

Distribution. Borders of woods in rich soil; western New York to southern Minnesota, central Iowa, southeastern South Dakota, northwestern Nebraska, central Kansas, Oklahoma to the valley of the Canadian River (near Minton, Caddo County), southern Arkansas and eastern Texas (Dallas County), and southward to eastern Tennessee, and Jackson County, Alabama; in the valley of the upper Missouri River, Montana; arborescent only in southern Arkansas and Texas.

Occasionally cultivated as an ornament of gardens in the eastern United States and in Europe.

2. MAYTENUS Molina.

Small unarmed trees or shrubs with slender branchlets and minute buds. **Leaves** alternate often in two ranks, coriaceous, petiolate, persistent; stipules minute, deciduous. Flowers polygamous, small, white, yellow or red, axillary, solitary or in cymose or fascicled clusters; calyx 5-lobed; petals 5, spreading; stamens 5, inserted under the orbicular disk, with undulate margins; filaments filiform; anthers ovoid-cordate; ovary immersed and confluent with the disk, 2–4-celled; style 0 or columnar; stigma 2–4-lobed, usually sessile; ovules erect, solitary or in pairs in each cell. Fruit capsular, coriaceous, 2–4-valved; seed erect, surrounded at base or entirely in a pulpy aril; testa crustaceous; albumen fleshy or wanting; cotyledons foliaceous.

Maytenus with some seventy species is widely distributed in the tropical and subtropical regions of America from southern Florida, where one species occurs, to Brazil and Chile.

The Chilean *Maytenus boaria* Molina, a handsome tree of graceful habit, is occasionally cultivated in California.

The generic name is from Mayten, the Chilean name of one of the species.

1. Maytenus phyllanthoides Benth.

Leaves oblong-obovate to elliptic, rounded and rarely emarginate or acute at apex, gradually narrowed and cuneate at base and entire, deeply tinged with red when they unfold and at maturity, $1'-1\frac{1}{2}'$ long and $\frac{1}{2}'-\frac{3}{4}'$ wide, with thickened often slightly undulate margins, a slender midrib, obscure primary veins, and conspicuous reticulate veinlets; petioles stout, $\frac{1}{6}'-\frac{1}{4}'$ in length. Flowers usually solitary or in compact fascicles, short-stalked, about $\frac{1}{12}'$ in diameter; calyx-lobes rounded at apex, often persistent under the fruit, reddish, shorter than the white petals; ovary 3–4-celled. Fruit solitary, short-

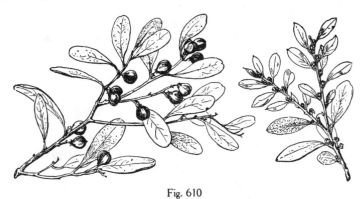

Fig. 610

stalked, broad-obovoid, 4-angled, rounded and minutely mucronate at apex, abruptly narrowed below, bright red, $\frac{1}{4}'-\frac{1}{3}'$ long and broad, 1-celled, 3–4-valved, the valves opening to the base, ridged down the inner surface with a low ridge developed from the dissepiment, 2–4-seeded; seed ellipsoid, acute at the ends, $\frac{1}{12}'$ long, surrounded at base by an open bright red aril.

A round-topped tree, rarely 20° high, with a trunk $1°-2°$ in diameter (teste *J. K. Small*), and slender alternate glabrous pale gray branchlets; usually a low shrub.

Distribution. Florida, west coast, Captiva Island, Lee County, to the neighborhood of Cape Sable; Cocoanut Grove, Dade County, and on many of the southern keys; on bluffs of Matagorda Bay near Corpus Christi, Nueces County, Texas; in northern Mexico and Lower California; probably of its largest size in Florida on Sands Key and on Captiva Island.

3. CANOTIA Torr.

A glabrous leafless tree, with light brown deeply furrowed bark, stout terete alternate branches terminating in rigid, pale green and striate spines, their base and those of the peduncles surrounded by black triangular persistent cushion-like processes minutely papillose on the surface. Flowers perfect, on slender spreading pedicels jointed below the middle, 3–7 together, in short-stemmed fascicles or corymbs near the end of the branches, from the axils of minute ovate subulate bracts; calyx 5-lobed, minute, persistent, much shorter than the oblong obtuse white hypogynous petals imbricated in the bud, reflexed at maturity above the middle, deciduous; stamens 5, hypogynous, opposite the lobes of the calyx; filaments awl-shaped, rather shorter than the petals, persistent on the fruit; anthers oblong, cordate, minutely apiculate, attached below the middle, grooved on the back; ovary raised upon and confluent with a fleshy slightly 10-angled gynophore, papillose-glandular on the surface, 5-celled, the cells opposite the petals, terminating in a fleshy elongated style; stigma slightly 5-lobed; ovules 6 in each cell, inserted in 2 ranks on its inner angle, subhorizontal; micropyle inferior.　Fruit a woody ovoid, acuminate capsule rounded at base, crowned with the subulate persistent style, septicidally 5-valved, the valves 2-lobed at apex; outer coat thin, fleshy; inner coat woody.　Seed solitary or in pairs, ascending, subovoid, flattened; seed-coat subcoriaceous, papillate, produced below into a subfalcate membranaceous wing; embryo surrounded by thin fleshy albumen, erect; cotyledons oval, compressed; radicle very short, inferior.

The genus is represented by a single species.

The generic name is that by which this plant was known to the Mexicans of Arizona at the time of its discovery.

1. Canotia holacantha Torr.

Leaves 0.　**Flowers** $\frac{1}{8}'-\frac{1}{4}'$ in diameter, appearing from June until October.　Capsule 1' long; **seed** about $\frac{3}{4}'$ in length.

A small shrub-like tree, sometimes 20°–30° high, with a short stout trunk rarely a foot in diameter; or often a low spreading shrub.

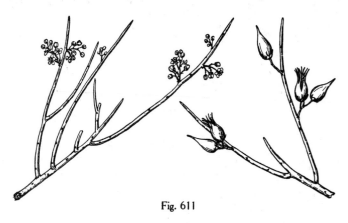

Fig. 611

Distribution.　Dry gravelly mesas on the Arizona foothills, from the White Mountain region to the valley of Bill Williams's Fork in the northwestern part of the state, and on Providence Mountain in southern California.

4. GYMINDA Sarg.

Trees or shrubs, with pale quadrangular branchlets and minute acuminate buds.　Leaves opposite, short-petiolate, oblong-obovate, rounded and sometimes emarginate at apex, entire or remotely crenulate-serrate above the middle with revolute thickened margins, feather-veined, coriaceous, persistent; stipules minute, acuminate, membranaceous, caducous.　Flowers unisexual, pedicellate, in axillary pedunculate few-flowered dichotomously branched cymes bibracteolate at apex; calyx minute, 4-lobed, persistent, with a short urceolate tube and rounded lobes; disk fleshy, filling the tube of the calyx, cupshaped, slightly 4-lobed; petals entire, obovate, white, rounded at apex, reflexed, much longer than the lobes of the calyx; stamens 4, opposite the sepals, inserted in the lobes of the disk, exserted, 0 in the pistillate flower; filaments slender, subulate, incurved; anthers oblong; ovary 2-celled, oblong, sessile, confluent with the disk, crowned with a large 2-lobed sessile stigma, rudimentary and deeply cleft in the staminate flower; ovule solitary, suspended from the apex of the cell; raphe dorsal; micropyle superior.　Fruit drupaceous, 2-celled, 1 or 2-seeded, black or dark blue, oval or obovoid, crowned with the remnants of the persistent stigma, often 1-celled by abortion; flesh thin; stone thick, crustaceous. Seed oblong, suspended; seed-coat membranaceous; albumen thin, fleshy; embryo axile; cotyledons ovate, foliaceous; radicle superior, next the hilum.

Gyminda with a single species is distributed from southern Florida to Trinidad and southern Mexico, and is represented in Central America by what is perhaps a second species.

The generic name is formed by transposing the first three letters of *Myginda,* to which this plant had been referred.

1. Gyminda latifolia Urb.

Gyminda Grisebachii Sarg.

Leaves 1½'–2' long, ¾'–1' broad, pale yellow-green. **Flowers** produced on shoots of the year from April to June. **Fruit** ripening in November, ¼' long.

A tree, sometimes 20°–25° high, with a trunk rarely more than 6' in diameter, and branchlets becoming terete during their third season and covered with thin slightly

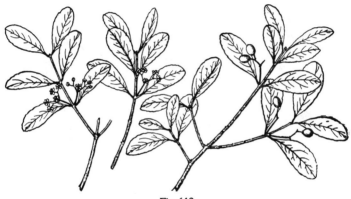

Fig. 612

grooved roughened bright red-brown bark. **Bark** of the trunk thin, brown tinged with red, separating into thin minute scales. **Wood** very heavy, hard, close-grained, dark brown or nearly black, with thick light brown sapwood of 75–80 layers of annual growth.

Distribution. Florida, common and generally distributed over the southern keys from the Marquesas group to Upper Matecombe Key; in Cuba, Porto Rico, Trinidad, and southern Mexico. A form (var. *glaucescens,* Small.) with smaller less coriaceous very glaucous leaves occurs in Cuba.

5. SCHÆFFERIA Jacq.

Glabrous trees or shrubs, with slender rigid terete branches and small obtuse buds. Leaves alternate, or fascicled on short spur-like branchlets, entire, obovate or spatulate, acute and minutely apiculate or gradually narrowed to the rounded or emarginate apex, cuneate below, persistent, without stipules. Flowers diœcious, pedicellate in axillary clusters from buds covered by scale-like persistent bracts; calyx 4-lobed, the lobes orbicular, persistent, much shorter than the 4 hypogynous, oblong, obtuse, white or greenish white petals; stamens 4, hypogynous, inserted under the margin of the small inconspicuous disk opposite the lobes of the calyx, wanting in the pistillate flower; filaments subulate, incurved; anthers oblong-ovoid; ovary 2-celled, ovoid, sessile, free, rudimentary in the staminate flower; style very short, gradually enlarged into the large 2-lobed stigma, with spreading lobes; ovule solitary, ascending; raphe thin, ventral; micropyle inferior. Fruit a small 2-seeded fleshy drupe, ovoid or obovoid, crowned with the remnants of the persistent style, indistinctly 2-lobed by longitudinal grooves, slightly flattened; flesh thin and tuberculate; nutlets 2, obovoid, rounded at the ends, with a thick bony shell. Seed solitary, ascending; seed-coat membranaceous; albumen fleshy; cotyledons broad, foliaceous; radicle very short, inferior, next the hilum.

Schæfferia with four or five species is confined to the New World, with one species in southern Florida, and another, a small shrub, *Schæfferia cuneifolia* A. Gray in the arid region of western Texas and northern Mexico.

The generic name is in honor of Jakob Christian Schaeffer (1718–1790), the distinguished German naturalist.

1. Schæfferia frutescens Jacq. Yellow Wood. Box Wood.

Leaves bright yellow-green, $2'-2\frac{1}{2}'$ long, $\frac{1}{2}'-1'$ wide, with thick revolute margins, appearing in Florida in April and persistent on the branches until the spring of the follow-

Fig. 613

ing year; petioles short and broad Flowers opening in spring on branchlets of the year, $\frac{1}{8}'$ across, the staminate generally 3 or 5 together on pedicels rarely more than $\frac{1}{8}'$ long, the pistillate solitary or 2 or 3 together on pedicels rather longer than the petioles. Fruit ripening in Florida in November, slightly grooved, compressed, bright scarlet, with an acrid disagreeable flavor.

A glabrous tree, $35°-40°$ high, with a trunk sometimes $8'-10'$ in diameter, erect branches, and slender many-angled branchlets pale greenish yellow during their first season, becoming light gray during their second year and then conspicuously marked by the remains of the persistent wart-like clusters of bud-scales; or often a tall or low shrub. Bark of the trunk rarely more than $\frac{1}{12}'$ thick, pale brown faintly tinged with red, the surface divided by long shallow fissures, and ultimately separating into long narrow scales. Wood heavy, close-grained, bright clear yellow, with thick rather lighter colored sapwood; sometimes used as a substitute for boxwood in wood engraving.

Distribution. Florida, upper Matecombe and Old Rhodes Keys, and eastward on the southern keys, and on the Everglade Keys, Dade County; on the Bahama Islands, and widely distributed through the West Indies to Venezuela.

XXXV. ACERACEÆ.

Trees or rarely shrubs, with limpid juice, terete branches, scaly buds, their inner scales accrescent and marking the base of the branchlets with ring-like scars, and fibrous roots. Leaves opposite, or on vigorous shoots rarely in whorls of 3, long-petiolate, simple, palmately 3–7-lobed and nerved or pinnately 3–7-foliolulate, usually without stipules, deciduous, in falling leaving small U-shaped narrow scars showing the ends of 3 equidistant fibro-vascular bundles. Flowers regular, diœciously or monœciously polygamous, rarely perfect or diœcious, in fascicles produced from separate lateral buds appearing in early spring before the leaves or in terminal and lateral racemes or panicles appearing with or later than the leaves; bracts minute, caducous; calyx colored, generally 5-parted, the lobes imbricated in the bud; petals usually 5, imbricated in the bud, or 0; disk annular, fleshy, more or less lobed, with a free margin; stamens 4–10, usually 7 or 8, inserted on the summit or inside of the disk, hypogynous; filaments distinct, filiform, commonly exserted in the staminate, shorter and generally abortive in the pistillate flower; anthers oblong or linear, attached at the base, introrse, 2-celled, the cells opening longitudinally; ovary 2-lobed, 2-celled, compressed contrary to the dissepiment, wing-margined on the back; styles 2, inserted between the lobes of the ovary, connate below and divided into 2 linear branches stigmatose on their inner surface; ovules 2 in each cell, collateral, rarely superposed, ascending, attached by their broad base to the inner angle of the cell, anatropous or amphitropous; micropyle inferior.   Fruit composed of 2 samaras separable from a small persistent axis, the nut-like carpels compressed laterally, produced on the back into a large chartaceous or coriaceous reticulated obovate wing thickened on the lower margin.   Seed solitary by abortion, or rarely 2 in each cell, ovoid, compressed, irregularly 3-angled, ascending obliquely, without albumen; seed-coat membranaceous, the inner coat often fleshy; embryo conduplicate; cotyledons thin, foliaceous or coriaceous, irregularly plicate, incumbent or accumbent on the elongated descending radicle turned toward the hilum.

A family of two genera, one widely distributed, the other, Dipteronia, distinguished by the broad wings encircling the mature carpels, and represented by a single Chinese species.

1. ACER L. Maple.

Characters of the family.

Acer with sixty or seventy species is widely distributed over the northern hemisphere, with a single species extending south of the equator to the mountains of Java. Acer produces light close-grained moderately hard wood valued for the interior finish of houses and in turnery. The bark is astringent, and the limpid sweet sap of some of the American species is manufactured into sugar.

Acer is the classical name of the Maple-tree.

CONSPECTUS OF THE NORTH AMERICAN ARBORESCENT SPECIES.

Leaves simple, usually palmately lobed (*sometimes 3-foliolate in 1, 3-lobed at apex in 4*).
  Flowers appearing with or after the leaves.
    Flowers with petals; sepals distinct.
      Inflorescence corymbose.
        Flowers in terminal drooping corymbs.
          Leaves 3-lobed or parted.   1. **A. glabrum** (B, F, G).
          Leaves palmately 3–5-lobed.   2. **A. circinatum** (B, G).
      Inflorescence racemose.
        Flowers in dense erect racemes.   3. **A. spicatum** (A).
        Flowers in drooping racemes.
          Ovary and young fruit glabrous; leaves 3-lobed at apex.
              4. **A. pennsylvanicum** (A).
          Ovary and young fruit hairy; leaves deeply 5-lobed. 5. **A. macrophyllum** (G).

Flowers without petals; sepals united; inflorescence corymbose; pedicels long, pendulous, mostly hairy.

Leaves pale or glaucescent, or green and glabrous beneath.

Leaves green or pale beneath, glabrous or in one form villose-pubescent on the under side of the veins and on the petioles.   6. **A. saccharum** (A, C).

Leaves pale and pubescent, rarely glabrous beneath, their lobes usually short and obtuse or acuminate.

Lobes of the leaves only slightly lobed or entire; bark of young trees smooth and pale.   7. **A. floridanum** (C).

Lobes of the leaves distinctly lobulate; bark of young trees dark brown and scaly.   8. **A. grandidentatum** (F, H).

Leaves green and pubescent, rarely glabrous beneath.

Leaves hirsute-pubescent beneath and on the petioles, the lobes entire or lobulate, the basal sinus often closed by the lower lobes; bark dark and furrowed.
                                                               9. **A. nigrum** (A).

Leaves pilose-pubescent, rarely glabrous beneath, the lobes slightly lobulate, the basal sinus open; petioles glabrous; bark pale and smooth.
                                                          10. **A. leucoderme** (C).

Flowers appearing before the leaves in dense lateral clusters from separate buds; leaves 5-lobed (*3-lobed in varieties of 12*); fruit ripening in May or June.

Flowers sessile or short-stalked, without petals; ovary and young fruit tomentose.
                                                          11. **A. saccharinum.**

Flowers on long pedicels, with petals; ovary and young fruit glabrous.
                                                          12. **A. rubrum.**

Leaves 3–7-foliolate; flowers diœcious, without petals.   13. **A. Negundo** (A, B, C, F, G, H).

1. Acer glabrum Torr.   Dwarf Maple.

Leaves glabrous, thin, rounded in outline, cordate-truncate or cuneate at base, 3–5-lobed, the middle lobe usually narrowed and entire below the middle, or often 3-parted or 3-foliolate (f. *trisecta* Sarg.), with acute or obtuse doubly serrate lobes, 3′–5′ in diameter, dark

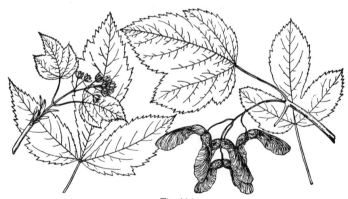

Fig. 614

green and lustrous on the upper, paler on the lower surface, with conspicuous veinlets; petioles stout, grooved, 1′–6′ in length, and often bright red. **Flowers** about ⅛′ long on short slender pedicels, in loose few-flowered glabrous racemose corymbs on slender drooping peduncles from the end of 2-leaved branchlets, the staminate and pistillate usually produced separately on different plants; sepals oblong, obtuse, petaloid, as long as the greenish yellow petals; stamens 7 or 8, with glabrous unequal filaments shorter than the petals, much shorter or rudimentary in the pistillate flower; ovary glabrous, with short obtuse lobes, rudimentary or 0 in the staminate flower; style divided to the base into 2 spreading stigmatic lobes as long as the petals. **Fruit** glabrous, with broad nearly erect or slightly spreading wings $\frac{3}{4}'-\frac{7}{8}'$ long, often rose-colored during the summer; **seeds** ovoid, bright chestnut-brown, **about** $\frac{1}{4}'$ long.

A small tree, occasionally 20°–30° high, with a short trunk 6′–12′ in diameter, small upright branches, and slender glabrous branchlets often slightly many-angled, pale greenish brown when they first appear, becoming bright red-brown during their first winter; often a shrub. **Winter-buds** acute, $\frac{1}{8}'$ long, with bright red or occasionally yellow scales, those of the inner ranks pale brown tinged with pink, tomentose on the inner surface, becoming $1\frac{1}{2}'$ long and narrow-spatulate. **Bark** of the trunk thin, smooth, and dark reddish brown. **Wood** heavy, hard, close-grained, light brown or often nearly white, with thick lighter colored sapwood.

Distribution. Borders of mountain streams usually at elevations of 5000°–6000°; Rocky Mountains from Montana to Wyoming, the Black Hills of South Dakota, Sioux County, Nebraska, Colorado, Utah, Nevada, northern Arizona, and to the Sacramento Mountains, New Mexico; in California from the Siskiyou Mountains along the Sierra Nevada to the East Fork of the Kaweah River, Kern County, at altitudes of 5000°–6000° at the north and of 8000°–9000° at the south. Passing into

Acer glabrum var. Douglasii Dippel.

Acer Douglasii Hook.

Leaves ovate or oblong-ovate, slightly cordate by a wide shallow sinus, truncate or rarely rounded at base, 3-lobed with acuminate lobes often slightly divided into acuminate lobules, the terminal leaflet usually ovate from a broad base, or occasionally gradually narrowed

Fig. 615

below and rhombic in outline and sharply serrate to the base or nearly to the base of the lobe with long-acuminate teeth pointing forward, dark green above, paler and often glaucescent below, $3\frac{1}{2}'-4'$ long and 3′–4′ wide, with 3 prominent nerves extending to the points of the lobes, and slender veins; petioles glabrous, 1′–3$\frac{1}{2}'$ in length. **Flowers** as in the species. **Fruit** with erect or nearly erect wings, $\frac{3}{4}'-1'$ long and $\frac{1}{3}'-\frac{1}{2}'$ wide.

A tree, occasionally 40° high, with a short trunk 12'–18' in diameter, small upright branches and slender bright red-brown branchlets.

Distribution.   Coast of southern Alaska (head of Lynn Canal), southward near the coast to Vancouver Island and western Washington, and eastward on the high mountains of Washington to the Blue Mountains of eastern Oregon, western Idaho and northern Montana; on Loomis Creek, Natrona County, Wyoming.

2. Acer circinatum Pursh.   Vine Maple.

Leaves almost circular in outline, cordate at base by a broad shallow sinus, or sometimes almost truncate, palmately 7–9-lobed occasionally nearly to the middle, with acute lobes sharply and irregularly doubly serrate, and conspicuously palmately nerved, with

Fig. 616

prominent veinlets, when they unfold tinged with rose color, and puberulous, especially on the lower surface and on the petioles, and at maturity glabrous with the exception of tufts of pale hairs in the axils of the large veins, thin and membranaceous, dark green above, pale below, and 2'–7' in diameter; in the autumn turning orange and scarlet; petioles stout, grooved, 1'–2' in length, clasping the stem by their large base.   **Flowers** appearing when the leaves are about half grown, in loose 10–20-flowered umbel-like corymbs pendent on long stems from the end of slender 2-leaved branchlets, the staminate and pistillate flowers produced together; sepals oblong to obovate, acute, villose, purple or red, much longer than the greenish white broad, cordate petals folded together at apex; stamens 6–8, with slender filaments villose at base, exserted in the staminate flower, much shorter than the petals in the pistillate flower; ovary glabrous, with spreading lobes, in the staminate flower reduced to a small point surrounded by a tuft of pale hairs; style divided nearly to the base into long exserted stigmas.   **Fruit** with thin wings, 1½' long, spreading almost at right angles, red or rose color like the nutlets in early summer, ripening late in the autumn; seeds smooth, pale chestnut-brown, ⅛'–¼' long.

A tree, rarely 30°–40° high, often vine-like or prostrate, with a trunk 10'–12' in diameter, and glabrous pale green or reddish brown branchlets frequently covered during their first winter with a glaucous bloom, and occasionally marked by small lenticels; often a low wide-spreading shrub.   **Winter-buds** ⅛' long, rather obtuse, with thin bright red outer scales rounded on the back, and obovate-spatulate inner scales rounded at apex, contracted into a long narrow claw, bright rose-colored and more or less pubescent, especially on the outer surface, and when fully grown often 2' long and ¼' broad.   **Bark** of the trunk thin, smooth, bright red-brown, marked by numerous shallow fissures.   **Wood** heavy, hard, close-grained, not strong, light brown, sometimes nearly white, with thick lighter colored sapwood; used for fuel, the handles of axes and other tools, and by the Indians of the northwest coast for the bows of their fishing-nets.

Distribution. Banks of streams; coast of British Columbia through western Washington and Oregon to Mendocino County, and the cañon of the upper Sacramento River, California; one of the most abundant of the deciduous-leaved trees of western Washington and Oregon up to altitudes of 4000° above the sea, and of its largest size on the rich alluvial soil of bottom-lands, its vine-like stems in such situations springing 4 or 5 together from the ground, spreading in wide curves and sending out long slender branches rooting when they touch the ground and forming impenetrable thickets of contorted and interlaced trunks, often many acres in extent; in California smaller and less abundant, growing along streams in the coniferous forest or rarely on dry ridges up to an altitude of 4000° in the northeastern part of the state.

Occasionally cultivated as an ornamental plant in Europe, and in the eastern states, and hardy as far north as eastern Massachusetts.

3. Acer spicatum Lam. Mountain Maple.

Leaves subcordate or sometimes truncate at base, conspicuously 3-nerved, 3 or slightly 5-lobed, with gradually narrowed pointed lobes, and sharply and coarsely glandular-serrate, when they unfold puberulous on the upper surface and densely tomentose on the

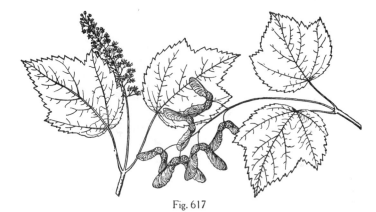

Fig. 617

lower surface, and at maturity thin, 4′–5′ long and broad; turning in the autumn to various shades of orange and scarlet; petioles slender, enlarged at base, 2′–3′ in length, often becoming scarlet in summer. **Flowers** opening in June after the leaves are fully grown, $\frac{1}{4}$′ diameter, on slender pedicels $\frac{1}{2}$′–$\frac{3}{4}$′ long, the pistillate toward the base and the staminate at the apex of a narrow many-flowered long-stemmed upright slightly compound pubescent raceme; calyx-lobes narrow-obovate, yellow, pubescent on the outer surface, much shorter than the linear-spatulate pointed yellow petals; stamens 7 or 8, inserted immediately under the ovary, with slender glabrous filaments as long as the petals in the sterile flower, about as long as the sepals in the pistillate flower, and glandular anthers; ovary hoary-tomentose, reduced to a minute point surrounded by a tuft of pale hairs in the staminate flower; style columnar, almost as long as the petals, with short stigmatic lobes. **Fruit** fully grown and bright red or yellow in July, turning brown late in the autumn, almost glabrous, with more or less divergent wings about $\frac{1}{2}$′ long; **seeds** smooth, dark red-brown, $\frac{1}{8}$′ long.

A bushy tree, occasionally 25°–30° high, with a short trunk 6′–8′ in diameter, small upright branches, and slender branchlets light gray and pubescent when they first appear.

becoming glabrous during the summer, bright red during their first winter, gray or pale brown the following season, and blotched or streaked with green toward the base; more often a tall or low shrub. **Winter-buds** acute; the terminal $\frac{1}{8}'$ long, with bright red outer scales more or less coated with hoary tomentum, those of the inner ranks becoming at maturity 1' or more in length and then lanceolate, pale and papery; axillary buds much smaller and glabrous or puberulous. **Bark** of the trunk very thin, reddish brown, smooth or slightly furrowed. **Wood** light, soft, close-grained, light brown tinged with red, with thick lighter colored sapwood.

Distribution. Moist rocky hillsides usually in the shade of other trees, and really arborescent only on the western slopes of the high mountains of Tennessee and North Carolina; Newfoundland and Labrador to Hudson Bay, Manitoba, and Saskatchewan, and southward through the northern states, and westward to Minnesota and northeastern Iowa, and along the Appalachian Mountains.

Occasionally cultivated as an ornament of parks and gardens in the northern states.

4. Acer pennsylvanicum L.   Striped Maple.   Moose Wood.

Leaves rounded or cordate at base, palmately 3-nerved, 3-lobed at apex, with short lobes contracted into a tapering serrate point, and finely and sharply doubly serrate, when they unfold thin, pale rose color and coated with ferrugineous pubescence, especially on the

Fig. 618

lower surface and on the petioles, and at maturity glabrous with the exception of tufts of ferrugineous hairs in the axils of the principal nerves on the two surfaces, thin, pale green above, rather paler below, 5'–6' long and 4'–5' wide; turning in the autumn clear light yellow; petioles stout, grooved, $1\frac{1}{2}'$–2' in length, with an enlarged base nearly encircling the branch. **Flowers** bright canary-yellow, opening toward the end of May or early in June when the leaves are nearly fully grown, on slender pedicels $\frac{1}{4}'$–$\frac{1}{2}'$ long, in slender drooping long-stemmed racemes 4'–6' in length, the staminate and pistillate usually in different racemes on the same plant; sepals linear-lanceolate to obovate, $\frac{1}{4}'$ long and a little shorter and narrower than the obovate petals; stamens 7–8, shorter than the petals in the staminate flower, rudimentary in the pistillate flower; ovary purplish brown, glabrous, in the staminate flower reduced to a minute point; styles united nearly to the top, with spreading recurved stigmas. **Fruit** in long drooping racemes, glabrous, with thin spreading wings $\frac{3}{4}'$ long, and marked on one side of each nutlet by a small cavity; **seeds** $\frac{1}{4}'$ long, dark red-brown, and slightly rugose.

A tree, 30°–40° high, with a short trunk 8'–10' in diameter, small upright branches, and slender smooth branchlets pale greenish yellow at first, bright reddish brown during their first winter, and at the end of two or three years striped like the trunk with broad pale lines; or often much smaller and shrubby in habit. **Winter-buds:** the terminal conspicuously stipitate, sometimes almost $\frac{1}{2}'$ long, much longer than the axillary buds, covered by two thick bright red spatulate boat-shaped scales prominently keeled on the back, the inner scales green and foliaceous, becoming $1\frac{1}{2}'$–$2'$ long, $\frac{1}{2}'$ wide, pubescent, and bright yellow or rose color. **Bark** of the trunk $\frac{1}{8}'$–$\frac{1}{4}'$ thick, reddish brown, marked longitudinally by broad pale stripes, and roughened by many oblong horizontal excrescences. **Wood** light, soft, close-grained, light brown, with thick lighter colored sapwood of 30–40 layers of annual growth.

Distribution. Usually in the shade of other trees, often forming in northern New England a large part of their shrubby undergrowth; shores of Ha-Ha Bay, Quebec, westward along the shores of Lake Ontario and the islands of Lake Huron to northern Wisconsin, and southward through the Atlantic states and along the Appalachian Mountains to northern Georgia; ascending to altitudes of 5000°; common in the north Atlantic states, especially in the interior and elevated regions; of its largest size on the slopes of the Big Smoky Mountains, Tennessee, and of the Blue Ridge in North and South Carolina.

Sometimes cultivated as an ornamental tree in the northern states, and occasionally in Europe.

5. Acer macrophyllum Pursh. Broad-leaved Maple.

Leaves more or less cordate at the broad base, deeply 5-lobed by narrow sinuses acute in the bottom, the lobes acute or acuminate, the terminal lobe often 3-lobed, the others usually furnished with small lateral lobules, the lower lobes much smaller than the others, promi-

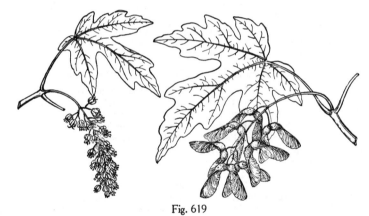

Fig. 619

nently 3–5-nerved, puberulous when they unfold, especially on the upper surface along the principal veins, and at maturity subcoriaceous, dark green and lustrous on the upper surface, pale on the lower surface, $8'$–$12'$ in diameter; turning in the autumn bright orange color before falling; petioles stout, $10'$–$12'$ in length, with enlarged bases united and encircling the stem and often furnished on the inside with small tufts of white hairs. **Flowers** bright yellow, fragrant, $\frac{1}{4}'$ long, on slender pubescent often branched pedicels $\frac{1}{2}'$–$\frac{3}{4}'$ in length, the staminate and pistillate together in graceful pendulous slightly puberulous racemes $4'$–$6'$ long, appearing in April and May after the leaves are fully grown; sepals petaloid, obovate, obtuse and a little longer and broader than the spatulate petals; stamens 9–10, with long slender filaments hairy at base, exserted in the staminate flower and included in the pistillate flower, and orange-colored anthers; ovary hoary-tomentose, reduced in the staminate flower to a minute point; styles united at base only; stigmas long and exserted. **Fruit** fully grown by the 1st of July and ripening late in the autumn; nutlets covered with long pale hairs, their wings $1\frac{1}{2}'$ long, $\frac{1}{2}'$ wide, slightly divergent and glabrous with the exception of a few hairs on the thickened edge; **seeds** dark-colored, rugose and pitted, $\frac{1}{4}'$ long.

A tree, 80°–100° high, with a tall straight trunk 2°–3° in diameter, stout often pendulous branches forming a compact handsome head, and stout branchlets smooth and pale green at first, becoming bright green or dark red in their first winter, covered more or less thickly with small longitudinal white lenticels, and in their second summer gray or grayish brown. **Winter-buds** obtuse; terminal $\frac{1}{4}'$ long, with short broad slightly spreading dark red ciliate outer scales rounded on the back, those of the inner ranks green and foliaceous, and at maturity $1\frac{1}{2}'$ long, colored and puberulous; axillary buds minute. **Bark** of the trunk $\frac{1}{2}'-\frac{3}{4}'$ thick, brown faintly tinged with red or bright reddish brown, deeply furrowed and broken on the surface into small square plate-like scales. **Wood** light, soft, not strong, close-grained, rich brown tinged with red, with thick lighter colored often nearly white sapwood of 60–80 layers of annual growth; more valuable than the wood produced by other deciduous-leaved trees of western North America, and in Washington and Oregon used in the interior finish of buildings, for furniture, and for axe and broom-handles.

Distribution. Banks of streams or on rich bottom-lands or the rocky slopes of mountain valleys; coast of Alaska south of latitude 55° north, southward along the islands and coast of British Columbia, through Washington and Oregon west of the Cascade Mountains, and southward along the coast ranges and the western slopes of the Sierra Nevada to the San Bernardino Mountains, and to Hot Spring Valley, San Diego County, California; on the Sierra Nevada usually between altitudes of 2000° and 5000° and on the southern mountains rarely above 3000°; most abundant and of its largest size in the humid climate and rich soil of the bottom-lands of southwestern Oregon, forming extensive forests; in California usually much smaller, especially on the coast ranges.

Generally planted in the Pacific States for shade and as a street tree, and occasionally in the Eastern States as far north as Long Island, New York, and in western Europe; not hardy in Massachusetts.

6. Acer saccharum Marsh. Sugar Maple. Rock Maple.

Leaves rarely in whorls of 3, heart-shaped by a broad sinus, truncate or sometimes cuneate at base, 3–5-lobed, the lobes usually acute sparingly sinuate-toothed usually 3-lobulate at apex, with 3–5 conspicuous nerves, and reticulate veinlets, when they unfold coated below with pale pubescence, glabrous or more or less pubescent on the nerves below (var. *Schneckii* Rehd.) and at maturity, $4'-5'$ in diameter, often rather coriaceous, dark green and opaque on the upper surface, green or pale (var. *glaucum* Sarg.) on the lower surface; turning in the autumn brilliant shades of deep red, scarlet and orange or clear yellow; petioles slender, glabrous, $1\frac{1}{2}'-3'$ in length. **Flowers** appearing with the leaves on slender more or less hairy pedicels $\frac{3}{4}'-3'$ long, in nearly sessile umbel-like corymbs from terminal leaf-buds and lateral leafless buds, the staminate and pistillate in the same or in separate clusters on the same or on different trees; calyx broad-campanulate, 5-lobed by the partial union of the obtuse sepals, greenish yellow, hairy on the outer surface; corolla 0; stamens 7–8, with slender glabrous filaments twice as long as the calyx in the staminate flower and much shorter in the pistillate flower; ovary obtusely lobed, pale green, covered with long scattered hairs, in the staminate flower reduced to a minute point; styles united at base only, with 2 long exserted stigmatic lobes. **Fruit** ripening in the autumn, glabrous, with broad thin and usually divergent wings $\frac{1}{2}'-1'$ long; **seeds** smooth, bright red-brown, $\frac{1}{4}'$ long.

A tree, 100°–120° high, with a trunk often 3°–4° in diameter, rising sometimes in the forest to the height of 60°–70° without branches, or in open situations developing 8°–10° from the ground stout upright branches forming while the tree is young a narrow egg-shaped head, ultimately spreading into a broad round-topped dome often 70°–80° across, and slender glabrous branchlets green at first, becoming reddish brown by the end of their first season, lustrous, marked by numerous large pale oblong lenticels, and in their second winter pale brown tinged with red. **Winter-buds** acute, $\frac{1}{4}'$ long, with purple slightly puberulous outer scales, and inner scales becoming 1½′ long, narrow-obovate, short-pointed at apex, thin, pubescent, and bright canary yellow. **Bark** of young stems and of large branches pale, smooth or slightly fissured, becoming on large trunks ½′–¾′ thick and broken into deep longitudinal furrows, the light gray-brown surface separating into small plate-like scales. **Wood** heavy, hard, strong, close-grained, tough, light brown tinged with red, with thin sapwood of 30–40 layers of annual growth; largely used for the interior finish of buildings, especially for floors, in the manufacture of furniture, in turnery, shipbuilding, for shoe-lasts and pegs, and largely as fuel. Accidental forms with the grain curled and contorted, known as curly maple and bird's-eye maple, are common and are highly prized in cabinet-making. The ashes of the wood are rich in alkali and yield large quantities of potash. Maple sugar is principally made from the sap of this tree.

Distribution. Newfoundland and Nova Scotia, westward to the Lake of the Woods, Ontario, and southward through eastern Canada and the northern states, and along the Appalachian Mountains to northern Georgia; in central Alabama and Mississippi, and

Fig. 620

westward in the United States to Minnesota, northeastern South Dakota (coulées of Little Minnesota River, Roberts County), central and northwestern Iowa, eastern Kansas, central Oklahoma, and eastern Louisiana; most abundant northward; ascending in North Carolina the Alleghany Mountains to altitudes of 3000°; the var. *glaucum* rare and local in the north from Prince Edwards Island and Lake St. John, Quebec, to Iowa and southward to Pennsylvania, Ohio and central Tennessee; more abundant southward; apparently the only form but not common in South Carolina, Alabama, Mississippi, Louisiana and southern Arkansas; the var. *Schneckii* with leaves glaucous or glaucescent below and more or less densely pubescent with spreading hairs, on the under side of the midrib and veins and on the petioles, southern Indiana and Illinois to western Kentucky and western and middle Tennessee, northwestern Georgia (near Rome, Floyd County), and to eastern Missouri southward to Williamsville, Wayne County.

Commonly planted as a shade and ornamental tree in the northern states. A form of columnar habit (var. *monumentale* Schwerin) is occasionally cultivated.

More distinct are the following varieties:

Acer saccharum var. Rugelii Rehd.

Leaves thick, 3′–5′ long and 4′–6′ wide, pale and glabrous below, 3-lobed by broad rounded sinuses, rounded or slightly cordate at base, the lobes long-acuminate, usually entire, the middle lobe occasionally slightly undulate, the lateral lobes spreading, sometimes furnished near the base with a short acute lobule.

Distribution. Southeastern Ohio to western Pennsylvania (Kittaning, **Armstrong** County) and eastern and middle Tennessee, and to southern Ontario, the southern penin-

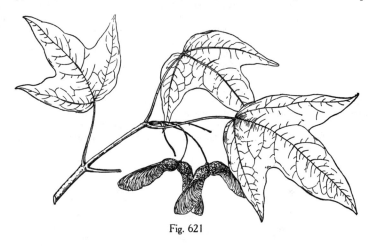

Fig. 621

sula of Michigan, eastern and central Indiana, southern Illinois, eastern Missouri and northwestern Arkansas (Eureka Springs, Carroll County); rare and local in its extreme form; its 3-lobed leaves sometimes appearing on upper branches of trees bearing on lower branches leaves of the typical Sugar Maple.

Acer saccharum var. sinuosum Sarg.

Acer sinuosum Rehd.

Leaves suborbicular, broader than long, 3–5-lobed with short triangular-ovate to triangular-oblong obtuse lobes, entire or on vigorous shoots occasionally dentate, usually broad-cordate at base, often with the nerves of the two lateral lobes projecting into the

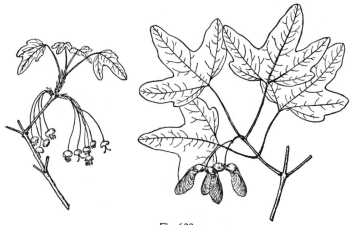

Fig. 622

broad sinus and forming its base, when they unfold glabrous and purplish above, loosely hairy below, soon glabrous, and at maturity dark yellow-green and lustrous on the upper surface, pale, reticulate-venulose and glabrous except in the axils of the principal veins on the lower surface, 3–5-nerved, usually not more than $1\frac{1}{2}'$ long, occasionally up to $2\frac{3}{4}'$ long and $3'$ wide; petioles slender, glabrous, $\frac{1}{2}$–$1\frac{1}{2}'$ in length. **Flowers** appearing with the leaves, on slender glabrous pedicels, $\frac{1}{2}'$–$1\frac{1}{4}'$ long, in 3–8-flowered nearly sessile corymbs; calyx broad-campanulate or cupulate, with short semiorbicular lobes ciliate on the margins; petals 0; stamens usually 6, with slender filaments longer than the calyx of the staminate flower; style divided to below the middle, with two spreading stigmas. **Fruit** glabrous, with long and broad almost horizontally spreading nutlets, convex, smooth, pale yellow-brown, the wing curved upward.

A tree, rarely more than $20°$ high with a short trunk $8'$–$10'$ in diameter, small branches forming an open irregular head, and slender glabrous branchlets light green above when they first appear, becoming pale red-brown and marked by pale lenticels during their first season and ultimately dull gray-brown. **Bark** of the trunk smooth, pale gray. **Winter-buds** small, obtuse, covered with dark brown scales, those of the inner ranks accrescent, linear-oblong, scarlet or pink, up to $1\frac{1}{8}'$ in length when fully grown.

Distribution. Edwards Plateau of western Texas, banks and bluffs of Cibelo Creek, near Boerne, Kendall County, on the rocky banks of upper Saco Creek, Bandera County, and at the base of a high limestone bluff near Utopia, Uvalde County; rare and local.

7. Acer floridanum Pax.   Sugar Maple.

Leaves rounded, truncate or slightly cordate at the broad base, 3–5-lobed, with short obtuse or acute entire or lobulate lobes, when they unfold sparingly hairy on the upper surface and hoary-tomentose on the lower surface, and at maturity thin, dark green and lustrous

Fig. 623

above, pale or glaucescent and pubescent below, $1\frac{1}{2}'$–$3'$ in diameter, and prominently 3–5-nerved, with stout spreading lateral veins and conspicuous reticulate veinlets; turning yellow and scarlet in the autumn before falling; petioles slender, glabrous, or pubescent generally becoming glabrous, $1\frac{1}{4}'$–$3'$ in length, with an enlarged base nearly encircling the branchlet. **Flowers** appearing with the leaves on slender elongated sparingly hairy ultimately glabrous or villose-tomentose (var. *villipes* Rehd.) pedicels, in many-flowered drooping nearly sessile corymbs; calyx campanulate, yellow, about $\frac{1}{8}'$ long, persistent under the fruit, the short lobes ciliate on the margins with long pale hairs; corolla 0. **Fruit** green, sparingly villose until fully grown, usually becoming glabrous, with spreading occasionally erect wings $\frac{3}{8}'-\frac{3}{4}'$ long; **seeds** smooth, bright red-brown, about $\frac{1}{4}'$ long.

A tree, occasionally 50°–60° high, with a trunk rarely 3° in diameter, small erect and spreading branches, and slender glabrous or more or less densely villose-tomentose (var. *villipes* Rehdr.) branchlets, light green when they first appear, becoming rather light red-brown during their first season, and covered with minute pale lenticels; usually smaller. **Winter-buds** obtuse, about $\frac{1}{8}'$ long, with dark chestnut-brown obtuse scales and bright rose-colored linear-spatulate inner scales often 1' long when fully grown. **Bark** of the trunk thin, smooth, pale, becoming near the base of old trees thick, dark, and deeply furrowed.

Distribution. River banks and low wet woods, southeastern Virginia (near McKinney, Dinwiddie County, *W. W. Ashe*), valley of the Roanoke River near Weldon, Halifax County, North Carolina, and southward to southern Georgia and western Florida to La-fayette County; near Selma, Dallas County, Alabama; West Feliciana Parish and through western Louisiana to eastern Texas (Harrison and San Augustine Counties), and southern Arkansas (Fulton, Hempstead County); the var. *villipes* near Raleigh, Wake County, North Carolina, Calhoun Falls, Abbeville County, South Carolina, Shell Bluff on the Savannah River, Burke County, Cuthbert, Randolph County, and Columbus, Muscogee County, Georgia; River Junction, Gadsden County, Florida, and on the San Luis Mountains, southern New Mexico (*A. brachypterum* Woot. & Stanl.).

Sometimes planted as a shade-tree; the prevailing tree in the streets and squares of Raleigh, North Carolina.

8. Acer grandidentatum Nutt. Sugar Maple.

Leaves cordate or truncate at base, 3-lobed by broad shallow sinuses, the lobes acute or obtuse, entire or slightly lobulate, sparingly hairy on the upper surface and thickly coated

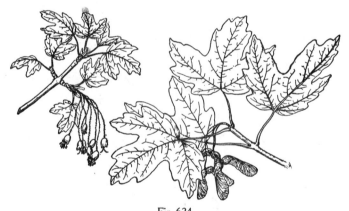

Fig. 624

with dense pale tomentum on the lower surface when they unfold, and at maturity thick and firm, dark green and lustrous above, pale and pubescent below, especially on the stout nerves and veins, or rarely glabrous, 2'–5' in diameter; turning in the autumn before falling yellow and scarlet; petioles stout, 1'–2' in length, glabrous, often red after midsummer, encircling the branchlet with their large base villose on the inner surface. **Flowers** appearing with the leaves on long slender drooping villose pedicels, in short-stalked corymbs; calyx cam-panulate, yellow, sparingly hairy with long pale hairs, about $\frac{1}{4}'$ long, with broad rounded lobes, often persistent under the fruit; corolla 0; stamens 7 or 8, much longer than the calyx, in the pistillate flower shorter than the calyx; ovary usually glabrous, with long spreading stigmatic lobes, rudimentary in the staminate flower. **Fruit** often rose-colored at mid-summer, green at maturity, glabrous or rarely sparingly hairy, with spreading or erect wings $\frac{1}{2}'$–1' long; **seeds** smooth, light red-brown, about $\frac{1}{4}'$ long.

A tree, occasionally 30°–40° high, with a trunk 8'–10' in diameter, stout usually erect branches, and slender glabrous bright red branchlets marked by numerous small pale lenticels and nearly encircled by the narrow leaf-scars, with conspicuous bands of long pale hairs in their axils. **Winter-buds** acute or acuminate, about $\frac{1}{16}'$ long, bright red-brown, with puberulous-ciliate outer scales and obovate apiculate inner scales sometimes $\frac{1}{2}'$ long when fully grown. **Bark** of the trunk thin, dark brown, separating on the surface into plate-like scales. **Wood** heavy, hard, close-grained, bright brown or nearly white, with thick sapwood.

Distribution. Banks of mountain streams usually at altitudes of 5000°–6000 above the sea; on the Salt River Mountains, western Wyoming; valley of the Columbia River in northern Montana, southeastern Idaho (Pocatello, Oneida County), Wasatch Mountains, Utah, mountains of Arizona and of southern New Mexico; on the Guadalupe Mountains, western Texas, and on the Wichita Mountains, southwestern Oklahoma (*G. W. Stevens*); in Coahuila; rare and local.

Occasionally cultivated; hardy in the Arnold Arboretum.

9. Acer nigrum Michx. Black Maple.

Leaves generally 3 or occasionally 5-lobed, with abruptly short-pointed acute or acuminate lobes, undulate and narrowed from broad shallow sinuses and rarely furnished with short lateral spreading lobules, cordate at base with a broad sinus usually more or less closed

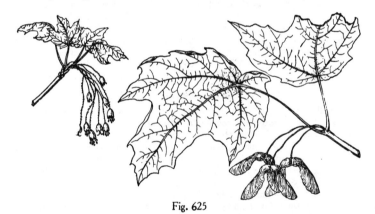

Fig. 625

by the approximation or imbrication of the basal lobes, occasionally 3-lobed with a broad long-acuminate nearly entire terminal lobe, and rounded or slightly cordate at base (var. *Palmeri* Sarg.), covered below when they unfold with hoary tomentum and above with caducous pale hairs, and at maturity thick and firm in texture, dull green on the upper surface, yellow-green and soft-pubescent, especially along the yellow veins on the lower surface, and 5'–6' long and wide, with drooping sides; turning bright clear yellow in the autumn; petioles stout, tomentose or pubescent, sometimes becoming glabrous at maturity, usually pendent, 3'–5' in length, much enlarged at base, frequently nearly inclosing the buds, in falling leaving narrow scars almost encircling the branchlet and furnished in their axils with tufts of long pale hairs; stipules triangular and dentate or foliaceous, sessile or stipitate, oblong, acute, tomentose or pubescent, sometimes slightly lobed, frequently $1\frac{1}{2}'$ long. **Flowers** yellow, about $\frac{1}{4}'$ long, on slender hairy pedicels $2\frac{1}{2}'$–3' long, in many-flowered nearly sessile umbel-like corymbs, the staminate and pistillate in separate or in the same cluster on the same or on different trees; calyx broad-campanulate, 5-lobed by the partial union of the sepals, pilose on the outer surface near the base; corolla 0; stamens 7 or 8, with slender glabrous filaments, in the staminate flower nearly twice as long as the calyx and in the pistillate flower shorter than the calyx; ovary obtusely lobed, pale green, covered with long scattered hairs, minute in the sterile flower. **Fruit** glabrous, with convergent or wide-spreading wings $\frac{1}{2}'-1'$ long; **seeds** smooth, bright red-brown, $\frac{1}{4}'$ long.

A tree, sometimes 80° high, with a trunk frequently 3° in diameter, stout spreading or often erect branches, and stout branchlets marked by oblong pale lenticels, orange-green and pilose with scattered pale caducous hairs when they appear, orange or orange-brown and lustrous during their first year, becoming dull pale gray-brown the following season. **Winter-buds** sessile, ovoid, acute, $\frac{1}{8}'$ long, with dark red-brown acute scales hoary-pubescent on the outer surface and often slightly ciliate on the margins, and yellow puberulous inner scales, $\frac{1}{2}'-1'$ long at maturity. **Bark** of young stems and of the branches thin, smooth, pale gray, becoming on old trunks thick, deeply furrowed, and sometimes almost black.

Distribution. Valley of the St. Lawrence River in the neighborhood of Montreal, Quebec, southward to the valley of Cold River, New Hampshire, through western Vermont and Massachusetts and northwestern Connecticut (near Salisbury, Litchfield County), and westward through northern and western New York, southern Ontario, Ohio, the southern peninsula of Michigan, Indiana, Illinois, and Iowa to southeastern Minnesota, northeastern South Dakota, western and southern Missouri, eastern Kansas, and southward through western Pennsylvania, West Virginia and eastern Kentucky; comparatively rare near Montreal and in New England, more abundant farther west; almost entirely replacing *Acer saccharum* in Iowa, and the only Sugar Maple of South Dakota; easily distinguished in summer by its heavy drooping leaves, and at all seasons of the year by the orange color of the branchlets; the var. *Palmeri* in a single grove at Tunnel Hill, Johnson County, Illinois; southern Indiana (Shelby, Putnam and Lawrence Counties), and in Clark, Jackson and Dunklin Counties, Missouri; rare and local.

Occasionally planted in the region where it grows naturally as a shade-tree.

10. Acer leucoderme Small. Sugar Maple.

Leaves usually truncate or slightly cordate at base, more or less deeply divided into 3–5 acute caudate-acuminate lobes coarsely and sinuately dentate or undulate, when they unfold coated below with long matted pale caducous hairs, and at maturity thin, dark yellow-green above, bright yellow-green and pilose-pubescent below, $2'-3\frac{1}{2}'$ in diameter; often turning in the autumn bright scarlet on the upper surface before falling; petioles slender, glabrous, $1'-1\frac{1}{2}'$ in length. **Flowers** yellow, about $\frac{1}{8}'$ long, on slender, glabrous pedicels, in nearly sessile clusters; calyx campanulate, glabrous or slightly villose, with rounded ciliate lobes; corolla 0; stamens 7 or 8; filaments villose, longer than the calyx, much shorter than the calyx in the pistillate flower; ovary villose; style elongated, with short spreading lobes. **Fruit** villose, with long scattered pale hairs until nearly grown, becoming glabrous at maturity, the wings wide-spreading or divergent, $\frac{1}{2}'-\frac{3}{4}'$ long; **seeds** smooth, light red-brown, about $\frac{1}{4}'$ long.

A tree, usually 20°–25° high, with a trunk a foot in diameter, occasionally 40° high, with a trunk 18'–20' in diameter, short slender branches forming a rather compact round-topped head, and slender glabrous branchlets dark green when they first appear, becoming bright red-brown and lustrous during their first summer, and marked by numerous small oblong pale lenticels, gradually growing darker in their second year and finally light gray-green. **Winter-buds** ovoid, acute, dark brown, glabrous, rather more than $\frac{1}{16}'$ long, the inner scales becoming bright crimson and very conspicuous when the tree is in flower. **Bark** of young stems and large branches close, light gray or grayish brown, becoming near the base of old trees dark brown or often nearly black and broken by deep furrows into narrow ridges covered by closely appressed scales.

Distribution. Banks of streams, rocky gorges, and woods in moist soil; valley of the Yadkin River, Stanley County, North Carolina; southeastern Tennessee (Polk County); valley of the Savannah River (Abbeville County, South Carolina, and Richmond County,

Fig. 626

Georgia) to central and northwestern Georgia (near Rome, Floyd County, and Walker County) and to the valley of the Chattahoochee River to Muscogee County; northern and central Alabama; western Louisiana (Natchitoches and Sabine Parishes); southern Arkansas (Baker Springs, Howard County); rare and local; most abundant in northwestern and central Georgia and northern Alabama.

Occasionally planted as a street tree in the towns of northern Georgia and Alabama; hardy as far north as eastern Massachusetts.

11. Acer saccharinum L.   Silver Maple.   Soft Maple.

Leaves truncate or somewhat cordate at base, deeply 5-lobed by narrow sinuses, with acute irregularly and remotely dentate lobes, the middle lobe often 3-lobed, rarely laciniately divided (var. *Wieri* Schwerin), 6′–7′ long and nearly as broad, thin, bright pale green above, silvery white and at first slightly hairy below, especially in the axils of the primary veins; turning pale yellow in the autumn before falling; petioles slender, drooping, bright red, 4′–5′ in length. **Flowers** greenish yellow, opening during the first warm days of the late winter or early spring long before the appearance of the leaves, on short pedicels, in sessile axillary fascicles on shoots of the previous year, or on short spur-like branchlets developed the year before from wood of the preceding season, the staminate and pistillate in separate clusters, on the same or on different trees, and produced from clustered obtuse buds covered with thick ovate pubescent red and green scales ciliate on the margins with a thick fringe of long rufous hairs; calyx slightly 5-lobed, more or less pubescent on the outer surface, long and narrow in the staminate and short and broad in the pistillate flower; corolla 0; stamens 3–7, with slender filaments, three times as long as the calyx of the staminate flower and about as long as the calyx of the pistillate flower; ovary covered, like the young fruit, with a thick coat of pubescence, rudimentary in the sterile flower; styles united at base only, with long exserted stigmatic lobes. **Fruit** ripening in April and May when the leaves are nearly grown, on slender drooping pedicels, 1½′–2′ long, glabrous, 1½′ to nearly 3′ long, with thin almost straight conspicuously falcate divergent wings sometimes ¾′ broad, prominently reticulate-veined and pale chestnut-brown or rarely bright red; **seeds** ½′ long, with a pale reddish brown wrinkled coat, germinating as soon as they fall to the ground, and producing plants with several pairs of leaves before the end of the summer.

A tree, 90°–120° high, with a trunk 3°–4° in diameter, generally dividing 10°–15° from the ground into 3 or 4 stout upright secondary stems destitute of branches for a considerable length, brittle pendulous branchlets light green and covered with lenticels when they first appear, soon becoming darker, bright chestnut-brown, smooth and lustrous in the autumn and winter of their first year, and in their second season pale rose color or gray faintly tinged with red. **Winter-buds** ⅛′ long, with thick ovate bright red outer scales rounded on the back, minutely apiculate, and ciliate on the margins, and acute inner scales pubescent on the inner surface, becoming pale green or yellow and about 1′ long. **Bark** of young stems and large branches smooth and gray faintly tinged with red, becoming on old trunks ½′–¾′ thick, reddish brown and more or less furrowed, the surface separating into large thin scales. **Wood** hard, strong, close-grained, easily worked, rather brittle,

Fig. 627

pale brown, with thick sapwood of 40–50 layers of annual growth; now sometimes used for flooring and in the manufacture of furniture. Sugar is occasionally made from the sap.

Distribution. Sandy banks of streams, rarely in deep often submerged swamps; valley of the St. John's River (near Fredericton), New Brunswick, to that of the St. Lawrence in Quebec, and southward through western Vermont and central Massachusetts to western Florida (valley of the Apalachicola River), Alabama, and south central Mississippi, and westward through Ontario, New York, Ohio, the southern peninsula of Michigan and southern Indiana to Minnesota, southeastern South Dakota, and eastern Nebraska, and through Kentucky, Tennessee, Missouri, eastern Kansas, northwestern Arkansas, and eastern Oklahoma; in western Louisiana (swamp near Alexandria, Rapides Parish); rare in the immediate neighborhood of the Atlantic coast and on the high Appalachian Mountains; probably of its largest size in the valley of the lower Ohio River.

Often cultivated with several forms differing in habit and in the lobing of the leaves; fast-growing, and largely planted in the eastern states as a park and street tree.

12. Acer rubrum L. Red Maple. Scarlet Maple.

Leaves truncate, more or less cordate by a broad shallow sinus, rounded or cuneate at base, 3–5-lobed by acute sinuses, with irregularly doubly serrate or toothed lobes, the middle lobe often longer than the others, when they unfold pubescent especially beneath, and at maturity light green and glabrous on the upper surface and white or glaucescent and more or less pubescent or densely tomentose (var. *tomentosum* Kirch. [var. *rubrocarpum* Detmars]) on the lower surface, particularly along the principal veins, chartaceous or sometimes almost coriaceous, 1½′–6′ long and rather longer than broad; turning in the early autumn to brilliant shades of scarlet and orange, or clear bright yellow; petioles slender, glabrous or puberulous, red or green, 2′–4′ in length. **Flowers** opening in March and April before the appearance of the leaves, bright scarlet, dull yellowish red or sometimes yellow (var. *pallidiflorum* Pax.), on long slender pedicels, in few-flowered fascicles on branches of the previous year, from clustered obtuse buds, the staminate and pistillate flowers in separate clusters on the same or on different trees; sepals oblong, obtuse, as long as and broader than the oblong or linear petals; stamens 5–8, scarlet or yellow, with slender filaments exserted in the staminate and included in the pistillate flower; ovary glabrous on a narrow slightly lobed glandular disk; styles slightly united above the base, with long exserted stigmatic lobes. **Fruit** ripening in the spring or early summer on drooping stems 3′–4′ long, scarlet, dark red or brown or yellow, with thin erect wings, convergent at first, divergent at ma-

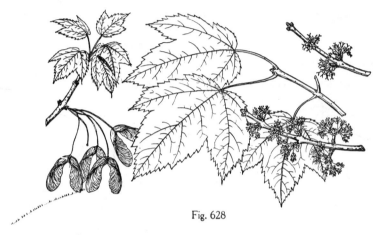

Fig. 628

turity, ½′–1′ long and ¼′–½′ wide; **seeds** dark red, with a rugose coat, ¼′ long, germinating as soon as it falls to the ground.

A tree, 80°–120° high, with a tall trunk 3°–4½° in diameter, upright branches usually forming a rather narrow head, and branchlets green or dark red when they first appear, becoming dark or bright red and lustrous at the end of their first summer and marked by numerous longitudinal white lenticels, and gray faintly tinged with red in their second year. **Winter-buds** obtuse, ⅛′ long, with thick dark red outer scales, rounded on the back and ciliate on the margins, and inner scales becoming ¾′–1′ long, narrow-oblong, rounded at apex and bright scarlet. **Bark** of young stems and of the branches smooth and light gray, becoming on old trunks ¼′–½′ thick, dark gray, and divided by longitudinal ridges separating on the surface into large plate-like scales. **Wood** very heavy, close-grained, not strong, light brown often slightly tinged with red, with thick rather lighter colored sapwood; used in large quantities in the manufacture of chairs and other furniture, in turnery, for wooden ware and gun-stocks. A form of fastigiate habit (var. *columnare* Rehd.) is occasionally cultivated.

Distribution. Borders of streams, wet swamps, upland forests and rarely on dry rocky hillsides and sand dunes; Newfoundland, southward to southern Florida (near the neighborhood of Fort Lauderdale, Broward County, *R. M. Harper*) and westward through Quebec to latitude 49° north, and Ontario to the sandy shores of the Upper Peninsula of Michigan (Brevort, Mackinac County, on Lake Michigan and White Fish Point, Chippewa County, on Lake Superior), western Wisconsin, northwestern Minnesota (Buckeye County), southeastern Iowa (Johnson County), central Oklahoma, and the valley of the Trinity River, Texas; on the mountains of North Carolina to altitudes of 4500°; one of the commonest and most generally distributed trees of eastern North America, ranging between more degrees

of latitude than any other American tree; most abundant southward especially in the valley
of the Mississippi River, and of its largest size in the river swamps of the lower Ohio and
its tributaries; in the north often covering with small trees low wet swamps; on the sand
dunes and ridges of northern Michigan reduced to a low shrub. On var. *tomentosum* leaves
usually 5-lobed, cordate or rarely rounded at base, with glabrous or pubescent petioles and
branchlets; widely distributed but rare; near Cranberry Island, Buckeye Lake, Licking
County, Ohio, Biltmore, Buncombe County, North Carolina; neighborhood of Augusta,
Richmond County, Georgia; top of Flagstaff Mountain, Barclay, Talladega County, Alabama; Panther Burn, Sharkey County, Mississippi; Crawford and Duvois Counties, Indiana, near Olney, Rutland County, and in Richland, Wayne and Johnson Counties, Illinois;
near Little Rock, Pulaski County, Arkansas; near Page, Leflore County, Oklahoma, and
Larissa, Cherokee County, Texas; connected by trees of this variety with pubescent branchlets and winter-buds, and broad-ovate 3–5-lobed slightly cordate leaves and pubescent
petioles with

Acer rubrum var. Drummondii Sarg.

Leaves often broader than long, usually 5-lobed, cordate or truncate at base, 3′–6′ long
and wide, with a stout midrib and veins, until nearly fully grown covered above with scattered hairs and clothed below with thick snow-white tomentum, and more or less pubescent

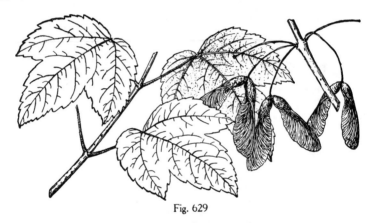

Fig. 629

during the season; petioles stout, hoary-tomentose, $1\frac{1}{4}$–4′ in length, becoming nearly
glabrous in the autumn. **Flowers** bright scarlet. **Fruit** ripening with or before the unfolding of the leaves late in March or in April, bright scarlet, with convergent wings $1\frac{1}{4}$–$2\frac{1}{2}$′
long and $\frac{1}{2}$–$\frac{3}{4}$′ wide.

A tree, usually not more than 30°–35° high, with small erect branches forming a narrow
head and slender branchlets coated when they first appear with matted pale hairs, becoming glabrous and dark reddish brown in their second season.

Distribution. Deep swamps, eastern Louisiana to the valley of the Neches River (Beaumont, Jefferson County, and Concord, Hardin County), eastern Texas and northward through
southern and eastern Arkansas to western Mississippi, western Tennessee and Kentucky,
southeastern Missouri (Butler, Stoddard, Dunklin and Mississippi Counties), southern Illinois (Gallatin, Pulaski and Richland Counties), and southwestern Indiana (swamp eighteen
miles west of Decker, Knox County, *C. C. Deam*). A form growing at Hattiesburg, Forrest County, Mississippi, at Glen Gordon, Covington, St. Tammany Parish, and Chopin,
Natchitoches Parish, Louisiana, near Beaumont, Jefferson County, Texas, and at Poplar
Bluff, Butler County, Missouri, with 3-lobed leaves rounded at base (f. *rotundatum* Sarg.)
shows in the shape of the leaves a transition from the var. *Drummondii* to

Acer rubrum var. tridens Wood. Red Maple.

Acer carolinianum Britt. not Walt.

Leaves obovate, usually narrowed from above the middle to the rounded or rarely cune-ate base, 3-lobed at apex, with acute or acuminate erect or slightly spreading lobes, simple or furnished with short lateral secondary lobes, remotely serrate except toward the base, with

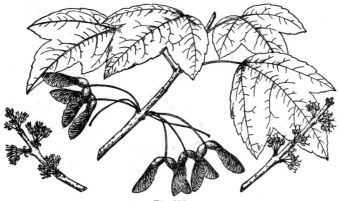

Fig. 630

incurved glandular teeth, and often ovate by the suppression of the lateral lobes and acute or acuminate, thick and firm in texture, glaucous and usually pubescent or rarely tomentose or tomentulose below, 2′–3′ long and 1½′–2½′ wide; petioles slender, glabrous or pubescent. **Flowers** sometimes tawny yellow. **Fruit** usually much smaller and rarely also yellow.

Distribution. Usually with the species; Massachusetts and central New York, south-ward usually in the coast region and the middle districts to western Florida, along the Gulf coast to the valley of the Trinity River, Texas, and through western Louisiana, and Arkansas to northeastern Mississippi, southern Missouri, Arkansas, western Tennessee and Kentucky and southern Illinois; in North Carolina occasionally ascending on the Appala-chian Mountains to altitudes of 3000°; often the prevailing Red Maple in southern Missouri and northwestern Louisiana; in the swamps of western Florida and southwestern Georgia the form with leaves densely tomentose below and pubescent petioles prevails.

13. Acer Negundo L. Box Elder. Ash-leaved Maple.

Leaves usually 3, rarely 5–7-foliolate, with a slender glabrous petiole 2′–3′ in length, the enlarged base often furnished with a minute rim of deciduous white hairs, and in falling leaving a large conspicuous scar surrounding the stem; leaflets ovate to elliptic or obovate, acuminate, and often long-pointed at apex, rounded or cuneate and often unsymmetrical at base, coarsely and irregularly serrate usually only above the middle or nearly entire, and occasionally slightly and irregularly lobulate; when they unfold more or less hoary-tomen-tose below and slightly pubescent above, and at maturity thin, light green, paler on the lower than on the upper surface, glabrous above, villose-pubescent along the under side of the midrib and veins, often furnished with conspicuous tufts of axillary hairs, otherwise glabrous or slightly pubescent below, 2½′–4′ long, and 1½′–2½′ wide, on slender glabrous petiolules, that of the terminal leaflet ¾′–1′ long and much longer than those of the smaller lateral leaflets. **Flowers** on slender glabrous or rarely hairy pedicels, minute, apetalous, yellow-green, the staminate and pistillate on separate trees, expanding just before or with the leaves from buds developed in the axils of the last leaves of the previous year, the stami-nate fascicled, the pistillate in narrow drooping racemes, sometimes furnished near the base with one or two smaller 3-lobed or rarely elliptic leaves; calyx 5-lobed, hairy, campanulate in the staminate flower, much smaller in the pistillate flower and divided to the base into 5 narrow sepals; corolla 0; stamens 4–6, with slender exserted hairy filaments and long linear anthers narrowed and apiculate at apex, 0 in the pistillate flower; ovary on a narrow rudimentary disk, pubescent, only partly inclosed by the calyx; style separating from the base into 2 long stigmatic lobes. **Fruit** attaining nearly its full size in summer, pendent on glabrous stems 1′–2′ long, in graceful racemes 6′–8′ in length, ripening in the autumn, deciduous from the stems persistent on the branches until the following spring, 1½′–2′ long, with narrow acute pubescent nutlets diverging at an acute angle and constricted below into a stipe-like base, and thin reticulate straight or falcate wings undulate toward the apex; **seeds** narrowed at the ends, smooth, bright red-brown, ½′ long.

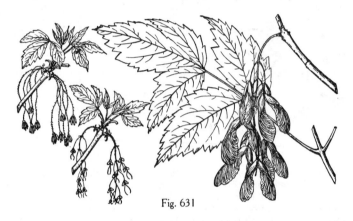

Fig. 631

A tree 50°–70° high, with a trunk 2°–4° in diameter, dividing near the ground into a number of stout wide-spreading or erect branches, and slender pale green lustrous glabrous branchlets. **Winter-buds** terminal acute, ⅛′ long, rather longer than the obtuse lateral buds, the scales tomentose, those of the inner pairs accrescent, becoming 1′ long at maturity, deciduous, leaving conspicuous scars visible at the base of the branchlet for two or three years. **Bark** of the trunk ¼′–½′ thick, pale gray or light brown and deeply divided into broad rounded ridges separating on the surface into short thick scales. **Wood** light, soft, close-grained, not strong, creamy white, with thick hardly distinguishable sapwood; occasionally manufactured into cheap furniture, and sometimes used for the interior finish of houses, for wooden ware, cooperage, and paper pulp. Small quantities of maple sugar are occasionally made from this tree.

Distribution. Banks of streams and lakes, and the borders of swamps; western Vermont, western Massachusetts and Connecticut, central New York and southwestern Ontario, and southward to west-central Florida (Hernando County) and westward to Minnesota, Iowa, Nebraska, Missouri, eastern Kansas, Arkansas, eastern Oklahoma, western Louisiana, and eastern and southern Texas to the valley of the lower Rio Blanco.

Often planted in the United States, especially in the western states and in eastern Canada, and in western and northern Europe, especially the varieties with variegated leaves.

Passing into the following varieties:

Var. **violaceum** Kirch., with slender pale or bluish violet glabrous branchlets covered with a glaucous bloom and rather larger winter-buds. **Leaves** 3–11, usually 3–7-foliolulate, the leaflets slightly thicker, lanceolate to oblong-ovate or obovate, often entire or irregularly dentate, occasionally lobed, the terminal leaflet sometimes 3-lobed, usually pubescent and furnished with tufts of axillary hairs on the lower surface. **Fruit** glabrous, usually constricted at the base. Western Massachusetts through Ohio to northern Wisconsin, Minnesota, Iowa and South Dakota, and to northern and southwestern Missouri; in Nez Perces County, Idaho.

Var. **texanum** Pax., with branchlets covered with pale tomentum. **Leaves** 3-foliate, the leaflets ovate, or the terminal obovate, acuminate, short-pointed at apex, rounded or cuneate at base, coarsely serrate above the middle or entire, only slightly and irregularly lobed, early in the season villose along the midrib and veins above and thickly coated below with matted pale hairs, and at maturity nearly glabrous on the upper surface and covered below with loose pubescence, 3′–4′ long and 2′–3′ wide. **Fruit** puberulous, constricted into a short stipe-like base. Western and southwestern Missouri, southeastern Kansas, Arkansas, Oklahoma and eastern Texas to the valley of the San Antonio River. Passing into forma *latifolia* Sarg. differing only in its glabrous branchlets, and distributed from eastern Texas through Louisiana to western Mississippi, western North Carolina, Virginia and southern Ohio.

Var. **interior** Sarg., with branchlets covered with close pale pubescence, or rarely nearly glabrous. **Leaves** trifoliate, with puberulous petioles, rachis and petiolules, the long-stalked leaflets ovate to lanceolate, or the terminal sometimes obovate, acuminate and long-pointed at apex, cuneate, rounded or cordate at base, coarsely serrate, sometimes distinctly 3-lobed at base, glabrous or villose on the midrib below, or in Arizona sometimes sparingly pubescent on the lower surface, 3′–4′ long and 1½–4′ wide. **Fruit** glabrous, not at all, slightly or at the north conspicuously constricted at the base. Southern Manitoba, Saskatchewan and Alberta to Wyoming, and through the mountain regions of Colorado and Utah to New Mexico and Arizona.

Var. **arizonicum** Sarg., with glabrous branchlets thickly covered with a glaucous bloom. **Leaves** thin, 3-foliolulate; petioles slender, glabrous, 1¾′–3′ long, often turning bright red late in summer; leaflets oblong-ovate to rhombic, acuminate and long-pointed at apex, rounded or cuneate at base, coarsely serrate, often slightly lobed near the middle, glabrous with the exception of conspicuous tufts of axillary hairs, 2½′–4′ long, 1½′–2′ wide; petiolules slender, glabrous, usually bright red, that of the terminal leaflet ¾′–1′ long, the others not more than ¼′ in length. **Fruit** in glabrous racemes 3′ or 4′ long, the body glabrous, spreading, not constricted at base. A tree, 20°–25° high. **Bark** fissured. Mountain cañons, central and southern Arizona up to 8000° altitude, and in Socorro County, New Mexico. More distinct is

Acer Negundo var. californicum Sarg.

Leaves trifoliate with tomentose or nearly glabrous rachis and petiolules; leaflets oblong-ovate to rhombic, acuminate and long-pointed at apex, cuneate or unsymmetrically

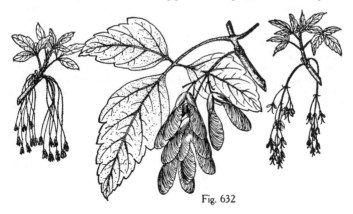

Fig. 632

rounded at base, coarsely serrate above the middle, or nearly entire, when they unfold hoary-tomentose below and densely pubescent above, occasionally deeply lobed, glabrous on the upper surface except along the midrib and veins, thickly coated on the lower surface with matted pale hairs and furnished with large axillary tufts. Fruit on pubescent pedicels, puberulous or nearly glabrous, not constricted or rarely slightly constricted at base.

A tree, 20°–50° high, with dark bark, hoary-tomentose branchlets and winter-buds.

Distribution. California, valley of the lower Sacramento River and the interior valleys of the coast ranges from the Bay of San Francisco to Santa Barbara County and in elevated cañons on the western slopes of the San Bernardino Mountains; widely distributed but nowhere abundant.

Occasionally planted in California.

XXXVI. HIPPOCASTANACEÆ.

Trees or rarely shrubs, with stout terete branchlets conspicuously marked by triangular leaf-scars, fetid bark, thick fleshy roots, and large scaly winter-buds, the inner scales accrescent with the young shoots and often brightly colored. Leaves opposite, digitately compound, without stipules, deciduous; leaflets 3–9, lanceolate or ovate, serrate, pinnately veined. Flowers polygamo-monœcious, showy, white, red, or pale yellow, on stout jointed pedicels from the axils of minute caducous bracts, racemose or nearly unilateral on the branches of large terminal thyrsi or panicles, appearing later than the leaves, only those near the base of the branches of the inflorescence perfect and fertile; calyx 5 or rarely 2-lobed, the lobes imbricated in the bud, unequal, campanulate or tubular, the lobes imbricated in the bud, mostly oblique or posteriorly gibbous at base; disk hypogynous, annular, depressed, lobed, more or less gibbous posteriorly; petals 4 or 5, imbricated in the bud, alternate with the lobes of the calyx, deciduous, the anterior petal often abortive, unguiculate, the margins of the claw commonly involute; stamens 6–8, rarely 5, generally 7, inserted on the disk, free, unequal; filaments filiform; anthers ellipsoid, glandular-apiculate, attached on the back below the middle, introrse, 2-celled, the contiguous cells opening longitudinally; ovary sessile, oblong or lanceolate, 3-celled, echinate or glabrous, rudimentary in the staminate flower; style slender, elongated, generally more or less curved; stigma terminal, entire, mostly acute; ovules 2 in each cell, borne on the middle of its inner angle, amphitropous, the upper ascending, the micropyle inferior, the lower pendulous, the micropyle superior. Fruit an echinate or smooth coriaceous capsule, 3-celled and loculicidally 3-valved, the cells 1-seeded by abortion, often by suppression 1 or 2-celled, and then 1 or 2-seeded, the remnants of the abortive cells and seeds commonly visible at its maturity. Seeds without albumen, round when one is developed, or, when more than one, flattened by mutual pressure; seed-coat coriaceous, dark chestnut-brown or pale orange-brown, smooth and lustrous, with a broad opaque light-colored hilum; embryo filling the cavity of the seed; cotyledons very thick and fleshy, often conferruminate, unequal, incurved on the short conic radicle, remaining under ground in germination; plumule conspicuously 2-leaved.

The Horsechestnut family is composed of the widely distributed genus Aesculus and of Billia Peyr., a genus of two species of Mexican and Central American trees, differing from Aesculus in its 3-foliolate leaves.

1. AESCULUS L.

Characters of the family; leaves 5–9-foliolate.

Aesculus with fifteen or sixteen species is represented in the floras of the three continents of the northern hemisphere and is most abundant in the southeastern United States. It produces soft straight-grained light-colored wood and bitter and astringent bark. The seeds contain a bitter principle, aesculin. *Aesculus Hippocastanum* L., of the mountains of Greece, the common Horsechestnut of gardens, is largely planted as an ornamental tree in all countries with temperate climates, and now occasionally grows spontaneously in the eastern states.

The generic name is the classical name of an Oak-tree.

CONSPECTUS OF THE ARBORESCENT SPECIES OF NORTH AMERICA.

Winter-buds without a resinous covering. PAVIA.

Calyx campanulate (*occasionally tubular in 3*); margins of the petals ciliate, eglandular; flowers usually yellow. OCTANDRÆ.

Fruit covered with prickles; flowers yellow; petals nearly equal in length, shorter than the stamens.   **1. A. glabra** (A, C).

Fruit without prickles; flowers yellow or red; petals unequal in length, longer than the stamens.

Pedicels and calyx glandular-villose.   **2. A. octandra** (A, C).

Pedicels and calyx without glandular hairs.   **3. A. georgiana** (C).

Calyx tubular; margins of the unequal petals without hairs, glandular; fruit without prickles. EUPAVIÆ.

Lower surface of the leaves glabrous or slightly pubescent along the midrib; flowers red; seeds dark chestnut-brown.   **4. A. Pavia** (C).

Lower surface of the leaves tomentose or pubescent; flowers red and yellow, red, or in one form yellow; seed light yellow-brown.   **5. A. discolor** (C).

Winter-buds resinous; petals nearly equal in length, shorter than the stamens; fruit without prickles. CALOTHYRSUS.   **6. A. californica** (G).

1. Aesculus glabra Willd.   Ohio Buckeye.   Fetid Buckeye.

Leaves with a slender petiole 4′–6′ long and enlarged at the end, a rachis often furnished on the upper side with clusters of dark brown chaff-like scales surrounding the base of the petiolules, and 5 rarely 7 (var. *Buckleyi* Sarg.) oval-oblong or obovate acuminate leaflets

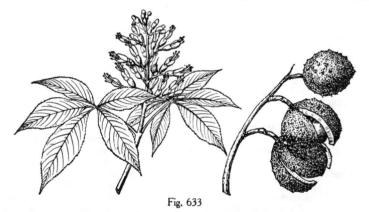

Fig. 633

gradually narrowed to the elongated entire base, finely and unequally serrate above, at first sessile, becoming slightly petiolulate at maturity, covered on the lower surface like the petioles when they first appear with floccose deciduous hairs most abundant on the midrib and veins, and at maturity glabrous with the exception of a few hairs along the under side of the conspicuous yellow midrib and in the axils of the principal veins, or rarely covered below with close dense pubescence persistent during the season (var. *pallida*, Kirch.), yellow-green, paler on the lower than on the upper surface, 4′–6′ long and $1\frac{1}{2}′$–$2\frac{1}{2}′$ wide; turning yellow in the autumn before falling. **Flowers** pale yellow-green, mostly unilateral, $\frac{1}{2}$-$1\frac{1}{2}'$ long or more than twice as long as the pedicels, appearing in April and May in clusters 5'-6' long and 2'-3' wide, and more or less densely covered with pubescence, with short usually 4-6-flowered branches; calyx campanulate; petals nearly equal, puberulous, the thin limb about twice as long as the claw, in the lateral pair broad-ovate or oblong, and in the superior pair oblong-spatulate, much narrower, sometimes marked with red stripes; stamens usually 7, with long exserted curved pubescent filaments and orange-colored slightly hairy anthers; ovary pubescent, covered with long slender deciduous prickles thickened and tubercle-like at base. **Fruit** on a stout stem $\frac{1}{2}$-1' long, ovoid or irregularly obovoid, pale brown, 1'-2' long, with thin or sometimes thick valves, roughened by the enlarged persistent bases of the prickles of the ovary; **seeds** 1'-1$\frac{1}{2}'$ broad.

A tree, occasionally 70° high, with a trunk rarely 2° in diameter, small spreading branches, and branchlets orange-brown and covered at first with short fine pubescence, soon glabrous, reddish brown, and marked by scattered orange-colored lenticels; usually much smaller, and rarely more than 30° high. **Winter-buds** $\frac{2}{3}'$ long, acuminate, with thin nearly triangular pale brown scales, the outer bright red on the inner surface toward the base, those of the inner pair strap-shaped, prominently keeled on the back, minutely apiculate and slightly ciliate along the margins, and at maturity 1$\frac{1}{2}'$-2' long and bright yellow. **Bark** of young stems and of the branches dark brown and scaly, becoming on old trees $\frac{3}{4}'$ thick, ashy gray, densely furrowed, and broken into thick plates roughened on the surface by numerous small scales. **Wood** light, soft, close-grained, not strong, often blemished by dark lines of decay, nearly white, with thin dark-colored sapwood of 10-12 layers of annual growth; used in the manufacture of artificial limbs, wooden ware, wooden hats, and paper pulp; occasionally sawed into lumber. An extract of the bark has been used as an irritant of the cerebro-spinal system.

Distribution. River-bottoms and the banks of streams in rich moist soil; western slopes of the Alleghany Mountains, western and southwestern Pennsylvania to northern Alabama, and westward to central and southern Iowa, southeastern Nebraska, northern and central Missouri and northeastern Kansas; nowhere abundant; most common and of its largest size in the valley of the Tennessee River in Tennessee and northern Alabama.

A shrubby form (var. *micrantha* Sarg.) with flowers not more than $\frac{1}{2}'$ long near Fulton, Hempstead County, Arkansas. In southern Missouri, Arkansas and probably Oklahoma *Aesculus glabra* is replaced by the var. *leucodermis* Sarg. with glabrous leaves pale green or glaucescent below. A tree occasionally 60° high, well distinguished from the type by the smooth pale nearly white bark of the trunk and large branches, becoming on old trunks light brown and separating into oblong flakes, and by its later flowers; the var. *pallida* in Iowa, Missouri and Arkansas; the var. *Buckleyi* in Jackson County, Missouri, eastern Kansas, Ohio and Mississippi.

The Ohio Buckeye is occasionally cultivated as an ornamental plant in the eastern United States and Europe; hardy as far north as eastern Massachusetts.

× *Aesculus Bushii* Schn., probably a hybrid of *Aesculus discolor* var. *mollis* Sarg. and *Aesculus glabra* var. *leucodermis* Sarg., has been found in the neighborhood of Fulton, Hempstead County, Arkansas; and what is evidently a hybrid of *Aesculus discolor* var. *mollis* and the typical form of *Aesculus glabra* occurs near Starkville, Oktibbeha County, Mississippi.

× *Aesculus mississippiensis* Sarg., a probable hybrid between *Aesculus glabra* and *Aesculus Pavia* with characters intermediate between those of its supposed parents, occurs near Brookville, Noxubee County, Mississippi. The mingling of a species of the Octandræ and of the Eupaviæ in these hybrids of Aesculus is shown by the presence of both hairs and glands on the margins of the petals.

2. Aesculus octandra Marsh. Sweet Buckeye.

Leaves with slender or slightly pubescent petioles 4'-6' long, and 5-7 elliptic or obovate-oblong leaflets, acuminate and usually abruptly long-pointed at apex, gradually narrowed and cuneate at base, sharply and equally serrate, glabrous above except on the midrib and veins sometimes clothed with reddish brown pubescence, when they unfold more or less canescent-pubescent on the lower surface, becoming glabrous at maturity, with the exception of a few pale or rufous hairs along the stout midrib and in the axils of the principal veins, dark yellow-green, duller on the lower than on the upper surface, 4'–6' long, and $1\frac{1}{2}'$–$2\frac{1}{2}'$ wide; petiolules $\frac{1}{12}'$–$\frac{1}{2}'$ in length; turning yellow in the autumn before falling. **Flowers** opening in early spring when the leaves are about half grown, $1'$–$1\frac{1}{2}'$ long, pale or dark yellow, rarely red, pink or cream-colored (var. *virginica* Sarg.), on short glandular-villose pedicels mostly unilateral on the branches of the pubescent clusters $5'$–$7'$ in length; calyx campanulate, glandular-villose; petals connivent, very unequal, puberulent, the claws villose within, limb of the superior pair spatulate, minute, the long claws exceeding the lobes of the calyx, those of the lateral pair obovate or nearly round and subcordate at base; stamens usually 7, rather shorter than the petals, with straight or inclining subulate villose filaments; ovary pubescent. **Fruit** $2'$–$3'$ long, generally 2-seeded, with thin smooth or slightly pitted pale brown valves; **seeds** $1\frac{1}{2}'$ to nearly $2'$ wide.

Fig. 634

A tree, sometimes 90° high, with a tall straight trunk $2\frac{1}{2}°$–$3°$ in diameter, small rather pendulous branches, and glabrous or nearly glabrous branchlets orange-brown when they first appear, becoming in their second year pale brown and marked by numerous irregularly developed lenticels. **Winter-buds** $\frac{3}{4}'$ long, rather obtuse, with broad-ovate pale brown outer scales rounded on the back, minutely apiculate, ciliate, and slightly covered with a glaucous bloom, the inner scales becoming sometimes $2'$ long, bright yellow or occasionally scarlet. **Bark** of the trunk about $\frac{3}{4}'$ thick, dark brown, divided by shallow fissures and separating on the surface into small thin scales. **Wood** light, soft, close-grained, difficult to split, creamy white, with thick hardly distinguishable sapwood; used in the manufacture of artificial limbs, for wooden ware, wooden hats, paper pulp, and occasionally sawed into lumber.

Distribution. Rich river-bottoms and mountain slopes; southwestern Pennsylvania (Alleghany, Greene and Fayette Counties), southward along the mountains to east Tennessee, and northwestern Georgia, and westward to north central Ohio (near Plymouth, Richard County), southeastern and southern Indiana (near Aurora, Dearborn County, and on the banks of Dry River near Leavenworth, Crawford County, *C. C. Deam*) and to southern Illinois (near Golconda, Pope County, shrub $6'$–$12'$ high, *E. J. Palmer*); the var. *virginica* at White Sulphur Springs, West Virginia.

Occasionally cultivated in the parks of the eastern United States and Europe.

× *Aesculus hybrida* DC., with red and yellow flowers, believed to be a hybrid of *Aesculus octandra* and *Aesculus Pavia*, appeared in the Botanic Garden at Montpelier in France early in the nineteenth century, and in many varieties is cultivated in Europe and occasionally in the eastern United States.

3. Aesculus georgiana Sarg.

Leaves with slender glabrous petioles $4\frac{1}{2}'-6'$ in length, and 5 leaflets oblong-obovate, abruptly acuminate and long-pointed at apex, gradually narrowed and acuminate at base, finely often doubly serrate with rounded teeth pointing forward, sparingly covered early in the season, especially on the upper side of the midrib and veins, with short caducous hairs, yellow-green above, green, glabrous and lustrous or pubescent (var. *pubescens* Sarg.) below, $4\frac{1}{2}'-6'$ long, $1\frac{1}{2}'-2\frac{1}{2}'$ wide, with a stout orange-colored midrib and 20–30 pairs of slender primary veins; petiolules stout, puberulous early in the season, $\frac{1}{4}'-\frac{1}{2}'$ in length. **Flowers**

Fig. 635

opening in April and May $1'-1\frac{1}{3}'$ long, on slender puberulous pedicels, in broad pubescent panicles, $4'-6'$ in length; calyx campanulate or tubular, puberulous, about $\frac{5}{12}'$ in diameter, red on the upper side, pale yellow on the lower side or entirely red or yellow, 5-lobed, the lobes oblong-ovate, narrowed and rounded at apex, finely serrate on the margins; petals connivent, obovate, rounded at apex, gradually narrowed below, those of the superior and lateral pairs very unequal in size, puberulous and glandular on the outer surface, pubescent on the inner surface, ciliate on the margins, bright yellow or red, their claws furnished on the margins with long white hairs, those of the superior pair as long as the lateral petals; stamens 7, shorter than the petals; filaments villose, especially below the middle; ovary covered with matted pale hairs; styles exserted, villose. **Fruit** on stout pendulous pedicels, globose, usually 1-seeded, $1'-1\frac{1}{4}'$ in diameter, with thin light brown slightly pitted valves; seed globose, dark chestnut-brown.

A tree, $25°-30°$ high, with a trunk $6'-10'$ in diameter, slender erect and spreading branches and stout glabrous branchlets, orange-green and marked by pale lenticels when they first appear, becoming light reddish brown in their first winter; more often a large or small round-topped shrub $3°-5°$ tall and broad. Bark of the trunk thin, dark brown, the surface separating into small thin scales. **Winter-buds** about $\frac{1}{3}'$ long, with light reddish brown scales, narrowed, rounded and short-pointed at apex. The common Buckeye of the Piedmont region of North and South Carolina and northern Georgia.

Distribution. Central North Carolina (Durham and Orange Counties), southward to eastern (Richmond County) and central Georgia; northern Alabama (Madison, Etowah and Tuscaloosa Counties), and near Pensacola, Escambia County, Florida. The var. *pubescens* occasionally arborescent in habit, common in the woods west of Augusta, Richmond County, and in De Kalb, Rabun and Floyd Counties, Georgia, ranging northward to Orange County, North Carolina, and ascending on the Blue Ridge to altitudes of 3000°; in northern Alabama.

× *Aesculus Harbisonii* Sarg., a probable hybrid between *A. discolor* var. *mollis* and *A. georgiana*, has appeared in the Arnold Arboretum among plants of *A. georgiana* raised from seeds collected near Stone Mountain, De Kalb County, Georgia.

A distinct form of *Aesculus georgiana* is

Aesculus georgiana var. lanceolata Sarg.

Leaves with glabrous petioles $3\frac{1}{2}'-5\frac{1}{2}'$ in length, and 5 lanceolate or slightly oblanceolate leaflets long-acuminate at apex, cuneate at base, and finely glandular-serrate, when the

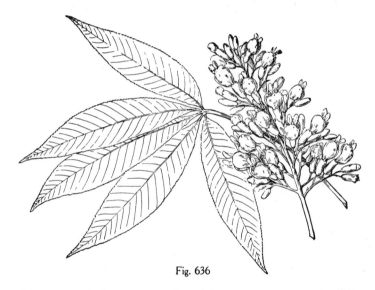

Fig. 636

flowers open early in May thin yellow-green above, pale below, glabrous with the exception of occasional hairs on the under side of the slender midrib and of minute axillary tufts, $6'-8'$ long and $1\frac{1}{4}'-1\frac{1}{2}'$ wide; petiolules $\frac{1}{12}'-\frac{1}{6}'$ in length. **Flowers** on stout puberulous pedicels, bright red, in narrow crowded clusters, $8'-10'$ long; calyx narrow-campanulate, otherwise as in the type. **Fruit** not seen.

A tree 25°-30° high, with a short trunk $6'-10'$ in diameter, small erect and spreading branches forming a narrow head, and slender glabrous branchlets orange-brown when they first appear, becoming dark gray-brown and marked by pale lenticels in their second year.

Distribution. Georgia, rich woods near Clayton, Rabun County.

4. Aesculus Pavia L. Red-flowered Buckeye.

Leaves with slender petioles glabrous or puberulous early in the season and $4'-7'$ long, and 5 short-petiolulate, oblong-obovate, acuminate leaflets, gradually narrowed at base, coarsely often doubly serrate above with incurved teeth, slightly pubescent early in the season along the upper side of the midrib and veins, and glabrous or slightly pubescent below, and at maturity thin, lustrous and glabrous, dark green on the upper surface, pale yellow-green on the lower surface, often furnished with conspicuous tufts of axillary hairs, $3\frac{1}{2}'-6'$ long and $1\frac{1}{4}'-1\frac{3}{4}'$ wide, with a thin midrib and from 18–30 pairs of slender primary veins. **Flowers** in narrow pubescent panicles, $4\frac{1}{2}'-8'$ in length, on slender pubescent pedicels; calyx tubular, dark red, puberulous on both surfaces, minutely lobed, the lobes rounded, much shorter than the light red petals; petals connivent, unequal, oblong-obovate,

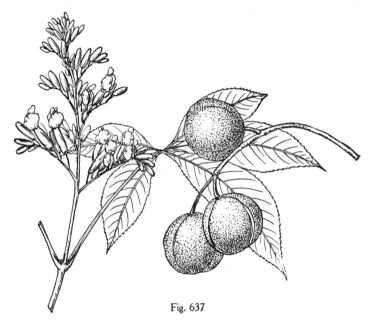

Fig. 637

rounded at apex, glandular on the outer surface and on the margins, gradually narrowed below into a long slender villose claw; claw of the lateral petals about as long or shorter than the calyx, those of the superior pair much longer than the calyx, their blades not more than one-third as large as the blades of the lateral pair; stamens exserted; filaments villose like the ovary. **Fruit** obovoid or subglobose, light brown, smooth, generally pitted, usually 1 or 2-seeded, pendulous on slender stems; **seeds** usually about $1'$ in diameter, dark chestnut-brown and lustrous with a small hilum.

Occasionally a tree, rarely $40°$ high, with a tall trunk $8'-10'$ in diameter covered with smooth dark bark, large erect branches forming an open head, and stout light orange-brown branchlets marked in their second year by conspicuous emarginate scars of fallen leaves showing the ends of 3 fibro-vascular bundles; usually a shrub, often flowering when not more than $3'$ high.

Distribution. Southeastern Virginia, southward to middle Florida to the valley of the Suwannee River (near Old Town, Dixie County), and westward to eastern Louisiana, usually in the neighborhood of the coast; in Alabama ranging inland to Jefferson and Dallas Counties and in Louisiana to West Feliciana Parish; in southern Kentucky (near Bowling Green, Warren County).

5. Aesculus discolor Pursh. Buckeye.

Leaves with slender grooved villose or pubescent usually ultimately glabrous petioles 4′ or 5′ long, and 5 oblong-obovate or elliptic leaflets, acuminate and usually long-pointed at apex, gradually narrowed and acuminate at the entire base, finely or coarsely and sometimes doubly crenulate-serrate above, dark green, lustrous and glabrous except along the slender yellow midrib and veins on the upper surface, lighter colored and tomentulose or tomentose on the lower surface, 4′–5′ long, 1½′–2′ wide, nearly sessile or raised on slender petiolules up to ½′ in length. **Flowers** opening from the first to the middle of April, usually ¾′–1′ long, on slender pubescent pedicels much thickened on the fruit, sometimes ¼′ long, and mostly aggregated toward the end of the short branches of the narrow pubescent inflorescence 6′–8′ in length; calyx red, rose color or yellow more or less deeply tinged with

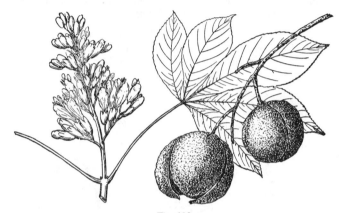

Fig. 638

red, tubular, short and broad or elongated, puberulous on the outer surface, tomentose on the inner surface, with rounded lobes; petals yellow, shorter than the stamens, connivent, unequal, oblong-obovate, rounded at apex, puberulous on the outer surface and glandular on the margins with minute dark glands, those of the superior pair about half as wide as those of the lateral pair, with claws much longer than the calyx; filaments and ovary villose. **Fruit** ripening and falling in October, usually only a few fruits maturing in a cluster, generally obovoid or occasionally subglobose, mostly 2-seeded, 1½′–2½′ long, with very thin, light brown slightly pitted valves; **seeds** light yellow-brown, sometimes 1½′ in diameter, with a comparatively small hilum and a thin shell.

Rarely arborescent and occasionally 25° high, with a straight trunk 6′ or 7′ in diameter, stout branches forming a narrow symmetric head, and slender branchlets marked by numerous small pale lenticels, green and puberulous at first, becoming gray slightly tinged with red during their first winter and only slightly darker in their second year; usually a small or large shrub. **Winter-buds** broad-ovoid, obtusely pointed, about ¼′ long, with rounded apiculate light red-brown scales. **Bark** thin, smooth, and pale.

Distribution. Rich woods; Shell Bluff on the Savannah River, Burke County, Georgia; near Birmingham, Jefferson County, and Selma, Dallas County, Alabama; near Campbell, Dunklin County, Missouri; Comal, Comal County, and Sutherland Springs, Wilson County, Texas; rare and local, and found as a tree only near Birmingham, Alabama; more abundant is the var. *mollis* Sarg. (*Aesculus austrina* Small) with bright red flowers; a tree up to 25° or 30° high, or more often a large or small shrub; valley of the lower Cape Fear River (near Wilmington, New Hanover County), North Carolina, southward near the coast to the neighborhood of Charleston, South Carolina, through Georgia to the neighborhood of Rome, Floyd County, and southward to western Florida; in Alabama widely distributed from Jefferson County southward; widely distributed in Mississippi except in the neighborhood of the Gulf coast, to West Feliciana Parish, eastern Louisiana; more common and generally distributed in western Louisiana, and through eastern Texas to the valley of the San Antonio River (neighborhood of San Antonio, Bexar County) and to that of the upper Guadalupe River (near Boerne, Kendall County), ranging northward through Arkansas to southern Missouri and western Tennessee.

On the Edwards Plateau of western Texas *Aesculus discolor* is represented by the var. *flavescens* Sarg., with yellow flowers, appearing a few days earlier than those of the var. *mollis;* a shrub 9′–12′ high, or often much smaller; interesting as the only form of Eupaviæ with yellow flowers; San Marcos, Hays County, common on the slopes above Comal Springs, near New Braunfels, Comal County, near Boerne, Kendall County (with the var. *mollis*), Kerrville, Kerr County, and Cancan, Uvalde County.

6. Aesculus californica Nutt. Buckeye.

Leaves with slender grooved petioles 3′–4′ long, and 4–7 usually 5 oblong-lanceolate acuminate leaflets narrowed and acuminate or rounded at base, sharply serrate, 4′–6′ long,

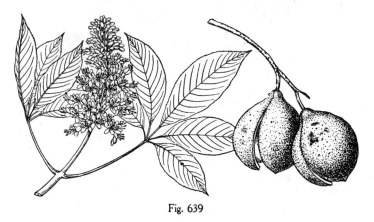

Fig. 639

1½′–2′ wide, dark green above, paler below, slightly pubescent when they first appear, becoming glabrous or nearly so, on petiolules ½′–1′ long; falling early, often by midsummer. Flowers white or pale rose color, 1′–1¼′ long, appearing from May to July when the leaves are fully grown, on short pedicels mostly unilateral on the long branches of the densely flowered long-stemmed pubescent cluster 3′–9′ in length; calyx 2-lobed, slightly toothed, much shorter than the narrow oblong petals; stamens 5–7, with long erect exserted slender filaments and bright orange-colored anthers; ovary densely pubescent. Fruit obovoid, often somewhat gibbous on the outer side, with thin smooth pale brown valves, usually 1-seeded, 2′–3′ long, on a slender stalk ¼′–½′ in length; seeds pale orange-brown, 1½′–2′ broad.

A tree, rarely 20°–30° high, with a short trunk occasionally 4°–5° in diameter, often much enlarged at base, stout wide-spreading branches, forming a round-topped head, and branchlets glabrous and pale reddish brown when they first appear, becoming darker in their second season; more often a shrub, with spreading stems 10°–15° high forming broad dense thickets. Winter-buds acute, covered with narrow dark brown scales rounded on the back and thickly coated with resin. Bark of the trunk about ¼′ thick, smooth, and light gray or nearly white. Wood soft, light, very close-grained, white or faintly tinged with yellow, with thin hardly distinguishable sapwood of 10–12 layers of annual growth.

Distribution. California, borders of streams, valley of the south fork of the Salmon River, Siskiyou County, south along the coast ranges to San Luis Obispo County and on the western slope of the Sierra Nevada, usually at altitudes between 2000° and 2500°, occasionally to 5000°, to the northern slopes of Tejon Pass, Kern County, and to Antelope Valley, Los Angeles County.

Occasionally cultivated as an ornamental plant in the Pacific states, and in western and southern Europe.

XXXVII. SAPINDACEÆ.

Trees or shrubs, with alternate pinnate petiolate persistent or deciduous leaves, without stipules. Flowers regular or irregular, polygamo-diœcious, polygamo-monœcious or polygamous; calyx of 4 or 5 sepals or lobes imbricated in the bud; petals 4 or 5 imbricated in the bud; disk annular, fleshy, 5-lobed, or unilateral and oblique; stamens usually 7-10, inserted on the disk; filaments free; anthers introrse, 2-celled, the cells opening longitudinally; ovary 2-4 or 3-celled; styles terminal; stigmas capitate or lobed; ovule solitary or 2 in each cell, anatropous or amphitropous. Fruit a drupe or capsule. Seed usually solitary, without albumen; seed-coat bony, coriaceous or crustaceous.

Of the one hundred and twenty-six genera of this family, which is chiefly confined to the tropics and is more abundant in the Old than in the New World, four have arborescent representatives in the United States.

CONSPECTUS OF THE ARBORESCENT GENERA OF THE UNITED STATES.

Fruit baccate.
　　Fruit dark orange-color or yellow, with thin semitranslucent coriaceous flesh; ovules 1 in
　　　　each cell of the ovary; leaflets subcoriaceous to coriaceous.　　　　1. **Sapindus.**
　　Fruit purple, with thick juicy flesh; ovules 2 in each cell of the ovary; leaflets large, per-
　　　　sistent.　　　　2. **Exothea.**
Fruit a drupe; leaves 3-foliolate, persistent.　　　　3. **Hypelate.**
Fruit a 3-valved capsule; leaves 4 or 5, rarely 3-foliolate, deciduous.　　　　4. **Ungnadia.**

1. SAPINDUS L.　Soapberry.

Trees or shrubs, with terete branches, without a terminal bud, marked by large obcordate leaf-scars showing the ends of 3 equidistant fibro-vascular bundles, small globose axillary buds often superposed in pairs, the upper bud the larger, and thick fleshy roots. Leaves equally or rarely unequally pinnate. Flowers regular, minute, polygamo-diœcious, on short pedicels from the axils of minute deciduous bracts, in ample axillary or terminal panicles; sepals 4 or 5, unequal, slightly united at base; petals 4 or 5, equal, alternate with the sepals, inserted under the thick edge of the annular fleshy entire crenately lobed disk, unguiculate, naked or furnished at the summit of the claw on the inside with a 2-cleft scale, deciduous; stamens usually 8 or 10, inserted on the disk immediately under the ovary, equal; filaments subulate or filiform, often pilose, exserted in the staminate, much shorter in the pistillate flower; anthers oblong, attached near the base; pistils 2 or 3, united; ovary sessile, entire or 2-4-lobed, 2-4-celled, narrowed into a short columnar style, rudimentary in the staminate flower; stigma 2-4-lobed, the lobes spreading; ovule solitary in each cell, ascending from below the inner angle of the cell; raphe ventral; micropyle inferior. Fruit baccate, coriaceous, 1-3-seeded, usually formed of 1 globose coriaceous carpel, with the rudiments of the others remaining at its base, or of 2 or sometimes 3 carpels more or less connate by their base and then 2-3-lobed. Seed solitary in each carpel, obovoid or globose; seed-coat bony, smooth, black or dark brown; tegmen membranaceous or fleshy; hilum oblong, surrounded by an ariloid tuft of long pale silky hairs; embryo incurved or straight; cotyledons thick and fleshy, incumbent; radicle very short, inferior, near the hilum.

Sapindus is widely distributed through the tropics, especially in Asia, occasionally extending into colder regions. About forty species have been distinguished; of these three are found within the territory of the United States.

Sapindus contains a detersive principle which causes the pulp of the fruit to lather in water, and makes it valuable as a substitute for soap. The bark, which is bitter and astringent, has been used as a tonic. The seeds of several of the species are strung for chaplets and bracelets and are used as buttons.

The generic name, from *sapo* and *Indus*, refers to the detersive properties and use of the first species known to Europeans, a native of the West Indies.

CONSPECTUS OF THE SPECIES OF THE UNITED STATES.

Leaves persistent.
    Rachis of the leaf interrupted-winged, with usually broad wings; leaflets 4–9, oblong-lanceolate and acute to elliptic-ovate or oblong, tomentulose below; petals without scales; fruit globose, orange-brown.   1. S. saponaria (D).
    Rachis of the leaf without wings narrow-margined or marginless; leaflets 7–13, oblong-lanceolate, acuminate, often somewhat falcate, glabrous below; petals with scales; fruit somewhat oblong, dorsally keeled, yellow.   2. S. marginatus (C).
Leaves deciduous, their rachis without marginal borders; leaflets 8–18, lanceolate, mostly falcate, soft-pubescent or ultimately glabrous below; petals with scales; fruit globose, not keeled, turning black in drying.   3. S. Drummondii (C, E).

1. Sapindus saponaria L.

Leaves 6′–7′ long, with a broad winged rachis, the wings narrow and often nearly obsolete below the lowest pair of leaflets, and sometimes nearly ½′ wide below the upper pair, and usually 7–9 elliptic to oblong-lanceolate leaflets, rounded or slightly emargi-

Fig. 640

nate at apex, gradually narrowed at base and very short-petiolulate, soft-pubescent on the lower surface when they unfold, and at maturity rather coriaceous, yellow-green, paler and tomentulose below, prominently reticulate-venulose, 3′–4′ long and 1½′ wide, with a yellow midrib and primary veins, those of the lowest pair smaller than the others; rarely reduced to a single leaflet. **Flowers** appearing in Florida in November, usually produced 3 together on short pedicels, in terminal panicles 7′–10′ in length, with an angulate peduncle and branches; calyx-lobes acute, concave, ciliate on the margins, the 2 outer rather smaller than those of the inner rank, much shorter than the white, ovate, short-clawed petals, without scales, rounded at apex and covered, especially toward the base, with long scattered hairs; ovary slightly 3-lobed; stamens included or slightly exserted, with hairy filaments broadened at base. **Fruit** ripening in spring or in early summer, globose, $\frac{2}{3}-\frac{3}{4}'$ in diameter, with thin orange-brown semitranslucent flesh; **seeds** obovoid, black, 1' in diameter.

A tree, sometimes 25°–30° high, with a trunk rarely exceeding 10'–12' in diameter, erect branches and slender branchlets at first slightly many-angled and puberulous, soon glabrous, orange-green and marked by white lenticels, becoming in their second season terete, pale brown faintly tinged with red. **Bark** of the trunk $\frac{1}{4}-\frac{1}{2}'$ thick, light gray and roughened by oblong lighter colored excrescences, the outer layer exfoliating in large flakes exposing the nearly black inner bark. **Wood** heavy, rather hard, close-grained, light brown tinged with yellow, with thick yellow sapwood.

Distribution. Florida, shores of Cape Sable, shores and islands of Caximbas Bay, Key Largo, Elliott's Key, and the shores of Bay Biscayne, Dade County; in Florida most common in the region of Cape Sable, and of its largest size on some of the Ten Thousand Islands, Lee County; generally distributed through the West Indies to Venezuela and Ecuador.

2. Sapindus marginatus Willd.

Sapindus manatensis Radlk.

Leaves 6'–7' long, with a slender wingless or narrow-margined or marginless rachis, and 7–13 lance-oblong acuminate more or less falcate leaflets, glabrous, dark green, and lustrous on the upper surface, paler and glabrous or puberulous on the lower surface along the slen-

Fig. 641

der midrib, sessile or very short-petiolulate, 2'–5' long, $\frac{3}{4}-1\frac{1}{4}'$ wide, the lower usually alternate, the upper opposite. **Flowers** appearing in early spring, more or less tinged with red and nearly $\frac{1}{8}'$ in diameter, on short stout tomentose pedicels, in panicles 4'–5' long and usually about 3' wide, with a villose stem and branches; sepals acute, concave, ciliate on the margins, much shorter than the ovate-oblong, short-clawed, ciliate petals furnished on the inner surface near the base with a 2-lobed villose scale; filaments villose; ovary 3-lobed. **Fruit** conspicuously keeled on the back, short-oblong to slightly obovoid, about $\frac{3}{4}'$ long, with thin light yellow translucent flesh; **seeds** obovoid, dark brown.

A tree, rarely more than 25°–30° high, with a trunk sometimes 1° in diameter, and stout pale brown or ultimately ashy gray branchlets.

Distribution. Hurricane Island at the mouth of Medway River, Liberty County,

Georgia (*Miss J. King*); hummocks, peninsula of Florida to Alachua and Manatee Counties; not common; in Cuba.

3. Sapindus Drummondii Hook. & Arn. Wild China-tree.

Leaves appearing in March and April, with a slender grooved puberulous rachis, without wings, and 4–9 pairs of alternate obliquely lanceolate acuminate leaflets, glabrous on the upper surface and covered with short pale pubescence on the lower surface, coriaceous,

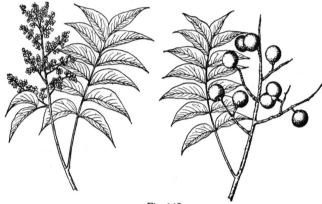

Fig. 642

prominently reticulate-venulose, pale yellow-green, 2′–3′ long, ½′–⅔′ wide, short-petiolulate; deciduous in the autumn or early winter. **Flowers** appearing in May and June in clusters 6′–9′ long and 5′–6′ wide, with a pubescent many-angled stem and branches; sepals acute and concave, ciliate on the margins, much shorter than the obovate white petals rounded at apex, contracted into a long claw hairy on the inner surface and furnished at base with a deeply cleft scale hairy on the margins; filaments hairy, with long soft hairs. **Fruit** ripening in September and October, persistent on the branches until the following spring, glabrous, not keeled, yellow, ½′ in diameter, turning black in drying; **seeds** obovoid, dark brown.

A tree, 40°–50° high, with a trunk sometimes 1½°–2° in diameter, usually erect branches, and branchlets at first slightly many-angled, pale yellow-green, pubescent, becoming in their second year terete, pale gray, slightly puberulous, and marked by numerous small lenticels. **Bark** of the trunk ⅓′–½′ thick, separating by deep fissures into long narrow plates broken on the surface into small red-brown scales. **Wood** heavy, strong, close-grained, light brown tinged with yellow, with lighter colored sapwood of about 30 layers of annual growth; splitting easily into thin strips and largely used in the manufacture of baskets used in harvesting cotton, and for the frames of pack-saddles.

Distribution. Moist clay soil or dry limestone uplands; southwestern Missouri to northeastern and southern Kansas, eastern Louisiana (Tangipahoa Parish *R. S. Cocks*), and to extreme western and southwestern Oklahoma, through eastern Texas to the Rio Grande, over the Edwards Plateau, and in the mountain valleys of western Texas, southern Colorado, and of southern New Mexico and Arizona; in northern Mexico.

2. EXOTHEA Macf.

A tree, with thin scaly bark, and terete branchlets covered with lenticels. **Leaves** petiolate, abruptly pinnate or 3 or rarely 1-foliolate, glabrous, without stipules, persistent; leaflets oblong or oblong-ovate, acute, rounded or emarginate at apex, with entire undulate margins, obscurely veined, thin, dark green and lustrous on the upper surface and slightly paler on the lower surface. Flowers regular, polygamo-diœcious, on short pedicels from the axils of minute deciduous bracts covered with thick pale tomentum, in ample terminal or axillary wide-branched panicles clothed with orange-colored pubescence; sepals 5, ovate, rounded at apex, ciliate on the margins, puberulous, persistent; petals 5, white, ovate, rounded at apex, short-unguiculate, alternate with and rather longer and narrower than the sepals; disk annular, fleshy, irregularly 5-lobed, puberulous; stamens 7 or 8, inserted on the disk, as long as the petals in the staminate flower, much shorter in the pistillate flower; filaments filiform, glabrous, anthers oblong, with a broad connective, rudimentary in the staminate flower; ovary sessile on the disk, conic, pubescent, 2-celled, contracted into a short thick style, rudimentary in the staminate flower, stigma large, declinate, obtuse; ovules 2 in each cell, suspended from the summit of the inner angle, collateral, anatropous, raphe ventral; micropyle superior. Fruit a nearly spherical 1-seeded berry containing the rudiment of the second cell and tipped with the short remnant of the style, surrounded at base by the persistent reflexed sepals; flesh becoming thick, dark purple, and juicy at maturity. Seed short-oblong to subglobose, solitary, suspended; seed-coat thin, coriaceous, orange-brown and lustrous; embryo subglobose, filling the cavity of the seed; cotyledons fleshy, plano-convex, puberulous; radicle superior, very short, uncinate, turned toward the small hilum and inclosed in a lateral cavity of the seed-coat.

The genus is represented by a single West Indian species.

The generic name is from ἐξωθέω, in allusion to its removal from a related genus.

1. Exothea paniculata Radlk. Ironwood. Ink Wood.

Leaves appearing in April, on stout grooved petioles $\frac{1}{2}'$–$1'$ in length; leaflets $4'$–$5'$ long and $1\frac{1}{2}'$–$2'$ wide. **Flowers** opening in Florida in April, $\frac{1}{4}'$ across when expanded, the staminate and pistillate on separate plants. **Fruit** fully grown by the end of June and then $\frac{1}{2}'$–$\frac{5}{8}'$

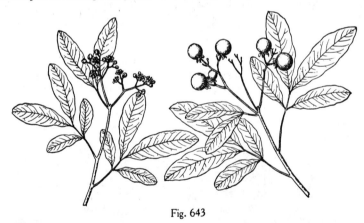

Fig. 643

long, and dull orange color, remaining on the branches during the summer, ripening in the autumn; seeds $\frac{1}{4}'$–$\frac{3}{8}'$ in diameter.

A tree, sometimes 40°–50° high, with a trunk $12'$–$15'$ in diameter, slender upright branchlets orange-brown when they first appear, becoming reddish brown in their second year and thickly covered by small white lenticels. **Bark** of the trunk $\frac{1}{8}'$–$\frac{1}{4}'$ thick, the bright red surface separating into large scales. **Wood** very hard and heavy, strong, close-grained, bright red-brown, with lighter colored sapwood of 10–12 layers of annual growth; valued for piles and also used in Florida in boatbuilding, for the handles of tools, and many small articles.

Distribution. Florida, Mosquito Inlet on the east coast to the shores of Bay Biscayne and on the Everglade Keys, Dade County, and on the southern keys; on the Bahamas, on many of the Antilles, and in Guatemala; on the Florida Keys generally distributed, but not common.

3. HYPELATE P. Br.

A glabrous tree or shrub, with smooth bark and slender terete branchlets. Leaves long-petioled, the petioles sometimes narrow-winged, 3-foliolate, the terminal leaflet rather larger than the others, persistent; leaflets sessile, obovate, rounded or rarely acute or emarginate at apex, entire, with thickened revolute margins and a prominent midrib, coriaceous, feather-veined, the veins arcuate and connected near the margins, dark green and lustrous on the upper surface, bright green on the lower surface. Flowers regular, polygamo-monœcious, minute, on slender pedicels from the axils of minute deciduous bracts, in few-flowered long-stemmed wide-branched terminal or axillary panicles; calyx 5-lobed, the lobes ovate, rounded at apex, slightly puberulous on the outer surface, ciliate on the margins, deciduous by a circumscissile line, petals 5, rather longer than the calyx-lobes; rounded, spreading, ciliate on the margins, white; stamens 7 or 8, inserted on the lobes of the annular fleshy disk; filaments filiform, as long as the petals in the staminate flower, much shorter in the pistillate flower; anthers oblong, attached on the back near the bottom, the cells spreading from above downward; ovary sessile on the disk, slightly 3-lobed, 3-celled, contracted into a short stout style, rudimentary in the staminate flower; stigma large, declinate, obscurely 3-lobed; ovules 2 in each cell, borne on the middle of its inner angle, superposed, amphitropous, the upper ascending, with the micropyle inferior, the lower pendulous, with the micropyle superior. Fruit an ovoid black drupe crowned with the remnants of the persistent style and supported on the persistent base of the disk; flesh thin and fleshy; walls of the stone thick and crustaceous. Seed solitary by the abortion of the upper ovule, suspended, obovoid; seed-coat thin, slightly wrinkled; embryo conduplicate, filling the cavity of the seed; cotyledons thin, foliaceous, irregularly folded, incumbent on the long radicle.

The genus with a single species is distributed from southern Florida to the Bahamas, Cuba, Porto Rico, St. Martin, Anguilla and Jamaica.

Hypelate is the ancient name of the Butcher's Broom.

1. Hypelate trifoliata Sw. White Ironwood.

Leaves unfolding in June and persistent until their second season or longer; petioles stout, $1\frac{1}{2}'$–$2'$ in length, with narrow green wings; leaflets $1\frac{1}{2}'$–$2'$ long and $\frac{3}{4}'$–$1\frac{1}{4}'$ wide.

Fig. 644

Flowers appearing in Florida in June, rather less than $\frac{1}{8}'$ in diameter, in few-flowered panicles $3'$–$4'$ long, on a slender peduncle, the staminate and pistillate in separate panicles on the same tree. **Fruit** ripening in September, $\frac{3}{4}'$ long, with a sweet rather agreeable flavor.

A tree, sometimes 35°–40° high, with a trunk occasionally 18′–20′ in diameter, and branchlets pale green when they first appear, becoming gray during their first season and bright red-brown the following year; generally much smaller. **Bark** of the trunk rarely $\frac{1}{8}'$ thick, marked by shallow depressions and numerous minute lenticels. **Wood** very heavy, hard, close-grained, rich dark brown, with thin darker colored sapwood of 4 or 5 layers of annual growth; very durable in contact with the soil and valued in Florida for posts; also used in shipbuilding and for the handles of tools.

Distribution. Southern Florida, Upper Metacombe, Umbrella and Windley's Keys; rare.

4. UNGNADIA Endl.

A tree or shrub, with thin pale gray fissured bark, slender terete slightly zigzag branchlets, without a terminal bud, marked by large conspicuous obcordate leaf-scars, small obtuse nearly globose winter-buds covered with numerous chestnut-brown imbricated scales, and thick fleshy roots. Leaves long-petioled, 5 or 7 or rarely 3-foliolate, deciduous; leaflets ovate-lanceolate, acuminate, rounded or cuneate, and often oblique at base, irregularly crenulate-serrate, coated when they first appear on the lower surface like the petiole with dense pale tomentum, and pilose above, glabrous at maturity with the exception of a few hairs on the lower surface along the principal veins, pinnately veined, reticulate-venulose, the terminal leaflet long-petiolulate, the others short-petiolulate to subsessile. Flowers irregular, polygamous, in small pubescent fascicles or corymbs appearing just before or with the leaves from the axils of those of the previous year, usually from separate buds, or occasionally from the base of leafy branches; calyx 5-lobed, hypogynous, the lobes oblong-lanceolate, somewhat united irregularly at base only, deciduous; petals 4 by the suppression of the anterior one, or 5 and then alternate with the lobes of the calyx, hypogynous on the margin of a thickened truncate torus, unguiculate, bright rose color, deciduous, the claw as long as the lobes of the calyx, nearly erect, clothed with tomentum, especially on the inner surface, conspicuously appendaged at the summit with a fimbricated crest of short fleshy tufted hairs, the blade obovate, spreading, often erose-crenulate; disk unilateral, oblique, tongue-shaped, surrounding and connate with the base of the stipe of the ovary; stamens 7–10, usually 8 or 9, inserted on the oblique edge of the disk, much exserted and unequal, the anterior ones shorter than the others, equal or almost so and shorter than the petals in the pistillate flower; filaments filiform; anthers oblong, attached near the base; ovary ovoid, 3-celled, pilose, raised on a long stipe, rudimentary in the staminate flower; style subulate, filiform, elongated, slightly curved upward; stigma minute, terminal; ovules 2, borne on the inner angle of the cell near its middle, ascending, the micropyle inferior. Fruit a coriaceous 3-celled loculicidally 3-valved broad-ovoid capsule, conspicuously stipitate, crowned with the remnants of the style, rugosely roughened and dark reddish brown, loculicidally 3-valved, the valves somewhat cordate, bearing the dissepiment on the middle. Seed generally solitary by abortion, almost globose; seed-coat coriaceous, very smooth and shining, dark chestnut-brown or almost black; hilum broad; tegmen thin; embryo filling the cavity of the seed; cotyledons thick and fleshy, nearly hemispheric, conferruminate, incumbent on the short conic descending radicle turned toward the hilum, remaining below ground in germination.

Ungnadia with a single species is confined to Texas, New Mexico, and northern Mexico. The name is in honor of Baron Ferdinand von Ungnad, Ambassador of the Emperor Rudolph II. at the Ottoman Porte who sent seeds of the Horsechestnut-tree from Constantinople to Vienna in the middle of the sixteenth century.

1. Ungnadia speciosa Endl. Spanish Buckeye.

Leaves appearing from March to April with or just after the flowers, 6′–12′ long, with a petiole 2′–6′ in length, rather coriaceous leaflets, dark green and lustrous on the upper sur-

face and pale and rugose on the lower surface, 3′–5′ long and 1½′–2′ wide, the terminal leaflet on a petiolule ¼′–1′ in length. **Flowers** 1′ across when expanded, in crowded clusters
1½′–2′ long. **Fruit** 2′ broad, opening in October, the empty pods often remaining on the
branches until the appearance of the flowers the following year; seeds ½′–⅝′ in diameter.

A tree, occasionally 25°–30° high, with a trunk 6′–8′ in diameter, dividing at some distance from the ground into a number of small upright branches, and branchlets light
orange-brown and covered during their first season with short fine pubescence, and pale
brown tinged with red, glabrous and marked by scattered lenticels in their second year;
more often a shrub, with numerous stems. **Winter-buds** about ⅛′ in diameter. **Bark** of

Fig. 645

the trunk rarely more than ¼′ thick, light gray and broken by numerous shallow reticulated
fissures. **Wood** heavy, close-grained, rather soft and brittle, red tinged with brown, with
lighter colored sapwood. The sweet seeds possess powerful emetic properties and are
reputed to be poisonous.

Distribution. Borders of streams, river-bottoms and limestone hills, and westward on
the sides of mountain cañons; valley of the Trinity River, Dallas County and of the lower
Brazos River, Texas, to the mountains of southeastern New Mexico, and southward into
Mexico; most common and of its largest size forty to fifty miles from the Texas coast west
of the Colorado River.

Occasionally cultivated as an ornamental plant in the southern United States.

XXXVIII. RHAMNACEÆ.

Trees or shrubs, with scaly or naked buds, watery bitter astringent juice, simple leaves,
and minute deciduous stipules (*persistent in Krugiodendron*). Flowers small, mostly greenish, perfect (*polygamo-diœcious in one species of Rhamnus*); calyx 4–5-lobed, the lobes valvate in the bud; petals 4–5, inserted on the calyx near the margin of the conspicuous disk
lining the short calyx-tube, and infolding the stamens, or 0; stamens as many as and alternate with the calyx-lobes, free, inserted at or below the margins of the disk; filaments
slender, subulate; anthers introrse, versatile, 2-celled, the cells opening longitudinally;
pistils of 2–3 united carpels; ovary 2–3-, or rarely 1-celled by abortion, partly immersed in
the disk; style terminal; stigma 2–4-lobed; ovules 1 in each cell, erect, anatropous; raphe
ventral; micropyle inferior. Fruit drupaceous, supported on the tube of the calyx and bearing the remnants of the style. Seed usually with scanty oily albumen; embryo with broad
cotyledons; radicle inferior, next the hilum.

CONSPECTUS OF THE ARBORESCENT GENERA OF THE UNITED STATES.

Fruit more or less fleshy.
  Fruit with a single stone; petals 0.
    Sepals without crests.
      Leaves alternate; branches spinescent.   **1. Condalia.**
      Leaves nearly opposite; branches not spinescent.   **2. Reynosia.**
    Sepals crested; leaves mostly opposite.   **3. Krugiodendron.**
  Fruit with 2 or 3 nutlets; petals 4 or 5, or 0; leaves alternate. **4. Rhamnus.**
Fruit crustaceous, 3-lobed, separating into 3 longitudinally 2-valved nutlets.
  Sepals inflexed; petals narrowed into a long slender claw. **5. Ceanothus.**
  Sepals spreading; petals sessile.   **6. Colubrina.**

1. CONDALIA Cav.

Trees or shrubs, with rigid spinescent branches and minute scaly buds. Leaves alternate, subsessile, obovate or oblong, entire, feather-veined. Flowers axillary, solitary or fascicled, greenish white, on short pedicels; calyx with a short broad-obconic tube and a 5-lobed limb, the lobes ovate, acute, membranaceous, spreading and persistent; disk fleshy, flat, slightly 5-angled, surrounding the free base of the ovary; petals 0; stamens 5, inserted on the free margin of the disk between the lobes of the calyx; filaments incurved, shorter than the calyx-lobes; ovary 1-celled, conic, gradually narrowed into a short thick style; stigma 3-lobed; ovule ascending from the base of the cell. Fruit ovoid or subglobose; flesh thin; stone thick-walled, crustaceous. Seed compressed; seed-coat thin and smooth; cotyledons oval, flat.

Condalia with nine or ten species is confined to the New World and is distributed from western Texas and southern California to Brazil and Argentina. Of the six species found within the territory of the United States one is a small tree.

The generic name commemorates that of Antonio Condal, a Spanish physician of the eighteenth century sent to South America on a scientific mission in 1754.

1. Condalia obovata Hook. Purple Haw. Log Wood.

Leaves often fascicled on short spinescent lateral branchlets, spatulate to oblong-cuneate, mucronate, when they first appear pubescent, especially on the lower surface, at

Fig. 646

maturity glabrous, rather thin, pale yellow-green, $1'-1\frac{1}{2}'$ long, and about $\frac{1}{3}'$ wide, with a conspicuous midrib and usually 3 pairs of prominent primary veins; unfolding in May and

June and falling irregularly during the winter.   **Flowers** in 2-4-flowered short-stemmed fascicles, on branchlets of the year.   **Fruit** ripening irregularly during the summer, $\frac{1}{4}'$ long, dark blue or black, with a sweet pleasant flavor.

A tree, sometimes 30° high, with a trunk 6′-8′ in diameter, erect rigid zigzag branchlets terminating in a stout spine and covered at first with soft velvety pubescence, becoming glabrous before the end of their first season, pale red-brown and often covered with thin scales; more often a shrub.   **Bark** of the trunk about $\frac{1}{8}'$ thick, divided into flat shallow ridges, the dark brown surface tinged with red separating into thin scales.   **Wood** very heavy, hard, close-grained, light red, with light yellow sapwood of 7-8 layers of annual growth; burning with an intense heat and valued as fuel.

Distribution.   Southwestern Texas from Jackson County (Vanderbilt) and Corpus Christi, Nueces County, to the Rio Grande and to Comal and Valverde Counties; in northeastern Mexico; of tree-like habit and of its largest size on the high sandy banks of the lower Rio Grande and its tributaries; often covering large areas with dense impenetrable chaparral.

2. REYNOSIA Griseb.

Trees or shrubs, with rigid unarmed terete branches, and scaly buds.   Leaves mostly opposite, entire, coriaceous, short-petiolate, reticulate-veined, persistent.   Flowers minute, on stout pedicels bibracteolate near the base and two or three times longer than the flower, in small axillary sessile umbels; calyx persistent, 5-lobed, the lobes deltoid or ovate, acute or acuminate, spreading, petaloid, deciduous; disk fleshy; petals 0; stamens 5, inserted on the margin of the disk, rather shorter than the calyx-lobes; filaments incurved; anthers oval; ovary free from the disk, almost superior, conic, 2-3-celled, contracted into a short erect thick style; stigma 2-3-lobed.   Fruit drupaceous; flesh thin; stone crustaceo-membranaceous.   Seed ovoid or subglobose; seed-coat very thin, conspicuously rugose and tuberculate; embryo axile in copious subcorneous ruminate albumen; cotyledons oblong.

Reynosia is distributed from southern Florida and the Bahama Islands to the Antilles. Four species are recognized; of these, one, a small tree, extends into southern Florida.

The generic name is in honor of Alvaro Reynoso (1830-1888), the distinguished Cuban chemist and writer on agriculture and scientific subjects.

1. Reynosia septentrionalis Urb.   Red Ironwood.   Darling Plum.

Leaves oblong to ovate or obovate, or sometimes nearly orbicular, rounded, truncate or

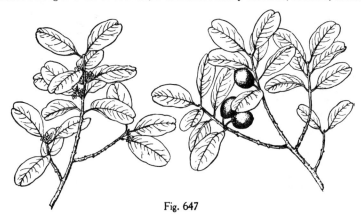

Fig. 647

frequently emarginate and usually minutely apiculate at apex, gradually narrowed at base into a short broad petiole, very thick and coriaceous, dark green on the upper, rather paler or often rufous on the lower surface, $1'-1\frac{1}{2}'$ long and $\frac{1}{2}'$ broad, with thickened revolute margins, a stout broad midrib, about five pairs of primary veins spreading nearly at right angles, and numerous reticulate veinlets; unfolding in April and remaining on the branches for one and sometimes for two years. **Flowers** yellowish green appearing in May, $\frac{1}{12}'$ long; sepals ovate, acute. **Fruit** ripening in Florida in November or frequently not until the following spring, short-obovoid, $\frac{1}{2}'$ long, purple or nearly black, edible, with an agreeable flavor.

A tree, $20°-25°$ high, with a trunk $6'-8'$ in diameter, stout terete rigid branchlets slightly puberulous when they first appear, soon becoming glabrous and gray faintly tinged with red, growing darker in their second season, then often covered by small tubercles and marked by the prominent elevated leaf-scars. **Winter-buds** minute, chestnut-brown. **Bark** of the trunk $\frac{1}{16}'-\frac{1}{8}'$ thick, dark-red-brown, and divided into large plate-like scales. **Wood** heavy, exceedingly hard, strong, close-grained, rich dark brown, with light brown sapwood of 15–20 layers of annual growth.

Distribution. Florida, coast and islands from the Marquesas group to the shores of Bay Biscayne and the Everglade Keys, Dade County; common and generally distributed; on the Bahama Islands.

3. KRUGIODENDRON Urb.

A small tree or shrub, with slender unarmed terete branches roughened by numerous small lenticels, and minute scaly buds. Leaves opposite or obliquely opposite, or sometimes alternate on lower branches, ovate or oval, often emarginate, coriaceous, entire, short-petiolate, feather-veined, persistent; stipules acuminate, persistent. Flowers greenish yellow, on short slender pedicels, in axillary simple or dichotomously branched cymes; calyx broad-obconic, 5-lobed, the lobes triangular, acute, erect or spreading, conspicuously crested on the inner surface, deciduous; disk annular, broad, fleshy, 5-lobed, surrounding the base of the ovary; petals 0; stamens 5, inserted under the margin of the disk; anthers ovoid or ovoid-orbicular, obtuse; ovary conic, imperfectly 2-celled; styles short and thick, united nearly to the apex, the branches spreading and stigmatic on the inner face; ovule ascending from the base of the cell. Fruit 1-seeded, oval or ovoid; flesh thin and black; wall of the stone thin and bony. Seed ellipsoid, compressed, without albumen; seed-coat membranaceous; embryo filling the cavity of the seed; cotyledons thick and fleshy, obovate or elliptic.

Krugiodendron, with a single species, is confined to southern Florida and the West Indies. The generic name is in honor of Leopold Krug (1833–1898), a student of the flora of the Antilles.

1. Krugiodendron ferreum Urb. Black Ironwood.

Leaves bright green and lustrous above, pale yellow-green below, glabrous with the exception of a few scattered hairs on the upper surface and on the petiole, $1'-1\frac{1}{2}'$ long and $\frac{3}{4}'-1'$ wide, with entire or slightly undulate margins; persistent for two or three years; petioles stout, $\frac{1}{4}'$ in length. **Flowers** on bibracteolate pedicels $\frac{1}{4}'$ long, in 3–5-flowered cymes on peduncles sometimes $\frac{1}{2}'$ in length, usually much shorter and often branched near the apex, on branchlets of the year; calyx about $\frac{1}{16}'$ long. **Fruit** generally solitary, $\frac{1}{3}'$ in length, on a stem $\frac{1}{3}'-\frac{1}{2}'$ long.

A tree, sometimes $30°$ high, with a trunk $8'-10'$ in diameter, and slender branchlets at first green and covered with dense velvety pubescence, becoming glabrous in their second year, and then gray faintly tinged with red and roughened by small crowded lenticels; generally much smaller and more often shrubby than arborescent. **Bark** of the trunk about $\frac{1}{4}'$ thick and divided into prominent rounded longitudinal ridges broken on the surface into short thick light gray scales. **Wood** exceedingly heavy, hard, strong, close-grained, brittle, rich orange-brown, with thin lighter colored sapwood.

Distribution. Florida, Cape Canaveral on the east coast to the shores of Bay Biscayne and on the Everglade Keys, Dade County, near Cape Sable, and on the southern keys; one of the commonest of the small trees of the region; on the Bahama Islands and on several of the Antilles.

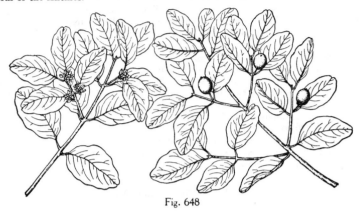

Fig. 648

4. RHAMNUS L.

Trees or shrubs, with terete often spinescent branches, without a terminal bud, scaly or naked axillary buds and acrid bitter bark. Leaves alternate or rarely obliquely opposite, conduplicate in the bud, petiolate, feather-veined, entire or dentate, stipulate. Flowers perfect or polygamo-diœcious, in axillary simple or compound racemes or fascicled cymes; calyx campanulate, 4-5-lobed, the lobes triangular-ovate, erect or spreading, keeled on the inner surface, deciduous; disk thin below, more or less thickened above; petals 5, inserted on the margin of the disk, ovate, unguiculate, emarginate, infolded round the stamens, deciduous, or 0; stamens 4 or 5; filaments very short; anthers oblong-ovoid or sagittate, rudimentary and sterile in the pistillate flower; ovary free, ovoid, included in the tube of the calyx, 2-4-celled, rudimentary in the staminate flower; styles united below, with spreading stigmatic lobes or terminating in a 2-3-lobed obtuse stigma; ovule erect from the base of the cell.   Fruit drupaceous, oblong or spherical; flesh thick and succulent, inclosing 2-4 separable cartilaginous 1-seeded nutlets.   Seeds erect, obovoid, grooved longitudinally on the back, with a cartilaginous seed-coat, the raphe in the groove, or convex on the back, with a membranaceous seed-coat, the raphe lateral next to one margin of the cotyledons; embryo large, surrounded by thin fleshy albumen; cotyledons oval, foliaceous, with revolute margins, or flat and fleshy.

Rhamnus with about sixty species is widely distributed in nearly all the temperate and in many of the tropical parts of the world with the exception of Australasia and the islands of the Pacific Ocean. Of the five species indigenous to the United States three attain the size of small trees. The fruit and bark of Rhamnus are drastic, and yield yellow and green dyes. The European *Rhamnus cathartica* L., the Buckthorn, has long been used as a hedge plant in northern Europe, and in eastern North America, where it has now become sparingly naturalized.

The generic name is from ῥάμνος, the classical name of the Buckthorn.

CONSPECTUS OF THE NORTH AMERICAN ARBORESCENT SPECIES.

Flowers polygamo-diœcious, in sessile umbels; calyx 4-lobed; petals 0; anthers oblong-ovoid; lobes of the stigma elongated, spreading; fruit red; seed grooved on the back; seed-coat cartilaginous; leaves often sharply toothed, persistent; winter-buds scaly.

1. **R. crocea** (G).

Flowers perfect, in pedunculate umbels; calyx 5-lobed; petals 5; anthers sagittate; lobes of the stigma short and obtuse; fruit black; seed rounded on the back; seed-coat membranaceous; leaves deciduous; winter-buds naked.

Peduncles shorter than the petioles.   2. R. caroliniana (C).
Peduncles longer than the petioles.   3. R. Purshiana (B, G).

1. Rhamnus crocea Nutt.

Leaves persistent, often in fascicles, elliptic, broad-ovate to suborbicular, rounded and often apiculate at apex, glandular-denticulate with minute teeth, coriaceous, yellow-green and lustrous on the upper surface, pale and frequently bronzed or copper color on the lower surface, glabrous or often puberulous while young, with a prominent midrib and slender primary veins, $\frac{1}{4}$'–$\frac{3}{4}$' long; petioles short and stout; stipules minute, acuminate. Flowers polygamo-diœcious, on slender often puberulous pedicels, in small clusters from the axils of the leaves or of small lanceolate persistent bracts on shoots of the year; calyx 4-lobed, with acuminate lobes, about $\frac{1}{8}$' long; petals 0; stamens rather shorter than the calyx, with short stout incurved filaments and large ovoid anthers, minute and rudimentary in the pistillate flower; ovary ovoid, contracted into a long slender style divided above the middle into two wide-spreading acuminate stigmatic lobes, rudimentary in the staminate flower. Fruit red, obovoid, slightly grooved or lobed at maturity, $\frac{1}{4}$' long, with thin dry flesh and 1–3 nutlets; seed broad-ovoid, pointed at apex, deeply grooved on the back and $\frac{1}{8}$' long, with a thin membranaceous pale chestnut-colored coat.

A shrub, 6'–3° high, with slender rigid often spinescent branchlets forming thickets.

Distribution. Coast mountains of central and southern California. Passing into

Rhamnus crocea var. ilicifolia Greene.

Leaves oval or orbicular, spinulose-dentate, often golden beneath and 1'–1$\frac{1}{2}$' long and $\frac{3}{4}$'–1' wide. Flowers with 4 or occasionally 5 calyx-lobes and stamens.

A tree, occasionally 25° high, with a trunk 6'–8' in diameter, stout spreading branches, and slender branchlets yellow-green and puberulous or glabrate when they first appear, be-

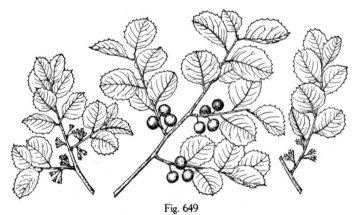

Fig. 649

coming dark red or reddish brown and glabrous in their second season. Winter-buds obtuse, barely more than $\frac{1}{16}$' long, with small puberulous apiculate imbricated scales ciliate on the margins. Bark of the trunk usually from $\frac{1}{16}$'–$\frac{1}{8}$' thick, the dark gray surface slightly roughened by minute tubercles.

Distribution. California, valley of the Sacramento River southward along the western slopes of the Sierra Nevada, and on the coast ranges and southern mountains to San Diego

County; Arizona, Oak Creek and Sycamore Cañons, near Flagstaff, Coconino County, (*P. Lowell*), Copper Cañon, west of Camp Verde, Yavapai County, and on the Pinal and Santa Catalina Mountains.

Passing into

Rhamnus crocea var. insularis Sarg.

A form with larger less prominently toothed leaves sometimes 3' long and 1½' wide, rather larger flowers, with shorter and broader calyx-lobes a less deeply divided style,

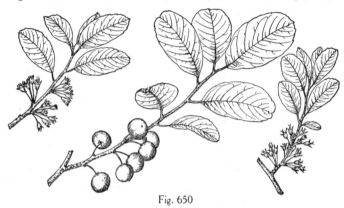

Fig. 650

and larger fruits. A tree often growing to the height of 25°–30°, flowering later than the var. *ilicifolia,* and not uncommon on the islands of the Santa Barbara group and on the mountains of the adjacent mainland. A form (f. *pilosa* Trel.) with narrow revolute leaves densely pilose throughout, occurs in the Santa Maria valley of the mountains near San Diego.

2. Rhamnus caroliniana Walt.   Indian Cherry.

Leaves deciduous, elliptic-oblong or broad-elliptic, acute or acuminate, cuneate or somewhat rounded at base, remotely and obscurely serrate, or crenulate, densely coated when they unfold with rusty brown tomentum, and at maturity thin, dark yellow-green above, paler below, glabrous or somewhat hairy on the lower surface, 2'–6' long and 1' to nearly 2' wide, with a prominent yellow midrib and about 6 pairs of conspicuous yellow primary veins; turning yellow in the autumn before falling; petioles slender, pubescent, ½' to nearly 1' in length; stipules nearly triangular.   **Flowers** appearing from April to June when the leaves are almost fully grown, on slender pedicels about ¼' long, in few-flowered pubescent umbels, on peduncles varying from ⅛'–½' in length; calyx 5-lobed, with a narrow turbinate tube and triangular lobes; petals 5, broad-ovate, deeply notched at apex and folded round the short stamens; ovary contracted into a long columnar style terminating in a slightly 3-lobed stigma.   **Fruit** ripening in September and sometimes remaining on the branches until the beginning of winter, globose, ⅓' in diameter, black, with thin sweet rather dry flesh and 2–4 nutlets: **seeds** obtuse at apex, rounded on the back, reddish brown, about ⅕' long.

A tree, 30°–40° high, with a trunk 6'–8' in diameter, small spreading unarmed branches, and slender branchlets light red-brown and puberulent or covered with a glaucous bloom when they first appear, becoming slightly angled, gray, and glabrous and marked during their second season by the small horizontal oval leaf-scars: more often a tall shrub, with numerous stems 15°–20° high.   **Winter-buds** naked, hoary-tomentose.   **Bark** of the trunk about ⅛' thick, slightly furrowed, ashy gray and often marked by large black blotches.   **Wood** rather hard, light, close-grained. not strong, light brown, with lighter colored sapwood of 5 or 6 layers of annual growth.

Distribution. Borders of streams on rich bottom-lands, and on limestone ridges; Virginia to western Florida and westward through the valley of the Ohio River to eastern

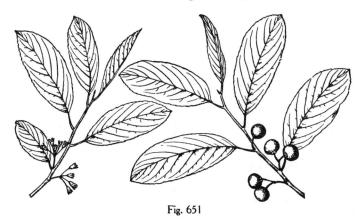

Fig. 651

Kansas, the valley of the Washita River, Oklahoma (Carter County), and to Kendall, Kerr and Uvalde Counties, western Texas; occasionally tree-like in western Florida and Mississippi, and of its largest size only in southern Arkansas and the adjacent portions of Texas; very abundant on the limestone barrens of central Kentucky and Tennessee.

3. Rhamnus Purshiana DC. Bearberry. Coffee-tree.

Leaves deciduous, broad-elliptic, obtuse or bluntly pointed at apex, rounded or slightly cordate at base, finely serrate, or often nearly entire, with undulate margins, thin, villose with short hairs on the lower surface and on the veins above, $1\frac{1}{2}'-7'$ long, $1\frac{1}{2}'-2'$ wide, conspicuously netted-veined, with a broad and prominent midrib and primary veins; turning pale yellow late in the autumn before falling; petioles stout, often pubescent, $\frac{1}{2}'-1'$ in length; stipules membranaceous, acuminate. **Flowers** on slender pubescent pedicels $\frac{1}{4}'-1'$ long, in axillary cymes on slender pubescent peduncles $\frac{1}{2}'-1'$ in length on shoots of the year; calyx nearly campanulate, with 5 spreading acuminate lobes; petals 5, minute, ovate, deeply notched at apex, and folded round the short stamens; stigma 2 or 3-lobed. **Fruit** globose or broad-obovoid, black, $\frac{1}{3}'-\frac{1}{2}'$ in diameter, slightly or not at all lobed, with thin rather juicy flesh, and 2 or 3 obovoid nutlets usually $\frac{1}{3}'$ long, rounded on the back, flattened on the inner surface, with 2 bony tooth-like enlargements at base, 1 on each side of the large scar of the hilum, and a thin gray or pale yellow-green shell; **seeds** obtuse at apex, rounded on the back; seed-coat thin and papery, yellow-brown on the outer surface, bright orange color on the inner surface like the cotyledons.

A tree, $35°-40°$ high, with a slender trunk often $18'-20'$ in diameter, separating $10°-15°$ from the ground into numerous stout upright or sometimes nearly horizontal branches, and slender branchlets coated at first with fine soft pubescence, pale yellow-green or reddish brown, and pubescent, glabrous, or covered with scattered hairs in their second season and then marked by the elevated oval horizontal leaf-scars; often shrubby and occasionally prostrate. **Winter-buds** naked, hoary-tomentose. **Bark** of the trunk rarely more than $\frac{1}{4}'$ thick, dark brown to light brown or gray tinged with red, broken on the surface into short thin scales. **Wood** light, soft, not strong, brown tinged with red, with thin lighter colored sapwood. The bark possesses the drastic properties peculiar to that of other species of the genus, and is a popular domestic remedy in Oregon and California, and under the name of Cascara Sagrada has been admitted into the American materia medica.

Distribution. Rich bottom-lands and the sides of cañons, usually in coniferous forests; shores of Puget Sound eastward along the mountain ranges of northern Washington to the Bitter Root Mountains of Idaho and the shores of Flat Head Lake, Montana, and southward to central California; Arizona, southern slope of the Grand Cañon of the Colorado

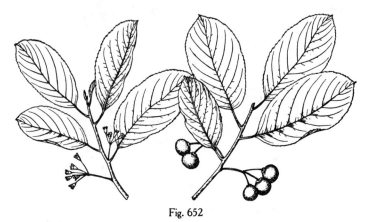

Fig. 652

River, Coconino County (*A. Rehder*), Cave Creek Cañon, Chiricahua Mountains, Cochise County (*J. W. Toumey*).

Occasionally cultivated in the gardens of western Europe and of the eastern United States.

5. CEANOTHUS L.

Small trees or shrubs, with slender terete branches, without a terminal bud, and small scaly axillary buds. Leaves petiolate, 3-ribbed from the base, or pinnately veined, persistent in the arborescent species. Flowers on colored pedicels, in umbellate fascicles collected in dense or prolonged terminal or axillary thyrsoid cymes or panicles, blue or white; calyx colored, with a turbinate or hemispheric tube and 5 triangular membranaceous petaloid lobes; disk fleshy, thickened above; petals 5, inserted under the margin of the disk, unguiculate, wide-spreading, deciduous, the long claw infolded round the stamens; stamens 5, inserted with and opposite the petals, persistent, filaments spreading; ovary partly immersed in and more or less adnate to the disk, 3-celled, sometimes 3-angled, the angles often surmounted by a fleshy gland persistent on the fruit; styles short, united below; stigmas 3-lobed with spreading lobes; ovule erect from the base of the cell. Fruit 3-lobed, subglobose, with a thin outer coat, soon becoming dry, and separating into 3 crustaceous or cartilaginous longitudinally 2-valved nutlets. Seeds erect, obovoid, lenticellate, with a broad basal excrescence surrounding the hilum; seed-coat thin, crustaceous; albumen fleshy; embryo axile; cotyledons oval or obovate.

Ceanothus is confined to the temperate and warmer regions of North America, with about thirty species, mostly belonging to California. The leaves, bark, and roots are astringent and tonic. Of the species of the United States three are small trees.

The generic name is from κεάνωθος, the classical name of some spiny plant.

CONSPECTUS OF THE ARBORESCENT SPECIES OF THE UNITED STATES.

Branchlets not spinose, leaves 3-ribbed.
Leaves broad-ovate to elliptic, subcordate or rounded at base, pale and tomentose below.
1. **C. arboreus** (G).

Leaves elliptic, acute at base, glabrous except on the veins below.
                                                                  2. C. thyrsiflorus (G).
Branchlets spinose; leaves with a single midrib, mostly elliptic, rounded or subcordate at
    base, glabrous.   3. C. spinosus (G).

1. Ceanothus arboreus Greene.

Leaves broad-ovate or elliptic, acute, conspicuously glandular-crenate, dark green and
softly puberulent on the upper surface, pale and densely tomentose on the lower surface,
$2\frac{1}{2}'$–$4'$ long and $1'$–$2\frac{1}{2}'$ wide, with prominent veins; petioles stout, pubescent, $\frac{1}{2}'$–$1'$ in length;
stipules subulate from a broad triangular base, $\frac{1}{4}'$ long. **Flowers** pale blue opening in July
and August, on slender hairy pedicels $\frac{1}{2}'$–$1'$ long, from the axils of large scarious caducous
bracts, in ample compound densely hoary-pubescent thyrsoid clusters $3'$–$4'$ long and
$1\frac{1}{2}'$–$2'$ wide, on a leafy or naked axillary peduncle at the end of young branches. **Fruit**
black, $\frac{1}{4}'$ across.
    A round-headed tree, $20°$–$25°$ high, with a straight trunk $6'$–$10'$ in diameter, dividing
$4°$–$5°$ from the ground into many stout spreading branches, and slender slightly angled
pale brown branchlets covered with short dense tomentum, becoming in their second season

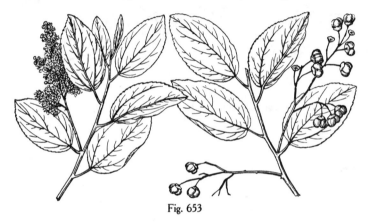

Fig. 653

terete, nearly glabrous, roughened with scattered lenticels and marked by large elevated
leaf-scars; often a shrub. **Bark** of the trunk dark brown, about $\frac{1}{8}'$ thick, and broken into
small square plates separating into thick scales.
    Distribution. Santa Catalina, Santa Cruz, and Santa Rosa Islands of the Santa Barbara
group off the coast of southern California; most abundant and of its largest size on the
northern slopes of Santa Cruz; on the other islands usually shrubby, with numerous slender
stems.

2. Ceanothus thyrsiflorus Eschs. Blue Myrtle. California Lilac.

Leaves oblong or oblong-ovate, minutely glandular-serrate, smooth and lustrous on the
upper surface and paler and slightly pubescent on the lower surface, especially along the 3
prominent ribs, $1'$–$1\frac{1}{2}'$ long and $\frac{1}{3}'$–$1'$ wide; petioles stout, $\frac{1}{3}'$–$\frac{1}{2}'$ in length; stipules membranaceous, acute. **Flowers** blue or white, appearing in early spring in small pedunculate
corymbs from the axils of minute deciduous bracts, and collected into slender rather loose
thyrsoid clusters $2'$–$3'$ long in the axils of upper leaves or of small scarious bracts, and
usually surmounted by the terminal leafy shoot of the branch. **Fruit** ripening from July
to December, black; **seeds** $\frac{1}{12}'$ long, smooth, dark brown or nearly black.
    A tree, occasionally $35°$ high, with a trunk $12'$–$14'$ in diameter, dividing $5°$–$6°$ from the

ground into many small wide-spreading branches, and conspicuously angled pale yellow-green branchlets slightly pubescent when they first appear, soon becoming glabrous; more often a tall or low shrub. **Bark** of the trunk thin, with a bright red-brown surface separating into thin narrow appressed scales. **Wood** close-grained, rather soft, light brown, with thin darker colored sapwood.

Distribution. Shady hillsides on the borders of the forest and often in the neighborhood of streams; coast mountains of California from Mendocino County to the valley of the San

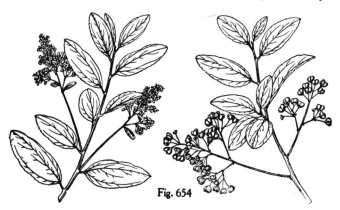

Fig. 654

Luis Rey River, San Diego County; of its largest size northward, and in the Redwood-forests of the Santa Cruz Mountains; southward often a low shrub, frequently flowering on the wind-swept shores of the ocean when only 1°–2° high.

3. Ceanothus spinosus Nutt. Lilac.

Leaves elliptic to oblong, full and rounded, apiculate or often slightly emarginate or gradually narrowed and pointed or rarely 3-lobed at apex, and rounded or cuneate at base, when

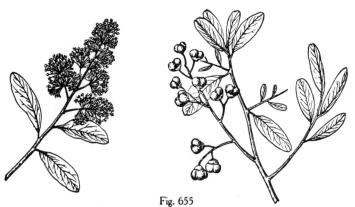

Fig. 655

they unfold villose-pubescent below along the stout midrib and obscure primary veins, soon glabrous, coriaceous, usually about 1′ long and ½′ wide; petioles stout, ⅛′–⅓′ in length, at first villose, becoming nearly glabrous; leaves on vigorous shoots sometimes ovate, conspicuously 3-nerved, irregularly serrate with incurved apiculate teeth, or coarsely dentate, and often $1\frac{1}{2}'$ long and $\frac{5}{8}'$ wide; stipules minute, acute. **Flowers** light or dark blue, very fragrant, opening from March until May, in lax corymbs from the axils of acute pubescent red caducous bracts on upper leafy branchlets of the year, the whole inflorescence forming an open thyrsus often $5'$–$6'$ long and $3'$–$4'$ thick, leafless toward the apex. **Fruit** depressed, obscurely lobed, crestless, black, $\frac{1}{4}'$–$\frac{1}{3}'$ in diameter.

A tree, 18°–20° high, with a trunk $5'$–$6'$ in diameter, upright branches forming a narrow open head, and slender divaricate angled branchlets pubescent or puberulous when they first appear, soon glabrous, bright green, ultimately reddish brown, frequently terminating in sharp leafless thorn-like points; more often shrubby. **Bark** of the trunk thin, red-brown, roughened by small closely appressed scales.

Distribution. California, common in mountain cañons near the coast of Santa Barbara, Ventura, and Los Angeles Counties; often forming a dense undergrowth in the forest, which it enlivens for many weeks in early spring by its large clusters of bright blue flowers.

6. COLUBRINA Brong.

Trees or shrubs, with terete branches and scaly buds. Leaves alternate, petiolate, pinnately veined or triple-veined from the base, often ferrugineo-tomentose on the lower surface, persistent. Flowers axillary, in contracted few-flowered cymes or fascicles, yellow or greenish yellow; calyx-tube hemispheric, persistent, 5-lobed, the lobes spreading, triangular-ovate, keeled on the inner surface, deciduous by a circumscissile line; disk fleshy, annular, 5-angled or indistinctly 5 or 10-lobed ; petals 5 yellow or white, inserted under the margin of the disk, shorter than the lobes of the calyx, cucullate, unguiculate, infolding the stamens; stamens 5, opposite to and inserted with the petals; filaments incurved; anthers ovoid; ovary surrounded by and confluent with the disk, 3-celled, subglobose, contracted into a slender 3-lobed style, the obtuse lobes stigmatic on the inner face; ovule erect, from the base of the cell. Fruit subglobose, 3-lobed, the outer coat thin and septicidally dehiscent into 3 1-seeded crustaceous nutlets 2-valved at apex. Seeds erect, broad-obovoid, compressed, 3-angled; seed-coat coriaceous, smooth and shining; embryo axile in thick fleshy albumen; cotyledons orbicular, flat or incurved, thin or fleshy.

Colubrina with about a dozen species is confined to the tropics, with the largest number of species in the New World. Of the four species found within the territory of the United States three are arborescent.

The generic name is from *coluber*, a serpent, probably on account of the peculiar twisting of the deep furrows on the stems of some of the species.

CONSPECTUS OF THE ARBORESCENT SPECIES OF THE UNITED STATES.

Leaves thin, elliptic, ovate or lanceolate, glabrous at maturity. 1. **C. reclinata** (D).
Leaves thick or coriaceous.
Leaves oblong to elliptic, rounded or acute at apex, densely soft-pubescent.
2. **C. cubensis** (D).
Leaves elliptic to ovate-lanceolate, bluntly pointed at apex, coriaceous, rusty-pubescent beneath. 3. **C. arborescens** (D).

1. Colubrina reclinata Brong. Naked Wood.

Leaves elliptic, ovate or lanceolate, usually contracted at apex into a blunt point, cuneate or somewhat rounded and furnished with 2 conspicuous marginal glands at base, and entire when they unfold in early summer thin, glabrous or finely puberulent below and along the principal veins, and at maturity thin, yellow-green, $2\frac{1}{2}'$–$3'$ long and $1\frac{1}{2}'$ to nearly $2'$ wide, with a stout midrib and arcuate primary veins; persistent until their second year; petioles slender, $\frac{1}{2}'$ in length. **Flowers** in cymes rather shorter than the petioles, on shoots of the year, pubescent, soon becoming glabrate. **Fruit** $\frac{1}{4}'$ in diameter and dark orange-red, ripening late in the autumn, on pedicels $\frac{1}{2}'$ in length; **seeds** light red-brown, $\frac{1}{8}'$ long.

A tree, 50°–60° high, with a trunk 3°–4° in diameter, divided by numerous irregular deep furrows multiplying and spreading in all directions, and branchlets slightly angled when they first appear, puberulent and reddish brown, soon becoming glabrate, and in their

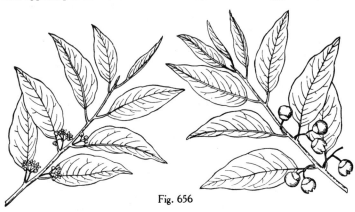

Fig. 656

second season nearly terete, gray or light brown, and marked by numerous small light-colored lenticels.   **Bark** of the trunk thin, orange-brown, exfoliating in large papery scales. **Wood** heavy, hard, very strong, dark brown tinged with yellow, with thin light yellow sap-wood of 8–10 layers of annual growth.

Distribution.   Florida, on Umbrella Key, the north end of Key Largo, and on some of the small keys south of Elliott's Key; of its largest size and forming a forest of considerable extent on Umbrella Key; on the Bahama Islands and on many of the Antilles.

2. Colubrina cubensis Brong.

Leaves oblong to elliptic, gradually narrowed and rounded or acute and apiculate at apex, rounded or cuneate at the often unsymmetric base, slightly crenulate-serrate with

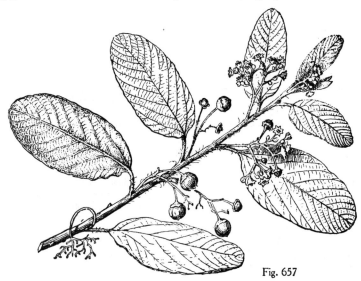

Fig. 657

broad rounded teeth, thick, dull dark green and soft-pubescent on the upper surface, pale
and pubescent on the lower surface, $3\frac{1}{2}'-5'$ long and $1\frac{1}{4}'-1\frac{1}{2}'$ wide, with a prominent pubescent yellow midrib and slender primary veins; petioles slender, yellow, densely pubescent,
$\frac{1}{4}'-\frac{1}{2}'$ in length; stipules linear-lanceolate, long-acuminate, pubescent, $\frac{1}{3}'$ in length. **Flowers**
minute on pedicels $\frac{1}{6}'$ long, from the axils of ovate acuminate villose caducous bracts, in
villose cymes on peduncles longer than the petioles; calyx densely pubescent, the lobes
triangular, ovate, acute, about as long as the yellow petals. **Fruit** globose, about $\frac{1}{3}'$ in diameter.

A tree in Florida from 20°–30° high, with a trunk $6'-8'$ in diameter (*teste J. K. Small*)
and slender light red-brown pubescent branchlets.

Distribution. Florida, hummocks of the Everglade Keys, Dade County; on the Bahama Islands and in Cuba and Hispaniola.

3. Colubrina arborescens Sarg.

Colubrina Colubrina Mills.

Leaves coriaceous, persistent, elliptic to ovate-lanceolate, gradually narrowed and
bluntly pointed at apex, narrowed and rounded or cuneate at base, entire, dark green,
glabrous and lustrous on the upper surface, pale and coated on the lower surface with thick
rusty pubescence and sometimes marked by conspicuous glands mostly at the end of small
veins, $2'-4\frac{1}{2}'$ long and $1\frac{1}{4}'-2\frac{1}{2}'$ wide, with a thick midrib; petioles stout, rusty-pubescent,
$\frac{1}{2}'-\frac{3}{4}'$ in length; stipules oblong, acuminate, rusty-pubescent, caducous. **Flowers** minute,
in axillary cymes shorter than the petioles, covered with persistent rusty pubescence and
generally produced on short axillary branches; petals white or nearly white. **Fruit** on a
stout rusty-pubescent pedicel, about $\frac{1}{2}'$ long, on a much thickened peduncle, obovoid to

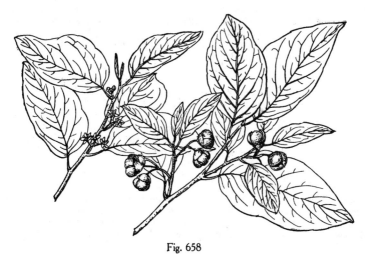

Fig. 658

subglobose, dark purple or nearly black, $\frac{5}{12}'$ in diameter; nutlets light yellow; **seed**
about $\frac{1}{6}'$ long.

A tree, sometimes 25° high, with a straight trunk $8'-12'$ in diameter, large erect branches
and stout branchlets densely rusty-pubescent when they first appear, and light gray, puberulous and marked by small dark lenticels in their second year; in Florida more often a shrub.

Distribution. Florida, on the Everglade and southern keys; on the Bahama Islands and
on several of the Antilles.

XXXIX. TILIACEÆ.

Trees, shrubs, or herbs, with alternate simple leaves, and free stipules. Flowers regular, perfect; sepals valvate in the bud, deciduous; corolla hypogynous; stamens numerous, with 2-celled anthers, the cells opening longitudinally; pistil compound; styles united into 1; stigma capitate. Fruit capsular or nut-like. Seeds with albumen; embryo with broad foliaceous cotyledons.

The Linden family with forty-four genera is chiefly tropical, with more representatives in the southern than in the northern hemisphere. Of the three North American genera only Tilia is arborescent.

1. TILIA L. Bass Wood. Linden.

Trees, with terete moderately stout branchlets, without a terminal bud, large compressed acute axillary buds, with numerous imbricated scales, those of the inner rank accrescent, mucilaginous juice, and tough fibrous inner bark. Leaves conduplicate in the bud, long-petiolate, 2-ranked, cordate or truncate at the oblique base, acute or acuminate, serrate, deciduous, their petioles in falling leaving large elevated horizontal leaf-scars displaying the ends of numerous fibro-vascular bundles; stipules ligulate, membranaceous, caducous. Flowers nectariferous, fragrant, on slender clavate pedicels, in axillary or terminal cymes, with minute caducous bracts at the base of the branches, their peduncle more or less connate with the axis of a large membranaceous light green ligulate often obovate persistent conspicuously reticulate-veined bract; sepals 5, distinct; petals 5, imbricated in the bud, alternate with the sepals, sometimes thickened and glandular at the narrow base, creamy white or yellow, deciduous; stamens inserted on a short hypogynous receptacle; filaments filiform, forked near the apex, collected into 5 clusters and united at base with each other and (in the American species) with a spatulate petaloid scale (staminodium) placed opposite each petal, the branches of the filament bearing oblong extrorse half anthers; ovary sessile, tomentose, 5-celled, the cells opposite the sepals; style erect, dilated at apex into 5 spreading stigmatic lobes; ovules 2 in each cell, ascending from the middle of its inner angle, semianatropous, the micropyle centripetal-inferior. Fruit nut-like, woody, subglobose to short-oblong or ovoid, sometimes ribbed, tomentose, 1-celled by the obliteration of the partitions, 1 or 2-seeded. Seeds obovoid, amphitropous, ascending; seed-coat cartilaginous, light reddish brown; embryo large, often curved, in fleshy albumen; cotyledons reniform or cordate, palmately 5-lobed, the margins irregularly involute or crumpled; radicle inferior.

Tilia with some thirty species is widely distributed in the temperate regions of the northern hemisphere with the exception of western America, central Asia, and the Himalayas. Tilia produces soft straight-grained pale-colored light wood, largely used for the interior finish of buildings, in cabinet-making, for the sounding-boards of pianos, wood-carving and wooden ware, and in the manufacture of paper. The tough inner bark is largely manufactured into mats, cords, fish-nets, coarse cloths, and shoes. Lime-flower oil, obtained by distilling the flowers of the European species, is used in perfumery. The flowers yield large quantities of nectar, and honey made near forests of Tilia is unsurpassed in flavor and delicacy. Many of the species are planted as shade and ornamental trees, and some of the European species are now common in the gardens and parks of the eastern United States.

CONSPECTUS OF THE SPECIES OF THE UNITED STATES.

Surface of the leaves glabrous at maturity.
    Leaves glabrous or almost glabrous when they unfold, coarsely serrate.
        Leaves furnished with conspicuous tufts of axillary hairs, their lower surface light
          green and lustrous; pedicels glabrous or nearly glabrous.   1. T. glabra (A).
        Leaves usually without tufts of axillary hairs, their lower surface not lustrous; pedicels
          densely hoary-tomentose.   2. T. nuda (C).

Leaves hoary-tomentose when they unfold.

Leaves soon glabrous.

Leaves coarsely serrate with stout teeth, their veinlets conspicuous; branchlets stout, bright red.　　　　　　　　　　　　　　　　　　　　　3. **T. venulosa** (A).

Leaves finely serrate with straight or incurved teeth, their veinlets less conspicuous; branchlets slender, pale reddish brown.　　　　　　　　4. **T. littoralis** (C).

Leaves crenately serrate, glaucescent on the lower surface.　　5. **T. crenoserrata** (C).

Leaves covered below early in the season with articulate hairs, becoming glabrous or nearly glabrous.

Leaves thin, coarsely serrate, green or glaucescent on the lower surface, with or without tufts of axillary hairs; summer shoots not pubescent.　　6. **T. floridana** (C).

Leaves subcoriaceous, finely serrate, bluish green and lustrous below early in the season; tufts of axillary hairs minute, usually wanting; summer shoots pubescent.　　　　　　　　　　　　　　　　　　　　　7. **T. Cocksii** (C).

Surface of the leaves pubescent below during the season.

Lower surface of the leaves covered with short gray firmly attached pubescence; tufts of axillary hairs not conspicuous.　　　　　　　　　　8. **T. neglecta** (A,C).

Lower surface of the leaves covered with articulate easily detached hairs.

Branchlets without straight hairs.

Leaves ovate, acuminate, usually obliquely truncate at base, glabrous above, their pubescence brownish or white.　　　　　　　　9. **T. caroliniana** (C).

Leaves oblong-ovate, cordate or obliquely cordate at base, pubescent above early in the season.　　　　　　　　　　　　　　　10. **T. texana** (C).

Leaves semiorbicular to broad-ovate, abruptly short-pointed, deeply and usually symmetrically cordate at base.　　　　　　　　　11. **T. phanera** (C).

Branchlets covered with straight hairs; leaves ovate, abruptly short-pointed, oblique and truncate at base.　　　　　　　　　　12. **T. lasioclada** (C).

Surface of the leaves tomentose below during the season with close firmly attached tomentum.

Tomentum white, gray, or brown; leaves usually glabrous on the upper surface; branchlets and winter-buds glabrous (*occasionally pubescent in varieties of 13*).

Branchlets slender; petioles not more than $1\frac{1}{2}'$ in length; leaves oblong-ovate, acuminate or abruptly pointed, oblique and truncate or cordate at base; tomentum on the leaves of upper branches often brown; flowers $\frac{1}{4}'-\frac{1}{3}'$ long. 13. **T. heterophylla** (A, C).

Branchlets stout; petioles up to $3'$ in length; leaves oblong-ovate, acuminate, obliquely truncate at base; tomentum always white; flowers $\frac{5}{12}'-\frac{1}{2}'$ long.

14. **T. monticola** (A).

Tomentum pale or brownish; leaves thickly covered above early in the season with fascicled hairs; branchlets tomentose; winter-buds pubescent. 15. **T. georgiana** (C).

1. Tilia glabra Vent.　Linden.　Bass Wood.

Tilia americana L.

Leaves broad-ovate, contracted at apex into a slender acuminate entire point, obliquely cordate or sometimes almost truncate at base, coarsely serrate with incurved glandular teeth, often slightly pubescent when they first appear soon glabrous with the exception of tufts of rusty brown hairs in the axils of the principal veins below, thick and firm, dark dull green on the upper surface, lighter, yellow-green and lustrous on the lower surface, $5'-6'$ long and $3'-4'$ wide; turning pale yellow in the autumn before falling; petioles slender, $1\frac{1}{2}'-2'$ in length.　**Flowers** $\frac{1}{2}'$ long, opening early in July on slender slightly angled pubescent pedicels, in few-flowered slender-branched glabrous cymes; peduncle slender, glabrous, the free portion $3\frac{1}{2}'-4'$ long, its bract rounded or pointed at apex, $4'-5'$ long, $1'-1\frac{1}{2}'$ wide, decurrent nearly to the base or to within $\frac{1}{2}'-1'$ of the base of the peduncle; sepals ovate, acuminate, densely hairy on the inner surface and slightly pubescent on the outer surface, a third shorter than the lanceolate petals; staminodia oblong-obovate, bluntly pointed at apex, a third shorter than the petals; ovary villose; style covered with rufous tomentum. **Fruit** short-oblong to oblong-obovoid, rounded or pointed at apex, $\frac{1}{3}'-\frac{1}{2}'$ long, and covered with short thick rufous tomentum.

A tree, usually 60°–70°, or sometimes 120°–130° high, with a tall trunk 3°–4° in diameter, small often pendulous branches forming a broad round-topped head, slender smooth gla-

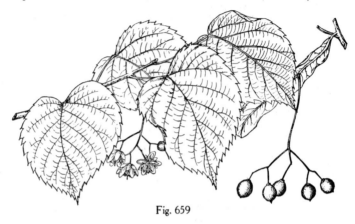

Fig. 659

brous light gray or light brown branchlets marked by numerous oblong dark lenticels, becoming darker in their second and dark gray or brown and conspicuously rugose in their third year. **Winter-buds** dark red, ovoid, about $\frac{1}{4}'$ long. **Bark** of the trunk about 1' thick, deeply furrowed, the light brown surface broken into small thin scales. **Wood** light brown faintly tinged with red, with thick hardly distinguishable sapwood of 55–65 layers of annual growth; employed in the manufacture of paper pulp, and under the name of white wood largely used in wooden ware, cheap furniture, the panels of carriages, and for the inner soles of shoes.

Distribution. Rich often moist soil, formerly often in nearly pure forests; northern New Brunswick to the eastern shores of Lake Superior, the southern shores of Lake Winnipeg and the valley of the Assiniboine River, and southward to Pennsylvania, Ohio, eastern Kentucky, southern Michigan, Indiana and Illinois, eastern Nebraska and northern Missouri.

Often cultivated as a shade and ornamental tree in the northeastern states, and occasionally in Europe.

2. Tilia nuda Sarg.

Leaves thin, ovate, abruptly pointed at apex, obliquely truncate or unsymmetrically cordate at base, and coarsely serrate with long slender straight or slightly curved conspicuously glandular teeth, as they unfold, dark red and sparingly pubescent on the midrib and veins, glabrous at the end of a few days, without or rarely with small axillary tufts, dark green on the upper surface, pale yellow-green or glaucous (var. *glaucescens* Sarg.) on the lower surface, $4'-4\frac{1}{2}'$ long and $2\frac{1}{2}'-3\frac{1}{2}'$ wide; petioles slender, glabrous, $2'-2\frac{1}{2}'$ in length. **Flowers** opening early in June, about $\frac{1}{3}'$ long, on hoary-tomentose pedicels, in broad usually 10 or 12, sometimes 30 or 40-flowered long-branched glabrous cymes; peduncle glabrous, the free portion $\frac{4}{5}'-1\frac{1}{4}'$ in length, its bract oblong, often slightly falcate, cuneate or rounded at base, rounded at apex, glabrous, $3'-4'$ long, $\frac{1}{2}'-1\frac{1}{4}'$ wide, decurrent nearly to the base of the peduncle; sepals acute, rusty-tomentose on the outer surface, glabrous on the inner surface; petals oblong-ovate, narrowed at the rounded apex; staminodia oblong-obovate rounded at the broad apex; style glabrous. **Fruit** ripening in September, subglobose to depressed-globose, covered with rusty tomentum, $\frac{1}{4}'-\frac{1}{3}'$ in diameter.

Usually a small tree with pale furrowed or sometimes checkered bark, small spreading branches forming a narrow round-topped head, and slender glabrous orange or red-brown branchlets. **Winter-buds** ovoid, obtusely pointed, dull red, glabrous, $\frac{1}{6}'-\frac{1}{5}'$ long.

Distribution. Central and southwestern Mississippi (Hinds and Adams Counties); Dallas County, Alabama; West Feliciana and Calcasieu Parishes, Louisiana, to the valley of the Brazos River, eastern Texas, and to Hempstead County (Fulton and McNab), southern Arkansas; the var. *glaucescens* with the type, and near Page, Le Flore County, Oklahoma; in wet woods subject to overflow at San Augustine, San Augustine County, Texas, a va-

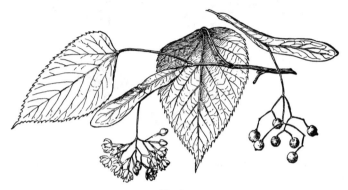

Fig. 660

riety (var. *brevipedunculata* Sarg.), differs from the type in the less coarsely serrate smaller leaves glaucescent below, in the shorter free portion of the peduncle of the inflorescence and its broader bract. A tree 25°–30° high, with slender glabrous dark red-brown branchlets.

3. Tilia venulosa Sarg.

Leaves broad-ovate, abruptly acuminate at apex, cordate or unsymmetrically cordate or obliquely truncate or cordate at base, coarsely serrate with gland-tipped teeth pointing forward, covered when they unfold with pale tomentum, soon becoming pubescent, and glabrous before the flowers open, dark yellow-green on the upper surface, paler on the lower surface, $4'-4\frac{3}{4}'$ long and broad, with a prominent pale yellow midrib slightly villose on the upper side near the base, and 9 or 10 pairs of remote primary veins without axillary tufts and connected by conspicuous cross veinlets; petioles stout, glabrous, $1\frac{3}{4}'-2'$ in length. **Flowers** opening early in July, $\frac{1}{3}'$ long, on slightly pubescent pedicels, in broad slender-branched nearly glabrous cymes; peduncle stout, glabrous, red, the free portion $1'-1\frac{1}{2}'$ in length, its bract oblong to slightly obovate, gradually narrowed and rounded at base, rounded at apex, glabrous on the upper surface, pubescent below on the midrib and veins, $3\frac{1}{2}'-6'$ long and $1\frac{1}{4}'-1\frac{1}{2}'$ wide, longer than the peduncle and decurrent nearly to its base or to within $1'-1\frac{1}{2}'$ of its base; sepals ovate, acute, pale pubescent on the outer surface, villose and furnished at base on the inner surface with a tuft of long white hairs, a third shorter than the lanceolate acuminate petals; staminodia oblong-obovate, rounded at apex, about as long as the sepals; stigma slightly villose at base. **Fruit** ripening the end of September, subglobose, $\frac{1}{4}'-\frac{1}{3}'$ in diameter, covered with loose light brown pubescence.

A tree, 60°–75° high, with stout red glabrous branchlets. **Winter-buds** ovoid, cylindric, obtusely pointed, dark red, $\frac{1}{4}'-\frac{1}{3}'$ in length.

Distribution. North Carolina, rocky "coves" in rich soil, Hickory Nut Gap, in the

Blue Ridge, and near Saluda, Polk County, passing into var. *multinervis* Sarg., differing from the type in its obliquely truncate, not cordate, leaves with 12 or 13 pairs of more

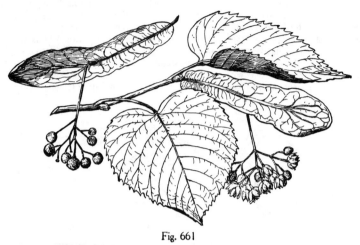

Fig. 661

crowded primary veins, ellipsoid fruit, slender branchlets, and smaller winter-buds; a single tree near Saluda, Polk County.

·4. Tilia littoralis Sarg.

Leaves ovate, abruptly short-pointed and acute or acuminate at apex, unsymmetric and rounded on one side and cuneate on the other, or symmetric and cuneate or oblique and truncate at base, and finely serrate with straight or incurved glandular teeth, covered above when they unfold with scattered fascicled hairs and tomentose below, soon glabrous,

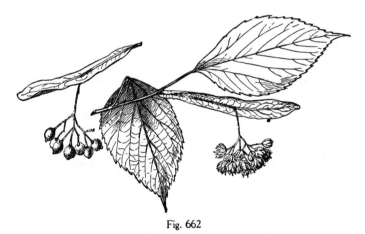

Fig. 662

and when the flowers open, thin, yellow-green, paler, rarely glaucous (var. *discolor* Sarg.) on the lower than on the upper surface, 3′–4′ long and 1¾′–2′ wide, with a slender midrib and primary veins and small conspicuous tufts of rusty brown axillary hairs; petioles slender, glabrous, $1'-1\frac{1}{4}'$ in length; leaves on young vigorous shoots broad-ovate, truncate or slightly cordate at base, more coarsely serrate, pubescent with fascicled hairs especially on the midrib and veins, $4'-5'$ long and $3'-4'$ wide; petioles densely pubescent. Flowers opening the middle of June, $\frac{1}{3}'$ long, on pale tomentose pedicels, in small, compact, mostly 9–15-flowered, pubescent cymes; peduncle covered with scattered fascicled hairs, the free portion $\frac{3}{5}'-1'$ long, its bract gradually narrowed and cuneate at base, rounded at apex, ciliate on the margins, pubescent on the midrib, otherwise glabrous, $2'-7'$ long, $\frac{1}{4}'-\frac{2}{3}'$ wide, longer or shorter than and decurrent to the base or nearly to the base of the peduncle; sepals acuminate, pale pubescent on the outer surface, villose on the inner surface along the margins and at the base with long white hairs; petals acuminate; staminodia oblong-obovate, rounded at apex. Fruit ellipsoid to depressed-globose, apiculate, covered with pale brown tomentum, $\frac{1}{4}'-\frac{1}{3}'$ in diameter.

A tree with slender glabrous branchlets densely coated when they first appear with pale pubescence, soon glabrous, light reddish brown during their first summer, often bright red during their first winter, becoming purple the following year and ultimately light gray-brown. Winter-buds ovoid, glabrous or puberulous, bright red, about $\frac{1}{5}'$ long and $\frac{1}{12}'-\frac{1}{8}'$ in diameter.

Distribution. Georgia, shore of Colonel's Island near the mouths of the North Newport and Medway Rivers, near Durham, Liberty County; the var. *discolor* with the type.

5. Tilia crenoserrata Sarg.

Tilia floridana Sarg., not Small.

Leaves ovate, abruptly narrowed and acuminate at apex, usually oblique and unsymmetrically cordate or truncate or occasionally symmetrical and cordate at base, crenately serrate, the teeth tipped with minute glands, covered when they unfold with pale caducous tomentum, and at maturity dark green and lustrous above, glaucescent below, glabrous with the exception of minute axillary tufts of rusty hairs, mostly $3\frac{1}{2}'-5\frac{1}{2}'$ long and $2\frac{3}{4}'-3'$ wide; petioles slender, glabrous, about $1\frac{1}{4}'$ in length. Flowers opening the middle of June, $\frac{1}{4}'$ long, on hoary-tomentose pedicels, in compact mostly 10–18-flowered tomentose cymes; peduncle glabrous, the free portion $1'-1\frac{1}{2}'$ in length, its bract oblong-obovate, cuneate at base, rounded at apex, glabrous, $3'-5'$ long, usually about $\frac{4}{5}'$ wide, decurrent nearly to the base of the peduncle; sepals acute, hoary-tomentose on the outer surface, coated with pale tomentum mixed with long white hairs on the inner surface; petals narrow-acuminate; staminodia oblong-obovate, notched at apex. Fruit ripening from the middle to the end of August, ellipsoid, conspicuously apiculate at apex, rusty-tomentose, $\frac{3}{8}'-\frac{5}{8}'$ long and $\frac{1}{4}'-\frac{1}{3}'$ in diameter.

A tree, $25°-30°$, rarely $60°$ high, with a trunk $10'-12'$ rarely $18'-20'$ in diameter, and slender glabrous red-brown branchlets. Winter-buds ovoid, acute, dark dull red, glabrous, $\frac{1}{6}'-\frac{1}{5}'$ long.

Distribution. Near Albany, Dougherty County, Georgia, to central Florida (Levy, Columbia, Alachua, Putnam, Seminole and Orange Counties).

6. Tilia floridana Small.

Leaves broad-ovate, acuminate or abruptly acuminate at apex, cordate or obliquely truncate at base and coarsely serrate with apiculate teeth, tinged with red and tomentose below when they unfold, fully grown and glabrous or nearly glabrous when the flowers open late in May or in early June, and at maturity thin, glabrous, dark yellow-green on the upper surface, pale or rarely covered below with a silvery white bloom (var. *hypoleuca* Sarg.), $3\frac{1}{2}'-5'$ long and $2\frac{1}{2}'-3\frac{1}{2}'$ wide, with a slender midrib and primary veins; in the east usually without axillary tufts, often present and sometimes conspicuous westward; petioles slender, glabrous, $\frac{3}{4}'-1'$ in length. Flowers opening in early summer $\frac{1}{5}'-\frac{1}{4}'$ long, on hoary-tomentose rarely puberulous (var. *australis* Sarg.) pedicels, in few-flowered rather compact pubescent corymbs; peduncle pubescent, the free portion $1\frac{1}{2}'-2\frac{1}{2}'$ in length, its bract oblong-obovate to oblong, rounded at apex, often falcate, glabrous, $3'-6'$ long, $\frac{1}{2}'-\frac{3}{4}'$ wide, decurrent nearly to the base of the peduncle; sepals narrow, ovate, acuminate, hoary-tomentose on the outer surface, sparingly villose on the inner surface, two-thirds as long as the lanceolate petals; staminodia oblong-obovate, acute, nearly as long as the petals; style glabrous. **Fruit** ripening in August and September, subglobose to ellipsoid, rusty-tomentose, $\frac{1}{2}'$ in diameter.

A tree, $40°-50°$ high, with a trunk $12'-15'$ in diameter, and slender glabrous red-brown or yellow branchlets. **Winter-buds** obtuse, dark red-brown, glabrous, about $\frac{1}{6}'$ long.

Distribution. North Carolina (Polk County) to western Florida and westward through northern and central Alabama, central Mississippi, northern and western Louisiana, eastern and over the Edwards Plateau to Kerr, Bandera and Uvalde Counties, Texas, and through

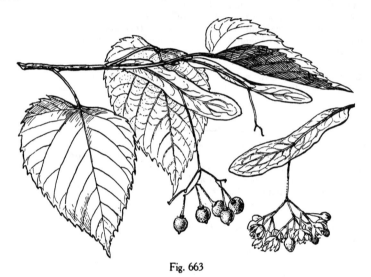

Fig. 663

southern and western Arkansas to eastern Oklahoma, Missouri and eastern Kentucky; in northeastern Mexico; the var. *australis* in Blount County, Alabama. A variety (var. *oblongifolia* Sarg.) with narrower more elongated leaves with more prominent tufts of axillary hairs occurs in Putnam, Leon and Gadsden Counties, Florida, on the bluffs of the Alabama River near Berlin, Dallas County, Alabama, in Hinds, Rankin and Adams Counties, Mississippi, in West Feliciana, Iberia (Avery Island) and Natchitoches Parishes, Louisiana, in Hempstead and Salina Counties, Arkansas, and in Harris, Anderson and Livingston Counties, Texas.

7. Tilia Cocksii Sarg.

Leaves ovate, abruptly acuminate at apex, very oblique at the truncate or rounded base, dentate with small remote glandular apiculate teeth, covered when they unfold with loose floccose pubescence, nearly glabrous when fully grown early in April, when the flowers open the middle of May dark green and lustrous on the upper surface, pale blue-green and lustrous below, and at mid-summer when the fruit ripens, subcoriaceous, dark green and lustrous on the upper surface, paler on the lower surface, with slender primary veins without or occasionally with minute axillary tufts, and connected by conspicuous straight or curved veinlets, $3\frac{1}{2}'-4'$ long and $2\frac{1}{2}'-3'$ wide; petioles slender, glabrous, $\frac{3}{4}'-1'$ in length;

leaves on leading summer branchlets sometimes obliquely cordate, more coarsely serrate, covered on the upper surface with short fascicled hairs, and floccose-pubescent on the lower surface, $4'-5'$ long and $4'-4\frac{3}{4}'$ wide, their petioles puberulous. **Flowers** opening the middle of May, $\frac{1}{4}'$ long, on tomentose pedicels, in compact pubescent many-flowered cymes; peduncle slender, glabrous, the free portion only $\frac{2}{3}'-\frac{4}{5}'$ in length, its bract oblong, occasionally

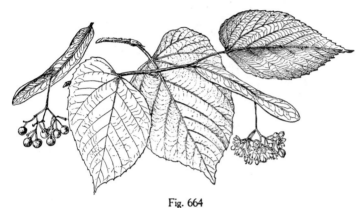

Fig. 664

slightly obovate, rounded at the ends, hoary-tomentose on the under surface and pubescent on the upper surface when it first appears, and when the flowers open puberulous below and glabrous above, $3\frac{1}{2}'-6'$ long, $\frac{1}{2}'-\frac{3}{5}'$ wide and shorter than and decurrent to the base of the peduncle; sepals ovate, acuminate, pale pubescent on the outer surface, villose at the base on the inner surface, a third shorter than the lanceolate acuminate petals; staminodia oblong-obovate, rounded at apex, about half the length of the petals; style glabrous. **Fruit** ripening the middle of July, globose to depressed-globose, covered with loose brown tomentum, $\frac{1}{4}'$ in diameter.

A small tree with slender dull red glabrous branchlets, the leading branchlets in summer more or less pubescent. **Winter-buds** ovoid, acute, dull red, glabrous or pubescent on leading shoots, $\frac{1}{3}'-\frac{1}{4}'$ long.

Distribution. Louisiana, river banks and low woods, Lake Charles and West Lake Charles, Calcasieu Parish.

8. Tilia neglecta Spach.

Tilia Michauxii Sarg., not Nutt.

Leaves thick and firm, acute or abruptly narrowed and long-pointed at apex, obliquely concave or unsymmetrically cordate at base, coarsely serrate with straight apiculate teeth pointing forward, dark green, smooth, glabrous and lustrous above, covered below except on the midrib and veins more or less thickly with short gray pubescence often slightly tinged with brown, and furnished with conspicuous tufts of axillary hairs, usually $4'-5\frac{1}{2}'$ long and $2\frac{1}{2}'-4\frac{1}{2}'$ wide; petioles stout, glabrous, $1\frac{1}{4}'-2\frac{1}{2}'$ in length. **Flowers** opening in June and July about $\frac{2}{5}'$ long, on pubescent or nearly glabrous pedicels, in long-branched slender glabrous mostly 5–15-flowered cymes; peduncle slender, glabrous, the free portion $1\frac{1}{4}'-1\frac{1}{2}'$ in length, its bract gradually narrowed and cuneate or unsymmetrically cuneate or rounded at base, rounded at apex, glabrous, $2\frac{3}{4}'-4\frac{1}{2}'$ long, $\frac{2}{5}'-\frac{4}{5}'$ wide and longer than and decurrent nearly to the base or to within $\frac{3}{5}'$ of the base of the peduncle; sepals broad-ovate, acute, ciliate on the margins, glabrous on the outer surface, covered on the inner surface with long white hairs, about half as long as the lanceolate petals rounded and notched at apex and rather longer than the spatulate staminodia; stamens included; style villose toward the base. **Fruit** ripening in September, ellipsoid, ovoid, obovoid, or depressed-globose, rounded or acute or rarely gradually narrowed and acuminate at apex, rarely 5-angled, covered with rusty or pale pubescence, usually about $\frac{1}{3}'$ in diameter.

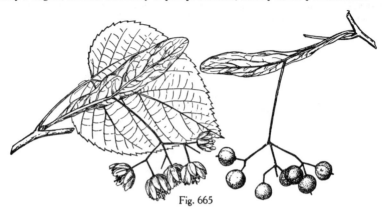

Fig. 665

A tree, 75°–90° high, with a trunk sometimes 3° in diameter, smooth often pendulous branches forming a broad round head, and slender glabrous branchlets. **Winter-buds** ovoid, rounded at the narrowed apex, about $\frac{1}{5}'$ long, with glabrous red-brown or light brown scales. **Bark** of the trunk about 1' thick, deeply furrowed, pale reddish brown and covered with small thin scales.

Distribution. Rich moist soil, Province of Quebec, near Montreal, to the coast of Massachusetts and New York, through the middle states to the valley of the Potomac River and along the Appalachian Mountains to those of North Carolina, and to Iuka, Tishomingo County, Mississippi, and from central and western New York to northern Missouri.

9. Tilia caroliniana Mill.

Leaves ovate, oblique and truncate or cordate at base, abruptly long-pointed at apex, coarsely dentate with broad apiculate glandular teeth pointing forward, and coated below

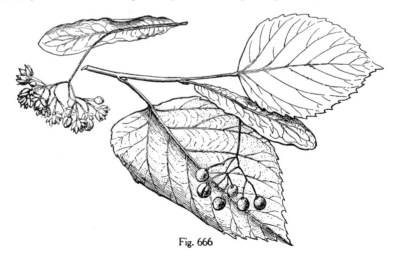

Fig. 666

with a rusty or pale easily detached pubescence of fascicled hairs, coated when they unfold with hoary tomentum, soon glabrous on the upper surface, and at maturity dark yellow-green and lustrous above, $2\frac{3}{4}'-4\frac{1}{2}'$ long and $2\frac{1}{2}-5'$ wide; petioles stout, glabrous, $1'-1\frac{1}{2}'$ in length. **Flowers** opening the middle of June, $\frac{1}{4}'$ long, on slender pubescent pedicels, in small stout-branched pubescent mostly 8–15-flowered cymes; peduncle slender, pubescent, the free portion $\frac{3}{4}'-1\frac{1}{4}'$ long, its bract oblong-obovate, cuneate at base, rounded or acute at apex, nearly glabrous on the upper surface when it first appears, pubescent becoming glabrous or almost glabrous below, $4'-5'$ long and $\frac{4}{5}'$ wide, longer or shorter than and decurrent to the base or nearly to the base of the peduncle; sepals ovate, acuminate, ciliate on the margins, brown and covered with pale pubescence on the outer surface, coated on the inner surface with long white hairs; petals lanceolate, acuminate, a third longer than the sepals; staminodia oblong-obovate, rounded at apex, rather shorter than the petals; style tomentose at base or glabrous. **Fruit** subglobose, ellipsoid or obovoid, $\frac{1}{3}'$ in diameter.

A large tree with slender red-brown glabrous or slightly pubescent branchlets. **Winter-buds** ovoid, acute, glabrous or rarely pubescent, about $\frac{1}{4}'$ long.

Distribution. Coast of North Carolina (Wrightsville Beach and the neighborhood of Wilmington, New Hanover County), southward in the immediate neighborhood of the coast to Liberty County, Georgia; western Louisiana to southern Arkansas (Hempstead and Clark Counties) common, and through eastern Texas to the Edwards Plateau (near Boerne, Kendall County); in Orizaba. Passing into

Tilia caroliniana var. rhoophila Sarg.

Differing from the type in its pubescent branchlets and winter-buds, its usually larger leaves, and in its tomentose corymbs of more numerous flowers. **Leaves** broad-ovate, abruptly short-pointed and acuminate at apex, oblique and truncate or cordate at base,

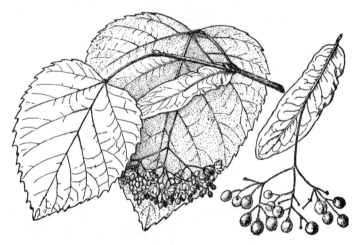

Fig. 667

coarsely serrate with broad apiculate teeth pointing forward, dark green and lustrous on the upper surface, pale and thickly covered on the lower surface with persistent white or brownish pubescence, $4'-5'$ long and $2\frac{1}{2}'-5'$ wide, with a slender midrib and primary veins pubescent on the lower side, and small conspicuous axillary tufts of pale hairs; petioles stout, thickly coated with pubescence, $1'-1\frac{3}{4}'$ in length; leaves on vigorous shoots often $6'$ long, and $5\frac{1}{2}'$ wide, and occasionally $10'$ long and $9'$ wide. **Flowers** $\frac{1}{4}'$ long, on short hoary-tomentose pedicels, in wide thin-branched pubescent many-flowered (sometimes 50) cymes; peduncle thickly covered with fascicled hairs, the free portion $\frac{1}{4}'$ long, its bract oblong, unequally rounded at base, rounded at apex, glabrous on the upper surface, pubescent on the lower surface, $4'-6'$ long, $1'-2'$ wide, usually shorter than and decurrent nearly to the base of the peduncle; sepals acuminate, coated on the outer surface with pale or slightly rusty pubescence, villose and furnished at base on the inner surface with tufts of long hairs; petals lanceolate, acuminate and ciliate at apex, about a third longer than the sepals; staminodia spatulate, acute, about half the length of the petals; style coated at base with long white hairs. **Fruit** subglobose, covered with rusty tomentum, about $\frac{1}{3}'$ in diameter.

A tree with slender branchlets thickly coated during their first year with pale pubescence, dark red-brown or gray and puberulous during their second season. **Winter-buds** covered with pale pubescence.

Distribution. Western Louisiana. (Calcasieu and Jefferson Davis Parishes) to Hempstead County, Arkansas, and through eastern Texas to the valley of the upper Guadalupe River, Kerr County.

10. Tilia texana Sarg.

Leaves thin, oblong-ovate, abruptly contracted into a long slender acuminate point, cordate or obliquely cordate at base, finely dentate with broad apiculate teeth, early in the

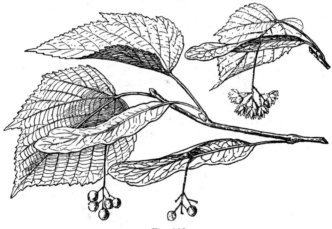

Fig. 668

season pubescent above with scattered fascicled hairs and covered below with brownish slightly attached pubescence, and in the autumn light yellow-green, lustrous and nearly glabrous on the upper surface, slightly pubescent on the lower surface, $4'-5\frac{1}{2}'$ long and $3\frac{1}{4}'-5'$ wide, with a slender midrib and primary veins sparingly villose on the upper side and nearly glabrous on the lower side, and small axillary tufts of brownish hairs; petioles slender, pubescent with fascicled hairs, $1'-1\frac{1}{2}'$ in length; leaves on vigorous shoots often furnished with one or two large lateral acuminate serrate lobes, more coarsely dentate and more thickly covered on the lower surface with pubescence, often $5\frac{1}{2}'-6'$ long and $3\frac{1}{2}'-6'$ wide. **Flowers** opening the middle of June, $\frac{1}{4}'$ long, on slender tomentose pedicels, in small villose-pubescent mostly 7–10-flowered cymes; peduncle slender, slightly villose-pubescent, the free portion $1\frac{1}{4}'-1\frac{1}{2}'$ in length, its bract oblong-ovate to slightly obovate, unsymmetrically cuneate at base, rounded and occasionally lobed at apex, glabrous on the upper surface, densely pubescent early in the season, later becoming nearly glabrous on the lower surface, 3'–6' long and $\frac{3}{4}$'–1$\frac{1}{4}$' wide, longer or shorter than the peduncle and decurrent to its base or to within 1$\frac{1}{2}$' of its base; sepals ovate, acute, pale pubescent on the outer surface, covered on the inner surface with white hairs longer and more abundant near the base; petals lanceolate, acuminate, a third longer than the sepals; staminodia linear-lanceolate, acuminate; style hoary-tomentose at base. **Fruit** ellipsoid, covered with rusty brown tomentum, $\frac{1}{3}$' long and $\frac{1}{4}$' broad.

A small tree with slender branchlets thickly covered during their first season with close pale pubescence, and pale and puberulous or glabrous in their second year; on vigorous terminal branchlets often with thicker, light rusty brown pubescence. **Winter-buds** ovoid, obtusely pointed, thickly covered with pale pubescence, $\frac{1}{4}$' long.

Distribution. Texas, Brazos and Cherokee Counties, on Spring Creek near Boerne, Kendall County, and on the rocky banks of the Guadalupe River at Kerrville, Kerr County.

11. Tilia phanera Sarg.

Leaves semiorbicular to broad-ovate, deeply and usually symmetrically cordate at base, abruptly short-pointed at apex, finely dentate with straight or incurved apiculate teeth, glabrous above when they unfold with the exception of a few hairs on the midrib and veins, and thickly coated below with hoary tomentum, and at maturity thin, blue-green, smooth and lustrous on the upper surface, paler and often brownish and coated with a floccose easily detached pubescence of fascicled hairs or scabrate (var. *scabrida* Sarg.) on the lower surface, 2'–4' wide and usually rather broader than long, with a slender midrib and primary veins pubescent on the lower side, and small axillary clusters of rusty brown hairs; petioles slender, coated when they first appear with hoary tomentum, glabrous or slightly pubescent in the autumn, 1'–1$\frac{1}{2}$' in length. **Flowers** opening the middle of June, $\frac{1}{5}$' long, on tomentose pedicels, in compact villose mostly 16–20-flowered cymes; peduncle villose, the free portion 1$\frac{1}{4}$' in length, its bract obovate, cuneate at base, broad and rounded at apex, floccose-pubescent on the lower surface, nearly glabrous on the upper surface, 3'–3$\frac{1}{2}$' long and

Fig. 669

$\frac{1}{2}$'–1' wide, longer than the peduncle and decurrent to its base or to within $\frac{1}{4}$' of its base; sepals acuminate, pale pubescent on the outer surface, villose on the margins and furnished at base on the inner surface with a tuft of long white hairs, broader and shorter than the lanceolate acuminate petals; staminodia oblong-obovate, rounded at apex, style glabrous except at the base. **Fruit** ripening the end of September, ellipsoid, covered with rusty tomentum, $\frac{1}{3}$'–$\frac{2}{5}$' long and $\frac{1}{4}$' wide, on a stout, densely floccose-pubescent pedicel.

A tree with slender light gray-brown often zigzag branchlets covered when they first appear with fascicled hairs and deciduous during their first summer. **Winter-buds** ovoid, obtusely pointed, terete, reddish brown, glabrous, $\frac{1}{8}'-\frac{1}{5}'$ long.

Distribution. Texas, banks of Spring Creek, near Boerne, Kendall County; the var. *scabrida* on a low limestone bluff of the Blanco River, near Blanco, Blanco County, near College Station, Brazos County, and at Velasco, Brazoria County.

12. Tilia lasioclada Sarg.

Leaves ovate, abruptly contracted at apex into a short acuminate point, oblique and truncate or on weak branchlets, often nearly symmetric and deeply cordate at base, and finely serrate with straight apiculate teeth, covered above when they unfold with soft cadu-

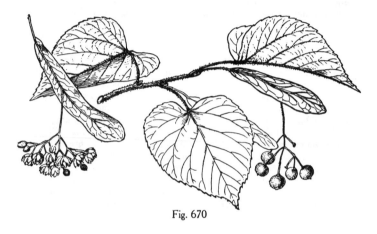

Fig. 670

cous hairs and pubescent below, and at maturity thick, bright green, smooth and lustrous on the upper surface, pale and covered on the lower surface with a thick floccose easily detached pubescence of fascicled hairs, pale on those of lower leaves and often rufous on those of upper branches, $4'-6'$ long and $3\frac{1}{4}'-5'$ wide, with a slender midrib and veins covered below with straight hairs mixed with fascicled hairs, and small conspicuous axillary tufts; petioles covered when they first appear with straight hairs mixed with fascicled hairs, soon glabrous, usually $1\frac{1}{4}'-1\frac{1}{2}'$ in length, those of the leaves of weak branchlets very slender and often $2'-2\frac{1}{2}'$ long. **Flowers** in May, $\frac{1}{6}'-\frac{1}{5}'$ long, on stout villose pedicels, in long-branched mostly 10-15-flowered cymes more or less thickly covered with straight white hairs; peduncle covered with long white hairs, the free portion $1'-1\frac{1}{4}'$ in length, its bract rounded and unsymmetric or acute at base, rounded or acute at apex, the midrib more or less thickly covered on the lower side with straight hairs, otherwise glabrous, $3\frac{1}{2}'-5'$ long and $1'$ wide, decurrent nearly to the base or to within $1'$ of the base of the peduncle; sepals narrow, acute. pubescent on the outer surface, villose on the inner surface, about one-third as long as the lanceolate acuminate petals; staminodia spatulate, rounded and often lobed at apex, about as long as the sepals; style slightly villose at base. **Fruit** ripening in September, globose or depressed-globose, covered with rusty tomentum, about $\frac{2}{5}'$ in diameter.

A tree, sometimes 60° high, with a trunk $12'-24'$ in diameter, heavy branches forming a broad round-topped head, and stout red-brown branchlets sometimes glabrous in early summer and sometimes covered more or less thickly during their first and second seasons with long straight hairs.

Distribution. Valley of the Savannah River, near Abbeville, South Carolina, to Shell Bluff, Burke County, Georgia; River Junction, Gadsden County, Florida.

13. Tilia heterophylla Vent.

Leaves ovate, obliquely truncate or rarely slightly cordate at base, gradually narrowed and acuminate at apex, finely dentate with apiculate gland-tipped teeth, pubescent above when they unfold with caducous fascicled hairs, and at maturity dark green and glabrous

Fig. 671

on the upper surface, covered on the lower surface with thick, firmly attached, white or on upper branches often brownish tomentum, and usually furnished with small axillary tufts of rusty brown hairs, $3\frac{1}{4}'-5\frac{1}{4}'$ long and $2\frac{1}{2}'-2\frac{3}{4}'$ wide; petioles slender, glabrous, $1\frac{1}{2}'-1\frac{3}{4}'$ in length. **Flowers** $\frac{1}{4}'$ long, opening in early summer, on pedicels pubescent with fascicled hairs, in wide mostly 10–20-flowered pubescent corymbs; peduncle glabrous, the free portion $\frac{1}{12}'-\frac{1}{6}'$ in length, its bract narrowed and rounded at apex, unsymmetrically cuneate at base, pubescent on the upper surface, tomentose on the lower surface when it first appears, becoming glabrous, $4'-6'$ long and $1'-1\frac{1}{2}'$ wide, nearly sessile or decurrent to within $1\frac{1}{2}'$ of the base of the peduncle; sepals acuminate, pale-pubescent on the outer surface, villose on the inner surface and furnished at base with a tuft of long white hairs; petals lanceolate, acuminate, a third longer than the sepals; staminodia oblong-ovate, acute, sometimes notched at apex; style villose at base with long white hairs. **Fruit** ellipsoid, apiculate at apex, covered with rusty brown tomentum, about $\frac{1}{3}'$ long.

A large tree with slender, glabrous, reddish or yellowish brown branchlets and oblong-ovate slightly flattened glabrous winter-buds $\frac{1}{5}'-\frac{1}{3}'$ in length, the outer scales slightly ciliate at apex.

Distribution. White Sulphur Springs, Greenbrier County, West Virginia; Piedmont region of North and South Carolina and Georgia; near Tallahassee, Leon County, River Junction, Gadsden County, and Rock Cave, Jackson County, Florida; near Selma and Berlin, Dallas County, Alabama; Vevay, Switzerland County, and near the Ohio River, Jefferson County, Indiana; not common. Passing into the var. *amphiloba* Sarg., differing from the type in the fascicled hairs on the upper surface of the young leaves and in the often pubescent branchlets; woods in sandy soil near River Junction, Gadsden County, Florida, and Valley Head, DeKalb County, Alabama; and into var. *nivea* Sarg., differing from the type in the white tomentum on the lower surface of the leaves, the glabrous styles, in the tomentum on the lower side of the floral bract when the flowers open, the pubescent gray or pale reddish brown branchlets and in the puberulous winter-buds; deep woods, River Junction, Gadsden County, Florida. More important is

Tilia heterophylla var. Michauxii Sarg.

Tilia Michauxii Nutt.

Leaves ovate to ovate-oblong, acute or abruptly short-pointed at the broad apex, cordate, obliquely cordate, or rarely obliquely truncate at base, and coarsely serrate with apiculate teeth, pubescent above when they unfold with caducous fascicled hairs, and hoary-tomentose beneath, and at maturity thin, dark green and lustrous on the upper surface and coated below with short white or grayish white tomentum, $3\frac{1}{2}'-6'$ long and $3\frac{1}{2}'-5'$ wide, with a slender yellow midrib and primary veins usually without axillary tufts; petioles slender, sparingly villose when they first appear, soon glabrous, $1\frac{1}{2}'-2\frac{1}{2}'$ in length. **Flowers** $\frac{1}{3}'$ long, opening about the 1st of July, on slender puberulous pedicels $\frac{1}{4}'$ in length, in wide long-stemmed puberulous cymes; peduncle pubescent, becoming glabrous, the free portion $1\frac{3}{4}'-2'$ in length, its bract obovoid, rounded or acute at apex, $3\frac{1}{2}'-5'$ long and $\frac{1}{2}'-1'$ wide, decurrent to within $\frac{1}{4}'-\frac{3}{4}'$ of the base of the peduncle; sepals ovate, acuminate, ciliate on the margins, puberulous on the outer surface, tomentose on the inner surface, $\frac{1}{4}'$ long, shorter than the lanceolate acuminate petals; staminodia oblong-obovoid, rounded or emarginate at apex; style glabrous. **Fruit** ripening in September, subglobose, rusty-tomentose, $\frac{1}{4}'-\frac{1}{3}'$ in diameter.

A large tree with slender glabrous light red-brown branchlets. **Winter-buds** ovoid, acute, slightly flattened, red, about $\frac{1}{4}'$ in length. **Bark** of the trunk 1' thick, deeply furrowed, reddish or grayish brown and covered with small thin scales.

Distribution. Pennsylvania, valley of the Susquehanna River (Lancaster County) to

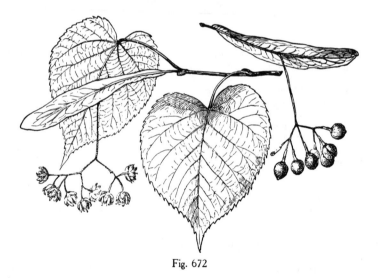

Fig. 672

southern and western New York and through southern Ohio, Indiana, and Illinois to northeastern Missouri (near Ilasco, Ralls County), and southward through eastern Kentucky and Tennessee to northeastern Mississippi, and along the Appalachian Mountains to northern Georgia; southern Georgia (Dougherty and Decatur Counties), Dallas County, Alabama; southwestern Missouri (Eagle Rock, Barry County), and northwestern Arkansas (Eureka Springs, Carroll County, and Cotter, Marion County).

14. Tilia monticola Sarg.

Tilia heterophylla Ṣạrg., in part, not **Vent.**

Leaves thin, gradually narrowed and acuminate at apex, ovate to oblong-ovate, very oblique and truncate or obliquely cordate at base, finely serrate with straight or incurved apiculate teeth, smooth, dark green and lustrous on the upper surface, thickly coated on the lower surface with hoary tomentum, $4'-7'$ long and $3'-5'$ wide; petioles slender, glabrous,

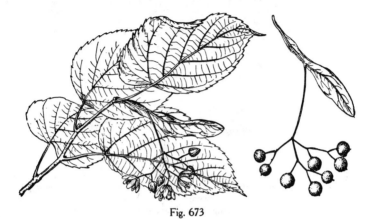

Fig. 673

$1\frac{1}{2}'-3'$ in length. **Flowers** from the middle to the end of July, $\frac{2}{3}'-\frac{1}{2}'$ long, on stout sparingly pubescent pedicels, in mostly 7–10-flowered thin-branched glabrous cymes; peduncle slender, glabrous, the free portion $1\frac{1}{3}'-1\frac{1}{2}'$ in length, its bract gradually narrowed and cuneate or rounded at base, narrowed and rounded at apex, glabrous, $4'-5\frac{1}{2}'$ long and $\frac{1}{4}'-1'$ wide, decurrent to within $\frac{1}{24}'-\frac{1}{8}'$ of the base of the peduncle; sepals ovate, acute, ciliate on the margins, covered on the outer surface with short pale pubescence and with silky white hairs on the inner surface; petals lanceolate, acuminate, twice longer than the sepals; staminodia oblong-lanceolate, rounded at the narrowed apex, as long or nearly as long as the petals; style clothed at the base with long white hairs. **Fruit** ripening in September, ovoid to ellipsoid, covered with pale rusty tomentum, $\frac{1}{4}'-\frac{1}{3}'$ long and about $\frac{1}{4}'$ in diameter.

A tree rarely exceeding 60° in height with a trunk $3°-4\frac{1}{2}°$ in diameter, slender branches forming a narrow rather pyramidal head, and stout glabrous branchlets usually bright red during their first year, becoming brown in their second season. **Winter-buds** compressed, ovoid, acute or rounded at apex, light red, covered with a glaucous bloom, $\frac{1}{3}'-\frac{1}{2}'$ long. **Bark** of the trunk $\frac{2}{3}'$ in thickness, deeply furrowed, the surface broken into small thin light brown scales.

Distribution. Appalachian Mountains at altitudes usually from 2500°–3000°, Farmer Mountain, on New River, Connell County, Virginia, to Johnson City, Washington County, Tennessee, and to Highlands, Macon County, North Carolina.

15. Tilia georgiana Sarg.

Leaves ovate, abruptly short-pointed at apex, slightly unsymmetric and usually cordate on lateral branches and often oblique or truncate on leading branches at base, and finely dentate with glandular teeth pointing forward, when they unfold deeply tinged with red, covered above by fascicled hairs and tomentose below, when the flowers open the middle of June dark yellow-green, dull and scabrate above and covered below with a thick coat of tomentum, pale on those of lower branches and tinged with brown on those from the top of the tree, and conspicuously reticulate-venulose, and at maturity thick, dull yellow-green, pubescent or glabrous above, rusty or pale tomentose below, sometimes becoming

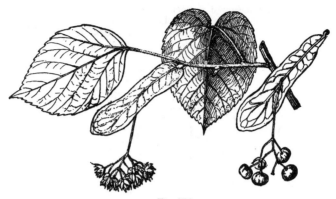

Fig. 674

nearly glabrous in the autumn, $2\frac{1}{2}'-4'$ long and $2'-3'$ wide; petioles slender, tomentose, $1'-1\frac{1}{2}'$ in length. **Flowers** $\frac{1}{4}'-\frac{1}{3}'$ long, on slender pubescent pedicels, in compact slender-branched pubescent mostly 10–15-flowered corymbs; peduncle slender, densely pubescent, the free portion $1'-1\frac{1}{2}'$ in length, its bract oblong to obovate, rounded at apex, rounded or cuneate at base, pubescent, becoming nearly glabrous, $2\frac{1}{2}'-4'$ long and $\frac{3}{4}'-1\frac{1}{2}'$ wide, decurrent to the base or to within $1'$ of the base of the peduncle; sepals ovate, acuminate, coated on the outer surface with pale pubescence and on the inner surface with pale hairs longest and most abundant at the base, not more than one-half the length of the lanceolate acuminate narrow petals; staminodia oblong-obovate to spatulate, acute, about two-thirds as long as the petals; style glabrous or furnished with a few hairs at the very base. **Fruit** ripens early in September on pubescent pedicels, depressed-globose, occasionally slightly grooved and ridged, covered with thick rusty tomentum, $\frac{1}{5}'-\frac{1}{4}'$ in diameter.

A small tree, with slender branchlets thickly coated during their first season with pale tomentum, and dark red-brown or brown and puberulous in their second year. **Winter-buds** covered with rusty brown pubescence, $\frac{1}{4}'-\frac{1}{3}'$ long.

Distribution. Coast of South Carolina, near Charleston; Colonel's Island near the mouths of the North Newport and Medway Rivers, near Dunham, Liberty County, and at Brunswick, Glynn County, Georgia, to central and western Florida; Magnet Cove, Hot Spring County, Arkansas (*E. J. Palmer*).

Tilia georgiana var. crinita Sarg.

Tilia pubescens Sarg., in part, not Vent.

Differing in the longer and more matted usually rusty brown hairs of the pubescence, usually less closely attached to the under surface of the leaves and often conspicuous on the young branches.

A tree, 30°–40° high, with a trunk rarely exceeding 15' in diameter, and slender branchlets densely rusty pubescent during their first season, and during their third year becoming glabrous, red-brown, rugose and marked by occasional small lenticels. **Winter-buds** acuminate, dark reddish brown and covered with short reddish pubescence. **Bark** of the trunk $\frac{1}{2}'-\frac{3}{4}'$ thick, furrowed and divided into parallel ridges, the red-brown surface broken into short thick scales.

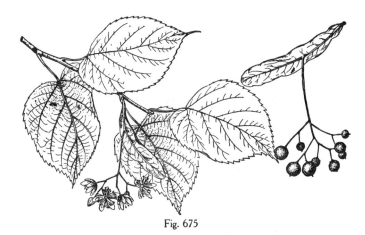

Fig. 675

Distribution. Sandy woods near Bluffton, Beaufort County, and in the neighborhood of Charleston, South Carolina, and on Colonel's Island near the mouth of the North Newport and Medway Rivers, near Dunham, Liberty County, Georgia.

XL. STERCULIACEÆ.

Trees or shrubs, with bitter astringent juice, mucilaginous bark, and alternate simple leaves, with stipules. Flowers perfect, regular; calyx of 5 sepals, imbricated in the bud; corolla 0 (in *Fremontia*); anthers extorse; pistil of 5 united carpels; ovary 5-celled; styles united; ovules anatropous.

A family of about fifty genera mostly confined to the tropics. Its most important species, *Theobroma Cacao* L., of the West Indies, produces chocolate from the cotyledons. *Firmiana simplex* F. N. Meyer, of this family and a native of southern China, is often planted as an ornamental tree in the southern states, where it has sometimes become naturalized, and in California.

1. FREMONTIA Torr.

A tree or shrub, with stellate pubescence and naked buds. Leaves broad-ovate, lobed, thick, prominently veined, usually rufous on the lower surface, persistent; stipules minute, deciduous. Flowers solitary, terminal or opposite the leaves, pedicellate, subtended by 3 or rarely 5 minute caducous bracts; calyx subcampanulate, hypogynous, deeply 5-lobed, the lobes imbricated in the bud, petaloid, yellow, spreading, obovate, often mucronate, 1' long, the 3 outer a little smaller than the others, pubescent on the outer surface, with a hairy cavity at the base of the inner surface; corolla 0; stamens 5; filaments alternate with the sepals, united to the middle into a column; anthers oblong-linear, incurved at the ends, 2-celled, the cells opening longitudinally; ovary 5-celled, the cells opposite the sepals; style filiform, elongated, terminated by an acute undivided stigmatic point; ovules numerous in each cell, horizontal. Fruit an ovoid acuminate 4 or 5-valved loculicidally dehiscent capsule densely coated with long matted hairs, the inner surface of the cells villose-pubescent. Seeds oval; seed-coat crustaceous, puberulous, with a small fleshy marginal deciduous ariloid appendage on the chalaza; embryo straight, in thick fleshy albumen; cotyledons oblong, foliaceous, three or four times longer than the short radicle.

Fremontia, named in honor of John C. Frémont, the distinguished explorer of western North America, is represented by a single species.

1. Fremontia californica Torr. Slippery Elm.

Fremontodendron californicum Cov.

Leaves usually 3-lobed, rarely entire or sometimes 5–7-lobed, $1\frac{1}{2}'$ in diameter; petioles stout, $\frac{1}{2}'-\frac{2}{3}'$ in length. **Flowers** appearing in July in great profusion on short spur-like lateral branchlets. **Fruit** 1′ long; seeds very dark red-brown, about $\frac{3}{16}'$ long.

A tree, 20°–30° high, with a short trunk 12′–14′ in diameter, stout rigid branches spreading almost at right angles, and stout terete branchlets thickly coated when they first appear with rufous pubescence, becoming glabrous and light red-brown; more often a low intri-

Fig. 676

cately branched shrub. **Bark** of the trunk rarely more than $\frac{1}{4}'$ thick, deeply furrowed, the dark red-brown surface broken into numerous short thick scales. **Wood** hard, heavy, close-grained, dark brown tinged with red, with thick lighter colored sapwood. The mucilaginous inner bark is sometimes used domestically in poultices.

Distribution. Lower slopes of the California mountains; western base of Mt. Shasta to the San Pedro Mártir Mountains, Lower California; nowhere common west of the Sierra Nevada, but of its largest size on their western foothills; most abundant east of the Sierra Nevada in the region of the Mohave Desert, growing as a low shrub and sometimes forming thickets several acres in extent.

Occasionally cultivated in western and southern Europe as an ornamental plant.

XLI. THEACEÆ.

Trees or shrubs, with simple alternate leaves, without stipules. Flowers perfect, regular, hypogynous; sepals and petals 5, imbricated in the bud; stamens numerous; anthers 2-celled, the cells opening longitudinally; pistil of 3–5 united carpels; ovary 3–5-celled; styles as many as the cells of the ovary, partly united. Fruit capsular; embryo with large cotyledons.

The Camellia family with eighteen genera is principally confined to the tropics of the New World and to southern and eastern Asia. Two genera are represented in the flora of the southern United States, and of these Gordonia is arborescent. Its most important genus, Camellia of eastern Asia, contains the Tea plant, *Camellia Thea* Link, and several species cultivated for the beauty of their flowers.

1. GORDONIA Ell.

Trees or shrubs, with terete branchlets, with an acuminate terminal bud, slender acuminate naked axillary buds, and watery juice. Leaves pinnately veined, entire or crenate, subcoriaceous and persistent, or thin and deciduous. Flowers axillary, solitary, long-stalked or subsessile; calyx subtended by 2–5 caducous bracts; sepals unequal, rounded, concave, coriaceous, persistent; petals free or slightly united, obovate, concave, white, deciduous; stamens numerous, filaments short, united at base into a fleshy cup adnate to the base of the petals and inserted with them, or long and inserted directly on the petals; anthers introrse, yellow; ovary sessile; style elongated, erect, 5-lobed at the stigmatic apex; ovules 4–8 in each cell, pendulous in 2 series from its inner angle, collateral, anatropous. Fruit a woody oblong or subglobose 5-celled capsule loculicidally 5-valved, with a persistent axis angled by the projecting placentas. Seeds 2–8 in each cell pendulous, flat, without albumen; seed-coat woody, usually produced upward into an oblong wing; embryo mostly straight or oblique, with oblong flat or oblique cotyledons; radicle short, superior.

Gordonia with sixteen species is confined to the south Atlantic states of North America and to tropical Asia and the Malay Archipelago.

The generic name is in honor of James Gordon (1728–1791), a well-known London nurseryman.

CONSPECTUS OF THE NORTH AMERICAN SPECIES.

Flowers long-pedicellate; filaments united into a cup; capsule ovoid, the valves not split-ting from the base; seeds winged; leaves persistent.   1. **G. Lasianthus** (C).

Flowers subsessile; filaments distinct; capsule globose, the valves septicidally splitting from the base; seeds without wings; leaves deciduous.   2. **G. alatamaha** (C).

1. Gordonia Lasianthus Ell.   Bay.   Loblolly Bay.

Leaves coriaceous, lanceolate to oblong, acute at apex, gradually narrowed to the cuneate base, finely or remotely crenately serrate, usually above the middle only, dark green, smooth and lustrous, 4'–5' long and $1\frac{1}{2}$'–2' wide, persistent; finally turning scarlet and

Fig. 677

dropping irregularly through the year; petioles stout, wing-margined toward the apex, channeled, about $\frac{1}{2}$' in length.   **Flowers** pungently fragrant, about $2\frac{1}{2}$' in diameter, expand-ing in July and continuing to open successively during two or three months, on stout red pedicels thickening from below upward, $2\frac{1}{2}$'–3' long, and usually furnished with 3 or 4 ovate minute subfloral bractlets; sepals ovate to oval, $\frac{1}{2}$' long, ciliate on the margins with long white hairs, and covered on the outer surface with dense velvety pale lustrous pubes-cence; petals rounded at apex, gradually contracted at base, silky-puberulent on the back, white, incurved, $1\frac{1}{4}$'–$1\frac{1}{2}$' long and 1' broad, stamens united into a shallow fleshy deeply 5-lobed cup pubescent on the inner surface and adnate to the base of the petals;

ovary ovoid, pubescent, gradually contracted into the stout style persistent on the fruit. **Fruit** ovoid, acute, pubescent, $\frac{3}{4}'$ long, and $\frac{1}{2}'$ in diameter, splitting to below the middle; **seeds** winged, nearly square, slightly concave on the inner surface and rounded on the outer surface, rugose, dotted with small pale brown excrescences, nearly $\frac{1}{16}'$ long and half the length of the thin membranaceous oblique pale brown wing pointed or rounded at apex; embryo filling the cavity of the seed, nearly straight; cotyledons subcordate, foliaceous.

A short-lived tree, 60°–75° high, with a tall straight trunk 18'–20' in diameter, small branches growing upward at first and ultimately spreading into a narrow compact head, and dark brown rugose branchlets marked during several years by the horizontal slightly obcordate leaf-scars; or rarely a low shrub. **Winter-buds** $\frac{1}{4}'-\frac{1}{3}'$ long, and covered with pale silky lustrous pubescence. **Bark** of the trunk nearly 1' thick, deeply divided into regular parallel rounded ridges, their dark red-brown scaly surface broken into many irregular shallow furrows. **Wood** light, soft, close-grained, not durable, light red, with lighter colored sapwood of 40–50 layers of annual growth; occasionally used in cabinet-making.

Distribution. Shallow swamps and moist depressions in Pine-barrens; South Carolina (Camden, Kershaw County, and Bluffton, Beaufort County) southward near the coast to the shores of Indian River on the east coast and to Cape Romano on the west coast of Florida, ranging to the interior of the peninsula from Lake to De Soto Counties, and westward along the Gulf coast to southern Mississippi; most abundant in Georgia and east Florida; gradually becoming less abundant westward.

2. Gordonia alatamaha Sarg. Franklinia.

Leaves obovate-oblong, rounded or pointed at apex, gradually narrowed to the long cuneate base, remotely serrate, usually above the middle only, with small glandular teeth, bright green and lustrous on the upper surface, pale on the lower surface, 5'–6' long and

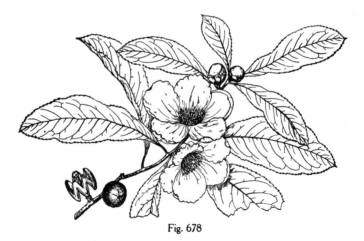

Fig. 678

$1\frac{1}{2}'-2'$ wide; turning scarlet in the autumn before falling; petioles stout, wing-margined above, $\frac{1}{4}'-\frac{1}{2}'$ in length. **Flowers** $3'-3\frac{1}{2}'$ in diameter, appearing about the middle of September, on short stout pedicels at first pubescent, finally glabrous, from the axils of crowded upper leaves, and marked by the broad conspicuous scars of 2 minute lateral subfloral pubescent bractlets; sepals nearly circular, $\frac{1}{2}'$ in diameter, ciliate on the margins, and covered on the outer surface with short lustrous silky pale hairs; petals obovate, crenulate, white, membranaceous, $1'-1\frac{1}{2}'$ long and 1' broad, and densely coated on the outer surface with fine pubescence; filaments distinct, inserted on the petals; ovary conspicuously ridged, pubescent, truncate, and crowned with a slender deciduous style nearly as long as the stamens. **Fruit** globose, slightly pubescent, $\frac{3}{4}'$ in diameter, the valves splitting nearly to the middle and septicidally from the base to the middle; **seeds** 6–8, or by abortion fewer in each cell, closely packed together on the whole length of the thick axile placenta, nearly $\frac{1}{2}'$ long, angled by mutual pressure, without wings.

A tree, 15°–20° high, with stout slightly angled dark red-brown branchlets covered with small pale oblong horizontal lenticels, and conspicuously marked by large prominent obcordate leaf-scars, with a marginal row of large fibro-vascular bundle-scars. **Winter-buds** compressed, reddish brown, puberulous, $\frac{1}{4}'-\frac{1}{3}'$ long. **Bark** of cultivated plants smooth, thin, dark brown.

Distribution. Near Fort Barrington on the Altamaha River, Georgia; not seen in a wild state since 1790, and now only known by cultivated plants.

Occasionally cultivated in the eastern states and hardy as far north as eastern New York and occasionally in eastern Massachusetts, and rarely in western and central Europe.

XLII. CANELLACEÆ.

Trees, with pungent aromatic bark, and alternate pellucid-punctate entire penniveined persistent leaves, without stipules. Flowers perfect, regular, cymose; sepals and petals imbricated in the bud; stamens numerous, hypogynous, with filaments united into a tube inclosing the pistil, and narrow extrorse anthers adnate to the tube and longitudinally 2-celled; pistil of 2–3 united carpels; ovary free, 1-celled, with 2–5 parietal placentas; styles thick; stigmas 2–5-lobed; ovules 2 or many. Fruit a berry; seeds 2 or several; seed-coat thick, crustaceous; embryo small in fleshy oily albumen.

The Wild Cinnamon family with five genera and a few species is confined to tropical America, south Africa and Madagascar, one species reaching the shores of southern Florida.

1. CANELLA P. Br.

A tree, with scaly bark, stout ashy gray branchlets conspicuously marked by large orbicular leaf-scars, and minute buds. Leaves obovate, rounded or slightly emarginate at apex, gradually narrowed to the cuneate base, petiolate, coriaceous. Flowers small, in many-flowered subcorymbose terminal or subterminal panicles of several dichotomously branched cymes from the axils of upper leaves or from minute caducous bracts; sepals 3, suborbicular, concave, coriaceous, erect, their margins ciliate, persistent; petals 5, hypogynous, in a single row on the slightly convex receptacle, oblong, concave, rounded at apex, fleshy, twice as long as the sepals, white or rose color; stamens about 20, staminal tube crenulate at the summit and slightly extended above the anthers; ovary cylindric or oblong-conic, 1-celled, with 2 parietal placentas; style short, fleshy, terminating in a 2 or 3-lobed stigma, ovules numerous, arcuate, horizontal or descending, attached by a short funicle, imperfectly anatropous; micropyle superior. Fruit globose or slightly ovoid, fleshy, minutely pointed with the base of the persistent style, 2–4-seeded. Seeds reniform, suspended; seed-coat black and shining; embryo curved in the copious albumen; cotyledons oblong; radicle next the hilum.

The genus consists of a single West Indian species, extending into southern Florida and to Venezuela.

The generic name is from *canella*, the diminutive of the Latin *cana* or *canna*, a cane or reed, first applied to the bark of some Old World tree from the form of a roll or quill which it assumed in drying.

1. Canella Winterana Gærtn. Cinnamon Bark. White Wood. Wild Cinnamon.

Leaves contracted into a short stout grooved petiole, $3\frac{1}{2}'-5'$ long and $1\frac{1}{2}'-2'$ wide, bright green and lustrous. **Flowers** about $\frac{1}{4}'$ in diameter, opening in the autumn. **Fruit** ripening in March and April, bright crimson, soft and fleshy, $\frac{1}{2}'$ in diameter; **seeds** about $\frac{3}{16}'$ long.

A tree, in Florida 25°–30° high, with a straight trunk 8'–10' in diameter, and slender

horizontal spreading branches forming a compact round-headed top. **Bark** of the trunk
⅛′ thick, light gray, broken on the surface into numerous short thick scales rarely more
than 2′–3′ long and about twice as thick as the pale yellow aromatic inner bark. **Wood**

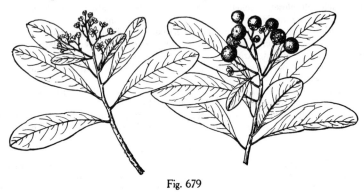

Fig. 679

very heavy, exceedingly hard, strong, close-grained, dark red-brown, with thick light
brown or yellow sapwood of 25–30 layers of annual growth.   The bitter acrid inner bark
is the wild cinnamon bark of commerce.   It has a pleasant cinnamon-like odor and is an
aromatic stimulant and tonic.

Distribution.   Florida, region of Cape Sable, Monroe County (Flamingo [*A. A. Eaton*],
East Cape, Madeira Hammock), and widely distributed on the southern keys, usually
growing in the shade of other trees; on the Bahama Islands and many of the Antilles.

XLIII. KŒBERLINIACEÆ.

An intricately branched almost leafless tree or shrub, with thin red-brown scaly bark,
stout alternate glabrous branchlets covered with pale green bark and terminating in a sharp
rigid straight or slightly curved spine.   Leaves minute, early deciduous, alternate, narrow-
obovate, rounded at apex.   Flowers perfect, on slender club-shaped puberulous pedicels
from the axils of minute scarious deciduous bracts, in short umbel-like racemes below the
end of the branches; calyx of 3 or 5 minute sepals imbricated in the bud, deciduous; petals
4, convolute in the bud, hypogynous, obovate or oblong, subunguiculate, white, much
longer than the sepals; disk 0; stamens 8, free, hypogynous, as long as the petals; filaments
thickened in the middle, subulate at the ends; anthers oval, attached on the back near the
base, 2-celled, the cells opening longitudinally; ovary ovoid, 2-celled, contracted at base
into a short stalk and above into a simple subulate style; stigma terminal, obtuse, slightly
emarginate; ovules numerous, adnate in several series to the fleshy placenta, horizontal or
dependent, anatropous.   Fruit a 2-celled berry, black at maturity, subglobose, tipped with
the remnants of the pointed style; flesh thin and succulent, the cells 1 or 2-seeded by abortion.   Seed vertical, circinate-cochleate; seed-coat crustaceous, slightly rugose, striate;
albumen thin; embryo annular; cotyledons semiterete; the radicle ascending.

The family is represented by a single genus.

1. KŒBERLINIA Zucc.

Characters of the family.

Kœberlinia with one species is North American.

The generic name is in honor of L. Koeberlin, a German botanist. .

1. Kœberlinia spinosa Zucc.

Leaves not more than ⅛′ long.   **Flowers** appearing in May and June, about ¼′ in diameter.   **Fruit** $\frac{3}{16}$′–¼′ in diameter.

A bushy tree, rarely 20°-25° high, with a short stout trunk sometimes 6°-8° long and a foot in diameter; more often a low branching shrub forming impenetrable thickets often of considerable extent. **Wood** very hard, heavy, close-grained, dark brown somewhat streaked with orange, becoming almost black on exposure, with thin yellow or nearly white sapwood of 12-15 layers of annual growth.

Distribution. Dry gravelly mesas and foothills; valleys of the upper Colorado River

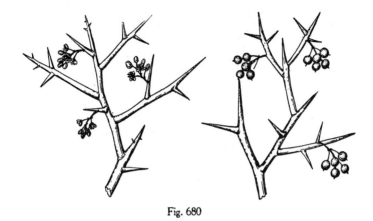

Fig. 680

(Big Springs, Howard County), and of the lower Rio Grande, Texas, westward through southern Texas and New Mexico to southern Arizona, and southward through northern Mexico, and in Lower California (San Jorge).

XLIV. CARICACEÆ.

Trees or shrubs, with bitter milky juice, and alternate long-petiolate persistent simple or digitately compound leaves, without stipules. Flowers unisexual or perfect, the perianth of the male and female flowers dissimilar; stamens in two series, inserted on the corolla; filaments free; anthers introrse. Fruit baccate.

The Pawpaw family with two genera is tropical American and Mexican, a single representative of the family reaching the shores of southern Florida.

1. CARICA L.

Short-lived trees, with erect simple or rarely branched stems composed of a thin shell of soft fibrous wood surrounding a large central cavity divided by thin soft cross partitions at the nodes, and covered with thin green or gray bark marked by the ring-like scars of fallen leaf-stalks, and stout soft fleshy roots. Leaves simple, palmately lobed or digitate, crowded toward the top of the stem and branches, large, flaccid, subpeltately palmately nerved, and usually deeply and often compoundly lobed. Flowers regular, monœcious or polygamo-diœcious, white, yellow, or greenish white, in axillary cymose panicles, the staminate elongated, pedunculate, and many-flowered, the pistillate abbreviated and few or usually 3-flowered, generally unisexual and diœcious, occasionally polygamo-diœcious, each flower in the axil of a minute ovate acute bract; calyx minute, 5-lobed, the lobes alternate with the petals; corolla of the staminate flower salverform, gamopetalous, the tube elongated, 5-lobed, the lobes oblong or linear, contorted in the bud; stamens 10; filaments free, those of the outer row alternate with the lobes of the corolla and elongated, the others alternate with them and abbreviated; anthers 2-celled, erect, opening longitudinally, often surmounted by their slightly elongated connective; ovary rudimentary, subulate; pistillate flower, calyx minute, 5-lobed, persistent under the fruit; corolla polypetalous, petals 5, linear-oblong, erect, ultimately spreading above the middle, deciduous; ovary free, sessile, 1-celled or more or less spuriously 5-celled; style 0 or abbreviated; stigmas 5, linear, radiating, dilated and subpalmately lobed at apex; ovules indefinite, inserted in two rows on the placenta, anatropous, long-stalked; micropyle superior; raphe ventral; hermaphrodite flower, corolla gamopetalous, tubular-campanulate, the lobes erect and spreading or subreflexed; stamens 10, in 2 ranks, or 5; ovary obovoid-oblong, longer than the tube of the corolla, more or less spuriously 5-celled below.   Fruit slightly 5-lobed, 1-celled or more or less completely 5-celled, filled with soft pulp, many-seeded, that produced from the hermaphrodite flower long-stalked, pendulous, usually unsymmetric, gibbous, and smaller than that from the pistillate flower.   Seeds ovoid, inclosed in membranaceous silvery white sac-like arils, occasionally germinating within the fruit; seed-coat crustaceous, closely investing the membranaceous inner coat, the outer coat becoming thick, rugose, succulent, and ultimately dry and leathery; embryo in the axis of fleshy albumen; cotyledons ovate, foliaceous, compressed, longer than the terete radicle turned toward the minute pale subbasilar hilum.

Carica with about twenty species is distributed from southern Florida through the West Indies to southern Brazil and Argentina, and from southern Mexico to Chili.   One species grows probably indigenously in Florida.   The milky juice of Carica contains papain, which has the power of digesting albuminous substances, and the leaves are often used in tropical countries to make meat tender.

The generic name is formed from the Carib name of one of the species.

1. Carica Papaya L. Pawpaw.

Leaves ovate or orbicular, deeply parted into 5–7 lobes divided more or less deeply into acute lateral lobes, these secondary divisions entire or rarely lobed, the lowest lobes form-

Fig. 681

ing a deep basal sinus, thin, flaccid, yellow-green, $15'$–$24'$ in diameter, with broad flat yellow or orange-colored primary veins radiating from the end of the petiole through the lobes, and small secondary veins extending to the point of the lateral lobes and connected by conspicuous reticulate veinlets; petioles stout, yellow, hollow, enlarged and cordate at base, sometimes becoming $3°$–$4°$ in length before the leaves fall.   **Flowers** often beginning to appear on plants only $3°$ or $4°$ high and a few months old, produced continuously throughout the year, the staminate in clusters on slender spreading or pendulous peduncles $4'$–$12'$ long, the pistillate in 1–3-flowered short-stalked cymes; staminate flowers fragrant, filled with nectar, their corolla $\frac{3}{4}'$–$1\frac{1}{4}'$ long, with a slender tube and acute lobes; anthers oblong, orange-colored, surmounted by the rounded thickened end of the connective, those of the inner row almost sessile and one third larger than those of the outer row, shorter than their flattened filaments covered, like the connectives, with long slender white hairs; pistillate flowers about 1′ long, with erect petals, without staminodia; ovary ovoid, ivory-white, slightly and obtusely 5-angled, 1-celled, and narrowed into a short slender style crowned by a pale green stigma divided to the base into 5 radiating lobes dilated and 3-nerved at apex. Fruits hanging close together against the stem at the base of the leaf-stalk, obovoid to ellipsoid, and obtusely short-pointed, yellowish green to bright orange color; in southern Florida not more than 4′ long and 3′ thick, and usually smaller, with a thick skin closely adherent to the sweet insipid flesh forming a thin layer outside the central cavity; seeds full and rounded, about $\frac{3}{16}′$ long; outer portion of the seed-coat rugose at first when the fruit is fully grown but still green, ivory-white, very succulent, and usually separable from the smooth paler chestnut-brown lustrous interior portion, the outer part turning black as the fruit ripens and becoming adherent to the inner portion closely investing the thin lustrous light red-brown inner coat.

A short-lived tree, in Florida attaining a height of 12°–15°, with a trunk seldom more than 6′ in diameter; in the West Indies and other tropical countries often twice as large, with a trunk occasionally dividing into a number of stout upright branches. Bark thin, light green, becoming gray toward the base of the stem.

Distribution. Florida from the southern shores of Bay Biscayne on the west coast and of Indian River on the east coast to the southern keys, growing sparingly in rich hummocks; common in all the West Indian islands, in southern Mexico, and in the tropical countries of South America; now naturalized in most of the warm regions of the world, where it is universally cultivated for its fruit, which is considered one of the most wholesome of all tropical fruits, and has been much improved by selection.

XLV. CACTACEÆ.

Succulent trees or shrubs, with copious watery juice, numerous spines springing from cushions of small bristles (areolæ), and minute caducous alternate leaves, or leafless. Flowers large and showy, perfect, usually solitary; calyx of numerous spirally imbricated sepals forming a tube, those of the inner series petal-like; corolla of numerous imbricated petals, in many series; stamens inserted on the tube of the calyx, very numerous, in several series, with slender filaments and introrse 2-celled oblong anthers, the cells opening longitudinally; pistil of several united carpels; ovary 1-celled, with several parietal placentas; styles united, terminal; stigmas as many as the placentas; ovules numerous, horizontal, anatropous. Fruit a fleshy berry. Seeds numerous, with albumen; cotyledons foliaceous; radicle turned toward the hilum.

The Cactus family with twenty genera and a very large number of species is most abundant in the dry region adjacent to the boundary of the United States and Mexico, with a few species ranging northward to the northern United States and southward to the West Indian islands, Brazil, Peru, Chili and the Galapagos Islands. Two of the genera have arborescent representatives in the flora of the United States.

CONSPECTUS OF THE ARBORESCENT GENERA OF THE UNITED STATES.

Branches and stems columnar, ribbed, continuous; leaves 0; flower-bearing and spine-bearing areolæ distinct; flowers close above spine-bearing areolæ; tube of the flower elongated; seeds dark-colored. 1. Cereus.
Branches jointed, tuberculate; leaves scale-like; flower-bearing and spine-bearing areolæ not distinct; tube of the flower short and cup-shaped; seeds pale. 2. Opuntia.

1. CEREUS Haw.

Trees or shrubs, with columnar ribbed stems, and buds on the back of the ridges from the axils of latent leaves, geminate, superposed, the upper producing a branch or flower, the lower arrested and developed into a cluster of spines surrounded by an elevated cushion or areola of chaffy tomentose scales.   Flowers lateral, elongated, the calyx-lobes forming an elongated tube, those of the outer ranks adnate to the ovary, scale-like, only their tips free, those of the inner ranks free, elongated; petals cohering by their base with the top of the calyx-tube, larger than its interior lobes, spreading, recurved; stamens numerous; filaments adnate by their base to the tube of the calyx, those of the interior ranks free, the exterior united into a tube; style filiform, divided into numerous radiating linear branches stigmatic on the inner face; stalks of the ovules long and slender, becoming thick and juicy in the fruit.   Seeds with very thin albumen; embryo straight; cotyledons abbreviated, hooked at apex; radicle conic.

Cereus with at least two hundred species inhabits the dry southwestern region of North America, the West Indies, tropical South America, and the Galapagos Islands.   Of the numerous species found within the territory of the United States only one assumes the habit and size of a tree.   The fruit of several species is edible, and the ribs of the durable woody frames of the stems of the large arborescent species are used for the rafters of houses and for fuel.   Many of the species are planted in warm dry countries in hedges to protect cultivated fields, and others are popular garden plants valued for their beautiful flowers, which are sometimes nocturnal and exceedingly fragrant.

The generic name relates to the candle-like form of the stem of some of the species.

1. Cereus giganteus Engelm.   Suwarro.

Leaves 0.   **Flowers** 4′–4½′ long and 2½′ wide, opening from May to July in great numbers near the top of the stem, each surrounded on the lower side by the radial spines of the cluster below it; ovary ovoid, 1′ long, rather shorter than the stout tube of the flower, and covered,

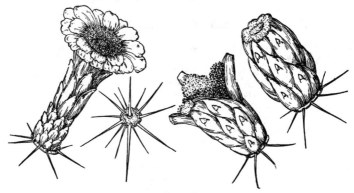

Fig. 682

like the base of the tube, by the thick imbricated green outer scale-like sepals, with small free triangular acute scarious mucronate tips, furnished in their axils with short tufts of rufous hairs and occasionally with clusters of chartaceous spines, gradually passing into thin oblong-ovate or obovate larger sepals, mucronate or rounded at apex and closely imbricated in many ranks; petals 25–35, obovate-spatulate, obtuse, entire, thick and fleshy, creamy white, ⅔′ long and much reflexed after anthesis; stamens, with linear anthers emarginate at the ends, and filaments united for half their length to the walls of the calyx-tube, those of the exterior rows joined below into a long tube, surrounding the stout columnar style glandular at base and divided at apex into 12–15 green stigmas.   **Fruit** ripening in August, ovoid or slightly obovoid, 2½′ long and 1½′ wide, truncate and covered at apex by the depressed pale scar left by the falling of the flower, light red at maturity, separating into 3 or 4 fleshy valves bright red on their inner surface and inclosing the bright scarlet juicy mass of the enlarged funiculi and innumerable seeds; seeds obovoid, rounded, $\frac{1}{6}'$ long, lustrous, dark chestnut-brown.

A tree, 50°–60° high, with a trunk sometimes 2° in diameter, thickest below the middle and tapering gradually toward the ends, marked by transverse superficial lines into rings 4'–8' long, representing the amount of annual longitudinal growth, 8–12-ribbed at base with obtuse ribs 4'–5' broad, and at summit 18–20-ribbed with obtuse deep compressed ribs, branchless or furnished above the middle with a few, usually 2 or 3, stout alternate or sometimes opposite upright branches shorter but otherwise resembling the principal stem composed of a thick tough green epidermis, a fleshy covering 3'–6' thick saturated with bitter juice, and a circle of bundles of woody fibres making, with annual layers of exogenous growth, dense tough elastic columns placed opposite the depressions between the ribs, $\frac{1}{2}'$–3' in diameter and frequently united by branches growing at irregular intervals between them, the woody frame remaining standing after the death of the plant and the decomposition of its fleshy covering. Areolæ pale, elevated, about $\frac{1}{2}'$ in diameter, bearing clusters of stout straight spines with a large dark fulvous base, sulcate or angled, tinged with red, with thick stout spines in the centre of each cluster, the 4 basal horizontal or slightly inclined downward, the lowest being the longest and stoutest and sometimes $1\frac{1}{2}'$ long and $\frac{1}{12}'$ thick, the upper shorter, more slender and slightly turned upward, with a row of shorter and thinner radial spines 12–16 in number surrounding the central group. Wood of the columns strong, very light, rather coarse-grained, with numerous conspicuous medullary rays, and light brown tinged with yellow; almost indestructible in contact with the ground, little affected by the atmosphere and largely used for the rafters of houses, for fences, and by Indians for lances, bows, etc. The fruit is consumed in large quantities by Indians.

Distribution. Low rocky hills and dry mesas of the desert; valley of the San Pedro River through central and southern Arizona to the valley of the Colorado River between Needles and Yuma, Yuma County, Arizona, and southward in Sonora.

2. OPUNTIA Adans.

Trees or usually shrubs, in the arborescent species of the United States with subcylindric or clavate articulate tuberculate branches, covered with small sunken stomata, and containing tubular reticulated woody skeletons, and thick fleshy or fibrous roots. Leaves scale-like, terete, subulate, caducous, bearing in their axils oblong or circular cushion-like areolæ of chaffy or woolly scales terminal on the branches and furnished above the middle with many short slender slightly attached sharp barbed bristles and toward the base with numerous stout barbed spines surrounded in some species, except at apex, by loose papery sheaths. Flowers diurnal, lateral, produced from areolæ on branches of the previous year between the bristles and spines, sessile, cup-shaped; sepals flat, erect, deciduous; corolla rotate; petals obovate, united at base, spreading; stamens shorter than the petals; filaments free or slightly united below; anthers oblong; style cylindric, longer than the stamens, obclavate below, divided at apex into 3–8 elongated or lobulate lobes stigmatic on the inner face. Fruit sometimes proliferous, covered by a thick skin, succulent and often edible, or dry, pyriform, globose or ellipsoid, concave at apex, surmounted by the marcescent tube of the flower, tuberculate, areolate, or rarely glabrous, truncate at base, with a broad umbilicus at apex. Seeds immersed in the pulpy placentas, compressed, discoid, often margined with a bony raphe; testa pale, bony, sometimes marked by a narrow darker marginal commissure; embryo coiled around the copious or scanty albumen; cotyledons large; radicle thin, obtuse.

Opuntia with many species is distributed from southern New England southward in the neighborhood of the coast to the West Indies, and through western North America to Chili, Brazil, and Argentina, the largest number of species occurring near the boundary of the United States and Mexico. Of the species of the United States at least three attain the size and habit of small trees. Cochineal is derived from a scale-insect which feeds on the juices of some of the Mexican species, and the fruit of several species is refreshing and is consumed in considerable quantities in semitropical countries. The large-growing species with flat branches are employed in many countries to form hedges for the protection of gardens and fields; and the branches saturated with watery juice are sometimes stripped of their spines and bristles and fed to cattle.

Opuntia is the classical name of some plant which grew in the neighborhood of the city of Opus in Bœotia.

CONSPECTUS OF THE ARBORESCENT SPECIES OF THE UNITED STATES.

Tubercles of the branches full and rounded below the areolæ.
  Joints pale olive color, easily separable, their tubercles broad, mammillate; spines yellow; flowers pink; fruit proliferous, usually spineless, often sterile.   1. O. fulgida (H).
  Joints green or purple, their tubercles narrow, ovoid; spines white to reddish brown; flowers purple; fruit yellow, sparingly spinescent, rarely proliferous.

                                                              2. O. spinosior (H).
Tubercles of the branches not full and rounded below the areolæ; joints elongated, dark green or purple, their tubercles elongated; spines brown or reddish brown; flowers green, tinted with red or yellow; fruit green, spinescent, rarely proliferous.

                                                              3. O. versicolor (H).

1. Opuntia fulgida Engelm.   Cholla.

Leaves light green, gradually narrowed to the acuminate apex, $\frac{1}{2}'$–$1'$ long. **Flowers** appearing from June to September, the earliest from tubercles at the end of the branches of the previous year the others from the terminal tubercles of the immature fruit developed from the earliest flowers of the season, $1'$ in diameter when fully expanded, with ovaries nearly $1'$ long, 8–10 obtuse crenulate sepals, 5 erect stigmas, and 8 light pink petals, those of the outer ranks cuneate, retuse, crenulate on the margins, shorter than the lanceolate acute petals of the inner ranks, the whole strongly reflexed at maturity. **Fruit** proliferous,

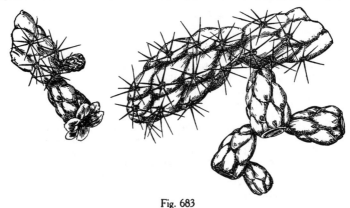

Fig. 683

oval, rounded, $1'$–$1\frac{1}{4}'$ long and nearly as broad, more or less tuberculate, conspicuously marked by large pale tomentose areolæ bearing numerous small bristles, usually spineless or occasionally armed with small weak spines, hanging in pendulous clusters usually of 6 or 7 and occasionally of 40–50 fruits in a cluster, one growing from the other in continuous succession, the first the largest and containing perfect seeds, the others frequently sterile, dull green when fully ripe, with dry flesh, falling usually during the first winter or occasionally persistent on the branches during the second season, and then developing flowers from the tubercles; **seeds** compressed, thin, very angular, $\frac{1}{12}'$–$\frac{1}{6}'$ in diameter.

A tree, with a more or less flexuous trunk occasionally 12° in height and sometimes a foot in diameter, a symmetric head of stout wide-spreading branches and thick pendulous joints sometimes almost hidden by the long conspicuous spines and beginning to develop their woody skeletons during their second or occasionally during their third season, the terminal or ultimate joints ovoid or ovoid-cylindric, tumid, crowded at the end of the limbs, pale olive color, $3'-8'$ long, often $2'$ in diameter, with broad ovoid-oblong tubercles, $\frac{1}{2}'-\frac{3}{4}'$ in length. **Areolæ** of pale straw-colored tomentum and short slender pale bristles, each areola bearing at first 5–15 stout stellate-spreading light yellow spines of nearly equal length, $\frac{3}{4}'-$ $1'$ long and inclosed in loose lustrous sheaths, additional spines developing in succeeding years at the upper margin of the areolæ, the tubercles of old branches being sometimes furnished with from 40–60 spines persistent on the branches for 4–6 years. **Bark** of the trunk and of the large limbs about $\frac{1}{4}'$ thick, separating freely on the surface into large thin loosely attached scales varying in color from brown to nearly black on the largest stems, and unarmed, the spines mostly falling with the outer layers from branches $3'-4'$ thick. **Wood** of old trunks light, hard, pale yellow, with broad conspicuous medullary rays, well marked layers of annual growth, and a thick pith.

Distribution. Plains of Arizona south of the Colorado plateau, and in the adjacent region of Sonora; not rare; apparently most abundant and of its largest size in the United States on the mesas near Tucson, Pima County, at altitudes between 2000° and 3000°.

2. Opuntia spinosior Toumey. Tassajo.

Leaves terete, tapering gradually to the setulose apex, about $\frac{1}{4}'$ long, remaining on the branches from four to six weeks. **Flowers** opening in April and May and remaining open

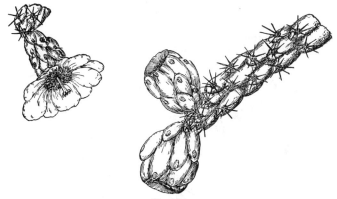

Fig. 684

for two or three days, $2'-2\frac{1}{2}'$ in diameter, with ovaries about $1'$ long, obovate sepals, broad-obovate dark purple petals, sensitive red stamens, and a 6–9-parted stigma. **Fruits** clustered at the end of the branches of the previous year, persistent during the winter and occasionally during the following summer and then sometimes proliferous, oval or rarely globose or hemispheric, frequently $2'$ long and $1\frac{1}{2}'$ thick, with yellow acrid flesh and 20–30 tubercles very prominent during the summer, nearly disappearing as the fruit ripens and enlarges, leaving it marked only by the small oval areolæ covered with short bristles, and bearing numerous slender spines deciduous in December as the fruit begins to turn yellow; **seeds** nearly orbicular, slightly or not at all beaked, $\frac{1}{6}'-\frac{1}{5}'$ in diameter, and marked by linear conspicuous commissures.

A tree, with an erect trunk occasionally 10° high and $5'-10'$ in diameter, numerous stout spreading limbs forming an open irregular head, and branches with joints $4'-12'$ long and

$\frac{3}{4}'$–$1'$ thick, covered with a thick epidermis varying from green to purple, and usually developing woody skeletons during their second season, their tubercles prominent, compressed, ovoid, $\frac{1}{3}'$–$\frac{1}{2}'$ long. Areolæ oval, clothed with pale tomentum and short light brown bristles, their spines 5–15 on the tubercles of young joints and 30–50 on those of older branches, and slender, white to light reddish brown, closely invested in white glistening sheaths, stellate-spreading, $\frac{1}{2}'$–$\frac{3}{4}'$ long, those in the interior sometimes considerably longer than the radial spines. Bark of the trunk and of the larger limbs about $\frac{1}{4}'$ thick, spineless, nearly black, broken into elongated ridges, and finally much roughened by numerous closely appressed scales. Wood light, soft, pale reddish brown, and conspicuously reticulate, with conspicuous medullary rays and well defined layers of annual growth; sometimes used in the manufacture of light furniture, canes, picture-frames, and other small articles.

Distribution. Widely scattered over the mesas of southern Arizona south of the Colorado plateau and of the adjacent regions of Sonora.

3. Opuntia versicolor Coult.

Leaves terete, abruptly narrowed to the spinescent apex, $\frac{1}{3}'$–$\frac{1}{2}'$ long, persistent on the branches from four to six weeks. Flowers opening in May, about $1\frac{1}{2}'$ in diameter, with ovaries $\frac{5}{8}'$ long, broad-ovate acute sepals, and narrow obovate petals rounded above and green tinged with red or with yellow. Fruit usually clavate, $2'$–$2\frac{1}{2}'$ long, nearly $1\frac{1}{2}'$ in diameter, with areolæ generally only above the middle and usually furnished with 1–3 slender reflexed persistent spines about $\frac{1}{2}'$ long, or occasionally spineless, rarely nearly spherical and only about $\frac{3}{4}'$ in diameter, ripening from December to February, and at maturity the same color as the joint on which it grows, usually withering, drying, and splitting open on the tree, or remaining fleshy and persistent on the branches until the end of the following summer, and sometimes through a second winter, or often becoming imbedded in the end of a more or less elongated joint; seeds irregularly angled, with narrow commissures.

A tree, with an erect trunk occasionally 6°–8° high and 8' in diameter, numerous stout irregularly spreading or often upright branches, and cylindric terminal joints generally

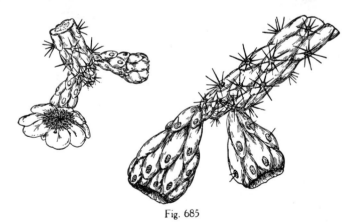

Fig. 685

$6'$–$12'$ but sometimes $2°$ in length, $\frac{3}{4}'$–$1'$ in diameter, and covered with a thick dark green or purple epidermis, marked by linear flattened tubercles, their woody skeletons usually formed during their second season. Areolæ large, oval, clothed with gray wool, generally bearing a cluster of small bristles, and slender stellate-spreading brown or reddish brown spines, with close early deciduous straw-colored sheaths, 4–14 and on old tubercles 20–25 in number, the inner 1–4 in number, usually deflexed and unequal in length, the longest about

$\frac{1}{3}'$ long and longer than the radial spines. **Bark** of the trunk and of the large branches smooth, light brown or purple, usually unarmed, $\frac{1}{2}'-\frac{3}{4}'$ thick, finally separating into small closely appressed black scales. **Wood** reticulate, hard, compact, light reddish brown and rather lustrous, with thin conspicuous medullary rays, well-defined layers of annual growth, and thick pale or nearly white sapwood.

Distribution. Foothills and low mountain slopes of southern Arizona and northern Sonora; very abundant.

XLVI. RHIZOPHORACEÆ.

Glabrous trees or shrubs, with terete branchlets, and usually opposite coriaceous entire persistent leaves, with interpetiolar stipules. Flowers in axillary clusters; calyx-lobes valvate in the bud, persistent; petals inserted on the tube of the calyx and as many as its lobes; stamens inserted at the base of a conspicuous disk; anthers 2-celled, the cells opening longitudinally; pistil of 2-5 united carpels; ovary 2-5-celled; ovules usually 2 in each cell, suspended from its apex, collateral, anatropous; raphe ventral; micropyle superior. Fruit usually indehiscent, 1-celled and 1-seeded.

The Mangrove family is tropical, with most of its seventeen genera confined to the Old World.

1. RHIZOPHORA L. Mangrove.

Trees, with pithy branchlets, thick astringent bark, and adventitious fleshy roots. Leaves ovate or elliptic, glabrous, petiolate; stipules elongated, acuminate, infolding the bud, caducous. Flowers perfect, yellow or creamy white, sessile or pedicellate, bibracteolate, the bractlets united into an involucral cup, in pedunculate dichotomously or trichotomously branched clusters, the base of their branches surrounded by an involucre of 2 ovate 3-lobed persistent bracts, or 1-flowered; calyx 4-lobed, the lobes acute, coriaceous, ribbed on the inner surface and thickened on the margins, two or three times longer than the turbinate globose tube, reflexed at maturity, persistent; petals 4, induplicate in the bud, alternate with and longer than the calyx-lobes, inserted on a fleshy disk-like ring in the mouth of the calyx-tube, involute on the margins, coated on the inner surface with long pale hairs, or flat and naked, caducous; stamens 8-12; filaments short or 0; anthers attached at the base, introrse, elongated, connivent, areolate; ovary partly inferior, conic, 2-celled, contracted into two subulate spreading styles stigmatic at apex. Fruit a conic coriaceous berry surrounded by the reflexed calyx-lobes and perforated at the apex by the germinating embryo. Seed germinating in the fruit before falling, the apex surrounded by a thin albuminous cuplike aril; seed-coat thick and fleshy; embryo surrounded by a thin layer of albumen; cotyledons dark purple; radicle elongated, clavate, and when fully grown separating from the narrow exserted woody tube inclosing the plumule and developed from the cotyledons after the ripening of the fruit.

Rhizophora with three species is widely and generally distributed on the shores of tidal marshes in the tropical regions of the two hemispheres, one specie reaching those of southern Florida. It possesses astringent properties; the bark has been used in tanning leather, in dyeing, and as a febrifuge. The wood is hard, durable, and dark-colored. By means of the aerial germination of its seeds and in its power to develop roots from trunks and branches, Rhizophora is especially adapted to maintain itself on low tidal shores and is an important factor in protecting and extending them into the ocean. Roots springing from the stems at a considerable distance above the ground and arching outward descend into the water and fix themselves in the mud beneath, while roots growing down from the branches enter the ground and gradually thicken into stems. The fully grown radicle ready to put forth roots and leaves, and often $10'-12'$ long, is thicker and heavier at the root end than at the other, and in detaching itself from the cotyledons and in falling the heavy end sticks in the mud, while the plumule at the other end, held above the shallow surface of the water, soon unfolds its leaves.

The generic name, from ῥίζα and φέρειν, was used by early authors to designate various climbing plants with thickened roots.

1. Rhizophora Mangle L.

Leaves ovate or elliptic, rounded or acute at apex, gradually narrowed at base, dark green and very lustrous on the upper surface, paler on the lower surface, $3\frac{1}{2}'-5'$ long and $1'-2'$ wide, with slightly thickened margins, a broad midrib, and reticulate veinlets; persistent for one or two years; petioles $\frac{1}{2}'-1\frac{1}{2}'$ in length; stipules lanceolate, acute, $1\frac{1}{2}'$ long, deciduous as the leaf unfolds. Flowers produced through the year, $1'$ in diameter, pedicellate, in

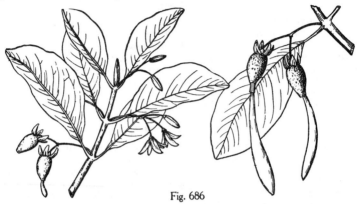

Fig. 686

2 or 3-flowered clusters on peduncles $1\frac{1}{2}'$ long from the axils of young leaves; petals pale yellow, coated on the inner surface with long pale hairs; stamens 8 with villose filaments. Fruit $1'$ long, rusty brown, slightly roughened by minute bosses, the hard woody thick-walled tube developed from the cotyledons protruding $\frac{1}{2}'-\frac{2}{3}'$ from its apex after the germination of the seed, covering the plumule, and holding the dark brown radicle marked with occasional orange-colored lenticels and when fully grown $10'-12'$ long and $\frac{1}{4}'-\frac{1}{3}'$ thick near the apex.

A round-topped bushy tree, with spreading branches usually $15°-20°$ high, forming almost impenetrable thickets with its numerous aerial roots, or occasionally $70°-80°$ high, with a tall straight trunk clear of branches for more than half its length, a narrow head, and stout glabrous dark red-brown branchlets, becoming lighter colored in their second year and then conspicuously marked by large oval slightly elevated leaf-scars. Bark of young stems and of the branches smooth, light reddish brown, becoming on old trunks $\frac{1}{3}'-\frac{1}{2}'$ thick, and gray faintly tinged with red, the surface irregularly fissured and broken into thin appressed scales. Wood exceedingly heavy, hard, close-grained, strong, dark reddish brown streaked with lighter brown, with pale sapwood of 40–50 layers of annual growth; u.ed for fuel and wharf-piles.

Distribution. Shores of Florida from Indian River on the east coast and shores of Tampa Bay on the west coast to the southern keys; most abundant south of latitude 29°, following the coast with wide thickets and ascending the rivers for many miles; on Cape Sable and the shores of Bay Biscayne sometimes growing at a little distance from the coast on ground not submerged by the tide, and here attaining its largest size, with tall straight trunks and few aerial roots; on Bermuda, the Bahamas, the Antilles, the west coast of Mexico, lower California, the Galapagos Islands, and from Central America along the northeast coast of South America to the limits of the tropics.

XLVII. COMBRETACEÆ.

Trees or shrubs, with astringent juice, naked buds, and alternate or opposite simple entire coriaceous persistent leaves, without stipules. Flowers regular, perfect, or polygamous; calyx 5-lobed, the lobes valvate in the bud; petals 5, valvate in the bud, inserted at the base of the calyx, or 0; disk epigynous; stamens 5–10, inserted on the limb of the calyx; filaments slender, filiform, distinct, exserted; anthers introrse, 2-celled, the cells opening longitudinally; ovary 1-celled; style slender, subulate; stigma minute, terminal, entire; ovules usually 2, suspended from the apex of the cell, collateral, anatropous; raphe ventral; micropyle superior. Fruit drupaceous, often crowned with the accrescent calyx. Seed solitary; albumen 0; embryo straight, with convolute cotyledons; radicle minute, turned toward the hilum.

Of the fifteen genera of this family, widely distributed through the tropics, three have arborescent representatives in southern Florida.

CONSPECTUS OF THE ARBORESCENT GENERA OF THE UNITED STATES.

Corolla 0; leaves alternate.
  Calyx persistent; flowers in spikes; seeds without wings.   **1. Bucida.**
  Calyx deciduous; flowers in capitate heads; seeds winged.   **2. Conocarpus.**
Corolla of 5 petals; calyx persistent; leaves opposite.   **3. Laguncularia.**

1. BUCIDA L.

A tree or shrub, with terete often spinescent branchlets. Leaves crowded at the end of spur-like lateral branchlets much thickened and roughened by the large elevated crowded leaf-scars, alternate, obovate to oblong-lanceolate, rounded and slightly emarginate or minutely apiculate at apex, gradually narrowed and cuneate at base, coriaceous, bluish green on the upper surface and yellow-green on the lower surface, pubescent while young, especially beneath, and glabrous at maturity with the exception of rufous hairs on the under surface of the stout midrib, and on the short stout petiole. Flowers perfect, greenish white, hairy on the outer surface, sessile in the axils of minute bracts, in lax elongated axillary clustered rufous-pubescent spikes; calyx-tube ovoid, constricted above the ovary, the limb campanulate, 5-lobed, the lobes valvate in the bud, persistent; petals 0; stamens 10, in two ranks, inflexed in the bud, unequal, 5 longer than the others and inserted opposite the calyx-lobes under the hairy 5-lobed disk, the others shorter, alternate with them and inserted higher on the calyx-tube; filaments incurved near the apex; anthers minute, sagittate; ovary included in the tube of the calyx; style thickened and villose at the base; ovules suspended on an elongated slender funiculus. Fruit ovoid, conic, oblique, and more or less falcate, irregularly 5-angled, coriaceous, light brown, puberulous on the outer surface, with thin membranaceous flesh inseparable from the crustaceous stone porous toward the interior. Seed ovoid, acute; seed-coat coriaceous, chestnut-brown; cotyledons fleshy; radicle superior.

Bucida with a single species is confined to tropical America, where it is distributed from southern Florida and the Bahama Islands through the West Indies to Guiana and Central America.

The generic name is from βοῦς, in allusion to the fancied resemblance of the fruit to the horns of an ox.

1. Bucida Buceras L.   Black Olive-tree.

Leaves 2′–3′ long, 1′–1½′ wide, their petioles ⅓′–½′ in length. **Flowers** appearing in Florida in April, ⅛′ long, on spikes 1½′–3′ in length. **Fruit** about ⅓′ long.

A tree, with a single straight trunk, or often with a short prostrate stem 2°–3° in diameter, producing several straight upright secondary stems 40°–50° high and 12′–18′ in diameter, stout branches spreading nearly at right angles with the trunk and forming a broad head, and branchlets clothed when they first appear with short pale rufous pubescence mostly persistent for two or three years, becoming light reddish brown and covered with bark separating into thin narrow shreds. **Bark** of the trunk and of the large branches thick, gray tinged with orange-brown, and broken into short appressed scales. **Wood** exceedingly heavy, hard, close-grained, light yellow-brown sometimes slightly streaked

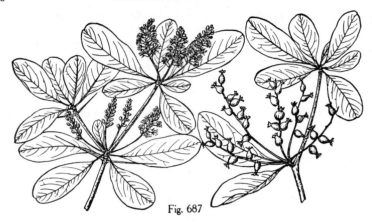

Fig. 687

with orange, with thick clear pale yellow sapwood of 30–40 layers of annual growth.   The bark has been used in tanning leather.

Distribution.   Florida, only on Elliott's Key; widely distributed in brackish marshes through the West Indies to the shores of the Caribbean Sea and the Bay of Panama.

2. CONOCARPUS L.

A tree or shrub, with angled branchlets.   Leaves alternate, short-petiolate, narrow-ovate or obovate, acute, gradually contracted and biglandular at base, glabrous or sericeous.   Flowers perfect, minute, in dense capitate heads in narrow leafy terminal panicles, with acute caducous bracts and bractlets coated with pale hairs, on stout hoary-tomentose peduncles bibracteolate near the middle; calyx-tube truncate, obliquely compressed at base, clothed with pale hairs, the limb campanulate, parted to the middle, the lobes ovate, acute, erect, pubescent on the outer and puberulous on the inner surface, deciduous; petals 0; disk 5-lobed, hairy; stamens usually 5, inserted in 1 rank, or rarely 7 or 8 in 2 ranks; anthers cordate, minute; style thickened and villose at base.   Fruits scale-like, broad-obovoid, pointed, recurved, and covered at apex with short pale hairs, densely imbricated in ovoid reddish heads; flesh coriaceous, corky, produced into broad lateral wings; stone thin-walled, crustaceous, inseparable from the flesh.   Seed irregularly ovoid; seed-coat membranaceous, pale chestnut-brown.

The genus consists of a single species of tropical America and Africa.

The generic name, from χῶνος and καρπὸς, is in allusion to the cone-like shape of the heads of fruits.

1. Conocarpus erecta L.   Buttonwood.

Leaves slightly puberulous on the lower surface when they first appear or coated with pale silky persistent pubescence (var. *sericea*, DC.), 2′–4′ long, ½′–1½′ wide, lustrous, dark green or pale on the upper surface, paler on the lower surface, with a broad orange-colored midrib, obscure primary veins, and reticulate veinlets; petioles stout, broad, ½′ in length. Flowers produced throughout the year, in heads ⅓′ in diameter on peduncles ½′–1½′ in length, in panicles 6′–12′ long.   Cone of fruit about 1′ in diameter.

A tree, 40°–60° high, with a trunk 20′–30′ in diameter, small branches forming a narrow regular head, and slender branchlets conspicuously winged, light red-brown, usually glabrous, or silky pubescent (var. *sericea*, DC.), becoming terete and marked by large orbicular leaf-scars in their second year; or sometimes a low shrub, with semiprostrate stems. Bark of the trunk dark brown, divided by irregular reticulating fissures into broad flat ridges broken on the surface into small thin appressed scales.   **Wood** very heavy, hard, strong, close-grained, dark yellow-brown, with thin darker colored sapwood of about 10 layers of annual growth; burning slowly like charcoal and highly valued for fuel. The

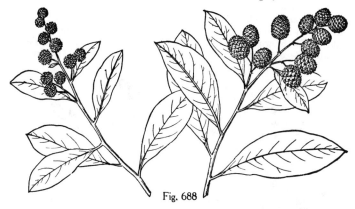

Fig. 688

bark is bitter and astringent, and has been used in tanning leather, and in medicine as an astringent and tonic.

Distribution. Low muddy tide-water shores of lagoons and bays; Florida, Cape Canaveral and shores of Tampa Bay to the southern keys; of its largest size in Florida on Lost Man's River near Cape Sable; at its northern limits a low shrub; common on the Bahama Islands, in the Antilles, on the shores of Central America and tropical South America, on the Galapagos Islands, and on the west coast of Africa.

3. LAGUNCULARIA Gærtn.

A tree, with scaly bark, terete pithy branchlets, and naked buds. Leaves opposite, glabrous, thick and coriaceous, oblong or elliptic, obtuse or emarginate at apex, marked toward the margin with minute tubercles; their petioles conspicuously biglandular. Flowers usually perfect or polygamo-monœcious, minute, flattened, greenish white, sessile, in simple terminal axillary tomentose spikes generally collected in leafy panicles, with ovate acute hoary-tomentose bracts and bractlets; calyx-tube turbinate, with 5 prominent ridges opposite the lobes of the limb and 5 intermediate lesser ridges, furnished near the middle with 2 minute appendages, and coated with dense pale tomentum, the limb urceolate, 5-parted to the middle, the divisions triangular, obtuse or acute, erect, persistent; disk epigynous, flat, 10-lobed, the 5 lobes opposite the petals broader than those opposite the calyx-lobes, hairy; petals 5, nearly orbicular, contracted into a short claw inserted on the bottom of the calyx-limb, ciliate on the margins, caducous; stamens 10, inserted in 2 ranks; anthers cordate, apiculate; ovary 1-celled; style short, crowned with a slightly 2-lobed capitate stigma. Fruit 10-ribbed, coriaceous, hoary-pubescent, elongated, obovoid, flattened, crowned with the calyx-limb, unequally 10-ribbed, the 2 lateral ribs produced into narrow wings, 1-seeded; flesh coriaceous, corky toward the interior, inseparable from the thin-walled crustaceous stone dark red and lustrous on the inner surface. Seed suspended, obovoid or oblong; seed-coat membranaceous, dark red; radicle elongated, slightly longer and nearly inclosed by the green cotyledons.

Laguncularia consists of a single species of tropical America and Africa.

The generic name is from *laguncula*, in allusion to the supposed resemblance of the fruit to a flask.

1. Laguncularia racemosa Gærtn. Buttonwood. White Mangrove.

Leaves slightly tinged with red when they unfold, and at maturity dark green on the upper and lighter green or pale on the lower surface, $1\frac{1}{2}'$–$2\frac{1}{2}'$ long and $1'$–$1\frac{1}{2}'$ wide; petioles red, ½′ in length. **Flowers** ¼′ long, in hoary-tomentose spikes produced throughout the year from the axils of young leaves and 1½′–2′ long. **Fruit** about ½′ long.

A tree, 30°–60° high, with a trunk 12′–20′ in diameter, stout spreading branches forming a narrow round-topped head, and slender glabrous branchlets somewhat angled at first, often marked with minute pale spots and dark red-brown, becoming in their second year terete, light reddish brown or orange color, thickened at the nodes, and marked by conspicuous ovate leaf-scars; or northward in Florida a low shrub. **Bark** of the trunk ¼′ thick,

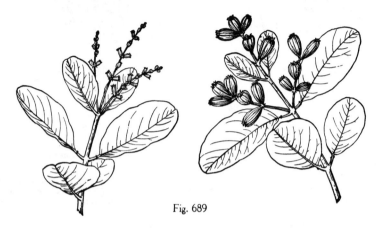

Fig. 689

brown slightly tinged with red, the surface broken into long ridge-like scales. **Wood** heavy, hard, strong, close-grained, dark yellow-brown, with lighter colored sapwood of 10–12 layers of annual growth. The bark contains a large amount of tannic acid and is sometimes used in tanning leather, and is astringent and tonic.

Distribution. Muddy tidal shores of bays and lagoons; southern Florida from Manatee County on the west coast and Brevard County on the east coast to the southern keys; common and of its largest size in Florida on the shores of Shark River, Monroe County; common in Bermuda, the Bahamas, the Antilles, tropical Mexico and Central America, tropical South America and western Africa.

XLVIII. MYRTACEÆ.

Trees or shrubs abounding in pungent aromatic volatile oil, with minute scaly buds. Leaves opposite, simple, mostly entire, pellucid-punctate, penniveined, persistent, the slender obscure veins arcuate and united within the thickened revolute margins; stipules 0. Flowers perfect, regular; calyx 4–5-lobed, the lobes imbricated in the bud, or lid-like and deciduous; petals 2–5, imbricated in the bud, inserted on the margin of the disk, or 0; stamens very numerous, inserted in many ranks with the petals; filaments slender, inflexed in the bud, exserted; anthers introrse, 2-celled, the cells opening longitudinally; ovary 2–4-celled; style simple, filiform, crowned with a minute stigma; ovules numerous or 2 or 3 in each cell, attached on a central placenta, anatropous or semianatropous; raphe ventral; micropyle superior. Fruit baccate, crowned with the persistent calyx-lobes, 1–4-seeded. Seeds without albumen; seed-coat membranaceous.

The Myrtle family with seventy-four genera is chiefly tropical and Australasian, with representatives in southern Europe, extratropical Africa, and extratropical South America. Two genera are represented by small trees in the flora of southern Florida. To this family, beside the Myrtle, belong the Australian Eucalypti, large and important timber-trees largely planted in California, and the Guava, cultivated in Florida for its fruit.

CONSPECTUS OF THE ARBORESCENT GENERA OF THE UNITED STATES.

Calyx closed in the bud by a lid-like deciduous limb; petals 0.   1. **Calyptranthes.**
Calyx 4 or 5-lobed with persistent lobes; petals 4 or 5.   2. **Eugenia.**

1. CALYPTRANTHES Sw.

Aromatic trees or shrubs, with terete or angled branchlets. Leaves complanate in the bud, penniveined, petiolate. Flowers minute, in subterminal and axillary pedunculate many-flowered panicles, their primary and secondary branches often racemose, the ultimate branches cymose; calyx-tube turbinate, produced above the ovary, closed in the bud by a slightly 4 or 5-lobed lid-like orbicular limb, opening in anthesis by a circumscissile line, the limb at first attached laterally, finally deciduous; disk lining the tube of the calyx; petals 2–5, minute, or 0; ovary 2 or 3-celled; ovules 2 or 3 in each cell, collateral, ascending, anatropous. Fruit 2–4-seeded. Seed subglobose or short-oblong; seed-coat shining; cotyledons foliaceous, contortuplicate; radicle elongated, incurved.

Calyptranthes with eighty species is confined to tropical America, with two species reaching southern Florida.

The generic name is from χαλύπτρα and ἄνθη, in reference to the peculiar lid-like limb which closes the calyx before the opening of the flower.

CONSPECTUS OF THE ARBORESCENT SPECIES OF THE UNITED STATES.

Leaves acuminate, pubescent below; petioles up to ½′ in length; inflorescence and young
  branchlets covered with silky rufous tomentum.   1. **C. pallens** (D).
Leaves abruptly pointed or obtuse at apex, glabrous; petioles not more than ⅙′ in
  length; inflorescence and young branchlets glabrous.   2. **C. Zuzygium** (D).

1. Calyptranthes pallens Griseb.

Chytraculia Chytraculia Sudw.

Leaves oblong or oblong-ovate, acuminate at apex, gradually narrowed and cuneate at base, pellucid-punctate above, marked with dark glands below, when they unfold pink or light red and covered with pale silky hairs, and at maturity coriaceous, dark green and lustrous on the upper surface, coated with pale pubescence on the lower surface, 2½′–3′ long and ½′–¾′ wide, with a broad midrib orange-colored beneath; petioles stout, ⅓′–½′ in length.

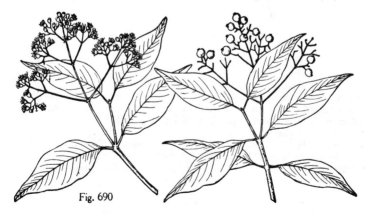

Fig. 690

Flowers sessile, ⅛′ long, in long-stalked many-flowered clusters 2½′–3′ long and wide, covered like their bracts and the flower-buds with silky rufous pubescence, with slender divaricate branches, the ultimate divisions 3-flowered; petals 0. **Fruit** short-oblong or nearly globose, dark reddish brown and puberulous, with thin dry flesh; seeds short-oblong, rounded at the ends.

A tree, in Florida 20°–25° high, with a trunk 3'–4' in diameter, small branches forming a narrow head, and slender branchlets at first wing-angled between the nodes and coated with short rufous silky tomentum, becoming in their second or third year terete, thickened at the nodes, light gray tinged with red and covered with small thin scales. **Bark** of the trunk about $\frac{1}{8}'$ thick, with a generally smooth light gray or almost white surface occasionally separating into irregular plate-like scales. **Wood** very heavy, hard, close-grained, brown tinged with red, with lighter colored sapwood of 30–40 layers of annual growth.

Distribution. Florida, shores of Lake Worth, in the neighborhood of Bay Biscayne, Dade County, and on Big Pine Key, Elliott's Key, Key Largo and Key West; on the Bahama Islands, on many of the Antilles and in southern Mexico.

2. Calyptranthes Zuzygium Sw.

Leaves elliptic, abruptly or gradually narrowed into a blunt point or obtuse at apex, cuneate at base, entire, covered with minute pellucid dots, glabrous, dark yellow-green

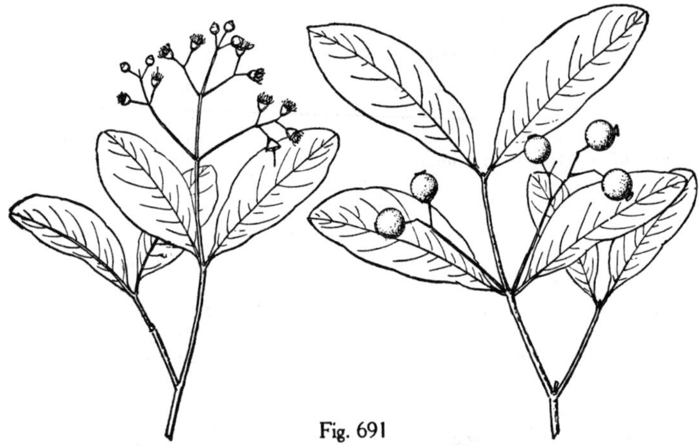

Fig. 691

and lustrous on the upper surface, paler on the lower surface, $1\frac{1}{2}'$–$2\frac{1}{4}'$ long and $\frac{3}{5}'$–$1\frac{1}{4}'$ wide, with a broad low midrib and slender primary veins arcuate and connected within the slightly revolute somewhat undulate margins; petioles deeply grooved, $\frac{1}{8}'$–$\frac{1}{6}'$ in length. **Flowers** on slender pedicels $\frac{1}{6}'$–$\frac{1}{5}'$ long, in axillary 1–3-branched few-flowered axillary cymes $\frac{3}{4}'$ long and $\frac{1}{2}'$ wide, on slender peduncles 1'–$1\frac{1}{4}'$ in length, the ultimate divisions of the inflorescence 1–3-flowered; petals wanting; style rather longer than the stamens. **Fruit** about $\frac{1}{3}'$ in diameter.

A tree, in Florida sometimes 40° high, with a tall trunk 4' or 5' in diameter, covered with smooth pale gray bark, small branches and slender terete ascending ashy gray branchlets.

Distribution. Florida, Paradise and Long Keys in the Everglades, Dade County; on the Bahama Islands and in Cuba, Jamaica and Hayti.

2. EUGENIA L.

Trees or shrubs, with hard durable wood and scaly bark. Flowers often large and conspicuous, on short bibracteolate pedicels, in axillary racemes or fascicles or dichotomously branched cymes, with minute caducous bracts and bractlets; calyx campanulate, scarcely produced above the ovary, the limb 4 or rarely 5-lobed; petals usually 4, free and spreading; ovary 2 or rarely 3-celled; ovules numerous in each cell, semianatropous. Fruit 1–4-seeded. Seeds globose or flattened; seed-coat membranaceous or cartilaginous; embryo thick and fleshy; cotyledons thick, more or less conferruminate into a homogeneous mass; radicle very short, turned toward the hilum.

Eugenia with some five hundred species is common in all tropical regions, with eight species reaching the shores of southern Florida, of these 6 are small trees. Several species are valued for their stimulant and digestive properties; some produce useful timber or edible fruit, and others are cultivated for the beauty of their flowers. Cloves are the flower-buds of *Eugenia aromatica* Baill., a native of the Molucca Islands; and *Eugenia Jambos* L., the Rose Apple, of southeastern Asia, is cultivated in all tropical countries as a shade-tree and for its delicately fragrant fruit.

The generic name commemorates the interest in botany and gardening taken by Prince Eugène of Savoy, who built the Belvidere Palace near Vienna in the beginning of the eighteenth century, and made a collection of rare plants in its gardens.

CONSPECTUS OF THE ARBORESCENT SPECIES OF THE UNITED STATES.

Flowers in axillary racemes or fascicles.
- Flowers in short solitary or clustered axillary racemes.
  - Leaves ovate or obovate, rounded at apex, short-petiolate; fruit subglobose to short-oblong, black, ⅓′ in diameter. 1. **E. buxifolia** (C, D).
  - Leaves ovate, contracted at apex into a broad point, distinctly petiolate; fruit globose, black, ½′ in diameter. 2. **E. axillaris** (C, D).
- Flowers in axillary fascicles.
  - Leaves usually broad-ovate, narrowed at apex into a short point, subcoriaceous; fruit subglobose, rather broader than high, ⅔′–1′ in diameter, becoming black at maturity. 3. **E. rhombea** (D).
  - Leaves oblong-ovate, narrowed at apex into a long point, coriaceous; fruit subglobose to obovoid, ¼′–⅓′ long, bright scarlet. 4. **E. confusa** (D).

Flowers in dichotomously branched cymes. (*Anamomis.*)
- Leaves ovate or obovate; cymes usually 3-flowered; flowers not more than ¼′ in diameter; fruit black. 5. **E. dicrana** (D).
- Leaves oblong or broad-elliptic; cymes 3–15-flowered; flowers up to ½′ in diameter; fruit red. 6. **E. Simpsonii** (D).

1. Eugenia buxifolia Willd. Gurgeon Stopper. Spanish Stopper.

Leaves ovate or obovate, rounded at apex, sessile or narrowed into a short thick petiole, occasionally slightly and remotely crenulate-serrate above the middle, thick and coriaceous, dark green on the upper surface, yellow-green and marked with minute black dots on the lower surface, 1′–1½′ long and about 1′ wide, with a narrow conspicuous midrib; usually unfolding in November and remaining on the branches until the end of their second winter, and often turning red or partly red before falling. **Flowers** appearing in Florida from midsummer until early autumn, ⅛′ in diameter, on short thick pedicels, in short rufous-pubescent racemes clustered in the axils of old or fallen leaves, with minute lanceolate acute persistent bracts, and broad-ovate acute bractlets immediately below the flowers; calyx glandular-punctate, pubescent on the outer surface, with 4 ovate rounded lobes much shorter than the 4 ovate white petals rounded at apex, ciliate on the margins, and glandular-punctate. **Fruit** subglobose to short-oblong, black, glandular-roughened, crowned with the large calyx-lobes, usually 1-seeded, and about ⅓′ in diameter, with thin aromatic flesh; **seeds** ⅛′ in diameter, with a thick pale brown lustrous cartilaginous coat and a pale olive-green embryo.

A shrubby tree, in Florida rarely 20° high, with a short trunk occasionally a foot in diameter, small mostly erect branches, and terete slender branchlets coated at first with rufous pubescence, becoming at the end of a few months ashy gray or gray tinged with red, and often more or less twisted or contorted.   **Bark** of the trunk rarely more than $\frac{1}{8}'$ thick, light brown tinged with red, and broken into small thick square scales.   **Wood** very heavy,

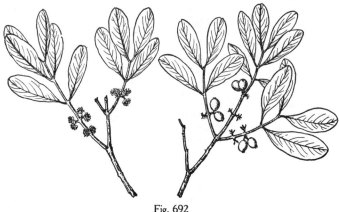

Fig. 692

exceedingly hard, strong, close-grained, dark brown shaded with red, with thick lighter colored sapwood of 15–20 layers of annual growth; sometimes used for fuel.

Distribution.   Florida, Cape Canaveral to the southern keys, and on the west coast from the banks of the Caloosahatchee River to Cape Sable; one of the commonest plants on the keys, forming on coral rock a large part of the shrubby second growth now occupying ground from which the original forest has been removed; on the Bahama Islands and on several of the Antilles.

2. Eugenia axillaris Willd.   Stopper.   White Stopper.

Leaves ovate, gradually or abruptly narrowed at apex into a short wide point, rounded at the narrowed base, thick and coriaceous, dark green on the upper surface, paler and

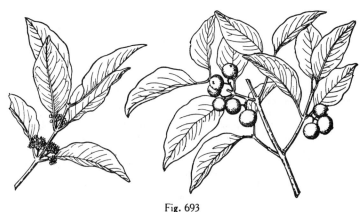

Fig. 693

covered with minute black dots on the lower surface, $1\frac{1}{2}'$–$2\frac{1}{2}'$ long and $\frac{1}{2}'$ wide, with a broad midrib deeply impressed above; petioles stout, slightly winged, about $\frac{1}{3}'$ in length.

Flowers appearing at midsummer, about $\frac{1}{8}'$ in diameter, in short axillary racemes, on stout pedicels $\frac{1}{16}'-\frac{1}{2}'$ long, covered with pale white hairs, and furnished near the middle or toward the apex with 2 acute minute persistent bractlets; calyx glandular-punctate, covered on the outer surface with pale hairs, 4-lobed, with ovate rounded lobes shorter than the 4 ovate glandular white petals. **Fruit** ripening in succession from November to April, globose, black, glandular-punctate, usually 1-seeded, $\frac{1}{2}'$ in diameter, edible, rather juicy, with a sweet agreeable flavor; seeds subglobose, $\frac{1}{4}'$ in diameter, with a pale brown chartaceous coat, and light olive-green cotyledons.

A tree, 20°–25° high, with a trunk occasionally a foot in diameter, small branches, and terete stout rigid ashy gray branchlets often slightly tinged with red and covered with small wart-like excrescences; or toward the northern limits of its range a low shrub. **Bark** of the trunk about $\frac{1}{8}'$ thick and divided by irregular shallow fissures into broad ridges finally separating on the surface into small thin light brown scales. **Wood** heavy, hard, strong, very close-grained, brown often tinged with red, with thin darker colored sapwood of 5–6 layers of annual growth.

Distribution. Florida, shores of the St. John's River to the southern keys; nowhere common; on the Bahama Islands and on several of the Antilles.

3. Eugenia rhombea Kr. & Urb. Stopper.

Leaves broad-ovate, narrowed into a broad point rounded at apex, and abruptly or gradually narrowed and cuneate at base, when they unfold thin and light red, and at maturity

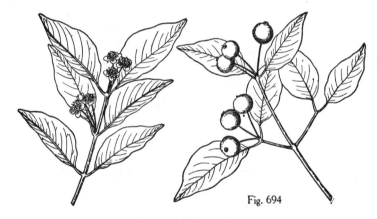

Fig. 694

subcoriaceous, conspicuously marked with black dots, olive-green on the upper surface and paler on the lower surface, $2'-2\frac{1}{2}'$ long and $1'-1\frac{1}{2}'$ wide, with a narrow midrib; unfolding in Florida in May; petioles narrow-winged, $\frac{1}{3}'-\frac{1}{2}'$ in length. **Flowers** $\frac{1}{2}'$ in diameter, appearing in Florida in April or May on slender glandular pedicels $\frac{1}{3}'-\frac{2}{3}'$ long and furnished at apex with 2 lanceolate acute persistent bractlets ciliate on the margins, in sessile axillary many-flowered clusters; calyx-tube much shorter than the limb divided into 4 glandular narrow lobes rounded at apex and one half the length of the broad-ovate rounded glandular white petals. **Fruit** ripening in Florida from September to November, $\frac{2}{3}'-1'$ in diameter, slightly glandular-roughened, orange color, with a bright red cheek when fully grown, becoming black at maturity; flesh thin and dry; seeds almost globose, nearly $\frac{1}{2}'$ in diameter, with a thick pale chestnut-brown lustrous coat and olive-green cotyledons.

A tree, 20°–25° high, with a trunk usually a foot in diameter, small branches, and slender terete branchlets at first light purple and covered with a glaucous bloom, becoming ashy gray or almost white. **Bark** of the trunk about $\frac{1}{16}'$ thick, with a smooth light gray surface slightly tinged with red. **Wood** heavy, hard, close-grained, light brown, with hardly distinguishable sapwood.

Distribution. Florida, Key West and Umbrella Key; on the Bahama Islands and on many of the Antilles.

4. Eugenia confusa DC. Red Stopper.

Leaves oblong-ovate, abruptly or gradually contracted into a long narrow point rounded or acute at apex, cuneate or occasionally rounded at base, thin and light red when they unfold, and at maturity dark green and very lustrous on the upper surface, paler and marked with minute black dots on the lower surface, $1\frac{1}{2}'-2'$ long and $\frac{1}{3}'-\frac{2}{3}'$ wide, with a thick orange-colored midrib barely impressed above and prominent reticulate veinlets; petioles stout, about $\frac{1}{4}'$ in length. **Flowers** barely $\frac{1}{8}'$ in diameter, appearing in September on slender pedicels $\frac{1}{4}'-\frac{1}{2}'$ long and furnished near the apex with 2 minute acute bractlets, in many-flowered axillary clusters; calyx glandular-punctate, with 4 ovate acute lobes much shorter than the 4 broad-ovate rounded white petals. **Fruit** ripening in March and April, sub-globose to obovoid, bright scarlet, $\frac{1}{4}'-\frac{1}{3}'$ long, glandular-roughened, usually solitary and

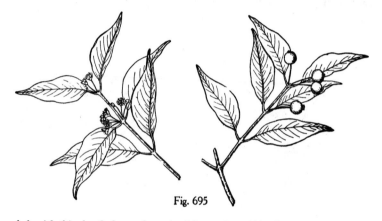

Fig. 695

1-seeded, with thin dry flesh; **seed** nearly globose, about $\frac{1}{8}'$ in diameter, with a thin crustaceous light brown lustrous coat and an olive-green embryo.

A tree, 50°–60° high, with a straight trunk 18'–20' in diameter, stout upright branches forming a narrow compact head, and slender terete ashy gray branchlets. **Bark** of the trunk about $\frac{1}{8}'$ thick, bright cinnamon-red, separating freely into small thin scales. **Wood** very heavy, exceedingly hard, strong, close-grained, bright red-brown, with thick dark-colored sapwood of 50–60 layers of annual growth.

Distribution. Florida, rich hummocks near the shores of Bay Biscayne, Dade County, and on Old Rhodes and Elliotts Keys; on the Bahama Islands and on several of the Antilles.

5. Eugenia dicrana Berg. Naked Wood.

Anamomis dichotoma Sarg.

Leaves ovate or obovate, acute or rounded and occasionally emarginate at apex, cuneate at base, chartaceous when they unfold, becoming subcoriaceous, glabrous, covered with minute black dots, $1'-1\frac{1}{4}'$ long and $\frac{1}{2}'-\frac{2}{3}'$ wide, with a stout midrib; petioles stout, enlarged at base, coated at first with silky hairs, finally glabrous. **Flowers** appearing in Florida in May, $\frac{1}{4}'$ in diameter, in cymes produced near the end of the branches, in the axils of leaves of the year, on slender peduncles coated with pale silky hairs, sometimes 1-

flowered and not longer than the leaves, more often longer than the leaves, dichotomously branched and 3-flowered, with 1 flower at the end of the principal division in the fork of its

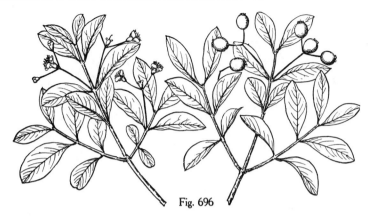

Fig. 696

branches, or occasionally 5–7-flowered by the development of peduncles from the axils of the bracts of the secondary divisions of the inflorescence, each branch of the inflorescence furnished immediately beneath the flower with 2 lanceolate acute bractlets nearly as long as the calyx-tube; calyx hoary-tomentose, the lobes ovate, rounded at apex and much shorter than the ovate acute glandular-punctate white petals. Fruit ripening in Florida in August, reddish brown, $\frac{1}{4}'$ long, obliquely oblong, obovate or subglobose, roughened by minute glands; flesh thin, rather dry and aromatic; seeds reniform, light brown, exceedingly fragrant.

A tree, 20°–25° high, with a trunk 6′–8′ in diameter, and slender terete branchlets light red and coated with pale silky hairs when they first appear, becoming glabrous in their second year and covered with light or dark brown bark separating into small thin scales; or often a shrub, with numerous slender stems. Bark of the trunk $\frac{1}{16}'-\frac{1}{8}'$ thick, with a smooth light red or red-brown surface separating into minute thin scales. Wood very heavy, hard, close-grained, light brown or red, with thick yellow sapwood of 40–50 layers of annual growth.

Distribution. Florida, rocky woods, Mosquito Inlet to Cape Canaveral on the east coast, and from the banks of the Caloosahatchee River to the shores of Cape Romano on the west coast, on Key West, and in the neighborhood of Bay Biscayne, Dade County; on the Bahama Islands and on several of the Antilles.

6. Eugenia Simpsonii Sarg.

Anamomis Simpsonii Small.

Leaves oblong, rounded and abruptly short-pointed or occasionally emarginate at apex, cuneate at base, or broad-elliptic, silky pubescent and ciliate on the margins when they unfold, soon glabrous, and at maturity coriaceous, dark yellow-green and lustrous on the upper surface, paler and dull on the lower surface, $1\frac{1}{2}'-2'$ long and $\frac{1}{2}'-1'$ wide, with a prominent midrib impressed on the upper side and obscure spreading primary veins united before reaching the thickened revolute entire margins of the leaf; petioles covered at first with snowy white tomentum, soon glabrous, slender, $\frac{1}{8}'-\frac{1}{4}'$ in length. Flowers fragrant, about $\frac{1}{2}'$ in diameter, sessile in lateral 3–15-flowered cymes on slender finely appressed-pubescent peduncles longer or shorter than the subtending leaves, their bractlets acuminate and $\frac{1}{3}'$ long; calyx-tube short-obconic, thickly covered with silky white hairs, the lobes rounded at apex, green, punctate, two of them orbicular-reniform, the others orbicular-ovate, shorter than the white concave, obovate to suborbicular erose ciliate sparingly punctate petals. **Fruit** ellipsoid, red, mostly $\frac{1}{3}'-\frac{2}{5}'$ long; seed reniform, usually solitary.

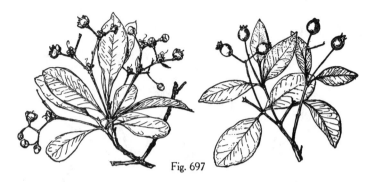

Fig. 697

A tree, occasionally 60°–70° high, with a trunk 15'–16' in diameter, small erect and spreading smooth gray-brown or reddish brown branches forming a narrow round-topped head, and slender branchlets covered when they first appear with snowy white tomentum, soon glabrous, and bright or dull reddish brown, and marked in their second year with the nearly orbicular elevated conspicuous scars of fallen leaves. **Bark** of the trunk thin, smooth, reddish, marked by pale blotches.

Distribution. Florida, Arch Creek Hummock north of Little River, and on Paradise and Long Keys in the Everglades, Dade County.

XLIX. MELASTOMACEÆ.

Trees, shrubs, or herbs with watery juice. Leaves opposite, rarely verticellate, 3–9-nerved, usually petiolate; stipules 0. Flowers regular, perfect, usually showy, rarely fragrant, in terminal clusters; calyx usually 4 or 5-lobed, the lobes imbricated in the bud; petals as many as the lobes of the calyx, inserted on its throat, imbricated or convolute in the bud; stamens as many or twice as many as the petals, inserted in 1 series with them, often inclined or declinate; anthers 2-celled, attached at the base, opening by a terminal pore; ovary 2 or many-celled; style terminal, simple, straight or declinate; stigma capitate, simple or lobed; ovules numerous, minute, anatropous. Fruit capsular or baccate, inclosed in the calyx-tube; seeds minute; testa coriaceous or crustaceous; hilum lateral or basal; embryo without albumen.

This family with 164 genera and a large number of species is chiefly confined to the tropics, and is most abundant in those of South America.

1. TETRAZYGIA A. Rich.

Trees or shrubs, with terete branchlets. Leaves opposite, petiolate, oblong-ovate to ovate-lanceolate, entire or denticulate, 3–5-nerved, persistent, scurfy, like the young branchlets, peduncles and calyx-tube. Flowers perfect in many-flowered terminal panicles or corymbs; calyx-tube urceolate or globose, adnate to the ovary, the limb constricted above the ovary and dilated below the apex, the lobes short or elongated; petals obovate, obtuse, convolute in the bud; stamens twice as many as the petals; filaments subulate; anthers linear-subulate, erect or slightly recurved, attached at base, 2-celled, opening by a minute pore at apex, their connective not extended below the cells; ovary 3–6-celled; style filiform, curved, exserted, surrounded at base by a short sheath 8–10-toothed at apex; ovules indefinite, minute, sessile on an axile placenta. Fruit a 3 or 4-celled berry, crowned by the persistent tube of the calyx; seeds numerous, minute, obpyramidal, thickened and incurved at apex; testa coriaceous, slightly pitted; hilum basal; cotyledons thick; radicle short, turned toward the hilum.

Tetrazygia with 14 species is confined to the West Indies and southern Florida where one species has been discovered, the only tree of the great family of the Melastomaceæ found in the United States.

The generic name is from τέτρα and ζυγόν in allusion to the often 4-parted flowers.

1. Tetrazygia bicolor Cogn.

Leaves oblong-lanceolate, acuminate, gradually narrowed and rounded at base, 3-nerved, entire, undulate and slightly thickened on the revolute margins, dark green on the upper surface, paler on the lower surface, $3'-4\frac{1}{2}'$ long and $1'-1\frac{3}{4}'$ wide; petioles stout, $\frac{3}{4}'-1'$ in

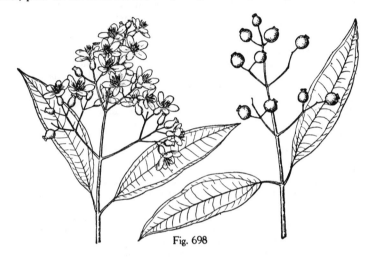

Fig. 698

length. **Flowers** appearing from March to May, $\frac{4}{5}'$ in diameter, short-stalked, in open cymose panicles; calyx urceolate, 4 or 5-lobed, the lobes nearly obsolete; petals 4 or 5, oblong-obovate, reflexed after anthesis, white; ovary 3-celled, style surrounded at base by a short sheath 10-toothed at apex. **Fruit** ripening in late autumn or early winter, oblong to ovoid, conspicuously constricted at apex, $\frac{1}{4}'-\frac{1}{3}'$ in length and $\frac{1}{6}'-\frac{1}{5}'$ in diameter.

In Florida a shrub, or in the dense woods of the keys of the Everglades a slender tree, often 30° high, with an erect trunk 3' o. 4' in diameter, covered with thin light gray-brown slightly fissured bark, small spreading branches becoming erect toward their apex and gracefully drooping leaves; or in the sandy soil of open Pine-woods often less than 3° in height.

Distribution. Florida, on the Everglade Keys, Dade County; on the Bahama Islands and in Cuba.

L. ARALIACEÆ.

Trees, shrubs, or herbs, with watery juice and scaly buds. Leaves alternate, compound or simple, petiolate, with stipules. Flowers in racemose or panicled umbels; parts of the flower in 5's; disk epigynous; ovule solitary, suspended from the apex of the cell, anatropous; raphe ventral, the micropyle superior. Fruit baccate. Seeds, with albumen.

The Aralia family with fifty-four genera is chiefly tropical, with a few genera extending beyond the tropics into the northern hemisphere, especially into North America and eastern Asia. The widely distributed and largely extratropical genus Aralia is represented by one arborescent species in the flora of the United States. Hedera, the Ivy, of this family, is commonly cultivated in the temperate parts of the United States, and some species of Panax and Acanthopanax from eastern Asia are found in gardens in the northeastern states.

1. ARALIA L.

Aromatic spiny trees and shrubs, with stout pithy branchlets, and thick fleshy roots, or bristly or glabrous perennial herbs. Leaves digitate or once or twice pinnate, the pinnæ serrulate; stipules produced on the expanded and clasping base of the petiole. Flowers perfect, polygamo-monœcious or polygamo-diœcious, on slender jointed pedicels, small, greenish white; calyx-tube coherent with the ovary, the limb truncate, repand or minutely toothed, the teeth valvate in the bud; petals imbricated in the bud, inserted by their broad base on the margin of the disk, ovate, obtuse or acute and slightly inflexed at apex; stamens inserted on the margin of the disk, alternate with the petals; filaments filiform; anthers oblong or rarely ovoid, attached on the back, introrse, 2-celled, the cells opening longitudinally; ovary 2–5-celled; styles 2–5, in the fertile flower distinct and erect or slightly united at base, spreading and incurved above the middle, or incurved from the base and sometimes inflexed at apex, crowned with large capitate stigmas, in the sterile flower short and united. Fruit fleshy, laterally compressed or 3–5-angled, crowned with the remnants of the style; nutlets 2–5, orbicular, ovoid or oblong, compressed, crustaceous, light reddish brown, 1-seeded. Seed compressed; seed-coat thin, light brown, adnate to the thin fleshy albumen; cotyledons ovate-oblong, as long as the straight radicle.

Aralia with forty species is confined to North America and Asia.

The name is of obscure meaning.

1. Aralia spinosa L.   Hercules' Club.   Prickly Ash.

Leaves clustered at the end of the branches, twice pinnate, $3°$–$4°$ long and $2\frac{1}{2}°$ wide, with a stout light brown petiole $18'$–$20'$ in length, clasping the stem with an enlarged base and armed with slender prickles, or occasionally unarmed; pinnæ unequally pinnate, usually with 5 or 6 pairs of lateral leaflets and a long-stalked terminal leaflet, and often furnished at base with a pinnate or simple leaflet; leaflets ovate, acute, dentate or crenate, cuneate or more or less rounded at base, short-petiolulate, when they unfold lustrous, bronze-green, and slightly pilose on the midrib and primary veins, and at maturity thin, dark green above, pale beneath, $2'$–$3'$ long a1d $1\frac{1}{2}'$ wide, with a thin midrib occasionally furnished with small prickles and slender primary veins nearly parallel with their margins; in the autumn turning light yellow before falling; stipules acute, about $1'$ long, at first puberulous on the back and ciliate on the margins. Flowers $\frac{1}{16}'$ long, appearing at midsummer on long slender pubescent straw-colored pedicels, in many-flowered umbels arranged in compound panicles, with light brown puberulous branches becoming purple in the autumn, forming a terminal racemose cluster $3°$–$4°$ long, and rising solitary or 2 or 3 together above the spreading leaves; bracts and bractlets lanceolate, acute, scarious, persistent; petals white, acute, inflexed at apex; ovary often abortive; styles connivent. Fruit ripening in autumn, black, $\frac{1}{8}'$ in diameter, globose, 3–5-angled, crowned with the blackened styles, with thin purple very juicy flesh; seeds oblong, rounded at the ends, about $\frac{1}{10}'$ long.

A tree, $30°$–$35°$ high, with a trunk $6'$–$8'$ in diameter, stout wide-spreading branches, and branchlets $\frac{1}{2}'$–$\frac{2}{3}'$ in diameter, armed like the branches and young trunks with stout straight or slightly incurved orange-colored scattered prickles, and nearly encircled by the conspicuous narrow leaf-scars marked by a row of prominent fibro-vascular bundle-scars, light orange-colored in their first season, lustrous and marked irregularly with oblong pale lenticels, becoming light brown in their second year, with bright green inner bark; more often a shrub, with a cluster of unbranched stems $6°$–$20°$ tall. Winter-buds: terminal conic, blunt at apex, $\frac{1}{2}'$–$\frac{3}{4}'$ long, with thin chestnut-brown scales; axillary triangular, flattened, about $\frac{1}{4}'$ long and broad. Bark of the trunk dark brown, about $\frac{1}{8}'$ thick, and divided by broad shallow fissures into wide rounded ridges irregularly broken on the surface. Wood close-grained, light, soft, brittle, brown streaked with yellow, with lighter colored sapwood

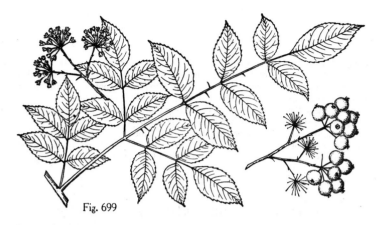

Fig. 699

of 2 or 3 layers of annual growth. The bark of the roots and the berries are stimulant and diaphoretic, and are sometimes used in medicine and in domestic practice.

Distribution. Deep moist soil in the neighborhood of streams; southern Pennsylvania to southern Indiana, southeastern Iowa and southeastern Missouri, and southward to northern Florida, western Louisiana, and eastern Texas; probably of its largest size on the foot-hills of the Big Smoky Mountains in Tennessee.

Occasionally cultivated as an ornamental plant in the eastern states and in western Europe; hardy in eastern Massachusetts.

LI. NYSSACEÆ.

Trees or shrubs, with terete branchlets, scaly buds, alternate entire dentate or serrate deciduous leaves, without stipules. Flowers dioecious, polygamo-dioecious or perfect; staminate, calyx minute, 5-toothed or lobed; petals 5 or more, imbricated in the bud, or 0; stamens as many, twice as many, or fewer than the petals, usually in 2 series; filaments sometimes of 2 lengths, elongated, filiform or subulate; disk fleshy, depressed at apex; pistillate flowers, calyx-tube adnate to the ovary; petals 5 or more, imbricated in the bud; ovary 1-celled or 6–10-celled; ovule solitary, pendulous from the apex of the cell, anatropous; micropyle superior; disk epigynous, pulvinate, the apex depressed or convex, or 0; style subulate, curved or spirally involute at apex, or 2-parted, or conic and divided into as many stigmatic lobes as the cells of the ovary. Fruit drupaceous or subsamaroid, crowned with the remnants of the calyx, 1-celled and 1-seeded, or 3–5-celled, the cells thin, 4-seeded; seed pendent, testa membranaceous or thin, albumen fleshy; cotyledons foliaceous or thin; radicle cylindric.

Nyssaceæ with 3 genera, Nyssa L., Camptotheca Decne. and Davidia Baill. and 8 species is confined to eastern North America, western China, Thibet, the Himalayas and the Malay Archipelago.

1. NYSSA L.

Trees, with leaves conduplicate in the bud, petiolate, sometimes remotely angulate or toothed, mostly crowded at the end of the branches. Flowers polygamo-dioecious, minute, greenish white; staminate on slender pedicels from the axils of minute caducous bracts, in simple or compound clusters on long axillary peduncles bibracteolate near the middle or at the apex or sometimes without bractlets; calyx disciform or cup-shaped, the limb 5-toothed; petals 5, imbricated in the bud, equal or unequal, ovate or linear-oblong, thick, inserted on the margin of the conspicuous pulvinate entire or lobed disk, erect; stamens 5–12, exserted;

filaments filiform; anthers oblong; ovary 0; pistillate flowers on axillary peduncles, in 2 or few-flowered clusters, sessile or nearly so, in the axils of conspicuous bracts and furnished with 1 or 2 small lateral bractlets, or solitary and surrounded by 2–4 bractlets; calyx-tube campanulate, sometimes slightly urceolate, the limb 5-toothed; petals small, thick, and spreading; stamens 5–10; filaments short; anthers fertile or sterile; disk less developed than in the staminate flower, depressed in the centre; ovary 1 or 2-celled; style terete, elongated, recurved, stigmatic toward the apex or the inner face; raphe ventral.   Fruit drupaceous, short-oblong, fleshy, urceolate at apex; flesh thin, oily, acidulous; stone thick-walled, bony, terete or compressed, ribbed or winged, 1 or rarely 2-celled, usually 1-seeded.   Seed filling the cavity of the stone; seed-coat pale; embryo straight.

Nyssa with six species is confined to the eastern United States and to southern and eastern Asia, where one species is distributed from the eastern Himalayas to the island of Java and another occurs in central and western China.   The American species produce tough wood, with intricately contorted and twisted grain.

Nyssa, the name of a nymph, was given to this genus from the fact that one of the species grows in water.

CONSPECTUS OF THE NORTH AMERICAN SPECIES.

Pistillate flowers in 2 or few-flowered clusters, their calyx disciform; fruit blue, not more
    than ⅔′ long; stone with broad rounded ribs.
  Stone indistinctly ribbed; leaves linear-oblong to oval or obovate.
                                       1. N. sylvatica (A, C).
  Stone prominently ribbed; leaves oblanceolate to oblong or elliptic.
                                       2. N. biflora (C).
Pistillate flowers solitary, their calyx cup-shaped; fruit 1′ or more long.
  Fruit red; stone with prominent wings; leaves oblong-oval or obovate, usually obtuse at
    apex.   **3. N. ogeche** (C).
  Fruit purple; stone with acute ridges; leaves oval or oblong, acute or acuminate at apex.
                                      4. N. aquatica (A, C).

1. Nyssa sylvatica Marsh. Tupelo. Pepperidge. Sour Gum.

Leaves crowded at the end of lateral branchlets or remote on vigorous shoots, linear-oblong, lanceolate, oval or obovate, acute or acuminate or sometimes contracted into a

Fig. 700

short broad point at apex, cuneate or occasionally rounded at base, entire, with slightly thickened margins, or rarely coarsely dentate, coated when they unfold with rufous tomentum, especially on the lower surface, or pubescent or sometimes nearly glabrous, and at maturity thick and firm, dark green and lustrous above, pale and often villose below, principally along the broad midrib and on the primary veins, 2'–5' long and $\frac{1}{2}$'–3' wide; turning early in autumn bright scarlet on the upper surface only; petioles slender or stout, terete or wing-margined, ciliate, $\frac{1}{4}$'–1$\frac{1}{2}$' in length, and often bright red. **Flowers** appearing in early spring when the leaves are about one third grown on slender pubescent or tomentose peduncles $\frac{1}{2}$'–1$\frac{1}{2}$' long, staminate in many-flowered dense or lax compound heads, pistillate in 2 to several-flowered clusters, sessile in the axils of conspicuous often foliaceous bracts, and furnished with 2 smaller acute hairy bractlets; calyx of the staminate flower disciform; petals thick, ovate-oblong, acute, rounded at apex, erect or slightly spreading, early deciduous; stamens exserted in the staminate flower, shorter than the petals in the pistillate flower; stigma stout, exserted, reflexed above the middle, 0 in the staminate flower. **Fruit** ripening in October, 1–3 from each flower-cluster, ovoid, $\frac{1}{3}$'–$\frac{2}{3}$' long, dark blue, with thin acrid flesh; **stone** light brown, ovoid, rounded at base, pointed at apex, terete or more or less flattened, and 10–12-ribbed, with narrow indistinct pale ribs rounded on the back.

A tree, with thick hard roots and few rootlets, often surrounded by root-sprouts, occasionally 100° or rarely 125° high, with a trunk sometimes 5° in diameter, numerous slender pendulous tough flexible branches forming a head sometimes short, cylindric and flat-topped, sometimes low and broad, or on trees crowded in the forest narrow, pyramidal or conic, and sometimes inversely conic and broad and flat at the top, and branchlets when they first appear light green to orange color, and in their first winter nearly glabrous or pale or rufous-pubescent, light red-brown marked by minute scattered pale lenticels and by small lunate leaf-scars displaying the ends of 3 conspicuous groups of fibro-vascular bundles, later becoming darker and developing short stout spur-like lateral branchlets; generally in the northern and extreme southern states much smaller, and rarely more than 50°–60° tall. **Winter-buds** obtuse, $\frac{1}{4}$' long, with ovate acute apiculate dark red puberulous imbricated scales, those of the inner ranks accrescent, bright-colored at maturity, and marking the base of the branchlet with obscure ring-like scars. **Bark** of the trunk $\frac{3}{4}$'–1$\frac{1}{2}$' thick, light brown often tinged with red, and deeply fissured, the surface of the ridges covered with small irregularly shaped scales. **Wood** heavy, soft, strong, very tough, not durable, light yellow or nearly white, with thick lighter colored sapwood of 80–100 layers of annual growth; used for the hubs of wheels, rollers in glass factories, ox-yokes, wharf-piles, and sometimes for the soles of shoes.

Distribution. Borders of swamps in wet imperfectly drained soil, and often especially southward on high wooded mountain slopes; valley of the Kennebec River, Maine, to southern Ontario, central Michigan, southern Missouri and eastern Oklahoma, and southward to northern Florida, and to the valley of the Brazos River, Texas; of its largest size on the southern Appalachian Mountains.

Occasionally cultivated as an ornamental tree in the eastern states, but difficult to transplant except when very young. The first tree in the eastern states to assume autumn colors of the leaves.

2. Nyssa biflora Walt.

Leaves oblanceolate, oblong, elliptic or rarely ovate, acute or acuminate or occasionally rounded at the narrow apex, cuneate or rounded at the gradually narrowed base, and entire, when they unfold silky-villose above and hoary-tomentose beneath, soon becoming glabrous, dark yellow-green and lustrous on the upper surface, paler and sometimes glaucous on the lower surface, 2'–4' long and $\frac{3}{4}$'–1' wide, with a prominent midrib and numerous slender veins; petioles stout, $\frac{1}{4}$'–$\frac{1}{2}$' in length. **Flowers** appearing when the leaves are nearly fully grown; staminate on slender villose pedicels, in many-flowered loose clusters on slender hairy peduncles 1'–1$\frac{1}{2}$' in length; pistillate in pairs on rather stouter peduncles usually about 1' long; calyx of the staminate flower disciform; petals oblong-ovate, rounded at apex, white, erect or slightly spreading, early deciduous. **Fruit** solitary or in pairs, on peduncles 1'–1$\frac{1}{2}$' in length, oval or ellipsoid, dark blue, lustrous, about $\frac{1}{4}$' long, with acrid pulp; **stone** oval, compressed, narrowed at the ends, and prominently ribbed.

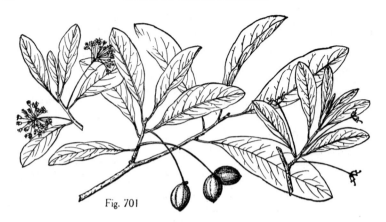

Fig. 701

A tree, rarely more than 30° high, with a slender trunk gradually tapering upward from a swollen and much enlarged base, small spreading branches forming a narrow pyramidal or round-topped head, branchlets slightly villose when they first appear, soon glabrous, bright reddish brown in their first winter, becoming darker the following year, and numerous erect thick roots rising above the surface of the water. **Winter-buds** acute, dark red-brown, puberulous, and about ⅛' long, the inner scales hoary-tomentose. **Bark** about 1' thick, deeply furrowed, gray to very dark reddish brown.

Distribution. Small Pine-barren ponds of the coastal plain from North Carolina to central and eastern Florida, southern Alabama and Mississippi, and western Louisiana (near Lake Charles, Calcasieu Parish).

3. Nyssa ogeche Marsh. Ogeechee Lime. Sour Tupelo.

Leaves oblong, oval or obovate, acute, rounded or rarely obtuse, and apiculate at apex, gradually or abruptly cuneate or sometimes rounded at base, and entire, covered on the lower surface when they unfold with thick hoary tomentum and on the upper surface with short scattered pale hairs, and at maturity thick and firm, dark green, lustrous and slightly pilose above, pale below, 4'–6' long and 2'–2½' wide, with a stout midrib, 9 or 10 pairs of primary veins covered on the lower side with rufous pubescence or often nearly glabrous, and obscure reticulate veinlets; petioles stout, grooved, ½'–1' in length. **Flowers** appearing in March and April; staminate in capitate clusters on slender hairy peduncles ½' long, bibracteolate near the middle, and developed from the axils of the inner scales of the terminal bud, covered with long pale hairs on the outer surface of the short obscurely 5-toothed cup-shaped calyx and on the oblong petals rounded at apex; filaments longer than the petals; anthers oval and conspicuously tuberculate-roughened; pistillate solitary, $\frac{1}{16}$' long, on short stout woolly peduncles from the axils of bud-scales, and furnished at apex with 2 acute hairy bractlets; calyx coated, like the minute rounded spreading petals, with hoary tomentum; stamens included, with short filaments, and small mostly fertile anthers; style stout, exserted, reflexed from near the base. **Fruit** bright or dull red, on slender tomentose stems enlarged at apex and ½'–¾' long, ripening in July and August, and sometimes persistent on the branches until after the falling of the leaves, oblong or obovoid, 1'–1½' in length, tipped with the thickened and pointed remnants of the style; flesh thick, juicy, very acid; **stone** oblong, compressed, narrowed at the ends, rounded at base, acute at apex, with walls produced into 10 or 12 broad thin papery white wings, about 1' long, and 1 or rarely 2-seeded.

A tree, usually not more than 30° high with one or several stems 2°–3° in diameter, or often only a shrub, and with spreading branches forming a narrow round-topped head, and slender branchlets coated when they first appear with rufous tomentum, light reddish brown or green tinged with red and puberulous during their first summer, turning gray or reddish brown in their first winter, and marked by large lunate or nearly triangular leaf-scars displaying the ends of 3 groups of fibro-vascular bundles; often a shrub, with numerous slender clustered diverging stems. **Winter-buds** obtuse, $\frac{1}{8}'$ long, with ovate apiculate imbricated scales rounded on the back and clothed with thick hoary tomentum, those of the inner ranks becoming at maturity ovate-oblong or obovate, rounded at apex, bright red, and

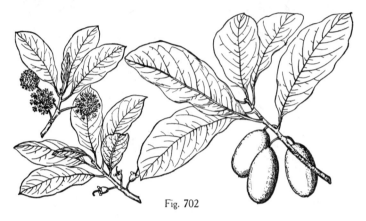

Fig. 702

$\frac{1}{2}'-\frac{3}{4}'$ long. **Bark** of the trunk about $\frac{1}{8}'$ thick, irregularly fissured, with a dark brown surface broken into thick appressed persistent plate-like scales. **Wood** light, soft, tough, not strong, white, with thin hardly distinguishable sapwood of about 10 layers of annual growth. A preserve with an agreeable subacid flavor, known as Ogeechee limes, is sometimes made from the fruit in Georgia and South Carolina. The flowers abound in nectar, and are much visited by bees.

Distribution. Deep often inundated river swamps or their borders and ponds; southern South Carolina in the neighborhood of the coast, widely and generally distributed in the Altamaha region of eastern Georgia (*R. M. Harper*); in northern and in western Florida to the mouth of the Choctawhatchee River (*R. H. Harper*), and in the valley of the lower Apalachicola River; rare and local.

4. Nyssa aquatica Marsh. Cotton Gum. Tupelo Gum.

Leaves oblong-ovate, acute or acuminate and often long-pointed at apex, cuneate, rounded, or subcordate at base, entire or remotely and irregularly angulate-toothed, the teeth often tipped with a long slender mucro, when they unfold light red and coated below and on the petioles with pale tomentum and pubescent above, especially on the broad thick midrib, and at maturity thick and firm, dark green and lustrous on the upper surface, pale and more or less downy-pubescent on the lower surface, $5'-7'$ long and $2'-4'$ wide, with 10–12 pairs of primary veins forked near the margins and connected by conspicuous cross veins; petioles stout, grooved, hairy, enlarged at base, $1\frac{1}{2}'-2\frac{1}{2}'$ in length. **Flowers** appearing in March and April on a long slender hairy peduncle from the axil of an inner scale of the terminal bud; staminate in dense capitate clusters, their peduncle furnished near the middle and occasionally at apex with long linear ciliate bractlets; calyx-tube cup-shaped, obscurely 5-toothed, one third as long as the oblong erect petals rounded at apex and much shorter than the stamens; pistillate solitary, surrounded by 2–4 strap-shaped scarious ciliate bractlets often $\frac{1}{2}'$ long and more or less united below into an involucral cup; calyx-tube oblong and much longer than the ovate minute spreading petals; stamens included, with small mostly fertile anthers; style stout, tapering, reflexed above the middle, and revolute into a close coil. **Fruit** ripening early in the autumn, on slender drooping stalks $3'-4'$ in length, oblong or slightly obovoid, crowned with the pointed remnants of the style, dark purple, marked by conspicuous scattered pale dots, and 1' long, with thick tough skin and thin acid flesh; stone obovoid, rounded at the narrow apex, pointed at base, flattened, light

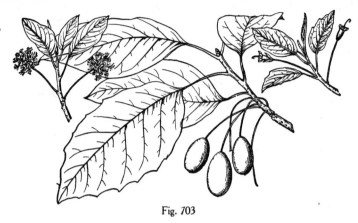

Fig. 703

brown or nearly white, and about 10-ridged, the ridges acute and wing-like, with thin separable margins, and sometimes united by short intermediate ridges.

A tree, 80°–100° high, with a trunk 3°–4° in diameter above the greatly enlarged tapering base, comparatively small spreading branches forming a narrow oblong or pyramidal head, stout pithy branchlets dark red and coated with pale tomentum when they first appear, soon becoming glabrous or nearly so, and in their first winter light or bright red-brown and marked by small scattered pale lenticels and by the conspicuous elevated nearly orbicular leaf-scars displaying the ends of 3 large fibro-vascular bundles, and thick corky roots. Winter-buds; terminal nearly globose, with broad ovate light chestnut-brown scales keeled on the back and rounded and apiculate at apex, those of the inner ranks accrescent and at maturity oblong-ovate or oblong-obovate, rounded at apex, 1' or more long, and bright yellow; axillary minute, obtuse, nearly imbedded in the bark. Bark of the trunk about ¼' thick, dark brown, longitudinally furrowed, and roughened on the surface by small scales. Wood light, soft, not strong, close-grained, difficult to split, light brown or often nearly white, with thick sapwood sometimes composed of more than 100 layers of annual growth; used in the manufacture of wooden-ware, broom-handles, and wooden shoes, and largely for fruit and vegetable boxes. The wood of the roots is sometimes employed instead of cork for the floats of nets.

Distribution. Deep swamps inundated during a part of every year; coast region of the Atlantic states from southeastern Virginia to northern Florida, through the Gulf states to the valley of the Nueces River, Texas, and through Arkansas and southeastern Missouri to western Kentucky and Tennessee, and to the valley of the lower Wabash River, Illinois; of its greatest size in the Cypress-swamps of western Louisiana and eastern Texas.

LII. CORNACEÆ.

Trees or shrubs, with terete branchlets, scaly buds, and alternate or opposite deciduous leaves, without stipules. Flowers perfect or polygamo-diœcious; calyx 4 or 5-toothed, petals 4 or 5; stamens inserted on the margin of the epigynous disk; anthers oblong; introrse, 2-celled, the cells opening longitudinally; ovary 1 or 2-celled; ovule solitary, suspended from the interior angle of the apex of the cell, anatropous; micropyle superior. Fruit drupaceous, 1 or 2-seeded. Seed oblong-ovoid; seed-coat membranaceous;

embryo in copious fleshy albumen; cotyledons foliaceous; radicle terete, turned toward the hilum.

The widely distributed Cornel family with ten genera, more numerous in temperate than in tropical regions, has arborescent representatives of the genus Cornus in North America.

1. CORNUS L. Dogwood.

Trees and shrubs, with astringent bark, opposite or rarely alternate deciduous leaves conduplicate or involute in the bud. Flowers small, perfect, white, greenish white or yellow; calyx-tube minutely 4-toothed, the teeth valvate in the bud; disk pulvinate, depressed in the centre, or obsolete; petals 4, valvate in the bud, oblong-ovate, inserted on the margin of the disk; stamens 4, alternate with the petals; filaments slender, exserted; ovary 2-celled; style exserted, simple, columnar, crowned with a single capitate or truncate stigma; raphe dorsal. Fruit ovoid or oblong; flesh thin and succulent; nut bony or crustaceous, 2-celled, 2 or sometimes 1-seeded. Seed compressed; embryo straight or slightly incurved.

Cornus with nearly fifty species is widely distributed through the three continents of the northern hemisphere, and south of the equator is represented in Peru by a single species. Of the sixteen or seventeen species of the United States four are arborescent. Cornus is rich in tannic acid, and the bark and occasionally the leaves and unripe fruit are used as tonics, astringents, and febrifuges. Of exotic species, *Cornus mas*, L., is often planted in the eastern states as an ornamental tree, and its edible fruit is used in Europe in preserves and cordials. The wood of Cornus is hard, close-grained, and durable, and is used in turnery and for charcoal.

The generic name, from *cornu*, relates to the hardness of the wood produced by plants of this genus.

CONSPECTUS OF THE ARBORESCENT SPECIES OF THE UNITED STATES.

Flowers greenish, in a dense cymose head surrounded by a conspicuous corolla-like involucre of 4–6 white or rarely red scales, from terminal buds formed the previous summer; fruit ovoid, bright red, rarely yellow.

Heads of flower-buds inclosed by the involucre during the winter; involucral scales 4, obcordate or notched at apex; leaves ovate to elliptic.   1. C. florida (A, C).

Heads of flower-buds inclosed only at base by the involucre during the winter; involucral scales 4–6, oblong to obovate, usually acute at apex; leaves ovate or rarely obovate.   2. C. Nuttallii (B, G).

Flowers cream color, in a flat cymose head, without involucral scales, terminal on shoots of the year; fruit subglobose, white or dark blue.

Leaves opposite, scabrous above; fruit white.   3. C. asperifolia (A, C).

Leaves mostly alternate and clustered at the end of the branches, smooth above; fruit dark blue or rarely yellow.   4. C. alternifolia (A, C).

1. Cornus florida L. Flowering Dogwood.

Leaves ovate to elliptic or rarely slightly obovate, acute and often contracted into a slender point at apex, gradually narrowed at base, remotely and obscurely crenulate-toothed on the somewhat thickened margins, and mostly clustered at the end of the branches, when they unfold pale and pubescent below and puberulous above, and at maturity thick and firm, bright green and covered with minute appressed hairs on the upper surface, pale or sometimes almost white and more or less pubescent on the lower surface, 3′–6′ long and $1\frac{1}{2}′$–2′ wide, with a prominent light-colored midrib deeply impressed above, and 5 or 6 pairs of primary veins connected by obscure reticulate veinlets; in the autumn turning bright scarlet on the upper surface, remaining pale on the lower surface; petioles grooved, $\frac{1}{2}′$–$\frac{3}{4}′$ in length. **Flowers**: head of flower-buds appearing during the summer between the upper pair of lateral leaf-buds, inclosed by 4 involucral scales remaining light brown and more or less covered with pale hairs during the winter, and borne on a stout club-shaped puberulous peduncle $\frac{1}{4}′$ long or less during the winter and becoming $1′$–$1\frac{1}{2}′$ in length; involucral scales beginning to unfold, enlarge and grow white in early spring and when the flowers open in March at the south to May at the north, when the leaves are nearly fully grown, forming a flat corolla-like cup 3′–4′ in diameter, becoming at maturity obovoid, 1′–

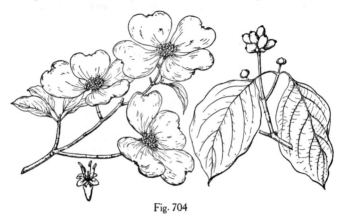

Fig. 704

1½′ wide, gradually narrowed below the middle and notched at the rounded apex, reticulate-veined, pure white, pink, or rarely bright red, deciduous after the fading of the flowers; flowers in dense many-flowered cymose heads, in the axils of broad-ovate nearly triangular minutely apiculate glabrous light green deciduous bracts, ⅛′ in diameter; calyx terete, slightly urceolate, puberulous, obtusely 4-lobed, light green; corolla-lobes strap-shaped, rounded or acute at apex, slightly thickened on the margins, puberulous on the outer surface, reflexed after anthesis, green tipped with yellow; disk large and orange-colored; style crowned with a truncate stigma.   Fruit ripening in October, ovoid, crowned with the remnants of the narrow persistent calyx and with the style, bright scarlet or rarely yellow (f. *xanthocarpa* Rehd.), lustrous, ½′ long and ¼′ broad, with thin mealy flesh, and a smooth thick-walled slightly grooved stone acute at the ends, and 1 or 2-seeded; seeds oblong, pale brown.

A bushy tree, rarely 40° high, with a short trunk 12′–18′ in diameter, slender spreading or upright branches, and divergent branchlets turning upward near the end, pale green or green tinged with red when they first appear, glabrous or slightly puberulous, bright red or yellow-green during their first winter and nearly surrounded by the narrow ring-like leaf-scars, later becoming light brown or gray tinged with red; frequently toward the northern limits of its range a much-branched shrub.   Winter-buds formed in midsummer; the terminal covered by 2 opposite acute pointed scales rounded on the back and joined below for half their length, and accompanied by 2 pairs of lateral buds, each covered by a single scale, those of the lower pair shedding their scales in the autumn and remaining undeveloped. **Bark** of the trunk ⅛′–¼′ thick, with a dark red-brown surface divided into quadrangular or many-sided plate-like scales.   **Wood** heavy, hard, strong, close-grained, brown sometimes changing to shades of green and red, with lighter colored sapwood of 30–40 layers of annual growth; largely used in turnery, for the bearings of machinery, the hubs of small wheels, barrel-hoops, the handles of tools, and occasionally for engravers' blocks.

Distribution.   Usually under the shade of taller trees in rich well-drained soil; southern Maine to southern Ontario, southern Michigan, southeastern Kansas and eastern Oklahoma, and southward to central Florida and the valley of the Brazos River, Texas; on the mountains of northern Mexico; comparatively rare at the north; one of the commonest and most generally distributed inhabitants of the deciduous-leaved forests of the middle and southern states, ranging from the coast nearly to the summits of the high Alleghany

Mountains. Trees with rose-colored or with pink involucral scales occasionally occur (var. *rubra* André). A variety with pendulous branches is known in gardens (var. *pendula* Dipp.); the var. *xanthocarpa* near Oyster Bay, Nassau County, Long Island, New York, and at Saluda, Polk County, North Carolina.

Often planted as an ornament of parks and gardens in the eastern states.

2. Cornus Nuttallii Aud. Dogwood.

Leaves ovate or slightly obovate, acute and often contracted into a short point at the apex, cuneate at base, faintly crenulate-serrate, and generally clustered toward the end of the branches, when they unfold coated below with pale tomentum and puberulous above, and at maturity thin, bright green and slightly puberulous, with short appressed hairs on the upper surface, and woolly pubescent on the lower surface, $4'-5'$ long and $1\frac{1}{2}'$ $-3'$ wide, with a prominent midrib impressed above, and about 5 pairs of slender primary veins connected by remote reticulate veinlets; in the autumn turning bright orange and scarlet before falling; petioles stout, grooved, pubescent, $\frac{1}{2}'-\frac{2}{3}'$ in length, with a large clasping base. **Flowers:** head of flower-buds appearing during the summer between the upper pair of lateral leaf-buds, surrounded at base but not inclosed by the involucral scales during the winter, hemispheric, $\frac{1}{2}'$ in diameter, usually nodding on a stout hairy peduncle $\frac{3}{4}'-1'$ long; involucral scales becoming when the flowers open $1\frac{1}{2}'-3'$ long and $1\frac{1}{2}'-2'$ wide, white or white tinged with pink, oblong to obovate or nearly orbicular, and acute, acuminate,

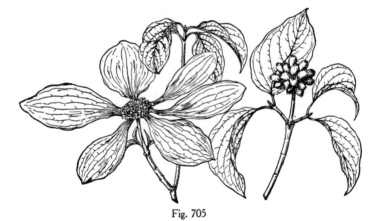

Fig. 705

or obtuse, entire and thickened at apex, puberulous on the outer surface, gradually narrowed below the middle and conspicuously 8-ribbed, the spreading ribs united by reticulate veinlets; flowers in dense cymose heads from the axils of minute acuminate scarious deciduous bracts; calyx terete, slightly urceolate, puberulous on the outer surface, yellow-green, or light purple, with dark red-purple lobes; petals strap-shaped, rounded at apex, spreading, somewhat puberulous on the outer surface, with thickened slightly inflexed margins, yellow-green; style crowned with a truncate stigma. **Fruit** ripening in October, in dense spherical heads of 30–40 drupes surrounded at base by a ring of abortive pendulous ovaries, $\frac{1}{2}'$ long, ovoid, much flattened, crowned with the broad persistent calyx, bright red or orange-colored, with thin mealy flesh, and a thick-walled 1 or 2-seeded stone obtuse at the ends and scarcely grooved; **seeds** oblong, compressed, with a very thin pale papery coat.

A tree, $40°-60°$, or exceptionally $100°$ high, with a trunk $1°-2°$ in diameter, small spreading branches forming an oblong conic or ultimately round-topped head, and slender light green branchlets coated while young with pale hairs, becoming glabrous or puberulous, dark reddish purple or sometimes green during their first winter and conspicuously marked by the elevated lunate leaf-scars, ultimately becoming light brown or brown tinged with red. **Winter-buds** formed in July; the terminal acute, $\frac{1}{3}'$ long, covered by 2 narrow-ovate acute long-pointed puberulous light green'opposite scales, accompanied by 2 pairs of lateral buds, each covered by a single scale, those of the lower pair shedding their scales in the autumn and remaining undeveloped, those of the upper pair clothed with pale hairs, especially toward the apex, their scales thickening, turning dark purple, lengthening in the spring with the inclosed shoot, finally becoming scarious and developing into small leaves, and in falling marking the base of the branchlets with ring-like scars. **Bark** of the trunk about $\frac{1}{4}'$ thick, brown tinged with red, and divided on the surface into small thin appressed scales. **Wood** heavy, exceedingly hard, strong, close-grained, light brown tinged with red, with lighter colored sapwood of 30–40 layers of annual growth; used in cabinet-making, for mauls and the handles of tools.

Distribution. Usually in moist well-drained soil under the shade of coniferous forests; valley of the lower Fraser River and Vancouver Island, British Columbia, southward through western Washington and Oregon, on the coast ranges of California to the San Bernardino Mountains, and on the western slopes of the Sierra Nevada; southward up to altitudes of 4000°–5000°, of its largest size near the shores of Puget Sound and in the Redwood-forests of northern California.

3. Cornus asperifolia Michx. Dogwood.

Leaves ovate or oblong, gradually or abruptly contracted at apex into a long slender point, gradually narrowed or rounded and cuneate at base, and slightly thickened on the

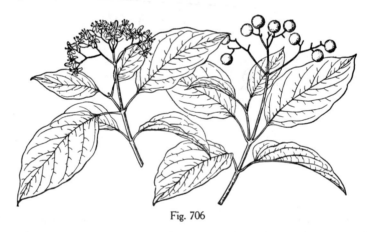

Fig. 706

undulate margins, coated with lustrous silvery tomentum when they unfold, and nearly fully grown when the flowers open from the middle of May in Texas to the middle of July at the north, and then dark green and roughened above by short rigid white hairs, and pale, often glaucous or rough-pubescent below, and at maturity thin, scabrous on the upper surface, pubescent or puberulous on the lower surface, $3'$–$4'$ long and $1\frac{1}{2}'$–$2'$ wide, with a thin midrib, and 4–6 pairs of slender primary veins parallel with their sides; petioles stout, grooved, pubescent, usually about $\frac{1}{2}'$ in length. **Flowers** cream color, on slender pedicels, in loose broad or narrow often panicled pubescent cymes, on peduncles frequently $1'$ in length; calyx oblong, cup-shaped, obscurely toothed, covered with fine silky white hairs; corolla-lobes narrow-oblong, acute, about $\frac{1}{8}'$ long, and reflexed after the flowers open; style thickened at apex into a prominent stigma. **Fruit** ripening from the end of August until the end of October, in loose spreading red-stemmed clusters, subglobose, white, tipped with the remnants of the style, about $\frac{1}{4}'$ in diameter, with thin dry, bitter flesh, and a full and rounded stone broader than high, somewhat oblique, slightly grooved on the edge, and 1 or 2-seeded; **seeds** nearly $\frac{1}{4}'$ long, with a pale brown coat.

A tree, sometimes nearly 50° high, with a short trunk 8′–10′ in diameter, thin erect wand-like branches forming a narrow irregular rather open head, and slender branchlets marked by numerous small pale lenticels, light green and puberulous when they first appear, pale red, lustrous, and puberulous during their first winter, light reddish brown in their second year, and ultimately light gray-brown or gray; usually shrubby. **Winter-buds** acute, compressed, pubescent, sessile, or stalked, about $\frac{1}{8}'$ long, with 2 pairs of opposite scales, the terminal bud nearly twice as large as the compressed lateral buds. **Bark** of the trunk about $\frac{1}{4}'$ thick, and divided by shallow fissures into narrow interrupted ridges broken into small closely appressed dark red-brown scales **Wood** close-grained, hard, pale brown, with thick cream-colored sapwood.

Distribution. Southwestern Ontario (Point Pelee and Pelee Island), southward through Ohio, Kentucky, Tennessee and Mississippi to western Florida (Gadsden and Levy Counties) and westward to southeastern South Dakota, southeastern Nebraska, central Kansas, northwestern Oklahoma (near Alva, Woods County) and western Texas (Kerr, Menard and Brown Counties); probably only arborescent on the rich bottomlands of southern Arkansas and eastern Texas.

4. Cornus alternifolia L. Dogwood.

Leaves mostly alternate, clustered at the end of the branches, rarely opposite, oval or ovate, gradually contracted at apex into a long slender point, cuneate or occasionally some-

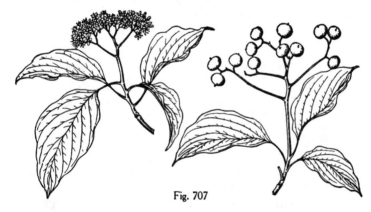

Fig. 707

what rounded at base, obscurely crenulate-toothed on the slightly thickened and incurved margins, coated when they unfold on the lower surface with dense silvery white tomentum, and faintly tinged with red and pilose above, and at maturity thin, bright yellow-green, glabrous or sparsely pubescent on the upper surface, pale or sometimes nearly white and covered with appressed hairs on the lower surface, 3′–5′ long and $2\frac{1}{2}'$–$3\frac{1}{2}'$ wide, with a broad orange-colored midrib slightly impressed above, and about 6 pairs of primary veins parallel with their sides; in the autumn turning yellow or yellow and scarlet; petioles slender, pubescent, grooved, $1\frac{1}{2}'$–2′ in length, with an enlarged clasping base. **Flowers** cream color, opening from the beginning of May to the end of June on slender jointed pedicels $\frac{1}{8}'$–$\frac{1}{4}'$ long, in terminal flat puberulous many-flowered cymes $1\frac{1}{2}'$–$2\frac{1}{2}'$ wide, mostly on lateral branchlets; calyx cup-shaped, obscurely toothed; corolla-lobes narrow, oblong, rounded at apex, $\frac{1}{8}'$ long, reflexed after anthesis; style enlarged into a prominent stigma. **Fruit** in loose spreading red-stemmed clusters, ripening in October, subglobose, dark blue-black, or rarely yellow (f. *ochrocarpa* Rehd.), ¾′ in diameter, tipped with the remnants of the style rising from the bottom of a small depression, with thin and bitter flesh; and an obovoid nutlet, pointed at base, gradually longitudinally many-grooved, thick-walled, and 1 or 2-seeded; seeds lunate. ¼′ long, with a thin membranaceous pale coat.

A flat-topped tree, rarely 25°–30° high, with a short trunk 6′–8′ in diameter, long slender alternate diverging horizontal branches, and numerous short upright slender branchlets pale orange-green or reddish brown when they first appear, mostly light green or sometimes brown tinged with green during their first winter, later turning darker green and marked by pale lunate leaf-scars and small scattered pale lenticels; often a shrub, with numerous stems. **Bark** of the trunk about ⅛′ thick, dark reddish brown, and smooth or divided by shallow longitudinal fissures into narrow ridges irregularly broken transversely. **Wood** heavy, hard, close-grained, brown tinged with red, with thick lighter colored sapwood of 20–30 layers of annual growth.

Distribution. Rich woodlands, the margins of the forest, and the borders of streams and swamps, in moist well-drained soil, New Brunswick and Nova Scotia, westward along the valley of the St. Lawrence River to the northern shores of Lake Superior and to Minnesota, and southward through the northern states to Iowa and southern Missouri (Monteer, Shannon County) and along the Appalachian Mountains to North Carolina, up to altitudes of 3500°–4000°; in Alabama to Covington County, southwestern Georgia, and western Florida (River Junction, Gadsden County, *T. G. Harbison*).

Occasionally cultivated as an ornamental plant in the eastern states.

Section 2. **Gamopetalæ.** Corolla of united petals (*divided in Elliottia in Ericaceæ 0 in some species of Fraxinus in Oleaceæ*).

A. Ovary superior (*inferior in Vaccinium in Ericaceæ, partly inferior in Symplocaceæ, partly superior in Styraceæ*)

LIII. ERICACEÆ.

Trees or shrubs, with scaly buds, and alternate simple leaves, without stipules. Flowers perfect, regular; calyx 4–5-lobed; corolla hypogynous, 5-lobed (*of 4 petals in Elliottia*), the lobes imbricated in the bud; stamens hypogynous, mostly free from the corolla, as many, or twice as many as its lobes; anthers introrse, 2-celled, opening by terminal pores, often appendaged; ovary 4–10-celled (*inferior in Vaccinium*); styles terminal, simple, stigma terminal; ovules numerous, anatropous or amphitropous; raphe ventral; micropyle superior. Fruit capsular, drupaceous, or baccate. Seeds with fleshy or horny albumen; embryo small; cotyledons small and short.

The Heath family with seventy-one genera is widely distributed over the temperate and tropical parts of the earth's surface. Of the twenty-one genera found in the United States seven have arborescent representatives.

CONSPECTUS OF THE ARBORESCENT GENERA OF THE UNITED STATES.

Ovary superior.
    Corolla of 4 petals; flowers in erect racemose panicles; leaves deciduous.   1. **Elliottia.**
    Corolla gamopetalous, 5-lobed.
        Fruit capsular.
            Capsule septicidal, the valves in opening separating from the persistent placentiferous axis; calyx-lobes imbricated in the bud; leaves persistent (*sometimes deciduous*).
            Flowers in terminal clusters; corolla 5-lobed; inflorescence-buds conic, covered with closely imbricated scales; leaves revolute on the margins.
                                                     2. **Rhododendron.**
            Flowers in axillary clusters; corolla saucer-shaped, with a short narrow tube and 10 pouches below the short limb, the anthers in the pouches in the bud: inflorescence-buds elongated, covered with loosely imbricated scales; leaves flat.
                                                    3. **Kalmia.**

Capsule loculicidal, the valves in opening bearing the partitions and separating from the persistent placentiferous axis; calyx-lobes valvate in the bud.

Capsule ovoid-pyramidal; flowers in terminal panicles of secund racemes; anther-cells opening longitudinally from the apex to the middle; leaves deciduous.

4. **Oxydendrum.**

Capsule oblong; flowers in axillary fascicles; anthers opening below the apex by 2 oblong pores; leaves persistent.

5. **Xolisma.**

Fruit drupaceous; flowers in terminal panicles; anthers bearing a pair of reflexed awns on the back, each cell opening at apex anteriorally by a terminal pore; leaves persistent.

6. **Arbutus.**

Ovary inferior; fruit baccate; flowers axillary, racemose or solitary; anther-cells terminating in tubular appendages and opening by terminal pores.

7. **Vaccinium.**

1. ELLIOTTIA Ell.

A glabrous tree or shrub, with slender terete branchlets, scaly buds, and fibrous roots. Leaves petiolate, oblong or oblong-obovate, acute at the ends or occasionally rounded at apex, entire, thin, dark green and glabrous above, pale and villose below, particularly on the thin yellow midrib and obscure forked veins; deciduous; petioles slender and flattened, with an abruptly enlarged base nearly covering the small axillary buds.   Flowers perfect, on slender elongated pedicels, in erect terminal elongated racemose panicles, with minute acute scarious caducous bracts and bractlets; calyx short, tubular, puberulous, dark red-brown, 4-toothed, the broad apiculate teeth erose on the margins and imbricated in the bud; petals 4, imbricated in the bud, spatulate-linear, sessile; stamens 8, hypogynous, shorter than the petals; filaments broad, flattened; anthers oblong-ovoid, the cells callous-mucronate, free at the apex of the spreading lobes, opening from above downward; disk much thickened, fleshy; ovary sessile, subglobose, 4-lobed, 4-celled, concave at apex; style elongated, slender, gradually enlarged and club-shaped above and incurved at apex; stigma 3-5-lobed, smaller than the thickened end of the style; ovules numerous in each cell, attached on the inner angle of a tumid placenta, ascending, anatropous.   Fruit unknown.

Elliottia with a single species is confined to the southern United States.

The genus is named in honor of Stephen Elliott (1771–1830), the distinguished botanist of South Carolina.

1. Elliottia racemosa Ell.

Leaves 3'-4' long, 1'-1½' wide; petioles ⅓'-½' in length.   **Flowers** about ½' long, opening from the middle to the end of June, in clusters 7'-10' in length.

A tree, 15°-20° high, with a trunk 4'-5' in diameter, short ascending branches forming

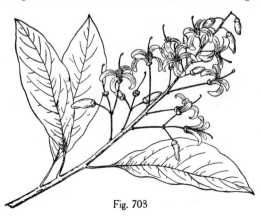

Fig. 703

a pyramidal head, and erect branchlets light red-brown and pilose when they first appear, bright orange-brown, lustrous, and nearly glabrous during their first winter, and roughened by slightly raised oblong-obovate leaf-scars with conspicuous central fibro-vascular bundle-scars, becoming light brown slightly tinged with red during their second season and dark gray-brown the following year; or more frequently shrubby. **Winter-buds:** terminal broad-ovoid, acute, about $\frac{1}{8}'$ long, with much thickened bright chestnut-brown shining scales conspicuously white-pubescent near the margins toward the apex; lateral buds smaller, ovoid, compressed, rounded or short-pointed at apex. **Bark** thin, smooth, pale gray.

Distribution. Sandy woods in a few isolated stations in the valley of the Savannah River, near Augusta, Richmond County, and in Burke and Bullock Counties, Georgia.

2. RHODODENDRON L.

Trees or shrubs, with scaly bark, terete branchlets, terminal buds formed in summer, and fibrous roots. Leaves usually clustered at the end of the branches, revolute and entire on the margin, persistent or deciduous. Flowers in terminal umbellate corymbs from buds with numerous caducous scales; calyx 5-parted or toothed, persistent under the fruit, corolla 5-10-lobed, deciduous; stamens 5 or 10, rarely more, more or less unequal, ultimately spreading; filaments subulate-filiform, pilose at the base; disk thick and fleshy, crenately lobed; ovary 5-10-celled; style slender, crowned with a capitate stigma and persistent on the fruit; ovules numerous in each cell, attached in many series to an axile 2-lipped placenta projected from the inner angle of the cell, anatropous. Fruit a woody many-seeded capsule. Seed scobiform; seed-coat loose, reticulate, produced at the ends beyond the nucleus into a short often laciniate appendage; embryo minute, cylindric, axile in fleshy albumen; cotyledons oblong, shorter than the radicle turned toward the hilum.

Rhododendron with some four or five hundred species occurs in eastern Thibet, on the Himalayas, in southwestern China, the Malay peninsula and Archipelago, New Guinea, northern China and Corea, Japan, the mountains of central Europe, on the Caucasus, and in eastern and western North America, the largest number of species being found in southwestern China and on the Himalayas. Of the twenty-three or twenty-four North American species one only is arborescent.

Rhododendron possesses astringent narcotic properties. It produces hard close-grained compact wood sometimes used in turnery and for fuel. Many of the species are cultivated in gardens for the beauty of their large and conspicuous flowers.

The generic name is from ῥόδον and δένδρον, the Rose-tree.

1. Rhododendron maximum L.   Great Laurel.   Rose Bay.

Leaves revolute in the bud, ovate-lanceolate or obovate-lanceolate, acute or short-pointed at apex, and narrowed, cuneate or rounded at base, when they unfold covered with a thick pale or ferrugineous tomentum of gland-tipped hairs, and at maturity glabrous, thick and coriaceous, dark green and lustrous on the upper surface, usually pale or whitish on the lower surface, $4'-12'$ long and $1\frac{1}{2}'-2\frac{1}{2}'$ wide, with a broad pale midrib and obscure reticulate veinlets; persistent for two or three years; petioles stout, ridged above, rounded below, $1'-1\frac{1}{2}'$ in length. **Flowers:** inflorescence-buds surrounded at first by several loose narrow leaf-like scales, and when fully grown in September cone-shaped, $1\frac{1}{2}'$ long and $\frac{1}{2}'$ broad, with many imbricated ovate scales rounded and contracted at apex into a long slender point, opening late in June after the shoots of the year from buds in the axils of upper leaves have reached their full length; flowers on slender pink pedicels covered with glandular white hairs and furnished at base with two linear scarious bractlets, from the axils of the scales of the inner ranks of the inflorescence-bud, in 16-24-flowered umbellate clusters $4'-5'$ in diameter, with accrescent scarious resinous puberulous bracts, those of the outer ranks becoming $1'$ long and $\frac{1}{3}'$ wide, and shorter than the lanceolate bracts of the inner ranks contracted into a long slender point; calyx light green and puberulous, with rounded remote lobes; corolla prominently 5-angled or ridged in the bud, campanulate, gibbous on the posterior side, puberulous in the throat, light rose color, purplish, or white, 1' long, cleft to the middle into 5 oval rounded lobes, with conspicuous central veins, the upper lobe marked on the inner face by a cluster of yellow-green spots, and

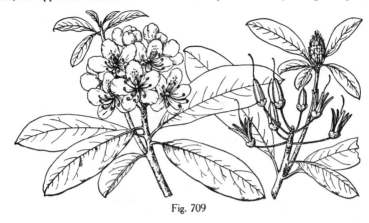

Fig. 709

furnished on the outer surface at the bottom of each sinus with a conspicuous dark red gland; stamens 8–12, white, inserted on the bright green disk; filaments enlarged and flattened at base, slightly bent inward above the middle, and bearded with stiff white hairs, the 4 or 5 short ones at the back of the flower for more than half their length and the others only near the base; ovary ovoid, green, coated with short glandular pale hairs, crowned with a long slender glabrous white declining style club-shaped and inflexed at apex, and terminating in a 5-rayed scarlet stigma.   **Fruit** dark red-brown, ovoid, $\frac{1}{2}'$ long, glandular-hispid, ripening and shedding its seeds in the autumn, the clusters of open capsules remaining on the branches until the following summer; **seeds** oblong, flattened, the coat prolonged at the ends into scarious fringed appendages.

A bushy tree, 30°–40° high, with a short crooked often prostrate trunk occasionally 10'–12' in diameter, stout contorted branches forming a round head, and branchlets green tinged with red and covered with dark red or slightly ferrugineous glandular-hispid hairs when they first appear, dark green and glabrous in their first winter, gradually turning bright red-brown in their second year, and ultimately gray tinged with red, the thin bark separating on branches four or five years old into persistent scales; more often a broad shrub, with many divergent twisted stems 10°-12° high.   **Winter-buds:** leaf-buds conic, dark green, axillary, or terminal on barren shoots, with many closely imbricated scales, those of the inner ranks accrescent, increasing in length from the outer to the inner, and at maturity $1\frac{1}{2}'$ long, $\frac{1}{4}'$ wide, gradually narrowed at base, and terminating at apex in a long slender point, light green, glabrous, closely held against the shoot by a resinous exudation from the glandular hairs, and in falling marking the branchlet with numerous conspicuous narrow remote scars persistent for three or four years.   **Bark** of the trunk about $\frac{1}{16}'$ thick, light red-brown, broken on the surface into small thin appressed scales.   **Wood** heavy, hard, strong, rather brittle, close-grained, light clear brown, with thin lighter colored sapwood; occasionally made into the handles of tools and used as a substitute for boxwood in engraving.   A decoction of the leaves is occasionally employed in domestic practice in the treatment of rheumatism.

Distribution.   Nova Scotia, Mt. Chocorua, New Hampshire, and southward in New England and eastern New York and along the Appalachian Mountains to northern Georgia and westward to the northern shores of Lake Erie and to southeastern Ohio (Hocking and Fairfield Counties); rare at the north and an inhabitant of deep cold swamps in a few isolated stations; more abundant on the mountains of western Pennsylvania, becoming exceedingly common farther south and occupying the steep banks of streams up to altitudes of 3000°; of its largest size on the high mountains of eastern Tennessee and the Carolinas, and here often forming thickets hundreds of acres in extent. Often cultivated as an ornament of parks and gardens in the United States, and in Europe, and one of the parents of a number of distinct and beautiful hybrids.

3. KALMIA L.

Trees or shrubs, with scaly bark, terete branchlets without a terminal bud, minute axillary leaf-buds, elongated axillary inflorescence-buds covered by imbricated scales, and fibrous roots. Leaves ovate-oblong or linear, short-petiolate, with flat entire margins, coriaceous, persistent or deciduous in one species. Flowers on slender pedicels bibracteolate at the base, from the axils of foliaceous coriaceous ovate or acute persistent bracts, in axillary umbels; calyx 5, rarely 6-parted, the divisions imbricated in the bud, persistent under the fruit; corolla 5, rarely 6-lobed, rose-colored, purple, or white, saucer-shaped, with a short tube and 10 pouches just below the 5 or 6-parted limb, the lobes ovate, acute, before anthesis prominently 10 or 12-ribbed from the pouches to the acute apex of the bud, the salient keel of the ribs running to the point of the lobes and to the sinuses; stamens 10, shorter than the corolla; filaments filiform; anthers oblong, each cell opening by a short apical oblong longitudinal pore, at first free in the bud, the filaments then erect, later received in the pouches of the corolla, the filaments becoming bent back by its enlargement and expansion, straightening elastically and incurving on the release of the anthers, and in straightening discharging the pollen-grains; disk prominently 10-lobed; ovary subglobose, 5-celled; style filiform, exserted, crowned with a capitate stigma; ovules numerous in each cell, inserted on a 2-lipped placenta, pendulous or spreading from near the top of the thin columella, few-ranked, anatropous. Fruit a woody many-seeded globose slightly 5-lobed 5-celled capsule, tardily septicidally 5-valved, the valves crustaceous, ultimately opening down the middle by a narrow slit and separating from the persistent placenta-bearing axis. Seeds oblong or subglobose, minute; seed-coat crustaceous or membranaceous; embryo in fleshy albumen, terete, near the hilum; radicle erect, rather shorter than the oblong cotyledons.

Kalmia with six species is North American and Cuban, one species occasionally becoming under favorable conditions a small tree.

The generic name is in honor of the Swedish traveler and botanist, Peter Kalm (1715–1779).

1. Kalmia latifolia L. Laurel. Mountain Laurel.

Leaves sometimes in pairs or in 3's, conduplicate in the bud, each leaf in the bud inclosed by the one immediately below it, oblong or elliptic-lanceolate, acute or rounded and tipped at apex with a callous point, and gradually narrowed at base, rarely oval to oblong-obovate and rounded at ends (f. *obtusata* Rehd.), when they unfold slightly tinged with pink and covered with glandular white hairs, and at maturity thick and rigid, dark rather dull green above, light yellow-green below, 3'–4' long and 1'–1½' wide, with a broad yellow midrib and obscure immersed veins; beginning to fall during their second summer; petioles stout, terete or slightly flattened, about ⅔' in length. **Flowers** opening from early in April in southern Mississippi to the 20th of June at the north; inflorescence-buds appearing in the autumn from the axils of upper leaves, beginning to lengthen with the first warm days of spring and usually developing 2 or several lateral branches, the whole forming a compound many-flowered corymb of numerous crowded fascicles more or less covered with dark scurfy scales, 4'–5' in diameter, and overtopped at the flowering time by the leafy branches of the year; flowers nearly 1' in diameter, on long slender red or green pedicels covered with glandular hairs, and furnished at base with 2 minute acute bractlets, developed from the axils of acute persistent bracts sometimes ⅓' long; calyx divided nearly to the base into narrow acute thin green lobes; corolla white (f. *alba* Rehd.), rose-color, or deep pink (f. *rubra* Rehd.) viscid-pubescent, marked on the inner surface with a waving dark rose-colored line and with delicate purple penciling above the sacs, rarely with a broad purple or chocolate-colored band (f. *fuscata* Rehd.). **Fruit** ripening in September, crowned with the persistent style, $\frac{3}{16}'$ in diameter, and covered with viscid hairs, remaining on the branches until the following year; **seeds** oblong, light brown, scattered by the, opening of the valves.

A tree, rarely 30°–40° high, with a short crooked and contorted trunk sometimes 18′–20′ in diameter, stout forked divergent branches forming a round-topped compact head, and slender branchlets light green tinged with red and covered with soft white glandular-viscid hairs when they first appear, soon becoming glabrous, and in their first winter green tinged with red and very lustrous, turning bright red-brown during their second year and paler the following season, the bark then separating into large thin papery scales exposing the cinnamon-red inner bark, and marked with large deeply impressed leaf-scars showing near the centre a crowded cluster of fibro-vascular bundle-scars; more often a dense broad shrub 6°–10° high, with numerous crooked stems. **Winter-buds** formed before midsummer in the axils of the leaves just below those producing the inflorescence-buds, their inner scales

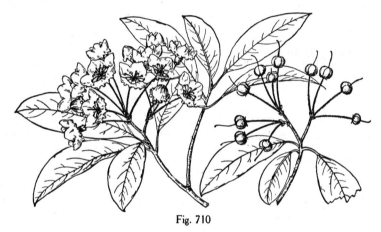

Fig. 710

accrescent, and at maturity often 1′ long and $\frac{1}{2}'$ wide, ovate, acute, light green, covered with glandular white hairs, and in falling marking the base of the shoots with conspicuous broad scars. **Bark** of the trunk hardly more than $\frac{1}{16}'$ thick, dark brown tinged with red, and divided by longitudinal furrows into narrow ridges separating into long narrow scales. **Wood** heavy, hard, strong, rather brittle, close-grained, brown tinged with red, with slightly lighter colored sapwood; used for the handles of tools, in turnery, and for fuel.

Distribution. New Brunswick to the northern shores of Lake Erie and southward in the Atlant c coast region to Virginia and to southern Ohio, Clark, Perry and Crawford Counties, Indiana and central Tennessee, along the Appalachian Mountains and their foot-hills to Georgia, and from western Florida through Alabama to eastern and southern Mississippi and the valley of the Bogue Lusa River, Washington Parish, Louisiana; often growing in low moist ground near the margins of swamps or on dry slopes under the shade of deciduous-leaved trees, or on rich rocky hillsides; most abundant and often forming dense impenetrable thickets on the southern Appalachian Mountains up to altitudes of 3000°–4000°; usually shrubby, and only arborescent in a few secluded valleys between the Blue Ridge and the Alleghany Mountains of North and South Carolina; abundant and of large size along small streams in Liberty County, middle Florida. The var. *myrtifolia* K. Koch with small lance-oblong leaves, and small compact clusters of small flowers, a compact dwarf shrub, and an old inhabitant of European gardens, is occasionally wild in Massachusetts; in an abnormal form (f. *polypetala* Rehd.) found in western Massachusetts the corolla is divided into 5 narrow petals.

Often cultivated as an ornament of parks and gardens in the eastern states, and in Europe.

4. OXYDENDRUM DC.

A tree, with thick deeply furrowed bark, slender terete glabrous light red or brown branchlets, without a terminal bud, marked by elevated nearly triangular leaf-scars displaying a lunate row of crowded fibro-vascular bundle-scars, and numerous elevated oblong dark lenticels, acid foliage, and fibrous roots.   Winter-buds axillary, minute, partly immersed in the bark, obtuse, covered with opposite broad-ovate dark red scales rounded at apex, those of the inner ranks accrescent.   Leaves alternate, revolute in the bud, oblong or lanceolate, acute, gradually contracted at base into a long slender petiole, serrate with minute incurved callous teeth, penniveined, with a conspicuous bright yellow midrib and reticulate veinlets, thin and firm, dark green and lustrous on the upper surface, pale and glaucous on the lower surface, glabrous or at first slightly puberulous, deciduous.   Flowers on erect clavate pedicels coated with hoary pubescence and bibracteolate above the middle, with linear acute caducous bractlets, in puberulous panicles of secund racemes appearing in summer and terminal on axillary leading shoots of the year, the lower racemes in the axils of upper leaves; calyx free, divided nearly to the base, the divisions valvate in the bud, ovate-lanceolate, acute, pubescent or puberulous on the outer surface, persistent under the fruit; corolla hypogynous, cylindric to ovate-cylindric, white, puberulous, 5-lobed, the lobes minute, ovate, acute, reflexed; stamens 10, included; filaments subulate, broad, pilose, inserted on the very base of the corolla; anthers linear-oblong, narrower than the filaments, the cells opening from the apex to the middle; disk thin, obscurely 10-lobed; ovary broad-ovoid, pubescent, 5-celled; style columnar, thick, exserted, crowned with a simple stigma; ovules attached to an axile placenta rising from the base of the cell, ascending, amphitropous.   Fruit a 5-celled ovoid-pyramidal many-seeded capsule crowned with the remnants of the persistent style, 5-lobed, puberulous, loculicidally 5-valved, the valves woody, separating from the central persistent placentiferous axis, many-seeded.   Seeds ascending, elongated; seed-coat membranaceous, loose, reticulated, produced at the ends into long slender points; embryo minute, axile in fleshy albumen, cylindric; radicle terete, next the hilum.

The genus consists of a single species.

The generic name is from ὀξύς and δένδρον, in allusion to the acid foliage.

1. Oxydendrum arboreum DC.   Sorrel-tree.   Sour Wood.

Leaves when they unfold bronze-green, very lustrous and glabrous with the exception of a slight pubescence on the upper side of the midrib and a few scattered hairs on the under side of the midrib and on the petioles, and at maturity 5′–7′ long and 1½′–2½′ wide; turning bright scarlet in the autumn; petioles ⅔′ in length.   **Flowers** opening late in July or early in August, ¼′ long, in panicles 7′–8′ in length.   **Fruit** ⅓′–½′ long, hanging in drooping clusters sometimes a foot in length, ripening in September, the empty capsules often persistent on the branches until late in the autumn; seeds about ⅛′ long, pale brown.

A tree, occasionally 50°–60° high, with a tall straight trunk 12′–20′ in diameter, slender spreading branches forming a narrow oblong round-topped head, and glabrous branchlets yellow-green and marked by orange-colored lenticels when they first appear, becoming in their first winter orange-colored to reddish brown.   **Winter-buds** about ₁/₁₆′ long, their inner scales at maturity 1′ in length, ⅛′ wide, spatulate, acute at apex, and slightly puberulous on the inner surface and on the margins.   **Bark** of the trunk ⅔′–1′ thick, gray tinged with red and divided by longitudinal furrows into broad rounded ridges covered with small thick appressed scales.   **Wood** heavy, hard, very close-grained, brown tinged with red, with lighter colored sapwood of 80–90 layers of annual growth; sometimes used locally for the handles of tools and the bearings of machinery. The leaves have a pleasant acidulous taste, and are reputed to be tonic, refrigerant, and diuretic, and are occasionally used in domestic practice in the treatment of fevers.

Distribution. Well-drained gravelly soil on ridges rising above the banks of streams; coast of Virginia (Accomac County) to that of North Carolina (near Newbern, Craven

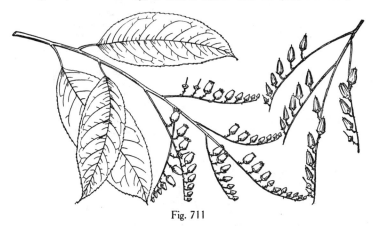

Fig. 711

County), southwestern Pennsylvania to southern Ohio and Indiana (Perry County), and to western Kentucky and Tennessee, along the Appalachian Mountains and their foothills, and southward to western Florida, the shores of Mobile Bay, the coast region of Mississippi, and West Feliciana Parish, Louisiana; up to altitudes of 3500° on the southern mountains; of its largest size on the western slopes of the Big Smoky Mountains, Tennessee.

Often cultivated as an ornamental plant in the eastern states and hardy as far north as eastern Massachusetts, and occasionally in western and central Europe.

5. XOLISMA. Raf.

Lyonia Nutt.

Trees or shrubs, with slender terete branchlets, and fibrous roots. Leaves petiolate, thin or coriaceous. Flowers on slender pedicels from the axils of ovate acute bracts, in axillary and terminal umbellate fascicles or panicled racemes; calyx persistent, 4–5-toothed or parted, the divisions valvate in the bud; corolla globular, 4 or 5-toothed or lobed, the lobes imbricated in the bud; stamens 8–10, included; filaments flat, incurved, usually slightly adnate to the base of the corolla, dilated and bearded at base, geniculate; anthers oblong, the cells opening below the apex by large oblong pores; disk 10-lobed; ovary 5-celled, depressed in the centre; style columnar, stigmatic at apex; ovules attached to a placenta borne near the summit of the axis, anatropous. Fruit ovoid, many-seeded, loculicidally 5-valved, the valves septiferous and separating from the placentiferous axis, 5-ribbed by the thickening of the valves at the dorsal sutures, the ribs more or less separable in dehiscence. Seeds minute, pendulous, narrow-oblong; seed-coat loose, thin, reticulate, produced at the ends beyond the nucleus into short fringe-like wings; embryo axile in fleshy albumen, cylindric, elongated: cotyledons much shorter than the terete radicle turned toward the hilum.

Lyonia with about twenty species is confined to North America, the West Indies, and Mexico. Of the four or five species which occur in the United States one is occasionally a small tree.

The derivation of the name Xolisma is obscure.

1. Xolisma ferruginea Hell.

Lyonia ferruginea Nutt.

Leaves cuneate-obovate, rhombic-obovate or cuneate-oblong, acute or rounded at apex, usually tipped with a cartilaginous mucro, gradually narrowed at base, and entire, with thickened revolute margins, scurfy when they unfold, and at maturity thick and firm, pale green, smooth and shining or sometimes obscurely lepidote above, covered below with ferrugineous or pale scales, 1′–3′ long and $\frac{1}{4}$′–$1\frac{1}{2}$′ wide, with a prominent midrib and primary veins; appearing in early spring and persistent until the summer or autumn of their second year; petioles short, thick, much enlarged at base. **Flowers** $\frac{1}{8}$′ in diameter, chiefly produced on branches of the year or occasionally on those of the previous year, opening from February until April when the leaves are fully grown, on slender recurved pedicels much shorter than the leaves, in crowded axillary short-stemmed or sessile ferrugineous-lepidote fascicles, with minute acute deciduous bracts and bractlets; calyx 5-lobed, with acute lobes, covered on the outer surface with ferrugineous scales, and about one third as long as the white pubescent corolla, with short reflexed acute teeth slightly thickened and ciliate on

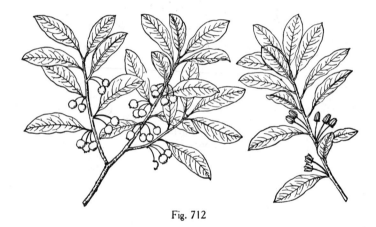

Fig. 712

the margins; filaments shortened by a conspicuous geniculate fold in the middle; ovary coated with thick white tomentum; style stout, as long or a little longer than the corolla. **Fruit** on a stout erect stem, oblong, 5-angled, $\frac{1}{4}$′ long; **seed** pale brown.

A tree, occasionally 20°–30° high, with a slender crooked or often prostrate trunk sometimes 10′ in diameter, thin rigid divergent branches forming a tall oblong irregular head, and slender branchlets coated when they first appear with minute ferrugineous scales and covered in their second year with glabrous or pubescent light or dark red-brown bark smooth or exfoliating in small thin scales. **Winter-buds** minute, acute, and covered with ferrugineous scales. **Bark** of the trunk $\frac{1}{8}$′–$\frac{1}{4}$′ thick, divided into long narrow ridges by shallow longitudinal furrows, reddish brown and separating into short thick scales. **Wood** heavy, hard, close-grained although not strong, light brown tinged with red, with thick lighter colored sapwood.

Distribution. Hummocks and sandy woods; coast region of South Carolina and Georgia, northern Florida to the centre of the peninsula, the shores of Tampa Bay, and to the neighborhood of Apalachicola (Franklin County); in the United States arborescent in the rich soil of the woody hummocks rising in the sandy Pine-covered coast plain, and as a low shrub in the dry sandy sterile soil of Pine-barrens; in the West Indies and Mexico.

6. ARBUTUS L.

Trees or shrubs, with astringent bark exfoliating from young stems in large thin scales, smooth terete red branches, and thick hard roots. Leaves petiolate, entire or dentate, obscurely penniveined, persistent. Flowers on clavate pedicels bibracteolate at base from the axils of ovate bracts, in simple terminal compound racemes or panicles, with scarious scaly persistent bracts and bractlets; calyx free from the ovary, 5-parted nearly to the base, the divisions imbricated in the bud, ovate, acute, scarious, persistent; corolla ovoid-urceolate, white, 5-toothed, the teeth obtuse and recurved; stamens 10, shorter than the corolla; filaments subulate, dilated and pilose at base, free, inserted in the bottom of the corolla; anthers short, compressed laterally, dorsally 2-awned, the cells opening at the top internally by a terminal pore; ovary glandular-roughened, glabrous or tomentose, sessile or slightly immersed in the glandular 10-lobed disk, 5 or rarely 4-celled; style columnar, simple, exserted; stigma obscurely 5-lobed; ovules attached to a central placenta developed from the inner angle of each cell, amphitropous. Fruit drupaceous, globose, smooth or glandular-coated, 5-celled, many-seeded; flesh dry and mealy; stone cartilaginous, often incompletely developed. Seeds small, compressed or angled, narrowed and often apiculate at apex; seed-coat coriaceous, dark red-brown, slightly pilose; embryo axile in copious horny albumen, clavate; radicle terete, erect, turned toward the hilum.

Arbutus with ten or twelve species inhabits southern and western North America, Central America, western, southern and eastern Europe, Asia Minor, northern Africa, and the Canary Islands. Three species occur within the territory of the United States. Arbutus produces hard close-grained valuable wood often made into charcoal, used in the manufacture of gunpowder. The fruit possesses narcotic properties, and the bark and leaves are astringent.

Arbutus is the classical name of the species of southern Europe.

CONSPECTUS OF THE SPECIES OF THE UNITED STATES.

Bark of old trunks dark red-brown.
Ovary glabrous; leaves oval or oblong.   1. **A. Menziesii** (B, G).
Ovary pubescent; leaves oval, ovate, or lanceolate.   2. **A. texana** (C).
Bark of old trunks ashy gray; ovary glabrous, conspicuously porulose; leaves lanceolate or
   rarely narrow-oblong.   3. **A. arizonica** (H).

1. Arbutus Menziesii Pursh. Madroña.

Leaves oval or oblong, rounded or contracted into a short point at apex, and rounded, subcordate or cuneate at base, with slightly thickened revolute entire or occasionally on young plants sharply serrate margins, when they unfold light green or often pink, especially on the lower surface, and glabrous or slightly puberulous, and at maturity thick and coriaceous, dark green and lustrous above, pale or often nearly white below, $3'-5'$ long and $1\frac{1}{2}'$–$3'$ wide, with a thick pale midrib and conspicuously reticulated veinlets; persistent until the early summer of their second year and then turning orange and scarlet and falling gradually and irregularly; petioles stout, grooved, $\frac{1}{4}'-1'$ in length, often slightly wing-margined toward the apex; often producing late in summer a second crop of smaller leaves. **Flowers** about $\frac{1}{3}'$ long, with a glabrous ovary, appearing from March to May on short slender puberulous pedicels from the axils of acute scarious bracts ciliate on the margins, in spicate pubescent racemes forming a cluster $5'-6'$ long and broad. **Fruit** ripening in the autumn, subglobose or occasionally obovoid or oval, $\frac{1}{2}'$ long, bright orange-red, with thin glandular flesh and a 5-celled more or less perfectly developed thin-walled cartilaginous stone; **seeds** several in each cell, tightly pressed together and angled, dark brown and pilose.

A tree, $80°-125°$ high, with a tall straight trunk $4°-5°$ in diameter, stout upright or spreading branches forming a narrow oblong or broad round-topped head, and slender branchlets light red, pea-green, or orange-colored and glabrous when they first appear, or on vigorous young plants sometimes covered with pale scattered deciduous hairs, becoming in their first winter bright reddish brown.   **Winter-buds obtuse,** $\frac{1}{3}'$ long, with numerous imbricated broadly-ovate bright brown scales keeled on the back, apiculate at apex, and slightly ciliate.   **Bark** of young stems and of the branches smooth, bright red, separating

Fig. 713

into large thin scales, becoming on old trunks $\frac{1}{3}'-\frac{1}{2}'$ thick, dark reddish brown, and covered with small thick plate-like scales.   **Wood** heavy, hard, strong, close-grained, light brown shaded with red, with thin lighter colored sapwood of 8–12 layers of annual growth; used for furniture and largely for charcoal.   The bark is sometimes employed in tanning leather.

Distribution. High well-drained slopes usually in rich soil or ocasionally in gravelly valleys; islands at Seymore Narrows, and southward through the coast region of British Columbia, Washington and Oregon; over the coast ranges of northern California, extending east to Mt. Shasta and south along the western slope of the Sierra Nevada from altitudes of 2500°-4000° to Placer County; on many of the coast ranges south of San Francisco Bay to the mountains of southern California; common and of its largest size in the Redwood-forests of northwestern California; much smaller north of California; rare on the Sierra Nevada and southward except on the Santa Cruz Mountains, and often shrubby in habit.

Occasionally cultivated in the gardens of western and southern Europe.

2. Arbutus texana Buckl. Madroña.

Arbutus xalapensis S. Watson, not H. B. K.

Leaves oval, ovate, or lanceolate, rounded, acute and often apiculate at apex, and rounded or cuneate at base, with slightly thickened usually entire or remotely crenulate-toothed or coarsely serrate margins, often tinged with red when they unfold and pubescent below, and at maturity thick and coriaceous, dark green and glabrous on the upper surface, pale and usually slightly pubescent on the lower surface, 1'–3' long and $\frac{2}{3}'-1\frac{1}{2}'$ wide, with a thick midrib often villose-pubescent below; petioles stout, pubescent, sometimes becoming nearly glabrous, 1'–1$\frac{1}{2}'$ in length.   **Flowers** $\frac{1}{4}'$ long, with ciliate calyx-lobes and a pubescent ovary, appearing in March on stout recurved hoary-tomentose club-shaped pedicels from the axils of ovate acute hoary-tomentose often persistent bracts, in compact conic hoary-tomentose panicles 2$\frac{1}{2}'$ long.   **Fruit** pubescent until half grown, becoming glabrous, usually produced very sparingly, ripening in summer, dark red, $\frac{1}{4}'$ in diameter, with thin granular flesh and a rather thick more or less completely formed stone; **seeds** numerous in each cell, compressed, puberulous.

A tree, in Texas rarely more than 18°-20° high, with a short often crooked trunk 8'–10' in diameter, separating a foot or two above the ground into several stout spreading branches, and branchlets light red and thickly coated with pubescence when they first appear, becoming dark red-brown and covered with small plate-like scales; often a broad irregularly shaped bush, with numerous contorted stems. **Winter-buds** about $\frac{1}{8}'$ long, with hoary tomentose scales, the outer ovate, acute, the inner obovate and rounded at apex. **Bark** of young stems and of the branches thin, tinged with red, separating into large papery scales exposing the light red or flesh-colored inner bark, becoming at the base of old trunks sometimes $\frac{1}{4}'$ thick, deeply furrowed, dark reddish brown, and broken into thick square plates. **Wood** heavy, hard, close-grained, brown tinged with red, with a lighter

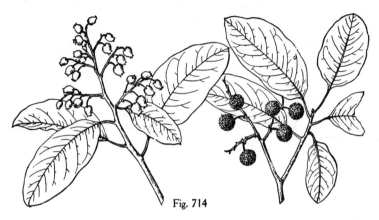

Fig. 714

colored sapwood of 10–12 layers of annual growth; sometimes used in Texas for the handles of small tools and in the manufacture of mathematical instruments.

Distribution. Texas, dry limestone hills, Travis, Comal, Blanco, Kendall and Bandera Counties, on the Guadalupe and Eagle Mountains, Culberson and El Paso Counties; southeastern New Mexico (Eddy County); on the mountains of Nuevo Leon in the neighborhood of Monterey.

3. Arbutus arizonica Sarg. Madroña.

Leaves lanceolate to rarely oblong, acute or rounded and apiculate at apex, and cuneate or occasionally rounded at base, with thickened entire or rarely denticulate margins, when

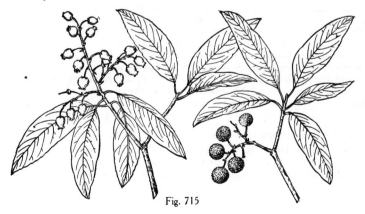

Fig. 715

they unfold, tinged with red, and slightly puberulous, especially on the petiole and margins, and at maturity thin, firm and rigid, light green on the upper surface, pale on the lower surface, $1\frac{1}{2}'$–$3'$ long and $\frac{1}{2}'$–$1'$ wide, with a slender yellow midrib and obscure reticulate veinlets; appearing in May and after the summer rains in September, and persistent for at least a year; petioles slender, often $1'$ in length. **Flowers** $\frac{1}{4}'$ long, with a corolla much contracted in the middle, and a glabrous porulose ovary, opening in May on short stout hairy pedicels from the axils of conspicuous ovate rounded scarious bracts, in rather loose clusters $2'$–$2\frac{1}{2}'$ long and broad, their lower branches from the axils of upper leaves. **Fruit** ripening in October and November, globose or short-oblong, dark orange-red, granulate, $\frac{1}{3}'$ in diameter, with thin sweetish flesh, and a papery usually incompletely developed stone; **seeds** compressed, puberulous.

A tree, 40°–50° high, with a tall straight trunk $18'$–$24'$ in diameter, stout spreading branches forming a rather compact round-topped head, and thick tortuous divergent branchlets reddish brown and more or less pubescent or light purple, pilose, and covered with a glaucous bloom when they first appear, becoming bright red at the end of their first season, their bark thin, separating freely into thin more or less persistent scales. **Winter-buds** $\frac{1}{8}'$ long, red, the two outer scales linear, acuminate a third longer than those of the next rank, acute and apiculate and ridged on the back. **Bark** of young stems and of the branches thin, smooth, dark red, exfoliating in large thin scales, becoming on old trunks $\frac{1}{3}'$–$\frac{1}{2}'$ thick, irregularly broken by longitudinal furrows and divided into square appressed plate-like light gray or nearly white scales faintly tinged with red on the surface. **Wood** heavy, close-grained, soft and brittle, light brown tinged with red, with lighter colored sapwood of 30–40 layers of annual growth.

Distribution. Dry gravelly benches at altitude of 6000°–8000° on the Santa Catalina and Santa Rita Mountains, southern Arizona, and on the San Luis and Animas Mountains of southwestern New Mexico (Grant County); on the Sierra Nevada of Chihuahua.

7. VACCINIUM L.

Shrubs or rarely small trees, with slender branchlets, and fibrous roots. Leaves thin or coriaceous, deciduous or persistent. Flowers small, on bibracteolate pedicels, in many-branched axillary racemes, or solitary, their bracts small or foliaceous; calyx-tube adnate to the ovary, 4–5-lobed, the lobes valvate in the bud, persistent; corolla epigynous, 4 or 5-toothed, the teeth imbricated in the bud, urceolate-campanulate; stamens 8–10, inserted on the base of the corolla under the thick obscurely lobed epigynous disk; filaments filiform, free, usually hirsute; anthers awned on the back, the cells produced upward into erect spreading tubes dehiscent by a terminal pore; ovary inferior, 4 or 5-celled, the cells sometimes imperfectly divided by the development from the back of a false partition; style filiform, erect; stigma minute; ovules attached to the interior angle of the cell by a 2-lipped placenta, anatropous. Fruit a berry crowned with the calyx-limb, 4 or 5 or imperfectly 8 or 10-celled, the cells many-seeded. Seed minute, compressed, ovoid or reniform; seed-coat crustaceous; embryo clavate, minute, surrounded by fleshy albumen, axile, erect; cotyledons ovate; radicle terete, turned toward the hilum.

Vaccinium with about one hundred species is distributed through the boreal and temperate regions of the northern hemisphere, and occurs within the tropics at high altitudes north and south of the equator. Of the twenty-five or thirty species which occur in North America one is small trees. The fruits of many of the species are edible, the most valuable being the North American *Vaccinium macrocarpum* L., the Cranberry.

Vaccinium is the classical name of one of the Old World species.

1. Vaccinium arboreum Marsh.   Farkleberry.   Sparkleberry.

Leaves obovate, oblong-oval or occasionally orbicular, acute, or rounded and apiculate at apex, gradually or abruptly cuneate at base, obscurely glandular-dentate or entire, with thickened slightly revolute margins, light red and more or less pilose or puberulous when they unfold, and at maturity coriaceous, dark green and lustrous above, paler below, glabrous or often puberulous on the midrib and veins, reticulate-venulose, $\frac{1}{2}'$–$2\frac{1}{2}'$ long, $\frac{1}{4}'$–$1'$ wide, and sessile or short-petiolate; southward persistent for a year, northward deciduous during the winter. **Flowers** appearing from March to May on slender drooping pedicels

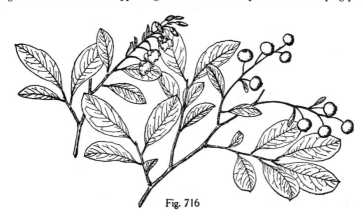

Fig. 716

$\frac{1}{2}'$ long, bibracteolate near the middle, with 2 minute acute scarious caducous bractlets, solitary in the axils of leaves of the year or arranged in terminal puberulous racemes $2'$–$3'$ long from the axils of leafy or minute acute scarious bracts; corolla white, open-campanulate, slightly 5-lobed, with acute reflexed lobes, longer than the 10 stamens; filaments hirsute; anther-cells opening by oblique elongated pores. **Fruit** ripening in October, sometimes persistent on the branches until the end of winter, globose, $\frac{1}{4}'$ in diameter, black and lustrous, with dry glandular slightly astringent flesh of a pleasant flavor.

A tree, $20°$–$30°$ high, with a short often crooked trunk occasionally $8'$–$10'$ in diameter, slender more or less contorted branches forming an irregular round-topped head, and slender branchlets light red and covered with pale pubescence when they first appear, glabrous or puberulous and bright red-brown in their first winter, later becoming dark red and marked by minute elevated nearly orbicular leaf-scars; or northward generally reduced to a low shrub, with numerous divergent stems. **Winter-buds** obtuse, nearly $\frac{1}{16}'$ long, with imbricated ovate acute chestnut-brown scales often persistent on the base of the branchlet throughout the season. **Wood** heavy, hard, very close-grained, light brown tinged with red, with thick hardly distinguishable sapwood; sometimes used for the handles of tools and in the manufacture of other small articles. Decoctions of the astringent bark of the root and of the leaves are sometimes employed domestically in the treatment of diarrhœa. The bark has been used by tanners.

Distribution. Usually in moist sandy soil along the banks of ponds and streams; southeastern Virginia and North Carolina, from the coast to the valleys of the high Appalachian Mountains, southward to the valley of the Caloosahatchee River, Florida, through the Gulf states to the shores of Matagorda Bay, Texas, and through eastern Oklahoma, Arkansas, and Missouri to southern Illinois, and the bluffs of White River, near Shoals, Martin County, and near Elizabeth, Harrison County, Indiana; common in the maritime Pinebelt of the south Atlantic and Gulf states, and of its largest size near the coast of eastern Texas; in the interior less abundant and usually of small size. Passing into

Vaccinium arboreum var. glaucescens Sarg.

Batodendron glaucescens Greene

Differing in its glaucescent, pubescent or glabrous leaves, in its usually larger leaf-like bracts of the inflorescence and often in its globose-campanulate corolla.

A tree, 10°–20° high, with a short often crooked trunk, pubescent or glabrous gray branch-lets, and winter-buds and bark like those of *Vaccinium arboreum* with which it often grows.

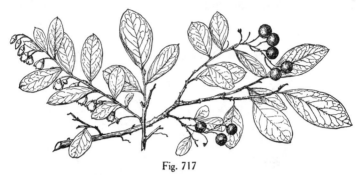

Fig. 717

Distribution. Tunnel Hill, Johnson County, Illinois, southern Missouri to eastern Oklahoma (Sapulpa, Creek County) and through Arkansas to western Louisiana (near Shreveport, Rapides Parish) and eastern Texas to Milam County.

LIV. THEOPHRASTACEÆ.

Trees or shrubs, with watery juice, and entire coriaceous persistent leaves. Flowers perfect, regular; calyx campanulate, with 5 sepals imbricated in the bud; corolla 5-lobed, the lobes imbricated in the bud, with 5 staminodia attached below the sinuses; stamens 5, attached to the base of the corolla-tube, opposite the lobes; ovary 1-celled, with a simple style and a slightly 5-lobed stigma; ovules peltate, numerous, attached to a central fleshy placenta, amphitropous. Fruit baccate, many-seeded. Seeds immersed in the thickened placenta filling the cavity of the fruit; seed-coat membranaceous; embryo surrounded by thick cartilaginous albumen.

A tropical American family of four genera with one species reaching the shores of southern Florida.

1. JACQUINIA Jacq.

Trees or shrubs, with terete or slightly many-angled branchlets, without a terminal bud, and fibrous roots. Leaves often punctate with pellucid dark glands. Flowers on slender ebracteolate pedicels from the axils of minute ovate acute persistent bracts, in terminal or axillary clusters; calyx slightly ciliate on the margins, rounded at apex, persistent under the fruit; corolla hypogynous, the lobes obtuse and spreading, furnished with 5 petal-like ovate obtuse spreading staminodia; stamens inserted on the corolla opposite its lobes near the base of the short tube; filaments flattened, broad at base; anthers oblong or ovoid, attached on the back above the base, extrorse, 2-celled, the cells opening longitudinally; ovary ovoid. Fruit ovoid or subglobose, crowned by the remnants of the persistent style, with a thin crustaceous outer coat, inclosing the thick enlarged mucilaginous placenta. Seeds oblong; seed-coat punctate; embryo eccentric; cotyledons ovate, shorter than the elongated inferior radicle turned toward the broad ventral hilum.

Jacquinia with five or six species is confined to tropical America, with one species reaching southern Florida.

The generic name is in honor of Nicholas Joseph Jacquin (1728–1818) the distinguished Austrian botanist.

1. Jacquinia keyensis Metz.   Joe Wood.   Sea Myrtle.

Leaves subverticillate, alternate or sometimes opposite, crowded near the end of the branches, cuneate-spatulate or oblong-obovate, rounded or emarginate or often apiculate at apex, gradually narrowed below, entire, with thickened slightly revolute margins, thick and coriaceous, yellow-green, nearly veinless, with a very obscure midrib, covered on the lower surface with pale dots, 1'–3' long and $\frac{1}{4}$'–1' wide; persistent on the branches until the appearance of the new leaves the following year; petioles short, stout, abruptly enlarged at base. **Flowers** appearing in Florida from November until June, $\frac{1}{4}$' in diameter, pale yellow, fragrant, on slender club-shaped pedicels $\frac{1}{2}$' long from the axils of minute ovate coriaceous, reddish bracts slightly ciliate on the margins, in terminal and axillary many-flowered glabrous racemes 2'–3' long; sepals ovate-orbicular, obtuse; corolla salverform, $\frac{2}{3}$' broad, the lobes longer than the tube; stamens shorter than the staminodia. **Fruit** ripening in the autumn, $\frac{1}{3}$' in diameter, orange-red when fully ripe; **seeds** light brown.

A tree, 12°–15° high, with a straight trunk 6'–7' in diameter, stout rigid spreading branches forming a compact regular round-topped head, and slightly many-angled branchlets yellow-green or light orange-colored and coated with short soft pale ferrugineous pubescence when they first appear, terete, darker and sometimes reddish brown and marked in their second year by orbicular depressed conspicuous leaf-scars and by many scattered pale lenticels, becoming glabrous and red-brown or ashy gray the following season. **Winter-buds** axillary, minute, nearly globose, immersed in the bark. **Bark** of the trunk

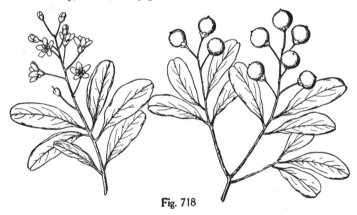

Fig. 718

thin, smooth, blue-gray, and usually more or less marked by pale or nearly white blotches. **Wood** heavy, hard, very close-grained, rich brown, beautifully marked by darker medullary rays.

Distribution. Florida, dry coral soil or silicious sand in the immediate neighborhood of the shore, Gasparilla Island, on the west coast to the southern keys, and to the borders of the Everglades; rare but most abundant and of its largest size in Florida on the Marquesas Keys; on the Bahama Islands and in Cuba and Jamaica.

LV. MYRSINACEÆ.

Trees or shrubs, with watery juice, alternate entire coriaceous punctate leaves, without stipules. Flowers regular, perfect or dimorphous; calyx persistent under the fruit; corolla, without staminodia, glandular-punctate; stamens inserted on the corolla, as many as and opposite its lobes; ovary 1-celled, with an undivided style and a minute terminal stigma; ovules peltate, immersed in the fleshy central placenta, amphitropous. Fruit a drupe. Seed solitary, globose, with copious cartilaginous or corneous albumen; seed-coat membranaceous.

A tropical family of thirty genera, with two arborescent species reaching the shores of southern Florida.

CONSPECTUS OF THE ARBORESCENT GENERA OF THE UNITED STATES.

Flowers perfect in terminal panicles; anthers on short broad filaments; style elongated.

                     1. Ardisia.

Flowers dimorphous in small axillary clusters; anthers sessile; stigma sessile or in one form of the staminate flower terminal on a slender style.   **2. Rapanea.**

1. ARDISIA Sw.

Glabrous trees or shrubs, with leaves punctate below with immersed resinous dots. Flowers resinous-punctate, pedicellate, the pedicels bibracteolate at base or ebracteolate, in terminal or rarely axillary branched panicles, with minute scarious deciduous or caducous bracts and bractlets; calyx free, 5 or rarely 4-lobed or parted, the divisions contorted or imbricated in the bud; corolla 5 or rarely 4–6-parted, the divisions extrorsely or sinistrorsely contorted in the bud, short or elongated, white or rose color; stamens exserted; filaments short or nearly obsolete, free, inserted on the throat of the corolla; anthers usually sagittate-lanceolate, attached on the back just above the base, introrse, 2-celled, the cells opening longitudinally sometimes nearly to the base; ovary globose; ovules numerous, immersed in the globose resinous-punctate placenta. Fruit globose, with thin usually dry flesh and a 1-seeded stone with a usually crustaceous or bony shell. Seed concave or more or less lobed at base, resinous-punctate; hilum basilar, concave, conspicuous; embryo cylindric, transverse; cotyledons flat on the inner face, rounded on the back, shorter than the slender radicle.

Ardisia with about two hundred species inhabits tropical and subtropical regions of the two hemispheres. The genus has few useful properties, but a number of species are cultivated for the beauty of their handsome evergreen foliage and bright-colored fruits.

The generic name is from ἀρδίς, in reference to the pointed anthers.

1. **Ardisia escallonioides** Cham. & Schlecht. **Marlberry.** **Cherry.**

   Icacorea paniculata Sudw. *Ardisia paniculata* Nutt.

Leaves ovate to oblong-lanceolate or lanceolate-obovate, acute or rounded at the narrow apex, cuneate and gradually contracted at base, entire, with thickened and slightly revo-

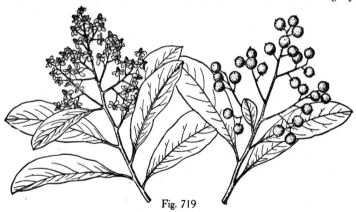

Fig. 719

lute margins, thick and coriaceous, glabrous, marked by minute scattered dark dots, dark yellow-green on the upper surface, pale on the lower surface, 3′–6′ long and 1′–1½′ wide, with a broad midrib yellow and conspicuous on the under side, slender primary veins and reticulate veinlets; appearing in the summer or early autumn and falling before the appearance of the flowers the following year; petioles stout, grooved, $\frac{1}{4}$–$\frac{1}{2}$ in length. **Flowers** fragrant, usually opening in November or occasionally as early as July, $\frac{1}{4}$ in diameter, on slender elongated pedicels without bractlets, from the axils of linear acute caducous bracts, in terminal rusty brown puberulous panicles 3′–4′ long and broad, their lower branches often from the axils of upper leaves; calyx ovoid, divided nearly to the base into 5 ovate acute lobes scarious and ciliate on the margins and marked on the back with dark lines; corolla 5-parted, with oblong rounded divisions sinistrorsely overlapping, or with 1 lobe wholly outside and 1 inside in the bud, conspicuously marked with red spots on the inner surface near the base, becoming reflexed; stamens, with short broad filaments, contracted by a geniculate fold in the middle, and large orange-colored anthers longer than the filaments, their cells opening almost to the base; ovary globose, glandular, gradually contracted into a long slender style ending in a simple stigma. **Fruit** ripening in early spring, globose, $\frac{1}{4}$ in diameter, tipped with the remnants of the style, and roughened by resinous glands, dark brown at first when fully grown, ultimately becoming black and lustrous; stone brown, thin-walled, crustaceous; **seed** conspicuously lobed at base, bright red-brown, about $\frac{1}{8}$ in diameter.

A slender tree, in Florida rarely more than 20° high, with a short trunk 4′–5′ in diameter, numerous thin upright branches forming a narrow head, and stout terete often contorted branchlets, rusty brown or dark orange-colored and slightly puberulous when they first appear, becoming in their second year dark brown or ashy gray, and marked by many minute circular lenticels and by thin nearly orbicular flat leaf-scars displaying in the centre a group of fibro-vascular bundle-scars. **Winter-buds** rusty brown; terminal slender, acuminate, $\frac{1}{8}$–$\frac{1}{4}$ long; axillary globose, minute, nearly immersed in the bark. **Bark** of the trunk about $\frac{1}{8}$ thick, light gray or nearly white, roughened by minute lenticels, and separating into large thin papery plates. **Wood** heavy, hard, very close-grained, rich brown beautifully marked by darker medullary rays, with thick lighter colored sapwood.

Distribution. Florida, usually in low damp hammocks, from Mosquito Inlet to the southern keys on the east coast, and from the shores of the Caloosahatchee River to Cape Romano on the west coast, ranging northward in the interior to Lake Okeechobee (*R. M. Harper*); usually a shrub, occasionally arborescent on the shores of Bay Biscayne and on some of the southern keys; on the Bahama Islands, in Cuba, and southern Mexico.

2. RAPANEA Aubl.

Trees or shrubs, with watery juices and terete branchlets. Leaves alternate, entire or rarely dentate, usually distinctly lepidote, persistent, without stipules. Flowers perfect or unisexual by abortion, minute, 4 or 5, or rarely 6 or 7-merous, sessile or pedicellate, in small axillary sessile or pedunculate fascicles, their bracts deciduous; calyx free, persistent, the sepals imbricate-valvate in the bud, ciliate, usually glandular-punctate; corolla hypogynous, the lobes more or less connate at base, ovate or elliptic, spreading or recurved, glandular-punctate, papillate on the margins, imbricate or rarely convolute in the bud; stamens inserted on the base of the corolla opposite its lobes; filaments 0; anthers short, connate to the corolla, acuminate and papillate at apex, introrse, 2-celled, the cells opening longitudinally; ovary globose or ellipsoidal, 1-celled; stigma capitate, irregularly lobed; ovules few, peltate, immersed in one series near the middle of the free fleshy globose placenta. Fruit dry or fleshy, seed filling the cavity of the fruit, globose, intruded at base; testa thin; albumen copious, corneous, rarely slightly ruminate; embryo cylindric, elongated, transverse, usually curved; cotyledons small, radicle elongated.

Rapanea, with nearly one hundred and fifty species, is widely distributed through the tropical and subtropical regions of the two hemispheres, one species reaching southern Florida.

The generic name is formed from the native name of *Rapanea guianensis* in British Guiana.

1. Rapanea guianensis Aubl.

Leaves crowded at the end of the branches, oblong-obovate, obtuse or retuse at apex, gradually narrowed and contracted at base, coriaceous, bright green and lustrous on the upper surface, paler on the lower surface, $2\frac{3}{4}'-3\frac{1}{2}'$ long and $1'-1\frac{1}{2}'$ wide, with thickened revolute margins, a thick midrib and obscure veins; petioles stout, narrowly wing-margined, $\frac{1}{4}'-\frac{1}{3}'$ in length. **Flowers** in November, minute, short-pedicellate in short pedunculate clus-

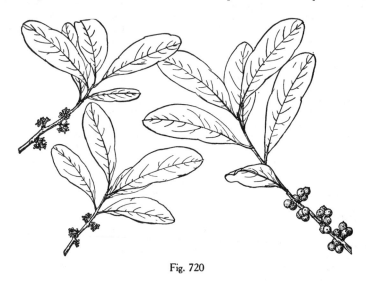

Fig. 720

ters usually 5, rarely 4-merous, white more or less marked with purple, about $\frac{1}{6}'$ in diameter; calyx divided to the middle, the lobes broad-ovate, acute or rounded at apex, slightly ciliate, persistent under the fruit; corolla 2 or 3 times longer than the calyx, the lobes spreading, narrowed and rounded at apex, slightly ciliate on the margins; staminate flowers dimorphous; anthers sagittate-apiculate, inserted below the middle of the petals; ovary in one form crowned by a minute discoid sessile stigma and probably abortive, in the other form gradually narrowed into a slender style, terminating in an oblique stigma and fertile; pistillate flowers, anthers smaller and rudimentary; ovary crowned by a large nearly sessile irregularly lobed papillate stigma deciduous from the fruit. **Fruit** in clusters crowded on the elongated somewhat thickened spur-like peduncle of the flower-cluster covered with imbricated persistent bracts, dark blue or nearly black, tipped with the persistent style, $\frac{1}{6}'-\frac{1}{5}'$ in diameter; exocarp thin and fleshy; endocarp crustaceous, white.

A tree, in Florida occasionally $18°-20°$ high, with a tall usually more or less crooked trunk $2'-3'$ in diameter, small ascending branches forming an open irregular head, and slender gray or light red-brown branchlets roughened for a year or two by the persistent spur-like peduncles of the fallen fruit and later marked by circular scars in the axils of the small transverse leaf-scars; more often a shrub. **Bark** of the trunk thin, close, pale gray.

Distribution. Florida, usually in low damp hammocks, shores of Indian River on the east coast and Palmetto, Manatee County, on the west coast, southward to the southern keys, ranging in the interior northward to Lake Okeechobee; common; on the Bahama Islands, Cuba, Porto Rico, Jamaica and Trinidad, to southern Brazil, and to Mexico and Bolivia.

LVI. SAPOTACEÆ.

Trees or shrubs, with milky juice. Leaves alternate, simple, entire, pinnately veined, mostly coriaceous, petiolate, without stipules. Flowers perfect, regular, small, in axillary clusters; calyx of 5–8 sepals imbricated in the bud, persistent under the fruit; corolla hypogynous, 5–8-cleft, the divisions imbricated in the bud, often with as many or twice as many internal appendages borne on its throat; disk 0; fertile stamens as many as and opposite the divisions of the corolla and inserted on its short tube, often with sterile filaments (*staminodia*) alternate with them; anthers generally extrorse, 2-celled, the cells opening longitudinally; pistil of united carpels; ovary sessile, usually 5-celled; style simple; ovules solitary in each cell, attached to an axile placenta, ascending, anatropous; raphe ventral; micropyle inferior. Fruit baccate, bearing at apex the remnant of the style, usually 1-celled and 1-seeded. Seed with or without albumen; embryo large; radicle terete, inferior.

This family with fifty genera is chiefly tropical and subtropical, with only Bumelia extending in North America into temperate regions. Some of the species produce valuable timber or edible and agreeable fruits. From *Palaquium gutta* Burkh., of the Malay Peninsula, gutta-percha is obtained. Five genera are represented by trees in the flora of the United States.

CONSPECTUS OF THE GENERA OF THE UNITED STATES.

Calyx of 5 sepals in a single series.
  Staminodia 1 in each sinus of the corolla.
    Appendages of the corolla 0; staminodia slender, scale-like.   **1. Sideroxylum.**
    Appendages of the corolla present; staminodia petaloid.
      Staminodia linear, fimbriate; seeds, with copious albumen.   **2. Dipholis.**
      Staminodia petaloid, entire or denticulate; seeds, without albumen.   **3. Bumelia.**
  Staminodia and appendages of the corolla 0; leaves covered below with lustrous copper-colored or golden pubescence.   **4. Chrysophyllum.**
Calyx of 6–8 sepals in 2 series; corolla 6–8-lobed, with 2 appendages in each sinus inside of a scale-like or petaloid staminodia.   **5. Mimusops.**

1. SIDEROXYLUM L.

Trees, with terete branchlets, naked buds, and long-petiolate persistent leaves, the veins remote and connected by reticulate veinlets. Flowers minute, on ebracteolate pedicels from the axils of minute deciduous bracts, in crowded many-flowered axillary fascicles; calyx 5-parted, the divisions in one series, nearly equal, corolla furnished with 5 or 6 staminodia, and 5 or rarely 6-lobed; filaments slender, elongated, bent outward at the apex; anthers oblong, the cells at first extrorse, sometimes becoming sublateral; staminodia linear, scale-like; ovary contracted into a subulate style tipped with a minute slightly 5-lobed stigma. Fruit dry, 1-seeded, oblong, with thin coriaceous flesh. Seed obovoid or oblong; seed-coat lustrous, light brown, folded on the inner face into 2 obscure lobes rounded at apex; hilum elevated, subbasilar or lateral, oblong or linear; embryo erect in thick fleshy albumen; radicle much shorter than the oblong fleshy cotyledons.

Sideroxylum with a hundred species is widely distributed through the tropics of the two hemispheres, and occurs also with a few species in Australia, Madeira, southern Africa, New Zealand, and Norfolk Island, a single species reaching the shores of southern Florida. Some of the species are large and valuable timber-trees, producing hard handsome durable wood.

The generic name, from σίδηρος and ξύλον, is in reference to the hardness of the wood.

1. Sideroxylum fœtidissimum Jacq. Mastic.
Sideroxylum Mastichodendron Jacq.

Leaves mostly clustered near the end of the branches, appearing irregularly from early spring until autumn, oval, acute or rounded and slightly emarginate at apex, and gradually narrowed at base, with thickened cartilaginous slightly involute margins, silky-canescent beneath when they unfold, and at maturity thin and firm, glabrous, bright green and lustrous above, lustrous and yellow-green below, 3′–5′ long and $1\frac{1}{2}$′–2′ wide, with a broad pale conspicuous midrib deeply impressed on the upper side and inconspicuous primary veins arcuate near the margins; petioles slender, 1′–$1\frac{1}{2}$′ in length. **Flowers** usually appearing in Florida in the autumn and also in early spring and during the summer on stout orange-colored puberulous pedicels from the axils of minute acute scarious bracts usually deciduous before the opening of the flower-buds, from the axils of young leaves or on the branches of the previous year from leafless nodes; calyx yellow-green, puberulous on the outer surface and deeply divided into broad-ovate rounded lobes rather shorter than the oblong-ovate rounded divisions of the light yellow corolla; staminodia lanceolate, nearly entire, tipped with a subulate point and much shorter than the stamens; ovary oblong-ovoid, glabrous, gradually contracted into an elongated style stigmatic at apex. **Fruit** ripening in March and April on a much thickened woody stem erect or nearly at right angles to the branch, 1′

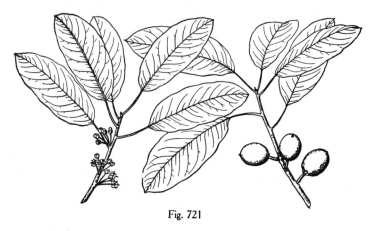

Fig. 721

long, separating from the calyx in falling, with tough yellow skin, and thick juicy flesh of a pleasant subacid flavor; **seed** obovoid, rounded above, narrowed at base, $\frac{1}{2}′$ long and $\frac{1}{3}′$ wide.

A tree, in Florida 60°–70° high, with a massive straight trunk 3°–4° in diameter, stout upright branches forming a dense irregular head, and thick terete branchlets orange-colored and slightly puberulous when they first appear, becoming glabrous, brown more or less tinged with red, and marked by the conspicuous nearly orbicular leaf-scars displaying 3 large fibro-vascular bundle-scars, and conspicuously roughened by the thickened persistent bases of the fruit stalks. **Bark** of the trunk $\frac{1}{4}′–\frac{1}{2}′$ thick, dark gray to light brown tinged with red and broken into thick plate-like scales separating into thin layers. **Wood** heavy, hard, strong, bright orange-colored, with thick yellow sapwood of 40–50 layers of annual growth; in Florida used in boat-building.

Distribution.   Florida, Cape Canaveral and Cape Romano to the southern keys; on the Bahama Islands and many of the Antilles.

2. DIPHOLIS A. DC.

Trees or shrubs, with naked buds, and persistent leaves, the slender veins arcuate and united near the margins.   Flowers minute, on clavate ebracteolate pedicels from the axils of minute deciduous bracts, in the axils of existing leaves or from the leafless nodes of previous years; calyx ovoid, deeply 5-lobed, the lobes nearly equal, ovate, rounded at apex; corolla campanulate, white, 5-lobed, the spreading lobes furnished on each side at the base with a linear or subulate appendage; stamens exserted; filaments filiform; anthers oblong-sagittate, extrorse; staminodia 5, petaloid, ovate, acute, fimbriately cut on the margins, oblique, keeled on the back, inserted in the same rank and alternate with the stamens; ovary oblong or narrow-ovoid, gradually contracted into a slender style shorter than the corolla and stigmatic at the apiculate apex.   Fruit oblong-ovoid, with thin dry flesh.

Seed ovoid; seed-coat thick, coriaceous and lustrous; hilum oblong, basilar or slightly lateral; embryo erect in thick fleshy albumen; cotyledons ovate, flat, much longer than the short radicle turned toward the hilum.

Dipholis with three species is confined to the West Indies and southern Florida. The generic name, from δίς and φολίς, relates to the appendages of the corolla.

1. Dipholis salicifolia A. DC.   Bustic.   Cassada.

Leaves oblong-lanceolate or narrow-obovate, acute, acuminate, or rounded at apex, gradually contracted at base, with slightly thickened cartilaginous wavy margins, thickly coated when they unfold with lustrous rufous pubescence, and at maturity thin and firm, dark green and lustrous above, pale yellow-green below, 3′–5′ long, ½′–1½′ wide, and glabrous, or slightly puberulous on the lower side of the narrow pale midrib, with inconspicuous veins and reticulate veinlets; appearing in Florida in the spring and remaining on the branches between one and two years; petioles slender, ½′–1′ in length.   **Flowers** opening during March and April, ⅛′ long, on thick pedicels ¼′ in length from the axils of minute ovate acute scarious bracts, and coated with rufous pubescence, in dense many-flowered fascicles crowded on branchlets of the year or of the previous year for a distance of 8′–12′; calyx half the length of the corolla, coated on the outer surface with rusty silky pubescence; appendages of the corolla as long as the oval acute irregularly toothed staminodia; ovary narrow-ovoid, glabrous, gradually contracted into a slender style shorter than the corolla and stigmatic at apex.   **Fruit** solitary or rarely clustered, ripening in the autumn, short-oblong to subglobose, black, ¼′ in length; **seed** pale brown, about $\frac{3}{16}$′ in length.

A tree, in Florida sometimes 40°–50° high, with a straight trunk 18′–20′ in diameter, small upright branches forming a narrow graceful head, and slender branchlets coated with

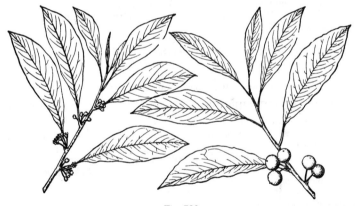

Fig. 722

rufous pubescence when they first appear, becoming ashy gray or light brown tinged with red and marked by numerous circular pale lenticels and by small elevated orbicular leaf-scars displaying near the centre a compact cluster of fibro-vascular bundle-scars.   **Bark** of the trunk about ¼′ thick and broken into thick square plate-like brown scales tinged with red.   **Wood** very heavy, exceedingly hard, strong, close-grained, dark brown or red, with thin sapwood of 4 or 5 layers of annual growth.

Distribution.   Florida, rich hummock soil, shores of Bay Biscayne and on the Everglade Keys, Dade County, and on several of the southern keys; on the Bahama Islands and on many of the Antilles.

3. BUMELIA Sw.

Small trees or shrubs, with terete usually spinescent branchlets, scaly buds, and fibrous roots.   Leaves often fascicled on spur-like lateral branchlets, conduplicate in the bud, coriaceous or thin, short-petiolate, obovate and obtuse or elliptic, silky-pubescent or tomentose below, or nearly glabrous, with rather inconspicuous veins arcuate near the entire margins and conspicuous reticulate veinlets, deciduous or persistent.   Flowers minute, on slender clavate ebracteolate pedicels from the axils of lanceolate acute scarious deciduous bracts, in many-flowered crowded fascicles in the axils of existing leaves or from the leafless nodes of previous years; calyx ovoid to subcampanulate, 5-lobed, the lobes in one series, imbricated in the bud, ovate or oblong, rounded at apex, nearly equal; corolla campanulate, white, with 5 spreading broad-ovate lobes rounded at apex and furnished on each side at base with a minute acute ovate or lanceolate appendage; stamens 5; filaments filiform; anthers ovoid-sagittate, attached on the back below the middle, the cells opening by subextrorse slits; staminodia petal-like, ovate or ovate-lanceolate, entire or obscurely denticulate, flattened or keeled on the back, sometimes furnished at base with a pair of minute scales; ovary hirsute, ovoid to ovoid-conic, gradually or abruptly contracted into a slender short or elongated simple style stigmatic at the acute apex.   Fruit oblong-obovoid or globose, black, solitary or in 2 or 3-fruited clusters; flesh thin and dry or succulent.   Seed ovoid or oblong, apiculate or rounded at apex, without albumen; seed-coat thick, crustaceous, light brown, smooth and shining, folded more or less conspicuously on the back into 2 lobes rounded at apex; embryo filling the cavity of the seed; cotyledons thick and fleshy, hemispheric, usually consolidated; radicle short, turned toward the basilar or subbasilar orbicular or elliptic hilum.

Bumelia, with about twenty-five species is confined to the New World, where it is distributed from the southern United States through the West Indies to Mexico, Central America, and Brazil.   Of the twelve species in the United States which have been distinguished five are small trees.

Bumelia produces hard heavy strong wood, that of the North American species containing bands of numerous large open ducts defining the layers of annual growth and connected by conspicuous branched groups of similar ducts, presenting in cross-section a reticulate appearance.

The generic name is from βουμελία, a classical name of the Ash-tree.

CONSPECTUS OF THE ARBORESCENT SPECIES OF THE UNITED STATES.

Lower surface of the leaves pubescent or lanuginose.

Leaves short-obovate to oblanceolate or elliptic, covered below with pale or ferrugineous silky pubescence.   1. B. tenax (C).

Leaves oblong-obovate, lanuginose below with ferrugineous or silvery white hairs.

2. B. lanuginosa (A, C, H).

Leaves glabrous or nearly so.

Leaves deciduous.

Leaves oblong-obovate, thick.   3. B. monticola.

Leaves elliptic to oblanceolate, usually acute or acuminate, thin. 4. B. lycioides (A, C).

Leaves persistent, obovate; fruit oblong.   5. B. angustifolia (C, D).

1. Bumelia tenax Willd.   Ironwood.   Black Haw.

Leaves oblong-obovate to oblanceolate or elliptic, rarely oval or ovate on leading shoots, rounded or acute at apex, cuneate at base, thin, dark dull green, and finally reticulate-venulose on the upper surface, thickly covered below with soft silky pale or gold-colored pubescence, usually becoming dark rusty brown by midsummer, 1'–3' long and 1⅛'–1½' wide, with slightly thickened and revolute margins and a prominent midrib; turning yellow and falling irregularly during the winter; petioles slender, hairy, grooved, ¼'–1' in length.   Flowers appearing from May in Florida to July in South Carolina, ⅛' long, on pedicels ½'–1' in length and coated like the calyx with rufous silky pubescence, in many-flowered crowded fascicles; calyx ovoid, with oblong lobes; appendages of the corolla large, ovate, acute, crenate, shorter than the ovate staminodia about as long as the lobes of the

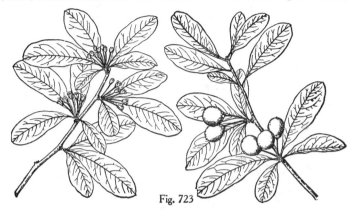

Fig. 723

corolla; ovary narrow-ovoid, gradually contracted into an elongated style. **Fruit** ripening and falling in the autumn, short-oblong to ellipsoid, ⅓'–½' in length; flesh sweet and edible; **seed** oblong, short-pointed at apex, ¼'–⅓' long.

A tree, 20°–30° high, with a trunk occasionally 5'–6' in diameter, straight spreading flexible tough branches unarmed or armed with straight stout rigid spines sometimes 1' in length, and slender branchlets coated when they first appear with silky pale pubescence often tinged with red and soon rusty brown, becoming glabrous before winter, and then dark red and slightly roughened by occasional minute dark lenticels; or often a shrub only a few feet high. **Winter-buds** minute, subglobose, with imbricated ovate scales rounded at apex and clothed with rusty brown tomentum. **Bark** of the trunk thick, brown tinged with red, and divided irregularly by deep fissures into narrow flat reticulate ridges covered with minute appressed scales. **Wood** heavy, hard, close-grained, light brown streaked with white, with lighter colored sapwood.

Distribution. Dry sandy soil; South Carolina (Saint Helena Island and Bluffton, Beaufort County), southward in the coast region of Georgia and east Florida to Cape Canaveral and through the interior of the peninsular to Cedar Keys on the west coast; near Bainbridge, Decatur County, southwestern Georgia.

2. Bumelia lanuginosa Pers. Gum Elastic. Chittam Wood.

Leaves oblong-obovate, rounded and often apiculate at apex and gradually narrowed at base, coated when they unfold with pale ferrugineous tomentum dense on the lower and loose on the upper surface, and at maturity thin and firm, dark green and lustrous above, more or less lanuginose below with rusty brown or silvery white (var. *albicans* Sarg.) hairs, 1'–2½' long and ⅓'–¾' wide; falling irregularly during the winter; petioles slender, rusty brown or pale pubescent, ⅛'–¾' in length. **Flowers** opening in summer on hairy pedicels ⅛' in length, in 16–18-flowered fascicles; calyx ovoid, with ovate rounded lobes coated on the outer surface with ferrugineous or pale tomentum and rather shorter than the tube of the corolla; appendages of the corolla small, ovate and acute; staminodia ovate, acute, remotely and slightly denticulate, as long as the corolla-lobes; ovary abruptly contracted into a slender elongated style. **Fruit** on a slender drooping stalk ripening and falling in the autumn, oblong or slightly obovoid, ½' long, with thick flesh; **seed** short-oblong, rounded at apex, about ¼' in length.

A tree, often 40°–50° high, with a tall straight trunk 1°–2° in diameter, short thick rigid branches forming a narrow-oblong round-topped head, unarmed, or armed with stout rigid straight or slightly curved spines frequently developing into spinescent leafy lateral branchlets, and slender often somewhat zigzag branchlets coated with thick rufous or pale tomentum when they first appear, becoming in their first winter red-brown to ashy gray and glabrous or nearly so, and marked by occasional minute lenticels and by small semi-orbicular leaf-scars displaying 2 clusters of fibro-vascular bundle-scars; of its largest size in the Texas coast region; much smaller east of the Mississippi River, and there rarely more than 20° tall.   Winter-buds obtuse, ⅛′ long, covered with broad-obovate rusty-tomentose scales.   Bark of the trunk ½′ thick, dark gray-brown and usually divided into narrow ridges

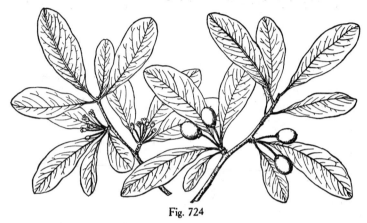

Fig. 724

broken into thick appressed scales.   **Wood** heavy, rather soft, not strong, close-grained, light brown or yellow, with thick lighter colored sapwood; producing in Texas considerable quantities of clear viscid gum from the freshly cut wood.

Distribution.   Southern and southeastern Georgia, western Florida southward to the neighborhood of Lake City, Columbia County and to Cedar Key, coast of Alabama and inland to Dallas County, southern Mississippi, Louisiana, and Texas to the valley of the San Antonio River and over the Edwards Plateau (Kendall, Kerr and Brown Counties) to the valley of the upper Brazos River (Palo Pinto County), and northward through western Louisiana and Arkansas to western Oklahoma (Seiling, Dewey County), and to south-eastern Kansas (Cherokee County) and southern Missouri as far north as the valley of the Meramec River (near Allenton, St. Louis County), and southern Illinois; at Calcasieu Pass, on the sandy beaches of the Louisiana coast forming thickets of plants 6°–8° high, and un-injured by salt spray; the var. *albicans* in eastern Texas from the valley of the lower Brazos to that of the San Antonio River and in the neighborhood of Monterey, Nuevo Leon; most distinct and of its largest size on the bottoms of the Guadalupe River, near Victoria, Vic-toria County, and here occasionally 70°–80° high, with a trunk 3° in diameter.

Passing into the var. *rigida* A. Gray, with smaller rather narrower leaves and often more spinescent branches.   Brown and Uvalde Counties, Texas; in Coahua and Nuevo Leon, and in the cañons of the mountains of southern Arizona up to altitudes of at least 4000°–5000°; in Texas shrubby in habit; in Arizona forming dense thickets of slender stems often 20°–25° tall and only 2′–3′ in diameter.

3. Bumelia monticola Buckl.

Leaves oblong-obovate, narrowed and acute or rounded and rarely slightly emarginate at apex, cuneate at base, entire, covered above with matted pale hairs and densely below with snow white pubescence when they unfold, and at maturity coriaceous, dark yellow-green, lustrous and glabrous on the upper surface, paler on the lower surface, $1\frac{1}{4}'-3'$ long and $\frac{1}{3}'-1\frac{1}{4}'$ wide, with slightly revolute margins, a slender yellow midrib glabrous or slightly pubescent below toward the base and conspicuous reticulate veinlets, deciduous; petioles slender pubescent early in the season, becoming glabrous. **Flowers** opening from the middle of June to the middle of July, on villose pedicels, becoming sometimes nearly glabrous in the autumn, $\frac{1}{8}'-\frac{1}{4}'$ in length; calyx pale green, villose-pubescent, its lobes ovate, ciliate on the margins, shorter than the lobes of the corolla, their appendages lanceolate; staminodia rounded at apex, longer than the corolla-lobes. **Fruit** ripening in September, subglobose to oblong-obovoid, $\frac{1}{4}'-\frac{1}{3}'$ long and $\frac{1}{4}'-\frac{1}{3}'$ in diameter; seed oblong, rounded at the ends, about $\frac{2}{5}'$ long.

A tree, in favorable positions 20°–25° high, with spinose branches forming an irregular open head, and slender often zigzag red-brown lustrous branchlets, the lateral branchlets

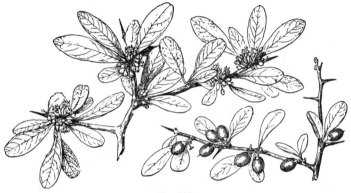

Fig. 725

often ending in stout spines; more often an irregularly branched shrub 10°–15° high, spreading on the banks of streams into great thickets. **Bark** of the trunk thick, pale and dark gray, rough and scaly, exfoliating in large scales.

Distribution. Texas, dry limestone cliffs and cañon bottoms and by streams dry during a large part of the year, valley of the upper Guadalupe River (Comal, Kendall and Kerr Counties) to the valley of the Rio Grande (Uvalde County), and northward to the valley of the upper Brazos River (Palo Pinto County); in Cohahuila (near Saltillo).

4. Bumelia lycioides Gærtn. f. Ironwood. Buckthorn.

Leaves elliptic to oblanceolate, acute, acuminate, or rarely rounded at apex, gradually narrowed at base, covered when they unfold especially below with silky villose pubescence, soon glabrous, and at maturity bright green and glabrous on the upper surface, light green and sometimes coated on the lower surface with pale pubescence, thin and rather firm, finely reticulate-venulose, $3'-6'$ long and $\frac{1}{2}'-2'$ wide, with a pale thin conspicuous midrib sometimes slightly pubescent below near the base, deciduous in the autumn; petioles slender, slightly grooved, mostly pubescent early in the season, usually becoming glabrous, $\frac{1}{2}'-1'$ in length. **Flowers** appearing at midsummer on slender glabrous pedicels $\frac{1}{2}'$ long, in crowded many-flowered fascicles; calyx glabrous, ovoid-campanulate, with rounded lobes rather shorter than the corolla; staminodia broad-ovate, denticulate, nearly as long as the narrow appendages; ovary ovoid, slightly hairy toward the base only, gradually contracted into a short thick style. **Fruit** ripening and falling in the autumn, ovoid or obovoid, about

$\frac{2}{3}'$ in length; flesh thick; **seed** short-oblong to subglobose, rounded at apex, nearly $\frac{1}{4}'$ long, with a pale conspicuous hilum.

A tree, 25°–30° high, with a short trunk rarely more than 6′ in diameter, stout flexible branches usually unarmed or furnished with short stout slightly curved spines occasionally

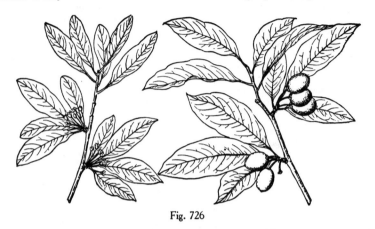

Fig. 726

developing into leafy spinescent branches, and short thick spur-like lateral branchlets slightly puberulous when they first appear, soon becoming glabrous, light red-brown, rather lustrous, and marked by numerous pale lenticels, and in their second year dark or light brown tinged with red or ashy gray. **Winter-buds** minute, obtuse, nearly immersed in the bark, with pale dark brown glabrous scales. **Bark** of the trunk thin, light red-brown, the generally smooth surface broken into small thin persistent scales. **Wood** heavy, hard, not strong, close-grained, light brown or yellow, with thick lighter colored sapwood.

Distribution. Usually in low moist soil on the borders of swamps and streams; rocky bluffs of the Ohio River near Cannelton, Perry County, southern Indiana, southern Illinois (Hardin, Pope and Pulaski Counties), to southeastern Missouri (Butler County) and to western Kentucky, western and central Tennessee, central Mississippi and northern Louisiana (West Feliciana Parish); and through Arkansas (Helena, Phillips County, and McNab, Hempstead County) to the coast region of eastern Texas (Beaumont, Jefferson County, and Columbia, Brazoria County); central Alabama; Florida southward to St. Mark's, Wakulla County, and to Taylor, Alachua and Volusia Counties, and to northwestern Georgia (Catoosa County), and the valley of the Savannah River in Georgia and South Carolina, and northward through eastern North Carolina to southeastern Virginia (Norfolk County).

5. Bumelia angustifolia Nutt. Ants' Wood. Downward Plum.

Leaves obovate, rounded at apex, and gradually narrowed and cuneate at base, with slightly thickened revolute margins, glabrous, thick and coriaceous, pale blue-green on the upper surface, paler on the lower surface, 1′–1½′ long and ¼′–1¼′ wide, with a pale slender midrib, and very obscure veins and veinlets; usually persistent on the branches until the end of their second winter; petioles stout, grooved, rarely ¼′ in length. **Flowers** generally appearing in October and November, on slender glabrous pedicels seldom more than ½′ in length, in few or many-flowered crowded fascicles; calyx glabrous, divided nearly to the base into narrow-ovate lobes rounded at apex and half as long as the divisions of the corolla furnished with linear-lanceolate appendages as long as the ovate acute denticulate staminodia; ovary narrow-ovoid, slightly hairy at base only, gradually contracted into an elongated style. **Fruit** ripening in the spring, on slender drooping stems, usually 1 fruit only being developed from a fascicle of flowers, oblong or slightly obovoid, rounded at the ends, $\frac{1}{2}'-\frac{3}{4}'$ long and $\frac{1}{4}'$ in diameter, with thick sweet flesh; **seed** oblong, rounded at apex, $\frac{1}{2}'$ long. A tree, sometimes 20° high, with a short trunk rarely exceeding 6′–8′ in diameter, graceful pendulous branches forming a compact round head, and rigid spinescent divergent lateral branchlets often armed with acute slender spines sometimes 1′ in length, and when they first appear thickly coated with loose pale or dark brown deciduous tomentum, becoming light brown tinged with red or ashy gray. **Winter-buds** ovoid, acute, and covered with rufous tomentum. **Bark** of the trunk $\frac{1}{3}'-\frac{1}{2}'$ thick, gray tinged with red, and deeply

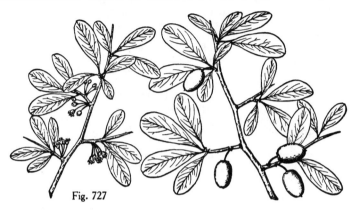

Fig. 727

divided by longitudinal and cross fissures into oblong or nearly square plates. **Wood** heavy, hard, although not strong, very close-grained, light brown or orange-colored, with thick lighter colored sapwood.

Distribution. Florida, shores of Indian River to the southern keys, and on the west coast from Cedar Keys to East Cape, and here less abundant and usually on rocky shores and in the interior of low barren islands; on the Bahama Islands and in Cuba.

4. CHRYSOPHYLLUM L.

Trees, with terete branchlets usually coated while young with dense tomentum, and naked buds. Leaves short-petiolate, bright green and glabrous on the upper surface and coated on the lower surface with brilliant silky pubescence or tomentum, persistent. Flowers on pedicels from the axils of minute acute bracts, in dense many-flowered fascicles; calyx usually 5-parted, the divisions nearly equal, obtuse; corolla 5 or rarely 6 or 7-lobed, tubular, campanulate or subrotate, white or greenish white; filaments short, subulate or filiform, enlarged into broad connectives; anthers ovoid or triangular, extrorse or rarely partly introrse, the cells spreading below; ovary usually 5-celled, style crowned by a 5-lobed stigma. Fruit short-oblong, ovoid or globose. Seed ovoid; seed-coat coriaceous, dull or lustrous; hilum subbasilar, elongated, conspicuous; embryo erect, surrounded by more or less pungent fleshy albumen; cotyledons oblong, foliaceous.

Chrysophyllum is tropical, with fifty or sixty species most abundant in the New World, with a small number of species in western and southern tropical Africa, southern Asia, Australia, and the Hawaiian Islands, and with one species in southern Florida. The most valuable species, *Chrysophyllum Cainito* L., a native of the West Indies and now cultivated in all tropical countries and naturalized in many parts of Central and South America, produces the so-called star-apple, a succulent edible blue or purple and green fruit the size and shape of a small apple.

The generic name, from χρυσός and φύλλον is in allusion to the golden covering of the under surface of the leaves.

1. Chrysophyllum oliviforme Lam. Satin-leaf.

Leaves revolute in the bud, oval, acute or contracted into a short broad point or sometimes rounded at apex, abruptly cuneate at base, thick and coriaceous, bright blue-green on the upper surface and covered on the lower surface and on the petiole with brilliant copper-colored pubescence, $2'-3'$ long and $1\frac{1}{2}'-2'$ wide, with a broad prominent midrib deeply impressed on the upper side and numerous straight veins arcuate near the margins; petioles stout, $\frac{1}{2}'-\frac{2}{3}'$ in length. **Flowers** appearing in Florida irregularly throughout the year and often found on a branch with ripe or half-grown fruits, on stout pedicels shorter than the petioles, covered like the calyx with rufous tomentum, in few or many-flowered fascicles in the axils of leaves or at the base of lateral branchlets in those of earlier years; calyx divided nearly to the base into broad rounded lobes rather shorter than the tube of the subrotate white corolla with short spreading rounded lobes; ovary 5-celled, pubescent, gradually contracted into a short style crowned by a broad 5-lobed stigma. **Fruit** usually 1-seeded by abortion, on stems $1'$ long, usually only a single fruit being produced from a flower-cluster, ovoid or sometimes nearly globose, dark purple, roughened by occasional excrescences, with a thick tough skin inclosing the juicy sweet mawkish flesh light purple on the exterior, lighter toward the interior, and quite white in the centre; seed narrowed at the ends, $\frac{1}{2}'$ long, covered with a thin light brown coat closely invested with a white glutinous aril-like pulpy mass.

A tree, $25°-30°$ high, with a tall straight trunk sometimes a foot in diameter, upright branches forming a compact oblong head, and slender slightly zigzag branchlets coated when they first appear with ferrugineous tomentum, becoming in their second year light

Fig. 728

red-brown or ashy gray and covered with small pale elevated circular lenticels; in sandy soil under the shade of Pine-trees in the Everglade Keys a shrub $6°$ high or less. **Bark** of the trunk $\frac{1}{4}'$ thick, light brown slightly tinged with red, and broken by shallow fissures into large irregularly shaped plates separating on the surface into small thin scales. **Wood** very heavy, hard, strong, close-grained, light brown shaded with red, with thin lighter colored sapwood.

Distribution. Florida, rich hummocks, from Mosquito Inlet on the east coast to the Everglade Keys, Dade County and to the southern keys, and on the west coast from the shores of the Caloosahatchee River to the neighborhood of Cape Sable; local and nowhere common; on the Bahama Islands, and in Cuba, Porto Rico and Jamaica.

5. MIMUSOPS L.

Trees or rarely shrubs, with stout terete branchlets, small naked buds, and sweet juice. Leaves usually clustered at the end of the branches, with slender inconspicuous transverse veins and minute reticulate veinlets, persistent. Flowers on clavate pedicels from the axils of minute deciduous bracts; calyx 6–8-parted, the divisions in 2 series, those of the exterior series almost valvate in the bud; corolla white, barely longer than the calyx, subrotate, usually dilated at the throat, 6–8-lobed, the lobes furnished at base with a pair of petal-like appendages; stamens as many as the lobes of the corolla; filaments short, dilated; anthers lanceolate, their connectives excurrent, acute, or sometimes aristate at apex; staminodia as many as the lobes of the corolla, scale-like or petaloid, entire, 2-lobed or laciniate; ovary ovoid, hirsute or puberulous, gradually narrowed into a slender style stigmatic at apex. Fruit globose, 1 or 2-seeded, tipped with the much thickened elongated style; skin crustaceous, indurate; flesh thick and dry. Seed oblong-ovoid, slightly compressed; seed-coat crustaceous, chestnut-brown and lustrous; hilum elongated, lateral or minute, basilar; embryo surrounded by thick fleshy albumen; cotyledons flat, thick and fleshy, much longer than the short erect radicle.

Mimusops with thirty or forty species is widely distributed through the tropics of the two hemispheres, a single species reaching the shores of southern Florida. Several species produce hard heavy timber, edible fruits, or valuable milky juices.

The significance of the generic name, from μιμώ and ὄψις in allusion to the shape of the corolla, is not apparent.

1. Mimusops emarginata Britt. Wild Dilly.

Mimusops Sieberi Chap., not A. DC.

Leaves clustered at the end of the branches, involute in the bud oblong-elliptic, or occasionally slightly obovate, rounded or retuse at apex, rounded or cuneate at base, with slightly thickened revolute margins, bright red when they unfold, and slightly puberulous on the under surface of the midrib, and at maturity thick and coriaceous, bright green and

Fig. 729

lustrous, covered on the upper surface with a slight glaucous bloom, conspicuously reticulate-venulose, 3′–4′ long and 1′–1½′ wide, with a stout midrib glabrous, or puberulous with rusty hairs below, and deeply impressed above; appearing in Florida in April and May and deciduous during their second year; petioles slender, grooved, rusty-pubescent, especially while young, ½′–1′ in length. Flowers opening in the spring on slender pedicels near the end of the branches, coated with rusty tomentum and 1' or more long, from the axils of leaves of the year or from those of fallen leaves of the previous year; calyx narrow-ovoid, divided nearly to the base into 6 lobes, those of the outer row lanceolate, acute, covered on the outer surface with rusty brown tomentum and on the inner surface with pale pubescence, thickened and usually marked at the base on the outer surface by black spots, those of the inner row ovate, acute, keeled toward the base, light greenish yellow and pale-pubescent; corolla light yellow tinged with green, $\frac{2}{3}'$ in diameter, with 6 spreading lanceolate acute divisions entire or erosely toothed toward the apex, their appendage slender, acute and from one half to two thirds their length; staminodia minute, nearly triangular, entire; ovary narrow-ovoid, dark red, puberulous toward the base with pale hairs, and gradually narrowed into an elongated exserted style stigmatic at apex. Fruit ripening at the end of a year, in the spring or in early autumn, on a stout erect stem about 1' long, and persistent until after the tree flowers the following year, subglobose to slightly obovoid, flattened and compressed at apex, $1'-1\frac{1}{2}'$ in diameter, usually 1-seeded by abortion, with a thick dry outer coat roughened by minute rusty brown scales, and thick spongy flesh filled with milky juice; seed $\frac{1}{2}'$ long, with an elongated lateral hilum.

A tree, in Florida rarely more than 30° high, with a short gnarled trunk 12'–15' in diameter and usually hollow and defective, thick branches forming a compact round head, and stout branchlets clustered at the end of the branches of the previous year, coated when they first appear with dark rufous pubescence, becoming glabrous and light orange-brown at the end of a few weeks, and in their second year covered with thick ashy gray or light red-brown scaly bark and marked by elevated obcordate leaf-scars displaying 3 large dark conspicuous fibro-vascular bundle-scars. Winter-buds ovoid, acute, rusty-tomentose. Bark of the trunk about $\frac{1}{4}'$ thick and irregularly divided by deep fissures into ridges rounded on the back and broken into small nearly square plates. Wood very heavy, hard, strong, close-grained, rich very dark brown, with light-colored sapwood.

Distribution. Florida, only on the southern keys; not common; on the Bahama Islands and in Cuba.

LVII. EBENACEÆ.

Trees or shrubs, with watery juice, and alternate simple entire leaves, without stipules. Flowers diœcious or polygamous, regular, axillary, articulate with the bibracteolate pedicels; calyx persistent; corolla hypogynous, regular; disk 0; stamens more numerous than the lobes of the corolla, inserted on its base, fewer and rudimentary or 0 in the pistillate flower; filaments short; anthers introrse, 2-celled; ovary several-celled; ovules 2 in each cell, suspended from its apex, anatropous; raphe dorsal; micropyle superior. Fruit a 1 or several-seeded berry. Seeds with copious albumen; embryo axile.

The Ebony family with seven genera and a large number of species is widely distributed in tropical and temperate regions, with two representatives of its most important genus, Diospyros, in the flora of the United States.

1. DIOSPYROS L.

Trees or shrubs, with terete branchlets, without a terminal bud, scaly axillary buds, coriaceous leaves revolute in the bud, and fibrous roots. Flowers mostly diœcious, from the axils of leaves of the year or of the previous year; staminate smaller than the pistillate and usually in short few-flowered bracted cymes; pistillate generally solitary; calyx 4-lobed, the lobes valvate in the bud, accrescent under the fruit; corolla 4-lobed, the lobes sinistrorsely contorted in the bud, more or less contracted in the throat, the lobes spreading or recurved; stamens usually 16, inserted on the bottom of the corolla in two rows and in pairs, those of the outer row rather longer than and opposite those of the inner row; filaments free, slender; anthers oblong, apiculate, the cells opening laterally by longitudinal slits; stamens rudimentary or 0 in the pistillate flower; ovary usually 4-celled, each cell more or less completely divided by the development of a false longitudinal partition from its anterior face, rudimentary or 0 in the staminate flower; styles 4, spreading, 2-lobed at apex; stigmas 2-parted or lobed; ovule solitary in each of the divisions of the cells. Fruit globose, oblong or conic, 1–10-seeded, surrounded at base by the enlarged persistent calyx. Seeds pendulous, oblong, compressed; seed-coat thick and bony, dark, more or less lustrous; embryo axile, straight or somewhat curved; cotyledons foliaceous, ovate or lanceolate; radicle superior, cylindric, turned toward the small hilum.

Diospyros, which is chiefly tropical, is widely distributed with more than two hundred species in the two hemispheres, with a few species extending beyond the tropics into eastern North America, eastern Asia, southwestern Asia, and the Mediterranean region.

Diospyros produces hard close-grained valuable wood, with dark or black heartwood and thick soft yellow sapwood. The ebony of commerce is partly produced by different tropical species. The fruit is often edible, and some of the species are important fruit-trees in China and Japan.

The generic name, from Διός and πυρός, is in allusion to the life-giving properties of the fruit.

CONSPECTUS OF THE SPECIES OF THE UNITED STATES.

Flowers on branchlets of the year; anthers opening longitudinally nearly throughout their entire length; filaments pubescent; pistillate flowers with 8 rudimentary stamens; ovary nearly glabrous; leaves oval; fruit green, yellow, orange color or rarely black.
1. **D. virginiana** (A, C).

Flowers on branchlets of the previous year; anthers opening only near the apex; filaments glabrous; pistillate flowers without rudimentary stamens; ovary pubescent; leaves cuneate-oblong or obovate; fruit black. **2. D. texana** (C).

1. Diospyros virginiana L. Persimmon.

Leaves ovate-oblong to oval or elliptic, acuminate or abruptly acuminate at apex, narrowed and cuneate or rounded or rarely broad and rounded at base, coriaceous, glabrous, dark green and lustrous on the upper surface, pale on the lower surface, 4′–6′ long and 2′–3′

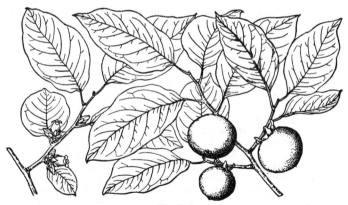

Fig. 730

wide, with a broad flat midrib, about six pairs of conspicuous primary veins arcuate near the margins and reticulate veinlets; falling in the autumn usually without much change of color; petioles stout, glabrous or slightly villose-pubescent, ½′–1′ in length. **Flowers** appearing when the leaves are more than half grown on branchlets of the year, from March in the extreme south to June in the north; the staminate in 2–3-flowered pubescent pedunculate cymes, on pedicels from the axils of minute lanceolate acute caducous bracts and furnished near the middle with two minute caducous bractlets; the pistillate solitary, on short recurved pedicels, bibracteolate with conspicuous acute bractlets ciliate on the margins and often $\frac{1}{4}'$ in length; corolla of the staminate flower tubular, $\frac{1}{3}'$ long, slightly contracted below the short acute reflexed lobes forming before expansion a pointed 4-angled bud rather longer than the broad-ovate acute foliaceous ciliate calyx-lobes inflexed on the margins; stamens with short slightly hairy filaments and linear-lanceolate anthers opening throughout their length; pistillate flower $\frac{3}{4}'$ long, with a greenish yellow or creamy white corolla nearly $\frac{1}{2}'$ broad; stamens 8, inserted in one row below the middle of the corolla, with short filaments and sagittate abortive or sometimes fertile anthers; ovary conic, pilose toward the apex, ultimately 8-celled, and gradually narrowed into the four slender styles hairy at the base. **Fruit** on a short thick stem, ripening at the north late in autumn or earlier southward, often persistent on the branches during the winter, depressed-globose to ovoid or slightly obovoid, rounded or pointed at apex, $\frac{3}{4}'$–$2'$ in diameter, yellow or pale orange color, often with a bright cheek, and covered with a glaucous bloom, turning yellowish brown when partly decayed by freezing, surrounded at base by the spreading calyx $1'$–$1\frac{1}{2}'$ in diameter, with broad ovate pointed lobes recurved on the margins; flesh austere while green, yellowish brown, sweet and luscious when fully ripened by the action of frost, or in some forms remaining hard and green during the winter; **seeds** oblong, rounded on the dorsal edge, nearly straight on the ventral edge, rounded at the ends, much flattened, $\frac{1}{2}'$ long and $\frac{1}{3}'$ wide, with a thick hard pale brown rugose testa, a narrow pale hilum and a slender raphe.

A tree, occasionally $50'$–$60'$ high, with a short trunk $16'$–$20'$ in diameter, spreading often pendulous branches forming a broad or narrow round-topped head, and slender slightly zigzag glabrous or rarely puberulous branchlets with a thick pith-cavity, light brown when they first appear, becoming during their first winter light brown or ashy gray and marked by occasional small orange-colored lenticels and by elevated semiorbicular leaf-scars, with deep horizontal lunate depressions; or in the primeval forest, under the most favorable conditions, sometimes $100°$–$130°$ high, with a long slender trunk free of branches for $70°$–$80°$ and rarely exceeding $2°$ in diameter; frequently not more than $15°$ or $20°$ high and sometimes shrubby in habit. **Winter-buds:** axillary, broad-ovoid, acute, $\frac{1}{4}'$ long, with thick imbricated dark red-brown or purple lustrous scales often persistent at the base of young branchlets during the season. **Bark** of the trunk $\frac{3}{4}'$–$1'$ thick, dark brown tinged with red, or dark gray, and deeply divided into thick square plates broken into thin persistent scales, with heavy strong dark brown sometimes nearly black heartwood often undeveloped until the tree is over one hundred years old; used in turnery, for shoe-lasts, plane-stocks, and preferred for shuttles to other American woods. The fruit contains tannin, to which it owes its astringent qualities, and is eaten in great quantities in the southern states. The inner bark is astringent and bitter.

Distribution. Light sandy well drained soil, or in the Mississippi basin sometimes on the deep rich bottom-lands of river valleys; Lighthouse Point, New Haven, New Haven County, Connecticut, and Long Island, New York, through southern Pennsylvania, southern Ohio, southern Indiana and Illinois, to southeastern Iowa, eastern Kansas, central Oklahoma, and southward to De Soto County, Florida, southern Alabama, Mississippi, Louisiana, and Texas to the valley of the Colorado River (Burnett County); very common in the south Atlantic and Gulf states, often covering with shrubby growth by means of the stoloniferous roots abandoned fields and springing up by the side of roads and fences; ascending on the Appalachian Mountains to altitudes of $3500°$; rare toward the western limits of its range in Texas. In southeastern Illinois, Missouri and Arkansas passing into the var. *platycarpa* Sarg. with larger broad-ovate leaves rounded or cordate at base or rarely elliptic, more or less densely pubescent on the lower surface, especially on the midrib and petiole, often $2\frac{1}{2}'$–$4'$ long and $2'$–$2\frac{1}{2}'$ wide, and at the end of vigorous shoots up to $6'$ in length, and depressed-globose, yellow, rarely nearly black (f. *atra* Sarg.), fruit much depressed at top and bottom, $1\frac{3}{4}'$–$3'$ wide and about $1'$ high, with sweet succulent flesh, ripening in September or early October, and seeds conspicuously rounded on the dorsal edge, much compressed, dark chestnut-brown and lustrous, only slightly rugose, $\frac{3}{4}'$ long and $\frac{1}{2}'$

wide.   A tree usually not more than 12°–25° high, with a trunk 16′–30′ in diameter and rather stouter branchlets densely villose-pubescent sometimes for two or three years, or becoming glabrate at the end of their first season.   Hills near Allenton, St. Louis County, and on the western slopes of the Ozark Mountains and the adjacent prairies of southeastern Missouri and prairies of northwestern Arkansas, eastern Kansas and Oklahoma.   In Dade County, Florida, *Diospyros virginiana* is replaced by the var. *Mosieri* Sarg. with smaller staminate flowers, nearly globose fruit with rather less compressed dark chestnut-brown lustrous only slightly rugose seeds.   A small tree with slightly fissured light gray bark.

Several named varieties of *Diospyros virginiana* are distinguished and cultivated by pomologists.

2. Diospyros texana Scheele.   Black Persimmon.   Chapote.

Leaves oblong-cuneate to obovate, rounded and often retuse at apex and cuneate at base, covered below when they unfold with thick pale tomentum and above with scattered long white hairs, and at maturity thick and coriaceous, dark green and lustrous,

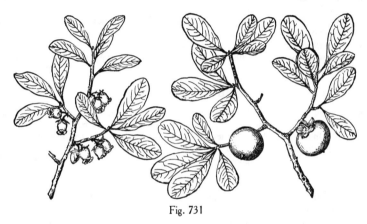

Fig. 731

glabrous or puberulous on the upper surface, paler and pubescent on the lower surface, $\frac{3}{4}$–$1\frac{1}{2}′$ long and nearly 1′ wide, with a broad midrib and about 4 pairs of arcuate primary veins and reticulate veinlets; unfolding in February and March, and falling during the following winter without change of color; petioles short, thick, and hairy.   Flowers appearing in early spring when the leaves are about one third grown, on branches of the previous year; staminate on slender drooping pedicels furnished near the middle with minute caducous bractlets, in 1–3-flowered crowded pubescent fascicles; pistillate on stouter club-shaped pedicels, solitary or rarely in pairs; calyx of the staminate flower $\frac{1}{8}′$ long and deeply divided into 5 ovate or lanceolate silky-tomentose lobes recurved after the opening of the flower, and much shorter than the corolla $\frac{1}{8}′$ long, creamy white, and slightly contracted below the 5 short spreading rounded lobes ciliate on the margins; stamens, with glabrous filaments shorter than the corolla, and linear-lanceolate anthers opening at apex only by short slits; pistillate flowers without rudimentary stamens, $\frac{1}{4}′$ long, with oblong acute silky-tomentose calyx-lobes half the length of the pubescent corolla nearly $\frac{1}{2}′$ across the short spreading lobes; ovary ovoid, pubescent like the young fruit, ultimately 8-celled.   Fruit ripening in August, subglobose, $\frac{1}{2}′$–1′ in diameter, and 3–8-seeded, surrounded at base by the large thickened leathery calyx sometimes 1′ in diameter, with oblong pubescent reflexed lobes, the thick tough black skin inclosing thin sweet insipid juicy dark flesh; seeds triangular, rounded on the back, narrowed and flattened at the pointed apex, $\frac{3}{8}′$ long, about $\frac{1}{8}′$ thick, with a bony lustrous light red pitted coat.

An intricately branched tree, occasionally 40°–50° high, with a trunk 18′–20′ in diameter, dividing at some distance above the ground into a number of stout upright branches forming a narrow round-topped head, and slender terete slightly zigzag branchlets, coated at first with pale or rufous tomentum, ashy gray, glabrous or puberulous during their first winter, later becoming brown and marked by minute pale lenticels and by small elevated semiorbicular leaf-scars displaying a lunate row of fibro-vascular bundle-scars; often much smaller, and toward the northern and western limits of its range a low many-stemmed shrub. **Winter-buds** obtuse, barely more than $\frac{1}{16}$′ long, with broad-ovate scales rounded on the back and coated with rufous tomentum. **Bark** of the trunk smooth, light gray slightly tinged with red, the outer layer falling away in large irregularly shaped patches displaying the smooth gray inner bark. **Wood** heavy, with black heartwood often streaked with yellow and clear bright yellow sapwood; used in turnery and for the handles of tools. The fruit, which is exceedingly austere until it is fully ripe, stains black, and is sometimes used by Mexicans in the valley of the Rio Grande to dye sheepskins.

Distribution. Southwestern Texas, Matagorda County (neighborhood of Matagorda and Bay City) to the lower Rio Grande, and northward to Brown County; in Coahuila, Nuevo Leon, and Tamaulipas; possibly in southern Lower California; abundant in southwestern Texas; in the neighborhood of the coast on the borders of prairies in rich moist soil; westward on dry rocky mesas and in isolated cañons; very common and of its largest size in the region between the Sierra Madre and the coast of the Gulf of Mexico in Nuevo Leon and Tamaulipas.

LVIII. STYRACACEÆ.

Trees or shrubs, with stellate pubescence or lepidote, watery juice, and scaly buds. Leaves alternate, simple, penniveined, without stipules. Flowers regular, perfect; calyx more or less adnate to the tube of the corolla; disk 0; anthers introrse, 2-celled, the cells opening longitudinally; ovary superior or partly superior, crowned with a simple style; ovules anatropous. Fruit drupaceous, with thin dry flesh, and a thick-walled 1-seeded bony stone. Seeds, with albumen.

The Storax family is confined to North and South America, the Mediterranean region, eastern Asia and the Malay Archipelago. Of the six genera of this family two are represented in the flora of North America.

CONSPECTUS OF THE GENERA OF THE UNITED STATES.

Calyx adherent to the whole surface of the ovary; corolla 4-lobed. Fruit oblong-obovoid,
   2 or 4-celled and 2 or 4-winged.   **1. Halesia.**
Calyx adherent to the base only of the ovary; corolla usually 5-parted. Fruit subglobose,
   1-celled.   **2. Styrax.**

1. HALESIA L. SILVER BELL TREE.

Trees or shrubs, with stellate pubescence, slender terete pithy branchlets, without a terminal bud, axillary buds with imbricated accrescent scales, and fibrous roots. Leaves involute in the bud, thin, elliptic, oblong-ovate or oblong-ovoid, denticulate, deciduous. Flowers opening in early spring, on slender elongated drooping ebracteolate pedicels from the axils of foliaceous acuminate or acute caducous bracts, in fascicles or short racemes from the axils of leaves of the previous year; calyx-tube obconic, adherent to the whole surface of the ovary, the limb short, 4-toothed, with minute triangular teeth, open in the bud; corolla epigynous, campanulate, 4-lobed, or divided nearly to the base, the lobes convolute or imbricated in the bud, thin and white or rarely tinged with rose; stamens 8–16; filaments elongated, shorter than the corolla, slightly attached at base, or sometimes free, flattened below; anthers oblong, adnate or free at the very base; ovary 2 or 4-celled, gradually contracted into an elongate glabrous or tomentose style stigmatic at apex; ovules 4 in each cell, attached by elongated funiculi at the middle of the axis, the 2 upper ascending, the 2 lower pendulous; raphe dorsal; micropyle inferior and superior. Fruit ripening in the autumn, elongated, oblong or obovoid and gradually narrowed at base; skin tough, separable, light green and lustrous, turning reddish brown late in the autumn; exocarp indehiscent, thick, becoming dry and corky at maturity, produced into 2 or 4 broad thin wings cuneate at base and rounded at apex; stone bony, cylindric, obovoid or ellipsoid, gradually narrowed at base into a slender stipe inclosed in the wings, narrowed above and terminating in the enlarged style protruding above the wings, usually obscurely and irregularly 8-angled or sulcate, 1–4-celled. Seed solitary in each cell, elongated, cylindric; seed-coat thin, light brown, lustrous, adherent to the walls of the stone, the delicate inner coat attached to the copious fleshy albumen; embryo terete, axile, erect; cotyledons oblong, as long as the elongated radicle turned toward the minute hilum.

Halesia inhabits the southeastern United States and eastern China.

The generic name is in honor of Stephen Hales (1677–1761), an English clergyman, author of "Vegetable Staticks."

CONSPECTUS OF THE SPECIES OF THE UNITED STATES.

Fruit 4-winged; flowers fascicled; corolla slightly lobed.
 Fruit oblong to slightly obovoid.
  Flowers hardly more than ½′ long; fruit 1½′ in length.   1. **H. carolina** (A, C).
  Flowers 2′ long; fruit up to 2′ in length.   2. **H. monticola** (A).
 Fruit clavate; flowers usually not more than ¼′ long.   3. **H. parviflora** (C).
Fruit 2-winged; flowers often racemose; corolla divided nearly to the base.
       4. **H. diptera** (C).

1. Halesia carolina L.

Mohrodendron carolinum Britt.

Leaves elliptic to oblong-obovate, abruptly acuminate and long-pointed at apex, gradually narrowed and rounded or cuneate at base, and dentate with small remote callous teeth, slightly pubescent or covered below when they unfold with thick hoary tomentum and

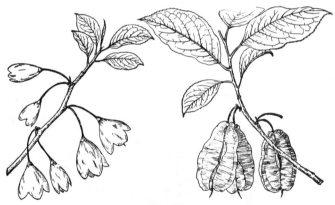

Fig. 732

densely stellate-pubescent above (var. *mollis* Perkins), and at maturity dark yellow-green and glabrous on the upper surface, pale and glabrous or slightly villose below on the slender yellow midrib and primary veins, 3′–4′ long and 1½′–2′ wide, and on leading shoots up to 6′–7′ in length; turning yellow in the autumn before falling; petioles slender, glabrous, pubescent or tomentose, early in the season, becoming nearly glabrous, ¼′–½′ in length.

Flowers about $\frac{1}{2}'$ long, on glabrous or densely or slightly villose pedicels $\frac{1}{2}'-\frac{3}{4}'$ in length, from the axils of ovate caducous serrate glabrous or pubescent bracts rounded at apex, in crowded fascicles; calyx obconic, glabrous, slightly pubescent or hoary-tomentose (var. *mollis* Lange), the lobes ciliate; corolla narrowed below into a short tube, $\frac{3}{4}'$ across, sometimes faintly tinged with rose, rarely divided nearly to the base (var. *dialypetala* Schn.); stamens 10–16; filaments villose with occasional white hairs; ovary 4-celled. **Fruit** oblong to oblong-obovate, 4-winged, $1\frac{1}{2}'$ long, $\frac{1}{2}'-\frac{3}{4}'$ in diameter; stone ellipsoid to slightly obovoid, narrowed below into a short stipe and above into the slender apex terminating in the elongated persistent style, slightly angled, $\frac{1}{2}'-\frac{5}{8}'$ long, usually 1-seeded by abortion; **seed** rounded at the narrow ends, $\frac{1}{4}'-\frac{1}{3}'$ long.

A round-headed tree, rarely 40° high, with a short trunk often divided near the ground into several spreading stems, and 12′–18′ in diameter, small branches, and slender branchlets glabrous or densely pubescent early in the season, becoming slightly pubescent or nearly glabrous and orange-brown, and marked by large obcordate leaf-scars during their first winter and dark red-brown the following year; more often a shrub with wide-spreading stems. **Winter-buds** ellipsoid to ovoid, $\frac{1}{8}'$ long, with thick broad-ovate dark red acute puberulous scales rounded on the back, those of the inner rows becoming strap-shaped, bright yellow and sometimes $\frac{1}{2}'$ long. **Bark** of the trunk $\frac{1}{2}'$ thick, slightly ridged, reddish brown, separating into thin closely appressed scales. **Wood** light, soft, close-grained, light brown with thick lighter-colored sapwood.

Distribution. Wooded slopes and the banks of streams, southern West Virginia (Fayette and Summers Counties); Piedmont region of North and South Carolina, ascending to altitudes of 2000′, through central Georgia to western Florida, and through Alabama south to Dallas County to western Kentucky and southern Illinois (near Metropolis, Massac County); the var. *mollis* with the type and the more common form in western Florida southward to Suwanee County. A seedling shrubby Halesia (var. *Meehanii* Perkins) with thicker smaller darker green rugose leaves, smaller cup-shaped flowers on shorter pedicels, appeared many years ago in the Meehan Nurseries at Germantown, Pennsylvania, and is possibly a hybrid but of obscure origin.

Often cultivated in the eastern United States, in California and in western and central Europe; hardy as far north as eastern Massachusetts.

2. Halesia monticola Sarg.

Leaves elliptic to oblong-obovate, abruptly acuminate at apex, cuneate or occasionally rounded at base, remotely dentate with minute blunt teeth, covered above when they unfold with short white hairs and below with thick hoary tomentum, half-grown and pubescent on the midrib below when the flowers open at the end of May, and at maturity thin, dark dull green on the upper surface, pale on the lower surface, glabrous with the exception of a few hairs on the lower side of the slender midrib and primary veins, 8′–11′ long and $1\frac{1}{2}'-2\frac{1}{2}'$ wide; turning yellow in the autumn before falling; petioles slender, villose-pubescent when they first appear, soon glabrous, $\frac{1}{2}'-\frac{3}{4}'$ in length. **Flowers** 2′ long on pedicels $\frac{1}{2}'-1'$ in length, from the axils of obovate or elliptic acute pubescent bracts $\frac{1}{2}'-\frac{3}{4}'$ long and $\frac{1}{4}'$ wide; calyx obconic, glabrous or slightly villose-pubescent; corolla 1′ in diameter, contracted below into a short limb; stamens 10–16; filaments slightly villose toward the base, ovary 4-celled. **Fruit** oblong-obovoid, cuneate at base, 4-winged, $1\frac{3}{4}'-2'$ long, 1′ in diameter; stone ovoid-ellipsoid, abruptly narrowed below into a short stipe, gradually narrowed above into the long apex, prominently angled about $1\frac{1}{4}'-1\frac{1}{2}'$ in length.

A tree, often 80°–90° high, with a trunk 3° in diameter and free of branches for 50°–60°, comparatively small spreading and erect branches forming a round-topped head and slender branchlets covered when they first appear with pale hairs, soon glabrous, lustrous, light red-brown or orange-brown during their first winter and dark red-brown in their second year. **Winter-buds** ovoid to ellipsoid, acuminate, much compressed, gibbous on the back, the outer scales thick, slightly keeled on the back, lustrous, bright red, $\frac{1}{3}'$ long. **Bark** of the trunk thick, separating freely into long broad loosely attached red-brown plates $\frac{1}{2}'-\frac{3}{4}'$ thick.

Distribution. Mountain slopes at altitudes from 3000°–4000°, western North Carolina, eastern Tennessee and western Georgia; passing into the var. *vestita* Sarg., with

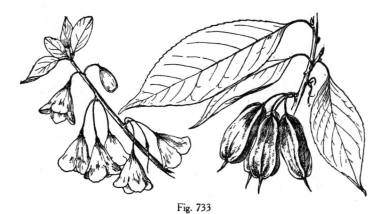

Fig. 733

leaves often rounded at base, coated below and on the petioles when they unfold with snow-white tomentum, and at maturity pubescent over the lower surface, especially on the midrib and veins, and occasionally pale rose-colored flowers (f. *rosea* Sarg.); banks of streams, near Marion, McDowell County, North Carolina, to Arkansas and eastern Oklahoma; occasionally cultivated with the var. *vestita* and hardy in the Arnold Arboretum and in Rochester, New York.

Halesia monticola in cultivation grows rapidly with a single trunk; and is hardy in eastern Massachusetts.

3 Halesia parviflora Michx.

Leaves oblong-ovate to slightly obovate or elliptic, abruptly long-pointed or acuminate at apex, narrowed and cuneate or rounded at base, finely serrate with minute glandular

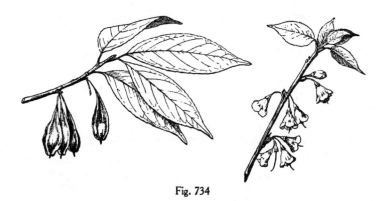

Fig. 734

teeth, densely covered when they unfold with hoary tomentum, becoming pubescent or glabrous, $2\frac{1}{2}'$–$3\frac{1}{4}'$ long and $1'$–$1\frac{1}{4}'$ wide, with a slender midrib and primary veins villose-pubescent below; petioles hoary-tomentose when they first appear, becoming glabrous, $\frac{1}{4}'-\frac{1}{3}'$ in length. **Flowers** opening the end of March or early in April, $\frac{1}{4}'-\frac{1}{3}'$ long, on pedicels more or less densely villose-pubescent with white hairs, becoming nearly glabrous, $\frac{1}{3}'-\frac{2}{3}'$ in length; calyx densely hoary-tomentose or rarely villose-pubescent; corolla $\frac{1}{3}'-\frac{1}{2}'$ in diameter; stamens 10–16, filaments slightly villose. **Fruit** ripening in August and September, clavate, gradually narrowed into the long stipitate base, $\frac{3}{4}'-1\frac{1}{2}'$ long, 4-winged, the wings narrow, of equal width or occasionally with the alternate wings narrower than the others; stone ovoid, abruptly narrowed below into a short stipe, gradually narrowed to the apex, obscurely angled, $\frac{3}{4}'-1\frac{1}{4}'$ long.

A slender tree, 25°–30° high, with a long trunk 8′–10′ in diameter, small light brown slightly ridged branches and slender branchlets hoary-tomentose when they first appear, becoming pubescent or nearly glabrous by the end of their first season and light gray-brown in their second year; or a shrub only a few feet tall. **Winter-buds** ovoid, acute, slightly compressed, villose, about $\frac{1}{8}'$ long. **Bark** of the trunk thick, dark brown or nearly black, and divided by deep longitudinal furrows into narrow rounded rough ridges.

Distribution. Northern Florida, in sandy uplands (St. John, Clay, Jackson, Gadsden and Lafayette Counties); not common; Alabama (Lee County); eastern Mississippi (Laurel, Jones County), and eastern Oklahoma (near Page, Le Flore County).

4. Halesia diptera Ellis.

Mohrodendron dipterum Britt.

Leaves ovate to obovate, oval or elliptic, abruptly long-pointed or rarely rounded at apex, gradually narrowed and cuneate or rounded at base, undulate-serrate with remote minute callous teeth, coated below with pale tomentum and pubescent above when they unfold, and at maturity thin, light green and glabrous or pubescent on the slender midrib on the upper surface and paler and soft-pubescent on the lower surface, 3′–4′ long and 2′–2½′ wide, and at the end of vigorous branches up to 8′ long and 3′ wide, with pale con-

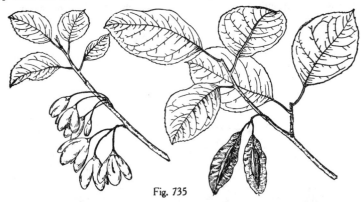

Fig. 735

spicuous arcuate veins and reticulate veinlets; petioles slender, pubescent, $\frac{1}{2}'-\frac{3}{4}'$ in length. **Flowers** opening from the middle of March to the end of April, usually nearly 1′ long, on slender tomentose pedicels $1\frac{1}{2}'-2'$ in length, from the axils of obovate puberulous bracts rounded or acute at apex and $\frac{1}{2}'-\frac{3}{4}'$ long, in few-flowered fascicles or in 4–6-flowered racemes; calyx thickly covered with hoary tomentum, the short lobes nearly glabrous on the inner surface; corolla puberulous on the outer surface, divided nearly to the base into slightly obovate or oval spreading lobes; stamens 8–16, usually 8, nearly as long as the corolla; filaments covered with pale hairs, and sometimes free from the corolla; ovary usually 2, rarely 4-celled and covered, like the style, with pale pubescence. **Fruit** oblong to slightly obovoid, compressed, $1\frac{1}{2}'$–$2'$ long, often nearly $1'$ wide, with two broad wings and often with 2 or rarely 3 narrow wings between them; stone ellipsoid, $1\frac{1}{2}'$–$1\frac{3}{4}'$ long, conspicuously ridged, gradually narrowed below into the short slender stipe and above into the thickened pubescent style; seed acuminate at the ends, about $\frac{3}{4}'$ in length.

A tree, occasionally 30° high, with a short or rarely a tall trunk $8'$–$10'$ in diameter, spreading branches forming a wide head and slender branchlets light green and more or less thickly covered with pale pubescence when they first appear, usually becoming glabrous, orange color, or reddish brown, lustrous and marked by the large elevated obcordate leaf-scars during their first winter, dark red-brown in their second season and dividing the following year into irregular pale longitudinal fissures; more often a shrub with numerous stout spreading stems. Winter-buds ovoid, obtuse, $\frac{1}{16}'$ long, with broad-ovate acute light red pubescent scales, those of the inner ranks becoming strap-shaped, scarious and $\frac{1}{4}'$ long. Bark of the trunk $\frac{1}{3}'$–$\frac{1}{2}'$ thick, brown tinged with red, and divided by irregular longitudinal often broad fissures, and separating into small thin closely appressed scales. Wood light, soft, strong, close-grained, light brown with thick lighter-colored sapwood.

Distribution. Low wet woods and the borders of swamps and streams; near Savannah (*Elliott*) and in southwestern Georgia, middle Florida (Leon and Gadsden Counties), southern Alabama, Mississippi and Louisiana to the valley of the lower Neches River, Texas.

Occasionally cultivated in the gardens of the eastern United States and western Europe. Doubtfully hardy in Massachusetts and western New York.

2. STYRAX L.

Trees or shrubs, lepidote or stellate-tomentose except on the upper surface of the leaves, with slender terete slightly zigzag branchlets, without a terminal bud, axillary buds, with imbricated scales, and fibrous roots. Leaves involute in the bud, entire or slightly serrate. Flowers usually white on short ebracteolate drooping pedicels from the axils of small bracts, in simple or branched usually drooping axillary racemes; calyx cup-shaped, adnate to the base of the ovary or nearly free, the margin truncate, obscurely or conspicuously 5-toothed or rarely 2 or 5-parted; corolla epigynous, campanulate, 5 or rarely 6 or 7-parted, with a short tube usually longer than the lanceolate oblong or spatulate erect and spreading or revolute lobes valvate or imbricated in the bud, stamens 8–13, usually 10, longer than the corolla slightly united below into a ring or short tube; filaments flattened above; cells of the anthers linear parallel, erect; ovary broad-conic, subglobose or depressed, densely villose or rarely glabrous, at first 3-celled, becoming 1-celled or nearly 1-celled after anthesis, crowned by a subulate or thickened style terminating in a small indistinctly 3-lobed or capitate stigma; ovules few or rarely solitary ascending; raphe dorsal, micropyle inferior. Fruit globose or slightly obovoid, drupaceous; pericarp hard and indehiscent or irregularly 3-valved or fleshy and irregularly dehiscent; endocarp glabrous, crustaceous or indurate; seed 1 by abortion or very rarely 2, filling the cavity of the stone, erect; testa membranaceous. mostly adherent to the walls of the stone; albumen fleshy or rarely horny; cotyledons usually broad. the elongated terete radicle turned toward the broad basal hilum.

Styrax is widely distributed in warm and tropical countries except in tropical and south Africa and in Australasia, extending northward into the southeastern United States and to California, southern Europe, central and western China and central Japan. Of nearly one hundred species which are now distinguished five are found within the territory of the United States; one of these occasionally becomes a small tree.

Storax and benzoin, aromatic resinous balsams, are obtained from *Styrax officinale* L. of southern Europe and Asia Minor. and from *Styrax Benzoin* Dryand. of Malaysia.

The generic name is that of the Greek name of *Styrax officinale*.

1. Styrax grandifolia Ait.

Leaves thin, deciduous, obovate, rounded and abruptly pointed or acute or acuminate or rarely rounded at apex, cuneate or rounded at the narrow base, entire or remotely serrate with small apiculate teeth, when they unfold ciliate on the margins, slightly stellate-pubescent on the midrib and veins above, and coated below with hoary tomentum, and at maturity pale green and glabrous or nearly glabrous above, pale tomentose and villose on the

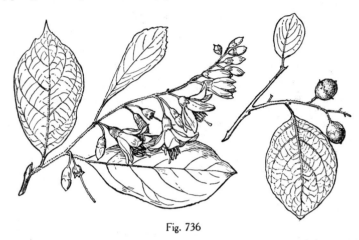

Fig. 736

midrib and veins below, $2\frac{1}{2}'-5'$ long and $1'-3'$ wide; petioles $\frac{1}{4}'$ in length, hoary-tomentose early in the season, becoming pubescent. **Flowers** opening in early spring after the leaves are more than half grown, $\frac{3}{4}'-1'$ long, on slender pubescent or tomentose pedicels $\frac{1}{4}'$ in length, in tomentose leafy erect or spreading axillary racemes $5'$ or $6'$ long, their bracts and bractlets linear, minute, tomentose, caducous; calyx more or less coarsely 5-toothed, membranaceous, tomentose on the outer surface; corolla 5-parted, the lobes longer than the tube, imbricated in the bud, membranaceous, oblong-obovate, rounded or acute at apex, stellate-pubescent on the outer surface; stamens 10, about as long as the corolla, villose-pubescent below the middle, united below into a short ring; ovary slightly inferior, obovoid, tomentose, 3-celled; style filiform, glabrous, exserted; ovules 3 or 4 in each cell. **Fruit** hoary-tomentose, slightly obovoid, rounded and tipped at apex with the remnants of the style, gradually narrowed and surrounded below by the calyx, $\frac{1}{3}'$ long, and $\frac{1}{4}'$ in diameter, the outer coat crustaceous, indehiscent; **seed** obovoid, dark orange-brown, filling the cavity of the fruit.

A tree, rarely $40°$ high, with a tall straight trunk sometimes $8'$ in diameter, short spreading branches forming a narrow round-topped head, and slender branchlets thickly coated when they first appear with hoary stellate pubescence more or less persistent during three seasons, ultimately glabrous and light or dark chestnut-brown; more often a broad shrub $6°-20°$ high. **Bark** of the trunk $\frac{1}{3}'-\frac{1}{2}'$ thick, close, smooth and dark red-brown. **Winter-buds: axillary,** often 3, superposed, acute, covered with hoary ultimately rusty tomentum, about $\frac{1}{8}'$ long.

Distribution. Low wet woods and the borders of swamps; southeastern Virginia, southward usually near the coast to the valley of the Apalachicola River, Florida, and through the Gulf states to western Louisiana, ranging inland to northern Georgia, northeastern Mississippi, and to the valley of the Red River at Natchitoches, Louisiana; of its largest size and perhaps only arborescent near Laurel Hill, West Feliciana Parish, Louisiana.

LIX. SYMPLOCACEÆ.

Trees or shrubs, with simple pubescence, watery juice, scaly buds, and fibrous roots. Leaves simple, alternate, coriaceous or thin, pinnately veined, usually becoming yellow in drying, without stipules. Flowers regular, perfect, or polygamo-diœcious, on ebracteolate pedicels, in dense or lax axillary spikes or racemes, with small caducous bracts; calyx campanulate, 5-lobed, open in the bud, the tube adnate to the ovary, enlarged after anthesis; corolla divided nearly to the base into 3–11 usually 5 lobes imbricated in the bud; disk 0; stamens usually numerous, inserted in many series on the base of the corolla or rarely 4 in one series; filaments filiform or flattened, more or less united below into clusters; anthers ovoid-globose, introrse, 2-celled, the cells lateral, opening longitudinally; ovary inferior or partly inferior, 2–5-celled, contracted into a simple style, with an entire or slightly lobed terminal stigma; ovules 2 or rarely 4 in each cell, suspended from its inner angle, anatropous; raphe ventral; micropyle superior. Fruit a drupe (in the North American species), crowned with the persistent lobes of the calyx, with thin dry flesh and a bony 1-seeded stone. Seed oblong, suspended; seed-coat membranaceous; embryo terete, erect in copious fleshy albumen; cotyledons much shorter than the long slender radicle turned toward the broad conspicuous hilum.

The family consists of the genus Symplocos.

1. SYMPLOCOS L'Her.

Characters of the family.

Symplocos with nearly three hundred species inhabits chiefly the warmer parts of America, Asia, and Australia, one species occurring in the southern United States.

Symplocos contains a yellow coloring matter, and the bark and leaves of some species have medical properties.

The generic name, from Σύμπλοκος, relates to the union of the filaments of some of the species.

1. Symplocos tinctoria L'Her.   Sweet Leaf.   Horse Sugar.

Leaves revolute in the bud, oblong, acute or acuminate at apex, gradually narrowed at base, obscurely crenulate-serrate with remote teeth, or sometimes nearly entire, coated below when they unfold with pale tomentum, glabrous or tomentose above, and furnished on the margins with minute dark caducous glands, and at maturity subcoriaceous, dark

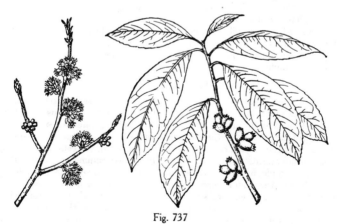

Fig. 737

green and lustrous on the upper surface, paler and pubescent on the lower surface, 5′–6′ long and 1′–2′ wide, with a broad midrib rounded and sometimes puberulous on the upper side, inconspicuous arcuate veins and reticulate veinlets; northward and at high altitudes falling in the autumn, and southward remaining on the branches until after the opening of the flowers the following spring; petioles stout, slightly winged, $\frac{1}{3}'$–$\frac{1}{2}'$ in length. **Flowers;** flower-clusters inclosed in the bud by ovate acute orange-colored scales brown and ciliate on the margins, each of the flower-buds surrounded by 3 imbricated oblong bracts rounded or pointed at apex and ciliate on the margins, the longest as long as the calyx and one third longer than the 2 lateral bracts; flowers fragrant, opening from the 1st of March at the south to the middle of May on the southern Appalachian Mountains, on short pedicels enlarged into thick hemispheric receptacles covered with long white hairs, in nearly sessile many-flowered clusters in the axils of leaves of the previous year; calyx oblong, cup-shaped, dark green and puberulous, with minute ovate scarious lobes rounded at apex; corolla creamy white, $\frac{1}{4}'$ long, with rounded lobes; stamens exserted, with slender filaments united at base into 5 clusters, and orange-colored anthers; ovary 3-celled, furnished on the top with 5 dark nectariferous glands placed opposite the lobes of the calyx, and abruptly contracted into a slender style gradually thickened toward the apex and longer than the corolla. **Fruit** ripening in the summer or early autumn, ovoid, $\frac{1}{4}'$ long, dark orange-colored or brown; seed ovoid, pointed, with a thin papery chestnut-brown coat.

A tree, occasionally 30°–35° high, with a short trunk barely exceeding 6'–8' in diameter, slender upright branches forming an open head, and stout terete pithy branchlets light green and coated with pale or rufous tomentum when they first appear, or sometimes glabrous, and covered with scattered white hairs, reddish brown to ashy gray, tinged with red and usually more or less pubescent or often covered with a glaucous bloom during their first and second years, later growing darker, roughened by occasional small elevated lenticels and marked by the low horizontal obcordate leaf-scars displaying a central cluster of large fibro-vascular bundle-scars; or more often a shrub. **Winter-buds** ovoid, acute, covered with broad-ovate nearly triangular acute scales, those of the inner rows accrescent on the young branchlets, and at maturity oblong-obovate, rounded and often apiculate at apex, light green, glabrous or pilose, ciliate on the margins, and often $\frac{1}{2}'$ in length. **Bark of** the trunk $\frac{1}{3}'$–$\frac{1}{2}'$ thick, ashy gray slightly tinged with red, divided by occasional narrow fissures and roughened by wart-like excrescences. **Wood** light, soft, close-grained, light red or brown, with thick lighter colored often nearly white sapwood of 18–20 layers of annual growth. The leaves are sweet to the taste and are devoured in the autumn by cattle and horses, and, like the bark, yield a yellow dye occasionally used domestically. The bitter aromatic roots have been used as a tonic.

Distribution. Moist rich soil, often in the shade of dense forests; peninsula of Delaware to northern Florida and from the coast to altitudes of nearly 4000° on the Blue Ridge in North and South Carolina, and to eastern Texas and southern Arkansas; in the Gulf states in hammocks and bluffs.

LX. OLEACEÆ.

Trees or shrubs, with watery juice, scaly buds, their inner scales accrescent, opposite leaves, without stipules, and fibrous roots. Flowers perfect, diœcious or polygamous, regular; calyx 4-lobed, or 0; corolla of 2–4 petals, or 0; disk 0; stamens 2–4, rudimentary or 0 in unisexual pistillate flowers; anthers attached on the back below the middle, often apiculate by the prolongation of the connective, introrse, 2-celled, the cells opening longitudinally usually by lateral slits; ovary free, 2 or rarely 3-celled, rudimentary or 0 in the staminate flower; style simple; ovules 2 in each cell, pendulous, anatropous; micropyle superior. Fruit (in the North American arborescent genera) a samara or berry. Seed pendulous; seed-coat membranaceous; embryo straight in copious fleshy albumen; cotyledons flat, much longer than the short terete superior radicle turned toward the minute hilum.

The Olive family with twenty-five genera is widely distributed in temperate and tropical regions chiefly in the northern hemisphere. Of the five genera indigenous to the United States four are arborescent. To this family belong *Olea europœa* L., the Olive-tree of the Mediterranean basin, now largely cultivated in California for its fruit, and the Lilacs, Forsythias, Privets, and Jasmines, favorite garden plants in all countries with temperate climates.

OLEACEÆ **833**

CONSPECTUS OF THE ARBORESCENT GENERA OF THE UNITED STATES.

Fruit a winged samara; leaves usually compound.   1. **Fraxinus.**
Fruit a drupe; leaves simple.
  Flowers usually without petals.   2. **Forestiera.**
  Flowers with petals.
    Corolla of 4 long linear petals united only at base; leaves deciduous.
                                   3. **Chionanthus.**
    Corolla tubular; leaves persistent.   4. **Osmanthus.**

1. FRAXINUS L. Ash.

Trees or shrubs, with thick furrowed or rarely thin and scaly bark, usually ash-colored branchlets, with thick pith, and compressed obtuse terminal buds much larger than the lateral buds. Leaves petiolate, unequally pinnate or rarely reduced to a single leaflet, deciduous; leaflets conduplicate in the bud, usually serrate, petiolulate or sessile. Flowers diœcious or polygamous, produced in early spring on slender elongated pedicels, without bractlets, in open or compact slender-branched panicles, with obovate linear or lanceolate caducous bracts, terminal on leafy shoots of the year, developed from the axils of new leaves, or from separate buds in the axils of leaves of the previous year, or at the base of young branchlets, and covered by 2 ovate scales; calyx campanulate, deciduous or persistent under the fruit, or 0; corolla 2–4-parted, the divisions conduplicate in the bud, united at base, or 0; stamens usually 2, rarely 3 or 4, inserted on the base of the corolla, or hypogynous; filaments terete, short or rarely elongated; anthers ovoid or linear-oblong, the cells opening by lateral slits; ovary 2 or rarely 3-celled, contracted into a short or elongated style terminating in a 2-lobed stigma; ovules suspended in pairs from the inner angle of the cell; raphe dorsal. Fruit a 1 or rarely 2 or 3-seeded winged samara; body terete or slightly flattened contrary to the septum, with a dry or woody pericarp produced into an elongated more or less decurrent wing, usually 1-celled by abortion or sometimes 2 or 3-celled and winged. Seed solitary in each cell, oblong, compressed, gradually narrowed and rounded at the ends, filling the cavity of the fruit; seed-coat chestnut-brown.

Fraxinus with thirty to forty species is widely distributed in the temperate regions of the northern hemisphere, and within the tropics occurs on the islands of Cuba and Java. Of the eighteen North American species here recognized all, with the exception of *Fraxinus dipetala* Hook., of California, are large or small trees.

Fraxinus produces tough straight-grained valuable wood, and some of the species are large and important timber-trees. The waxy exudations from the trunk and leaves of *Fraxinus Ornus* L., of southern Europe and Asia Minor furnish the manna of commerce used in medicine as a gentle laxative; and the Chinese white wax is obtained from the branches of *Fraxinus chinensis* Roxb.

Fraxinus is the classical name of the Ash-tree.

CONSPECTUS OF THE NORTH AMERICAN ARBORESCENT SPECIES.

Flowers with a corolla, in terminal panicles on lateral leafy branchlets of the year; leaflets
  3–7, lanceolate to ovate-lanceolate (ORNUS).   1. **F. cuspidata** (E, H).
Flowers without a corolla, diœcious or polygamous, in axillary panicles, from separate buds,
  in the axils of leaves of the previous year (FRAXINASTRUM).
  Flowers with a calyx.
    Leaflets with obscure veins, not more than ¾′ long; fruit narrow-spatulate to oblong-
    obovate; rachis slightly winged.   2. **F. Greggii** (E).
    Leaflets with distinct veins, more than ¾′ long; rachis without a wing.
      Body of the fruit compressed, its wing extending to the base.
        Branchlets 4-sided.
          Leaves usually 5-foliolate, with ovate acute leaflets; flowers unknown.
                                    3. **F. Lowellii** (F).

Leaves usually reduced to a single ovate or orbicular leaflet; flowers polygamous. 4. **F. anomala** (F).
Branchlets terete.
Leaflets 5–7, oblong-ovate; fruit oblong-elliptic to spatulate, often 3-winged, long-stipitate. 5. **F. caroliniana** (A, C).
Leaflets 3–5, oblong; fruit lanceolate to oblanceolate, the body extending to the base of the fruit. 6. **F. pauciflora** (C).
Body of the fruit nearly terete.
Wing of the fruit terminal or slightly decurrent on the body.
Leaves and branchlets glabrous (*tomentose in one form of* 7).
Leaflets sessile or nearly sessile 5–7 rarely 5, ovate to oblong-ovate, rarely elliptic, acute or short-acuminate, glaucescent below.
7. **F. Standleyi** (H).
Leaflets stalked.
Leaflets 5–7, ovate to lanceolate, abruptly pointed or acuminate, usually pale below. 8. **F. americana** (A, C)
Leaflets usually 5, ovate to obovate, rounded or acute at apex.
9. **F. texensis** (C).
Leaves and branches pubescent; leaflets oblong-ovate to lanceolate, pale below; fruit linear-oblong. 10. **F. biltmoreana** (A, C).
Wing of the fruit decurrent to below the middle of the body.
Leaflets 7–9, usually 7; leaves and branches pubescent (*glabrous in one form of 12*).
Fruit 2′–3′ in length. 11. **F. profunda** (A, C).
Fruit 1′–2½′ in length. 12. **F. pennsylvanica** (A, E).
Leaflets 3–5.
Leaves and branchlets glabrous; fruit up to 1½′ in length.
13. **F. Berlandieriana** (C, E).
Leaves and branchlets pubescent or glabrous; fruit not more than ½′ in length. 14. **F. velutina** (F, H).
Leaflets 5–7, usually 7, the lateral generally sessile; leaves and branchlets pilose-pubescent, rarely glabrous. 15. **F. oregona** (B, G).
Flowers without a calyx; leaflets 5–11; wing of the fruit decurrent to the base of the body.
Branchlets quadrangular; lateral leaflets short-stalked. 16. **F. quadrangulata** (A, C).
Branchlets terete; lateral leaflets sessile. 17. **F. nigra** (A, C).

1. Fraxinus cuspidata Torr.

Leaves 5′–7′ long, with a slender pale petiole sometimes slightly wing-margined, and 3–7 lanceolate or ovate-lanceolate long-stalked leaflets gradually narrowed at apex into a long slender point, cuneate at base nearly entire or coarsely and remotely serrate above the middle with recurved teeth (var. *serrata* Rehd.), or with 3–5, rarely 7-foliolate leaves, with broader often ovate entire leaflets occasionally with simple leaves at the base of the branchlets (var. *macropetala* Rehd.); slightly puberulous when they unfold on the lower surface, and at maturity thin, dark green above, paler below, 1½′–2½′ long and ¼′–¾′ wide, with a pale midrib and obscure veins; petiolules slender, sometimes nearly 1′ in length. **Flowers** perfect, extremely fragrant, appearing in April, in open glabrous panicles 3′–4′ long and broad, terminal on lateral leafy branchlets developed from the axils of leaves of the previous year, calyx cup-shaped, ¹⁄₁₆′ long, with acute apiculate attenuate teeth of unequal length, deciduous, corolla ¾′ long, thin and white, divided to below the middle into 4 linear-oblong lobes pointed at apex, and much longer than the nearly sessile oblong long-pointed anthers; ovary 2-celled, with a thick 2-lobed nearly sessile stigma. **Fruit** elliptic to oblong-obovate, 1′ long and ¼′ wide, the wing round and slightly emarginate at apex, and decurrent nearly to the base of the flat nerveless longer body.

A tree, rarely 20° high, with a short trunk 6′–8′ in diameter, and slender terete branchlets light red-brown when they first appear, soon becoming darker and marked by scattered pale lenticels, and ashy gray and roughened by the dark elevated lunate leaf-scars in their second year; more often a shrub or small shrubby tree, with numerous slender spreading

Fig. 738

stems 6°-8° tall. **Winter-buds:** terminal acute, nearly $\frac{1}{2}'$ long, with dark reddish brown glutinous scales.

Distribution. Rocky slopes and dry ridges; western Texas, valley of the Rio Grande (mouth of Devil's River, Valverde County) to the Chisos Mountains, and in southern New Mexico; in Coahuila, Nuevo Leon and Chihuahua; the var. *macropetala* in cañons of northern Arizona; the var. *serrata* (fig. 738) in Coahuila.

2. Fraxinus Greggii A. Gray.

Leaves $1\frac{1}{2}'-3'$ long, with a winged petiole and rachis, and 3-7 narrow spatulate to oblong-obovate leaflets entire or crenately serrate above the middle with remote teeth, a slender

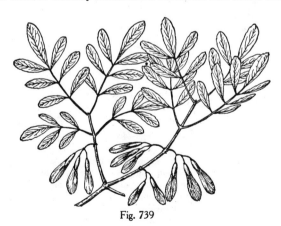

Fig. 739

midrib, and obscure reticulate veins, thick and coriaceous, dark green on the upper surface rather paler and covered with small black dots on the lower surface, $\frac{1}{2}'-\frac{3}{4}'$ long, $\frac{1}{8}'-\frac{1}{4}'$ wide, and nearly sessile. **Flowers** perfect or unisexual, on slender pedicels $\frac{1}{8}'-\frac{1}{4}'$ long, from the axils of ovate acuminate rusty-pubescent bracts, in pubescent panicles $\frac{1}{2}'-\frac{3}{4}'$ in length; calyx campanulate, scarious; stamens 1 or 2, filaments longer than the calyx, anthers declinate, nearly $\frac{1}{8}'$ long; ovary broad-ovate, rounded at apex, longer than the calyx, the short style terminating in large reflexed stigmatic lobes. **Fruit** narrow-spathulate to oblong-obovate, $\frac{1}{2}'-\frac{2}{3}'$ long and about $\frac{1}{4}'$ wide, the thin wing decurrent on the short terete body, rounded and emarginate at apex and tipped with the elongated persistent conspicuous style.

A tree, rarely 20°–25° high, with a trunk 8°–10° long and occasionally 8' in diameter, and slender terete branchlets dark green and puberulous when they first appear, soon becoming ashy gray and roughened by numerous minute pale elevated lenticels, gradually turning dark gray, or brown in their second and third years; more often a shrub, with numerous slender erect stems 4°–12° tall. **Winter-buds:** terminal, about $\frac{1}{8}'$ long, obtuse, with thick ovate light brown pubescent scales rounded on the back. **Bark** of the trunk thin, gray or light brown tinged with red, separating on the surface into large papery scales. **Wood** heavy, hard, close-grained, brown, with thick lighter-colored sapwood.

Distribution. Western Texas, along rocky beds of streams and deep ravines, Valverde County (near Devil's River, Del Rio and Comstock); on the mountains of northeastern Mexico; apparently most common and of its largest size on the Sierra Nevada of Nuevo Leon.

3. Fraxinus Lowellii Sarg.

Leaves $3\frac{1}{2}'-6'$ long, with a stout glabrous or slightly villose petiole, and 5 or rarely 3 ovate stalked leaflets, acuminate and long-pointed, acute or rarely rounded at apex, cuneate at base, serrate, often only above the middle, with small remote teeth, yellow-green, glabrous,

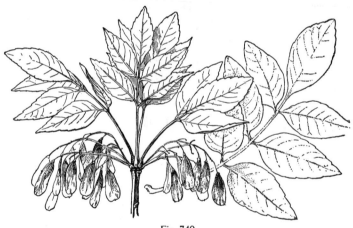

Fig. 740

or puberulous along the midrib above, glabrous or rarely sparingly villose near the base of the slender pale midrib below, $2\frac{1}{4}'-3'$ long and $1'-1\frac{1}{2}'$ wide, with thin primary veins arching and united near the slightly thickened and revolute margins; on vigorous shoots occasionally 1-foliolate with a broad-ovate or semi-orbicular leaflet. **Flowers** unknown. **Fruit** ripening in July, in long glabrous panicles, oblong-obovate to oblong-elliptic, surrounded at base by the minute slightly dentate calyx, $1'-1\frac{1}{2}'$ long, $\frac{1}{4}'-\frac{1}{3}'$ wide, the wing broad or gradually narrowed and rounded, and often emarginate at apex and extending to the base of the thin compressed many-rayed body about three-quarters the length of the fruit.

A tree, 20°–25° high, with dark deeply furrowed bark, stout quadrangular often winged branchlets orange-brown in their first season and dark gray-brown the following year.

Distribution. Arizona, rocky slopes of Oak Creek Cañon about twenty miles south of Flagstaff, Coconino County, and in Copper Cañon, west of Camp Verde, Yavapai County.

4. Fraxinus anomala S. Wats.

Leaves mostly reduced to a single leaflet but occasionally 2 or 3-foliolate, the leaflets broad-ovate or orbicular, rounded or acute or rarely obcordate at apex, cuneate or cordate at base, and entire, or sparingly crenately serrate above the middle, covered above when they unfold with short pale hairs and pubescent beneath, and at maturity thin but rather coriaceous, dark green above, paler below, $1\frac{1}{2}'-2'$ long and $1'-2'$ wide, or when more than one much smaller, with a broad rather conspicuous midrib and obscure veins, and when solitary raised on a stout grooved petiole rusty-pubescent early in the season, becoming

Fig. 741

glabrous, and often $1\frac{1}{2}'$ long, or short-petiolulate in the compound leaves. **Flowers** appearing when the leaves are about two thirds grown, in short compact pubescent panicles, with strap-shaped or lanceolate acute bracts $\frac{1}{2}'$ long and covered with thick brown villose tomentum, perfect or unisexual by the abortion of the stamens, the 2 forms occurring in the same panicle; calyx cup-shaped, minutely 4-toothed; anthers linear-oblong, orange colored, raised on slender filaments nearly as long as the stout columnar style. **Fruit** obovate, $\frac{1}{2}'$ long, the wing rounded and often deeply emarginate at apex, surrounding the short flattened striately nerved body, and $\frac{1}{4}'$ wide.

A tree, 18°–20° high, with a short trunk 6'–7' in diameter, stout contorted branches forming a round-topped head, and branchlets at first quadrangular, dark green tinged with red and covered with pale pubescence, orange colored and puberulous in their first winter and marked by elevated pale lenticels and narrow lunate leaf-scars, and in their second or third year terete and ashy gray; often a low shrub, with numerous spreading stems. **Winter-buds:** terminal broad-ovoid, acuminate or obtuse, covered with thick orange-colored tomentum, and $\frac{1}{8}'-\frac{1}{4}'$ long. **Bark** of the trunk dark brown slightly tinged with red, $\frac{1}{4}'$ thick and divided by shallow fissures into narrow ridges separating into small thin appressed scales. **Wood** heavy, hard, close-grained, light brown, with thick lighter colored sapwood of 30–50 layers of annual growth.

Distribution. In the neighborhood of streams; valley of the McElmo River, southwestern Colorado; Carriso Mountains, San Juan County, northwestern New Mexico; northeastern (Apache County), and the Grand Cañon of the Colorado River, Coconino County, Arizona; southern Utah to the Charleston Mountains, southwestern Nevada and adjacent California (Inyo County).

5. Fraxinus caroliniana Mill.　Water Ash.　Swamp Ash.

Leaves 7′–12′ long, with an elongated stout terete pale petiole, and 5–7 long-stalked ovate to oblong acute or acuminate leaflets rarely rounded at apex, cuneate or sometimes rounded or subcordate at base, and coarsely serrate with acute incurved teeth, or entire, pilose above and more or less hoary-tomentose below when they unfold, and at maturity thick and firm, 3′–6′ long and 2′–3′ wide, dark green above, paler or sometimes yellow-green and glabrous or pubescent (var. *Rehderiana* Sarg.) beneath, particularly along the conspicuous midrib and the numerous arcuate veins connected by obscure reticulate veinlets. **Flowers** diœcious, appearing in February and March in short or ultimately elongated panicles inclosed in the bud by chestnut-brown pubescent scales; staminate flower with a minute or nearly obsolete calyx, and 2 or sometimes 4 stamens, with slender filaments and linear apiculate anthers; calyx of the pistillate flower cup-shaped, deeply divided and laciniate, as long as the ovary gradually narrowed into an elongated slender style. **Fruit** elliptic to oblong-obovate, frequently 3-winged, surrounded at base by the persistent calyx, 2′ long, ⅓′–¾′ wide, often marked on the 2 faces by a conspicuous impressed midvein, the body short, compressed, and surrounded by the broad thin many-nerved sometimes bright violet-colored wing, acute or acuminate, or rounded and emarginate at apex and usually narrowed below into a stalk-like base.

A tree, rarely more than 40° high, with a trunk sometimes 12′ in diameter, small branches forming a narrow often round-topped head, and slender terete branchlets light green and glabrous or tomentose when they first appear, light brown tinged with red and sometimes covered with a glaucous bloom or rarely pubescent or tomentose (var. *Rehderiana* Sarg.) in their first winter, becoming in their second year light gray or yellow, occasionally marked

Fig. 742

by large pale lenticels, and by the elevated semiorbicular leaf-scars displaying a short row of conspicuous fibro-vascular bundle-scars. **Winter-buds:** terminal, ⅛′ long, with 3 pairs of ovate acute chestnut-brown puberulous scales, those of the outer rank thickened at base, rounded on the back, and shorter than the others. **Bark** of the trunk 1/16′–⅛′ thick, light gray, more or less marked by large irregularly shaped round patches, and separating on the surface into small thin closely appressed scales. **Wood** light, soft, weak, close-grained, nearly white sometimes tinged with yellow, with thick lighter colored sapwood.

Distribution. Deep river swamps inundated during several months of the year, usually under the shade of larger trees, or rarely in drier ground; coast region of the Atlantic and Gulf states, valley of the Potomac River, Virginia, near Washington, D.C., to Florida southward to Lake County and on the west coast to the valley of the lower Apalachicola

River, and to the valley of the Neches River (Beaumont, Jefferson County), Texas, and northward through western Louisiana to southwestern (Malvern, Hot Springs County) Arkansas; east of the Mississippi River occasionally appearing in isolated stations remote from the coast (Anson County, North Carolina, *C. L. Boynton*, Pike County, Georgia, *R. M. Harper*, Forrest County, Mississippi, *T. G. Harbison*); in Cuba.

6. Fraxinus pauciflora Nutt. Water Ash.

Fraxinus floridana Sarg.

Leaves 5′–9′ long, with an elongated stout terete petiole, and 3–7, usually 5, elliptic to oblong-obovate or ovate leaflets, acuminate or rarely abruptly pointed at apex, gradually narrowed and rounded at the often unsymmetric base, finely or coarsely serrate, scurfy-pubescent above and hoary-tomentose below when they unfold, and at maturity thick and

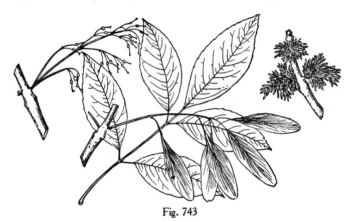

Fig. 743

firm, dark green and glabrous or puberulous on the upper surface and more or less tomentose on the lower surface, 3′–4′ long and 1′–1¼′ wide, with a slender midrib, and thin primary veins arcuate and united within the thickened revolute margins; petiolules of the lateral leaflets ¼′–½′ long, much shorter than those of the terminal leaflet. Flowers diœcious, appearing late in February or early in March, in elongated panicles inclosed in the bud by chestnut-brown pubescent scales; staminate flower composed of an annular disk and 2 or 3 stamens, with short filaments and apiculate anthers; calyx of the pistillate flower cup-shaped, slightly lobed, as long as the ovary gradually narrowed into the slender style. Fruit oblong to lanceolate or oblanceolate, surrounded at base by the persistent calyx, 1′–2′ long, ¼′–½′ wide, marked on each of the 2 faces by a broad impressed midvein, the body near the base of the many-nerved wing narrowed, rounded, and emarginate at apex.

A tree, 30°–40° high, with a trunk sometimes 12′ in diameter, small spreading branches, and slender terete branchlets light orange-brown and occasionally marked by large pale lenticels during their first season, ashy gray and roughened the following year by the large horizontal obcordate elevated leaf-scars displaying a central ring of fibro-vascular bundle-scars. Winter-buds terminal, broad-ovoid, acute, rusty-pubescent, about ¼′ long. Bark of the trunk ¹⁄₁₆′–⅛′ thick, light gray, and broken on the surface into small thin closely appressed scales.

Distribution. Deep swamps; valleys of the St. Mary's and Flint Rivers (Albany), southern Georgia; Florida, near Jacksonville, Duval County, valley of the Caloosahatchee River, and Bonita Springs, Lee County, to the shores of Lake Okeechobee, and in the valley of the lower Apalachicola River; most abundant in Florida.

7. Fraxinus Standleyi Rehd.

Leaves 5′–7′ long, with a slender glabrous petiole flattened, or slightly concave on the upper side, and 7–9 ovate to oblong-ovate rarely elliptic leaflets, acute or short-acuminate or rarely rounded at apex, broad-cuneate at base, slightly and irregularly ser-

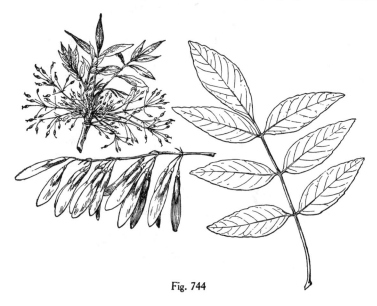

Fig. 744

rate, yellow-green and glabrous above, glaucescent, slightly reticulate, minutely punctulate, glabrous or slightly villose on the slender midrib below, or rarely closely villose over the entire lower surface, $1\frac{1}{2}′-2\frac{1}{2}′$ long and 1′–2′ wide, with usually 5–7 primary veins, the terminal leaflet raised on a petiolule up to $\frac{1}{2}′$ long, the lateral short-petiolulate, or nearly sessile. **Flowers** not seen. **Fruit** ripening in September, on slender pedicels, in glabrous panicles 3′–5′ long, oblong-obovate, acute, rarely obtuse and occasionally emarginate at apex, surrounded at base by the minute calyx deeply divided into acuminate lobes, $\frac{3}{4}′-1\frac{1}{2}′$ long and $\frac{1}{8}′-\frac{1}{4}′$ wide, the wing decurrent nearly to the middle of the subterete or slightly compressed ellipsoid or oblong body.

A tree, sometimes 30° high, usually smaller, with a trunk only a few inches in diameter, and slender terete glabrous branches orange-brown or rarely on vigorous shoots dark red-brown and lustrous. **Winter-buds:** terminal ovoid, gradually narrowed and acute at apex, $\frac{1}{3}′$ long.

Distribution. Mountain cañons at altitudes of 5500°–8000°; Now Mexico (Lincoln, Grant and Luna Counties); Arizona (Cochise, Pima and Coconino Counties); on the San José Mountains, Sonora, at an altitude of 7200°; passing into var. *lasia* Rehd. with branchlets, lower surface of the 7 leaflets and petioles densely tomentose; in Oak Creek and Sycamore cañons south of Flagstaff, Coconino County, at Fort Apache, Navajo County, on the White Mountains, Graham County, and on the Chiricahua Mountains, Cochise County, Arizona; and near Santa Rita, Grant County, New Mexico. A single plant, possibly a shrub, of the Mexican *Fraxinus papilosa* Ling. differing chiefly from *F. Standleyi* in the glaucous papillose under surface of the leaves, has been seen at an altitude of 6750° on the west sides of the San Luis Mountains, Grant County, New Mexico.

8. Fraxinus americana L. White Ash.

Leaves 8′–12′ long, with a stout grooved petiole, and 5–9, usually 7, ovate to oblanceolate or oval, often falcate abruptly pointed or acuminate leaflets, cuneate or rounded at base, crenulate-serrate or nearly entire, thin but firm, dark green above, pale or light green and glabrous or slightly pubescent below, or rarely thicker, lanceolate, long-acuminate, entire, glabrous and silvery white below (var. *subcoriacea* Sarg.), 3′–5′ long and 1½′–3′ wide, with a broad midrib, and numerous conspicuous veins arcuate near the margins; falling early in the autumn after turning on some individuals deep purple and on others clear bright yellow; petiolules ¼′–½′ or that of the terminal leaflet up to 1′ in length. **Flowers** diœcious, opening before the leaves late in the spring, in compact ultimately elongated glabrous panicles from buds covered with dark ovate scales rounded at apex and slightly keeled on the back; calyx campanulate, slightly 4-lobed in the staminate flower, and deeply lobed or laciniately cut in the pistillate flower; stamens 2 or occasionally 3, with short stout filaments, and large oblong-ovate apiculate anthers at first nearly black, later becoming

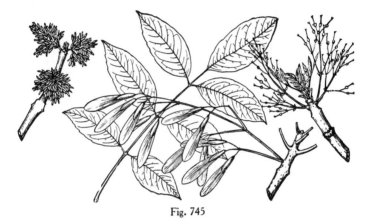

Fig. 745

reddish purple; ovary contracted into a long slender style divided into 2 spreading dark purple stigmatic lobes. **Fruit** rarely deeply tinged with purple (f. *iodocarpa* Fern.), 1′–2½′ long and usually about ¼′ wide, or sometimes not more than ½′ long (var. *microcarpa* A. Gray), in crowded clusters 6′–8′ in length, lanceolate or oblanceolate, surrounded at base by the persistent calyx, the wing pointed or emarginate at apex and terminal or slightly decurrent on the terete body.

A tree. sometimes 120° high, with a tall massive trunk 5°–6° in diameter, stout upright or spreading branches forming in the forest a narrow crown, or with sufficient space a round-topped or pyramidal head, and thick terete branchlets dark green or brown tinged with red and covered with scattered pale caducous hairs when they first appear, soon becoming light orange color or ashy gray and marked by pale lenticels, becoming in their first winter gray or light brown, lustrous, often covered with a glaucous bloom and roughened by the large pale semiorbicular leaf-scars displaying near the margins a line of conspicuous fibro-vascular bundle-scars. **Winter-buds: terminal** broad-ovoid, obtuse, with 4 pairs of scales, those of the outer pair ovate, acute, apiculate, conspicuously keeled on the back, nearly black, slightly puberulous, about one half the length of the scales of the second pair rather shorter than those of the third pair, lengthening with the young shoots, and at maturity oblong-ovate, narrowed and rounded at apex, keeled, ½′ long, and rusty-pubescent, the scales of the inner pair becoming ⅔′ long, ovate, pointed, keeled, sometimes slightly pinnatifid, green tinged with brown toward the apex, covered with pellucid dots and very lustrous. **Bark** of the trunk 1'–3' thick, dark brown or gray tinged with red, and deeply divided by narrow fissures into broad flattened ridges separating on the surface into thin appressed scales. **Wood** heavy, hard, strong, close-grained, tough, and brown, with thick lighter colored sapwood; used in large quantities in the manufacture of agricultural implements, for the handles of tools, in carriage-building, for oars and furniture, and in the interior finish of buildings; the most valuable of the American species as a timber-tree.

Distribution. Common in rich rather moist soil on low hills, and in the neighborhood of streams; Nova Scotia, New Brunswick, southern Quebec and Ontario and the southern peninsula of Michigan, and westward and southward to eastern Minnesota, central Iowa, southeastern Nebraska, Missouri and Arkansas, eastern Kansas, and northern Oklahoma to the valley of the Salt Fork of the Arkansas River in Woods County (near Alva, *G. W. Stevens*), and to Florida to Taylor County and the valley of the lower Apalachicola River, and through the Gulf states to the valley of the Trinity River, Texas; of its largest size on the bottom-lands of the basin of the lower Ohio River; southward and west of the Mississippi River less common and of smaller size; on the Appalachian Mountains up to altitudes of 3800°; the var. *crassifolia* at Mt. Victory, Harding County, Ohio, Campbell, Dunklin County, Missouri, and near Texarkana, Bowie County, Texas.

Often planted in the eastern states as a shade and ornamental tree, and occasionally in western and northern Europe.

A form with the wing of the fruit extending nearly to the middle of the body distinguished as *Fraxinus Smallii* Britt. has the appearance of a hybrid between *F. americana* and *F. pennsylvanica* var. *lanceolata;* individuals of this form have been found near McGuire's Mill, on the Yellow River, Guinnett County, Georgia; near Rochester, Monroe County, New York; and near Lake Wingra, Dane County, Wisconsin.

9. Fraxinus texensis Sarg. Mountain Ash.

Leaves 5'–8' long, with a long slender terete petiole, and 5 or occasionally 7 usually long-stalked ovate broad-oval or obovate leaflets, rounded or acute, or often abruptly pointed at apex, cuneate, rounded or slightly cordate at base, and coarsely crenulate-serrate, chiefly above the middle, light green slightly tinged with red and pilose with occa-

Fig. 746

sional pale caducous hairs when they unfold, and at maturity thick and firm, glabrous, dark green on the upper surface, pale on the lower surface, 1'–3' long and ¾'–2' wide, and occasionally furnished below with tufts of long white hairs at the base of the broad midrib, and in the axils of the numerous conspicuous veins forked near the margins and connected by coarse reticulate veinlets; petiolules slender, $\frac{1}{4}'-\frac{1}{2}'$ and on the terminal leaflet up to 1' in length. **Flowers** diœcious, appearing in March as the leaves begin to unfold, in compact glabrous panicles from the axils of leaves of the previous year, and covered in the bud by ovate rounded orange-colored scales; staminate flower composed of a minute or nearly obsolete 4-lobed calyx and 2 stamens, with short filaments and linear-oblong light purple apiculate anthers; calyx of the female flower deep cup-shaped, and divided to the base into 4 acute lobes; ovary gradually narrowed into a long slender style. **Fruit** in short compact clusters, spatulate to oblong, surrounded at base by the persistent calyx, $\frac{1}{2}'-1'$ long and $\frac{1}{8}'-\frac{1}{4}'$ wide, the wing rounded or occasionally emarginate at apex, and terminal on the short terete many-rayed body; very rarely with 3 or 4 wings extending to the base of the fruit.

A tree, rarely 50° high, with a short trunk occasionally 2°-3° in diameter, thick spreading often contorted branches, and stout terete branchlets dark green tinged with red and slightly puberulous when they first appear, becoming light yellow-brown or light orange color during the summer, and in their first winter light brown marked by remote oblong pale lenticels and by large elevated lunate leaf-scars displaying a row of conspicuous fibrovascular bundle-scars, and dark or reddish brown in their second or third season; usually much smaller. **Winter-buds:** terminal acute, with 3 pairs of scales, those of the first pair broad-ovate, rounded at the apex, dark orange color, pilose toward the base, and rather shorter than the ovate rounded scales of the second pair coated with rufous tomentum and becoming $\frac{1}{2}'$ long or about one half the length of the linear strap-shaped scales of the inner pair truncate or emarginate at the apex and orange color. **Bark** of the trunk $\frac{1}{2}'-\frac{3}{4}'$ thick, dark gray and deeply divided by narrow fissures into broad scaly ridges. **Wood** heavy, hard, strong, light brown, with thin lighter colored sapwood; valued as fuel and occasionally used for flooring.

Distribution. Texas, high dry limestone bluffs and ridges, in the neighborhood of Dallas, Dallas County, and Fort Worth, Tarrant County, to the valley of the Colorado River near Austin, Travis County, and over the Edwards Plateau to Bandera, Kerr, Edwards and Palo Pinto Counties.

Hardy in the Arnold Arboretum.

10. Fraxinus biltmoreana Beadl.

Leaves 10'-12' long, with a stout pubescent or puberulous petiole, and 7-9 oblong-ovate to ovate-lanceolate or oval often falcate entire or obscurely toothed leaflets acuminate at apex, rounded or cuneate and often inequilateral at base, yellow-bronze color and nearly glabrous above, coated beneath, particularly on the midrib and veins, with long white hairs when they unfold, and at maturity 3'-6' long, $1\frac{1}{4}'-2'$ wide, thick and firm in texture, dark green and slightly lustrous on the upper surface, pale or glaucous and puberulous on the lower surface and villose along the slender yellow midrib, and primary veins arcuate near the slightly thickened and incurved margins; petiolules pubescent, $\frac{1}{4}'-\frac{1}{2}'$ or that of the terminal leaflet up to 2' in length. **Flowers** diœcious, appearing with the leaves about the 1st of May, in a rather compact pubescent panicle, with scarious caducous bracts and bractlets; staminate flower with a minute cup-shaped very obscurely dentate calyx and nearly sessile oblong acute anthers; calyx of the pistillate flower much larger and deeply lobed; ovary oblong, gradually narrowed into the slender style divided at apex into 2 short stigmatic lobes. **Fruit** linear-oblong, in elongated glabrous or puberulous clusters, $1\frac{1}{2}'-1\frac{3}{4}'$ long and about $\frac{1}{4}'$ wide, the wing terminal, only slightly narrowed at the ends, emarginate at apex, and two and a half to three times longer than the short ellipsoid terete manynerved body.

A tree, 40°-50° high, with a trunk 12'-18' in diameter, stout ascending or spreading branches forming an open symmetrical head, and stout light or dark gray branchlets softpubescent usually during two seasons, much roughened during their first winter and often for two or three years by the large elevated mostly obcordate or sometimes orbicular leafscars displaying a marginal line of fibro-vascular bundle-scars. **Winter-buds:** terminal ovoid, usually broader than long, and covered with bright brown scales, those of the outer pair keeled on the back and apiculate at apex, the others rounded, accrescent, and slightly villose. **Bark** of the trunk rough, dark gray, and slightly furrowed.

Distribution. Banks of streams and on low river benches; western New Jersey (Bordentown, Burlington County); eastern Pennsylvania (Bucks County); near Arlington, Alex-

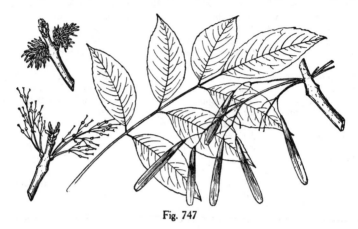

Fig. 747

andria County, Great Falls, Fairfax County, Woodbridge, Prince William County, and Clifton Forge, Alleghany County, Virginia; near Easton, Monongalia County, West Virginia, and along the Appalachian Mountains up to altitudes of 2200° to northern Georgia; in northern Alabama (St. Bernard, Cullman County), and westward to eastern Kentucky, central Tennessee and through Ohio northward to Erie County; northern Indiana and Illinois (Richland County), to southeastern Missouri (Campbell, Dunklin County).

11. Fraxinus profunda Bush. Pumpkin Ash.

Leaves 9′–18′ long, with a stout tomentose petiole, and usually 7 but occasionally 9 lanceolate or elliptic entire or slightly serrate leaflets acuminate or abruptly long-pointed at apex, rounded, cuneate and often unsymmetric at base, coated below when they unfold with hoary tomentum, and pilose on the upper surface with short pale hairs, particularly on the midrib and veins, and at maturity thick and firm in texture, dark yellow-green and nearly glabrous on the upper surface, soft-pubescent on the lower surface, 5′–10′ long and $1\frac{1}{2}′$–5′ wide, with a stout yellow midrib deeply impressed and puberulous above and numerous slender primary veins; petiolules stout, tomentose early in the season, usually becoming glabrous or nearly glabrous, $\frac{1}{4}′$–$\frac{1}{2}′$ or that of the terminal leaflet up to 2′ in length. **Flowers** diœcious, in elongated much-branched pubescent panicles, with oblong or oblong-obovate scarious bracts and bractlets; staminate flower with a minute campanulate obscurely 4-toothed calyx, and 2 or 3 stamens, with comparatively long slender filaments and oblong apiculate anthers; pistillate flower with a large deeply lobed calyx accrescent and persistent under the fruit, and an ovary gradually contracted into a slender style. **Fruit** in long drooping many-fruited pubescent clusters, oblong, 2′–3′ in length and often $\frac{1}{2}′$ wide, the wing sometimes falcate, rounded, apiculate, or emarginate at apex, and decurrent to below the middle or nearly to the base of the thick terete many-rayed body.

A tree, occasionally 120° high, with a slender trunk 3° in diameter above the much enlarged and buttressed base, small spreading branches forming a narrow rather open head, and stout branchlets marked by large pale lenticels, coated at first with hoary tomentum, tomentose and pubescent during their first winter and light gray and pilose or glabrous the following year, and marked by the oblong slightly raised obconic leaf-scars nearly surrounding the lateral buds; usually much smaller. **Winter-buds** terminal, broad-ovate,

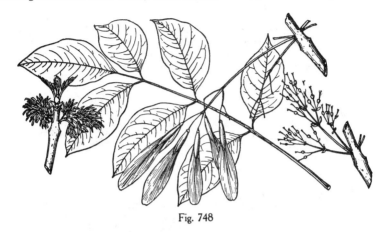

Fig. 748

obtuse, light reddish brown, and covered with close pale pubescence. **Bark** of the trunk $\frac{1}{2}'-\frac{3}{4}'$ thick, light gray and divided by shallow fissures into broad flat or rounded ridges broken on the surface into thin closely appressed scales.

Distribution. Deep river swamps often inundated during several months of the year; western New York (*H. F. Sartwell*); southern Indiana and Illinois; western Kentucky (Caldwell and McCracken Counties) and Tennessee (Henderson County); southeastern Missouri, eastern Arkansas (Moark and Corning, Clay County, and Varner, Lincoln County); near New Orleans, Louisiana, eastern Mississippi (near Columbus, Lowndes County), and in the valley of the lower Apalachicola River, western Florida.

Occasionally cultivated; hardy in the Arnold Arboretum.

12. Fraxinus pennsylvanica Marsh. Red Ash.

Leaves 10'-12' long, with a stout slightly grooved pubescent petiole, and 7-9 oblong-lanceolate, ovate-elliptic or slightly obovate leaflets gradually narrowed at apex into a long slender point, unequally cuneate at base, and obscurely serrate, or often entire below the middle, when they unfold coated below and on the petiole with hoary tomentum, and lustrous and puberulous on the upper surface, and at maturity thin and firm, 4'-6' long, $1'-1\frac{1}{2}'$ wide, light yellow-green above and pale and covered below with silky pubescence, with a conspicuous midrib and branching veins; in the autumn turning yellow or rusty brown before falling; petiolules thick, grooved, pubescent, $\frac{1}{8}'-\frac{1}{4}'$ or that of the terminal leaflet up to 1' in length. **Flowers** diœcious, appearing late in spring as the leaves begin to unfold, in a rather compact tomentose panicle, covered in the bud with ovate rusty-tomentose scales; staminate flower with a minute obscurely toothed cup-shaped calyx, and 2 stamens, with short slender filaments and linear-oblong light green anthers tinged with purple; calyx of the pistillate flower cup-shaped, deeply divided, as long as the ovary gradually narrowed into an elongated style divided at apex into 2 green stigmatic lobes. **Fruit** in an open glabrous or pubescent panicle, lanceolate to slightly oblanceolate or oblong-obovate or elliptic, $1'-2\frac{1}{2}'$ long, $\frac{1}{4}'-\frac{1}{3}'$ wide, surrounded at base by the persistent calyx, the thin wing narrowed, rounded and occasionally emarginate or acute or acuminate and often apiculate at apex, decurrent to below the middle or nearly to the gradually tapering base of the slender terete many-rayed body.

A tree, 40°-60° high, with a trunk rarely exceeding 18'-20' in diameter, stout upright branches forming a compact irregularly shaped head, and slender terete branchlets more or less coated when they first appear with pale tomentum sometimes persistent until their second or third year or often disappearing during the first summer, ultimately becoming ashy gray or light brown tinged with red, frequently covered with a glaucous bloom and marked by pale lenticels, and in their first winter by the semicircular leaf-scars displaying a short row of large fibro-vascular bundle-scars. **Winter-buds:** terminal, about $\frac{1}{8}'$ long, with 3 pairs of scales coated with rufous tomentum, those of the outer pair acute, rounded on the back, truncate at apex, and rather shorter than those of the other pairs $1'-1\frac{1}{2}'$ long

Fig. 749

at maturity and sometimes pinnately cut toward the apex. **Bark** of the trunk $\frac{1}{2}'-\frac{2}{3}'$ thick, brown tinged with red, and slightly furrowed, the surface of the ridges separating into thin appressed scales. **Wood** heavy, hard, rather strong, brittle, coarse-grained, light brown, with thick lighter brown sapwood streaked with yellow; sometimes confounded commercially with the more valuable wood of the White Ash. Variable in the length of the petiolules and in the shape of the fruit and the width of its wing; a form with short-stalked or nearly sessile leaflets, found chiefly in Nebraska has been described as *F. campestris* Britt. and a form with the wing of the spatulate fruit sometimes $\frac{1}{4}'$ wide as *F. Michauxii* Britt.

Distribution. Low rich moist soil near the banks of streams and lakes; Nova Scotia to Manitoba, and southward to central Georgia, northern Alabama (St. Bernard, Cullman County, and Attalla, Etowah County), northeastern Mississippi (Tishomingo County), southern Indiana and Illinois, northern Missouri, eastern Kansas and southwestern Oklahoma (Cache, Comanche County); usually confined in the Carolinas to the Piedmont region and foothills of the high mountains. Passing into

Fraxinus pennsylvanica var. lanceolata Sarg.   Green Ash.

Leaves with rather narrower and shorter and usually more sharply serrate leaflets lustrous and bright green on both surfaces, and glabrous or pubescent along the midrib below.

A round-topped tree, rarely more than 60° high, or with a trunk more than 2° in diameter, slender spreading branches, ashy gray terete glabrous branchlets marked by pale lenticels, and rusty-pubescent bud-scales.

Distribution. Banks of streams; valley of the Penobscot River (Orono, Penobscot County), Maine, to northern Vermont and the valley of the St. Lawrence River, near Montreal, Province of Quebec, and to the valley of the Saskatchewan (Saskatoon, Saskatchewan), and in the United States westward to North Dakota, eastern Wyoming to the base of the Bighorn Mountains, and on the mountains of northern Montana, and southward to western Florida to the valley of the lower Apalachicola River, Dallas County, Alabama, central Mississippi, Louisiana, Oklahoma to Comanche County, and Texas to the valley of the Guadalupe River; most abundant in the basin of the Mississippi River;

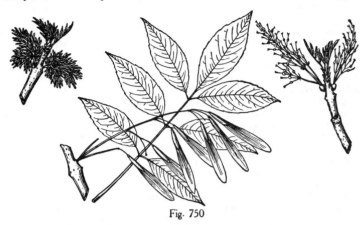

Fig. 750

attaining its largest size on the rich bottom-lands of eastern Texas and here often 60°–70° high, with a trunk 2°–3° in diameter; on the southern Appalachian Mountains ascending to altitudes of 2000°–2500°. As it usually grows in the east with its bright green glabrous leaves and glabrous branchlets the Green Ash appears distinct from the Red Ash, but trees occur over the area which it inhabits, but more often westward, with slightly pubescent leaves and branchlets which may be referred as well to one tree as to the other and make it impossible to distinguish satisfactorily as species the Green and Red Ash.

Often planted as a shade and ornamental tree in the middle western and occasionally in the eastern states, but less valuable than the White Ash.

13. Fraxinus Berlandieriana DC.

Leaves 3′–7′ long, with a slender petiole, and 3–5 lanceolate, elliptic or obovate leaflets, acuminate or abruptly acuminate or acute at apex, cuneate or rarely rounded at base,

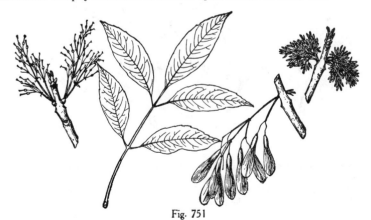

Fig. 751

mostly entire or remotely serrate, thin, dark green and glabrous on the upper surface, rather paler and glabrous or furnished with small axillary tufts of white hairs on the lower surface, 3′–4′ long and ½′–1½′ wide; petiolules slender, 1¼′–1½′ or that of the terminal leaflet up to 1½′ in length.   Flowers diœcious, in a short glabrous panicle inclosed in the bud by broad-ovate rounded chestnut-brown pubescent scales; staminate flower with a minute obscurely lobed calyx and 2 stamens, with short filaments and linear-oblong apiculate anthers; calyx of the pistillate flower cup-shaped, deeply divided, and as long as the ovary gradually narrowed into the slender style.   Fruit ripening in May, oblong-obovate to spatulate, acute or acuminate at apex, 1′–1½′ long and ¼′ wide, the wing decurrent nearly to the base of the compressed many-rayed clavate body gradually narrowed into a long slender base surrounded by the enlarged deeply lobed calyx.

A tree, rarely more than 30° high, or with a trunk more than a foot in diameter, and terete slender branchlets light green when they first appear, becoming in their first winter light brown tinged with red or ashy gray, and marked by occasional lenticels and by the small elevated nearly circular leaf-scars displaying a short row of large fibro-vascular bundle-scars.   Winter-buds: terminal acute, with dark brown puberulous scales.   Bark of the trunk dark gray tinged with red, 1′–1½′ thick, and divided by shallow interrupted fissures into narrow ridges.   Wood light, soft, close-grained, light brown, with thick lighter colored sapwood.

Distribution.   Texas, banks of streams and mountain cañons, valley of the Colorado River (Bastrop and Travis Counties), and those of the San Antonio and Nueces Rivers to the lower Rio Grande, and over the Edwards Plateau to Palo Pinto County; in northeastern Mexico.

14. Fraxinus velutina Torr.

Leaves 4′–5′ long, with a broad densely villose petiole grooved like the slender rachis on the upper side, and 3–5 elliptic to ovate or slightly obovate leaflets acute at apex, narrowed and rounded or cuneate at base, finely crenulate-serrate above the middle, pubescent above

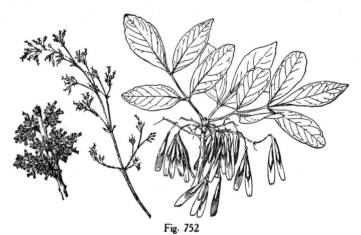

Fig. 752

and tomentose below when they unfold, and at maturity thick, pale green, glabrous on the upper surface, tomentose on the lower surface, 1′–1½′ long and ¾′–1′ wide, with a prominent midrib and primary veins, and conspicuous reticulate veinlets; petiolules of the lateral leaflets ⅛′ or less or that of the terminal leaflet up to ½′ in length.   Flowers diœcious, appearing in March and April with the unfolding of the leaves, on long slender pedicels. in elongated pubescent panicles, covered in the bud by broad-ovate tomentose scales rounded at apex; calyx cup-shaped, densely pubescent; stamens, with short slender filaments and oblong apiculate anthers; ovary nearly inclosed in the calyx, shorter than the nearly sessile lobes of the stigma.   **Fruit** ripening in September, on slender villose pedicels, in large many-fruited clusters, oblong-obovate to elliptic, surrounded at base by the enlarged deeply divided calyx, rarely more than $\frac{3}{4}'$ long and $\frac{1}{6}'$ wide, the wing terminal, rounded and often emarginate or acute at apex, shorter than the terete many-rayed clavate body attenuate at base and $\frac{5}{12}'-\frac{1}{2}'$ in length.

A slender tree, $25°-30°$, rarely $40°-50°$ high, with a trunk $12'-18'$ in diameter, stout often spreading branches forming a round-topped head, and slender terete branchlets coated during their first season with hoary tomentum, and ashy gray, glabrous and marked by large obcordate dark leaf-scars in their second year.   **Winter-buds:** terminal acute, $\frac{1}{8}'$ long, with 3 pairs of broad-ovate pointed tomentose scales, those of the inner pair strap-shaped and $\frac{1}{2}'$ long when fully grown.   **Bark** of the trunk $\frac{1}{3}'-\frac{1}{2}'$ thick, gray slightly tinged with red, and deeply divided into broad flat broken ridges separating on the surface into small thin scales.   **Wood** heavy, rather soft, not strong, close-grained, light brown, with thick lighter colored sapwood; used locally for axe-handles and in the manufacture of wagons.

Distribution.   Mountain cañons up to altitudes of 6000°, central and southern Arizona and southern New Mexico.   Passing into the following varieties: var. *coriacea* Rehd. (*Fraxinus coriacea* S. Wats.) differing in its thicker more coriaceous often more coarsely serrate leaflets and in the less densely pubescent or glabrescent branchlets; southern Utah (St. George, Washington County) to southeastern California; var. *glabra* Rehd. with glabrous 3-7-foliolate leaves and glabrous branchlets; common with the species; occasionally cultivated in the cities of Arizona; more distinct is

Fraxinus velutina var. Toumeyi Rehd.

Fraxinus Toumeyi Britt.

Leaves $3\frac{1}{2}'-6'$ long, with a villose-pubescent petiole, and 5-7 lanceolate to elliptic or rarely obovate acuminate and long-pointed or acute leaflets, finely serrate above the middle, glabrous on the upper surface, covered on the lower surface with close fine pubescence,

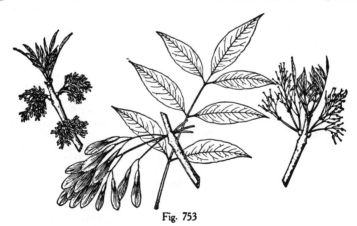

Fig. 753

$1\frac{1}{2}'-3'$ long and $\frac{1}{3}'-1'$ wide; petiolules slender, pubescent, $\frac{1}{8}'-\frac{1}{2}'$ or that of the terminal leaflet up to $1'$ in length; occasionally on vigorous shoots reduced to a single leaflet.   **Flowers** as in the species.   **Fruit** narrow-oblong, $1'$ long and often not more than $\frac{1}{12}'$ wide, or spatulate with the wing longer or shorter than the body, and sometimes only about $\frac{3}{4}'$ long and $\frac{1}{16}'$ wide, with the wing longer or not more than half the length of the body.

A tree, usually 20°–30° high, with a trunk 6'–8' in diameter, and ashy gray branchlets pale pubescent when they first appear, becoming glabrous or puberulous during their second season.

Distribution. Mountain cañons at altitudes of 5000°–6000°; in Arizona more common than *F. velutina;* less abundant in southern New Mexico; in Sonora.

Often used to shade the streets in the towns of southern Arizona.

15. Fraxinus oregona Nutt.

Leaves 5'–14' long, with a stout grooved and angled pubescent, tomentose or glabrous petiole, and usually 5–7, rarely 3, or on young trees occasionally 9, ovate to elliptic or rarely oval or obovate leaflets usually contracted at apex into a short broad point, gradually nar-

Fig. 754

rowed at base, and entire or remotely and obscurely serrate, usually coated below and on the petioles with thick pale tomentum when they unfold and pubescent above, or nearly glabrous or pilose with a few scattered hairs, and at maturity light green on the upper surface, paler and usually tomentose, puberulous or rarely glabrous (var. *glabra* Rehd.), on the lower surface, 3'–7' long and 1'–1$\frac{1}{2}'$ wide, with a broad pale midrib, conspicuous veins arcuate near the margins, and reticulate veinlets, the lateral usually sessile, rarely on petiolules up to $\frac{1}{2}'$, or that of the terminal leaflet up to 1' in length; turning yellow or russet brown in the autumn before falling.   **Flowers** diœcious, appearing in April or May when the leaves begin to unfold, in compact glabrous panicles covered in the bud by broad-ovate scales coated with rufous pubescence; staminate flower composed of a minute calyx, short filaments, and short-oblong apiculate anthers; calyx of the pistillate flower lacini-ately cut and shorter than the ovary narrowed into a stout style divided into long conspic-uous stigmatic lobes.   **Fruit** in ample crowded clusters, oblong, obovate to oblanceolate or elliptic, rounded and often emarginate or acute at apex, 1'–2' long and $\frac{1}{4}'$–$\frac{1}{3}'$ wide, the wing decurrent to the middle or nearly to the attenuate base of the clavate or ellipsoid slightly compressed many-rayed body.

A tree, frequently 70°–80° high, with a long trunk occasionally 4° in diameter, stout branches forming a narrow upright head or a broad shapely crown, and thick terete branch-lets more or less densely coated with pale or rarely rufous silky pilose tomentum per-sistent during their second year or occasionally deciduous during their first summer, be-coming light red-brown or orange color, glabrous or puberulous, often covered with a slight glaucous bloom, marked by small remote pale lenticels, and during their first and second winters by the large elevated semiorbicular leaf-scars displaying a short row of conspicuous fibro-vascular bundle-scars, rarely always glabrous (var. *glabra* Rehd.). **Winter-buds:** terminal acute, $\frac{1}{8}$–$\frac{1}{4}'$ long, with 4 pairs of scales covered with pale hairs or with rusty pubescence, those of the inner rows often foliaceous at maturity. **Bark** of the trunk 1'–1½' thick, dark gray, or brown slightly tinged with red, and deeply divided by interrupted fissures into broad flat ridges separating on the surface into thin scales. **Wood** light, hard, brittle, coarse-grained, brown, with thick lighter colored sapwood; largely used in the manufacture of furniture, for the frames of carriages and wagons, in cooperage, the interior finish of houses, and for fuel.

Distribution. Usually in rich moist soil in the neighborhood of streams; coast region of southern British Columbia, southward through western Washington and Oregon and the California coast region to the Bay of San Francisco and the Santa Cruz Mountains, and along the western foothills of the Sierra Nevada to those of the mountains of San Bernardino and San Diego Counties, California; the var. *glabra* in Los Angeles and San Bernardino Counties, and east of the Sierra Nevada in Inyo County (Ash Creek, near Owens Lake), and occasionally northward in California; most abundant and of its largest size on the bottom-lands of the rivers of southwestern Oregon; one of the most valuable of the deciduous-leaved timber-trees of Pacific North America.

Occasionally cultivated; hardy in the Arnold Arboretum.

16. Fraxinus quadrangulata Michx. Blue Ash.

Leaves 8'–12' long, with a slender petiole glabrous, or puberulous toward the base, and 5–11 oblong-ovate to lanceolate long-pointed coarsely serrate leaflets unequally rounded or cuneate at base, and coated when they unfold on the lower surface with thick brown to-

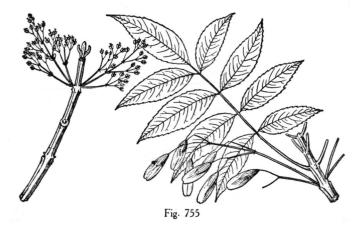

Fig. 755

mentum, and at maturity thick and firm, yellow-green and glabrous above, pale and glabrous or sometimes furnished with tufts of pale hairs along the base of the conspicuous midrib below, 3'–5' long and 1'–2' wide, with short stout petiolules and 8–12 pairs of veins arcuate near the margins; turning pale yellow in the autumn before falling. **Flowers** perfect, appearing as the terminal buds begin to expand, in loose-branched panicles from small obtuse buds with scales keeled on the back, apiculate at apex, and covered with thick brown tomentum; calyx reduced to an obscure ring; corolla 0; stamens 2, with nearly sessile broad connectives and dark purple oblong obtuse anther-cells; ovary oblong-ovoid, gradually narrowed into a short style divided at apex into 2 light purple stigmatic lobes generally maturing and withering before the anthers open. **Fruit** oblong to oblong-cuneate, 1'–2' long and $\frac{1}{3}'-\frac{1}{2}'$ wide, the wing rounded and often emarginate or acute at apex, surrounding the flat body faintly many-rayed on both surfaces.

A tree, usually 60°–70° or occasionally 120° high, with a trunk 2°–3° in diameter, small spreading branches forming a slender head, and stout 4-angled branchlets more or less 4-winged between the nodes, dark orange color and covered with short rufous pubescence when they first appear, becoming gray tinged with red in their second year and marked by scattered pale lenticels and by the large elevated obcordate leaf-scars displaying a lunate row of fibro-vascular bundle-scars, and in their third year light brown or ashy gray and then gradually becoming terete.   **Winter-buds:** terminal about $\frac{1}{4}'$ long, with 3 pairs of scales, those of the outer row thick, rounded on the back, usually obscurely pinnate toward the apex, dark reddish brown, slightly puberulous or often hoary-tomentose, partly covering the bud, those of the inner rows strap-shaped, coated with light brown tomentum, often pinnate, becoming $1'-1\frac{1}{2}'$ long.   **Bark** of the trunk $\frac{1}{2}'-\frac{2}{3}'$ thick, irregularly divided into large plate-like scales, the light gray surface slightly tinged with red separating into thin minute scales.   **Wood** heavy, hard, close-grained, rather brittle, light yellow streaked with brown, with thick lighter colored sapwood of 80–90 layers of annual growth; largely used for flooring and in carriage-building, and not often distinguished commercially from that of other species of the northern and middle states.   A blue dye is obtained by macerating the inner bark in water.

Distribution.   Rich limestone hills, occasionally descending into the bottom-lands of fertile valleys; southwestern Ontario through southern Michigan to southwestern Iowa and southward through western Ohio and southeastern Indiana to eastern and central Kentucky (near Clarksville, Montgomery County), eastern Tennessee and northern Alabama (near Huntsville, Madison County), and through Missouri to southeastern Kansas, southwestern Arkansas and northeastern Oklahoma (near Pawhuska, Osage County); nowhere very abundant; of its largest size in the basin of the lower Wabash River, Illinois, and on the western slopes of the Big Smoky Mountains, Tennessee.

Occasionally cultivated as an ornament of parks and gardens in the eastern United States.

17. Fraxinus nigra Marsh.   Black Ash.   Brown Ash.

Leaves 12'–16' long, with a stout pale petiole, and 7–11 oblong or oblong-lanceolate long-pointed leaflets, unequally cuneate or sometimes rounded at base, serrate with small incurved apiculate teeth, the lateral sessile, the terminal on a petiolule up to 1' in length, covered especially below when they unfold with rufous hairs, and at maturity thin and firm,

Fig 756

dark green above, paler below, glabrous with the exception of occasional tufts of rufous hairs along the under side of the broad pale midrib, 4'–5' long and 1'–2' wide, with many conspicuous primary veins arcuate near the margins and obscurely reticulate veinlets; turning rusty brown and falling early in the autumn. **Flowers** polygamous, without a perianth, appearing before the leaves in a compact or ultimately elongated panicle 4'–5' long, and covered in the bud by broad-ovate dark brown or nearly black scales rounded at apex; staminate flowers on separate trees or mixed with perfect flowers, and consisting of 2 large deeply pitted oblong dark purple apiculate anthers attached on the back to short broad filaments; pistillate flower consisting of a long slender style deeply divided into 2 broad purple stigmas and often accompanied by 1 or 2 perfect or globose rudimentary pink anthers sessile or borne on long or short filaments. **Fruit** in open panicles 8'–10' in length, oblong to slightly oblong-obovate, 1'–1½' long and ¼' wide, with a thin wing, surrounding the short flat faintly nerved body, rounded and emarginate at apex and narrowed and rounded or cuneate at base.

A tree, occasionally 80°–90° high, with a tall trunk rarely exceeding 20' in diameter, slender mostly upright branches forming a narrow head, and stout terete branchlets dark green and slightly puberulous when they first appear, soon becoming ashy gray or orange color and marked by large pale lenticels, growing darker during their first winter and then roughened by the large suborbicular leaf-scars displaying a semicircular row of conspicuous fibro-vascular bundle-scars; usually much smaller. **Winter-buds**: terminal broad-ovate, acute, rather less than ¼' long, with 3 pairs of scales, those of the outer pair thick and rounded on the back at base, gradually narrowed and acute at apex, dark brown, slightly puberulous, falling as the bud begins to enlarge in the spring, and shorter than the scales of the inner rows coated on the outer surface with rufous pubescence, those of the second pair becoming strap-shaped, 1' long, ¼' wide, and about half as long as the pinnate usually foliaceous inner scales. **Bark** of the trunk gray slightly tinged with red, ⅓'–½' thick, and divided into large irregular plates separating into thin papery scales. **Wood** heavy, rather soft, not strong, tough, coarse-grained, durable, easily separable into thin layers, dark brown, with thin light brown often nearly white sapwood; largely used for the interior finish of houses and in cabinet-making, and for fences, barrel hoops, and in the manufacture of baskets.

Distribution. Deep cold swamps and the low banks of streams and lakes; southern Newfoundland and the northern shores of the Gulf of St. Lawrence to Lake Winnipeg, and southward to New Castle County, Delaware, the mountains of West Virginia, southwestern Indiana (Knox County; now probably exterminated by drainage), and central Iowa.

2. FORESTIERA Poir. Swamp Privet.

Adelia Michx.

Trees or shrubs, with thin close bark, slender branchlets, and small scaly buds. Leaves simple, entire or serrulate, petiolate, deciduous or persistent. Flowers diœcious or polygamous, minute, on slender ebracteolate pedicels, in fascicles or panicles, their bracts caducous, from buds in the axils of leaves of the previous year and covered with numerous scales; calyx reduced to a narrow ring or cup-shaped, 5 or 6-lobed; corolla 0; stamens hypogynous, filaments 2–4, anthers ovoid, opening by lateral slits; ovary 2-celled, gradually narrowed into a slender style terminating in an abruptly enlarged 2-lobed stigma; ovules 2 in each cell, suspended from its apex; raphe dorsal. Fruit 1 or very rarely 2-celled, drupaceous, oblong or subglobose, with thin flesh and a thin-walled stone; seed 1 in each cell, pendulous, testa membranaceous; albumen fleshy; cotyledons plane, nearly filling the cavity of the stone.

Forestiera with 14 species is distributed from the southern United States and Mexico through Central America to Paraguay, and through the West Indies to Brazil.

The generic name is in memory of the French physician and botanist Charles Leforestière.

1. Forestiera acuminata Poir.

Leaves elliptic, acuminate and long-pointed at apex, gradually narrowed and cuneate at base, serrate above the middle with small remote incurved teeth, glabrous with the exception of occasional hairs on the upper side of the slender midrib, yellow-green on the upper surface, paler on the lower surface, $2\frac{1}{2}'-4\frac{1}{2}'$ long and $1'-1\frac{1}{2}'$ wide, with usually 5 or 6 pairs of slender primary veins and slightly thickened and incurved margins, deciduous; petioles slender, often slightly winged above the middle, $\frac{1}{4}'-\frac{1}{2}'$ in length.   **Flowers** appearing in April and May before the leaves from ovoid pointed buds $\frac{1}{8}'$ long, with thickened pale chestnut-brown scales; calyx reduced to a narrow slightly lobed ring; corolla 0; staminate in many-flowered fascicles, on short pedicels from the axils of broad-obovate thin yellow apiculate conspicuous bracts; stamens 4, on long slender filaments; anthers bright yellow; ovary reduced to a minute ovoid body; pistillate flowers on slender pedicels $\frac{1}{8}'$ long, in glabrous pedunculate several-flowered panicles $\frac{3}{4}'-1\frac{1}{4}'$ long, their bracts caducous; stamens with shorter filaments and abortive or rarely fertile anthers, or usually 0; ovary oblong-ovoid, slightly unsymmetric, gradually narrowed into the long slender style enlarged into the thickened imperfectly 2-lobed terminal stigma.   **Fruit** falling as soon as ripe in June and July, oblong-ovoid, gradually narrowed, acute and tipped with the remnants of the style at apex, gradually narrowed and rounded at base, slightly compressed and unsymmetric, dark blue-purple, $1'-1\frac{1}{4}'$ long, about $\frac{1}{4}'$ thick, with thin dry flesh, and a striate stone rounded at base, straight on one side and rounded on the other, its wall covered with thin vertical scales spongy in appearance, and conspicuously longitudinally ridged on the inner surface the ridges terminating in long slender tips forming the acuminate apex of the stone; **seeds** ellipsoid, slightly compressed, striate, light brown, about $\frac{1}{3}'$ in length.

Fig. 757

A tree, rarely 50° high, with a short trunk $8'-10'$ in diameter, small spreading branches, and slender light brown branchlets becoming darker in their second year, and marked by numerous lenticels and by the small elevated nearly orbicular leaf-scars. **Winter-buds:** terminal ovoid, pointed, about $\frac{1}{16}'$ long, with numerous scales increasing in size from the outer to the inner ranks; usually much smaller, and generally a shrub 10°–15° high and broad.   **Bark** close, slightly ridged, dark brown.

Distribution.   Borders of streams and swamps in low moist soil; valley of the lower Wabash River, southwestern Indiana, southern Illinois northward along the Mississippi River to Pike County, and to central Tennessee, and from southern Missouri through Arkansas to eastern Oklahoma (near Muskogee, Muskogee County) and eastern Texas to the valley of the lower Colorado River inland to Colorado County (shores of Eagle Lake), and through Louisiana, central and southern Mississippi and Alabama to western Florida (Branford, Suwanee County) and on the Savannah River, near Augusta, Richmond County, Georgia; most abundant in Missouri, Arkansas and Texas; comparatively rare east of the Mississippi River, but probably of its largest size in eastern Louisiana.

Occasionally cultivated; hardy in the Arnold Arboretum.

3. CHIONANTHUS L.

Trees or shrubs, with stout terete or slightly angled branchlets, thick pith, and buds with numerous opposite scales. Leaves simple, conduplicate in the bud, deciduous. Flowers diœcious or rarely polygamous, on elongated ebracteolate pedicels, in 3-flowered clusters terminal on the slender opposite branches, of ample loose panicles, with foliaceous persistent bracts, from separate buds in the axils of the upper leaves of the previous year; calyx minute, deeply 4-parted, the divisions imbricated in the bud, persistent under the fruit; corolla white, deeply divided into 4 or rarely 5 or 6 elongated linear lobes conduplicate-valvate in the bud, united at base into a short tube, or rarely separate; stamens 2, inserted on the base of the corolla opposite the axis of the flower, or rarely 4 in the staminate flower, included; filaments terete, short; anthers ovoid, attached on the back below the middle, apiculate by the elongation of the connective, 2-celled, the cells opening by longitudinal lateral or subextrorse slits; ovary ovoid, abruptly contracted into a short columnar style; stigma thick and fleshy, slightly 2-lobed; in the staminate flower of the Asiatic species reduced to a minute subglobose body; ovules laterally attached near the apex of the cell; raphe ventral. Fruit an ovoid or oblong, usually 1 or rarely 2 or 3-seeded thick-skinned drupe tipped with the remnants of the style; flesh thin and dry; stone thick-walled, crustaceous. Seed filling the cavity of the stone, ovoid; seed-coat chestnut-brown.

Chionanthus inhabits the middle and southern United States with one species, and northern and central China with another.

The specific name, from χιών and ἄνθος, is in allusion to the light and graceful clusters of snow-white flowers.

1. Chionanthus virginica L. Fringe-tree. Old Man's Beard.

Leaves ovate or oblong, acuminate, short-pointed or sometimes rounded at apex, gradually narrowed and cuneate below, entire, with undulate margins, and coarsely reticulate-

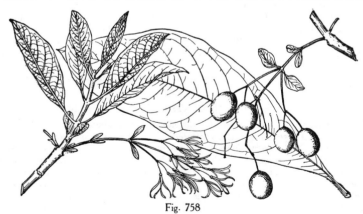

Fig. 758

venulose, yellow-green and lustrous above, pubescent below, and ciliate on the margins when they unfold, and at maturity 4'–8' long, ½'–4' wide, thick and firm, dark green on the upper surface, pale and glabrous on the lower surface except on the stout midrib and conspicuous arcuate primary veins more or less covered with short white hairs; turning bright clear yellow before falling early in the autumn; petioles stout, puberulous, $\frac{1}{2}'$–$1'$ in length. **Flowers** slightly and agreeably fragrant, appearing when the leaves are about one third grown, in loose pubescent drooping panicles $4'$–$6'$ in length, the bracts at the base of the lower branches of the inflorescence oblong, glabrous on the upper surface, pubescent on the lower surface, and sometimes $1'$ long, those at the base of the upper branches oval, successively smaller, and gradually passing into the minute laciniate bracts subtending the lateral pedicels of the 3-flowered clusters terminating the last divisions of the panicle; some individuals bearing occasional perfect flowers among others functionally diœcious, some with sterile or rarely perfect anthers and a well-developed stigma, and others with an imperfectly developed stigma and fertile anthers; calyx light green, glabrous, with acute entire or laciniately cut lobes; corolla $1'$ long, marked on the inner surface near the base by a row of bright purple spots; anthers light yellow, with a green connective. **Fruit** ripening in September, in loose few-fruited clusters, their bracts leaf-like and sometimes $2'$ in length, oval or short-oblong, $1'$ long, dark blue or nearly black, and often covered with a glaucous bloom; seeds $\frac{1}{3}'$ long, ovoid, narrowed at apex and covered with a thin light chestnut-brown coat marked by reticulate veins radiating from the hilum.

A tree, $20°$–$30°$ high, with a short trunk $8'$–$10'$ in diameter, stout ashy gray or light brown branches forming an oblong rather narrow head, and stout branchlets light green and covered with pale pubescence or sometimes glabrous when they first appear, terete or slightly angled in their first winter, often much thickened below the nodes, light brown or orange color, and marked by large scattered darker colored lenticels and by the elevated semiorbicular leaf-scars displaying a semicircular row of conspicuous fibro-vascular bundle-scars; often a shrub, with several stout thick spreading stems. **Winter-buds** broad-ovoid, acute, $\frac{1}{8}'$ long, with about 5 pairs of scales increasing in length from the outer to the inner pair, ovate, acute, keeled on the back, light brown and slightly pilose on the outer surface, bright green and lustrous on the inner surface, and ciliate on the margins with scattered white hairs, those of the inner pair at maturity obovate, gradually narrowed below, foliaceous, and $1'$–$1\frac{1}{2}'$ long. **Bark** of the trunk $\frac{1}{4}'$–$\frac{1}{2}'$ thick, and irregularly divided into small thin appressed brown scales tinged with red. **Wood** heavy, hard, close-grained, and light brown, with thick lighter colored sapwood. The bark is tonic and is sometimes used in decoctions and in the treatment of intermittent fevers, or as an aperient and diuretic, and in homœopathic practice.

Distribution. Banks of streams in rich moist soil; southeastern Pennsylvania to northeastern Kentucky, and to the Manatee River region, western Florida, and through the Gulf states to northern Arkansas (Baxter and Cleburne Counties), southwestern Oklahoma (near Page, Leflore County) and the valley of the Brazos River, Texas; ascending on the southern Appalachian Mountains to altitudes of $4000°$.

Often cultivated as an ornamental plant in the eastern United States, and in western and central Europe.

4. OSMANTHUS Lour.

Trees or shrubs, with terete or slightly angled branches, and fibrous roots. Leaves simple, persistent. Flowers fragrant, polygamo-diœcious or perfect, on ebracteolate pedicels subtended by scale-like bracts, in short axillary racemes or in short axillary or rarely terminal fascicles; calyx minute, 4-toothed or divided, the divisions imbricated in the bud, persistent under the fruit; corolla tubular, 4-lobed, the lobes imbricated in the bud, ovate, obtuse, spreading after anthesis; stamens 2, inserted on the tube of the corolla opposite the lateral lobes of the calyx, or rarely 4; filaments terete, short; anthers ovoid or linear-oblong, blunt, or apiculate by the prolongation of the connective, attached on the back below the middle, 2-celled, the cells opening longitudinally by marginal slits, sometimes rudimentary or 0 in the pistillate flower; ovary subglobose; style columnar, short or elongated, crowned with an entire capitate stigma; ovules laterally attached near the apex of the cell; raphe ventral. Fruit a fleshy 1-seeded ovoid or globose drupe tipped with the remnants of the style; flesh thin and succulent; stone hard and bony. Seed filling the cavity of the stone; cotyledons flat, much longer than the short superior radicle turned toward the hilum.

Osmanthus with ten species inhabits eastern North America, the Hawaiian Islands, Polynesia, Japan, China, and the Himalayas. *Osmanthus fragrans* Lour., a native of China and the temperate Himalayas, is cultivated in China for its fragrant minute cream-colored or yellow flowers used by the Chinese to perfume tea, and is everywhere a favorite garden plant.

The generic name, from ὀσμή and ἄνθος, relates to the fragrance of the flowers.

1. Osmanthus americanus B. & H.   Devil Wood.

Leaves oblong-lanceolate or obovate, acute or rarely rounded and occasionally emarginate at apex, and gradually narrowed and cuneate at base, with thickened revolute margins, when they unfold coated beneath with pale tomentum, and at maturity thick and coriaceous, glabrous, bright green, lustrous above, obscurely reticulate-venulose, 4'–5' long

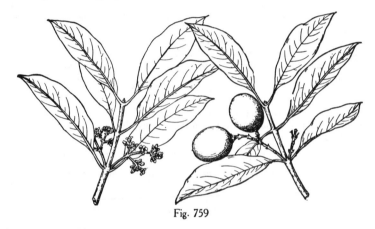

Fig. 759

and $\frac{1}{2}'-2\frac{1}{2}'$ wide, with a broad pale midrib and remote forked primary veins arcuate near the margins; persistent until their second year; petioles stout, $\frac{1}{2}'-\frac{3}{4}'$ in length. **Flowers** opening in March from pilose inflorescence-buds formed the previous autumn in the axils of the leaves of the year, the staminate, pistillate, and perfect flowers on different individuals in 3-flowered clusters, sessile or short-pedicellate, in pedunculate cymes or short racemes, with scale-like nearly triangular acute persistent bracts; calyx puberulous, with acute rigid lobes, and much shorter than the creamy white corolla $\frac{1}{8}'$ long when expanded, with an elongated tube and short spreading ovate rounded lobes; stamens inserted on the middle of the tube of the corolla, included or slightly exserted, small and often rudimentary in the pistillate flower; ovary abruptly contracted into a stout columnar style crowned with a large exserted capitate stigma, reduced in the staminate flower to a minute point. **Fruit** ripening early in the autumn, oblong or obovoid, 1' long, dark blue, with thin flesh and a thick or sometimes thin-walled brittle ovoid pointed stone; seed ovoid, covered with a chestnut-brown coat marked by broad conspicuous pale veins radiating from the short broad ventral hilum and encircling the seed.

A tree, occasionally 60°–70° high, with a trunk sometimes a foot in diameter, and slender slightly angled ultimately terete branchlets light or red-brown and marked by minute pale lenticels, becoming ashy gray in their second year and roughened by the small elevated orbicular leaf-scars displaying a ring of minute fibro-vascular bundle-scars; usually much smaller and often shrubby. **Winter-buds** narrow-lanceolate, $\frac{1}{2}'$ long, with 2 thick lanceolate reddish brown puberulous scales. **Bark** of the trunk thin, dark gray or gray tinged with red, and roughened by small thin appressed scales displaying in falling the dark cinnamon red inner bark. **Wood** heavy, very hard and strong, close-grained, difficult to work, dark brown, with thick light brown or yellow sapwood.

Distribution. Usually in hammocks and other places protected from fires near the borders of streams and Pine-barren ponds and swamps, and occasionally on dry sandy uplands; coast region of the south Atlantic and Gulf states from the valley of the lower Cape Fear River, North Carolina, to Lake and Orange Counties, the shores of Tampa Bay, Florida, and westward to eastern Louisiana.

LXI. BORRAGINACEÆ.

Scabrous-pubescent trees or shrubs, with watery juice, and terete branchlets. Leaves simple, alternate or subverticillate, penniveined, persistent or tardily deciduous, without stipules. Flowers regular, perfect, in terminal or axillary dichotomous often scorpioid-branched cymes; calyx usually 5-lobed, persistent under the fruit; corolla hypogynous, 5-lobed, the lobes imbricated in the bud; stamens 5, inserted on the tube of the corolla opposite its lobes; filaments filiform; anthers introrse, 2-celled, the cells opening longitudinally; pistil of 2 carpels; ovary undivided (in the arborescent genera of the United States), sessile on the hypogynous inconspicuous disk, more or less completely 4-celled; style single, 2-branched or parted toward the apex; stigmas clavate or capitate; ovule solitary in each cell. Fruit drupaceous (in the arborescent genera of the United States), tipped with the remnants of the style, with 2–4 nutlets or cells. Seeds ascending; seed-coat membranaceous.

The Borage family with ninety-five genera, mostly of herbaceous plants, is widely distributed and most abundant in temperate regions, especially in the Mediterranean basin and central Asia.

CONSPECTUS OF THE ARBORESCENT GENERA OF THE UNITED STATES.

Branches of the style 2-branched; fruit partly or entirely inclosed in the enlarged calyx.

1. **Cordia.**

Branches of the style not branched; fruit not inclosed in the calyx.

Calyx valvately splitting into 5 minute teeth; fruit with 2–4 1-seeded nutlets.

2. **Beureria.**

Calyx 5-parted or cleft, the divisions imbricated in the bud; fruit with 2 2-seeded nutlets.

3. **Ehretia.**

1. CORDIA L.

Trees or shrubs, with petiolate entire persistent leaves and naked buds. Flowers in terminal scorpioid-branched cymes; calyx tubular or campanulate, conspicuously many-ribbed or rayed, the teeth valvate in the bud; corolla funnel form; anthers oblong-ovate; ovary 4-celled; style slender, elongated, 2-branched above the middle, the branches 2-parted, their division stigmatic to the base; ovule ascending, laterally attached below the middle to the inner angle of the cell, suborthotropous; micropyle superior. Fruit entirely or partly inclosed in the thickened calyx; flesh dry and corky or sweet and juicy; stone thick-walled, hard and bony, 1–4-celled, usually 1 or 2-seeded. Seeds without albumen; embryo filling the cavity of the seed; cotyledons thick and fleshy or membranaceous, longitudinally plicate or corrugated, much shorter than the superior radicle turned toward the hilum.

Cordia with two hundred and fifty species inhabits the tropical and warm extratropical regions of the two hemispheres, the largest number of species being American. Of the four species found within the territory of the United States two are trees. Some of the species are valuable timber-trees, and others are cultivated for their edible fruits.

The generic name is in honor of Valerius Cordus (1515–1544), the German writer on pharmacy and botany.

CONSPECTUS OF THE ARBORESCENT SPECIES OF THE UNITED STATES.

Corolla orange or flame color; fruit inclosed in the smooth glabrous thickened ivory-white calyx; leaves ovate. 1. C. Sebestena (D).

Corolla white with a yellow centre; fruit entirely or partly inclosed in the thin many-ribbed tomentose orange-brown calyx; leaves oval or oblong-ovate.

2. C. Boissieri (E, H).

1. Cordia Sebestena L. Geiger-tree.

Leaves unfolding through a large part of the year, ovate, short-pointed or rounded at apex, rounded, subcordate, or cuneate at base, entire or remotely and coarsely serrate above the middle, covered when they unfold, like the branches of the inflorescence, the outside of the calyx, and the young branchlets, with thick dense rusty tomentum and with short rigid

Fig. 760

pale hairs, and at maturity thick and firm, dark green, scabrous-pubescent, or often nearly glabrous below, reticulate-venulose, 5′–6′ long and 3′–4′ wide, with a broad midrib usually covered below with pale hairs, especially in the axils of remote primary veins connected by conspicuous cross veinlets; petioles stout, pubescent, 1′–1½′ in length. **Flowers** appearing throughout the year on slender pedicels, in open flat cymes 6′–7′ in diameter, some individuals producing flowers with short included stamens and elongated styles, and others with exserted stamens and included styles; calyx tubular, ½′–⅔′ long, and obscurely many-rayed, with short nearly triangular rigid teeth; corolla orange or flame color, puberulous on the outer surface, with a slender tube about twice as long as the calyx and spreading rounded lobes, irregularly undulate on the margins and 1′–1½′ in diameter when fully expanded; ovary conic, glabrous, contracted into a slender style branched near the apex. **Fruit** broad-ovate, rather abruptly narrowed and pointed at apex, concave at base, 1¼′–1½′ long and about ¾′ broad, inclosed in the thickened fibrous calyx smooth and ivory-white on the outer surface; flesh thin, pale, and corky, separable from the irregularly sulcate thick-walled stone gradually narrowed and acuminate at apex, and deeply lobed at base; seeds linear-lanceolate, ½′ long, with a delicate white seed-coat.

A tree, in Florida 25°–30° high, with a tall trunk 5′–6′ in diameter, slender upright branches forming a narrow close round-topped head, and stout branchlets with thick pith, dark green at first, becoming ashy gray and marked by large nearly orbicular cordate leaf-scars displaying 2 central circular clusters of fibro-vascular bundle-scars. **Bark** of the trunk ½′–¾′ thick, dark brown, frequently nearly black, and deeply and irregularly divided into narrow ridges broken on the surface into short thick appressed scales. **Wood** heavy, hard, close-grained, dark brown, with thick light brown or yellow sapwood.

Distribution. Florida, Flamingo near Cape Sable (*A. A. Eaton*) and Madeira Hammock, **Monroe** County, and on the southern keys; on the Bahama Islands, on most of the Antilles, and in Guiana and New Granada.

Often planted in tropical countries as an ornament of gardens.

2. Cordia Boissieri A. DC. Anacahuita.

Leaves oval to oblong-ovate, acute or rounded at apex, rounded or subcordate at base, entire or obscurely crenulate-serrate, covered when they unfold like the branches of the inflorescence, both surfaces of the calyx and the young branchlets with rusty or dark brown tomentum and short white usually matted hairs, thick and firm, dark green, minutely rugose and more or less scabrous above, coated below with thick soft pale or rufous tomentum, 4'–5' long and 3'–4' wide, with a broad midrib, and conspicuous primary veins forked near the margins and connected by cross veinlets; deciduous at the end of their first year; petioles stout, tomentose, 1'–1½' in length. **Flowers** opening from April to June, slightly fragrant, sessile or short-pedicellate, in open terminal dichotomous cymes; calyx tubular or subcampanulate, conspicuously many-ribbed, with 5 linear acute teeth, and about half as long as the tube of the white corolla puberulous on the outer surface, marked in the throat by a large light yellow spot, the lobes rounded, imbricated in the bud, and 2' across when

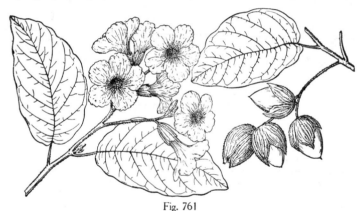

Fig. 761

fully expanded; ovary glabrous, gradually narrowed into a slender 2-branched style. **Fruit** ovoid, 1' long, about ¾' broad, pointed at apex, lustrous, bright red-brown, and inclosed entirely or partly by the thin fibrous now conspicuously rayed orange-brown calyx coated on the outer surface with thick short pale tomentum, and often splitting nearly to the base; flesh thin, sweet, and pulpy, separating easily from the ovoid smooth light brown stone gradually narrowed from above the middle, faintly reticulate-veined, and marked by 4 longitudinal lines and at the acuminate apex by a deeply 4-lobed thin cap, thick-walled, hard and bony, deeply lobed at base; seeds ovoid, acute, ¼' long, with a thin delicate pure white coat.

A tree, occasionally 20°–25° high, with a short often crooked trunk 6'–8' in diameter, stout spreading branches forming a low round-topped head, and stout branchlets, becoming in their second year dark gray or brown, slightly puberulous, and marked by occasional large lenticels and by elevated obcordate leaf-scars; or often a shrub, with numerous stems sometimes only 2° or 3° tall. **Bark** of the trunk thin, gray tinged with red, and irregularly divided into broad flat ridges, the surface ultimately separating into long thin papery scales. **Wood** light, rather soft, close-grained, and dark brown, with thick light brown sapwood.

Distribution. Dry limestone ridges, and depressions in the desert; valley of the Rio Grande, Texas, and southern New Mexico, southward into Mexico; most abundant and of its largest size in Tamaulipas and Nuevo Leon between the mouth of the Rio Grande and the base of the Sierra Madre.

2. BEURERIA Jacq.

Trees or shrubs, with oblong-obovate or ovate leaves involute in the bud, persistent. Flowers on slender bracteolate pedicels, in terminal corymbose many-flowered cymes, with linear-lanceolate caducous bracts and bractlets; calyx campanulate, 5-toothed, the divisions closed and valvate in the bud; corolla white, campanulate, the lobes broad-ovate, spreading after anthesis; anthers ovoid, rugulose, apiculate; ovary incompletely 4-celled by the development of the 2 parietal placentas, narrowed into a terminal style 2-parted at apex, the divisions more or less coalescent; stigmas capitate; ovules attached on the back near the middle of the inner face of the revolute placentas, anatropous; raphe ventral; micropyle superior. Fruit subglobose, flesh thin; stone somewhat 4-lobed and separable into 4 thick-walled bony 1-seeded nutlets rounded and furnished on the back with a thick spongy longitudinal many-ridged appendage, flattened on their converging inner faces and attached at apex to a filiform column. Seed terete, filling the seminal cell, longitudinally incurved round a rather small cavity opposite an elevated oblong scar on one of the inner faces of the nutlet and connected with the hilum by a narrow passage; seed-coat membranaceous, light brown; embryo axile in fleshy albumen; cotyledons plane; radicle slender, elongated, turned toward the hilum.

Beureria with forty species is confined to tropical America, two species reaching the shores of southern Florida; of these one is a tree and the other *Beureria revoluta* H. B. K. is an arborescent shrub.

The generic name is in honor of J. A. Beurer, an apothecary at Nuremberg.

1. Beureria ovata Meyers.

Beureria havanensis Hitch., not Meyers.

Leaves elliptic to oval or broad-obovate, acute and often apiculate or rounded and then occasionally emarginate at apex, gradually narrowed and cuneate at base entire, densely

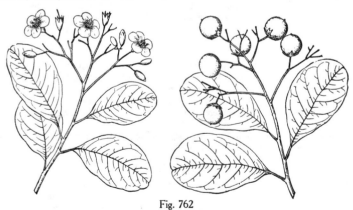

Fig. 762

covered when they unfold with white caducous hairs, and at maturity thick, dark yellow-green and lustrous above, paler below, $2\frac{1}{2}'-3'$ long and $1\frac{1}{4}'-2'$ wide, with slightly thickened undulate margins, a slender orange-colored midrib, thin primary veins and conspicuous reticulate veinlets more prominent above than below; usually persistent through their second summer; petioles slender, covered when they first appear like the very young branchlets with long white hairs, very soon glabrous, $\frac{1}{2}'-1'$ in length. **Flowers** opening in spring and late in autumn on pedicels $\frac{1}{2}'$ long and furnished near the middle with an acuminate scarious bractlet $\frac{1}{4}'$ in length and caducous from a persistent base, in open glabrous 15–20-flowered long-stalked cymes $3'-4'$ in diameter, with slender branches, and small bracts; calyx gradually narrowed into a stipe-like base, the lobes acuminate, ciliate on the margins; corolla subcampanulate, creamy white, with a short tube somewhat enlarged in the throat, and broad-ovate spreading lobes $\frac{3}{4}'$ across when expanded; stamens rather longer than the tube of the corolla, anthers much shorter than the filaments; ovary conic, glabrous, gradually contracted into a slender exserted style divided only toward the apex or sometimes nearly entire, and crowned with 2 capitate stigmas. **Fruit** ripening in early autumn or early spring from autumnal flowers, bright orange-red, $\frac{1}{2}'$ in diameter, with a thick tough skin and thin dry flesh inclosing the 4 nutlets, the enlarged spreading calyx becoming sometimes $\frac{1}{2}'$ across.

A tree, in Florida occasionally 40°–50° high, with a buttressed and often fluted trunk $8'-10'$ in diameter, and slender branchlets light red and pilose with caducous hairs when they first appear, becoming in their first winter dark red, orange color or ashy gray, and sometimes roughened by pale lenticels, their thin bark often separating into delicate scales; usually much smaller and often a shrub, with numerous spreading stems. **Winter-buds** minute, globose, covered with hoary tomentum, nearly immersed in the bark. **Bark** of the trunk $\frac{1}{16}'-\frac{1}{8}'$ thick, light brown tinged with red, more or less fissured and divided on the surface into thick plate-like irregular scales. **Wood** hard, strong, very close-grained, brown streaked with orange, with thick hardly distinguishable sapwood.

Distribution. Florida, Cocoanut Grove, Dade County (*Miss O. Rodham*), and on the southern keys; common; on the Bahama Islands and on many of the Antilles.

3. EHRETIA P. Br.

Trees or shrubs, with entire or dentate leaves, and scaly buds. Flowers small, in terminal and axillary scorpioid clusters; calyx open or closed in the bud, the divisions imbricated, ovate or linear; corolla usually white, with a short or cylindric tube and spreading obtuse lobes; ovary oblong-conic, 1-celled before anthesis, becoming incompletely 4-celled by the development of the 2 parietal placentas; style columnar, parted into 2 divisions terminating in capitate stigmas; ovules attached laterally near the middle on the inner face of the revolute placentas, anatropous; raphe ventral; micropyle superior. Fruit fleshy, small, globose, with thin flesh; stone separable into 2 2-celled thick-walled bony nutlets rounded on the back, plane on the inner face, and attached to a thin axile column. Seed terete, usually erect, filling the longitudinally incurved seminal cavity; seed-coat thin, membranaceous, light brown; embryo axile in thin albumen; cotyledons ovate, plane; shorter than the elongated superior radicle turned toward the hilum.

Ehretia with about forty species is widely distributed through tropical and warm extratropical regions of the two hemispheres, with a single species extending into southeastern Texas.

The generic name commemorates the artistic and scientific labors of the German botanical artist, George Dionysius Ehret (1708–1770).

1. Ehretia elliptica DC. Anaqua. Knackaway.

Leaves oval or oblong, pointed and apiculate at apex, gradually rounded or cuneate at base, entire or occasionally furnished above the middle with a few broad teeth, conspicuously reticulate-venulose, unfolding late in winter and then thin, light green, lustrous, minutely tuberculate and pilose above, and covered below like the branches of the inflorescence, the outer surface of the calyx, and the young branchlets with rigid pale hairs, often furnished with axillary tufts of white hairs, and at maturity subcoriaceous, dark green and roughened on the upper surface by the enlarged circular crowded pale tubercles, and more or less covered with soft pale or rufous pubescence on the lower surface, especially on the narrow midrib, and numerous primary veins arcuate near the margins; irregularly deciduous during the winter; petioles stout, grooved, pubescent, $\frac{1}{8}'-\frac{1}{4}'$ in length. **Flowers** opening from autumn to early spring, in compact racemose scorpioid-branched panicles $2'-3'$ long and

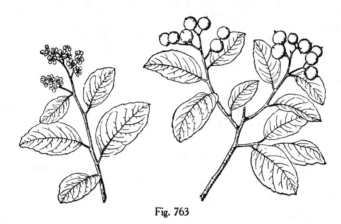

Fig. 763

broad, on short leafy branches of the year, with linear acute deciduous bracts about $\frac{1}{4}'$ long; calyx open in the bud, divided to the base into 5 linear acute divisions and nearly as long as the campanulate tube of the corolla, with ovate thin white lobes $\frac{1}{2}'$ across when expanded. **Fruit** ripening in autumn and spring, light yellow, $\frac{1}{4}'$ in diameter, with thin sweet rather juicy edible flesh, and 2 2-seeded nutlets.

A tree, sometimes $40°-50°$ high, with a trunk occasionally $3°$ in diameter, stout spreading branches forming a handsome compact round-topped head, and slender branchlets, without a terminal bud, covered when they first appear, like the under surface of the leaves, the branches of the inflorescence, and the outer surface of the calyx of the flower, with rigid hirsute pale hairs, becoming in their first winter light brown tinged with red, sometimes puberulous, often roughened by numerous pale lenticels, and by small depressed obcordate leaf-scars displaying a short lunate row of fibro-vascular bundle-scars; usually much smaller within the territory of the United States, and often a low shrub. **Winter-buds:** axillary, minute, 1 or 2 together, superposed, buried in the bark, and covered by 2 pairs of dark scales persistent on the base of the growing branchlet and at maturity acute, dark chestnut-brown, coated with pale hairs, and sometimes $\frac{1}{4}'$ in length. **Bark** of young stems and of the branches thin, light brown, and broken into thick appressed scales, becoming on old trunks sometimes $1'$ thick, deeply furrowed and divided into long thick irregular plate-like scales gray or reddish brown on the surface and separating into thin flakes. **Wood** heavy, hard, not strong, close-grained, difficult to split, light brown, with thick slightly lighter colored sapwood.

Distribution. River valleys in fertile soil, or as a shrub on dry barren ridges; valleys of the upper Marcos and of the Guadalupe Rivers, Texas, to the Rio Grande; often extremely common on the bottom-lands, and probably of its largest size in the United States on the Guadalupe and Nueces Rivers sixty or seventy miles from the coast; through Nuevo Leon and Coahuila to the mountains of San Luis Potosí.

Often planted as a shade-tree in the streets of the cities and towns of western Texas and northeastern Mexico.

LXII. VERBENACEÆ.

Trees or shrubs, with opposite simple entire persistent leaves, without stipules. Flowers perfect; calyx 5-toothed or parted, persistent under the fruit; corolla 4 or 5-lobed, the lobes imbricated in the bud; stamens 4, inserted on the tube of the corolla in pairs of different lengths, anthers 2-celled, introrse, the cells opening longitudinally; ovary sessile on the annular disk; style simple, 2-lobed and stigmatic at apex.   Fruit a fleshy drupe or a capsule. The Verbena family with seventy-eight genera, largely composed of herbaceous plants, is widely scattered through temperate and tropical regions.   Some of the species are important timber-trees, the most valuable being the Teak, *Tectoria grandis* L. f., of southeastern Asia and the Malay Archipelago, and some of the tropical species of Vitex.

CONSPECTUS OF THE ARBORESCENT GENERA OF THE UNITED STATES.

Flowers in axillary or terminal racemes; staminodium 1; ovary imperfectly 4-celled; fruit a fleshy drupe.   **1. Citharexylon.**

Flowers cymose in pedunculate spikes or heads; staminodium 0; ovary 1-celled; fruit a capsule.   **2. Avicennia.**

1. CITHAREXYLON L.

Trees or shrubs, with coriaceous lustrous leaves, slightly angled branchlets, without a terminal bud, and with minute axillary buds.   Flowers small, on short ebracteolate pedicels, alternate or scattered on the filiform rachis of a slender raceme; calyx membranaceous, tubular-campanulate, truncate, minutely 5-toothed, spreading and cup-shaped under the fruit; corolla salver-form, usually white, the spreading limb somewhat oblique, 5-lobed, the lobes broad-ovate, rounded, slightly unequal, the 2 posterior exterior, sometimes reduced to staminodia; stamens included; filaments short, filiform, slightly thickened at base, the 2 anterior filaments longer than the others; anthers oblong; staminodium 1, posterior, linear, acute, rarely fertile; ovary ovoid, incompletely 4-celled by the development of two parietal placentas, gradually narrowed into a short included style; ovule solitary in each cell, erect, attached laterally near the base, ascending, anatropous; micropyle inferior.   Fruit a 2-stoned 4-seeded fleshy drupe tipped with the remnants of the style, with thin flesh and a thick-walled bony stone separable into 2 2-seeded compressed smooth light brown nutlets rounded on the back and concave on the inner face.   Seed erect, without albumen, filling the seminal cavity; seed-coat membranaceous, light brown; embryo subterete, straight; cotyledons thick and fleshy, oblong, much longer than the short inferior radicle turned toward the oblong basal hilum.

Citharexylon with about twenty species is confined to tropical America, where it is distributed from southern Florida through the West Indies to southern Mexico, Lower California, Bolivia, and Brazil.

The generic name, from κιθάρα and ξύλον, is a translation of the English West Indian name Fiddle Wood, a corruption of the earlier French-colonial Bois Fidèle, in allusion to the strength and toughness of the wood of the trees of this genus.

1. Citharexylon fruticosum L.   Fiddle Wood.

Citharexylon villosum Jacq.

Leaves oblong-obovate to oblong, acute, acuminate, rounded or emarginate at apex, and gradually narrowed at base, with thickened slightly revolute margins, and glabrous or coated with short pubescence (var. *villosum* Schulz); conspicuously reticulate-venulose, pale green, 3′–4′ long and 1′–1½′ wide, with a broad pale midrib rounded on the upper side and remote prominent arcuate veins; petioles stout, grooved, ¾′ in length, separating in falling from an elevated nearly circular persistent woody base.   **Flowers** fragrant, appearing throughout the year on slender pedicels from the axils of scarious pubescent bracts, in drooping axillary pubescent racemes crowded near the end of the branches and 2′–4′ long; calyx coated with pale hairs, or sometimes nearly glabrous; corolla ⅛′ across the expanded lobes of the limb, and covered on the inner surface of the tube with pale hairs; staminodium minute. **Fruit** subglobose to oblong-ovoid, light red-brown, very lustrous, $\frac{1}{3}'$ in

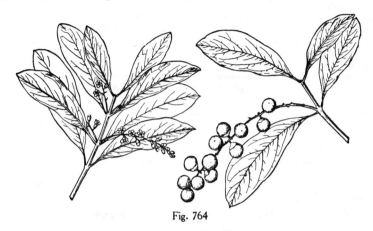

Fig. 764

diameter, with thin sweet rather juicy flesh, and inclosed nearly to the middle in the cuplike pale brown slightly and irregularly lobed or sometimes nearly entire calyx; **seeds** oblong, narrowed at the rounded ends, about $\frac{1}{8}'$ long.

A tree, in Florida rarely more than 30° high, with a trunk $4'-7'$ in diameter, slender upright branches forming a narrow irregularly shaped head, and slender slightly many-angled branchlets light yellow and covered with pale simple caducous hairs or pubescent when they first appear, becoming in their second year terete and ashy gray; or often a shrub, with numerous low stems. **Winter-buds** globose, nearly immersed in the bark, and covered with hoary pubescence. **Bark** of the trunk $\frac{1}{16}'-\frac{1}{8}'$ thick, light brown tinged with red, the surface separating into minute appressed scales. **Wood** heavy, exceedingly hard, strong, close-grained, clear bright red, with thin lighter colored sapwood.

Distribution. Florida, Cape Canaveral to the southern keys; common and of its largest size in the United States on the shores of Bay Biscayne near the mouth of the Miami River, Dade County; northward usually a low shrub; on the Bahama Islands and on many of the Antilles.

2. AVICENNIA L.

Trees, with coriaceous persistent leaves, stout pithy branches thickened at the nodes and marked by interpetiolar lines, and long thick horizontal roots producing numerous short vertical thick and fleshy leafless stems rising above the surface of the soil. Flowers opposite, cymose, in centripetal pedunculate spikes or heads, closely invested by a bract and **2** bractlets, the peduncles solitary or in pairs in the axils of upper leaves and ternate on the end of the branches, their bracts and bractlets concave, acute, apiculate, keeled on the back, scarious, slightly ciliate on the margins, shorter than the corolla, persistent under the fruit; calyx cup-shaped, coated like the bracts and bractlets with canescent pubescence, divided nearly to the base into 5 concave ovate rounded lobes imbricated in the bud; corolla campanulate, white, with a straight cylindric tube shorter than the glabrous or tomentose spreading 4-lobed limb, the posterior lobe usually larger than the others; stamens exserted; filaments short, filiform, slightly thickened at base; anthers ovoid; ovary ovoid, pubescent, 1-celled, gradually narrowed into an elongated slender style divided at apex into **2** lobes stigmatic on their inner face; ovules 4, suspended from the summit of a free central placenta, orthotropous, naked. Fruit an ovoid oblique compressed 1-seeded capsule apiculate at apex; pericarp thin, light green, villose-pubescent on the outer surface, longitudinally veined on the inner surface, opening by the ventral suture and displaying the embryo enlarging before separating from the branch, ultimately 2-valved.   Seed naked, without albumen; embryo filling the cavity of the fruit, light green; cotyledons thick and fleshy, broader than long, slightly pointed, deeply cordate at base, unequal, conduplicate; radicle elongated, clavate, retrorsely hirsute, inferior, descending obliquely and included between the lobes of the cotyledons slightly attached near the apex in the bottom of the capsule to the withered columella by a minute papillose point; plumule hairy.

Avicennia with three species is widely distributed on maritime shores of the tropics of the two worlds, with one species reaching those of the southern United States.   Avicennia produces hard strong wood.   The bark is rich in tannic acid, and is used for tanning leather. The chief value of these trees is in their ability to live on low tidal shores by the structure of the embryo, which is growing and ready to take root as soon as it falls into the soft mud, and in the long horizontal roots furnished with short vertical fleshy leafless branches or aerating roots, forming a close network which holds the soil together and prevents it from being washed away by outflowing tides, and extends the growth of the tree by numerous stems which soon form dense thickets.

The generic name is in honor of the illustrious physician of the Orient, Avicenna of Bokhara (980–1036).

1. Avicennia nitida Jacq.   Black Mangrove.

Leaves oblong or lanceolate-elliptic, rounded or acute at apex and gradually narrowed at base, dark green and often lustrous above, hoary-tomentulose below, 2′–3′ long and $\frac{3}{4}$′– 1$\frac{1}{2}$′ wide, with slightly thickened revolute margins, a broad midrib thickened and grooved

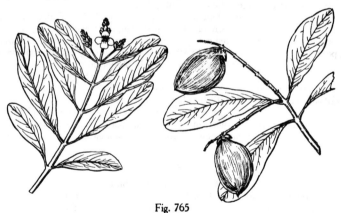

Fig. 765

toward the base on the upper side, and oblique primary veins arcuate and joined close to the margins, conspicuous on the 2 surfaces, and connected by prominent reticulate veinlets; appearing irregularly and falling early in their second season; petioles broad, channeled, enlarged at base, and about $\frac{1}{4}$′ in length.   **Flowers** produced continuously throughout the year, their bracts and bractlets nearly $\frac{1}{4}$′ long, coated with pale or slightly rufous pubescence and about as long as the lobes of the calyx, in few-flowered short spikes on stout 4-angled canescent peduncles $\frac{1}{2}$′–1$\frac{1}{2}$′ in length, the lateral peduncles of the ternate terminal cluster subtended by oblong acute bracts $\frac{1}{2}$′ long; corolla $\frac{1}{2}$′ across the expanded slightly tomentose lobes, and nearly closed in the throat.   **Fruit** 1′–1$\frac{1}{2}$′ long and $\frac{3}{4}$′–1′ wide.

A tree, occasionally 60°–70° high, with a short trunk rarely 2° in diameter, spreading branches forming a broad round-topped head, and branchlets at first slightly angled, coated with fine hoary deciduous pubescence, and light orange color, becoming in their second year more or less contorted, light or dark gray, conspicuously marked by the interpetiolar lines and by horizontal leaf-scars displaying a central row of fibro-vascular bundle-scars; usually not more than 20°-30° tall, with a short slender stem, and toward the northern limit of its range a low shrub. **Bark** of the trunk $\frac{1}{4}'-\frac{1}{2}'$ thick, roughened with thin irregularly appressed dark brown scales tinged with red, and in falling displaying the bright orange-red inner bark. **Wood** very heavy, hard, rather coarse-grained, with numerous medullary rays and eccentric layers of annual growth, dark brown or nearly black, with thick brown sapwood.

Distribution. Florida, St. Augustine to the southern keys on the east coast, and from Cedar Keys to Cape Sable on the west coast; on some of the islands in Mississippi Sound, and on the shore of Terrebonne and Cameron Parishes, and on most of their islands, Louisiana; on the Bahama Islands, on many of the Antilles, and southward to Brazil; and on the west coast of Africa; in the United States of its largest size in Florida just north of Cape Sable; north of Matanzas Inlet on the east coast of Florida usually with stems only a few feet tall.

LXIII. SOLANACEÆ.

Trees, shrubs or herbs, with colorless juice and rank smelling foliage, alternate rarely opposite leaves, without stipules, and perfect regular yellow, white or purple flowers on ebracteolate pedicels in usually dichotomous cymes; calyx campanulate, usually 5-lobed, the lobes slightly imbricated or valvate, usually persistent; corolla gamopetalous, usually 5, rarely 4-lobed, the lobes induplicate-valvate or plicate in the bud; stamens inserted on the tube of the corolla and alternate with and as many as its lobes, equal or unequal; filaments filiform or dilated at base; anthers 2-celled, introrse, opening by apical or longitudinal slits, disk pulvinate or annular, entire, sinuate or 2-lobed or 0; ovary sessile or stipitate on the disk, 2 or rarely 3-5-celled; style slender, terminating in a small or more or less dilated stigma; ovules numerous, attached in many series on the axile placenta, rarely few or solitary, anatropous or slightly amphitropous. Fruit baccate or capsular. Seeds numerous; testa membranaceous or crustaceous; embryo usually slender and curved in fleshy albumen; cotyledons semiterete, shorter than the radicle turned toward the hilum.

A family of 83 genera widely distributed in tropical and temperate regions; often producing fruit with narcotic or poisonous properties, and containing among its useful members the Potato and the Tomato.

1. SOLANUM L.

Herbs, shrubs or rarely trees. Leaves alternate, lobed or pinnatifid, persistent or deciduous. Flowers in mostly lateral, extra-axillary or axillary clusters; calyx and corolla 5, rarely 4-10-parted, the calyx persistent under the fruit, corolla rotate in the bud; stamens 5, rarely 4-6, exserted; filaments short; anthers oblong or acuminate, rarely ovoid, converging round the style, opening at apex by two pores; disk not conspicuous, or annular; ovary usually 2, rarely 3 or 4-celled; style simple; stigma usually small; ovules numerous. Fruit baccate, often surrounded by the enlarged calyx, usually globose and juicy; seeds compressed, orbicular or subreniform.

Solanum with some 1200 species is widely distributed through the tropics, with a few species extending into cooler regions, the larger number of species occurring in the New World.

The name is of uncertain derivation.

1. Solanum verbascifolium L.

Leaves ovate to elliptic or oblong, acute or acuminate at apex, rounded or cuneate at base, entire, thickly coated when they unfold with hoary tomentum, and at maturity thin, yellow-green and stellate-pubescent on the upper surface, paler and more densely stellate-pubescent on the lower surface, $5'-7'$ long and $1'-3'$ wide, with slightly undulate margins, a prominent midrib and slender primary veins; persistent; petioles slender, densely stellate-pubescent, $\frac{3}{4}'$–1' in length. **Flowers** appearing throughout the year on pedicels $\frac{1}{4}'$ long and much thickened at maturity, in broad many-flowered dichotomous stellate-

Fig. 766

pubescent cymes on peduncles 1'–4' in length from the axils of upper leaves; calyx about $\frac{1}{2}'$ long, densely stellate, the lobes triangular-ovate; corolla about $\frac{3}{4}'$–1' wide after the expansion of the oblong-ovate lobes; stamens exserted. **Fruit** globose, yellow, $\frac{1}{2}'$–$\frac{3}{4}'$ in diameter, surrounded at base by the densely stellate calyx, with ovate acute lobes about $\frac{1}{8}'$ long; **seeds** nearly orbicular to obovoid, much compressed, yellow, $\frac{1}{12}'$ in diameter.

A tree, rarely 20° high, with a trunk 4' or 5' in diameter, spreading branches forming a flat-topped head, and stout unarmed branchlets densely stellate-tomentose during their first season, becoming glabrous and light orange-brown or gray-brown in the following year; usually smaller and generally a shrub. **Bark** of the trunk thin, close, much roughened by many wart-like excrescences, light greenish or yellowish gray.

Florida, rich hummocks, Merritt's Island on the east coast, southward to the shores of Bay Biscayne, and to the Cape Sable region; on the Bahama Islands, and many of the Antilles, in Mexico and Central America, in the tropics of the Old World and in southeastern China; now thoroughly established but more probably introduced than indigenous in Florida.

LXIV. BIGNONIACEÆ.

Trees or shrubs, with watery juice, and opposite or rarely alternate simple (in the arborescent genera of the United States) leaves, without stipules. Flowers perfect, large and showy; calyx closed in the bud, bilabiately splitting in anthesis; corolla hypogynous, 2-lipped, 5-lobed, the lobes imbricated in the bud; stamens 2 or 4, inserted on the corolla, introrse; anthers 2-celled, the cells opening longitudinally; staminodia 1 or 3; ovary sessile, 1 or 2-celled, gradually narrowed into a slender simple style 2-lobed and stigmatic at apex; ovules numerous, horizontal, anatropous; raphe ventral; micropyle superior. Fruit a linear woody loculicidally 2-valved capsule, or a berry. Seeds without albumen; embryo filling the cavity of the seed.

The Bignonia family with about one hundred genera, many of them of scandent plants, is widely distributed in the tropics and most abundant in the New World, with a few genera extending into temperate regions. Of the five genera of the United States three are arborescent. Many of the species are important timber-trees.

CONSPECTUS OF THE ARBORESCENT GENERA OF THE UNITED STATES.

Fruit a linear woody capsule; ovary 2-celled; leaves thin, deciduous.
    Stamens 4; staminodium 1; leaves linear, often alternate or scattered.   **1. Chilopsis.**
    Stamens 2; staminodia 3; leaves oblong-ovate, mostly opposite.   **2. Catalpa.**
Fruit a berry; stamens 4; staminodium 1; ovary 1-celled; leaves coriaceous, persistent.
    3. Enallagma.

1. CHILOPSIS D. Don.

A tree, with slender terete branches, without a terminal bud, minute compressed rusty-pubescent axillary buds covered by several imbricated scales, those of the inner rows accrescent, deeply furrowed bark, soft coarse-grained dark-colored wood, and fibrous roots. Leaves opposite, alternate or scattered, involute in the bud, linear or linear-lanceolate, long-pointed, entire, 3-nerved, the lateral nerves obscure, reticulate-venulose, thin, light green, smooth or glutinous, short-petiolate or sessile from an enlarged base, deciduous, in falling leaving small elevated suborbicular scars. Flowers on slender pedicels from the axils of ovate acute scarious tomentose deciduous bracts and bibracteolate near the middle, in short puberulous crowded racemes or rarely panicles terminal on leafy branches of the year; calyx pale pubescent, puberulous or rarely glabrous, closed before anthesis into an ovoid rounded apiculate bud splitting to the base into 2 ovate divisions, minutely toothed or long-pointed at apex, the upper with 3, the lower with 2 rigid teeth, membranaceous, dark green; corolla white shaded into pale purple or rarely white, slightly oblique, enlarged and blotched with yellow in the throat, the limb undulate-margined, the upper lip 2-lobed, the lower unequally 3-lobed, the central lobe much longer than the others; stamens 4, inserted in 1 row near the base of the corolla in pairs, introrse; filaments filiform, glabrous, the anterior nearly twice as long as the posterior; anther oblong, the cells divergent in anthesis; staminodium 1, posterior, linear, acute; disk thin, nearly obsolete; ovary 2-celled, conic, glabrous, divided at apex into 2 ovate flat rounded lobes; ovules inserted in many series on a central placenta. Fruit a slender elongated thin-walled capsule gradually narrowed from the middle to the ends, splitting into 2 concave valves. Seeds numerous, inserted in 2 ranks near the margin of the thin flat woody septum free from the walls of the capsule, compressed, oblong; seed-coat thin, light brown, longitudinally veined, produced into broad lateral wings divided at their rounded ends into a long fringe of thin soft white hairs; cotyledons plane, broader than long, slightly 2-lobed, and rounded laterally; radicle short, erect, turned toward the oblong basal hilum.

The genus is represented by a single species, a native of the region adjacent to the boundary between the United States and Mexico.

The generic name, from χεῖλος and ὄψις, is without special significance.

1. Chilopsis linearis DC. Desert Willow.

Leaves unfolding in early spring, 6′–12′ long and ¼′–⅓′ wide; deciduous during the following winter. **Flowers** appearing in early summer in racemes or narrow panicles 3′–4′ long, and continuing to open for several months in succession, ¾′–1½′ long and ¾′–1¼′ across the expanded lobes of the corolla. **Fruit** ripening in the autumn, 7′–12′ long, ¼′ thick in the middle, persistent on the branches during the winter; **seeds** ⅓′ long and ⅛′ wide.

A tree, 20°–30° high, with a trunk usually more or less reclining, often hollow, and sometimes a foot in diameter, slender upright branches forming a narrow head, and branchlets glabrous or covered with dense tomentum when they first appear, light chestnut-brown during their first season, later becoming darker and tinged with red, or sometimes ashy gray; or often a straggling shrub. **Bark** of the trunk ⅛′–¼′ thick, dark brown, and divided into broad branching ridges broken on the surface into small thick plate-like scales. **Wood** soft, not strong, close-grained, brown streaked with yellow, with thin light-colored sapwood of 2 or 3 layers of annual growth.

Distribution. Banks of streams, and depressions in the desert, usually in dry gravelly

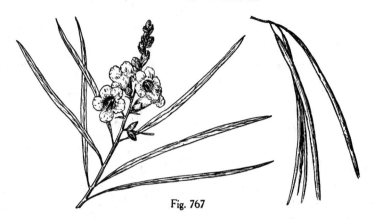

Fig. 767

porous soil; valley of the lower Rio Grande, and through western Texas, southern New Mexico, Arizona, southern Utah and Nevada to San Jacinto Valley, San Diego County, California; in northern Mexico and Lower California (Calamujuit).

Occasionally cultivated as an ornamental plant in the southern states, and in Mexico.

2. CATALPA Scop.

Trees, with stout terete branchlets, without a terminal bud, minute globose axillary buds nearly immersed in the bark and covered by numerous scales, the inner accrescent, thick pith, thin scaly bark, soft light-colored wood very durable in contact with the soil, and fibrous roots. Leaves opposite or in verticels of 3, involute in the bud, entire or lobed, oblong-ovate, often cordate, long-petiolate, deciduous. Flowers on slender bracte-olate pedicels, in terminal compound trichotomously branched panicles or corymbs, with linear-lanceolate deciduous bracts and bractlets; calyx membranaceous, subglobose, closed and apiculate in the bud, in anthesis splitting nearly to the base into 2 broad-ovate entire pointed apiculate lobes; corolla thin, variously marked and spotted on the inner surface, inserted on the nearly obsolete disk, the tube broad, campanulate, occasionally furnished on the upper side near the base with an external lobed appendage, and oblique and enlarged above into a broad limb, with spreading lips undulate on the margin, the posterior 2-parted, the anterior deeply 3-lobed; stamens and staminodia inserted near the base of the corolla; stamens 2, anterior, included or slightly exserted; filaments flattened, arcuate; anthers ob-long, carried to the rear of the corolla and face to face on either side of the stigma by a half turn of the filaments near their base, the cells divergent in anthesis; staminodia 3, free, filiform, minute or rudimentary; ovary 2-celled, sessile on the hypogynous nearly obsolete disk, abruptly contracted into an elongated filiform style divided at apex into 2 stigmatic lobes exserted above the anthers; ovules inserted in many series on a central placenta. Fruit an elongated subterete capsule tapering from the middle to the ends, persistent on the branches during the winter, ultimately splitting into 2 valves. Seeds numerous, com-pressed, oblong, inserted in 2–4 ranks near the margin of the flat or more or less thickened woody septum free from the walls of the capsule; seed-coat thin, light brown or silvery gray, longitudinally veined, produced into broad lateral wings notched at base of the seed and divided at their narrowed or rounded ends into tufts of long coarse white hairs; cotyledons plane, broader than long, slightly 2-lobed, rounded laterally; radicle short, erect, turned toward the oblong conspicuous basal hilum.

Catalpa with seven species is confined to the eastern United States, the West Indies, and eastern China, two of the species being North American. Catalpa contains a bitter princi-ple and is a tonic and diuretic.

The generic name is that by which one of the North American species was known among the Cherokee Indians.

CONSPECTUS OF THE NORTH AMERICAN SPECIES.

Flowers in many-flowered crowded panicles; calyx glabrous; corolla thickly spotted on the inner surface; fruit slender, thin-walled; leaves short-acuminate.

1. C. **bignonioides** (C).

Flowers in few-flowered open panicles; calyx often sparingly villose or pubescent; corolla inconspicuously spotted; fruit stout, thick-walled; leaves caudate-acuminate.

2. C. **speciosa** (A, C).

1. Catalpa bignonioides Walt. Catalpa. Indian Bean.

Catalpa Catalpa Karst.

Leaves broad-ovate, rather abruptly contracted into a slender point or sometimes rounded at apex, cordate at base, entire or often laterally lobed, coated below when they unfold with pale tomentum and pilose above, and at maturity thin and firm, light green and glabrous on the upper surface, pale and pubescent on the lower surface, 5'–6' long and 4'–5' wide, with a prominent midrib, and primary veins arcuate near the margins, connected by reticulate veinlets and furnished in the axils with clusters of dark hairs; turning black and falling after the first severe frost in the autumn; petioles stout, terete, 5'–6' in length. **Flowers** opening at the end of May or in June, on slender sparingly villose or glabrous pedicels, in compact many-flowered panicles 8'–10' long and broad, with light green branches tinged with purple; calyx ½' long, glabrous, green or light purple; corolla white, nearly 2' long, 1½' wide, marked on the inner surface on the lower side by 2 rows of yellow blotches following 2 parallel ridges or folds, and in the throat and on the lower lobes

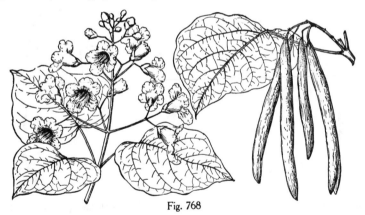

Fig. 768

of the limb by crowded conspicuous purple spots. **Fruit** ripening in the autumn, in thick-branched orange-colored panicles, remaining unopened during the winter, 6'–20' long and ¼'–⅓' thick in the middle, with a thin wall bright chestnut-brown on the outer surface and light olive-brown and lustrous on the inner surface, splitting in the spring into 2 flat valves; **seeds** about 1' long, ¼' wide, silvery gray, with pointed wings terminating in long pencil-shaped tufts of white hairs.

A tree, rarely 60° high, with a short trunk 3°–4° in diameter, long heavy brittle branches forming a broad head, and dichotomous branchlets green shaded with purple when they first appear, and during their first winter thickened at the nodes, slightly puberulous, lustrous, light orange color or gray-brown, covered with a slight glaucous bloom, marked by large pale scattered lenticels, and by large oval elevated leaf-scars containing a circle of conspicuous fibro-vascular bundle-scars, becoming in their third or fourth year, reddish brown and marked by a network of thin flat brown ridges. **Winter-buds** covered by chestnut-brown broad-ovate rounded slightly puberulous loosely imbricated scales, those of the inner ranks when fully grown bright green, pubescent, and sometimes 2' in length. **Bark** of the trunk ¼'–⅓' thick, light brown tinged with red, and separating on the surface into large thin irregular scales. **Wood** not strong, coarse-grained, light brown, with lighter colored often nearly white sapwood of 1 or 2 layers of annual growth; used and highly valued for fence-posts and rails.

Distribution. Usually supposed to be indigenous on the banks of the rivers of southwestern Georgia, western Florida, and central Alabama and Mississippi, and now widely naturalized through the south Atlantic states and in Kentucky and Tennessee.

Often planted for the decoration of parks and gardens in the eastern United States, and hardy as far north as eastern New England, and in western, central, and southern Europe. A dwarf round-headed form (var. *nana* Bur.) of unknown origin is often cultivated under the erroneous name of *C. Bungei* Hort. not C. A. Meyer.

× *Catalpa hybrida* Spaeth a hybrid of this species and the Chinese *C. ovata* G. Don is occasionally cultivated.

2. Catalpa speciosa Engelm. Western Catalpa.

Leaves oval, long-pointed, cordate at base, and usually entire or furnished with 1 or 2 lateral teeth, pilose above when they unfold and covered below and on the petioles with pale or rufous tomentum, and at maturity thick and firm, dark green on the upper surface and covered with soft pubescence on the lower surface, especially on the stout midrib and

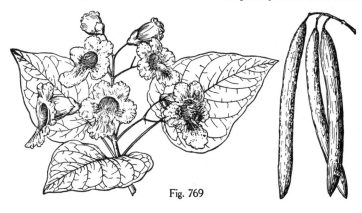

Fig. 769

the primary veins furnished in their axils with large clusters of dark glands, 10'–12' long and 7'–8' wide; turning black and falling after the first severe frost of the autumn; petioles stout, terete, 4'–6' in length. **Flowers** appearing late in May or early in June, on slender purple glabrous pedicels furnished near the middle with 1–3 bractlets, in open few-flowered panicles 5'–6' long and broad, with green or purple branches marked by orange-colored lenticels, the lowest branches often in the axils of small leaves; calyx purple, often sparingly villose or pubescent on the outer surface; corolla white, often spotted externally with purple near the base, about 2' long and 2½' wide, and marked internally on the lower side by 2 bands of yellow blotches following 2 lateral ridges and by occasional purple spots spreading over the lobes of the lower lip of the limb; filaments marked near the base by oblong purple spots. **Fruit** 8'–20' long, ½'–¾' in diameter near the middle, with a thick wall splitting toward spring into 2 concave valves; **seeds** 1' long and ⅓' wide, with a light brown coat, and wings rounded at the ends and terminating in a fringe of short hairs.

A tree, in the forest occasionally 120° high, with a tall straight trunk rarely 4½° in diameter, slender branches forming a narrow round-topped head, and branchlets light green often tinged with purple and pilose with scattered pale hairs when they first appear, light orange color or reddish brown, covered with a slight bloom during their first winter, and marked by numerous conspicuous pale lenticels and by the elevated oval leaf-scars ¼′ long and displaying a circular row of large fibro-vascular bundle-scars, becoming darker in their second and third years; usually smaller, and in open situations rarely more than 50° high, with a short trunk and a broad head of spreading branches. Winter-buds covered by loosely imbricated ovate chestnut-brown scales keeled on the back, slightly apiculate at apex, those of the inner ranks at maturity foliaceous, obovate, acute, gradually narrowed below to a sessile base, many-nerved with dark veins, pubescent on the lower surface, and sometimes 2½′ long and ¾′ wide. Bark of the trunk ¾′–1′ thick, brown tinged with red, and broken on the surface into thick scales. Wood light, soft, not strong, coarse-grained, light brown, with thin nearly white sapwood of 1 or 2 layers of annual growth; largely used for fence-posts, rails, telegraph and telephone poles, and occasionally for furniture and the interior finish of houses.

Distribution. Borders of streams and ponds, and fertile often inundated bottom-lands; valley of the Vermilion River, Illinois, through southern Illinois and Indiana, western Kentucky and Tennessee, southeastern Missouri and northeastern Arkansas; very abundant and probably of its largest size in southern Illinois and Indiana; naturalized through cultivation in southern Arkansas, western Louisiana, and eastern Texas.

Often planted in the prairie region of the Mississippi basin as a timber-tree, and as an ornament of parks and gardens in the eastern states, and now in many other countries with a temperate climate.

3. ENALLAGMA Bail.

Trees, with scaly bark, and stout slightly angled branchlets. Leaves alternate, short-petiolate, persistent. Flowers solitary, or in few-flowered fascicles on long bibracteolate peduncles from the axils of upper leaves or from the sides of the branches; calyx coriaceous, splitting in anthesis into 2 unequal broad divisions, or sometimes slightly 5-lobed, deciduous; corolla inserted under the hypogynous pulvinate fleshy disk, yellow streaked with purple, or dingy purple, tubular-campanulate, more or less ventricose on the lower side by a transverse fold, abruptly dilated into an oblique 2-lipped obscurely 5-lobed laciniately toothed limb; stamens 4, inserted in 2 ranks on the tube of the corolla, in pairs of different lengths, introrse, included or slightly exserted; filaments filiform; anthers oblong, the cells divergent; staminodium solitary, posterior, often 0; ovary sessile, 1-celled, ovate-conic, gradually narrowed into an elongated simple exserted style; stigma terminal, 2-lobed, the lobes stigmatic on their inner face, or entire; ovules in many ranks on 2 thickened 2-lobed lateral parietal placentas. Fruit baccate, oblong or ovoid; indehiscent, umbonate at apex, many-seeded; pericarp thin and brittle; becoming hard, light brown and separable into 2 layers, the inner membranaceous, filled with the united and thickened fleshy viscid placentas attached at base by a cluster of thick fibro-vascular bundles. Seeds imbedded irregularly in the placental mass, compressed, suborbicular, cordate above and below and deeply grooved on the convex faces; embryo filling the seminal cavity, flattened, thick and fleshy, deeply grooved, becoming black in drying; radicle minute, turned toward the lateral hilum.

Enallagma with three or four species is distributed from southern Florida through the Antilles to southern Mexico and Central America.

1. Enallagma cucurbitina Urb. Black Calabash Tree.

Crescentia cucurbitina L.

Leaves crowded near the end, of the branches, obovate-oblong or ovate-oblong, contracted into a short broad point or rarely rounded or emarginate at apex, gradually narrowed and cuneate at base, and entire, with cartilaginous slightly revolute margins, coriaceous, dark green and lustrous above, paler and yellow-green below, 6'–8' long and 1½'–4' wide, with a broad stout midrib deeply impressed on the upper side, conspicuous primary veins arcuate and united near the margins, and reticulate veinlets; unfolding in the

Fig. 770

spring, and persistent until their second year; petioles thick, covered with glands, and about ¼' in length.   **Flowers** appearing in April and May and also in autumn, bad-smelling, on thick drooping pedicels solitary in the axils of upper leaves, 1½'–2' long, furnished below the middle with 2 minute rigid acute bractlets and enlarged at apex into the thick oblique receptacle; calyx light green and slightly glandular at base, splitting nearly to the bottom into 2 ovate pointed lobes nearly as long as the tube of the corolla; corolla thick and leathery, dull purple or creamy white, and marked by narrow purple bands on the lower side, and 2' long, with a narrow tube creamy white within and slightly contracted above the base, the transverse fold near its apex, the limb erosely cut on the margins and obscurely 2-lipped, the upper lip slightly divided into 2 reflexed lobes, the lower obscurely 3-lobed; stamens inserted near the middle of the tube of the corolla, those of the anterior pair below the others and above the linear staminodium; ovary obliquely conic; stigma 2-lobed.   **Fruit** ovoid or oblong, 3'–4' long, 1½'–2' wide, dark green, minutely rugose-punctulate, and marked with 4 obscure longitudinal ridges corresponding with the margins and midrib of the carpellary leaves, raised on the thickened woody disk and pendent on a stout drooping stalk 1½'–2' long and much enlarged at apex; shell ¹⁄₁₆' thick, ultimately hard and brittle, lustrous on the outer surface and lined with a thin membranaceous shining light brown coat marked by the broad placental scars; **seeds** ⅝' long and broad and ¼' thick, with a minute lateral hilum just above the basal sinus; seed-coat of 2 layers, the outer thin, dark reddish brown, rugose, and separable from the thick pale felt-like inner layer; cotyledons with 2 ear-like folds near the base, inclosing the radicle in their lower sinus.

A tree, in Florida 18°–20° high, with a trunk 4'–5' in diameter, long slender drooping branches covered with wart-like excrescences, and stout slightly angled branchlets roughened and somewhat enlarged at the nodes by the thickening of the large crowded cup-shaped persistent woody bases of the leaves, and covered with thin creamy white bark becoming dark or ashy gray in their third year.   **Winter-buds** with linear acute apiculate scales becoming woody, and persistent for one or two years.   **Bark** of the trunk about ¼' thick, light brown tinged with red, and irregularly divided into large thin scales.   **Wood** heavy, hard, very close-grained, thin, light brown or orange color, with lighter colored sapwood.

Distribution.   Florida, only near the shores of Bay Biscayne on rich hummocks; common on the shores of many of the Antilles, and southward to southern Mexico, the Pacific coast of the Isthmus of Panama, and to Venezuela.

B. Ovary inferior (*partly superior in Caprifoliaceæ*).

LXV. RUBIACEÆ.

Trees or shrubs, with watery juice, and opposite simple entire leaves turning black in drying, with stipules. Flowers regular, perfect; calyx-tube adnate to the ovary, its limb 4 or 5-lobed or toothed; corolla 4 or 5-lobed; stamens inserted on the tube of the corolla, as many as and alternate with its lobes; filaments free, or united at base; anthers introrse, 2-celled, the cells opening longitudinally; disk epigynous, annular; ovary inferior; style slender; ovules numerous, or 1 in each cell; raphe ventral; micropyle superior. Fruit capsular, akene-like, or drupaceous. Seeds with albumen; seed-coat membranaceous.

The Madder family with some three hundred and fifty genera is chiefly tropical, with a few herbaceous genera confined exclusively to temperate regions. To this family belong the Coffee, the Cinchonas, South American trees yielding quinine from their bark, and the plant which produces ipecacuanha, a species of Cephaelis and a native of Brazil, the Gardenia and other plants cultivated for their fragrant flowers.

CONSPECTUS OF THE ARBORESCENT GENERA OF THE UNITED STATES.

Fruit a capsule; seeds numerous, surrounded by a wing; parts of the flower in 5's.
    Calyx 5-lobed, the lobes unequal, sometimes developing into rose-colored leaf-like bodies; filaments free; wing of the seed broad, oblong-ovate, unsymmetric on the sides; leaves deciduous.   1. **Pinckneya.**
    Calyx 5-toothed; filaments united into a short tube; wing of the seed narrow, symmetric; leaves persistent.   2. **Exostema.**
Fruit akene-like, 1 or 2-seeded; parts of the flower in 4's or rarely in 5's, flowers in pedunculate globose heads; leaves deciduous.   3. **Cephalanthus.**
Fruit drupaceous, with a 4-celled stone; parts of the flower in 4's; leaves persistent.
                                                   4. **Guettarda.**

1. PINCKNEYA Michx.

A tree, with fibrous roots, scaly light brown bitter bark, resinous scaly buds, stout terete pithy branchlets coated while young with hoary tomentum, becoming glabrous, and marked by scattered minute white lenticels and large nearly orbicular or obcordate leaf-scars displaying a lunate row of numerous crowded fibro-vascular bundle-scars. Leaves complanate in the bud, elliptic to oblong-ovate, acute at apex, cuneate at base, and gradually narrowed into a long stout petiole, thin, coated at first with pale pubescence, and at maturity dark green and puberulous above, paler and puberulous below, especially along the stout midrib and primary veins, deciduous; stipules interpetiolar, conspicuously glandular-punctate at base on the inner face, inclosing the leaf in the bud, triangular, subulate, pink, becoming oblong, acute, scarious, light brown, caducous. Flowers in pedunculate terminal and axillary pubescent trichotomous few-flowered cymes, with linear-lanceolate acute bracts and bractlets at first pink, becoming scarious, deciduous, or sometimes enlarging and rose-colored; flower-buds sulcate, coated with thick pale tomentum; calyx-tube clavate, bracteolate at base, covered with hoary tomentum, not closed in the bud, the limb 5-lobed, with subulate-lanceolate lobes green tinged with pink, scarious, or in the central flower of the ultimate division of the cyme with 1 or rarely with 2 of the lobes produced into oval or ovate acute rose-colored puberulous membranaceous leaf-like bodies, deciduous; corolla salver-form, light yellow, cinereo-tomentose, with a long narrow tube somewhat enlarged in the throat, 5-lobed, the lobes valvate in the bud, oblong, obtuse, marked by red lines and pilose with long white hairs on the inner surface, recurved after anthesis; stamens exserted; filaments filiform, free; anthers oblong, emarginate; ovary 2-celled; style filiform, exserted, slightly enlarged, 2-lobed and stigmatic at apex; ovules numerous, inserted in 2 ranks on a thin 2-lipped placenta longitudinally adnate to the inner face of the cell. Fruit a subglobose obscurely 2-lobed 2-celled capsule, loculicidally 2-valved, the valves thin and papery, light brown, puberulous, especially at the base, faintly rayed, marked by oblong pale spots and by the scars left by the falling of the deciduous calyx-limb and style, sometimes tardily septicidally 2-parted to the middle, persistent on the branches during the winter, the valves finally falling from the woody axis, their outer layer very thin, brittle, separable from the slightly thicker tough woody inner layer. Seeds horizontal, 2-ranked, minute, compressed; seed-coat thin, light brown, reticulate-veined, produced into a broad thin oblong-ovate wing, unsymmetrical on the sides, acute at apex, and longer above than below the seed; embryo elongated, immersed in the thick fleshy albumen; cotyledons ovate-oblong, foliaceous, longer than the terete radicle turned toward the hilum.

The genus is represented by a single species of the southeastern United States.

The generic name is in honor of Charles Cotesworth Pinckney (1746–1825) of South Carolina, the Revolutionary patriot.

1. Pinckneya pubens Michx. Georgia Bark.

Leaves unfolding in March, 5′–8′ long, 3′–4′ wide; petioles ⅔′–1½′ in length. **Flowers** 1½′ long appearing late in May and early in June, in open clusters 7′–8′ across, their petaloid

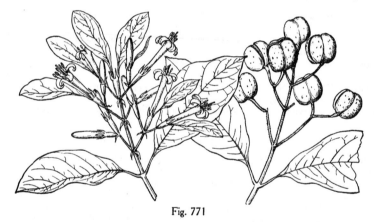

Fig. 771

calyx-lobes sometimes 2½′ long and ½′ wide. **Fruit** ripening in the autumn 1′ long and ⅔′ wide; **seeds** with their wings about ½′ long and ¼′ wide.

A tree, 20°–30° high, with a trunk occasionally 8′–10′ in diameter, slender spreading branches forming usually a narrow round-topped head, and branchlets coated when they first appear with hoary tomentum soon turning light red-brown, pubescent during the summer, and slightly puberulous during their first winter, ultimately becoming glabrous. **Winter-buds**: terminal ovoid, terete, ½′ long, contracted above the middle into a slender point, and covered by the dark red-brown lanceolate acute stipules of the last pair of leaves of the previous year, often persistent at the base of the growing shoots and marked at the base by 2 broadly ovate pale scar-like slightly pilose elevations; axillary buds obtuse, minute, nearly immersed in the bark. **Bark** of the trunk about ¼′ thick, with a light brown surface divided into minute appressed scales. **Wood** close-grained, soft, weak, brown, with lighter-colored sapwood of 8–10 layers of annual growth. The bark has been used in the treatment of intermittent fevers.

Distribution. Low wet sandy swamps on the borders of streams; coast region of South Carolina through southern Georgia and northern Florida from Leon to Washington County; rare and local.

2. EXOSTEMA Rich.

Trees or shrubs, with terete branchlets, and bitter bark. Leaves sessile or petiolate, persistent; stipules interpetiolar, deciduous. Flowers axillary and solitary or in terminal pedunculate cymes, fragrant, the peduncle bibracteolate above the middle; calyx-tube ovoid, clavate or turbinate, the limb short, 5-lobed, the lobes nearly triangular, persistent; corolla 5-lobed, white, salver-form, the tube long and narrow, erect, the lobes of the limb linear, elongated, spreading, imbricated in the bud; filaments filiform, exserted, united at base into a tube inserted on and adnate to the tube of the corolla; anthers oblong-linear; ovary 2-celled; style elongated, slender, exserted; stigma capitate, simple or minutely 2-lobed; ovules numerous, attached on the 2 sides of a fleshy oblong peltate placenta fixed to the inner face of the cell, ascending. Fruit a many-seeded 2-celled capsule septicidally 2-valved, the valves 2-parted, their outer layer membranaceous, separable from the crustaceous inner layer. Seeds compressed, oblong, imbricated downward on the placenta; seed-coat chestnut-brown, lustrous, produced into a narrow wing; embryo minute, in fleshy albumen; cotyledons flat; radicle terete, inferior.

Exostema with about twenty species is confined to the tropics of America, and is most abundant in the Antilles, one species reaching the shores of southern Florida. The bark contains active tonic properties, and has been used as a febrifuge.

The generic name, from ἔξω and στῆμα, relates to the long exserted stamens.

1. Exostema caribæum R. & S. Prince Wood.

Leaves oblong-ovate to lanceolate, contracted into a slender point and apiculate at apex, gradually narrowed and cuneate at base, entire, thick and coriaceous, dark green on the upper surface and yellow-green on the lower surface, $1\frac{1}{2}'-3'$ long and $\frac{1}{2}'-1\frac{1}{4}'$ wide, with a prominent orange-colored midrib and conspicuous reticulate veinlets; unfolding in the autumn and in early spring and summer, and persistent for 1 or 2 years; petioles slender,

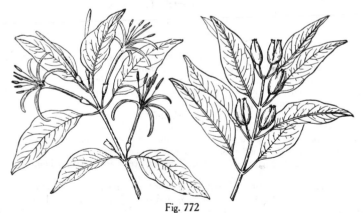

Fig. 772

orange-colored, $\frac{1}{4}'-\frac{1}{2}'$ in length; stipules nearly triangular, apiculate, with entire dentate or ciliate margins, about $\frac{1}{16}'$ long, and in falling marking the branchlets with ring-like scars. **Flowers** axillary, solitary, appearing from March until June, about $3'$ long, on slender pedicels spirally twisted before the flowers open; calyx-tube ovoid; corolla glabrous; filaments united into a short tube. **Fruit** $\frac{2}{3}'$ long, becoming black in drying; **seeds** oblong, $\frac{1}{8}'$ long, with a dark brown papillose coat and a light brown wing.

A glabrous tree, in Florida sometimes 20°–25° high, with a trunk 10′–12′ in diameter, slender erect branches forming a narrow head, and terete branchlets dark green at first, soon becoming dark red-brown and covered with pale lenticels, and in their second year ashy gray and conspicuously marked by the elevated leaf-scars. **Bark** of the trunk about ⅛′ thick, and divided by deep fissures into square smooth pale or nearly white plates. **Wood** very heavy, exceedingly hard, strong, close-grained, light brown handsomely streaked with different shades of yellow and brown, with bright yellow sapwood of 12–20 layers of annual growth.

Distribution. Florida, shores of Bay Biscayne and on the Everglade Keys, Dade County, and on the southern keys; abundant on Key West and Upper Metacombe Key: on many of the Antilles, in southern Mexico, and on the west coast of Nicaragua.

3. CEPHALANTHUS L.

Small trees or shrubs, with opposite or verticillate petiolate leaves, interpetiolar stipules, and scaly buds. Flowers nectariferous, yellow or creamy white, sessile in the axils of glandular bracts, in dense globose pedunculate terminal or axillary solitary or panicled heads; receptacle globose, setose; calyx-tube obpyramidal, with a short limb unequally 4 or 5-toothed or lobed; corolla tubular salver-form, divided into 4 or 5 short spreading or reflexed lobes usually furnished with a minute dark gland at the base or on the side of each sinus, puberulous on the inner surface of the tube, the lobes imbricated in the bud; stamens inserted on the throat of the corolla; filaments short; anthers linear-oblong, sagittate, apiculate at base; pistil of 2 carpels; ovary 2-celled; style filiform, elongated; stigma clavate, entire; ovule solitary in each cell, suspended from the apex of the cell on a short papillose funicle, anatropous. Fruit obpyramidal, coriaceous, 2-coccous. Seeds oblong, pendulous, covered at apex by a white spongy aril; embryo straight in cartilaginous albumen; cotyledons oblong, obtuse; radicle elongated, superior.

Cephalanthus with seven species is widely distributed in North and South America, and in southern and eastern Asia, and the Malay Archipelago.

The generic name, from κεφαλή and ἄνθος, relates to the capitate inflorescence.

1. Cephalanthus occidentalis L.   Button Bush.

Leaves ovate, lanceolate or elliptic, acute, acuminate or short-pointed at apex, rounded or cuneate at base, thin, dark green on the upper surface, paler and glabrous or puberulous on the lower surface, 2′–7′ long and ½′–3½′ wide, with a stout light yellow midrib often covered below with long white hairs and 5 or 6 pairs of slender primary veins nearly parallel with the sides of the leaf; deciduous, or persistent during the winter; petioles stout, grooved, glabrous, ½′–¾′ in length; stipules minute, nearly triangular. **Flowers**: flower-heads 1′–1½′ in diameter on slender peduncles 1′–2′ long, usually in panicles 4′–5′ in length, their lower peduncles from the axil of upper leaves; flowers creamy white, very fragrant, opening from the middle of May in Florida and Texas to the middle of August in Canada and on the mountains of California; calyx usually 4 or occasionally 5-lobed, with short rounded lobes, and slightly villose toward the base; corolla glandular or eglandular; anthers nearly sessile, included, discharging their pollen before the flowers open; disk thin and obscure. **Fruit** ripening late in the autumn in heads ⅝′–¾′ in diameter, green tinged with red and ultimately dark red-brown.

A tree, occasionally 40°–50° high, with a straight tapering trunk a foot in diameter, and frequently free of limbs for 15°–20°, ascending and spreading branches, and stout branchlets with a thick pith, glabrous and marked by large oblong pale lenticels, and developed mostly in verticels of 3's from the axillary buds of one of the upper nodes, without a terminal bud, light green when they first appear, pale reddish brown, covered with a glaucous bloom during their first winter and then marked by small semicircular leaf-scars displaying semilunate fibro-vascular bundle-scars, and connected by the persistent black stipules or by their subulate scars, darker the following season, and dark brown in their third year, the bark then beginning to separate into the large loose scales found on the large branches and on the stems of small plants; usually a shrub, only a few feet high. **Winter-buds** axillary, single or in pairs or in 3's one above the other, minute, nearly immersed in the bark. **Bark**

Fig. 773

of large trunks dark gray-brown or often nearly black, divided by deep fissures into broad flat ridges broken on the surface into elongated narrow scales. The bark contains tannin, and has been used in the treatment of fevers and in homœopathic practice.

Distribution. Swamps and the low wet borders of ponds and streams; New Brunswick to Ontario, southern Michigan, southern Minnesota, eastern Nebraska, Kansas and western Oklahoma (near Canton, Blaine County), southward to the shores of Bay Biscayne and the Everglade Keys, Dade County, Florida, eastern Texas to the valley of the Rio Grande, southern New Mexico, and Arizona, and widely distributed in California; in Mexico and Cuba; very rarely arborescent at the north and of its largest size on the margins of river-bottoms and swamps and in pond holes in southern Arkansas and eastern Texas; ascending on the southern Appalachian Mountains to altitudes of 2500°; passing into var. *pubescens* Rafn, with leaves soft pubescent below especially on the midrib and veins, and pubescent petioles, inflorescence and branchlets; southern Indiana, southeastern Missouri, southern Arkansas, western Louisiana and eastern Texas to the valley of the lower Brazos River.

Occasionally cultivated in the northeastern states as an ornamental plant.

4. GUETTARDA Endl.

Small trees or shrubs, with bitter bark, opposite or rarely verticellate persistent leaves, interpetiolar deciduous stipules, and scaly buds. Flowers sessile or short-pedicellate, with or without bractlets, in axillary forked pedunculate cymes, their bracts and bractlets lanceolate, acute, minute, deciduous; calyx globose, the limb produced above the ovary into an elongated 4–7-lobed tube; corolla salver-shaped, with an elongated cylindric tube naked in the throat, and a 4-lobed limb, the oblong lobes imbricated in the bud; stamens included; filaments free, short; anthers oblong-linear; ovary 4-celled, the cells elongated, tubular; style stout; stigma capitate; ovule solitary, suspended on the thickened funicle from the inner angle of the cell. Fruit a fleshy 1-stoned 2–9-seeded subglobose drupe, with thin flesh, and a bony or ligneous globose 4–9-celled stone obtusely angled or sulcate, the cells narrow and often curved upward. Seed compressed, suspended on the thick funicle closing the orifice of the wall of the stone, straight or excurved; albumen thin and fleshy; embryo elongated, cylindric or compressed; cotyledons flat, minute, not longer than the elongated terete radicle turned toward the hilum.

Guettarda with about fifty species is chiefly tropical American, with one species widely distributed on maritime shores from east tropical Africa to Australia and the islands of the Pacific Ocean. Of the species found within the territory of the United States two are arborescent. The bark of some of the species is occasionally employed as a tonic and febrifuge, and a few species are cultivated in tropical gardens for the delightful fragrance of their white flowers.

The generic name is in honor of Jean Étienne Guettard (1715–1786), the distinguished French botanist and mineralogist.

CONSPECTUS OF THE ARBORESCENT SPECIES OF THE UNITED STATES.

Leaves thin, pilose or glabrate above.   1. G. elliptica (D).
Leaves coriaceous, hispidulose-papillose and scabrate above.   2. G. scabra (D).

1. Guettarda elliptica Sw.

Leaves broad-oval to oblong-elliptic, acute or obtuse and apiculate at apex, and cuneate or rounded at base, covered with pale silky hairs when they unfold, and at maturity thin, dark green, pilose or glabrate on the upper surface, lighter colored and pubescent on the lower surface, especially along the stout midrib and in the axils of the 4–6 pairs of primary veins, $\frac{3}{4}'-2\frac{1}{2}'$ long and $\frac{1}{2}'-1'$ wide; unfolding in Florida in May and June and persistent on the branches until the trees begin their growth the following year; petioles stout, hairy,

Fig. 774

$\frac{1}{4}'-\frac{1}{2}'$ in length. **Flowers** pedicellate, appearing in Florida in June, yellowish white, $\frac{1}{4}'$ long, in slender hairy-stemmed cymes from the axils of leaves of the year near the end of branches, or from bud-scales at base of young shoots, their peduncle shorter than the leaves, forked near the apex, often with a flower in the fork and 3 at the end of each branch, or the lateral flowers of these clusters replaced by branches producing 3 flowers at their apex, the bractlets subtending the branches of the peduncle, and the lateral flowers of the ultimate divisions of the inflorescence linear-lanceolate, acute, coated with hairs, about $\frac{1}{16}'$ long, deciduous; calyx-lobes nearly triangular, acute, coated on the outer surface with long pale hairs, and half as long as the erect corolla canescent externally, with rounded lobes. **Fruit** ripening in November, dark purple, pilose, $\frac{1}{3}'$ in diameter, crowned with the remnants of the persistent calyx-tube, the flesh sweet and mealy; stone obscurely ridged and usually 2–4-seeded; **seeds** oblong-lanceolate, compressed, nearly straight, with a thin pale coat.

A slender tree, in Florida in hammocks occasionally 18°–20° high, with an irregularly buttressed or lobed trunk 5'–6' in diameter, the deep depressions between the lobes continuous or often interrupted, small upright branches, and thin terete branchlets coated when they first appear with long pale or rufous hairs and light red-brown or ashy gray and conspicuously marked by pale lenticels, and in their second year by large elevated orbicular leaf-scars; or often a shrub. **Winter-buds** acuminate, light brown, coated with pale pubescence, and about ⅛' long. **Bark** of the trunk about 1/16' thick, with a smooth dark brown surface covered with large irregularly shaped pale blotches and numerous small white spots. **Wood** heavy, hard, very close-grained, light brown tinged with red, with thin sapwood of 6–10 layers of annual growth.

Distribution. Florida, on the Everglade Keys (Royal Palm Hammock), and coast of the southern keys; on the Bahama Islands and in Jamaica.

2. Guettarda scabra Lam.

Leaves oval, oblong or ovate, acuminate or rounded and apiculate at apex, gradually narrowed or broad at the rounded or subcordate base, entire, coriaceous, dark green, hispidulose-papillose and scabrate on the upper surface, pale and soft-pubescent on the lower surface, 2'–5' long and 1¼'–3¼' wide, with thickened slightly revolute margins, a stout midrib, usually 8–11 pairs of prominent primary veins and conspicuous reticulate veinlets;

Fig. 775

petioles stout, rusty-pubescent, ⅓'–¾' in length; stipules concave at base, gradually narrowed above into a long slender point, pubescent, as long as the petioles. **Flowers** produced irregularly during the winter and early spring, sessile or short-pedicellate in the axils of acute bracts, in pedunculate cymes on slender rusty-pubescent peduncles 1½'–2' in length; calyx short-oblong, densely pubescent on the outer surface; corolla often 1' in length, the slender tube retrorsely silky-villose on the outer surface, the lobes 5–7, usually 5, oblong-obtuse; filaments free, short; anthers oblong-linear, included, style shorter than the tube of the corolla; stigma capitate. **Fruit** ripening in the autumn, subglobose, pubescent, ¼' in diameter, and crowned by the persistent tube of the calyx; flesh thin and dry; stone slightly angled thick-walled, 4–9-seeded.

A tree, in Florida sometimes 20°–25° high, with a tall trunk 2'–2½' in diameter, small ascending branches forming an open irregular head, and stout or slender branchlets densely covered during their first season with rufous pubescence, and light reddish brown, slightly pubescent and marked by conspicuous leaf-scars in their second year; often a shrub.

Distribution. Florida, near Miami and on the Everglade Keys, Dade County, and on the southern keys; on the Bahama Islands and on several of the Antilles.

LXVI. CAPRIFOLIACEÆ.

Trees or shrubs, with watery juice, opposite petiolate leaves involute in the bud, with or without stipules, scaly buds, and fibrous roots.   Flowers regular, perfect, with articulated pedicels, in terminal compound cymes; calyx-tube adnate to the ovary, 5-toothed; corolla epigynous, 5-lobed, the lobes imbricated in the bud; stamens 5, inserted on the tube of the corolla, as many as and alternate with its lobes; filaments slender, free; anthers oblong, introrse, 2-celled, the cells opening longitudinally; disk 0 (in the arborescent genera of the United States); ovary inferior or partly superior, 3–5 or 1-celled; style short, capitate, 3–5-lobed and stigmatic at apex; ovule solitary, suspended from the apex of the cell, resupinate; raphe dorsal; micropyle superior.   Fruit drupaceous, crowned with the remnants of the style.   Seeds with copious fleshy albumen; seed-coat membranaceous, adherent to the albumen; embryo minute, near the hilum; cotyledons ovoid or ovate; radicle terete, erect.

The Honeysuckle family with ten genera is most abundant in the temperate regions of the northern hemisphere, with a few species extending into the tropics and to beyond the tropics in the southern hemisphere.   Many of the species, especially of Lonicera, Sambucus, and Viburnum, are cultivated in gardens for the beauty of their flowers and fruits.

CONSPECTUS OF THE ARBORESCENT GENERA OF THE UNITED STATES.

Leaves unequally pinnate; fruit with 3–5 nutlets.   1. **Sambucus.**
Leaves simple; fruit with 1 stone.   2. **Viburnum.**

1. SAMBUCUS L. Elder.

Trees or shrubs, with stout branches containing thick white or brown pith, and buds with several scales.   Leaves petiolate, unequally pinnate, deciduous, with serrate or laciniate leaflets, the base of the petiole naked, glandular or furnished with a stipule-like leaflet; stipels small, leaf-like, usually setaceous, often 0; stipules small, rudimentary, usually 0 except on vigorous shoots.   Flowers small, in broad terminal corymbose cymes, their bracts and bractlets lanceolate, acute, scarious, caducous, sometimes ebracteolate; calyx-tube ovoid, the limb 3–5-lobed or toothed; corolla rotate or slightly campanulate, equally 3–5-parted; filaments filiform or subulate; ovary inferior or partly superior, 3–5-celled; style abbreviated, thick and conic, 3–5-lobed, stigmatic at apex.   Fruit subglobose, with juicy flesh, and 3–5 oblong cartilaginous punctate-rugulose or smooth 1-seeded nutlets full and rounded on the back and rounded at the ends.   Seeds filling the cavity of the nutlets, pale brown; cotyledons ovoid.

Sambucus with about twenty species is widely and generally distributed through the temperate parts of North America, Europe, and Asia, and inhabits high mountain ranges within the tropics, and in Australia, Tasmania, and New Zealand.   Of the nine or ten North American species three are arborescent.   Sambucus possesses cathartic and emetic properties in the bark; the flowers are excitant and sudorific, and the juice of the fruit is alterative and laxative.   The dried flowers of the European Sambucus nigra L., are used in the preparation of an aromatic distilled water and in flavoring lard, and the hard and compact wood is made into combs and mathematical instruments.   The large pithy shoots of Sambucus furnish children with pop-guns, pipes, and whistles; and the fruit of some of the species is cooked and eaten.

Sambucus, the name of the Elder-tree, is believed to have been derived from σαμβύκη, a musical instrument, probably in allusion to the use of the pithy stems.

CONSPECTUS OF THE ARBORESCENT SPECIES OF THE UNITED STATES.

Cymes flat-topped; pith usually white; fruit black; nutlets rugose.
    Fruit lustrous.   1. **S. Simpsonii** (C).
    Fruit appearing blue from a thick covering of bloom.   2. **S. coerulea** (B, F, G, H).
Cymes ovoid; pith pale brown; fruit red; nutlets smooth.   3. **S. callicarpa** (B, G).

1. Sambucus Simpsonii Rehd.

Sambucus intermedia Small, not Carrière.

Leaves 4′–7′ long, 3–7, usually 5-foliolulate, with a glabrous petiole and usually 5 dark yellow-green leaflets, frequently deciduous, lustrous and glabrous on the upper surface with the exception of a few scattered hairs on the midrib, and paler and glabrous on the lower surface, the terminal leaflet obovate or oblong-obovate, short-acuminate at apex, and gradually narrowed at base into a slender petiolule $\frac{1}{3}′–\frac{1}{2}′$ in length, the lateral leaflets broad-

Fig. 776

elliptic to oblong-elliptic, short-acuminate, broad-cuneate at base, those of the upper pair usually sessile, those of the lower pair on short stalks rarely more than $\frac{1}{12}′$ long, serrate except at the base with small slightly spreading teeth, $1\frac{1}{2}′–3′$ long and $1\frac{1}{2}′–2\frac{1}{2}′$ wide. **Flowers** slightly fragrant, on slender pedicels in convex or sometimes flat cymes 3′–8′ in diameter, with 4 or 5 rays, the terminal ray as long or longer than the lateral rays, rarely shorter; calyx-tube ovoid, the lobes oblong-ovate, acute, about as long as the tube and slightly exceeding the thick conic style; stamens about as long as the white corolla-lobes; ovary usually 5, rarely 4-celled. **Fruit** subglobose, dark purplish black, about $\frac{1}{4}′$ in diameter; nutlets rugose.

A tree, sometimes 15°–18° high, with a trunk often 8′ in diameter, and slightly angled branchlets greenish when they first appear, becoming light yellow-gray and sometimes covered during their second and third years with thick corky excrescences; pith white, on 2 or 3-year-old branches comparatively narrow, occupying only about one-third of the diameter of the stem.

Distribution. Florida, neighborhood of Jacksonville, Duval County, to Eustis, Lake County, Bradentown, Manatee County, and Sanibel Island, Lee County; Mississippi, Ocean Springs, Jackson County; Louisiana, Cameron, Cameron Parish.

2. Sambucus coerulea Raf.

Sambucus glauca Nutt.

Sambucus neomexicana Woot.

Leaves 5′–7′ long, with a stout grooved petiole much enlarged and naked or sometimes furnished at the base with leaf-like appendages, and 5–9 ovate or narrow-oblong leaflets contracted at apex into a long point, unequally cuneate or rounded at base, and coarsely serrate with spreading or slightly incurved callous-tipped teeth, the lower leaflets often 3-parted or pinnate, the terminal one sometimes furnished with 1 or 2 lateral stalked leaflets, yellow-green on the upper surface, pale on the lower surface, covered with scattered pale hairs when they unfold, and at maturity glabrous or soft pubescent beneath (var. *velutina* Rehd.), thin, rather firm in texture, bright green above and pale below, 1'-6' long and ⅓'-1½' wide, with a narrow pale midrib and inconspicuous veins; petiolules slender, those of the lateral leaflets ¼'-½' and of the terminal leaflet up to 2' in length; stipels linear, oblong-lanceolate to ovate, rounded or acute at apex, entire or sharply serrate and leaf-like, ₁₆'-½' long, caducous, often 0.   Flowers ⅛' in diameter, appearing from April in southern

Fig. 777

California to July in British Columbia, in flat long-branched glabrous or pubescent cymes 4'-10' wide, with linear acute green caducous bracts and bractlets, the lower branches often from the axils of upper leaves; flower-buds globose, covered with a glaucous bloom, sometimes turning red before opening; calyx ovoid, red-brown, with acute scarious lobes; corolla yellowish white, with oblong divisions rounded at apex, as long as the stamens. **Fruit** subglobose, ⅓' in diameter, black, appearing blue by its thick covering of mealy bloom; flesh rather sweet and juicy.

A tree, 30°-50° high, with a tall straight trunk sometimes enlarged at base and 12'-18' in diameter, stout spreading branches forming a compact round-topped head, and branchlets usually without a terminal bud, green tinged with red or brown when they first appear, and covered with short white caducous hairs, or densely soft pubescent during their first season (var. *velutina* Rehd.), stout, slightly angled, covered with lustrous red-brown bark in their first winter and nearly encircled by the large triangular leaf-scars marked by conspicuous fibro-vascular bundle-scars; pith white or rarely brownish; often a broad shrub, with numerous spreading stems. **Winter-buds** axillary generally in pairs, superposed or in clusters of 4 or 5, only the upper bud or sometimes the lower usually developing, covered with 2 or 3 pairs of opposite broad-ovate chestnut-brown scales, those of the inner rank accrescent, and at maturity acute, entire, green, 1' long, and sometimes developing into pinnate leaves 2'-3' in length. **Bark** of the trunk deeply and irregularly fissured, the dark brown surface slightly tinged with red and broken into small square appressed scales. **Wood** light, soft, weak, coarse-grained, yellow tinged with brown, with thin lighter colored sapwood.

Distribution. Gravelly rather dry soil of valleys and river-bottoms; western Montana (neighborhood of Flathead Lake and Missoula, Missoula County), through Idaho to the coast of British Columbia (Vancouver Island), and southward to the San Bernardino

Mountains and Santa Catalina Island, California, ascending on the Cascade and Sierra
Nevada Mountains to altitudes of 6000°–8000°; Nevada, King's Cañon, Ormsby County;
Utah, Juab, Juab County, and the neighborhood of Salt Lake City, Salt Lake County;
Colorado, near Trinidad, Las Animas County; New Mexico, Sacramento Mountains, Otero
County; very abundant in the coast region; comparatively rare in the interior; of its largest
size in the valleys of western Oregon; northward, and east of the Cascade and Sierra Ne-
vada Mountains rarely arborescent; in southern California often with smaller leaves and
flower-clusters than northward; the var. *velutina* rare and local, California, Goose Valley,
Shasta County; at altitudes of 6000°–7000° on the Sierra Nevada in Sierra, Madera and
Kern Counties, and on Santa Catalina Island; Nevada, on Hunter's Creek, Washoe County,
at an altitude of 6000°.

Occasionally planted as an ornamental plant in the Pacific states, passing into

Sambucus coerulea var. arizonica Sarg.

Sambucus mexicana Sarg., not Presl.

Differing from *Sambucus coerulea* in its 3–5, usually 3-foliate leaves with usually elliptic
long-acuminate leaflets glabrous or slightly pubescent when they appear, 1′–3′ long and
½′–1′ wide, their stipels minute or rudimentary, smaller flower-clusters and fruit not more
than ¼′ in diameter.

A tree, often 30° high, with stout spreading branches forming a compact round-topped
head, and slender branchlets glabrous or villose pubescent early in the season, usually be-

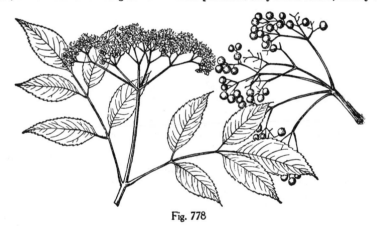

Fig. 778

coming glabrous. **Bark** of the trunk about ¼′ thick, the light brown surface tinged with red
and broken into long narrow horizontal ridge-like scales. **Wood** light, soft, close-grained,
light brown, with thin lighter-colored sapwood of 2 or 3 layers of annual growth.

Distribution. Banks of streams; Arizona, Grand View Trail, Grand Cañon of the Colorado River and near Flagstaff, Coconino County, Globe, Gila County, and banks of the
Rialta near Tucson, Pima County; common; New Mexico, near Silver City, Grant County;
southern California (San Diego, Los Angeles, Ventura and Kern Counties).

3. Sambucus callicarpa Greene.

Leaves 6′–10′ long, with a stout slightly grooved petiole and 5–7, usually 5, elliptic finely
or coarsely serrate leaflets, acuminate and long-pointed at apex, cuneate and often unsymmetric at base, dark green and glabrous on the upper surface, paler and more or less villose-
pubescent on the lower surface, especially along the slender midrib, 2½′–5′ long and ½′–2′

wide; petiolules $\frac{1}{8}'-\frac{1}{4}'$ or that of the terminal leaflet up to $1\frac{1}{2}'$ in length. **Flowers on pedicels** $\frac{1}{8}'$ long, in ovoid to semiorbicular cymes, usually $2\frac{1}{2}'-3'$ long and broad, often somewhat flattened at maturity, on stout peduncles $1\frac{1}{2}'-3'$ in length, about $\frac{1}{4}'$ in diameter, with white

Fig. 779

or yellow slightly obovate petals rounded at apex, and stamens rather shorter than the lobes of the corolla. **Fruit** about $\frac{1}{2}'$ in diameter, bright red or rarely chestnut color (f. *Piperi* Sarg.); nutlets smooth.

A tree, occasionally 25°–30° high, with a trunk 10'–12' in diameter, slender branchlets occasionally puberulous early in the season, becoming glabrous, light brown, separating on the surface into thin scales.

Distribution. River banks in low moist soil, from sea-level in the neighborhood of the coast up to altitudes of 7000°–8000°; coast of Alaska (Skagway), southward along the coast to Marin County, California, and inland to the western slopes of the Cascade and Sierra Nevada Mountains, southward to Amador County; the f. *Piperi* in western Washington.

2. VIBURNUM A. L. de Juss.

Trees or shrubs, with tough flexible branchlets, and large winter-buds naked or covered with scales, those of the arborescent North American species enclosed in one pair of valvate scales, the buds containing flower-bearing branches ovoid, swollen below the middle and contracted into a long or short point and subtended by 2 minute lateral generally abortive buds formed in the axils of the last leaves of the previous year, those containing sterile shoots narrow-lanceolate, slightly angled, acute; axillary buds acute, much flattened, and much smaller than the terminal bud. Leaves deciduous (in the American species), without or rarely with stipules, the first pair rudimentary, with small blades and broad boat-shaped petioles, caducous (in the North American arborescent species). Flowers on short bracteolate or bibracteolate pedicels, in terminal or axillary umbel-like flat or panicled cymes, their bracts and bractlets minute, lanceolate, acute, caducous; calyx-tube cylindric, the limb short, equally 5-lobed, persistent on the fruit; corolla rotate, equally 5-lobed, spreading and reflexed after anthesis; stamens inserted on the base of the corolla; filaments elongated, exserted; anthers bright yellow; ovary inferior, 1-celled; style conic, divided at apex into three stigmatic lobes. Fruit 1-celled, with thin sweet acidulous or oily flesh, stone (in the North American arborescent species) coriaceous, oval, short-pointed at apex; much flattened, dull reddish brown, slightly pitted. Seed filling the cavity of the stone, concave on the ventral face, bright reddish brown, the thin coat projected into a red narrow irregular often erose marginal border.

Viburnum with a hundred species is widely and generally distributed through the temperate regions of the northern hemisphere, and occurs on the mountains of central and western South America, on the Antilles, the islands of the Malay Archipelago, and Madagascar. Of the fifteen North American species four are small trees. Many of the species produce beautiful flowers and fruits, and are frequently cultivated as ornaments of parks and gardens.

Viburnum is the classical name of one of the European species.

CONSPECTUS OF THE NORTH AMERICAN ARBORESCENT SPECIES.

Leaves entire or obscurely crenulate; inflorescence long-stalked; winter-buds elongated, narrow-lanceolate, acuminate, covered with rusty scales. 1. **V. nudum** (A, C).
Leaves sharply serrate; inflorescence sessile or short-stalked.
Petioles wing-margined; inflorescence sessile; winter-buds long-pointed, scurfy pubescent. 2. **V. Lentago** (A, C, F).
Petioles usually without margins.
Petioles nearly glabrous; inflorescence short-stalked; winter-buds short-pointed or obtuse, rufous pubescent. 3. **V. prunifolium** (A, C).
Petioles of early leaves and the short-pointed winter-buds rusty tomentose, inflorescence sessile. 4. **V. rufidulum** (A, C).

1. Viburnum nudum L.

Leaves broad-elliptic to oval or slightly obovate, or in one form narrow-elliptic (var. *angustifolium* Torr. & Gray), acute, acuminate or abruptly short-pointed or rarely rounded at apex, cuneate or rounded at base, entire or slightly crenulate, covered when they unfold

Fig. 780

with rusty scales persistent on the lower side of the midrib and petioles and occasionally on the whole lower surface, thick, dark green and lustrous on the upper surface, paler on the lower surface, 4′–6′ long and 1½′–2′ wide, with a prominent midrib, slender veins, and slightly thickened and revolute margins; very variable in the size and shape of the leaves and in the amount of their scurfy covering, those of the southern tree form usually larger than the leaves of more northern shrubs; leaves of the var. *angustifolium* often not more than 2′ long and ½′ wide; petioles slender, ½′ in length. **Flowers** appearing from the first of May at the south to the middle of June at the north and occasionally also in the autumn, white or pale cream color, about $\frac{1}{4}'$ wide, in flat or slightly convex cymes with ovate acute bracts and bractlets, $2'-4'$ in diameter and about as long or rather shorter than their peduncle. **Fruit** ripening late in the autumn, globose, pink at first when fully grown, becoming bright blue, $\frac{1}{4}'$ in diameter.

A tree, rarely $18'-20'$ high, with a tall trunk $6'-8'$ in diameter, with spreading nearly horizontal branches forming an open head, and slender branchlets scurfy when they first appear, soon becoming glabrous, reddish brown and lustrous during their first season and greenish brown the following year; usually a small or large shrub, and perhaps only a tree on the borders of swamps near Gainesville, Alachua County, and Palatka, Putnam County, Florida. **Winter-buds** reddish brown, covered with rusty scales, those containing flower-bearing branches, abruptly long pointed, $\frac{1}{2}'-\frac{3}{4}'$ in length.

Distribution. Low moist soil usually in the neighborhood of swamps and streams, and on rich hillsides; southern Connecticut (Milford and Derby, New Haven County), southward through the coast and Piedmont region, to De Soto County (near Sebring), Florida, and westward usually in the neighborhood of the coast to the valley of the lower Brazos River, eastern Texas, and northward through western Louisiana to central Arkansas and western Tennessee; occasionally ascending the Appalachian Mountains to altitudes of $2000°$; the var. *angustifolium* from North Carolina up to altitudes of $3000°$ on the Blue Ridge, to northern Florida.

2. Viburnum Lentago L. Sheepberry. Nannyberry.

Leaves ovate, usually acuminate, with short or elongated points, or sometimes rounded at apex, cuneate, rounded or subcordate at base, and sharply serrate with incurved callous-tipped teeth, when they unfold bronze-green, lustrous, coated on both surfaces of the mid-rib and on the petioles with thick rufous pubescence, slightly pilose on the upper surface and covered on the lower with short pale hairs, and at maturity bright green and lustrous

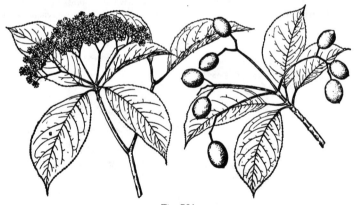

Fig. 781

above, yellow-green and marked by minute black dots below, $2\frac{1}{2}'-3'$ long and $1'-1\frac{1}{2}'$ wide, with a slender midrib, and primary veins connected by conspicuous reticulate veinlets; turning in the autumn before falling deep orange-red or red and orange color; petioles broad, grooved, more or less interruptedly winged or occasionally wingless, $1'-1\frac{1}{2}'$ long, those of the first pair of leaves covered with thick rufous tomentum. **Flowers** about $\frac{1}{4}'$ in diameter, slightly fragrant, appearing from the middle of April to the 1st of June in stout-branched scurfy sessile slightly convex cymes $3'-5'$ in diameter, with nearly triangular green caducous bracts and bractlets about $\frac{1}{16}'$ in length; corolla pale cream color or nearly white, with ovate lobes acute and slightly erose at apex. Fruit ripening in September on slender drooping stalks, in red-stemmed few-fruited clusters, oval or occasionally globose (var. *sphaerocarpum* A. Gray), thick-skinned, sweet and rather juicy, black or dark blue, and covered with a glaucous bloom; stone about $\frac{7}{8}'$ long and $\frac{5}{16}'$ wide.

A bushy tree, 20°–30° high, with a short trunk 8'–10' in diameter, slender rather pendulous branches forming a compact round-topped head, and thin divergent branchlets light green, slightly covered with rufous pubescence when they first appear, and in their first winter light red, scurfy, marked by occasional dark orange-colored lenticels and by narrow leaf-scars displaying 3 conspicuous fibro-vascular bundle-scars, becoming in their second year dark reddish brown and sometimes covered with a glaucous bloom. Winter-buds light red, generally covered with pale scurfy pubescence, those containing flower-bearing branchlets $\frac{3}{4}'$ in length, abruptly contracted into long narrow tapering points. Bark of the trunk reddish brown and irregularly broken into small thick plates divided on their surface into minute thin appressed scales. Wood bad-smelling, heavy, hard, close-grained, dark orange-brown, with thin nearly white sapwood.

Distribution. Rocky hillsides, along the borders of forests, or near the banks of streams and the margins of swamps, in moist soil; valley of the Rivière du Loup, Province of Quebec, to Saskatchewan, and southward through the northern states to southern Pennsylvania, central Ohio, northern Indiana and southern Wisconsin, northeastern Iowa and eastern Nebraska, and along the Appalachian Mountains up to altitudes of 2500° to West Virginia; on the Turtle Mountains of North Dakota, the Black Hills of South Dakota, on the eastern foothills of the Bighorn Mountains of Wyoming and on those of the Rocky Mountains of Colorado (Boulder, Boulder County).

Often cultivated as an ornament of parks and gardens in the eastern United States, and occasionally in Europe.

× *Viburnum Jackii* Rehd. with characters intermediate between *Viburnum Lentago* and V. *prunifolium* is now believed to be a hybrid between those species.

3. Viburnum prunifolium L. Black Haw. Stag Bush.

Leaves ovate or rarely obovate, oval or suborbicular, rounded, acute, or short-pointed at apex, cuneate or rounded at base, and usually rather remotely or sometimes finely serrate with rigid incurved callous-tipped teeth, lustrous and tinged with red, glabrous on the lower surface and covered on the upper side of the midrib and on the bright red petioles with scattered reddish hairs when they unfold, and at maturity thick or sometimes coriaceous, dark green and glabrous on the upper surface, pale and glabrous on the lower surface, 1'–3' long and $\frac{1}{2}'$–3' wide, with slender primary veins connected by reticulate veinlets; in the autumn turning brilliant scarlet or dark vinous red before falling; petioles terete, grooved, $\frac{1}{2}'$–$\frac{2}{3}'$ in length, and on vigorous shoots sometimes narrowly wing-margined. Flowers $\frac{1}{4}'$ in diameter on slender pedicels bibracteolate at apex, in glabrous short-stemmed flat cymes 2'–4' in diameter, with subulate caducous bracts about $\frac{1}{16}'$ long, usually red above the middle; corolla pure white, with oval to nearly orbicular lobes. Fruit ripening in October, in few-fruited red-stemmed clusters, persistent on the branches until the beginning of winter, oval or slightly obovoid, $\frac{1}{2}'$–$\frac{2}{3}'$ long or rarely globose, dark blue and covered with a glaucous bloom; stone about $\frac{1}{2}'$ long and $\frac{1}{4}'$ wide.

A bushy tree, occasionally 20°–30° high, with a short and usually crooked trunk 6'–8' in diameter, stout spreading rigid branches beset with slender spine-like branchlets, bright red and glabrous when they first appear, soon turning green, and in their first winter gray tinged with red, covered with a slight bloom, and marked by orange-colored lenticels and by the large lunate leaf-scars displaying 3 fibro-vascular bundle-scars, and ultimately dark brown tinged with red; or often a low intricately branched shrub. Winter-buds short-pointed or obtuse, brown, glabrous or scurfy, those containing flower-bearing branches about $\frac{1}{2}'$ long and $\frac{1}{4}'$ wide, and about twice as large as those containing sterile branchlets. Bark of the trunk $\frac{1}{4}'$–$\frac{1}{3}'$ thick, and broken into thick irregularly shaped plate-like red-brown scales.

Wood heavy, hard, strong, brittle, close-grained, browr tinged with red, with thick nearly white sapwood of 20-30 layers of annual growth.

Distribution. Dry rocky hillsides, fence-rows and the sides of roads; Fairfield County, Connecticut, and the valley of the lower Hudson River, New York, southward to south-

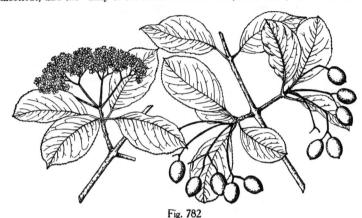

Fig. 782

eastern Virginia and to the Coast and Piedmont regions of North and South Carolina up to altitudes of 2000° to the valley of the Savannah River (near Augusta, Georgia, Richmond County, rare), and through southern Ohio, to central Michigan, Indiana, southern Illinois, southern and western Kentucky, Missouri and eastern Kansas; very abundant in Missouri from the northeastern counties southward through the state.

Often cultivated as an ornament of parks and gardens in the eastern United States, and occasionally in western and northern Europe.

4. Viburnum rufidulum Raf.   Black Haw.

Leaves elliptic to obovate or oval, rounded, acute, or short-pointed at apex, cuneate or rounded at base, and finely serrate with slender apiculate straight or incurved teeth, cov-

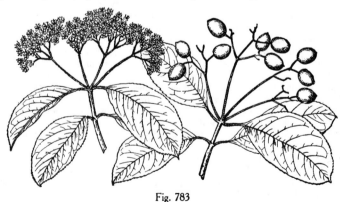

Fig. 783

ered below and on the wings of the petiole with thick ferrugineous tomentum when they unfold and at maturity coriaceous, dark green and very lustrous above, pale and dull below, usually about 3' long and $\frac{3}{4}$'–1$\frac{1}{2}$' wide, with a stout yellow midrib, numerous slender primary veins, and reticulate veinlets more or less covered below throughout the season with rufous tomentum also occasionally found on the upper side of the midrib; petioles stout, grooved, $\frac{1}{2}$'–$\frac{3}{4}$' long, and margined with broad or narrow wings. **Flowers** $\frac{1}{4}$' in diameter, in sessile 3–5 but usually 4-rayed thick-stemmed ferrugineo-pubescent flat corymbs often 5'–6' in diameter, with minute subulate bracts and bractlets; corolla creamy white, with orbicular or oblong rounded lobes. **Fruit** ripening in October, in few-fruited drooping red-stemmed clusters, short-oblong or slightly obovoid, bright blue covered with a glaucous bloom, and $\frac{1}{2}$'–$\frac{2}{3}$' long; stone $\frac{1}{2}$' long and about $\frac{1}{3}$' wide.

A tree, often 40° high, with a trunk 12'–18' in diameter, short thick branches forming an open irregular head, and stout branchlets marked by numerous small red-brown or orange lenticels, when they first appear more or less coated with ferrugineous tomentum, ashy gray during their first winter, and dark dull red-brown in their second season. **Winter-buds** ferrugineo-tomentose, those containing flower-bearing branchlets broad-ovoid, full and rounded at base, short-pointed and obtuse at apex, compressed, often $\frac{1}{2}$' long and $\frac{1}{3}$' wide, and rather larger than those containing sterile branchlets. **Bark** of the trunk $\frac{1}{4}$'–$\frac{1}{2}$' thick, separating into narrow rounded ridges divided by numerous cross fissures, and roughened by small plate-like dark brown scales tinged with red. **Wood** bad-smelling.

Distribution. Dry upland woods and the margins of river-bottom lands; southwestern Virginia and southern Indiana and Illinois to Hernando County, Florida, and through the Gulf States to the valleys of the upper Guadalupe River and of Clear Creek, Brown County, Texas, and to eastern and southwestern Oklahoma (on the Wichita Mountains, Comanche County), eastern Kansas and Central Missouri; most abundant and of its largest size in southern Arkansas, western Louisiana, and eastern Texas.

Occasionally cultivated in the eastern states, and hardy as far north as eastern Massachusetts.

GLOSSARY OF TECHNICAL TERMS

Accrescent. Increasing in size with age.

Accumbent. Lying against, as the radicle against the edges of the cotyledons.

Acuminate. Gradually tapering to the apex.

Acute. Pointed.

Adnate. Congenitally united to.

Adventitious. Said of buds produced without order from any part of a stem.

Æstivation. The arrangement of the parts of a flower in the bud.

Akene or *achene.* A small dry and hard, 1-celled, 1-seeded, indehiscent fruit.

Albumen. The deposit of nutritive material within the coats of a seed and surrounding the embryo.

Ament. A unisexual spike of flowers with scaly bracts, usually deciduous in one piece.

Amphitropous. Descriptive of an ovule with the hilum intermediate between the micropyle and chalaza.

Anatropous. Descriptive of a reversed ovule, with the micropyle close by the side of the hilum, and chalaza at the opposite end.

Androdiœcious. With perfect flowers on one individual and staminate flowers only on another.

Androgynous. Applied to an inflorescence composed of male and female flowers.

Angiospermæ. Plants with seeds borne in a pericarp.

Annular. In the form of a ring.

Anterior. The front side of a flower, that is averse from the axis of inflorescence.

Anther. The part of the stamen containing the pollen.

Anthesis. The act of opening of a flower.

Apetalous. Having no petals.

Apex. The top, as the end of the leaf opposite the petiole.

Apiculate. Ending in a short pointed tip.

Apophysis. An enlargement or swelling of the surface of an organ.

Arcuate. Moderately curved.

Areolate. Marked by areolæ or spaces marked out on a surface.

Aril. An extraneous seed-coat or covering, or an appendage growing about the hilum of a seed.

Ariloid. Furnished with an aril.

Aristate. Furnished with awns.

Articulate. Jointed or having the appearance of a joint.

Auricled or *auriculate.* Furnished with an auricle or ear-shaped appendage.

Autocarpus. A fruit consisting of pericarp alone, without adherent parts.

Axil. The angle formed on the upper side of the attachment of a leaf with a stem.

Axillary. In or from an axil.

Baccate. Berry-like.

Bark. The rind or cortical covering of a stem.

Berry. A fruit with a homogeneous fleshy pericarp.

Bipinnate. Doubly or twice pinnate.

Bract. The more or less modified leaf of a flower-cluster.

Bracteate. Furnished with bracts.

Bracteolate. Furnished with bractlets.

Bractlet. The bract of a pedicel or ultimate flower-stalk.

Branch. A secondary axis or division of a trunk.

Branchlet. An ultimate division of a branch.

Bud. The undeveloped state of a branch or flower-cluster with or without scales.

Bud-scales. Reduced leaves covering a bud.

Calyx. The flower-cup or exterior part of a perianth.

Campanulate. Bell-shaped, or elongated cup-shaped.

Campylotropous. Descriptive of an ovule or seed curved in its formation so as to bring the micropyle or apex down near the hilum.

Canescent. Hoary, with gray or whitish pubescence.

Capsule. A dry dehiscent fruit of more than one carpel.

Carpel. A simple pistil or an element of a compound pistil.

Catkin. The same as an ament.

Caudate. Furnished with a tail, or with a slender tip or appendage.

Centripetal. Developing from without toward the centre.

Chalaza. The part of an ovule where the coats and nucleus are confluent.

Chartaceous. Having the texture of paper.

Ciliate. Fringed with hairs.

Cinereous. Ashy gray.

Circinnate. Involute from the apex into a coil.

Circumscissile. Circularly and transversely dehiscent.

Clavate. Club-shaped.

Cocci. Portions into which a lobed fruit with 1-seeded cells splits up.

Cochleate. Shell-shaped, spiral like the shell of a snail.

Columella. The persistent axis of a capsule.

Commissure. The face by which 2 carpels unite.

Complanate. Flattened.

Conduplicate. Folded together lengthwise.

Cone. An inflorescence or fruit formed of imbricated scales.

Conferruminate. Stuck together by adjacent faces.

Connate. United congenitally.

Connective. The portion of a stamen which connects the two cells or lobes of an anther.

Contortuplicate. Twisted and plaited, or folded.

Convolute. Rolled up from the sides.

Cordate. Heart-shaped.

Coriaceous. Of the texture of leather.

Corymb. A flat-topped or convex open flower-cluster, the flowers opening from the outside inward.

Corymbose. Said of flowers arranged in a corymb.

Costate. Having ribs.

Cotyledons. The leaves of the embryo.

Crenate. Scalloped.

Crenulate. The diminutive of crenate.

Crispate. Curled.

Crustaceous. Of hard brittle texture.

Cucullate. Hooded or hood-shaped.

Cuneate. Wedge-shaped, or triangular with an acute angle downward.

Cyme. A flower-cluster, the flower opening from the centre outward.

Cymose. Bearing cymes or relating to a cyme.

Deciduous. Falling, said of leaves falling in the autumn, or of parts of a flower falling after anthesis.

Declinate. Bent or curved downward.

Decompound. Several times compound or divided.

Decurrent. Running down, as of the blades of leaves extending down their petioles.

Decussate. In pairs alternately crossing at right angles.

Dehiscent. The opening of an anther or capsule by slits or valves.

Deltoid. Having the shape of the Greek letter Δ.

Dentate. Toothed.

Denticulate. Minutely toothed.

Dextrorse. Turned or directed to the right.

Diadelphous Said of stamens combined by their filaments into 2 sets.

Dichotomous. Forked in pairs.

Digitate. Said of a compound leaf in which the leaflets are borne at the apex of the petiole.

Dimorphous. Said of flowers of two forms on the same plant, or on plants of the same species.

Diœcious. Unisexual, with the flowers of the 2 sexes borne by distinct individuals.

Disciferous. Bearing a disk.

Disciform. Depressed and circular like a disk.

Discoid. Appertaining to a disk.

Disk. The development of the torus or receptacle of a flower within the calyx or within the corolla and stamens.

Dissepiment. A partition in an ovary or pericarp.

Distichous. Said of leaves arranged alternately in two vertical ranks upon opposite sides of an axil.

Dorsal. Relating to the back.

Dorsal suture. The line of opening of a carpel corresponding to its midrib.

Drupaceous. Resembling or relating to a drupe.

Drupe. A stone fruit.

Duct. An elongated cell or tubular vessel found especially in the woody parts of plants.

Eglandular. Without glands.

Ellipsoidal. Of the shape of an elliptical solid.

Elliptic. Of the form of an ellipse.

Emarginate. Notched at the apex.

Embryo. The rudimentary plant formed in the seed.

Endocarp. The inner layer of a pericarp.

Endogenous. Descriptive of Endogens, monocotyledonous plants with stems increasing by internal accessions.

Epicarp. The thin filmy external layer of a pericarp.

Epigynous Placed on the ovary.

Epiphytal Said of a plant growing on another plant, but not parasitic.

Erose. Descriptive of an irregularly toothed or eroded margin.

Excurrent. Running through the apex or beyond.

Exocarp. The outer layer of a pericarp.

Exogenous. Descriptive of Exogens, plants with stems increasing by the addition of a layer of wood on the outside beneath the constantly widening bark.

Extrorse. Directed outward, descriptive of an anther opening away from the axis of the flower.

Falcate. Scythe-shaped.

Fascicle. A close cluster of leaves or flowers.

Fascicled. Arranged in fascicles.

Feather-veined. Having veins extending from the sides of the midrib.

Ferrugineous. The color of iron rust.

Fibro-vascular. Consisting of woody fibres and ducts.

Filament. The stalk of an anther.

Filamentose. Composed of threads.

Fimbriate. Fringed.

Fistulose. Hollow through the whole length.

Flabellate. Fan-shaped; much dilated from a wedge-shaped base with the broader end rounded.

Floccose. Bearing flocci or tufts of woody hairs.

Foliaceous. Leaf-like in texture or appearance.

Foliolate. Having leaflets.

Foliole. A leaflet.

Follicle. A dry 1-celled seed vessel consisting of a single carpel, and opening only by the ventral suture.

Funicle. The stalk of an ovule or seed.

Gamopetalæ. Plants with a corolla of coalescent petals.

Gamopetalous. Descriptive of a corolla of coalescent petals.

Geniculate. Bent abruptly like a knee.

Gibbous. Swollen on one side.

Glabrate. Nearly glabrous or becoming glabrous.

Glabrous. Smooth, not pubescent or hairy.

Gland. A protuberance on the surface, or partly imbedded in the surface of any part of a plant, either secreting or not.

Glandular. Furnished with glands.

Glaucescent. Nearly or becoming glaucous.

Glaucous. Covered or whitened with a bloom.

Glomerate. Said of flowers gathered into a compact head.

Gymnospermæ. Plants with naked seeds, that is, not inclosed in a pericarp.

Gynophore. The stipe of a pistil.

Heartwood. The mature and dead wood of an exogenous stem.

Hermaphrodite. With staminate and pistillate organs in the same flower, equivalent to perfect.

Hilum. The scar or place of attachment of a seed.

Hirsute. Hairy, with coarse or stiff hairs.

Hispidulous. Minutely hispid.

Hypogynous. Under or free from the pistil.

Imbricate. Overlapping, like the shingles on a roof.

Incumbent. Leaning or resting upon, as the radicle against the back of one of the cotyledons.

Induplicate. With edges folded in or turned inward.

Inferior. Said of an organ placed below another,

like a calyx below an ovary or an ovary below a superior calyx.

Inflorescence. Flower-cluster.

Infrapetiolar. Below the petioles.

Innate. Borne on the apex of the supporting part; in an anther the counterpart of adnate.

Interpetiolar. Between the petioles.

Introrse. Turned inward; descriptive of an anther opening toward the axis of the flower.

Inverse. Inverted.

Involucre. A circle of bracts surrounding a flower-cluster.

Involute. Rolled inward.

Laciniate. Cut into narrow incisions or lobes.

Lactescent. Yielding milky juice.

Lamellate. Composed of thin plates.

Lanceolate. Shaped like a lance; narrower than oblong and tapering to the ends, or at least to the apex.

Lanuginose. Clothed with soft reflexed hairs.

Leaf. Green expansions borne by the stem in which assimilation and the processes connected with it are carried on.

Leaflet. The separate division of a compound leaf.

Legume. The seed vessel of plants of the Pea family, composed of a solitary carpel normally dehiscent only by the ventral suture.

Lenticels. Lenticular corky growths on young bark.

Lenticellate. Having lenticels.

Lepidote. Beset with small scurfy scales.

Ligulate. Strap-shaped.

Linear. Said of a narrow leaf several times narrower than long, with parallel margins.

Lobe. The division of an organ.

Lobulate. Divided into small lobes.

Loculicidal. Dehiscent into the cavity of a pericarp by the back, that is through a dorsal suture.

Marcescent. Said of a part of a plant, withering without falling off.

Medullary rays. The rays of cellular tissue in a transverse section of an exogenous stem and extending from the pith to the bark.

Membranaceous. Thin and pliable like a membrane.

Micropyle. The spot or point in the seed at the place of the orifice of the ovule.

Midrib. The central or main rib of a leaf.

Monœcious. Unisexual, with the flowers of the two sexes borne by the same individual.

Mucro. A small and abrupt tip to a leaf.

Mucronate. Furnished with a mucro.

Muricate. Rough, with short rigid excrescences.

Naked buds. Buds without scales.

Nectar. The sweet secretion of various parts of a flower.

Nectariferous. Nectar-bearing.

Node. The portion of the stem which bears a leaf or whorl of leaves.

Nucleus. The kernel of an ovule or seed.

Nut. A hard and indehiscent 1-seeded pericarp produced from a compound ovary.

Nutlet. A diminutive nut or stone.

Obclavate. Inverted club-shape.

Obcordate. Inverted heart-shaped.

Oblanceolate. Lanceolate but tapering toward the base more than toward the apex.

Oblong. Longer than broad with nearly parallel sides.

Obovate. Ovate with the broader end toward the apex.

Obovoid. Solid obovate with the broader end toward the apex.

Obpyramidal. Inversely pyramidal.

Obtuse. Blunt or rounded at the apex.

Operculate. Furnished with a lid.

Orbicular. A flat body circular in outline.

Orthotropous. Descriptive of an ovule with a straight axis much enlarged at the insertion and the orifice at the other end.

Oval. Broad-elliptic, with round ends.

Ovate. Of the shape of the longitudinal section of a hen's egg, with the broad end basal.

Ovoid. Solid ovate or solid oval.

Ovule. The part of the flower which becomes a seed.

Palmate. Lobed or divided, with the sinuses pointing to or reaching the apex of the petiole or insertion.

Panicle. A loose compound flower-cluster.

Papilionaceous. Butterfly-like.

Papilliform. The shape of papillæ.

Papillate. Bearing papillæ, minute nipple-shaped papillose projections.

Parietal placenta. A placenta borne on the wall of the ovary.

Pedicel. The stalk of a flower in a compound inflorescence.

Pedicellate. Borne on a pedicel.

Peduncle. A general flower-stalk supporting either a cluster of flowers, or a solitary flower.

Pedunculate. Borne on a peduncle.

Peltate. Descriptive of a plane body attached by its lower surface to the stalk.

Penniveined. Same as pinnately veined.

Perfect. Said of a flower with both stamens and pistil.

Perianth. The envelope of a flower consisting of calyx, corolla, or both.

Pericarp. The fructified ovary.

Persistent. Said of leaves remaining on the branches over their first winter, and of a calyx remaining under on the fruit.

Petal. A division of the corolla.

Petiolate. Having a petiole.

Petiole. The footstalk of a leaf.

Petiolulate. Having a petiolule.

Petiolule. The footstalk of a leaflet.

Pilose. Hairy, with soft and distinct hairs.

Pinnæ. The primary divisions of a twice pinnate leaf.

Pinnate. A leaf with leaflets arranged along each side of a common petiole.

Pistil. The female organ of a flower, consisting of ovary, style, and stigma.

Pistillate. Said of a unisexual flower without fertile stamens.

Pith. The central cellular part of a stem.

Placenta. That part of the ovary which bears the ovules.

Plane. Used in describing a flat surface.

Plumule. The bud or growing part of the embryo.

Pollen. The fecundating cells contained in the anther.

Polygamodiœcious. Said of flowers sometimes perfect and sometimes unisexual, the 2 forms borne on different individuals.

Polygamomonœcious. Said of flowers sometimes perfect and sometimes unisexual, the 2 forms borne on the same individual.

Polygamous. Said of flowers sometimes perfect and sometimes unisexual.

Pome. An inferior fruit of 2 or several carpels inclosed in thick flesh.

Posterior. The side of an axillary flower next the axis of inflorescence.

Prickle. Outgrowth of the bark.

Proliferous. Bearing offshoots.

Puberulent. Very slightly pubescent.

Puberulous. Minutely pubescent.

Pubescence. A covering of short soft hairs.

Pubescent. Clothed with soft short hairs.

Pulvinate. Cushion-shaped.

Punctate. Dotted with depressions or translucent internal glands, or with colored dots.

Punctulate. Minutely punctate.

Raceme. An indeterminate or centripetal inflorescence with an elongated axis and flowers on pedicels of equal length.

Rachis. The axis of a spike or of a compound leaf.

Radial. Belonging to a ray.

Radicle. The initial stem in an embryo.

Receptacle. The axile portion of a blossom bearing sepals, petals, stamens, and pistils; the axis or rachis of the head, spike, or other flower-cluster.

Reniform. Kidney-shaped.

Resupinate. Upside down.

Reticulate. Netted.

Retrorse. Directed backward or downward.

Retuse. With a shallow notch at a rounded apex.

Revolute. Rolled backward from the margins or apex.

Rhaphe. The adnate cord or ridge connecting the hilum with the chalaza in an anatropous ovule.

Rhombic. Having the shape of a rhomb.

Rhomboidal. Approaching a rhombic outline; quadrangular with lateral angles obtuse.

Rind. The bark of some endogenous stems, like that of Palms.

Rostrate. Narrowed into a slender tip.

Rotate. Circular, flat and horizontally spreading.

Rugose. Wrinkled.

Rugulose. Slightly wrinkled.

Ruminate. Looking as if chewed, like the albumen of the nutmeg.

Sagittate. Shaped like an arrowhead.

Samara. An indehiscent winged fruit.

Sapwood. The young living wood of an exogenous stem.

Scales. Thin scarious bodies, usually degenerate leaves.

Scarious. Thin, dry and membranaceous, not green.

Scobiform. Having the appearence of sawdust.

Scorpioid. A form of unilateral inflorescence circinately coiled in the bud.

Scurfy. Covered with small bran-like scales.

Seed. The fertilized and mature ovule, the result of sexual reproduction in a flowering plant.

Segment. One of the divisions into which a leaf, calyx, or corolla may be divided.

Semianatropous. Same as amphitropous.

Sepals. The divisions of a calyx.

Septicidal. Descriptive of a capsule splitting through the lines of junction of the carpels.

Septum. A partition.

Serrate. Beset with teeth.

Serrulate. Serrate with small fine teeth.

Sessile. Without a stalk.

Setose. Beset with bristles.

Setulose. Beset with minute bristles.

Sheath. A tubular or enrolled part or organ.

Sinistrorse. Turned or directed to the left.

Sinus. A recess between the lobes of a leaf.

Spatulate. Oblong with the lower end attenuated.

Spike. An indeterminate inflorescence with flowers sessile on an elongated common axis.

Spine. A sharp-pointed woody body, commonly a modified branch or stipule.

Spinescent. Ending in a spine.

Spinose. Furnished with spines.

Stamen. One of the male organs of a flower.

Staminate. Said of unisexual flowers without pistils.

Staminodium. A sterile or much reduced stamen.

Stigma. The part or surface of a pistil which receives the pollen for the fecundation of the ovules.

Stigmatic. Relating to the stigma.

Stipe. A stalk-like support of a pistil or of a carpel.

Stipel. An appendage to a leaflet analagous to the stipules of a leaf.

Stipellate. Having stipels.

Stipitate. Having a stipe.

Stipulate. Having stipules.

Stipules. Appendages of a leaf, placed on one side of the petiole at its insertion with the stem.

Stomata. Breathing pores or apertures in the epidermis of leaves connecting internal cavities with the external air.

Stomatiferous. Furnished with stomata.

Stone. The hard endocarp of a drupe.

Strobile. The same as cone.

Strophiolate. Said of a seed bearing a strophiole or appendage at the hilum.

Style. The attenuated portion of a pistil between the ovary and the stigma.

Subcordate. Slightly cordate.

Subulate. Awl-shaped.

Sulcate. Grooved or furrowed.

Superior. Growing or placed above; also in a lateral flower for the side next the axis.

Suture. A junction, usually a line of opening of a carpel.

Syncarp. A multiple fruit.

Taproot. The primary descending root, a direct continuation from the radicle.

Tegmen. The inner coat of a seed.

Testa. The outer seed-coat.

Thyrsoidal. Relating to a thyrsus.

Thyrsus. A mixed inflorescence with the main axis indeterminate and the secondary or ultimate cluster cymose.

Tomentose. Densely pubescent with matted wool or tomentum.

Tomentulose. Slightly pubescent with matted wool.

Torose. Cylindric, with contractions or bulges at intervals.

Torulose. Slightly torose.

Torus. The receptacle of a flower.

Transverse. Horizontal.

Trichotomous. Three-forked.

Trifoliate. Three-leaved.

Trifoliolate. Descriptive of leaves, with 3 leaflets.

Truncate. As if cut off at the end.

Tubercle. A small tuber or excrescence.

Tuberculate. Beset with knobby excrescences.

Turbinate. Top-shaped.

Turgid. Swollen.

Umbel. An inflorescence with numerous pedicels springing from the same point like the rays of an umbrella.

Umbilicus. The hilum of a seed

Umbo. A boss or protuberance.

Umbonate. Bearing an umbo.

Uncinate. Hooked, bent, or curved at the ti in the form of a hook.

Unequally pinnate. Pinnate, with an odd terminal leaflet.

Unguiculate. Contracted at the base into a claw or stalk.

Unisexual. Said of flowers with either the stamens or pistil 0 or abortive.

Urceolate. Hollow and contracted at or below the mouth like an urn or pitcher.

Utricle. A small bladdery pericarp.

Valvate. Said of a bud in which the parts meet without overlapping.

Valve. One of the pieces into which a capsule splits.

Veinlet. One of the ultimate or smaller ramifications of a vein.

Veins. Ramifications or threads of fibro-vascular tissue in a leaf or other flat organ.

Ventral. Belonging to the anterior or inner face of a carpel.

Ventricose. Swelling unequally or inflated on one side.

Vernation. The disposition of parts in a leaf-bud.

Verrucose. Covered with wart-like elevations.

Versatile. Said of an anther turning freely on its filament.

Verticillate. Arranged in a circle or whorl round an axis.

Villose. Hairy, with long and soft hairs.

Whorl. An arrangement of branches or leaves in a circle round an axis.

Wood. The hard part of a stem mainly composed of wood-cells, wood fibre, or tissue.

TABLE OF CHANGES IN NOMENCLATURE

The text of this Dover edition is that of the second (1922) edition of Sargent's work. In the forty years since its initial publication, taxonomists, guided by established rules of botanical nomenclature, have made numerous changes in both the common and technical names of trees. Others, in careful study of certain generic groups, have developed new concepts of the validity and limitations of many species which are described in Sargent's *Manual*. In many instances this has led to combining closely related forms into one large polymorphic species.

Thus, in the interests of technical accuracy, and with a view toward making this work of even greater utility to the serious student of American arborescent vegetation, the publisher is happy to provide a supplementary listing of all genera, species and/or varieties where there have been significant changes in nomenclature. Included in this listing are the latest concepts of the limits of several species, most notable of which are in the genus *Cratægus* of the Rosaceae, *Tilia* of the Tiliaceæ, *Carya* of the Juglandaceæ, and *Salix* and *Populus* of the Salicaceæ.

This Table of Changes in Nomenclature has been prepared especially for this Dover edition by E. S. Harrar, Dean of the School of Forestry, Duke University.

Dover Publications, Inc.

1965

Vol. I Page	Vol. II Page	Line	For	Read
xvi	xiv	24	Acœlorraphe (p. 105)	Paurotis
xviii	xvi	17	Evonymus (p. 675)	Euonymus
xviii	xvi	54	Acer Negundo (p. 699)	Acer negundo,
xix	xvii	46	Heteromeles (p. 392)	Photinia
xx	xviii	4	Gordonia Lasianthus (p. 751)	Gordonia lasianthus
xx	xviii	15	Coccolobis (p. 338)	Coccoloba
xx	xviii	46	Ilex Cassine (p. 670)	Ilex cassine
xx	xviii	53	Ilex Krugiana (p. 672)	Ilex krugiana
xxi	xix	6	Misanteca (p. 364)	Licaria
xxi	xix	10	Ocotea (p. 359)	Nectandra
xxii	xx	4	Mimusops (p. 819)	Achras
xxii	xx	8	Beureria (p. 861)	Bourreria
xxv	xxiii	26	Pithecolobium unguis-cati (p. 586)	Pithecellobium var. unguiscate
xxv	xxiii	29	Pithecolobium (p. 586)	Pithecellobium
xxv	xxiii	44	Xanthoxylum coriaceum (p. 637)	Zanthoxylum coriaceum
xxvi	xxiv	2	Ichthyomethia (p. 628)	Piscidia
xxvi	xxiv	14	*Xanthoxylum flavum*	*Zanthoxylum flavum*
xxvi	xxiv	18	Xanthoxylum flavum (p. 636)	Zanthoxylum flavum
xxvi	xxiv	24	Xanthoxylum Fagara (p. 634)	Zanthoxylum fagara
xxvi	xxiv	36	Xanthoxylum clava-Herculis (p. 635)	Zanthoxylum clava-herculis
xxvi	xxvi	42	Sapindus Drummondii (p. 714)	Sapindus drummondii

Page	Item	Line	For	Read
3	–	9	P. Strobus	P. strobus
3	–	12	P. Lambertiana	P. lambertiana
3	–	23	P. Balfouriana	P. balfouriana
3	1	–	Pinus Strobus L.	Pinus strobus L.
4	2	–	Pinus monticola D. Don	Pinus monticola Dougl.
5	3	–	Pinus Lambertiana Dougl.	Pinus lambertiana Dougl.
6	4	–	Rocky Mountain White Pine	Limber Pine
6	5	–	White Pine	Whitebark Pine
7	6	–	Pinus Balfouriana Balf.	Pinus balfouriana (Grev. & Balf.)
8	7	–	Foxtail Pine, Hickory Pine	Bristlecone Pine
8	8	–	Nut Pine, Piñon	Mexican Pinyon
9	–	20	Pinus cembroides var. Parryana Voss.	Pinus quadrifolia Parl.
9	–	20	Nut Pine, Piñon	Parry Pinyon
9	–	46	Pinus cembroides var. edulis Voss.	Pinus edulis Engelm.
9	–	46	Nut Pine, Piñon	Pinyon
10	–	25	Pinus cembroides var. monophylla Voss.	Pinus monophylla Torr. & Frem.
10	–	25	Nut Pine, Piñon	Singleleaf Pinyon
11	–	10	P. leiophylla	P. leiophylla var. chihuahuana
11	–	19	P. caribaea	P. elliottii
11	–	29	P. Sabiniana	P. sabiniana
11	–	30	P. Coulteri	P. coulteri
11	–	40	P. Banksiana	P. banksiana
12	–	5	P. Torreyana	P. torreyana
12	9	–	Pinus leiophylla Schlecht. and Cham.	Pinus leiophylla var. chihuahuana (Engelm.) Shaw
12	9	–	Yellow Pine	Chihuahua Pine
12	10	–	Yellow Pine, Bull Pine	Ponderosa Pine
13	–	34	Note: Now generally regarded as a distinct species under the designation of Jeffrey Pine, *Pinus jeffreyi* Grev. & Balf.	
14	–	14	Yellow Pine	Arizona Pine

Page	Item	Line	For	Read
14	11	–	Long-leaved Pine	Longleaf Pine
15	12	–	Pinus caribæa Morelet	Pinus elliottii Engelm.
18	–	17	*Note:* Now generally regarded as a distinct species under the designation of Pond Pine, *Pinus serotina* Michx.	
19	16	–	Knob-cone Pine	Knobcone Pine
20	17	–	Pinus Sabiniana Dougl.	Pinus sabiniana Dougl.
21	18	–	Pinus Coulteri D. Don	Pinus coulteri D. Don
23	20	–	Scrub Pine	Lodgepole Pine
23	–	43	*Note:* Now regarded as the Rocky Mountain form of lodgepole pine (Pinus contorta) without benefit of variety ranking.	
24	21	–	Pinus Banksiana Lamb.	Pinus banksiana Lamb.
26	23	–	Short-leaved Pine	Shortleaf Pine
26	24	–	Jersey Pine	Virginia Pine
27	25	–	Pinus clausa Sarg.	Pinus clausa (Chapm.) Vasey
28	26	–	Prickle-cone Pine	Bishop Pine
30	28	–	Pinus Torreyana Carr.	Pinus torreyana Parry.
31	–	34	L. Lyallii	L. lyallii
31	1	–	Larix laricina K. Koch.	Larix laricina (DuRoi) K. Koch.
32	2	–	Tamarack	Western Larch
33	3	–	Larix Lyallii Parl.	Larix lyallii Parl.
33	3	–	Tamarack	Subalpine Larch
35	–	18	P. rubra	P. rubens
35	–	23	P. Engelmannii	P. engelmannii
35	–	28	P. Breweriana	P. breweriana
35	1	–	Picea mariana B. S. P.	Picea mariana (Mill.) B. S. P.
36	2	–	Picea rubra Link.	Picea rubens Sarg.
37	3	–	Picea glauca Voss.	Picea glauca (Moench.) Voss.
38	4	–	Picea Engelmannii Engelm.	Picea engelmannii Parry
40	6	–	Picea Breweriana S. Wats.	Picea breweriana S. Wats.
41	7	–	Picea sitchensis Carr.	Picea sitchensis (Bong.) Carr.
43	–	24	T. Mertensiana	T. mertensiana
43	1	–	Tsuga canadensis Carr.	Tsuga canadensis (L.) Carr.
43	1	–	Hemlock	Eastern Hemlock
44	2	–	Hemlock	Carolina Hemlock
45	3	–	Tsuga heterophylla Sarg.	Tsuga heterophylla (Raf.) Sarg.
45	3	–	Hemlock	Western Hemlock
46	4	–	Tsuga Mertensiana Sarg.	Tsuga mertensiana (Bong.) Carr.
48	1	–	Douglas Spruce	Douglas-fir
49	2	–	Pseudotsuga macrocarpa Mayr.	Pseudotsuga macrocarpa (Vasey) Mayr.
49	2	–	Hemlock	Bigcone Douglas-fir
51	–	10	A. Fraseri	A. fraseri
51	–	24	A. nobilis	A. procera
51	–	31	A. venusta	A. bracteata
51	1	–	Balsam Fir, She Balsam	Fraser Fir
52	2	–	Abies balsamea Mill.	Abies balsamea (L.) Mill.
53	3	–	Abies lasiocarpa Nutt.	Abies lasiocarpa (Hook.) Nutt.
53	3	–	Balsam Fir	Subalpine Fir
54	4	–	Abies grandis Lindl.	Abies grandis (Dougl.) Lindl.
54	4	–	White Fir	Grand Fir
55	5	–	Abies concolor Lindl. & Gord.	Abies concolor (Gord. & Glend.) Lindl.
56	6	–	Abies amabilis Forbes	Abies amabilis (Dougl.) Forbes
56	6	–	White Fir	Pacific Silver Fir
57	7	–	Abies Nobilis Lindl.	Abies procera Rehd.
57	7	–	Red Fir	Noble Fir
58	8	–	Red Fir	California Red Fir
59	–	36	Red Fir	Shasta Red Fir

Page	Item	Line	For	Read
60	9	–	Abies venusta K. Koch.	Abies bracteata D. Don
60	9	–	Silver Fir	Bristlecone Fir
61	1	–	Sequoia sempervirens Endl.	Sequoia sempervirens (D. Don) Endl.
62	2	–	Sequoia gigantea Decne.	Sequoia gigantea (Lindl.) Decne.
62	2	–	Big Tree	Giant Sequoia
63	8	–	Bald Cypress	Baldcypress
64	1	–	Taxodium distichum Rich.	Taxodium distichum (L.) Rich.
64	1	–	Bald Cypress	Baldcypress
65	–	19	*Note:* Taxonomists are now in general agreement that Sargent's *Taxodium distichum* var. *imbricarium*, which was later given species rank under the epithet *Taxodium ascendens* Brong., is in reality merely a variety of *Taxodium distichum*. Correctly distinguished, it is known as the pondcypress, *Taxodium distichum* var. *nutans* (Ait.) Sweet.	
65	1	–	Incense Cedar	Incense-cedar
67	1	–	White Cedar	Northern White-cedar
68	2	–	Thuja plicata D. Don	Thuja plicata Donn.
68	2	–	Red Cedar, Canoe Cedar	Western Redcedar
70	–	2	C. Goveniana	C. goveniana
70	–	4	C. Sargentii	C. sargentii
70	–	6	C. Macnabiana	C. macnabiana
70	1	–	Cupressus macrocarpa Gord.	Cupressus macrocarpa Hartw.
70	2	–	Cupressus Goveniana Gord.	Cupressus goveniana Gord.
70	2	–		*add:* Gowen Cypress
72	4	–	Cupressus Macnabiana A. Murr.	Cupressus macnabiana A. Murr.
72	4	–	Cypress	MacNab Cypress
73	6	–	Cypress	Arizona Cypress
75	–	40	C. Lawsoniana	C. lawsoniana
75	1	–	Chamæcyparis thyoides B. S. P.	Chamæcyparis thyoides (L.) B. S. P.
75	1	–	White Cedar	Atlantic White-Cedar
76	2	–	Chamæcyparis nootkatensis Sudw.	Chamæcyparis nootkatensis (D. Don) Spach
76	2	–	Yellow Cypress, Sitka Cypress	Alaska-cedar
77	3	–	Chamæcyparis Lawsoniana Parl.	Chamæcyparis lawsoniana (A. Murr.) Parl.
77	3	–	Port Orford Cedar	Port-Orford-cedar
79	–	34	J. Pinchotii	J. pinchotii
79	–	39	J. utahensis	J. osteosperma
79	–	44	J. pachyphlæa	J. deppeana
80	–	2	J. mexicana	J. ashei
80	–	9	J. lucayana	J. silicicola
80	1	–	Juniper	Common Juniper
81	2	–	Juniperus Pinchotii Sudw.	Juniperus pinchotii Sudw.
81	2	–		*add:* Pinchot Juniper
82	3	–	Desert White Cedar	California Juniper
82	4	–	Juniperus utahensis Lemm.	Juniperus osteosperma (Torr.) Little
82	4	–	Juniper	Utah Juniper
83	5	–	Juniper	Drooping Juniper
84	6	–	Juniperus pachyphlæa Torr.	Juniperus deppeana Steud.
84	6	–	Checker-bark Juniper	Alligator Juniper
85	7	–	Juniper	Western Juniper
86	8	–	Juniperus monosperma Sarg.	Juniperus monosperma (Engelm.) Sarg.
86	8	–	Juniper	One-seed Juniper

Page	Item	Line	For	Read
87	9	–	Juniperus mexicana Spreng.	Juniperus ashei Buckholz
87	9	–	Rock Cedar	Ashe Juniper
88	10	–	Red Cedar	Eastern Redcedar
89	11	–	Juniperus lucayana Britt.	Juniperus silicicola (Small) Bailey
89	11	–	Red Cedar	Southern Redcedar
90	12	–	Red Cedar	Rocky Mountain Redcedar
91	1	38	Stinking Cedar, Torreya	Florida Torreya
92	2	–	California Nutmeg	California Torreya
93	1	–	Yew	Pacific Yew
94	2	–	Yew	Florida Yew
96	–	33	Acœlorraphe	Paurotis
97	1	–	Thatch	Florida Thatchpalm
98	2	–	Thrinax Wendlandiana Becc.	Thrinax parviflora Su.
98	2	–	Thatch	Jamaica Thatchpalm
99	3	–	Thatch	Thatchpalm
100	1	–	Coccothrinax jucunda Sarg.	Coccothrinax argentata (Jacq.) Bailey
100	1	–	Brittle Thatch	Florida Silverpalm
102	–	19	S. Palmetto	S. palmetto
102	1	–	Sabal Palmetto R. & S.	Sabal palmetto (Walt.) Lodd.
103	2	–	Sabal texana Becc.	Sabal texana (O. F. Cook) Becc.
103	2	–	Palmetto	Texas Palmetto
104	1	–	Washingtonia filamentosa O. Kuntze.	Washingtonia filifera (Linden) H. Wendl.
104	1	–	Desert Palm	California Washingtonia
105	5	–	Acœlorraphe H. Wendl.	Paurotis Cook
106	–	4	A. Wrightii	P. wrightii
106	–	7	A. arborescens	P. arborescens
106	1	–	Acœlorraphe Wrightii Becc.	Paurotis wrightii (Griseb. & H. Wendl.) Britt.
106	1	–		*add:* Wright Parotis
106	2	–	Acœlorraphe arborescens Becc.	Paurotis arborescens (Sarg.) Becc.
106	2	–		*add:* Tree Parotis
108	1	–	Roystonea regia Cook	Roystonea elata (Bartr.) F. Harper.
108	1	–	Royal Palm	Florida Royal Palm
109	1	–	Pseudophœnix vinifera Becc.	Pseudophœnix sargentii H. Wendl.
109	1	–		*add:* Florida Cherrypalm
111	–	9	Y. Treculeana	Y. treculeana
111	–	11	Y. macrocarpa	Y. torreyi
111	–	14	Y. Schottii	Y. schottii
111	–	16	Y. Faxoniana	Y. faxoniana
111	1	–	Spanish Bayonet	Aloe Yucca
112	2	–	Yucca Treculeana Carr.	Yucca treculeana Carr.
112	2	–	Spanish Bayonet, Spanish Dagger	Trecul Yucca
113	3	–	Yucca macrocarpa Coville	Yucca torreyi Schafer
113	3	–	Spanish Dagger	Torrey Yucca
113	4	–	Spanish Dagger	Mohave Yucca
114	5	–	Yucca Schottii Engelm.	Yucca schottii Engelm.
114	5	–	Spanish Dagger	Schotts Yucca
115	6	–	Yucca Faxoniana Sarg.	Yucca faxoniana Sarg.
115	6	–	Spanish Dagger	Faxon Yucca
116	7	–	Joshua Tree	Joshua-tree
117	8	–	Spanish Dagger	Moundlily Yucca

Page	Item	Line	For	Read
117	9	–	Spanish Dagger	Soaptree Yucca
120	–	35	P. Fremontii	P. fremontii
120	–	41	P. McDougallii	P. mcdougallii
120	–	43	P. Wislizenii	P. fremontii var. wislizenii
120	–	47	P. Sargentii	P. sargentii
120	–	51	P. Palmeri	P. palmeri
123	2	–	Poplar	Bigtooth Aspen
125	4	–	*Note:* This form now included as a part of *Populus balsamifera* L.	
126	5	–	Populus trichocarpa Hook.	Populus trichocarpa Torr. & Gray
127	6	–	Narrow-leaved Cottonwood	Narrowleaf Cottonwood
128	7	–	Populus acuminata Rydb.	Populux × acuminata Rydb.
128	7	–	Cottonwood	Lanceleaf Cottonwood
129	8	–	Populus Fremontii S. Wats.	Populus fremontii S. Wats.
129	8	–	Cottonwood	Fremont Cottonwood
131	9	–	*Note:* This form now included as a part of *Populus fremontii* S. Wats.	
132	10	–	*Note:* This form now included as a part of *Populus sargentii* Dode.	
133	11	–	*Note:* This form now included as a part of *Populus fremontii* S. Wats.	
133	12	–	Populus Wislizenii Sarg.	Populus fremontii var. wislizenii S. Wats.
133	12	–	Cottonwood	Rio Grande Cottonwood
134	13	–	Populus Sargentii Dode	Populus sargentii Dode
134	13	–		*add:* Plains Cottonwood
135	14	–	Cottonwood	Balsam Poplar
136	–	6	*Note:* Now included in *Populus balsamifera* L. without benefit of variety ranking.	
137	15	–	Populus Palmeri Sarg.	Populus palmeri Sarg.
137	15	–		*add:* Palmer Cottonwood
139	–	21	S. Gooddingii	S. gooddingii
139	–	26	S. Harbisonii	S. caroliniana
139	–	32	S. Bonplandiana	S. bonplandiana
140	–	4	S. longifolia	S. interior
140	–	16	S. Mackenzieana	S. mackenzieana
140	–	18	S. missouriensis	S. eriocephala
140	–	29	S. Bebbiana	S. bebbiana
140	–	37	S. Scouleriana	S. scouleriana
140	–	40	S. Hookeriana	S. hookeriana
142	2	–	Salix Gooddingii Ball.	Salix gooddingii Ball.
142	2	–		*add:* Goodding Willow
143	3	–	Salix Harbisonii Schn.	Salix caroliniana Michx.
143	3	–		*add:* Coastal Plain Willow
144	4	–	Peach Willow	Peachleaf Willow
145	–	3	Salix amygdaloides var. Wrightii Schn.	Salix amygdaloides var. wrightii Schn.
145	5	–	Salix Bonplandiana var. Toumeyi Schn.	Salix bonplandiana H. B. K.
145	5	–		*add:* Bonpland Willow
147	7	–	*Note:* This form now included as a part of *Salix caroliniana* Michx.	
148	8	–	Yellow Willow	Pacific Willow
149	9	–	Salix lucida Muehl.	Salix lucida Mühl.
150	10	–		*add:* Yewleaf Willow
151	11	–		*add:* Northwest Willow
152	12	–		*add:* Coyote Willow
152	13	–	Salix longifolia Muehl.	Salix interior Rowlee
152	13	–	Sand Bar Willow	Interior Willow
154	15	–	Salix Mackenzieana Barr.	Salix mackenzieana (Hook.) Barr.
154	15	–		*add:* Mackenzie Willow

Page	Item	Line	For	Read
155	16	–	Salix missouriensis Bebb.	Salix eriocephala Michx.
155	16	–		*add:* Missouri River Willow
156	17	–		*add:* Balsam Willow
157	18	–		*add:* Yukutat Willow
158	20	–	Salix Bebbiana Sarg.	Salix bebbiana Sarg.
158	20	–		*add:* Bebb Willow
159	21	–	Salix discolor Muehl.	Salix discolor Mühl.
159	21	–	Glaucous Willow	Pussy Willow
160	22	–	Salix Scouleriana Barr.	Salix scouleriana Barr.
160	22	–	Black Willow	Scouler Willow
161	23	–	Salix Hookeriana Barr.	Salix hookeriana Barr.
161	23	–		*add:* Hooker Willow
162	24	–		*add:* Sitka Willow
164	1	–	Wax Myrtle	Southern Bayberry
165	2	–	Wax Myrtle	Odorless Bayberry
166	3	–	Wax Myrtle	Pacific Bayberry
167	1	–	Cork Wood	Corkwood
169	–	42	J. rupestris	J. microcarpa
169	–	46	J. Hindsii	J. hindsii
172	3	–	Juglans major Hell.	Juglans major (Torr.) Heller
172	3	–	Nogal	Arizona Walnut
173	4	–	Juglans rupestris Engelm.	Juglans microcarpa Berl.
173	4	–	Walnut	Little Walnut
174	5	–		*add:* California Walnut
175	6	–	Juglans Hindsii Rehd.	Juglans hindsii Jeps.
175	6	–		*add:* Hinds Walnut
176	–	47	C. pecan	C. illinoensis
176	–	48	C. texana	C. × lecontei
177	–	22	C. alba	C. tomentosa
177	–	50	C. Buckleyi	C. texana
177	1	–	Carya pecan Engl. & Graebn.	Carya illinoensis (Wangenh.) K. Koch.
179	2	–	Carya texana Schn.	Carya × lecontei Little
180	3	–	Pignut, Bitternut	Bitternut Hickory
183	6	–	Shellbark Hickory	Northern Shagbark Hickory
185	7	–	Shagbark Hickory	Southern Shagbark Hickory
186	8	–	Big Shellbark, King Nut	Shellbark Hickory
188	9	–	Carya alba K. Koch.	Carya tomentosa Nutt.
188	9	–	Hickory	Mockernut Hickory
189	10	–		*add:* Swamp Hickory
190	11	–		*add:* Sand Hickory
191	12	–	Pignut	Pignut Hickory
193	13	–	*Note:* This "species" and its several "varieties" now included with Carya glabra Sweet by several authorities.	
196	14	–		*add:* Scrub Hickory
197	15	–	Carya Buckleyi Durand	Carya texana Buck.
197	15	–		*add:* Black Hickory
201	1	1	Hornbeam	American Hornbeam
201	1	27	Hornbeam	American Hornbeam
202	2	–	Hop Hornbeam	Hophornbeam
203	–	3	O. Knowltonii	O. knowltonii
203	1	–	Hop Hornbeam	Eastern Hophornbeam
204	2	, –	Ostrya Knowltonii Cov.	Ostrya knowltonii Cov.
204	2	–	Ironwood	Knowlton Hophornbeam
206	–	9	B. lutea	B. alleghaniensis
206	–	23	B. cœrulea	B. × cœrulea
206	–	30	B. alaskana	B. papyrifera var. humilis

Page	Item	Line	*For*	*Read*
206	–	34	B. fontinalis	B. occidentalis
206	1	–	Cherry Birch, Black Birch	Sweet Birch
207	2	–	Betula lutea Michx.	Betula alleghaniensis Britt.
211	5	–	Betula cœrulea Blanch.	Betula × cœrulea Blanch.
213	–	33		*add:* Mountain Paper Birch
214	–	11		*add:* Northwestern Paper Birch
214	–	26	Betula papyrifera var. montanensis Sarg.	Betula papyrifera var. commutata (Reg.) Fern.
214	–	26		*add:* Western Paper Birch
215	–	12	*Note:* This form now included as a part of the water birch *Betula occidentalis* Hook.	
216	–	8	Red Birch, Black Birch	Kenai Birch
217	7	–	Betula alaskana Sarg.	Betula papyrifera var. humilis (Reg.) Fern. & Raup
217	7	–	White Birch	Alaska Paper Birch
218	8	–	Betula fontinalis Sarg.	Betula occidentalis Hook.
218	8	–	Black Birch	Water Birch
219	–	8	Betula fontinalis var. Piperi Sarg.	Betula occidentalis var. fecunda Fern.
219	–	8		*add:* Piper Birch
219	9	–	Betula Eastwoodæ Sarg.	Betula × eastwoodæ Sarg.
219	9	–		*add:* Yukon Birch
220	–	13	B. alaskana Sarg.	B. papyrifera var. humilis (Reg.) Fern. & Raup
221	1	–	Alder	Sitka Alder
222	2	–	Alder	Red Alder
223	3	–	Alder	Thinleaf Alder
224	4	–	Alder	White Alder
225	5	–	Alder	Arizona Alder
226	6	–	Alder	Seaside Alder
228	1	39	Beech	American Beech
231	1	–	Chestnut	American Chestnut
232	2	–	Chinquapin	Dwarf Chinkapin
233	3	–	Chinquapin	Trailing Chinkapin
233	–	32	Chinquapin	Florida Chinkapin
234	1	–	Chinquapin, Golden-leaved Chestnut	Golden Chinkapin
236	1	–	Tan Bark Oak	Tanoak
238	–	45	Q. borealis	Q. rubra
238	–	53	Q. texana	Q. shumardii var. texana
239	–	12	Q. Kelloggii	Q. kelloggii
239	–	13	Q. Catesbæi	Q. lævis
239	–	17	Q. rubra	Q. falcata
239	–	31	Q. Phellos	Q. phellos
239	–	35	Q. cinerea	Q. incana
239	–	40	Q. hypoleuca	Q. hypoleucoides
239	–	45	Q. Wislizenii	Q. wislizenii
240	–	8	Q. Emoryi	Q. emoryi
240	–	17	Q. Toumeyi	Q. toumeyi
240	–	24	Q. Engelmannii	Q. engelmannii
240	–	28	Q. Douglasii	Q. douglasii
240	–	31	Q. Vaseyana	Q. pungens var. vaseyana
240	–	33	Q. Mohriana	Q. mohriana
240	–	35	Q. Laceyi	Q. laceyi
240	2	40	Q. annulata	Q. durandii var. breviloba
240	–	41	Q. Durandii	Q. durandii
240	–	43	Q. Chapmanii	Q. chapmanii

Page	Item	Line	For	Read
240	–	55	Q. Garryana	Q. garryana
241	–	2	Q. utahensis	Q. gambelii
241	–	17	Q. Prinus	Q. michauxii
241	–	19	Q. montana	Q. prinus
241	–	22	Q. Muehlenbergii	Q. muehlenbergii
241	1	–	Quercus borealis Michx. f.	Quercus rubra L.
241	1	–	Red oak	Northern Red Oak
242	–	30	*Note:* This form now included with *Quercus rubra* L. without benefit of variety ranking.	
243	2	–	Quercus Shumardii Buckl.	Quercus shumardii Buckl.
243	2	–		*add:* Shumard Red Oak
244	–	27	*Note:* This form now included with *Quercus shumardii* Buckl. without benefit of variety ranking.	
245	3	–	Quercus texana Buckl.	Quercus shumardii var. texana (Buckl.) Ashe
245	3	–		*add:* Texas Oak
246	4	–	Black Oak	Northern Pin Oak
249	7	–		*add:* Georgia Oak
251	9	–	Quercus Kelloggii Newb.	Quercus kelloggii Newb.
251	9	–	Black Oak	California Black Oak
253	10	–	Quercus Catesbæi Michx.	Quercus lævis Walt.
255	12	–	Quercus rubra L.	Quercus falcata Michx.
255	12	–	Red Oak, Spanish Oak	Southern Red Oak
256	–	28	Quercus rubra var. pagodæfolia Ashe	Quercus falcata var. pagodæfolia Ell.
256	–	28	Swamp Spanish Oak	Cherrybark Oak
258	13	–	Black Jack, Jack Oak	Blackjack Oak
259	14	–		*add:* Arkansas Oak
261	16	–	*Note:* This form now included as a part of *Quercus laurifolia* Michx.	
262	17	–	Quercus Phellos L.	Quercus phellos L.
263	–	32	Quercus heterophylla Michx. f.	Quercus × heterophylla Michx. f.
263	–	32		*add:* Bartram Oak
265	19	–	Quercus cinerea Michx.	Quercus incana Bartr.
265	19	–	Blue Jack, Upland Willow Oak	Bluejack Oak
268	21	–	Quercus hypoleuca Engelm.	Quercus hypoleucoides A. Camas
268	21	–		*add:* Silverleaf Oak
269	22	–	Live Oak, Encina	California Live Oak
270	23	–	Quercus Wislizenii A. DC.	Quercus wislizenii A. DC.
270	23	–	Live Oak	Interior Live Oak
271	24	–		*add:* Myrtle Oak
272	25	–	Live Oak, Maul Oak	Canyon Live Oak
273	26	–		*add:* Island Live Oak
274	27	–	Quercus Emoryi Torr.	Quercus emoryi Torr.
274	27	–	Black Oak	Emory Oak
275	28	–	Scrub Oak	California Scrub Oak
277	–	30	Quercus virginiana var. geminata Sarg.	Quercus virginiana var. maritima (Michx.) Sarg.
277	–	30		*add:* Sand Live Oak
279	30	–		*add:* Netleaf Oak
280	31	–	Quercus Toumeyi Sarg.	Quercus toumeyi Sarg.
280	31	–		*add:* Toumey Oak
280	32	–	White Oak	Arizona White Oak
281	33	–	White Oak	Mexican Blue Oak
282	34	–	Quercus Engelmannii Greene	Quercus engelmannii Greene
282	34	–	Evergeen Oak	Engelmann Oak
283	35	–	Quercus Douglasii Hook. & Arn.	Quercus douglasii Hook. & Arn.
285	36	–	Quercus Vaseyana Buckl.	Quercus pungens var. vaseyana (Buckl.) C. H. Muller

Page	Item	Line	For	Read
285	36	–	Shin Oak	Vasey Oak
285	37	–	Quercus Mohriana Rydb.	Quercus mohriana Buckl.
285	37	–	Shin Oak	Mohrs Oak
286	38	–	Quercus Laceyi Small	Quercus laceyi Small
286	38	–		*add:* Lacey Oak
287	39	–	Quercus annulata Buckl.	Quercus durandii var. breviloba (Torr.) Palmer
288	40	–	Quercus Durandii Buckl.	Quercus durandii Buckl.
288	40	–		*add:* Durand Oak
289	41	–	Quercus Chapmanii Sarg.	Quercus chapmanii Sarg.
289	41	–		*add:* Chapman Oak
290	42	–	Burr Oak	Bur Oak
295	–	13	Quercus stellata var. Margaretta Sarg.	Quercus stellata var. margaretta (Ashe) Sarg.
295	–	13		*add:* Sand Post Oak
296	45	–	Quercus Garryana Hook.	Quercus garryana Dougl.
296	45	–	White Oak	Oregon White Oak
297	46	–	Quercus utahensis Rydb.	Quercus gambelii Nutt.
297	46	–		*add:* Gambel Oak
298	47	–	White Oak, Valley Oak	California White Oak
299	48	–	*Note:* This form now included as a part of *Quercus gambelii.*	
302	–	3	*Note:* This form included as a part of *Quercus alba* L. without benefit of variety ranking.	
304	52	–	Quercus Prinus L.	Quercus michauxii Nutt.
304	52	–	Basket Oak, Cow Oak	Swamp Chestnut Oak
305	53	–	Quercus montana Willd.	Quercus prinus L.
306	54	–	Quercus Muehlenbergii Engelm.	Quercus muehlenbergii Engelm.
306	54	–	Yellow Oak, Chestnut Oak	Chinkapin Oak
309	–	27	U. racemosa	U. thomasii
309	–	34	U. fulva	U. rubra
309	1	–	White Elm	American Elm
311	2	–	Ulmus racemosa Thomas	Ulmus thomasii Sarg.
313	4	–	Ulmus fulva Michx.	Ulmus rubra Mühl.
315	6	–	Red Elm	September Elm
317	1	–	Water Elm	Planertree
318	–	50	C. Douglasii	C. douglasii
319	–	4	C. Lindheimeri	C. lindheimeri
320	–	11	*Note:* This form now included as a part of *Celtis occidentalis* L. without benefit of variety ranking.	
320	–	22	*Note:* This form now included as a part of *Celtis occidentalis* L. without benefit of variety ranking.	
321	2	–	*Note:* This form now included as a part of *Celtis reticulata* Torr.	
322	3	–	Celtis Lindheimeri K. Koch.	Celtis lindheimeri Engelm.
322	3	–	Palo Blanco	Lindheimer Hackberry
323	4	–	Hackberry	Netleaf Hackberry
324	–	28	*Note:* This form now included as a part of *Celtis lævigata* Willd. without benefit of variety ranking.	
325	–	6	*Note:* This form now included as a part of *Celtis lævigata* Willd. without benefit of variety ranking.	
326	6	–	*Note:* Now regarded as merely a variation of *Celtis occidentalis* L.	
326	–	9	Celtis pumila var. georgiana Sarg.	Celtis tenuifolia Nutt.
326	–	9		*add:* Georgia Hackberry
327	1	–	Trema mollis Lour.	Trema micrantha (L.) Blume
327	1	–		*add:* Florida Trema
330	2	–	Mulberry, Mexican Mulberry	Texas Mulberry
332	1	–	Osage Orange, Bow Wood	Osage-orange

Page	Item	Line	For	Read
334	–	5	F. brevifolia	F. lævigata
334	1	–	Wild Fig	Florida Strangler Fig
335	2	–	Ficus brevifolia Nutt.	Ficus lævigata Vahl.
335	2	–	Fig, Wild Fig	Shortleaf Fig
336	1	31		*add:* Gulf Graytwig
337	1	–		*add:* Tallowwood
338	1	–	Coccolobis P. Br.	Coccoloba P. Br.
339	–	9	C. laurifolia	C. diversifolia
339	1	–	Coccolobis uvifera Jacq.	Coccoloba uvifera (L.) L.
339	1	–	Sea Grape	Seagrape
340	2	–	Coccolobis laurifolia Jacq.	Coccoloba diversifolia Jacq.
340	2	–	Pigeon Plum	Doveplum
341	1	14	Blolly	Longleaf Blolly
343	–	14	M. cordata	M. acuminata var. cordata
343	–	29	M. Fraseri	M. fraseri
343	1	–	Cucumber-tree, Mountain Magnolia	Cucumbertree
344	2	–	Magnolia cordata Michx.	Magnolia acuminata var. cordata Sarg.
344	2	–		*add:* Yellow Cucumbertree
345	3	–	Magnolia	Southern Magnolia
346	4	–	Sweet Bay, Swamp Bay	Sweetbay
347	5	–	Umbrella-tree, Elkwood	Umbrella Magnolia
348	6	–	Large-leaved Cucumber-tree	Bigleaf Magnolia
349	7	–	Magnolia Fraseri Walt.	Magnolia fraseri Walt.
349	7	–	Mountain Magnolia, Long-leaved Cucumber-tree	Fraser Magnolia
350	8	–	Magnolia pyramidata Pursh.	Magnolia pyramidata Bartr.
350	8	–		*add:* Pyramid Magnolia
352	1	–	Yellow Poplar, Tulip-tree	Yellow-poplar
355	1	–	Pond Apple	Pond-apple
356	–	27	Ocotea	Nectandra
356	–	33	Misanteca	Licaria
357	–	17	P. Borbonia	P. borbonia
357	1	–	Persea Borbonia Spreng.	Persea borbonia (L.) Spreng.
357	1	–	Red Bay	Redbay
358	2	–	*Note:* This form now included as a part of *Persea borbonia* (L.) Spreng.	
359	2	–	OCOTEA Aubl.	NECTANDRA Roland
359	1	–	Ocotea Catesbyana Sarg.	Nectandra coriacea (Sw.) Griseb.
359	1	–		*add:* Jamaica Nectandra
361	1	–	Umbellularia californica Nutt.	Umbellularia californica (Hook. & Arn.) Nutt.
361	1	–	California Laurel, Spice-tree	California-laurel
363	11	–	Sassafras officinale Nees & Ebermaier	Sasafras albidum (Nutt.) Nees
363	11	–		*add:* Sassafras
364	–	12	MISANTECA Cham. & Schl.	LICARIA Aubl.
364	1	–	Misanteca triandra Mez.	Licaria triandra (Sw.) Kosterm.
364	1	–		*add:* Gulf Licaria
365	1	43	Capparis jamaicensis Jacq.	Capparis cynophallophora L.
365	1	43		*add:* Jamaica Caper
367	1	–	Liquidambar Styraciflua L.	Liquidambar styraciflua L.
367	1	–	Sweet Gum, Bilsted	Sweetgum
369	1	–		*add:* Witch-hazel
370	2	–	*Note:* This form now included as a part of *Hamamelis virginiana* L.	
371	1	–	Plane-tree	Sycamore

Page	Item	Line	For	Read
372	–	16	P. Wrightii	P. wrightii
372	1	–	Sycamore, Buttonwood	American Sycamore
373	1	–	*Note:* This form now included as a part of *Platanus occidentalis* L. without benefit of variety ranking.	
374	2	–	Sycamore	California Sycamore
375	3	–	Platanus Wrightii S. Wats.	Platanus wrightii S. Wats.
375	3	–	Sycamore	Arizona Sycamore
376	–	33	Heteromeles	Photinia
377	1	26	Vauquelinia california Sarg.	Vauquelinia californica (Torr.) Sarg.
377	1	26		*add:* Torrey Vauquelinia
378	1	–	Ironwood	Lyontree
380	–	13	M. platycarpa	M. × platycarpa
380	–	25	M. fusca	M. diversifolia
380	1	–	Crab Apple	Biltmore Crab Apple
381	2	–	*Note:* This form now included as a part of *Malus coronaria* L.	
382	3	–	Crab Apple, Garland Tree	Sweet Crab Apple
383	–	14	*Note:* This form now included as a part of *Malus coronaria* L. without variety ranking.	
383	4	–	Malus platycarpa Rehd.	Malus × platycarpa Rehd.
383	4	–	Crab Apple	Bigfruit Crab Apple
384	5	–	*Note:* This form now included as a part of *Malus coronaria* L.	
385	6	–	Crab Apple	Southern Crab Apple
386	7	–	*Note:* This form now included as a part of *Malus coronaria* L.	
387	8	–	Crab Apple	Prairie Crab Apple
389	9	–	Malus fusca Schn.	Malus diversifolia (Bong.) Roem.
389	9	–	Crab Apple	Oregon Crab Apple
390	1	–		*add:* American Mountain-ash
391	–	27	Sorbus americana var. decora Sarg.	Sorbus decora (Sarg.) Schneid.
391	–	27		*add:* Showy Mountain-ash
392	5	–	HETEROMELES Roem.	PHOTINIA Lindl.
392	1	–	Heteromeles arbutifolia Roem.	Photinia arbutifolia Lindl.
392	1	–	Tollon, Toyon	Christmasberry
394	–	12	A. canadensis	A. arborea
394	1	–	Amelanchier canadensis Med.	Amelanchier arborea (Michx. F.) Fern.
394	1	–	Service Berry, Shad Bush	Downy Serviceberry
395	2	–	Service Berry	Allegheny Serviceberry
396	3	–	Service Berry	Pacific Serviceberry
400	–	43	C. Crus-galli	C. crus-galli
401	–	20	C. arborea	C. pyracanthoides
401	–	28	C. montivaga	C. tracyi
402	1	–	Cratægus Crus-galli L.	Cratægus crus-galli L.
402	1	–	Cock-spur Thorn	Cockspur Hawthorn
403	2	–		*add:* Canby Hawthorn
403	3	–		*add:* Prairie Hawthorn
404	4	–		*add:* St. Claire Hawthorn
405	5	–		*add:* Piedmont Hawthorn
406	6	–	*Note:* This form now included as a part of *Cratægus crus-galli* L.	
407	7	–	*Note:* This form now included as a part of *Cratægus crus-galli* L.	
408	8	–	Cratægus Palmeri Sarg.	Cratægus palmeri Sarg.
408	8	–		*add:* Palmer Hawthorn
408	9	–	*Note:* This form now included as a part of *Cratægus acutifolia* Sarg.	
409	10	–		*add:* St. Louis Hawthorn
410	11	–	Cratægus Bushii Sarg.	Cratægus bushii Sarg.
410	11	–		*add:* Bush Hawthorn

Page	Item	Line	For	Read
411	12	–	Cratægus Cocksii Sarg.	Cratægus cocksii Sarg.
411	12	–		add: Cocks Hawthorn
412	13	–	Cratægus arborea Beadl.	Cratægus pyracanthoides Beadl.
413	15	–	Cratægus Engelmannii Sarg.	Cratægus engelmannii Sarg.
413	15	–		add: Engelmann Hawthorn
414	16	–	Cratægus montivaga Sarg.	Cratægus tracyi Ashe
414	16	–		add: Tracy Hawthorn
415	17	–	Note: This form now included as a part of *Cratægus mohrii* Beadl.	
415	18	–		add: Pineland Hawthorn
417	20	–		add: Opelousas Hawthorn
418	21	–		add: Barberryleaf Hawthorn
421	25	–	Cratægus Mohrii Beadl.	Cratægus mohrii Beadl.
421	25	–		add: Mohrs Hawthorn
423	26	–		add: Dotted Hawthorn
424	27	–	Note: This form now included as a part of *Cratægus punctata* Jacq.	
425	28	–		add: Sandhill Hawthorn
429	33	–	Note: This form now included as a part of *Cratægus collina* Chapm.	
430	34	–		add: Brazoria Hawthorn
431	35	–		add: Dallas Hawthorn
432	36	–	Note: This form now included as a part of *Cratægus collina* Chapm.	
433	37	–	Note: This form now included as a part of *Cratægus peoriensis* Sarg.	
434	38	–	May Haw, Apple Haw	May Hawthorn
435	39	–	Note: This form now included as a part of *Cratægus æstivalis* Sarg.	
436	40	–		add: Riverflat Hawthorn
438	–	16	C. micracantha	C. succulenta
438	41	–		add: Green Hawthorn
439	42	–	Note: This form now included as a part of *Cratægus viridis* L.	
442	46	–	Note: This form now included as a part of *Cratægus viridis* L.	
443	47	–	Note: This form now included as a part of *Cratægus viridis* L.	
444	48	–		add: Glossy Hawthorn
445	49	–	Note: This form now included as a part of *Cratægus acutifolia* Sarg.	
446	50	–	Note: This form now included as a part of *Cratægus viridis* L.	
448	53	–	Cratægus micracantha Sarg.	Cratægus succulenta Schrad.
448	53	–		add: Fleshy Hawthorn
449	–	27	C. callicarpa	C. coccinioides
449	54	–		add: Frosted Hawthorn
450	55	–		add: Georgia Hawthorn
451	56	–	Note: This form now included as a part of *Cratægus coccinioides* Ashe	
453	–	13	C. drymophila	C. iracunda
453	–	15	C. diffusa	C. populnea
453	–	16	C. luxuriosa	C. gravis
453	58	–	Cratægus drymophila Sarg.	Cratægus iracunda Beadl.
454	59	–	Cratægus diffusa Sarg.	Cratægus populnea Ashe
455	60	–	Cratægus luxuriosa Sarg.	Cratægus gravis Ashe
456	–	23	C. apiomorpha	C. flabellata
456	–	25	C. paucispina	C. macrosperma
457	61	–	Cratægus apiomorpha Sarg.	Cratægus flabellata (Bosc.) K. Koch
457	61	–		add: Fanleaf Hawthorn
458	62	–	Cratægus paucispina Sarg.	Cratægus macrosperma Ashe
458	62	–		add: Large-seed Hawthorn
458	63	–	Note: This form now included as a part of *Cratægus macrosperma* Ashe.	
459	64	–	Note: This form now included as a part of *Cratægus macrosperma* Ashe.	
463	–	52	C. corusca	C. × corusca
464	–	2	C. Kelloggii	C. × kelloggii

Page	Item	Line	For	Read
464	–	31	C. Ellwangeriana	C. ellwangeriana
464	–	33	C. Robesoniana	C. robesoniana
464	68	–	Red Haw	Downy Hawthorn
465	69	–	*Note:* This form now included as a part of *Cratægus mollis* Scheele.	
466	70	–	*Note:* This form now included as a part of *Cratægus mollis* Scheele.	
467	71	–	*Note:* This form now included as a part of *Cratægus mollis* Scheele.	
468	72	–	*Note:* This form now included as a part of *Cratægus induta* Sarg.	
470	74	–		*add:* Viburnum Hawthorn
471	75	–	*Note:* This form now included as a part of *Cratægus texana* Buckl.	
472	77	–	*Note:* This form now included as a part of *Cratægus lanuginosa* Sarg.	
473	78	–		*add:* Canada Hawthorn
474	79	–	Cratægus corusca Sarg.	Cratægus × corusca Sarg.
475	80	–	Cratægus Kelloggii Sarg.	Cratægus × kelloggii Sarg.
476	81	–	Turkey Apple	Turkey Hawthorn
477	82	–		*add:* Texas Hawthorn
478	83	–	*Note:* This form now included as a part of *Cratægus texana* Buckl.	
479	84	–	*Note:* This form now included as a part of *Cratægus lanuginosa* Sarg.	
481	86	–		*add:* Arnold Hawthorn
482	87	–	*Note:* This form now included as a part of *Cratægus submollis* Sarg.	
483	88	–		*add:* Pennsylvania Hawthorn
484	89	–		*add:* Quebec Hawthorn
484	90	–	*Note:* This form now included as a part of *Cratægus pedicellata* Sarg.	
485	91	–	*Note:* This form now included as a part of *Cratægus pedicellata* Sarg.	
486	92	–	*Note:* This form now included as a part of *Cratægus pedicellata* Sarg.	
487	93	–		*add:* Noel Hawthorn
488	–	24	C. Hillii	C. hillii
488	–	31	C. Pringlei	C. pringlei
489	–	5	C. Holmesiana	C. holmesiana
489	–	13	C. Eamesii	C. eamesii
489	94	–	*Note:* This form now included as a part of *Cratægus dilatata* Sarg.	
490	95	–	*Note:* This form now included as a part of *Cratægus pedicellata* Sarg.	
491	96	–	*Note:* This form now included as a part of *Cratægus pedicellata* Sarg.	
492	97	–	Cratægus Pringlei Sarg.	Cratægus pringlei Sarg.
492	97	–		*add:* Pringle Hawthorn
493	98	–	*Note:* This form now included as a part of *Cratægus pringlei* Sarg.	
494	99	–		*add:* Scarlet Hawthorn
495	100	–		*add:* Holmes Hawthorn
496	101	–	*Note:* This form now included as a part of *Cratægus pedicellata* Sarg.	
497	102	–	*Note:* This form now included as a part of *Cratægus pedicellata* Sarg.	
498	103	–	*Note:* This form now included as a part of *Cratægus pedicellata* Sarg.	
499	104	–	*Note:* This form now included as a part of *Cratægus pedicellata* Sarg.	
503	108	–		*add:* Kansas Hawthorn
504	–	17	C. rotundifolia	C. chrysocarpa
504	–	19	C. Jonesæ	C. jonesiæ
504	–	22	C. Margaretta	C. margaretta
504	109	–	Cratægus rotundifolia Moen.	Cratægus chrysocarpa Ashe
504	109	–		*add:* Fireberry Hawthorn
505	110	–	Cratægus Jonesæ Sarg.	Cratægus jonesiæ Sarg.
505	110	–		*add:* Jones Hawthorn
506	111	–	Cratægus Margaretta Ashe	Cratægus margaretta Ashe
506	111	–		*add:* Margaret Hawthorn
508	–	5	C. Boyntonii	C. boyntonii
508	–	7	C. Buckleyi	C. buckleyi
508	–	13	C. Sargentii	C. sargentii
508	112	–	Cratægus Boyntonii Beadl.	Cratægus boytonii Beadl.
508	112	–		*add:* Boynton Hawthorn
509	113	–	*Note:* This form now included as a part of *Cratægus boyntonii* Beadl.	

Page	Item	Line	For	Read
510	115	–	Cratægus Sargentii Beadl.	Cratægus sargentii Beadl.
510	115	–		*add:* Sargent Hawthorn
513	–	25	C. Harbisonii	C. harbisonii
513	–	27	C. Ashei	C. ashei
513	118	–	Cratægus Harbisonii Beadl.	Cratægus harbisonii Beadl.
513	118	–		*add:* Harbison Hawthorn
514	119	–	Cratægus Ashei Beadl.	Cratægus ashei Beadl.
514	119	–		*add:* Ashe Hawthorn
516	–	16	C. Ravenelii	C. ravenelii
516	120	–		*add:* Yellow Hawthorn
521	125	–		*add:* Jacksonville Hawthorn
522	126	–		*add:* Pensacola Hawthorn
523	127	–	Cratægus Ravenelii Sarg.	Cratægus ravenelii Sarg.
523	127	–		*add:* Ravenel Hawthorn
526	131	–	*Note:* This form now included as a part of *Cratægus floridana* Sarg.	
530	–	15	C. apiifolia	C. marshallii
530	–	18	C. Phænopyrum	C. phænopyrum
530	135	–	Cratægus apiifolia Michx.	Cratægus marshallii Eggl.
530	135	–	Parsley Haw	Parsley Hawthorn
531	136	–	Cratægus Phænopyrum Med.	Cratægus phænopyrum (L. f.) Med.
531	136	–	Washington Thorn	Washington Hawthorn
532	137	–		*add:* Littlehip Hawthorn
533	138	–	Pomette Bleue	Blueberry Hawthorn
534	139	–		*add:* Willow Hawthorn
535	–	27	C. tomentosa	C. calpodendron
535	–	29	C. Chapmanii	C. chapmanii
535	–	36	C. Deweyana	C. brainerdii
536	140	–	Cratægus tomentosa L.	Cratægus calpodendron (Ehrh.) Med.
536	140	–		*add:* Pear Hawthorn
537	141	–	Cratægus Chapmanii Ashe	Cratægus chapmanii Ashe
537	142	–	*Note:* This form now included as a part of *Cratægus succulenta* Schrad.	
538	143	–	*Note:* This form now included as a part of *Cratægus succulenta* Schrad.	
539	144	–	Cratægus Deweyana Sarg.	Cratægus brainerdii Sarg.
539	144	–		*add:* Brainerd Hawthorn
540	145	–	Cratægus succulenta Link.	Cratægus succulenta Schrad.
540	145	–		*add:* Fleshy Hawthorn
541	146	–	*Note:* This form now included as a part of *Cratægus succulenta* Schrad.	
542	147	–	*Note:* This form now included as a part of *Cratægus succulenta* Schrad.	
543	148	–	*Note:* This form now included as a part of *Cratægus succulenta* Schrad.	
544	149	–	*Note:* This form now included as a part of *Cratægus succulenta* Schrad.	
545	–	19	C. Douglasii	C. douglasii
545	150	–	Cratægus Douglasii Lindl.	Cratægus douglasii Lindl.
545	150	–		*add:* Black Hawthorn
546	151	–		*add:* River Hawthorn
547	152	–	*Note:* This form now included as a part of *Cratægus brainerdii* Sarg.	
548	153	–	*Note:* This form now included as a part of *Cratægus succulenta* Schrad.	
549	1	–		*add:* Cliffrose
550	9	–	Mountain Mahogany	Cercocarpus

Page	Item	Line	For	Read
551	–	17	C. Traskiæ	C. betuloides var. traskiæ
551	–	19	C. alnifolius	C. betuloides var. blancheæ
551	–	26	C. paucidentatus	C. breviflorus
551	2	–	Cercocarpus Traskiæ Eastw.	Cercocarpus betuloides var. traskiæ (Eastw.) Dunkle.
551	2	–		add: Catalina Cercocarpus
552	2	–	Cercocarpus alnifolius Rydb.	Cercocarpus betuloides var. blancheæ (Schneid.) Little
552	2	–		add: Alderleaf Cercocarpus
553	3	–		add: Curlleaf Cercocarpus
553	4	–		add: Hairy Cercocarpus
554	5	–	Cercocarpus paucidentatus Britt.	Cercocarpus breviflorus A. Gray
556	–	35	P. lanata	P. americana var. lanata
556	–	50	P. Munsoniana	P. munsoniana
557	–	16	P. alabamensis	P. serotina var. alabamensis
557	–	21	P. virens	P. serotina var. rufula
557	–	36	P. Lyonii	P. lyonii
557	1	–	Wild Plum	Klamath Plum
558	2	–	Black Sloe	Flatwoods Plum
561	4	–	Wild Plum	American Plum
563	5	–	Prunus lanata Mack. & Bush	Prunus americana var. lanata Swdw.
563	5	–		add: Inch Plum
564	6	–	Note: This form now included as a part of Prunus mexicana S. Wats.	
565	7	–	Big Tree Plum	Mexican Plum
566	8	–	Sloe	Allegheny Plum
567	9	–	Wild Plum	Hortulan Plum
568	10	–	Prunus Munsoniana Wight & Hedrick	Prunus munsoniana Wight & Hedr.
568	10	–		add: Wildgoose Plum
571	12	–	Wild Red Cherry, Bird Cherry	Pin Cherry
572	13	–	Wild Cherry	Bitter Cherry
573	14	–	Choke Cherry	Common Chokecherry
575	15	–	Wild Black Cherry, Rum Cherry	Black Cherry
576	16	–	Prunus alabamensis Mohr.	Prunus serotina var. alabamensis (Mohr.) Little
576	16	–		add: Alabama Black Cherry
577	17	–	Note: This form now included as a part of Prunus serotina var. alabamensis (Mohr.) Little	
578	18	–	Prunus virens Shrive.	Prunus serotina var. rufula (Woot. & Standl.) McVaugh
578	18	–	Wild Cherry	Southwestern Black Cherry
579	19	–	Wild Orange, Mock Orange	Carolina Laurelcherry
580	20	–		add: Myrtle Laurelcherry
581	21	–	Islay	Hollyleaf Cherry
582	22	–	Prunus Lyonii Sarg.	Prunus lyonii Sarg.
582	22	–		add: Catalina Cherry
583	1	–	Cocoa Plum	Icaco coco-plum
584	–	26	Chrysobalanus icaco var. pellocarpa DC.	Chrysobalanus icaco var. pellocarpus (G. F. W. May) DC.
584	–	26		add: Smallfruit Coco-plum
585	–	20	Pithecolobium	Pithecellobium
586	–	16	Ichthyomethia	Piscidia
586	1	17	PITHECOLOBIUM Mart.	PITHECELLOBIUM Mart.
586	–	42	P. brevifolium	P. pallens
586	1	45	Pithecolobium unguis-cati Mart.	Pithecellobium unguis-cati Mart.
586	1	45	Cat's Claw	Catclaw Blackbead
587	2	–	Pithecolobium brevifolium Benth.	Pithecellobium pallens (Benth.) Standl.

Page	Item	Line	For	Read
588	3	–	Pithecolobium flexicaule Coult.	Pithecellobium flexicale (Benth.) Coult.
588	3	–	Ebony	Ebony Blackbead
590	1	–	Wild Tamarind	Bahama Lysiloma
591	–	44	A. Farnesiana	A. farnesiana
591	–	48	A. Emoriana	A. emoryana
592	–	3	A. Wrightii	A. wrightii
592	–	6	A. Greggii	A. greggii
592	1	–	Acacia Farnesiana Willd.	Acacia farnesiana (L.) Willd.
592	1	–	Huisache, Cassie	Sweet Acacia
593	2	–		add: Twisted Acacia
593	3	–	Acacia Emoriana Benth.	Acacia emoryana Benth.
593	3	–		add: Emory Acacia
594	4	–	Acacia Wrightii Benth.	Acacia wrightii Benth.
594	4	–	Cat's Claw	Wright Acacia
595	5	–	Acacia Greggii A. Gray	Acacia greggii A. Gray
595	5	–	Cat's Claw, Una de Gato	Catclaw Acacia
597	–	4	L. Greggii	L. greggii
597	1	–	Leucæna Greggii S. Wats.	Leucæna greggii S. Wats.
597	1	–		add: Gregg Leadtree
598	2	–		add: Littleaf Leadtree
598	3	–	Mimosa	Great Leadtree
600	1	–	Prosopis juliflora DC.	Prosopis juliflora (Sw.) DC.
601	–	18		add: Honey Mesquite
601	–	29		add: Velvet Mesquite
602	2	–	Screw Bean, Screw Pod Mesquite	Screwbean Mesquite
603	–	50	C. reniformis	C. canadensis var. texensis
604	2	–	Cercis reniformis Engl.	Cercis canadensis var. texensis (S. Wats.) Hopkins
604	2	–	Redbud	Texas Redbud
606	1	–	Kentucky Coffee-tree, Mahogany	Kentucky Coffeetree
608	–	5	G. texana	G. × texana
608	1	–	Honey Locust	Honeylocust
609	2	–	Gleditsia texana Sarg.	Gleditsia × texana Sarg.
609	2	–	Locust	Texas Honeylocust
610	3	–	Water Locust	Waterlocust
611	1	–	Retama, Horse Bean	Jerusalem-thorn
614	–	8	C. Torreyanum	C. torreyanum
614	1	–	Green-barked Acacia	Blue Paloverde
615	2	–	Note: This form now included as a part of Cercidium floridum Benth.	
616	1	–	Frijolito, Coral Bean	Mescalbean
617	2	–		add: Texas Sophora
619	1	–	Yellow Wood, Virgilia	Yellowwood
620	1	–	Eysenhardtia orthocarpa S. Wats.	Eysenhardtia polystachya (Ortega) Sarg.
620	1	–		add: Kidneywood
621	1	–	Smoke Tree	Smokethorn
623	–	15	R. Pseudoacacia	R. pseudoacacia
623	–	17	R. neo-Mexicana	R. neomexicana
623	1	–	Robinia Pseudoacacia L.	Robinia pseudoacacia L.
623	1	–	Locust, Acacia, Yellow Locust	Black Locust
624	2	–	Robinia neo-mexicana A. Gray	Robinia neomexicana A. Gray
624	2	–	Locust	New-Mexican Locust
626	1	–	Ironwood	Tetosa
628	1	–	Erythrina herbacea var. arborea Chapm.	Erythrina herbacea L.
628	1	–		add: Eastern Coralbean
628	18	–	ICHTHYOMETHIA P. Brown	PISCIDIA L.

Page	Item	Line	For	Read
629	1	–	Ichthyomethia piscipula A. S. Hitch.	Piscidia piscipula (L.) Sarg.
629	1	–	Jamaica Dogwood	Florida Fishpoison-tree
631	1	–		*add:* Holywood Lignumvitæ
632	1	23	Byrsonima lucida DC.	Byrsonima lucidum DC.
632	1	23		*add:* Long Key Byrsonima
633	–	32	Xanthoxylum	Zanthoxylum
633	1	–	XANTHOXYLUM L.	ZANTHOXYLUM L.
634	–	11	X. Fagara	Z. fagara
634	–	14	X. clava-Herculis	Z. clava-herculis
634	1	–	Xanthoxylum Fagara Sarg.	Zanthoxylum fagara Sarg.
634	1	–	Wild Lime	Lime Prickly-ash
635	2	–	Xanthoxylum clava-Herculis L.	Zanthoxylum clava-herculis L.
635	2	–	Toothache-tree	Hercules-club
636	3	–	Xanthoxylum flavum Vahl.	Zanthoxylum flavum Vahl.
636	3	–	Satinwood	Yellowheart
637	4	–	Xanthoxylum coriaceum A. Richard	Zanthoxylum coriaceum A. Rich.
637	4	–		*add:* Biscayne Prickly-ash
638	1	–		*add:* Baretta
639	1	–	Hop-tree, Wafer Ash	Common Hoptree
640	1	–	Torch Wood	Sea Amyris
643	1	–		*add:* Bitterbush
644	1	–		*add:* Mexican Alvaradoa
646	–	10	B. Simaruba	B. simaruba
646	1	–	Bursera Simaruba Sarg.	Bursera simaruba Sarg.
646	1	–	Gumbo Limbo, West Indian Birch	Gumbo-limbo
647	2	–		*add:* Elephanttree
648	1	–	Mahogany	West Indies Mahogany
650	1	–	White Wood	Milkbark
651	2	–	Guiana Plum	Guianaplum
653	1	–	Hippomane Mancinella L.	Hippomane mancinella L.
654	1	–	Crab Wood	Oysterwood
656	1	29		*add:* Texas Pistache
657	1	–	Cotinus americanus Nutt.	Cotinus obovatus Raf.
657	1	–	Chittam Wood	American Smoketree
659	1	–	Poison Wood, Hog Gum	Florida Poisontree
660	–	34	R. vernix	T. vernix
660	1	–	Staghorn Sumach	Staghorn Sumac
662	2	–	Sumach	Shining Sumac
663	3	–	Rhus vernix L.	Toxicodendron vernix (L.) Kuntze.
663	3	–	Poison Dogwood, Poison Sumach	Poison-sumac
664	4	–	Mahogany	Lemonade Sumac
666	1	23	Ironwood, Leather Wood	Swamp Cyrilla
667	1	–	Titi, Ironwood	Buckwheat-tree
669	–	3	I. Cassine	I. cassine
669	–	7	I. Krugiana	I. krugiana
669	–	13	I. monticola	I. montana
669	1	–	Holly	American Holly
670	2	–	Ilex Cassine L.	Ilex cassine L.
672	4	–	Ilex Krugiana Loesen.	Ilex krugiana Loesen.
672	4	–		*add:* Tawnyberry Holly
673	5	–		*add:* Possumhaw
673	6	–	Ilex monticola Gray	Ilex montana Torr. & Gray
673	6	–		*add:* Mountain Winterberry

Page	Item	Line	For	Read
675	–	3	Evonymus	Euonymus
675	1	14	EVONYMUS L.	EUONYMUS L.
675	1	41	Burning Bush, Wahoo	Eastern Wahoo
677	1	–		add: Guttapercha Mayten
678	1	–		add: Canotia
679	1	–		add: West Indies Falsebox
680	1	–	Yellow Wood, Box Wood	Florida-Boxwood
682	–	9	A. floridanum	A. barbatum
682	–	25	A. Negundo	A. negundo
682	1	–	Dwarf Maple	Rocky Mountain Maple
683	–	21	Acer glabrum var. Douglasii	Acer glabrum var. douglasii
			Dippel	(Hook.) Dipp.
683	–	21		add: Douglas Maple
687	5	–	Broad-leaved Maple	Bigleaf Maple
689	–	30	Acer saccharum var. Rugelii	Acer saccharum var. rugelii
			Rehd.	Rehd.
691	7	–	Acer floridanum Pax	Acer barbatum Michx.
691	7	–	Sugar Maple	Florida Maple
692	8	–	Sugar Maple	Bigtooth Maple
694	10	–	Sugar Maple	Chalk Maple
698	–	15	Acer rubrum var. Drummondii	Acer rubrum var. drummondii
			Sarg.	(Hook. & Arn.) Sarg.
698	–	15		add: Drummond Red Maple
699	–	1	Red Maple	Trident Red Maple
699	13	–	Acer Negundo L.	Acer negundo L.
699	13	–	Box Elder, Ash-leaved Maple	Boxelder
701	–	34	Acer Negundo var. californicum	Acer negundo var. californicum
			Sarg.	Sarg.
703	–	14	A. georgiana	A. sylvatica
703	–	–	A. Pavia	A. pavia
704	2	–	Sweet Buckeye	Yellow Buckeye
706	3	–	Aesculus georgiana Sarg.	Aesculus sylvatica Bartr.
707	–	10	Aesculus × Harbisonii Sarg.	Aesculus × harbisonii Sarg.
707	–	14	Aesculus georgiana var. lanceolata	Aesculus sylvatica var. lanceolata
			Sarg.	(Sarg). Bartr.
707	4	–	Aesculus Pavia L.	Aesculus pavia L.
707	4	–	Red-flowered Buckeye	Red Buckeye
709	5	–	Note: This form now included as a part of Aesculus pavia L.	
710	6	–	Buckeye	California Buckeye
712	–	20	S. Drummondii	S. drummondii
712	1	–		add: Twinleaf Soapberry
713	2	–		add: Florida Soapberry
714	3	–	Sapindus Drummondii Hook.	Sapindus drummondii Hook.
			& Arn.	& Arn.
714	3	–	Wild China-tree	Western Soapberry
715	1	–	Ironwood, Ink Wood	Butterbough
716	1	–	White Inkwood	Inkwood
717	1	–	Spanish Buckeye	Mexican-buckeye
719	1	28	Purple Haw, Log Wood	Bluewood
720	1	–	Red Ironwood, Darling Plum	Darling-plum
721	1	–	Black Ironwood	Leadwood
723	–	5	R. Purshiana	R. purshiana
723	–	23		add: Hollyleaf Buckthorn
724	–	5	Rhamnus crocea var. insularis	Rhamnus crocea var. pirifolia
			Sarg.	(Greene) Little.
724	–	5		add: Great Redberry Buckthorn
724	2	–	Indian Cherry	Carolina Buckthorn

Page	Item	Line	For	Read
725	3	–	Rhamnus Purshiana DC.	Rhamnus purshiana DC.
725	3	–	Bearberry, Coffee-tree	Cascara Buckthorn
727	1	–		add: Feltleaf Ceanothus
727	2	–	Blue Myrtle, California Lilac	Blueblossom
728	3	–	Lilac	Spiny Ceanothus
729	1	–	Naked Wood	Soldierwood
730	2	–		add: Cuba Colubrina
731	3	–		add: Coffee Colubrina
732	–	10	Bass Wood	Basswood
732	–	49	T. glabra	T. americana
733	1	–	Tilia glabra Vent.	Tilia americana L.
733	–	14	T. Cocksii	T. cocksii
733	1	–	Linden, Bass Wood	American Basswood
734	2	–	Note: This form now included as a part of Tilia floridana Small.	
735	3	–	Note: This form now included as a part of Tilia americana L.	
736	4	–	Note: This form now included as a part of Tilia floridana Small.	
737	5	–	Note: This form now included as a part of Tilia floridana Small.	
737	6	–		add: Florida Basswood
738	7	–	Note: This form now included as a part of Tilia americana L.	
739	8	–	Note: This form now included as a part of Tilia americana L.	
740	9	–		add: Carolina Basswood
742	10	–	Note: This form now included as a part of Tilia caroliniana Mill.	
743	11	–	Note: This form now included as a part of Tilia caroliniana Mill.	
744	12	–	Note: This form now included as a part of Tilia heterophylla Vent.	
745	13	–		add: White Basswood
746	–	1	Tilia heterophylla var. Michauxii Sarg.	Tilia heterophylla var. michauxii Sarg.
747	14	–	Note: This form now included as a part of Tilia heterophylla Vent.	
747	15	–	Note: This form now included as a part of Tilia caroliniana Mill.	
748	–	23	Note: This form now included as a part of Tilia caroliniana Mill.	
750	1	1	Slippery Elm	California Fremontia
751	–	18	G. Lasianthus	G. lasianthus
751	1	–	Gordonia Lasianthus Ell.	Gordonia lasianthus (L.) Ellis
751	1	–	Bay, Loblolly Bay	Loblolly-bay
753	1	46	Canella Winterana Gærtn.	Canella winterana (L.) Gærtn.
753	1	46	Cinnamon Bark, White Wood	Canella
754	1	33		add: Allthorn
756	1	–	Carica Papaya L.	Carica papaya L.
756	1	–	Pawpaw	Papaya
758	1	–	Suwarro	Saguaro
760	1	–	Cholla	Jumping Cholla
764	1	–	Rhizophora Mangle L.	Rhizophora mangle L.
764	1	–		add: Mangrove
765	1	41	Bucida Buceras L.	Bucida buceras L.
765	1	41	Black Olive-tree	Oxhorn Bucida
766	1	–	Buttonwood	Button-mangrove
767	1	–	Buttonwood, White Mangrove	White-mangrove
769	–	22	C. Zuzygium	C. zuzygium
769	1	23		add: Pale Lidflower
770	2	14	Calyptranthes Zuzygium Sw.	Calyptranthes zuzygium Sw.
770	2	14		add: Myrtle-of-the-river
771	–	20	E. buxifolia	E. myrtoides
771	–	33	E. Simpsonii	E. simpsonii
771	1	–	Eugenia buxifolia Willd.	Eugenia myrtoides Poir.
771	1	–	Gurgeon Stopper, Spanish Stopper	Boxleaf Eugenia
772	2	–	Stopper, White Stopper	White-stopper Eugenia
773	3	–	Stopper	Spiceberry Eugenia

Page	Item	Line	For	Read
774	4	–	Red Stopper	Redberry Eugenia
774	5	–	Naked Wood	Twinberry Eugenia
775	6	–	Eugenia Simpsonii Sarg.	Eugenia simpsonii
775	6	–		add: Simpson Eugenia
777	1	–		add: Florida Tetrazygia
778	1	23		delete: Prickly Ash
				add: Devils-walkingstick
				(insert before Hercules' Club)
780	–	23	N. biflora	N. sylvatica var. biflora
780	1	–	Tupelo, Pepperidge, Sour Gum	Black Tupelo, Blackgum
781	2	–	Nyssa biflora Walt.	Nyssa sylvatica var. biflora
				(Walt.) Sarg.
781	2	–		add: Swamp Tupelo
782	3	–	Ogeechee Lime, Sour Tupelo	Ogeechee Tupelo
783	4	–	Cotton Gum, Tupelo Gum	Water Tupelo
785	–	32	C. Nuttallii	C. nuttallii
785	–	35	C. asperifolia	C. drummondii
787	2	–	Cornus Nuttallii Aud.	Cornus nuttallii Aud.
787	2	–		add: Pacific Dogwood
738	3	–	Cornus asperifolia Michx.	Cornus drummondii C. A. Meyer
788	3	–	Dogwood	Roughleaf Dogwood
789	4	–	Dogwood	Alternate-leaf Dogwood
791	–	7	Xolisma	Lyonia
791	1	32		add: Elliottia
792	1	–	Great Laurel, Rose Bay	Rosebay Rhododendron
794	1	–	Laurel, Mountain Laurel	Mountain-laurel
796	1	–	Sorrel-tree, Sour Wood	Sourwood
797	5	–	XOLISMA Raf.	LYONIA Nutt.
798	1	–	Xolisma ferruginea Hell.	Lyonia ferruginea Nutt.
798	1	–		add: Lyonia
799	–	28	A. Menziesii	A. menziesii
799	1	–	Arbutus Menziesii Pursh.	Arbutus menziesii Pursh.
799	1	–	Madroña	Pacific Madrone
800	2	–	Madroña	Texas Madrone
801	3	–	Madroña	Arizona Madrone
802	1	–	Farkleberry, Sparkleberry	Tree sparkleberry
804	1	34	Joe Wood, Sea Myrtle	Joewood
807	1	–		add: Guiana Rapanea
809	–	23	Mimusops	Achras
809	1	42		add: False-mastic
811	1	–	Bustic, Cassada	Willow Bustic
812	–	41	B. monticola	B. lanuginosa var. rigida
812	–	43	B. angustifolia	B. celastrina
812	1	–	Ironwood, Black Haw	Tough Bumelia
813	2	–	Gum Elastic, Chittam Wood	Gum Bumelia
814	3	–	Bumelia monticola Buckl.	Bumelia lanuginosa var. rigida
				A. Gray
814	3	–		add: Gum Bumelia
815	4	–	Ironwood, Buckthorn	Buckthorn Bumelia
816	5	–	Bumelia angustifolia Nutt.	Bumelia celastrina H. K. B.
816	5	–	Ant's Wood, Downward Plum	Saffron-plum
818	1	–	Satin-leaf	Satinleaf
819	5	–	MIMUSOPS L.	ACHRAS L.
819	1	–	Mimusops emarginata Britt.	Achras emarginata (L.) Little
819	1	–	Wild Dilly	Wild-dilly
821	1	–	Persimmon	Common Persimmon
823	2	–	Black Persimmon, Chapote	Texas Persimmon

Page	Item	Line	For	Read
825	–	19	H. monticola	H. carolina var. monticola
825	1	–		add: Carolina Silverbell
826	2	–	Halesia monticola Sarg.	Halesia carolina var. monticola Redh.
826	2	–		add: Mountain Silverbell
827	3	–		add: Little Silverbell
828	4	–		add: Two-wing Silverbell
829	1	–		add: Bigleaf Snowbell
831	1	24	Sweet Leaf, Horse Sugar	Common Sweetleaf
833	–	46	F. Greggii	F. greggii
833	–	51	F. Lowellii	F. anomala var. lowellii
834	–	13	F. Standleyi	F. standleyi
834	–	27	F. Berlandieriana	F. berlandieriana
834	–	31	F. oregona	F. latifolia
834	1	–		add: Fragrant Ash
835	2	–	Fraxinus Greggii A. Gray	Fraxinus greggii A. Gray
835	2	–		add: Fragrant Ash
836	3	–	Fraxinus Lowellii Sarg.	Fraxinus anomola var. lowellii (Sarg.) Little
836	3	–		add: Lowell Ash
837	4	–		add: Singleleaf Ash
838	5	–	Water Ash, Swamp Ash	Carolina Ash
839	6	–	Note: This form now included as a part of Fraxinus caroliniana Mill.	
840	7	–	Note: This form now included as a part of Fraxinus velutina Torr.	
842	9	–	Mountain Ash	Texas Ash
843	10	–	Note: This form now included as a part of Fraxinus americana L.	
845	12	–	Red Ash	Green Ash
846	–	23	Note: This form now included as a part of Fraxinus pennsylvanica Marsh. without benefit of variety ranking.	
847	13	–	Fraxinus Berlandieriana DC.	Fraxinus berlandieriana DC.
847	13	–		add: Berlandier Ash
848	14	–		add: Velvet Ash
849	–	26	Note: This form now included as a part of Fraxinus velutina Torr. without benefit of variety ranking.	
850	15	–	Fraxinus oregona Nutt.	Fraxinus latifolia Benth.
854	1	–		add: Swamp-privet
855	1	–	Chionanthus virginica L.	Chionanthus virginicus L.
855	1	–	Fringe-tree, Old Man's Beard	Fringetree
857	1	–	Devil Wood	Devilwood
858	–	32	Beureria	Bourreria
859	–	3	C. Sebestena	C. sebestena
859	–	6	C. Boissieri	C. boissieri
859	1	–	Cordia Sebestena L.	Cordia sebestena L.
860	2	–	Cordia Boissieri A. DC.	Cordia boissieri A. DC.
861	2	–	BEURERIA Jacq.	BOURRERIA P. Br.
861	1	–	Beureria ovata Meyers.	Bourreria ovata Miers.
861	1	–		add: Bahama Strongbark
862	1	–	Ehretia elliptica DC.	Ehretia anacua (Mier. & Berland.) Johnst.
864	1	40	Fiddle Wood	Florida Fiddlewood
867	1	47		add: Mullein Nightshade
869	1	37	Desert Willow	Desertwillow
871	1	–	Catalpa, Indian Bean	Southern Catalpa
872	2	–	Western Catalpa	Northern Catalpa
873	1	–	Enallagma cucurbitina Urb.	Enallagma latifolia (Mill.) Small
873	1	–	Black Calabash Tree	Black-calabash
876	1	–	Georgia Bark	Pinckneya

Page	Item	Line	For	Read
877	1	–	Prince Wood	Caribbean Princewood
878	1	–	Button Bush	Buttonbush
880	1	–		*add:* Everglades Velvetseed
881	2	–		*add:* Roughleaf Velvetseed
882	–	47	S. Simpsonii	S. simpsonii
882	–	48	S. coerulea	S. glauca
883	1	–	Sambucus Simpsonii Rehd.	Sambucus simpsonii
883	1	–		*add:* Florida Elder
883	2	–	Sambucus coerulea Raf.	Sambucus glauca Nutt.
883	2	–		*add:* Blueberry Elder
885	–	13	Sambucus coerulea var. arizonica Sarg.	Sambucus glauca var. arizonica (Sarg.) Nutt.
885	3	–		*add:* Pacific Red Elder
887	–	18	V. Lentago	V. lentago
887	1	–		*add:* Possumhaw Virburnum
888	2	–	Viburnum Lentago L.	Viburnum lentago L.

INDEX

This comprehensive index covers both volumes of the work. Volume One contains pages 1 through 433 and Volume Two contains pages 434 through 891.

A CATALOG OF SELECTED
DOVER BOOKS
IN ALL FIELDS OF INTEREST

A CATALOG OF SELECTED DOVER
BOOKS IN ALL FIELDS OF INTEREST

DRAWINGS OF REMBRANDT, edited by Seymour Slive. Updated Lippmann, Hofstede de Groot edition, with definitive scholarly apparatus. All portraits, biblical sketches, landscapes, nudes. Oriental figures, classical studies, together with selection of work by followers. 550 illustrations. Total of 630pp. 9⅛ × 12¼.
21485-0, 21486-9 Pa., Two-vol. set $25.00

GHOST AND HORROR STORIES OF AMBROSE BIERCE, Ambrose Bierce. 24 tales vividly imagined, strangely prophetic, and decades ahead of their time in technical skill: "The Damned Thing," "An Inhabitant of Carcosa," "The Eyes of the Panther," "Moxon's Master," and 20 more. 199pp. 5⅜ × 8½. 20767-6 Pa. $3.95

ETHICAL WRITINGS OF MAIMONIDES, Maimonides. Most significant ethical works of great medieval sage, newly translated for utmost precision, readability. Laws Concerning Character Traits, Eight Chapters, more. 192pp. 5⅜ × 8½.
24522-5 Pa. $4.50

THE EXPLORATION OF THE COLORADO RIVER AND ITS CANYONS, J. W. Powell. Full text of Powell's 1,000-mile expedition down the fabled Colorado in 1869. Superb account of terrain, geology, vegetation, Indians, famine, mutiny, treacherous rapids, mighty canyons, during exploration of last unknown part of continental U.S. 400pp. 5⅜ × 8½. 20094-9 Pa. $6.95

HISTORY OF PHILOSOPHY, Julián Marías. Clearest one-volume history on the market. Every major philosopher and dozens of others, to Existentialism and later. 505pp. 5⅜ × 8½. 21739-6 Pa. $8.50

ALL ABOUT LIGHTNING, Martin A. Uman. Highly readable non-technical survey of nature and causes of lightning, thunderstorms, ball lightning, St. Elmo's Fire, much more. Illustrated. 192pp. 5⅜ × 8½. 25237-X Pa. $5.95

SAILING ALONE AROUND THE WORLD, Captain Joshua Slocum. First man to sail around the world, alone, in small boat. One of great feats of seamanship told in delightful manner. 67 illustrations. 294pp. 5⅜ × 8½. 20326-3 Pa. $4.95

LETTERS AND NOTES ON THE MANNERS, CUSTOMS AND CONDITIONS OF THE NORTH AMERICAN INDIANS, George Catlin. Classic account of life among Plains Indians: ceremonies, hunt, warfare, etc. 312 plates. 572pp. of text. 6⅛ × 9¼. 22118-0, 22119-9 Pa. Two-vol. set $15.90

ALASKA: The Harriman Expedition, 1899, John Burroughs, John Muir, et al. Informative, engrossing accounts of two-month, 9,000-mile expedition. Native peoples, wildlife, forests, geography, salmon industry, glaciers, more. Profusely illustrated. 240 black-and-white line drawings. 124 black-and-white photographs. 3 maps. Index. 576pp. 5⅜ × 8½. 25109-8 Pa. $11.95

THE BOOK OF BEASTS: Being a Translation from a Latin Bestiary of the Twelfth Century, T. H. White. Wonderful catalog real and fanciful beasts: manticore, griffin, phoenix, amphivius, jaculus, many more. White's witty erudite commentary on scientific, historical aspects. Fascinating glimpse of medieval mind. Illustrated. 296pp. 5⅜ × 8¼. (Available in U.S. only) 24609-4 Pa. $5.95

FRANK LLOYD WRIGHT: ARCHITECTURE AND NATURE With 160 Illustrations, Donald Hoffmann. Profusely illustrated study of influence of nature—especially prairie—on Wright's designs for Fallingwater, Robie House, Guggenheim Museum, other masterpieces. 96pp. 9¼ × 10¾. 25098-9 Pa. $7.95

FRANK LLOYD WRIGHT'S FALLINGWATER, Donald Hoffmann. Wright's famous waterfall house: planning and construction of organic idea. History of site, owners, Wright's personal involvement. Photographs of various stages of building. Preface by Edgar Kaufmann, Jr. 100 illustrations. 112pp. 9¼ × 10.
23671-4 Pa. $7.95

YEARS WITH FRANK LLOYD WRIGHT: Apprentice to Genius, Edgar Tafel. Insightful memoir by a former apprentice presents a revealing portrait of Wright the man, the inspired teacher, the greatest American architect. 372 black-and-white illustrations. Preface. Index. vi + 228pp. 8¼ × 11. 24801-1 Pa. $9.95

THE STORY OF KING ARTHUR AND HIS KNIGHTS, Howard Pyle. Enchanting version of King Arthur fable has delighted generations with imaginative narratives of exciting adventures and unforgettable illustrations by the author. 41 illustrations. xviii + 313pp. 6⅛ × 9¼. 21445-1 Pa. $5.95

THE GODS OF THE EGYPTIANS, E. A. Wallis Budge. Thorough coverage of numerous gods of ancient Egypt by foremost Egyptologist. Information on evolution of cults, rites and gods; the cult of Osiris; the Book of the Dead and its rites; the sacred animals and birds; Heaven and Hell; and more. 956pp. 6⅛ × 9¼.
22055-9, 22056-7 Pa., Two-vol. set $21.90

A THEOLOGICO-POLITICAL TREATISE, Benedict Spinoza. Also contains unfinished *Political Treatise*. Great classic on religious liberty, theory of government on common consent. R. Elwes translation. Total of 421pp. 5⅜ × 8½.
20249-6 Pa. $6.95

INCIDENTS OF TRAVEL IN CENTRAL AMERICA, CHIAPAS, AND YUCATAN, John L. Stephens. Almost single-handed discovery of Maya culture; exploration of ruined cities, monuments, temples; customs of Indians. 115 drawings. 892pp. 5⅜ × 8½. 22404-X, 22405-8 Pa., Two-vol. set $15.90

LOS CAPRICHOS, Francisco Goya. 80 plates of wild, grotesque monsters and caricatures. Prado manuscript included. 183pp. 6⅝ × 9⅝. 22384-1 Pa. $4.95

AUTOBIOGRAPHY: The Story of My Experiments with Truth, Mohandas K. Gandhi. Not hagiography, but Gandhi in his own words. Boyhood, legal studies, purification, the growth of the Satyagraha (nonviolent protest) movement. Critical, inspiring work of the man who freed India. 480pp. 5⅜ × 8½. (Available in U.S. only)
24593-4 Pa. $6.95

ILLUSTRATED DICTIONARY OF HISTORIC ARCHITECTURE, edited by Cyril M. Harris. Extraordinary compendium of clear, concise definitions for over 5,000 important architectural terms complemented by over 2,000 line drawings. Covers full spectrum of architecture from ancient ruins to 20th-century Modernism. Preface. 592pp. 7½ × 9⅝. 24444-X Pa. $14.95

THE NIGHT BEFORE CHRISTMAS, Clement Moore. Full text, and woodcuts from original 1848 book. Also critical, historical material. 19 illustrations. 40pp. 4⅝ × 6. 22797-9 Pa. $2.50

THE LESSON OF JAPANESE ARCHITECTURE: 165 Photographs, Jiro Harada. Memorable gallery of 165 photographs taken in the 1930's of exquisite Japanese homes of the well-to-do and historic buildings. 13 line diagrams. 192pp. 8⅜ × 11¼. 24778-3 Pa. $8.95

THE AUTOBIOGRAPHY OF CHARLES DARWIN AND SELECTED LETTERS, edited by Francis Darwin. The fascinating life of eccentric genius composed of an intimate memoir by Darwin (intended for his children); commentary by his son, Francis; hundreds of fragments from notebooks, journals, papers; and letters to and from Lyell, Hooker, Huxley, Wallace and Henslow. xi + 365pp. 5⅜ × 8. 20479-0 Pa. $5.95

WONDERS OF THE SKY: Observing Rainbows, Comets, Eclipses, the Stars and Other Phenomena, Fred Schaaf. Charming, easy-to-read poetic guide to all manner of celestial events visible to the naked eye. Mock suns, glories, Belt of Venus, more. Illustrated. 299pp. 5¼ × 8¼. 24402-4 Pa. $7.95

BURNHAM'S CELESTIAL HANDBOOK, Robert Burnham, Jr. Thorough guide to the stars beyond our solar system. Exhaustive treatment. Alphabetical by constellation: Andromeda to Cetus in Vol. 1; Chamaeleon to Orion in Vol. 2; and Pavo to Vulpecula in Vol. 3. Hundreds of illustrations. Index in Vol. 3. 2,000pp. 6⅛ × 9¼. 23567-X, 23568-8, 23673-0 Pa., Three-vol. set $37.85

STAR NAMES: Their Lore and Meaning, Richard Hinckley Allen. Fascinating history of names various cultures have given to constellations and literary and folkloristic uses that have been made of stars. Indexes to subjects. Arabic and Greek names. Biblical references. Bibliography. 563pp. 5⅜ × 8½. 21079-0 Pa. $7.95

THIRTY YEARS THAT SHOOK PHYSICS: The Story of Quantum Theory, George Gamow. Lucid, accessible introduction to influential theory of energy and matter. Careful explanations of Dirac's anti-particles, Bohr's model of the atom, much more. 12 plates. Numerous drawings. 240pp. 5⅜ × 8½. 24895-X Pa. $4.95

CHINESE DOMESTIC FURNITURE IN PHOTOGRAPHS AND MEASURED DRAWINGS, Gustav Ecke. A rare volume, now affordably priced for antique collectors, furniture buffs and art historians. Detailed review of styles ranging from early Shang to late Ming. Unabridged republication. 161 black-and-white drawings, photos. Total of 224pp. 8⅜ × 11¼. (Available in U.S. only) 25171-3 Pa. $12.95

VINCENT VAN GOGH: A Biography, Julius Meier-Graefe. Dynamic, penetrating study of artist's life, relationship with brother, Theo, painting techniques, travels, more. Readable, engrossing. 160pp. 5⅜ × 8½. (Available in U.S. only) 25253-1 Pa. $3.95

HOW TO WRITE, Gertrude Stein. Gertrude Stein claimed anyone could understand her unconventional writing—here are clues to help. Fascinating improvisations, language experiments, explanations illuminate Stein's craft and the art of writing. Total of 414pp. 4⅜ × 6⅜. 23144-5 Pa. $5.95

ADVENTURES AT SEA IN THE GREAT AGE OF SAIL: Five Firsthand Narratives, edited by Elliot Snow. Rare true accounts of exploration, whaling, shipwreck, fierce natives, trade, shipboard life, more. 33 illustrations. Introduction. 353pp. 5⅜ × 8½. 25177-2 Pa. $7.95

THE HERBAL OR GENERAL HISTORY OF PLANTS, John Gerard. Classic descriptions of about 2,850 plants—with over 2,700 illustrations—includes Latin and English names, physical descriptions, varieties, time and place of growth, more. 2,706 illustrations. xlv + 1,678pp. 8½ × 12¼. 23147-X Cloth. $75.00

DOROTHY AND THE WIZARD IN OZ, L. Frank Baum. Dorothy and the Wizard visit the center of the Earth, where people are vegetables, glass houses grow and Oz characters reappear. Classic sequel to *Wizard of Oz*. 256pp. 5⅜ × 8. 24714-7 Pa. $4.95

SONGS OF EXPERIENCE: Facsimile Reproduction with 26 Plates in Full Color, William Blake. This facsimile of Blake's original "Illuminated Book" reproduces 26 full-color plates from a rare 1826 edition. Includes "The Tyger," "London," "Holy Thursday," and other immortal poems. 26 color plates. Printed text of poems. 48pp. 5¼ × 7. 24636-1 Pa. $3.50

SONGS OF INNOCENCE, William Blake. The first and most popular of Blake's famous "Illuminated Books," in a facsimile edition reproducing all 31 brightly colored plates. Additional printed text of each poem. 64pp. 5¼ × 7. 22764-2 Pa. $3.50

PRECIOUS STONES, Max Bauer. Classic, thorough study of diamonds, rubies, emeralds, garnets, etc.: physical character, occurrence, properties, use, similar topics. 20 plates, 8 in color. 94 figures. 659pp. 6⅛ × 9¼. 21910-0, 21911-9 Pa., Two-vol. set $15.90

ENCYCLOPEDIA OF VICTORIAN NEEDLEWORK, S. F. A. Caulfeild and Blanche Saward. Full, precise descriptions of stitches, techniques for dozens of needlecrafts—most exhaustive reference of its kind. Over 800 figures. Total of 679pp. 8⅛ × 11. Two volumes. Vol. 1 22800-2 Pa. $11.95
Vol. 2 22801-0 Pa. $11.95

THE MARVELOUS LAND OF OZ, L. Frank Baum. Second Oz book, the Scarecrow and Tin Woodman are back with hero named Tip, Oz magic. 136 illustrations. 287pp. 5⅜ × 8½. 20692-0 Pa. $5.95

WILD FOWL DECOYS, Joel Barber. Basic book on the subject, by foremost authority and collector. Reveals history of decoy making and rigging, place in American culture, different kinds of decoys, how to make them, and how to use them. 140 plates. 156pp. 7⅞ × 10¾. 20011-6 Pa. $8.95

HISTORY OF LACE, Mrs. Bury Palliser. Definitive, profusely illustrated chronicle of lace from earliest times to late 19th century. Laces of Italy, Greece, England, France, Belgium, etc. Landmark of needlework scholarship. 266 illustrations. 672pp. 6⅛ × 9¼. 24742-2 Pa. $14.95

ILLUSTRATED GUIDE TO SHAKER FURNITURE, Robert Meader. All furniture and appurtenances, with much on unknown local styles. 235 photos. 146pp. 9 × 12. 22819-3 Pa. $7.95

WHALE SHIPS AND WHALING: A Pictorial Survey, George Francis Dow. Over 200 vintage engravings, drawings, photographs of barks, brigs, cutters, other vessels. Also harpoons, lances, whaling guns, many other artifacts. Comprehensive text by foremost authority. 207 black-and-white illustrations. 288pp. 6 × 9. 24808-9 Pa. $8.95

THE BERTRAMS, Anthony Trollope. Powerful portrayal of blind self-will and thwarted ambition includes one of Trollope's most heartrending love stories. 497pp. 5⅜ × 8½. 25119-5 Pa. $8.95

ADVENTURES WITH A HAND LENS, Richard Headstrom. Clearly written guide to observing and studying flowers and grasses, fish scales, moth and insect wings, egg cases, buds, feathers, seeds, leaf scars, moss, molds, ferns, common crystals, etc.—all with an ordinary, inexpensive magnifying glass. 209 exact line drawings aid in your discoveries. 220pp. 5⅜ × 8½. 23330-8 Pa. $4.50

RODIN ON ART AND ARTISTS, Auguste Rodin. Great sculptor's candid, wide-ranging comments on meaning of art; great artists; relation of sculpture to poetry, painting, music; philosophy of life, more. 76 superb black-and-white illustrations of Rodin's sculpture, drawings and prints. 119pp. 8⅜ × 11¼. 24487-3 Pa. $6.95

FIFTY CLASSIC FRENCH FILMS, 1912–1982: A Pictorial Record, Anthony Slide. Memorable stills from Grand Illusion, Beauty and the Beast, Hiroshima, Mon Amour, many more. Credits, plot synopses, reviews, etc. 160pp. 8¼ × 11. 25256-6 Pa. $11.95

THE PRINCIPLES OF PSYCHOLOGY, William James. Famous long course complete, unabridged. Stream of thought, time perception, memory, experimental methods; great work decades ahead of its time. 94 figures. 1,391pp. 5⅜ × 8½. 20381-6, 20382-4 Pa., Two-vol. set $19.90

BODIES IN A BOOKSHOP, R. T. Campbell. Challenging mystery of blackmail and murder with ingenious plot and superbly drawn characters. In the best tradition of British suspense fiction. 192pp. 5⅜ × 8½. 24720-1 Pa. $3.95

CALLAS: PORTRAIT OF A PRIMA DONNA, George Jellinek. Renowned commentator on the musical scene chronicles incredible career and life of the most controversial, fascinating, influential operatic personality of our time. 64 black-and-white photographs. 416pp. 5⅜ × 8¼. 25047-4 Pa. $7.95

GEOMETRY, RELATIVITY AND THE FOURTH DIMENSION, Rudolph Rucker. Exposition of fourth dimension, concepts of relativity as Flatland characters continue adventures. Popular, easily followed yet accurate, profound. 141 illustrations. 133pp. 5⅜ × 8½. 23400-2 Pa. $3.50

HOUSEHOLD STORIES BY THE BROTHERS GRIMM, with pictures by Walter Crane. 53 classic stories—Rumpelstiltskin, Rapunzel, Hansel and Gretel, the Fisherman and his Wife, Snow White, Tom Thumb, Sleeping Beauty, Cinderella, and so much more—lavishly illustrated with original 19th century drawings. 114 illustrations. x + 269pp. 5⅜ × 8½. 21080-4 Pa. $4.50

SUNDIALS, Albert Waugh. Far and away the best, most thorough coverage of ideas, mathematics concerned, types, construction, adjusting anywhere. Over 100 illustrations. 230pp. 5⅜ × 8½. 22947-5 Pa. $4.50

PICTURE HISTORY OF THE NORMANDIE: With 190 Illustrations, Frank O. Braynard. Full story of legendary French ocean liner: Art Deco interiors, design innovations, furnishings, celebrities, maiden voyage, tragic fire, much more. Extensive text. 144pp. 8⅜ × 11¾. 25257-4 Pa. $9.95

THE FIRST AMERICAN COOKBOOK: A Facsimile of "American Cookery," 1796, Amelia Simmons. Facsimile of the first American-written cookbook published in the United States contains authentic recipes for colonial favorites—pumpkin pudding, winter squash pudding, spruce beer, Indian slapjacks, and more. Introductory Essay and Glossary of colonial cooking terms. 80pp. 5⅜ × 8½. 24710-4 Pa. $3.50

101 PUZZLES IN THOUGHT AND LOGIC, C. R. Wylie, Jr. Solve murders and robberies, find out which fishermen are liars, how a blind man could possibly identify a color—purely by your own reasoning! 107pp. 5⅜ × 8½. 20367-0 Pa. $2.50

THE BOOK OF WORLD-FAMOUS MUSIC—CLASSICAL, POPULAR AND FOLK, James J. Fuld. Revised and enlarged republication of landmark work in musico-bibliography. Full information about nearly 1,000 songs and compositions including first lines of music and lyrics. New supplement. Index. 800pp. 5⅜ × 8¼. 24857-7 Pa. $14.95

ANTHROPOLOGY AND MODERN LIFE, Franz Boas. Great anthropologist's classic treatise on race and culture. Introduction by Ruth Bunzel. Only inexpensive paperback edition. 255pp. 5⅜ × 8½. 25245-0 Pa. $5.95

THE TALE OF PETER RABBIT, Beatrix Potter. The inimitable Peter's terrifying adventure in Mr. McGregor's garden, with all 27 wonderful, full-color Potter illustrations. 55pp. 4¼ × 5½. (Available in U.S. only) 22827-4 Pa. $1.75

THREE PROPHETIC SCIENCE FICTION NOVELS, H. G. Wells. *When the Sleeper Wakes, A Story of the Days to Come* and *The Time Machine* (full version). 335pp. 5⅜ × 8½. (Available in U.S. only) 20605-X Pa. $5.95

APICIUS COOKERY AND DINING IN IMPERIAL ROME, edited and translated by Joseph Dommers Vehling. Oldest known cookbook in existence offers readers a clear picture of what foods Romans ate, how they prepared them, etc. 49 illustrations. 301pp. 6⅛ × 9¼. 23563-7 Pa. $6.50

SHAKESPEARE LEXICON AND QUOTATION DICTIONARY, Alexander Schmidt. Full definitions, locations, shades of meaning of every word in plays and poems. More than 50,000 exact quotations. 1,485pp. 6½ × 9¼. 22726-X, 22727-8 Pa., Two-vol. set $27.90

THE WORLD'S GREAT SPEECHES, edited by Lewis Copeland and Lawrence W. Lamm. Vast collection of 278 speeches from Greeks to 1970. Powerful and effective models; unique look at history. 842pp. 5⅜ × 8½. 20468-5 Pa. $11.95

THE BLUE FAIRY BOOK, Andrew Lang. The first, most famous collection, with many familiar tales: Little Red Riding Hood, Aladdin and the Wonderful Lamp, Puss in Boots, Sleeping Beauty, Hansel and Gretel, Rumpelstiltskin; 37 in all. 138 illustrations. 390pp. 5⅜ × 8½.   21437-0 Pa. $5.95

THE STORY OF THE CHAMPIONS OF THE ROUND TABLE, Howard Pyle. Sir Launcelot, Sir Tristram and Sir Percival in spirited adventures of love and triumph retold in Pyle's inimitable style. 50 drawings, 31 full-page. xviii + 329pp. 6½ × 9¼.   21883-X Pa. $6.95

AUDUBON AND HIS JOURNALS, Maria Audubon. Unmatched two-volume portrait of the great artist, naturalist and author contains his journals, an excellent biography by his granddaughter, expert annotations by the noted ornithologist, Dr. Elliott Coues, and 37 superb illustrations. Total of 1,200pp. 5⅜ × 8.
Vol. I 25143-8 Pa. $8.95
Vol. II 25144-6 Pa. $8.95

GREAT DINOSAUR HUNTERS AND THEIR DISCOVERIES, Edwin H. Colbert. Fascinating, lavishly illustrated chronicle of dinosaur research, 1820's to 1960. Achievements of Cope, Marsh, Brown, Buckland, Mantell, Huxley, many others. 384pp. 5¼ × 8¼.   24701-5 Pa. $6.95

THE TASTEMAKERS, Russell Lynes. Informal, illustrated social history of American taste 1850's–1950's. First popularized categories Highbrow, Lowbrow, Middlebrow. 129 illustrations. New (1979) afterword. 384pp. 6 × 9.
23993-4 Pa. $6.95

DOUBLE CROSS PURPOSES, Ronald A. Knox. A treasure hunt in the Scottish Highlands, an old map, unidentified corpse, surprise discoveries keep reader guessing in this cleverly intricate tale of financial skullduggery. 2 black-and-white maps. 320pp. 5⅜ × 8½. (Available in U.S. only)   25032-6 Pa. $5.95

AUTHENTIC VICTORIAN DECORATION AND ORNAMENTATION IN FULL COLOR: 46 Plates from "Studies in Design," Christopher Dresser. Superb full-color lithographs reproduced from rare original portfolio of a major Victorian designer. 48pp. 9¼ × 12¼.   25083-0 Pa. $7.95

PRIMITIVE ART, Franz Boas. Remains the best text ever prepared on subject, thoroughly discussing Indian, African, Asian, Australian, and, especially, Northern American primitive art. Over 950 illustrations show ceramics, masks, totem poles, weapons, textiles, paintings, much more. 376pp. 5⅜ × 8. 20025-6 Pa. $6.95

SIDELIGHTS ON RELATIVITY, Albert Einstein. Unabridged republication of two lectures delivered by the great physicist in 1920–21. *Ether and Relativity* and *Geometry and Experience*. Elegant ideas in non-mathematical form, accessible to intelligent layman. vi + 56pp. 5⅜ × 8½.   24511-X Pa. $2.95

THE WIT AND HUMOR OF OSCAR WILDE, edited by Alvin Redman. More than 1,000 ripostes, paradoxes, wisecracks: Work is the curse of the drinking classes, I can resist everything except temptation, etc. 258pp. 5⅜ × 8½.   20602-5 Pa. $4.50

ADVENTURES WITH A MICROSCOPE, Richard Headstrom. 59 adventures with clothing fibers, protozoa, ferns and lichens, roots and leaves, much more. 142 illustrations. 232pp. 5⅜ × 8½.   23471-1 Pa. $3.95

PLANTS OF THE BIBLE, Harold N. Moldenke and Alma L. Moldenke. Standard reference to all 230 plants mentioned in Scriptures. Latin name, biblical reference, uses, modern identity, much more. Unsurpassed encyclopedic resource for scholars, botanists, nature lovers, students of Bible. Bibliography. Indexes. 123 black-and-white illustrations. 384pp. 6 × 9. 25069-5 Pa. $8.95

FAMOUS AMERICAN WOMEN: A Biographical Dictionary from Colonial Times to the Present, Robert McHenry, ed. From Pocahontas to Rosa Parks, 1,035 distinguished American women documented in separate biographical entries. Accurate, up-to-date data, numerous categories, spans 400 years. Indices. 493pp. 6½ × 9¼. 24523-3 Pa. $9.95

THE FABULOUS INTERIORS OF THE GREAT OCEAN LINERS IN HISTORIC PHOTOGRAPHS, William H. Miller, Jr. Some 200 superb photographs capture exquisite interiors of world's great "floating palaces"—1890's to 1980's: *Titanic, Ile de France, Queen Elizabeth, United States, Europa,* more. Approx. 200 black-and-white photographs. Captions. Text. Introduction. 160pp. 8⅞ × 11¾. 24756-2 Pa. $9.95

THE GREAT LUXURY LINERS, 1927–1954: A Photographic Record, William H. Miller, Jr. Nostalgic tribute to heyday of ocean liners. 186 photos of Ile de France, Normandie, Leviathan, Queen Elizabeth, United States, many others. Interior and exterior views. Introduction. Captions. 160pp. 9 × 12. 24056-8 Pa. $9.95

A NATURAL HISTORY OF THE DUCKS, John Charles Phillips. Great landmark of ornithology offers complete detailed coverage of nearly 200 species and subspecies of ducks: gadwall, sheldrake, merganser, pintail, many more. 74 full-color plates, 102 black-and-white. Bibliography. Total of 1,920pp. 8⅝ × 11¼. 25141-1, 25142-X Cloth. Two-vol. set $100.00

THE SEAWEED HANDBOOK: An Illustrated Guide to Seaweeds from North Carolina to Canada, Thomas F. Lee. Concise reference covers 78 species. Scientific and common names, habitat, distribution, more. Finding keys for easy identification. 224pp. 5⅜ × 8½. 25215-9 Pa. $5.95

THE TEN BOOKS OF ARCHITECTURE: The 1755 Leoni Edition, Leon Battista Alberti. Rare classic helped introduce the glories of ancient architecture to the Renaissance. 68 black-and-white plates. 336pp. 8⅜ × 11¼. 25239-6 Pa. $14.95

MISS MACKENZIE, Anthony Trollope. Minor masterpieces by Victorian master unmasks many truths about life in 19th-century England. First inexpensive edition in years. 392pp. 5⅜ × 8½. 25201-9 Pa. $7.95

THE RIME OF THE ANCIENT MARINER, Gustave Doré, Samuel Taylor Coleridge. Dramatic engravings considered by many to be his greatest work. The terrifying space of the open sea, the storms and whirlpools of an unknown ocean, the ice of Antarctica, more—all rendered in a powerful, chilling manner. Full text. 38 plates. 77pp. 9¼ × 12. 22305-1 Pa. $4.95

THE EXPEDITIONS OF ZEBULON MONTGOMERY PIKE, Zebulon Montgomery Pike. Fascinating first-hand accounts (1805–6) of exploration of Mississippi River, Indian wars, capture by Spanish dragoons, much more. 1,088pp. 5⅜ × 8½. 25254-X, 25255-8 Pa. Two-vol. set $23.90

A CONCISE HISTORY OF PHOTOGRAPHY: Third Revised Edition, Helmut Gernsheim. Best one-volume history—camera obscura, photochemistry, daguerreotypes, evolution of cameras, film, more. Also artistic aspects—landscape, portraits, fine art, etc. 281 black-and-white photographs. 26 in color. 176pp. 8⅜ × 11¼. 25128-4 Pa. $12.95

THE DORÉ BIBLE ILLUSTRATIONS, Gustave Doré. 241 detailed plates from the Bible: the Creation scenes, Adam and Eve, Flood, Babylon, battle sequences, life of Jesus, etc. Each plate is accompanied by the verses from the King James version of the Bible. 241pp. 9 × 12. 23004-X Pa. $8.95

HUGGER-MUGGER IN THE LOUVRE, Elliot Paul. Second Homer Evans mystery-comedy. Theft at the Louvre involves sleuth in hilarious, madcap caper. "A knockout."—Books. 336pp. 5⅜ × 8½. 25185-3 Pa. $5.95

FLATLAND, E. A. Abbott. Intriguing and enormously popular science-fiction classic explores the complexities of trying to survive as a two-dimensional being in a three-dimensional world. Amusingly illustrated by the author. 16 illustrations. 103pp. 5⅜ × 8½. 20001-9 Pa. $2.25

THE HISTORY OF THE LEWIS AND CLARK EXPEDITION, Meriwether Lewis and William Clark, edited by Elliott Coues. Classic edition of Lewis and Clark's day-by-day journals that later became the basis for U.S. claims to Oregon and the West. Accurate and invaluable geographical, botanical, biological, meteorological and anthropological material. Total of 1,508pp. 5⅜ × 8½.
21268-8, 21269-6, 21270-X Pa. Three-vol. set $25.50

LANGUAGE, TRUTH AND LOGIC, Alfred J. Ayer. Famous, clear introduction to Vienna, Cambridge schools of Logical Positivism. Role of philosophy, elimination of metaphysics, nature of analysis, etc. 160pp. 5⅜ × 8½. (Available in U.S. and Canada only) 20010-8 Pa. $2.95

MATHEMATICS FOR THE NONMATHEMATICIAN, Morris Kline. Detailed, college-level treatment of mathematics in cultural and historical context, with numerous exercises. For liberal arts students. Preface. Recommended Reading Lists. Tables. Index. Numerous black-and-white figures. xvi + 641pp. 5⅜ × 8½.
24823-2 Pa. $11.95

28 SCIENCE FICTION STORIES, H. G. Wells. Novels, *Star Begotten* and *Men Like Gods,* plus 26 short stories: "Empire of the Ants," "A Story of the Stone Age," "The Stolen Bacillus," "In the Abyss," etc. 915pp. 5⅜ × 8½. (Available in U.S. only)
20265-8 Cloth. $10.95

HANDBOOK OF PICTORIAL SYMBOLS, Rudolph Modley. 3,250 signs and symbols, many systems in full; official or heavy commercial use. Arranged by subject. Most in Pictorial Archive series. 143pp. 8⅛ × 11. 23357-X Pa. $5.95

INCIDENTS OF TRAVEL IN YUCATAN, John L. Stephens. Classic (1843) exploration of jungles of Yucatan, looking for evidences of Maya civilization. Travel adventures, Mexican and Indian culture, etc. Total of 669pp. 5⅜ × 8½.
20926-1, 20927-X Pa., Two-vol. set $9.90

DEGAS: An Intimate Portrait, Ambroise Vollard. Charming, anecdotal memoir by famous art dealer of one of the greatest 19th-century French painters. 14 black-and-white illustrations. Introduction by Harold L. Van Doren. 96pp. 5⅜ × 8½.
25131-4 Pa. $3.95

PERSONAL NARRATIVE OF A PILGRIMAGE TO ALMANDINAH AND MECCAH, Richard Burton. Great travel classic by remarkably colorful personality. Burton, disguised as a Moroccan, visited sacred shrines of Islam, narrowly escaping death. 47 illustrations. 959pp. 5⅜ × 8½.   21217-3, 21218-1 Pa., Two-vol. set $17.90

PHRASE AND WORD ORIGINS, A. H. Holt. Entertaining, reliable, modern study of more than 1,200 colorful words, phrases, origins and histories. Much unexpected information. 254pp. 5⅜ × 8½.   20758-7 Pa. $5.95

THE RED THUMB MARK, R. Austin Freeman. In this first Dr. Thorndyke case, the great scientific detective draws fascinating conclusions from the nature of a single fingerprint. Exciting story, authentic science. 320pp. 5⅜ × 8½. (Available in U.S. only)   25210-8 Pa. $5.95

AN EGYPTIAN HIEROGLYPHIC DICTIONARY, E. A. Wallis Budge. Monumental work containing about 25,000 words or terms that occur in texts ranging from 3000 B.C. to 600 A.D. Each entry consists of a transliteration of the word, the word in hieroglyphs, and the meaning in English. 1,314pp. 6⅛ × 10.
23615-3, 23616-1 Pa., Two-vol. set $27.90

THE COMPLEAT STRATEGYST: Being a Primer on the Theory of Games of Strategy, J. D. Williams. Highly entertaining classic describes, with many illustrated examples, how to select best strategies in conflict situations. Prefaces. Appendices. xvi + 268pp. 5⅜ × 8½.   25101-2 Pa. $5.95

THE ROAD TO OZ, L. Frank Baum. Dorothy meets the Shaggy Man, little Button-Bright and the Rainbow's beautiful daughter in this delightful trip to the magical Land of Oz. 272pp. 5⅜ × 8.   25208-6 Pa. $4.95

POINT AND LINE TO PLANE, Wassily Kandinsky. Seminal exposition of role of point, line, other elements in non-objective painting. Essential to understanding 20th-century art. 127 illustrations. 192pp. 6½ × 9¼.   23808-3 Pa. $4.50

LADY ANNA, Anthony Trollope. Moving chronicle of Countess Lovel's bitter struggle to win for herself and daughter Anna their rightful rank and fortune— perhaps at cost of sanity itself. 384pp. 5⅜ × 8½.   24669-8 Pa. $6.95

EGYPTIAN MAGIC, E. A. Wallis Budge. Sums up all that is known about magic in Ancient Egypt: the role of magic in controlling the gods, powerful amulets that warded off evil spirits, scarabs of immortality, use of wax images, formulas and spells, the secret name, much more. 253pp. 5⅜ × 8½.   22681-6 Pa. $4.50

THE DANCE OF SIVA, Ananda Coomaraswamy. Preeminent authority unfolds the vast metaphysic of India: the revelation of her art, conception of the universe, social organization, etc. 27 reproductions of art masterpieces. 192pp. 5⅜ × 8½.
24817-8 Pa. $5.95

CHRISTMAS CUSTOMS AND TRADITIONS, Clement A. Miles. Origin, evolution, significance of religious, secular practices. Caroling, gifts, yule logs, much more. Full, scholarly yet fascinating; non-sectarian. 400pp. 5⅜ × 8½.
23354-5 Pa. $6.50

THE HUMAN FIGURE IN MOTION, Eadweard Muybridge. More than 4,500 stopped-action photos, in action series, showing undraped men, women, children jumping, lying down, throwing, sitting, wrestling, carrying, etc. 390pp. 7⅞ × 10⅝.
20204-6 Cloth. $19.95

THE MAN WHO WAS THURSDAY, Gilbert Keith Chesterton. Witty, fast-paced novel about a club of anarchists in turn-of-the-century London. Brilliant social, religious, philosophical speculations. 128pp. 5⅜ × 8½.
25121-7 Pa. $3.95

A CEZANNE SKETCHBOOK: Figures, Portraits, Landscapes and Still Lifes, Paul Cezanne. Great artist experiments with tonal effects, light, mass, other qualities in over 100 drawings. A revealing view of developing master painter, precursor of Cubism. 102 black-and-white illustrations. 144pp. 8¾ × 6⅜.
24790-2 Pa. $5.95

AN ENCYCLOPEDIA OF BATTLES: Accounts of Over 1,560 Battles from 1479 b.c. to the Present, David Eggenberger. Presents essential details of every major battle in recorded history, from the first battle of Megiddo in 1479 b.c. to Grenada in 1984. List of Battle Maps. New Appendix covering the years 1967–1984. Index. 99 illustrations. 544pp. 6½ × 9¼.
24913-1 Pa. $14.95

AN ETYMOLOGICAL DICTIONARY OF MODERN ENGLISH, Ernest Weekley. Richest, fullest work, by foremost British lexicographer. Detailed word histories. Inexhaustible. Total of 856pp. 6½ × 9¼.
21873-2, 21874-0 Pa., Two-vol. set $17.00

WEBSTER'S AMERICAN MILITARY BIOGRAPHIES, edited by Robert McHenry. Over 1,000 figures who shaped 3 centuries of American military history. Detailed biographies of Nathan Hale, Douglas MacArthur, Mary Hallaren, others. Chronologies of engagements, more. Introduction. Addenda. 1,033 entries in alphabetical order. xi + 548pp. 6½ × 9¼. (Available in U.S. only)
24758-9 Pa. $11.95

LIFE IN ANCIENT EGYPT, Adolf Erman. Detailed older account, with much not in more recent books: domestic life, religion, magic, medicine, commerce, and whatever else needed for complete picture. Many illustrations. 597pp. 5⅜ × 8½.
22632-8 Pa. $8.95

HISTORIC COSTUME IN PICTURES, Braun & Schneider. Over 1,450 costumed figures shown, covering a wide variety of peoples: kings, emperors, nobles, priests, servants, soldiers, scholars, townsfolk, peasants, merchants, courtiers, cavaliers, and more. 256pp. 8⅜ × 11¼.
23150-X Pa. $7.95

THE NOTEBOOKS OF LEONARDO DA VINCI, edited by J. P. Richter. Extracts from manuscripts reveal great genius; on painting, sculpture, anatomy, sciences, geography, etc. Both Italian and English. 186 ms. pages reproduced, plus 500 additional drawings, including studies for *Last Supper*, *Sforza* monument, etc. 860pp. 7⅞ × 10¾. (Available in U.S. only) 22572-0, 22573-9 Pa., Two-vol. set $25.90

THE ART NOUVEAU STYLE BOOK OF ALPHONSE MUCHA: All 72 Plates from "Documents Decoratifs" in Original Color, Alphonse Mucha. Rare copyright-free design portfolio by high priest of Art Nouveau. Jewelry, wallpaper, stained glass, furniture, figure studies, plant and animal motifs, etc. Only complete one-volume edition. 80pp. 9⅜ × 12¼. 24044-4 Pa. $8.95

ANIMALS: 1,419 COPYRIGHT-FREE ILLUSTRATIONS OF MAMMALS, BIRDS, FISH, INSECTS, ETC., edited by Jim Harter. Clear wood engravings present, in extremely lifelike poses, over 1,000 species of animals. One of the most extensive pictorial sourcebooks of its kind. Captions. Index. 284pp. 9 × 12. 23766-4 Pa. $9.95

OBELISTS FLY HIGH, C. Daly King. Masterpiece of American detective fiction, long out of print, involves murder on a 1935 transcontinental flight—"a very thrilling story"—NY Times. Unabridged and unaltered republication of the edition published by William Collins Sons & Co. Ltd., London, 1935. 288pp. 5⅜ × 8½. (Available in U.S. only) 25036-9 Pa. $4.95

VICTORIAN AND EDWARDIAN FASHION: A Photographic Survey, Alison Gernsheim. First fashion history completely illustrated by contemporary photographs. Full text plus 235 photos, 1840–1914, in which many celebrities appear. 240pp. 6½ × 9¼. 24205-6 Pa. $6.00

THE ART OF THE FRENCH ILLUSTRATED BOOK, 1700–1914, Gordon N. Ray. Over 630 superb book illustrations by Fragonard, Delacroix, Daumier, Doré, Grandville, Manet, Mucha, Steinlen, Toulouse-Lautrec and many others. Preface. Introduction. 633 halftones. Indices of artists, authors & titles, binders and provenances. Appendices. Bibliography. 608pp. 8⅜ × 11¼. 25086-5 Pa. $24.95

THE WONDERFUL WIZARD OF OZ, L. Frank Baum. Facsimile in full color of America's finest children's classic. 143 illustrations by W. W. Denslow. 267pp. 5⅜ × 8½. 20691-2 Pa. $5.95

FRONTIERS OF MODERN PHYSICS: New Perspectives on Cosmology, Relativity, Black Holes and Extraterrestrial Intelligence, Tony Rothman, et al. For the intelligent layman. Subjects include: cosmological models of the universe; black holes; the neutrino; the search for extraterrestrial intelligence. Introduction. 46 black-and-white illustrations. 192pp. 5⅜ × 8½. 24587-X Pa. $6.95

THE FRIENDLY STARS, Martha Evans Martin & Donald Howard Menzel. Classic text marshalls the stars together in an engaging, non-technical survey, presenting them as sources of beauty in night sky. 23 illustrations. Foreword. 2 star charts. Index. 147pp. 5⅜ × 8½. 21099-5 Pa. $3.50

FADS AND FALLACIES IN THE NAME OF SCIENCE, Martin Gardner. Fair, witty appraisal of cranks, quacks, and quackeries of science and pseudoscience: hollow earth, Velikovsky, orgone energy, Dianetics, flying saucers, Bridey Murphy, food and medical fads, etc. Revised, expanded In the Name of Science. "A very able and even-tempered presentation."—The New Yorker. 363pp. 5⅜ × 8. 20394-8 Pa. $6.50

ANCIENT EGYPT: ITS CULTURE AND HISTORY, J. E Manchip White. From pre-dynastics through Ptolemies: society, history, political structure, religion, daily life, literature, cultural heritage. 48 plates. 217pp. 5⅜ × 8½. 22548-8 Pa. $4.95

SIR HARRY HOTSPUR OF HUMBLETHWAITE, Anthony Trollope. Incisive, unconventional psychological study of a conflict between a wealthy baronet, his idealistic daughter, and their scapegrace cousin. The 1870 novel in its first inexpensive edition in years. 250pp. 5⅜ × 8½. 24953-0 Pa. $5.95

LASERS AND HOLOGRAPHY, Winston E. Kock. Sound introduction to burgeoning field, expanded (1981) for second edition. Wave patterns, coherence, lasers, diffraction, zone plates, properties of holograms, recent advances. 84 illustrations. 160pp. 5⅜ × 8¼. (Except in United Kingdom) 24041-X Pa. $3.50

INTRODUCTION TO ARTIFICIAL INTELLIGENCE: SECOND, ENLARGED EDITION, Philip C. Jackson, Jr. Comprehensive survey of artificial intelligence—the study of how machines (computers) can be made to act intelligently. Includes introductory and advanced material. Extensive notes updating the main text. 132 black-and-white illustrations. 512pp. 5⅜ × 8½. 24864-X Pa. $8.95

HISTORY OF INDIAN AND INDONESIAN ART, Ananda K. Coomaraswamy. Over 400 illustrations illuminate classic study of Indian art from earliest Harappa finds to early 20th century. Provides philosophical, religious and social insights. 304pp. 6⅝ × 9⅜. 25005-9 Pa. $8.95

THE GOLEM, Gustav Meyrink. Most famous supernatural novel in modern European literature, set in Ghetto of Old Prague around 1890. Compelling story of mystical experiences, strange transformations, profound terror. 13 black-and-white illustrations. 224pp. 5⅜ × 8½. (Available in U.S. only) 25025-3 Pa. $5.95

ARMADALE, Wilkie Collins. Third great mystery novel by the author of *The Woman in White* and *The Moonstone*. Original magazine version with 40 illustrations. 597pp. 5⅜ × 8½. 23429-0 Pa. $9.95

PICTORIAL ENCYCLOPEDIA OF HISTORIC ARCHITECTURAL PLANS, DETAILS AND ELEMENTS: With 1,880 Line Drawings of Arches, Domes, Doorways, Facades, Gables, Windows, etc., John Theodore Haneman. Sourcebook of inspiration for architects, designers, others. Bibliography. Captions. 141pp. 9 × 12. 24605-1 Pa. $6.95

BENCHLEY LOST AND FOUND, Robert Benchley. Finest humor from early 30's, about pet peeves, child psychologists, post office and others. Mostly unavailable elsewhere. 73 illustrations by Peter Arno and others. 183pp. 5⅜ × 8½. 22410-4 Pa. $3.95

ERTÉ GRAPHICS, Erté. Collection of striking color graphics: *Seasons, Alphabet, Numerals, Aces* and *Precious Stones*. 50 plates, including 4 on covers. 48pp. 9⅜ × 12¼. 23580-7 Pa. $6.95

THE JOURNAL OF HENRY D. THOREAU, edited by Bradford Torrey, F. H. Allen. Complete reprinting of 14 volumes, 1837-61, over two million words; the sourcebooks for *Walden*, etc. Definitive. All original sketches, plus 75 photographs. 1,804pp. 8½ × 12¼. 20312-3, 20313-1 Cloth., Two-vol. set $80.00

CASTLES: THEIR CONSTRUCTION AND HISTORY, Sidney Toy. Traces castle development from ancient roots. Nearly 200 photographs and drawings illustrate moats, keeps, baileys, many other features. Caernarvon, Dover Castles, Hadrian's Wall, Tower of London, dozens more. 256pp. 5⅜ × 8¼. 24898-4 Pa. $5.95

CATALOG OF DOVER BOOKS

AMERICAN CLIPPER SHIPS: 1833–1858, Octavius T. Howe & Frederick C. Matthews. Fully-illustrated, encyclopedic review of 352 clipper ships from the period of America's greatest maritime supremacy. Introduction. 109 halftones. 5 black-and-white line illustrations. Index. Total of 928pp. 5⅜ × 8½.
25115-2, 25116-0 Pa., Two-vol. set $17.90

TOWARDS A NEW ARCHITECTURE, Le Corbusier. Pioneering manifesto by great architect, near legendary founder of "International School." Technical and aesthetic theories, views on industry, economics, relation of form to function, "mass-production spirit," much more. Profusely illustrated. Unabridged translation of 13th French edition. Introduction by Frederick Etchells. 320pp. 6⅛ × 9¼. (Available in U.S. only)
25023-7 Pa. $8.95

THE BOOK OF KELLS, edited by Blanche Cirker. Inexpensive collection of 32 full-color, full-page plates from the greatest illuminated manuscript of the Middle Ages, painstakingly reproduced from rare facsimile edition. Publisher's Note. Captions. 32pp. 9⅜ × 12¼.
24345-1 Pa. $4.95

BEST SCIENCE FICTION STORIES OF H. G. WELLS, H. G. Wells. Full novel *The Invisible Man*, plus 17 short stories: "The Crystal Egg," "Aepyornis Island," "The Strange Orchid," etc. 303pp. 5⅜ × 8½. (Available in U.S. only)
21531-8 Pa. $4.95

AMERICAN SAILING SHIPS: Their Plans and History, Charles G. Davis. Photos, construction details of schooners, frigates, clippers, other sailcraft of 18th to early 20th centuries—plus entertaining discourse on design, rigging, nautical lore, much more. 137 black-and-white illustrations. 240pp. 6⅛ × 9¼.
24658-2 Pa. $5.95

ENTERTAINING MATHEMATICAL PUZZLES, Martin Gardner. Selection of author's favorite conundrums involving arithmetic, money, speed, etc., with lively commentary. Complete solutions. 112pp. 5⅜ × 8½.
25211-6 Pa. $2.95

THE WILL TO BELIEVE, HUMAN IMMORTALITY, William James. Two books bound together. Effect of irrational on logical, and arguments for human immortality. 402pp. 5⅜ × 8½.
20291-7 Pa. $7.50

THE HAUNTED MONASTERY and THE CHINESE MAZE MURDERS, Robert Van Gulik. 2 full novels by Van Gulik continue adventures of Judge Dee and his companions. An evil Taoist monastery, seemingly supernatural events; overgrown topiary maze that hides strange crimes. Set in 7th-century China. 27 illustrations. 328pp. 5⅜ × 8½.
23502-5 Pa. $5.95

CELEBRATED CASES OF JUDGE DEE (DEE GOONG AN), translated by Robert Van Gulik. Authentic 18th-century Chinese detective novel; Dee and associates solve three interlocked cases. Led to Van Gulik's own stories with same characters. Extensive introduction. 9 illustrations. 237pp. 5⅜ × 8½.
23337-5 Pa. $4.95

Prices subject to change without notice.
Available at your book dealer or write for free catalog to Dept. GI, Dover Publications, Inc., 31 East 2nd St., Mineola, N.Y. 11501. Dover publishes more than 175 books each year on science, elementary and advanced mathematics, biology, music, art, literary history, social sciences and other areas.